XSLT Cookbook

XSLT Cookbook

Sal Mangano

O'REILLY®

Beijing · Cambridge · Farnham · Köln · Paris · Sebastopol · Taipei · Tokyo

XSLT Cookbook
by Sal Mangano

Published by O'Reilly & Associates, Inc., 1005 Gravenstein Highway North, Sebastopol, CA 95472.

O'Reilly & Associates books may be purchased for educational, business, or sales promotional use. Online editions are also available for most titles (*safari.oreilly.com*). For more information, contact our corporate/institutional sales department: (800) 998-9938 or *corporate@oreilly.com*.

Editor:	Simon St.Laurent
Production Editor:	Jeffrey Holcomb
Cover Designer:	Ellie Volckhausen
Interior Designer:	David Futato

Printing History:

December 2002:   First Edition.

ISBN: 0-596-00372-2
[M]

Table of Contents

Preface

Extensible Stylesheet Language Transformations (XSLT) is a powerful technology for transforming XML documents into other useful forms, but it is sometimes considered difficult to learn. Its template-based approach makes it a prime candidate for learning by example, and XSLT examples are often easily repurposed.

When I first began working with XSLT, I longed for a cookbook that would accelerate my productivity by providing ready-made solutions to the challenges I faced. My first experience with such a book was O'Reilly's *Perl Cookbook*. This book was more influential to my reluctant learning and ultimate appreciation of Perl than the original camel book (*Programming Perl*) by Larry Wall. I believe cookbooks are important because most software developers are not satisfied with simply figuring out how to make something work: they are interested in mastering the technology and using the best-known techniques, and they want answers fast. There is no better way to master a subject than by borrowing from those who already discovered better ways to do things.

Longing for a cookbook soon turned into a desire to write one, especially since I collected several useful recipes—some that were developed by others and some that I created. However, I did not want to write an XSLT book simply packaged in an alternate form; I wanted to provide a useful resource that also highlighted some less-obvious ways to apply XSLT. In the process, I hoped to attract XML developers who have not yet been motivated to learn XSLT and who, in my opinion, are missing out on one of XML's best productivity tools. If you are one of these folks who has not yet experienced XSLT, please bear with me for a few more paragraphs while I pitch the value of XSLT and the role of this book in helping you realize its potential.

XSLT is a language that lives simultaneously on the fringes and in the mainstream of current software-development technology. While working on this project, I often found myself explaining to friends what XSLT was and why it was important enough to spend time writing a whole book about it. These same friends have heard of Java, Perl, and even XML, but not XSLT. I also observed an increasing number of requests for XSLT assistance on XSLT mailing lists and more industry attention in the form of books, articles, and sophisticated XSLT development tools. The XSLT user base is clearly growing daily; however, many software professionals and technology enthusiasts do not understand what it is and why it is important.

I would estimate that more that half of all companies and individuals working with XML do not use XSLT. Not so long ago, a colleague who is otherwise well-versed in all the latest technologies described XSLT as just another styling language. One can certainly forgive such a blatant misunderstanding because XSLT advertises itself through the first three words in its name (Extended Stylesheet Language) and with the keyword that begins most XSLT programs (xsl:stylesheet). However, the last word in the XSLT acronym, *Transformations*, is what makes XSLT so important and is what drew me to the language in the first place. One of my goals in writing this book is to show how XSLT is relevant to a wide variety of problems. I also want to provide both novice and intermediate users of XSLT a one-stop shopping place for some of the most commonly requested XSLT techniques. Finally, I want to push the envelope of what one can do with XSLT so current users can go even further and the unconvinced can join the fold of highly productive XML transformers.

Over the years, I have heard many sweeping statements about computer science. Opinions like, "All computation is simply fancy bit manipulation," "Computers are really just sophisticated number crunchers," or "Everything a computer does can be understood in terms of symbol manipulation" are true to some extent. However, I would like to make a sweeping generalization of my own: "Every problem we solve with software can be understood in terms of transformations." Mastery of computer science is mastery of transformation. Transformation is what CPUs do, it is what algorithms do, and it is what software developers do. And transformation is what XSLT does, at least when the input is XML (and sometimes when it is not). Of course, XSLT is not the only transformational game in town, and as with the thousands of languages that came before it, it is unclear whether it will evolve as an independent language or be absorbed into the next "big thing." What is clear is that the ideas behind XSLT will not go away because many of these ideas are as old as computer science itself. This book helps the reader master and apply these ideas to specific problems.

Structure of This Book

One of transformation's most primitive forms is the transformation of character sequences otherwise known as strings. Unlike the ancient language SNOBOL or the relatively modern Perl, XSLT was not specifically designed with string manipulation in mind. However, Chapter 1, *Strings*, shows that almost anything one wants to do with strings can be done within the confines of XSLT.

Numerical transformation (commonly referred to as mathematics) is another crucial form of low-level transformation that pervades all software development simply because measurement and counting pervades life itself. Chapter 2, *Numbers and Math*, shows how to push the limits of XSLT's mathematical capabilities even though XSLT was not designed to be the next great Fortran replacement.

Manipulating dates and times is a quintessentially human activity and a large part of our technological progress has been driven by an obsession with clocks, calendars, and accurate forecasting. Chapter 3, *Dates and Times*, contains date and time recipes that augment an area standard XSLT currently lacks. This chapter does not cover XSLT per se. However, it presents fascinating and difficult problems arising in date conversion and transformation, ready-made XSLT solutions, and important links to external date- and calendar-related resources.

All transformations begin by identifying the target you want to transform. If that target is a compound object, you need to traverse the objects constituent parts as the transformation proceeds. Chapter 4, *Selecting and Traversing*, covers these topics and explores the problems XSLT was specifically designed to solve. This chapter describes XML as a tree and shows how XSLT can manipulate such trees. It also provides pointers for getting the best performance out of XML processing tasks.

Before there were word processors, HTML, PDF, or other forms of sophisticated textual presentation, there was plain old text. The problem of transforming data used for computer consumption to data organized for human consumption is important. When the source data is XML, then the problem is perfect for XSLT. Chapter 5, *XML to Text*, provides recipes that control how text extracted from XML is rendered for layout on the terminal, on the text editor, or for import to programs that require delimited data, such as comma-separated values.

XML is quickly becoming the universal syntax for information transfer, and there is every indication that this trend will accelerate rather than abate. Therefore, a vast amount of XML transformation has XML as the destination as well as the source. Chapter 6, *XML to XML*, covers these types of transformations. It shows how XML documents can be split, merged, flattened, cleaned up, and otherwise reorganized with relatively little XSLT code.

Much of transformation simply extracts information from raw data to answer questions. Chapter 7, *Querying XML*, presents a treasure trove of recipes that demonstrate XSLT as a query language. It provides solutions to a wide variety of query-use cases that will probably resemble queries you'll need to ask of your own XML data.

HTML is an important target of XSLT transformation. Chapter 8, *XML to HTML*, demonstrates solutions to problems that arise when generating web content, including links, tables, frames, forms, and other client-side transformation issues.

Graphics programming transforms data to the visual domain. You would not think of XSLT as a graphics programming language, and it is not. However, when Scalable Vector Graphics (SVG) is the target of the transformation, XSLT can achieve impressive results. Chapter 9, *XML to SVG*, describes the transformation of raw data into bar charts, pie charts, line plots, and other graphical components. It also covers the transformation of XML to a hierarchical tree diagram. This chapter emphasizes how transformations are structures that can be mixed and matched to create many different outputs.

Generating code is an automation task that I have always been interested in. Of all the transformations, humans still do this one best (lucky for us who make a living at it). However, sometimes it is better to write a program that generates code rather write the code ourselves. Chapter 10, *Code Generation*, shows the advantage gained from representing the data that drives code generation in XML and illustrates how XSLT is ideal for writing code generators for C++, Java, and XSLT itself. The chapter also includes a code-generation recipe taken from a design pattern represented in UML via XMI.

XSLT can enable some sophisticated applications. Chapter 11, *Vertical XSLT Application Recipes*, includes some advanced uses of XSLT. The chapter is an eclectic mix that includes Visio VDX to SVG conversion, Microsoft Excel XML transformation, topic maps, and WSDL processing.

Although XSLT is powerful in its own right, we can really do some wicked things with extensions or by embedding it in programs written in other languages. Chapter 12, *Extending and Embedding XSLT*, provides extensive coverage of XSLT extensibility using Java and JavaScript. It also shows how XSLT can be used within Perl and Java programs.

Testing and debugging are essential to any software development effort, and XSLT development is no exception. Chapter 13, *Testing and Debugging*, demonstrates useful techniques that can help you transform misbehaved XSLT programs into functional ones even if you don't have a native XSLT debugger handy.

Chapter 14, *Generic and Functional Programming*, pushes the XSLT envelope to show how XSLT is far more than just another styling language. This chapter focuses on using XSLT as a generic and functional programming language. If nothing else, this chapter will open your eyes and stimulate your thoughts on the power of XSLT and how it can be used to create generic solutions.

Conventions Used in This Book

The following font conventions are used in this book:

Italic is used for:

- Pathnames, filenames, and program names
- Internet addresses, such as domain names and URLs
- New items where they are defined

`Constant width` is used for:

- Command lines and options that should be typed verbatim
- Names and keywords in programs, including method names, variable names, and class names
- XML element tags

`Constant-width bold` is used for emphasis in program code line.

`Constant-width italic` is used for replaceable arguments within program code.

 This icon designates a note relating to the surrounding text.

 This icon designates a warning related to the surrounding text.

How to Contact Us

Please address comments and questions concerning this book to:

O'Reilly & Associates, Inc.
1005 Gravenstein Highway North
Sebastopol, CA 95472
(800) 998-9938 (in the United States or Canada)
(707) 829-0515 (international or local)
(707) 829-0104 (fax)

There is a web page for this book, which lists errata, examples, or any additional information. You can access this page at:

http://www.oreilly.com/catalog/xsltckbk

To comment or ask technical questions about this book, send email to:

bookquestions@oreilly.com

For more information about books, conferences, Resource Centers, and the O'Reilly Network, see the O'Reilly web site at:

http://www.oreilly.com/

Acknowledgments

Writing a book has always been a dream of mine, and I am very pleased that O'Reilly was the publisher that helped me realize this dream. However, this was far from a solo effort. Many people helped me achieve this goal, and I would like to take some time to acknowledge their contributions.

First, I want to thank Simon St.Laurent, my editor at O'Reilly. Simon was with me every step of the way, from the initial hastily written email proposal through the final stages of production. Simon was always there to reassure me and share in the joy and frustration that is inevitable in any creative endeavor.

Second, I want to thank Jeni Tennison, my primary technical editor. Jeni's technical expertise and attention to detail are unparalleled. Not only did Jeni correct both my boneheaded and less-obvious mistakes, but she graciously contributed code and ideas to this book as she so generously does each day in the many XML-related mail groups she belongs to. (Any mistakes that remain are most definitely the fault of my own latent boneheadedness.) Jeni is truly unique, and I am sure the XML community will join me in thanking her for all her contributions and unselfish help.

Third, I would like to thank all my colleagues at Morgan Stanley for providing encouragement and praise for this work—especially my boss Farid Khalili for being understanding when I had to rush or stay home to make a deadline, and his boss John Reynolds for promoting my book to the entire Fixed Income Development department that he heads. I would also like to thank to my former client SIAC and especially Karen Halbert for allowing me to spearhead a project that first honed my XSLT skills.

Fourth, I would like to thank those who graciously contributed material to this book, including Steve Ball, John Breen, Jason Diamond, Nikita Ogievetsky, and Jeni Tennison. I also want to thank the later technical editors Micah Dubinko and Jirka Kosek, whose comments and suggestions were extremely helpful, as well as the O'Reilly production staff who helped bring this work to fruition.

Finally, I want to thank my parents, family, and friends. As always, you have sustained and nourished me and helped me keep a balanced life. Most of all, I want to thank my wife, Wanda, and son, Leonardo, without whose moral support and numerous sacrifices this book would have not been possible. Thank you Wanda for all the things you did that should have rightly been mine to do as I slaved in the dungeon! Thank you Leonardo for saying, "Daddy, you work" when I know you really wanted to say, "Daddy, we play!" Both of you and our child to be will always be my greatest success story.

CHAPTER 1

Strings

I believe everybody in the world should have guns.
Citizens should have bazookas and rocket launchers
too. I believe that all citizens should have their
weapons of choice. However, I also believe that only I
should have the ammunition. Because frankly, I
wouldn't trust the rest of the goobers with anything
more dangerous than [a] string.

—Scott Adams

When it comes to manipulating strings, XSLT certainly lacks the heavy artillery of Perl. XSLT is a language optimized for processing XML markup, not strings. However, since XML is simply a structured form of text, string processing is inevitable in all but the most trivial transformation problems. Unfortunately, XSLT has only nine standard functions for string processing. Java, on the other hand, has about two dozen, and Perl, the undisputed king of modern text-processing languages, has a couple dozen plus a highly advanced regular-expression engine.

XSLT programmers have two choices when they need to perform advanced string processing. First, they can call out to external functions written in Java or some other language supported by their XSLT processor. This choice is wise if portability is not an issue and fairly heavy-duty string manipulation is needed. Second, they can implement the advanced string-handling functionality directly in XSLT. This chapter shows that quite a bit of common string manipulation can be done within the confines of XSLT. Advanced string capabilities are implemented in XSLT by combining the capabilities of the native string functions and by exploiting the power of recursion, which is an integral part of all advanced uses of XSLT. In fact, recursion is such an important technique in XSLT that it is worthwhile to look through some of these recipes even if you have no intention of implementing your string-processing needs directly in XSLT.

This book also refers to the excellent work of EXSLT.org, a community initiative that helps standardize extensions to the XSLT language. You may want to check out their site at *http://www.exslt.org*.

1.1 Testing if a String Ends with Another String

Problem

You need to test if a string ends with a particular substring.

Solution

```
substring($value, (string-length($value) - string-length($substr)) + 1) = $substr
```

Discussion

XSLT contains a native starts-with( ) function but no ends-with( ). However, as the previous code shows, ends-with can be implemented easily in terms of substring( ) and string-length( ). The code simply extracts the last string-length($substr) characters from the target string and compares them to the substring.

 Programmers used to having the first position in a string start at index 0 should note that XSLT strings start at index 1.

1.2 Finding the Position of a Substring

Problem

You want to find the index of a substring within a string rather than the text before or after the substring.

Solution

```
<xsl:template name="index-of">
    <xsl:param name="input"/>
    <xsl:param name="substr"/>
<xsl:choose>
    <xsl:when test="contains($input, $substr)">
        <xsl:value-of select="string-length(substring-before($input, $substr))+1"/>
    </xsl:when>
    <xsl:otherwise>0</xsl:otherwise>
</xsl:choose>
</xsl:template>
```

Discussion

The position of a substring within another string is simply the length of the string preceding it plus 1. If you are certain that the target string contains the substring, then you can simply use string-length(substring-before($value, $substr))+1. However, in general, you need a way to handle the case in which the substring is not present. Here, zero is chosen as an indication of this case, but you can use another value such as -1 or NaN.

1.3   Removing Specific Characters from a String

Problem

You want to strip certain characters (e.g., whitespace) from a string.

Solution

Use translate with an empty replace string. For example, the following code can strip whitespace from a string:

```
translate($input," &#x9;&#xa;&xd;", "")
```

Discussion

translate( ) is a versatile string function that is often used to compensate for missing string-processing capabilities in XSLT. Here you use the fact that translate( ) will not copy characters in the input string that are in the from string but do not have a corresponding character in the to string.

You can also use translate to remove all but a specific set of characters from a string. For example, the following code removes all non-numeric characters from a string:

```
translate($string,
          translate($string,'0123456789',''),'')
```

The inner translate( ) removes all characters of interest (e.g., numbers) to obtain a from string for the outer translate( ), which removes these non-numeric characters from the original string.

Sometimes you do not want to remove all occurrences of whitespace, but instead want to remove leading, trailing, and redundant internal whitespace. XPath has a built-in function, normalize-space( ), which does just that. If you ever needed to normalize based on characters other than spaces, then you might use the following code (where C is the character you want to normalize):

```
translate(normalize-space(translate($input,"C "," C")),"C "," C")
```

However, this transformation won't work quite right if the input string contains whitespace characters other than spaces, i.e., tab (#x9), newline (#xA), and carriage return (#xD). The reason is that the code swaps space with the character to normalize and then normalizes the resulting spaces and swaps back. If nonspace whitespace remains after the first transformation, it will also be normalized, which might not be what you want. Then again, the applications of nonwhitespace normalizing are probably rare anyway. Here you use this technique to remove extra - characters.

```
<xsl:template match="/">
  <xsl:variable name="input"
        select=" '---this --is-- the way we normalize non-whitespace---' "/>
 <xsl:value-of
      select="translate(normalize-space(
                                translate($input,'- ',' -')),'- ',' -')"/>
</xsl:template>
```

The result is:

```
this -is- the way we normalize non-whitespace
```

1.4 Finding Substrings from the End of a String

Problem

XSLT does not have any functions for searching strings in reverse.

Solution

Using recursion, you can emulate a reverse search with a search for the last occurrence of substr. Using this technique, you can create a substring-before-last and a substring-after-last.

```
<xsl:template ="substring-before-last">
  <xsl:param name="input" />
  <xsl:param name="substr" />
  <xsl:if test="$substr and contains($input, $substr)">
    <xsl:variable name="temp" select="substring-after($input, $substr)" />
    <xsl:value-of select="substring-before($input, $substr)" />
    <xsl:if test="contains($temp, $substr)">
      <xsl:value-of select="$substr" />
      <xsl:call-template name="substring-before-last">
        <xsl:with-param name="input" select="$temp" />
        <xsl:with-param name="substr" select="$substr" />
      </xsl:call-template>
    </xsl:if>
  </xsl:if>
</xsl:template>

<xsl:template name="substring-after-last">
<xsl:param name="input"/>
<xsl:param name="substr"/>
```

```
<!-- Extract the string which comes after the first occurence -->
<xsl:variable name="temp" select="substring-after($input,$substr)"/>

<xsl:choose>
    <!-- If it still contains the search string the recursively process -->
    <xsl:when test="$substr and contains($temp,$substr)">
        <xsl:call-template name="substring-after-last">
            <xsl:with-param name="input" select="$temp"/>
            <xsl:with-param name="substr" select="$substr"/>
        </xsl:call-template>
    </xsl:when>
    <xsl:otherwise>
        <xsl:value-of select="$temp"/>
    </xsl:otherwise>
</xsl:choose>
</xsl:template>
```

Discussion

Both XSLT string-searching functions (`substring-before` and `substring-after`) begin searching at the start of the string. Sometimes you need to search a string from the end. The simplest way to do this in XSLT is to apply the built-in search functions recursively until the last instance of the substring is found.

 There was a nasty "gotcha" in my first attempt at these templates, which you should keep in mind when working with recursive templates that search strings. Recall that `contains($anything,'')` will always return true! For this reason, I make sure that I also test the existence of a non-null `$substr` value in the recursive invocations of `substring-before-last` and `substring-after-last`. Without these checks, the code will go into an infinite loop for null search input or overflow the stack on implementations that do not handle tail recursion.

Another algorithm is *divide and conquer*. The basic idea is to split the string in half. If the search string is in the second half, then you can discard the first half, thus turning the problem into a problem half as large. This process repeats recursively. The tricky part is when the search string is not in the second half because you may have split the search string between the two halves. Here is a solution for `substring-before-last`:

```
<xsl:template name="str:substring-before-last">

<xsl:param name="input"/>
<xsl:param name="substr"/>

<xsl:variable name="mid" select="ceiling(string-length($input) div 2)"/>
<xsl:variable name="temp1" select="substring($input,1, $mid)"/>
<xsl:variable name="temp2" select="substring($input,$mid +1)"/>
<xsl:choose>
```

```
  <xsl:when test="$temp2 and contains($temp2,$substr)">
    <!-- search string is in second half so just append first half -->
    <!-- and recuse on second -->
    <xsl:value-of select="$temp1"/>
    <xsl:call-template name="str:substring-before-last">
      <xsl:with-param name="input" select="$temp2"/>
      <xsl:with-param name="substr" select="$substr"/>
    </xsl:call-template>
  </xsl:when>
  <!--search string is in boundary so a simple  substring-before -->
  <!-- will do the trick-->
  <xsl:when test="contains(substring($input,
                            $mid - string-length($substr) +1),
                            $substr)">
    <xsl:value-of select="substring-before($input,$substr)"/>
  </xsl:when>
  <!--search string is in first half so through away second half-->
  <xsl:when test="contains($temp1,$substr)">
    <xsl:call-template name="str:substring-before-last">
    <xsl:with-param name="input" select="$temp1"/>
    <xsl:with-param name="substr" select="$substr"/>
    </xsl:call-template>
  </xsl:when>
  <!-- No occurances of search string so we are done -->
  <xsl:otherwise/>
  </xsl:choose>

</xsl:template>
```

As it turns out, divide and conquer is of little or no advantage unless you search large texts (roughly 4,000 characters). You might have a wrapper template that chooses the appropriate algorithm based on the length or switches from divide and conquer to the simpler algorithm when the subpart becomes small enough.

1.5 Duplicating a String N Times

Problem

You need to duplicate a string N times, where N is a parameter. For example, you might need to pad out a string with spaces to achieve alignment.

Solution

A nice solution is a recursive approach that doubles the input string until it is the required length while being careful to handle cases in which $count is odd:

```
<xsl:template name="dup">
    <xsl:param name="input"/>
    <xsl:param name="count" select="1"/>
    <xsl:choose>
        <xsl:when test="not($count) or not($input)"/>
        <xsl:when test="$count = 1">
```

```
                <xsl:value-of select="$input"/>
            </xsl:when>
            <xsl:otherwise>
                <!-- If $count is odd append an extra copy of input -->
                <xsl:if test="$count mod 2">
                    <xsl:value-of select="$input"/>
                </xsl:if>
                <!-- Recursively apply template after doubling input and
                halving count -->
                <xsl:call-template name="dup">
                    <xsl:with-param name="input"
                        select="concat($input,$input)"/>
                    <xsl:with-param name="count"
                        select="floor($count div 2)"/>
                </xsl:call-template>
            </xsl:otherwise>
        </xsl:choose>
    </xsl:template>
```

Discussion

The most obvious way to duplicate a string $count times is to figure out a way to
concatenate the string to itself $count-1 times. This can be done recursively by the
following code, but this code will be expensive unless $count is small, so it is not rec-
ommended:

```
<xsl:template name="slow-dup">
    <xsl:param name="input"/>
    <xsl:param name="count" select="1"/>
    <xsl:param name="work" select="$input"/>
    <xsl:choose>
        <xsl:when test="not($count) or not($input)"/>
        <xsl:when test="$count=1">
            <xsl:value-of select="$work"/>
        </xsl:when>
        <xsl:otherwise>
            <xsl:call-template name="slow-dup">
                <xsl:with-param name="input" select="$input"/>
                <xsl:with-param name="count" select="$count - 1"/>
                <xsl:with-param name="work"
                    select="concat($work,$input)"/>
            </xsl:call-template>
        </xsl:otherwise>
    </xsl:choose>
</xsl:template>
```

A better approach is shown in the "Solution" section. The solution limits the number
of recursive calls and concatenation to the order of log2($count) by repeatedly dou-
bling the input and halving the count as long as count is greater than 1. The slow-dup
implementation is awkward since it requires an artificial work parameter to keep track
of the original input. It may also result in stack growth due to recursion of $count-1
and requires $count-1 calls to concat( ). Contrast this to dup that limits stack growth
to floor(log2($count)) and requires only ceiling(log2($count)) calls to concat( ).

The slow-dup technique has the redeeming quality of also being used to duplicate structure in addition to strings if we replace xsl:value-of with xsl:copy-of. The faster dup has no advantage in this case because the copies are passed around as parameters, which is expensive.

Another solution based on, but not identical to, code from EXSLT str:padding is the following:

```
<xsl:template name="dup">
  <xsl:param name="input"/>
  <xsl:param name="count" select="1"/>
  <xsl:choose>
    <xsl:when test="not($count) or not($input)" />
    <xsl:otherwise>
      <xsl:variable name="string"
                    select="concat($input, $input, $input, $input,
                                   $input, $input, $input, $input,
                                   $input, $input)"/>
      <xsl:choose>
        <xsl:when test="string-length($string) >=
                        $count * string-length($input)">
          <xsl:value-of select="substring($string, 1,
                                $count * string-length($input))" />
        </xsl:when>
        <xsl:otherwise>
          <xsl:call-template name="dup">
            <xsl:with-param name="input" select="$string" />
            <xsl:with-param name="count" select="$count div 10" />
          </xsl:call-template>
        </xsl:otherwise>
      </xsl:choose>
    </xsl:otherwise>
  </xsl:choose>
</xsl:template>
```

This implementation makes ten copies of the input. If this approach accomplishes more than is required, it trims the result to the required size. Otherwise, it applies the template recursively. This solution is slower because it will often do more concatenations than necessary and it uses substring( ), which may be slow on some XSLT implementations. See Recipe 1.7 for an explanation. It does have an advantage for processors that do not optimize tail recursion since it reduces the number of recursive calls significantly.

See Also

The so-called *Piez Method* can also duplicate a string without recursion. This method is discussed at *http://www.xml.org/xml/ xslt_efficient_programming_techniques.pdf*. It uses a for-each loop on any available source of nodes (often the stylesheet itself). Although this method can be highly effective in practice, I find it deficient because it assumes that enough nodes will be available to satisfy the required iteration.

1.6   Reversing a String

Problem

You need to reverse the characters of a string.

Solution

This template reverses $input in a subtle yet effective way:

```
<xsl:template name="reverse">
    <xsl:param name="input"/>
    <xsl:variable name="len" select="string-length($input)"/>
    <xsl:choose>
        <!-- Strings of length less than 2 are trivial to reverse -->
        <xsl:when test="$len &lt; 2">
            <xsl:value-of select="$input"/>
        </xsl:when>
        <!-- Strings of length 2 are also trivial to reverse -->
        <xsl:when test="$len = 2">
            <xsl:value-of select="substring($input,2,1)"/>
            <xsl:value-of select="substring($input,1,1)"/>
        </xsl:when>
        <xsl:otherwise>
            <!-- Swap the recursive application if this template to
            the first half and second half of input -->
            <xsl:variable name="mid" select="floor($len div 2)"/>
            <xsl:call-template name="reverse">
                <xsl:with-param name="input"
                    select="substring($input,$mid+1,$mid+1)"/>
            </xsl:call-template>
            <xsl:call-template name="reverse">
                <xsl:with-param name="input"
                    select="substring($input,1,$mid)"/>
            </xsl:call-template>
        </xsl:otherwise>
    </xsl:choose>
</xsl:template>
```

Discussion

The algorithm shown in the solution is not the most obvious, but it is efficient. In fact, this algorithm successfully reverses even very large strings, whereas other more obvious algorithms either take too long or fail with a stack overflow. The basic idea behind this algorithm is to swap the first half of the string with the second half and to keep applying the algorithm to these halves recursively until you are left with strings of length two or less, at which point the reverse operation is trivial. The following example illustrates how this algorithm works. At each step, I placed a + where the string was split and concatenated.

1. reverse("abcdef") (input)
2. reverse(def)+reverse("abc")
3. reverse("ef") + "d" + reverse("bc") + "a"
4. "f" + "e" + "d" + "c" + "b" + "a"
5. fedcba (result)

Considering more obvious XSLT implementations of reverse is instructive because they provide lessons in how and how not to implement recursive solutions in other contexts.

One of the worst algorithms is probably the one that many would think of on their first try. The idea is to swap the first and last character of the string, continue to the second and next to last, and so on until you reach the middle, at which point you are done. A C programmer might come up with this solution, since it is a perfectly efficient iterative solution in a language like C in which you can read and write individual characters of the string randomly and iteration rather than recursion is the norm. However, in XSLT you must implement this algorithm, shown in Example 1-1, in a recursive fashion, and you do not have the luxury of manipulating variables in place.

Example 1-1. A very poor implementation of reverse

```
<xsl:template name="reverse">
    <xsl:param name="input"/>
    <xsl:variable name="len" select="string-length($input)"/>
    <xsl:choose>
        <!-- Strings of length less than 2 are trivial to reverse -->
        <xsl:when test="$len &lt; 2">
            <xsl:value-of select="$input"/>
        </xsl:when>
        <!-- Strings of length 2 are also trivial to reverse -->
        <xsl:when test="$len = 2">
            <xsl:value-of select="substring($input,2,1)"/>
            <xsl:value-of select="substring($input,1,1)"/>
        </xsl:when>
        <xsl:otherwise>
            <!-- Concatenate the last + reverse(middle) + first -->
            <xsl:value-of select="substring($input,$len,1)"/>
            <xsl:call-template name="reverse">
                <xsl:with-param name="input"
                    select="substring($input,2,$len - 2)"/>
            </xsl:call-template>
            <xsl:value-of select="substring($input,1,1)"/>
        </xsl:otherwise>
    </xsl:choose>
</xsl:template>
```

A major problem with this solution makes it useless for all but very short strings. The problem is that the solution is not tail recursive (see the "Tail Recursion" sidebar for an explanation of tail recursion). Many XSLT processors (such as Saxon) optimize for tail recursion, so you are advised to structure your code to benefit from this significant optimization. Example 1-2 makes this version of reverse tail recursive by moving only the last character in the string to the front on each recursive call. This puts the recursive call at the end and thus subject to the optimization.

Example 1-2. An inefficient tail recursive implementation

```
<xsl:template name="reverse">
    <xsl:param name="input"/>
    <xsl:variable name="len" select="string-length($input)"/>
    <xsl:choose>
        <!-- Strings of length less than 2 are trivial to reverse -->
        <xsl:when test="$len &lt; 2">
            <xsl:value-of select="$input"/>
        </xsl:when>
        <!-- Strings of length 2 are also trivial to reverse -->
        <xsl:when test="$len = 2">
            <xsl:value-of select="substring($input,2,1)"/>
            <xsl:value-of select="substring($input,1,1)"/>
        </xsl:when>
        <!-- Concatenate the last + reverse(rest) -->
        <xsl:otherwise>
            <xsl:value-of select="substring($input,$len,1)"/>
            <xsl:call-template name="reverse">
                <xsl:with-param name="input" select="substring($input,1,$len - 1)"/>
            </xsl:call-template>
        </xsl:otherwise>
    </xsl:choose>
</xsl:template>
```

This change prevents reverse from overflowing the stack, but it is still inefficient for large strings. First, notice that each step results in the movement of only a single character. Second, each recursive call must process a string that is just one character shorter than the current string. For very large strings, this call will potentially overstress the memory management subsystem of the XSLT implementation. In editing this recipe, Jeni Tennison pointed out that another method of making the version tail recursive would pass the remaining (reverse) string and $len as a parameter to the template. This, in general, is a good strategy for achieving tail recursion. In this particular case, it improved matters but did not do as well as the solution.

An important goal in all recursive implantations is to try to structure the algorithm so that each recursive call sets up a subproblem that is at least half as large as the current problem. This setup causes the recursion to "bottom out" more quickly. Following this advice results in the solution to reverse, shown in Example 1-3.

Example 1-3. An efficient (but not ideal) implementation

```
<xsl:template name="reverse">
    <xsl:param name="input"/>

    <xsl:variable name="len" select="string-length($input)"/>
    <xsl:choose>
        <xsl:when test="$len &lt; 2">
            <xsl:value-of select="$input"/>
        </xsl:when>
        <xsl:otherwise>
            <xsl:variable name="mid" select="floor($len div 2)"/>
            <xsl:call-template name="reverse">
                <xsl:with-param name="input"
                    select="substring($input,$mid+1,$mid+1)"/>
            </xsl:call-template>
            <xsl:call-template name="reverse">
                <xsl:with-param name="input"
                    select="substring($input,1,$mid)"/>
            </xsl:call-template>
        </xsl:otherwise>
    </xsl:choose>
</xsl:template>
```

This solution is the first one I came up with, and it works well even on large strings (1,000 characters or more). It has the added benefit of being shorter than the implementation shown in the "Solution" section. The only difference is that this implementation considers only strings of length zero or one as trivial. The slightly faster implementation cuts the number of recursive calls in half by also trivially dealing with strings of length two.

All the implementations shown here actually perform the same number of concatenations, and I do not believe there is any way around this without leaving the confines of XSLT. However, my testing shows that on a string of length 1,000, the best solution is approximately 5 times faster than the worst. The best and second-best solutions differ by only a factor of 1.3.

Tail Recursion

A recursive call is *tail recursive* if, when the call returns, the returned value is immediately returned from the fuction. The term "tail" is attributed to the recursive call, which comes at the end. Tail recursion is important because it can be implemented more efficiently than general recursion. A general recursive call must establish a new stack frame to store local variables and other bookkeeping items. Thus a general recursive implementation can quickly exhaust the stack space on large inputs. However, tail-recursive implementations can be transformed internally into iterative solutions by an XSLT processor capable of recognizing tail recursion.

1.7   Replacing Text

Problem

You want to replace all occurrences of a substring within a target string with another string.

Solution

The following recursive template replaces all occurrences of a search string with a replacement string.

```
<xsl:template name="search-and-replace">
    <xsl:param name="input"/>
    <xsl:param name="search-string"/>
    <xsl:param name="replace-string"/>
    <xsl:choose>
        <!-- See if the input contains the search string -->
        <xsl:when test="$search-string and
                        contains($input,$search-string)">
        <!-- If so, then concatenate the substring before the search
        string to the replacement string and to the result of
        recursively applying this template to the remaining substring.
        -->
            <xsl:value-of
                select="substring-before($input,$search-string)"/>
            <xsl:value-of select="$replace-string"/>
            <xsl:call-template name="search-and-replace">
                <xsl:with-param name="input"
                select="substring-after($input,$search-string)"/>
                <xsl:with-param name="search-string"
                select="$search-string"/>
                <xsl:with-param name="replace-string"
                    select="$replace-string"/>
            </xsl:call-template>
        </xsl:when>
        <xsl:otherwise>
            <!-- There are no more occurences of the search string so
            just return the current input string -->
            <xsl:value-of select="$input"/>
        </xsl:otherwise>
    </xsl:choose>
</xsl:template>
```

If you want to replace only whole words, then you must ensure that the characters immediately before and after the search string are in the class of characters considered word delimiters. We chose the characters in the variable $punc plus whitespace to be word delimiters:

```
<xsl:template name="search-and-replace-whole-words-only">
  <xsl:param name="input"/>
  <xsl:param name="search-string"/>
  <xsl:param name="replace-string"/>
  <xsl:variable name="punc"
    select="concat('.,;:()[]!?$@&amp;&quot;',&quot;&apos;&quot;)"/>
    <xsl:choose>
      <!-- See if the input contains the search string -->
      <xsl:when test="contains($input,$search-string)">
      <!-- If so, then test that the before and after characters are word
      delimiters. -->
        <xsl:variable name="before"
         select="substring-before($input,$search-string)"/>
        <xsl:variable name="before-char"
         select="substring(concat(' ',$before),string-length($before) +1, 1)"/>
        <xsl:variable name="after"
         select="substring-after($input,$search-string)"/>
        <xsl:variable name="after-char"
         select="substring($after,1,1)"/>
        <xsl:value-of select="$before"/>
        <xsl:choose>
        <xsl:when test="(not(normalize-space($before-char)) or
                   contains($punc,$before-char)) and
               (not(normalize-space($after-char)) or
                   contains($punc,$after-char))">
          <xsl:value-of select="$replace-string"/>
        </xsl:when>
        <xsl:otherwise>
          <xsl:value-of select="$search-string"/>
        </xsl:otherwise>
        </xsl:choose>
        <xsl:call-template name="search-and-replace-whole-words-only">
         <xsl:with-param name="input" select="$after"/>
         <xsl:with-param name="search-string" select="$search-string"/>
         <xsl:with-param name="replace-string" select="$replace-string"/>
        </xsl:call-template>
      </xsl:when>
    <xsl:otherwise>
      <!-- There are no more occurences of the search string so
         just return the current input string -->
      <xsl:value-of select="$input"/>
    </xsl:otherwise>
    </xsl:choose>
  </xsl:template>
</xsl:template>
```

Notice how we construct $punc using concat( ) so it contains both single and double quotes. It would be impossible to do this in any other way because XPath and XSLT, unlike C, do not allow special characters to be escaped with a backslash (\). XPath 2.0 will allow the quotes to be escaped by doubling them up.

Discussion

Searching and replacing is a common text-processing task. The solution shown here is the most straightforward implementation of search and replace written purely in terms of XSLT. When considering the performance of this solution, the reader might think it is inefficient. For each occurrence of the search string, the code will call `contains( )`, `substring-before( )`, and `substring-after( )`. Presumably, each function will rescan the input string for the search string. It seems like this approach will perform two more searches than necessary. After some thought, you might come up with one of the following, seemingly more efficient, solutions shown in Examples 1-4 and 1-5.

Example 1-4. Using a temp string in a failed attempt to improve search and replace

```
<xsl:template name="search-and-replace">
    <xsl:param name="input"/>
    <xsl:param name="search-string"/>
    <xsl:param name="replace-string"/>
    <!-- Find the substring before the search string and store it in a
    variable -->
    <xsl:variable name="temp"
        select="substring-before($input,$search-string)"/>
    <xsl:choose>
        <!-- If $temp is not empty or the input starts with the search
        string then we know we have to do a replace. This eliminates the
        need to use contains( ). -->
        <xsl:when test="$temp or starts-with($input,$search-string)">
            <xsl:value-of select="concat($temp,$replace-string)"/>
            <xsl:call-template name="search-and-replace">
                <!-- We eliminate the need to call substring-after
                by using the length of temp and the search string
                to extract the remaining string in the recursive
                call. -->
                <xsl:with-param name="input"
                select="substring($input,string-length($temp)+
                    string-length($search-string)+1)"/>
                <xsl:with-param name="search-string"
                    select="$search-string"/>
                <xsl:with-param name="replace-string"
                    select="$replace-string"/>
            </xsl:call-template>
        </xsl:when>
        <xsl:otherwise>
            <xsl:value-of select="$input"/>
        </xsl:otherwise>
    </xsl:choose>
</xsl:template>
```

Example 1-5. Using a temp integer in a failed attempt to improve search and replace

```
<xsl:template name="search-and-replace">
    <xsl:param name="input"/>
    <xsl:param name="search-string"/>
    <xsl:param name="replace-string"/>
    <!-- Find the length of the sub-string before the search string and
    store it in a      variable -->
    <xsl:variable name="temp"
    select="string-length(substring-before($input,$search-string))"/>
    <xsl:choose>
    <!-- If $temp is not 0 or the input starts with the search
    string then we know we have to do a replace. This eliminates the
    need to use contains(). -->
        <xsl:when test="$temp or starts-with($input,$search-string)">
            <xsl:value-of select="substring($input,1,$temp)"/>
            <xsl:value-of select="$replace-string"/>
                <!-- We eliminate the need to call substring-after
                by using  temp and the length of the search string
                to extract the remaining string in the recursive
                call. -->
            <xsl:call-template name="search-and-replace">
                <xsl:with-param name="input"
                    select="substring($input,$temp +
                        string-length($search-string)+1)"/>
                <xsl:with-param name="search-string"
                    select="$search-string"/>
                <xsl:with-param name="replace-string"
                    select="$replace-string"/>
            </xsl:call-template>
        </xsl:when>
        <xsl:otherwise>
            <xsl:value-of select="$input"/>
        </xsl:otherwise>
    </xsl:choose>
</xsl:template>
```

The idea behind both attempts is that if you remember the spot where substring-before() finds a match, then you can use this information to eliminate the need to call contains() and substring-after(). You are forced to introduce a call to starts-with() to disambiguate the case in which substring-before() returns the empty string; this can happen when the search string is absent or when the input string starts with the search string. However, starts-with() is presumably faster than contains() because it doesn't need to scan past the length of the search string. The idea that distinguishes the second attempt from the first is the thought that storing an integer offset might be more efficient than storing the entire substring.

Alas, these supposed optimizations fail to produce any improvement when using the Xalan XSLT implementation and actually produce timing results that are an *order of magnitude* slower on some inputs when using either Saxon or XT! My first hypothesis regarding this unintuitive result was that the use of the variable $temp in the recursive call interfered with Saxon's tail-recursion optimization (see Recipe 1.6).

However, by experimenting with large inputs that have many matches, I failed to cause a stack overflow. My next suspicion was that for some reason, XSLT substring( ) is actually slower than the substring-before( ) and substring-after( ) calls. Michael Kay, the author of Saxon, indicated that Saxon's implementation of substring( ) was slow due to the complicated rules that XSLT substring must implement, including floating-point rounding of arguments, handling special cases where the start or end point are outside the bounds of the string, and issues involving Unicode surrogate pairs. In contrast, substring-before( ) and substring-after( ) translate more directly into Java.

The real lesson here is that optimization is tricky business, especially in XSLT where there can be a wide disparity between implementations and where new versions continually apply new optimizations. Unless you are prepared to profile frequently, it is best to stick with simple solutions. An added advantage of obvious solutions is that they are likely to behave consistently across different XSLT implementations.

1.8 Converting Case

Problem

You want to convert an uppercase string to lowercase or vice versa.

Solution

Use the XSLT translate( ) function. This code, for example, converts from upper- to lowercase:

```
translate($input,'ABCDEFGHIJKLMNOPQRSTUVWXYZ','abcdefghijklmnopqrstuvwxyz')
```

This example converts from lower- to uppercase:

```
translate($input, 'abcdefghijklmnopqrstuvwxyz','ABCDEFGHIJKLMNOPQRSTUVWXYZ')
```

Discussion

This recipe is, of course, trivial. However, I include it as an opportunity to discuss the solution's shortcomings. Case conversion is trivial as long as your text is restricted to a single locale. In English, you rarely, if ever, need to deal with special characters containing accents or other complicated case conversions in which a single character must convert to two characters. The most common example is German, in which the lowercase "ß" is converted to an uppercase "SS". Many modern programming languages provide case-conversion functions that are sensitive to locale, but XSLT does not support this concept directly. This is unfortunate, considering that XSLT has other features supporting internationalization.

A slight improvement can be made by defining general XML entities for each type conversion, as shown in the following example:

```
<?xml version="1.0" encoding="UTF-8"?>
<!DOCTYPE stylesheet [
      <!ENTITY UPPERCASE "ABCDEFGHIJKLMNOPQRSTUVWXYZ">
      <!ENTITY LOWERCASE "abcdefghijklmnopqrstuvwxyz">
      <!ENTITY UPPER_TO_LOWER " '&UPPERCASE;' , '&LOWERCASE;' ">
      <!ENTITY LOWER_TO_UPPER " '&LOWERCASE;' , '&UPPERCASE;' ">
]>
<xsl:stylesheet version="1.0" xmlns:xsl="http://www.w3.org/1999/XSL/Transform">
      <xsl:output method="xml" version="1.0" encoding="UTF-8" indent="yes"/>

      <xsl:template match="/">
      <xsl:variable name="test"
            select=" 'The rain in Spain falls mainly in the plain' "/>
      <output>
            <lowercase>
                  <xsl:value-of
                        select="translate($test,&UPPER_TO_LOWER;)"/>
            </lowercase>
            <uppercase>
                  <xsl:value-of
                        select="translate($test,&LOWER_TO_UPPER;)"/>
            </uppercase>
      </output>
      </xsl:template>

</xsl:stylesheet>
```

These entity definitions accomplish three things. First, they make it easier to port the stylesheet to another locale because only the definition of the entities UPPERCASE and LOWERCASE need be changed. Second, they compact the code by eliminating the need to list all letters of the alphabet twice. Third, they make the intent of the translate call obvious to someone inspecting the code. Some purists might object to the macro-izing away of translate( )'s third parameter, but I like the way it makes the code read. If you prefer to err on the pure side, then use translate($test, &UPPERCASE;, &LOWERCASE;).

I have not seen entities used very often in other XSLT books; however, I believe the technique has merit. In fact, one benefit of XSLT being written in XML syntax is that you can exploit all features of XML, and entity definition is certainly a useful one. If you intend to use this technique and plan to write more than a few stylesheets, then consider placing common entity definitions in an external file and include them as shown in Example 1-6.

Example 1-6. Standard.ent

```
<!ENTITY UPPERCASE "ABCDEFGHIJKLMNOPQRSTUVWXYZ">
<!ENTITY LOWERCASE "abcdefghijklmnopqrstuvwxyz">
<!ENTITY UPPER_TO_LOWER " '&UPPERCASE;' , '&LOWERCASE;' ">
<!ENTITY LOWER_TO_UPPER " '&LOWERCASE;' , '&UPPERCASE;' ">
<!-- others... -->
```

Then use a parameter entity defined in terms of the external *standard.ent* file, as shown in Example 1-7.

Example 1-7. A stylesheet using standard.ent

```
<?xml version="1.0" encoding="UTF-8"?>
<!DOCTYPE stylesheet [
    <!ENTITY % standard SYSTEM "standard.ent">
    %standard;
]>
<xsl:stylesheet version="1.0"
<!-- ... -->
</xsl:stylesheet>
```

Steve Ball's implementation of case conversion works in virutally all cases by including all the most common Unicode characters in the upper- and lowercase strings and taking special care to handle the German ß ("eszett") correctly.

See Also

Steve Ball's solution is available in the "Standard XSLT Library" at *http://xsltsl. sourceforge.net/*.

1.9   Tokenizing a String

Problem

You want to break a string into a list of tokens based on the occurrence of one or more delimiter characters.

Solution

Jeni Tennison implemented this solution (but the comments are my doing). The tokenizer returns each token as a node consisting of a <token> element text. It also defaults to character-level tokenization if the delimiter string is empty.

```
<xsl:template name="tokenize">
    <xsl:param name="string" select="''" />
  <xsl:param name="delimiters" select="' &#x9;&#xA;'" />
  <xsl:choose>
    <!-- Nothing to do if empty string -->
    <xsl:when test="not($string)" />

    <!-- No delimiters signals character level tokenization. -->
    <xsl:when test="not($delimiters)">
      <xsl:call-template name="_tokenize-characters">
        <xsl:with-param name="string" select="$string" />
      </xsl:call-template>
    </xsl:when>
```

```
        <xsl:otherwise>
          <xsl:call-template name="_tokenize-delimiters">
            <xsl:with-param name="string" select="$string" />
            <xsl:with-param name="delimiters" select="$delimiters" />
          </xsl:call-template>
        </xsl:otherwise>
      </xsl:choose>
  </xsl:template>

<xsl:template name="_tokenize-characters">
  <xsl:param name="string" />
  <xsl:if test="$string">
    <token><xsl:value-of select="substring($string, 1, 1)" /></token>
    <xsl:call-template name="_tokenize-characters">
      <xsl:with-param name="string" select="substring($string, 2)" />
    </xsl:call-template>
  </xsl:if>
</xsl:template>

<xsl:template name="_tokenize-delimiters">
  <xsl:param name="string" />
  <xsl:param name="delimiters" />
  <xsl:param name="last-delimit"/>
  <!-- Extract a delimiter -->
  <xsl:variable name="delimiter" select="substring($delimiters, 1, 1)" />
  <xsl:choose>
      <!-- If the delimiter is empty we have a token -->
    <xsl:when test="not($delimiter)">
      <token><xsl:value-of select="$string"/></token>
    </xsl:when>
      <!-- If the string contains at least one delimiter we must split it -->
    <xsl:when test="contains($string, $delimiter)">
        <!-- If it starts with the delimiter we don't need to handle the -->
        <!-- before part -->
        <xsl:if test="not(starts-with($string, $delimiter))">
            <!-- Handle the part that comes befor the current delimiter -->
            <!-- with the next delimiter. If ther is no next the first test -->
            <!-- in this template will detect the token -->
            <xsl:call-template name="_tokenize-delimiters">
              <xsl:with-param name="string"
                             select="substring-before($string, $delimiter)" />
              <xsl:with-param name="delimiters"
                             select="substring($delimiters, 2)" />
            </xsl:call-template>
        </xsl:if>
        <!-- Handle the part that comes after the delimiter using the -->
        <!-- current delimiter -->
        <xsl:call-template name="_tokenize-delimiters">
          <xsl:with-param name="string"
                         select="substring-after($string, $delimiter)" />
          <xsl:with-param name="delimiters" select="$delimiters" />
        </xsl:call-template>
    </xsl:when>
```

```
      <xsl:otherwise>
        <!-- No occurances of current delimiter so move on to next -->
        <xsl:call-template name="_tokenize-delimiters">
          <xsl:with-param name="string"
                          select="$string" />
          <xsl:with-param name="delimiters"
                          select="substring($delimiters, 2)" />
        </xsl:call-template>
      </xsl:otherwise>
    </xsl:choose>
  </xsl:template>

</xsl:stylesheet>
```

Discussion

Tokenization is a common string-processing task. In languages with powerful regular-expression engines, tokenization is trivial. In this area, languages such as Perl, Python, JavaScript, and Tcl currently outshine XSLT. However, this recipe shows that XSLT can deal with tokenization if you must stay within the bounds of pure XSLT. If you are willing to use extensions, then you can defer to another language for low-level string manipulations such as tokenization.

If you use the XSLT approach and your processor does not optimize for tail-recursion, then you may want to use a divide-and-conquer algorithm for character tokenization:

```
<xsl:template name="_tokenize-characters">
  <xsl:param name="string" />
  <xsl:param name="len" select="string-length($string)"/>
  <xsl:choose>
      <xsl:when test="$len = 1">
      <token><xsl:value-of select="$string"/></token>
      </xsl:when>
      <xsl:otherwise>
      <xsl:call-template name="_tokenize-characters">
        <xsl:with-param name="string"
                        select="substring($string, 1, floor($len div 2))" />
        <xsl:with-param name="len" select="floor($len div 2)"/>
      </xsl:call-template>
      <xsl:call-template name="_tokenize-characters">
        <xsl:with-param name="string"
                        select="substring($string, floor($len div 2) + 1)" />
        <xsl:with-param name="len" select="ceiling($len div 2)"/>
      </xsl:call-template>
      </xsl:otherwise>
    </xsl:choose>
</xsl:template>
```

See Also

Chapter 12 shows how to access the RegEx facility in JavaScript if your XSLT processor allows JavaScript-based extensions. Java also has a built-in tokenizer (`java.util.StringTokenizer`).

1.10 Making Do Without Regular Expressions

Problem

You would like to perform regular-expression-like operations but you don't want to resort to nonstandard extensions.

Solution

Several common regular-expression-like matches can be emulated in native XSLT. Table 1-1 lists the regular-expression matches by using Perl syntax along with their XSLT/XPath equivalent. The single character "C" is a proxy for any user-specified single character, and the string "abc" is a proxy for any user supplied-string of non-zero length.

Table 1-1. Regular-expression matches

`$string =~ /^C*$/`	`translate($string,'C','') = ''`
`$string =~ /^C+$/`	`$string and translate($string,'C', '') = ''`
`$string =~ /C+/`	`contains($string,'C')`
`$string =~ /C{2,4}/`	`contains($string,'CC') and not(contains($string,'CCCCC'))`
`$string =~ /^abc/`	`starts-with($string,'abc')`
`$string =~ /abc$/`	`substring($string, string-length($string) - string-length('abc') + 1) = 'abc'`
`$string =~ /abc/`	`contains($string,'abc')`
`$string =~ /^[^C]*$/`	`translate($string,'C','') = $string`
`$string =~ /^\s$/`	`not(normalize-space($string))`
`$string =~ /\s/`	`translate(normalize-space($string),' ','') != $string`
`$string =~ /^\S$/`	`translate(normalize-space($string),' ','') = $string`

Discussion

When it comes to brevity and power, nothing beats a good regular-expression engine. However, many simple matching operations can be emulated by more cumbersome yet effective XPath expressions. Many of these matches are facilitated by `translate( )`, which removes extraneous characters so the match can be implemented as an equality test. Another useful application of translate is its ability to count the number of occurrences of a specific character or set of characters. For example, the following code counts the number of numeric characters in a string:

```
string-length(translate($string,
           translate($string,'0123456789',''),''))
```

If it is unclear what this code does, refer to Recipe 1.3. Alternatively, you can write:

```
string-length($string) -
string-length(translate($string,'0123456789',''))
```

This code trades a `translate( )` call for an additional `string-length( )` and a subtraction. It might be slightly faster.

An important way in which these XPath expressions differ from their Perl counterparts is that in Perl, special variables are set as a side effect of matching. These variables allow powerful string-processing techniques that are way beyond the scope of XSLT. If anyone attempted to mate Perl and XSLT into a hybrid language, I would want to be one of the first alpha users!

The good news is that XPath 2.0 will support regular expressions.

1.11   Using the EXSLT String Extensions

Problem

You have good reason to use extension functions for string processing, but you are concerned about portability.

Solution

You may find that your XSLT processor already implements string functions defined by the EXSLT community (*http://www.exslt.org/*). At the time of publication, these functions are:

`node-set str:tokenize(string input, string delimiters?)`
> The `str:tokenize` function splits up a string and returns a node set of token elements, each containing one token from the string.
>
> The first argument is the string to be tokenized. The second argument is a string consisting of a number of characters. Each character in this string is taken as a delimiting character. The string given by the first argument is split at any occurrence of any character.
>
> If the second argument is omitted, the default is the string `&#x9;&#xA;&#xD;&#x20;` (i.e., whitespace characters).
>
> If the second argument is an empty string, the function returns a set of token elements, each of which holds a single character.

```
node-set str:replace(string, object search, object replace)
```
The str:replace function replaces any occurrences of search strings within a string with replacement nodes to create a node set.

The first argument gives the string within which strings are to be replaced.

The second argument is an object that specifies a search string list. If the second argument is a node set, then the search string list shows the result of converting each node in the node set to a string with the string() function, listed in document order. If the second argument is not a node set, then the second argument is converted to a string with the string() function, and the search string list consists of this string only.

The third argument is an object that specifies a replacement node list. If the third argument is a node set, then the replacement node list consists of the nodes in the node set in document order. If the third argument is not a node set, then the replacement node list consists of a single text node whose string value is the same as the result of converting the third argument to a string with the string() function.

```
string str:padding(number, string?)
```
The str:padding function creates a padding string of a certain length.

The first argument gives the length of the padding string to be created.

The second argument gives a string necessary to create the padding. This string is repeated as many times as is necessary to create a string of the length specified by the first argument; if the string is more than a character long, it may have to be truncated to produce the required length. If no second argument is specified, it defaults to a space (" "). If the second argument is an empty string, str:padding returns an empty string.

```
string str:align(string, string, string?)
```
The str:align function aligns a string within another string.

The first argument gives the target string to be aligned. The second argument gives the padding string within which it will be aligned.

If the target string is shorter than the padding string, then a range of characters in the padding string are replaced with those in the target string. Which characters are replaced depends on the value of the third argument, which gives the type of alignment. It can be left, right, or center. If no third argument is given or if it is not one of these values, then it defaults to left alignment.

With left alignment, the range of characters replaced by the target string begins with the first character in the padding string. With right alignment, the range of characters replaced by the target string ends with the last character in the padding string. With center alignment, the range of characters replaced by the target string is in the middle of the padding string so that either the number of unreplaced characters on either side of the range is the same or there is one less on the left than on the right.

If the target string is longer than the padding string, then it is truncated to be the same length as the padding string and returned.

string str:encode-uri(string)

The str:encode-uri function returns an encoded URI. The str:encode-uri method does not encode the following characters: ":", "/", ";", and "?".

A URI-encoded string converts unsafe and reserved characters with "%", immediately followed by two hexadecimal digits (0–9, A–F) giving the ISO Latin 1 code for that character.

string str:decode-uri(string)

The str:decode-uri function decodes a string that has been URI-encoded. See str:encode-uri for an explanation.

string str:concat(node-set)

The str:concat function takes a node set and returns the concatenation of the string values of the nodes in that set. If the node set is empty, it returns an empty string.

node-set str:split(string, string?)

The str:split function splits up a string and returns a node set of token elements, each containing one token from the string. The first argument is the string to be split. The second is a pattern string. The string given by the first argument is split at any occurrence of this pattern.

If the second argument is omitted, the default is the string   (i.e., a space).

If the second argument is an empty string, the function returns a set of token elements, each of which holds a single character.

Discussion

Using the EXSLT string functions does not guarantee portability, since currently no XSLT implementation supports them all. In fact, according to the EXSLT web site, some functions have no current implementation. The EXSLT team makes up for this by providing native XSLT implementations, JavaScript, and/or MSXML implementations whenever possible.

A good reason for using EXSLT is that the members of the EXSLT team are very active in the XSLT community and many implementations will probably support most of their extensions eventually. It is also possible that some of their work will be incorporated into a future standard XSLT release.

CHAPTER 2
Numbers and Math

Arithmetic is being able to count up to twenty
without taking off your shoes.
—Mickey Mouse

Chapter 1 lamented the absence of sophisticated string-processing facilities in native XSLT. By comparison, XSLT's handling of numerical computation is truly "Mickey Mouse"! XSLT 1.0 gives you facilities for basic arithmetic, counting, summing, and formatting numbers, but the remaining mathematics is up to your sheer wit. Fortunately, as with strings, XSLT's recursive powers permit reasonable mathematical feats with reasonable effort.

Do not expect to find matrix multiplication or Fast-Fourier transform recipes in this section. If you really need them to perform on XML-encoded data then XSLT is not the language for you. Instead, bring the data into a C, C++, or Fortran program using an XSLT frontend converter or native SAX or DOM interface. Nevertheless, a web page called "Gallery of Stupid XSL and XSLT Tricks" (*http://www. incrementaldevelopment.com/xsltrick/*) contains some interesting mathematical XSLT curiosities such as computing primes and differentiating polynomials. These tricks can be instructive because they might extend your understanding of XSLT. Instead, this chapter concentrates on recipes that demonstrate commonly used mathematics that can be implemented economically within the confines of XSLT.

Some of this section's early examples read more like tutorials on how to use native functionality in XSLT. I include these examples because they represent XSLT facilities that are sometimes misunderstood.

Many of the recipes shown here are implementations of EXSLT's math definitions. When a pure XSLT implementation is available at EXSLT.org, we will discuss that first and then consider alternative solutions.* Pure XSLT implementations are

---

* The EXSLT implementations shown are as they existed at the time of this writing. Naturally, these may be improved over time or deprecated as new version of XPath and XSLT emerge.

provided for all extensions defined in EXSLT math except for trigonometric functions (sin, cos, etc.). If you desperately need a pure XSLT implementation of trigonometric functions, then Recipe 2.5 will point you in one general direction.

Many discussion sections in this chapter will explore alternative implementations of the solution. Readers uninterested in technical details are encouraged simply to use the example shown in the solution section since it will be the best solution or as good as the alternatives.

2.1   Formatting Numbers

Problem

You need to display numbers in various formats.

Solution

This problem has two general solutions.

Use xsl:decimal-format in conjunction with format-number( )

The top-level element xsl:decimal-format is establishes a named formatting rule that can be referenced by the format-number( ) function whenever that format rule is required. xsl:decimal-format has a rich set of attributes that describe the formatting rules. Table 2-1 explains each attribute and shows its default value in parentheses.

Table 2-1. Attributes of the xsl:decimal-format element

Attribute	Purpose
name	An optional name for the rule. If absent, this rule becomes the default rule. There can be only one default, and all names must be unique (even when there is a difference in import precedence).
decimal-separator (.)	The character used to separate the whole and fractional parts of a number.
grouping-separator (,)	The character used to separate groups of digits.
infinity (Infinity)	The string that represents infinity.
minus-sign (-)	The character used as a minus sign.
NaN (NaN)	The string representing the numerical value "not a number."
percent (%)	The percent sign.
per-mille (‰)	The per-mille sign.
zero-digit (0)	The character used in formatting pattern to indicate where a leading or trailing zero should be placed. Setting this character resets the origin of the numbering system. See Example 2-1 in the "Discussion" section.
digit (#)	The character used in a formatting pattern to indicate where a digit will appear, provided it is significant.
pattern-separator (;)	The character used in a formatting pattern to separate the positive subpattern from the negative subpattern.

The format-number( ) function takes the arguments shown in Table 2-2.

Table 2-2. Arguments for format-number()

Argument	Purpose
value	The value to be formatted
format	A format string
name (optional)	A name of an xsl:decimal-format element

Use xsl:number

The most common use of xsl:number is to number nodes sequentially. However, it can also format numbers. When used to perform the later, the relevant attributes are shown in Table 2-3.

Table 2-3. Attributes of xsl:number

Name	Purpose
value	The number to be formatted.
format	A format string (see later).
lang	A language code as defined by the the xml:lang attribute.
letter-value	Must be either alphabetic or traditional and is used to distinguish between different numbering schemes.
grouping-separator	A single character used to separate groups. For example, in the US, the comma (,) is standard.
grouping-size	The number of digits in each group.

Table 2-4 shows how formatting tokens are used with a format attribute.

Table 2-4. Example behavior of formatting tokens used with a format attribute

Format token	Example value	Resulting output
1	1	1
1	99	99
01	1	01
001	1	001
a	1	a
a	10	j
a	27	aa
A	1	A
A	27	AA
i	1	i
i	10	x
I	1	I
I	11	XI

The format string is an alternating sequence of format and punctuation tokens. Using multiple format tokens makes sense only when the value contains a set of numbers.

Discussion

Given the formatting machinery defined earlier, almost any numeric-formatting task can be handled.

Formatting numbers into columns using a fixed number of decimal places

Here we can take advantage of leading and trailing zero padding and then map the leading zeros to spaces and use a trailing minus sign. This solution gives a nice columnar, right-justified output when the final display medium uses a fixed-width font. Examples 2-1 through 2-3 show more conventional ways of padding. The examples illustrate the behavior of the 0 digit when used as a format character.

Example 2-1. Input

```
<numbers>
   <number>10</number>
   <number>3.5</number>
   <number>4.44</number>
   <number>77.7777</number>
   <number>-8</number>
   <number>1</number>
   <number>444</number>
   <number>1.1234</number>
   <number>7.77</number>
   <number>3.1415927</number>
   <number>10</number>
   <number>9</number>
   <number>8</number>
   <number>7</number>
   <number>666</number>
   <number>5555</number>
   <number>-4444444</number>
   <number>22.33</number>
   <number>18</number>
   <number>36.54</number>
   <number>43</number>
   <number>99999</number>
   <number>999999</number>
   <number>9999999</number>
   <number>32</number>
   <number>64</number>
   <number>-64.0001</number>
</numbers>
```

Example 2-2. format-numbers-into-columns.xslt

```
<xsl:stylesheet version="1.0" xmlns:xsl="http://www.w3.org/1999/XSL/Transform">
    <xsl:output method="text" />
```

Example 2-2. format-numbers-into-columns.xslt (continued)

```
<xsl:variable name="numCols" select="4"/>

<xsl:template match="numbers">
  <xsl:for-each select="number[position( ) mod $numCols = 1]">
    <xsl:apply-templates
        select=". | following-sibling::number[position( ) &lt; $numCols]"
        mode="format"/>
    <xsl:text>&#xa;</xsl:text>
  </xsl:for-each>
</xsl:template>

<xsl:template match="number" name="format" mode="format">
  <xsl:param name="number" select="." />
  <xsl:call-template name="leading-zero-to-space">
    <xsl:with-param name="input"
                select="format-number($number,
                                      '0000000.0000   ;0000000.0000- ')"/>
  </xsl:call-template>
</xsl:template>

<xsl:template name="leading-zero-to-space">
  <xsl:param name="input"/>
  <xsl:choose>
    <xsl:when test="starts-with($input,'0')">
    <xsl:value-of select="' '"/>
    <xsl:call-template name="leading-zero-to-space">
      <xsl:with-param name="input" select="substring-after($input,'0')"/>
    </xsl:call-template>
    </xsl:when>
    <xsl:otherwise>
      <xsl:value-of select="$input"/>
    </xsl:otherwise>
  </xsl:choose>
</xsl:template>

</xsl:stylesheet>
```

Example 2-3. Output

```
     10.0000       3.5000      4.4400
     77.7777       8.0000-     1.0000
    444.0000       1.1234      7.7700
      3.1416      10.0000      9.0000
      8.0000       7.0000    666.0000
   5555.0000 4444444.0000-    22.3300
     18.0000      36.5400     43.0000
  99999.0000  999999.0000 9999999.0000
     32.0000      64.0000     64.0001-
```

Formatting money like U.S. accountants

Example 2-4 gives a variation of the previous format template that will make your accountant happy.

Example 2-4. Accountant-friendly format

```
<xsl:template match="number" name="format" mode="format">
  <xsl:param name="number" select="." />
  <xsl:text> $ </xsl:text>
  <xsl:call-template name="leading-zero-to-space">
    <xsl:with-param name="input"
                    select="format-number($number,
                                         ' 0000000.00 ;(0000000.00)')"/>
  </xsl:call-template>
</xsl:template>
```

Output:

```
$      10.00  $        3.50  $        4.44
$      77.78  $       (8.00) $        1.00
$     444.00  $        1.12  $        7.77
$       3.14  $       10.00  $        9.00
$       8.00  $        7.00  $      666.00
$    5555.00  $ (4444444.00) $       22.33
$      18.00  $       36.54  $       43.00
$   99999.00  $   999999.00  $  9999999.00
$      32.00  $       64.00  $      (64.00)
```

Formatting numbers for many European countries

Example 2-5 demonstrates the use of a named format.

Example 2-5. European-number format

```
<xsl:stylesheet version="1.0"
    xmlns:xsl="http://www.w3.org/1999/XSL/Transform"
    xmlns:str="http://www.ora.com/XSLTCookbook/namespaces/strings">

<xsl:output method="text" />

<!-- From Recipe 1.5 ... -->
<xsl:include href="../strings/str.dup.xslt"/>

<xsl:variable name="numCols" select="3"/>

<xsl:decimal-format name="WesternEurope"
                    decimal-separator="," grouping-separator="."/>

<xsl:template match="numbers">
  <xsl:for-each select="number[position() mod $numCols = 1]">
    <xsl:apply-templates
        select=". | following-sibling::number[position() &lt; $numCols]"
        mode="format"/>
    <xsl:text>&#xa;</xsl:text>
  </xsl:for-each>
</xsl:template>

<xsl:template match="number" name="format" mode="format">
  <xsl:param name="number" select="." />
  <xsl:call-template name="pad">
```

Example 2-5. European-number format (continued)

```
    <xsl:with-param name="string"
                    select="format-number($number,'#.###,00','WesternEurope')"/>
  </xsl:call-template>
</xsl:template>

<xsl:template name="pad">
  <xsl:param name="string"/>
  <xsl:param name="width" select="16"/>
  <xsl:call-template name="str:dup">
    <xsl:with-param name="input" select="' '"/>
    <xsl:with-param name="count" select="$width - string-length($string)"/>
  </xsl:call-template>
  <xsl:value-of select="$string"/>
</xsl:template>

</xsl:stylesheet>
```

Output:

10,00	3,50	4,44
77,78	-8,00	1,00
444,00	1,12	7,77
3,14	10,00	9,00
8,00	7,00	666,00
5.555,00	-4.444.444,00	22,33
18,00	36,54	43,00
99.999,00	999.999,00	9.999.999,00
32,00	64,00	-64,00

Converting numbers to Roman numerals

Example 2-6 uses xsl:number as a Roman numeral formatter to label columns as rows:

Example 2-6. Roman-numeral format

```
<xsl:stylesheet version="1.0" xmlns:xsl="http://www.w3.org/1999/XSL/Transform"
 xmlns:str="http://www.ora.com/XSLTCookbook/namespaces/strings">
    <xsl:output method="text" />

<xsl:include href="../strings/str.dup.xslt"/>

<xsl:variable name="numCols" select="3"/>

<xsl:template match="numbers">
  <xsl:for-each select="number[position() &lt;= $numCols]">
    <xsl:text>              </xsl:text>
    <xsl:number value="position()" format="I"/><xsl:text>   </xsl:text>
  </xsl:for-each>
    <xsl:text>&#xa;    </xsl:text>
  <xsl:for-each select="number[position() &lt;= $numCols]">
    <xsl:text>---------------   </xsl:text>
  </xsl:for-each>
    <xsl:text>&#xa;</xsl:text>
```

Example 2-6. Roman-numeral format (continued)

```
  <xsl:for-each select="number[position( ) mod $numCols = 1]">
    <xsl:call-template name="pad">
      <xsl:with-param name="string">
        <xsl:number value="position( )" format="i"/>
      </xsl:with-param>
      <xsl:with-param name="width" select="4"/>
    </xsl:call-template>|<xsl:text/>
    <xsl:apply-templates
        select=". | following-sibling::number[position( ) &lt; $numCols]"
        mode="format"/>
    <xsl:text>&#xa;</xsl:text>
  </xsl:for-each>
</xsl:template>

<xsl:template match="number" name="format" mode="format">
  <xsl:param name="number" select="." />
  <xsl:call-template name="pad">
    <xsl:with-param name="string" select="format-number(.,'#,###.00')"/>
  </xsl:call-template>
</xsl:template>

<xsl:template name="pad">
  <xsl:param name="string"/>
  <xsl:param name="width" select="16"/>
  <xsl:call-template name="str:dup">
    <xsl:with-param name="input" select="' '"/>
    <xsl:with-param name="count" select="$width - string-length($string)"/>
  </xsl:call-template>
  <xsl:value-of select="$string"/>
</xsl:template>

</xsl:stylesheet>
```

Output:

```
            I               II              III
      ---------------  ---------------  ---------------
    i|         10.00            3.50             4.44
   ii|         77.78           -8.00             1.00
  iii|        444.00            1.12             7.77
   iv|          3.14           10.00             9.00
    v|          8.00            7.00           666.00
   vi|      5,555.00   -4,444,444.00            22.33
  vii|         18.00           36.54            43.00
 viii|     99,999.00      999,999.00     9,999,999.00
   ix|         32.00           64.00           -64.00
```

Creating column numbers like a spreadsheet

Spreadsheets number columns in the alpha sequence A, B, C ... ZZ, and we can do the same using xsl:number (see Example 2-7).

Example 2-7. Spreadsheet-like column numbers

```
<xsl:template match="numbers">
  <xsl:for-each select="number[position( ) &lt;= $numCols]">
    <xsl:text>            </xsl:text>
    <xsl:number value="position( )" format="A"/><xsl:text>    </xsl:text>
    <xsl:text>        </xsl:text>
  </xsl:for-each>
    <xsl:text>&#xa;</xsl:text>
  <xsl:for-each select="number[position( ) &lt;= $numCols]">
    <xsl:text> ---------------- </xsl:text>
  </xsl:for-each>
    <xsl:text>&#xa;</xsl:text>
  <xsl:for-each select="number[position( ) mod $numCols = 1]">
    <xsl:value-of select="position( )"/><xsl:text>|</xsl:text>
    <xsl:apply-templates
        select=". | following-sibling::number[position( ) &lt; $numCols]"
        mode="format"/>
    <xsl:text>&#xa;</xsl:text>
  </xsl:for-each>
</xsl:template>

<xsl:template match="number" name="format" mode="format">
  <xsl:param name="number" select="." />
  <xsl:call-template name="pad">
    <xsl:with-param name="string" select="format-number(.,'#,###.00')"/>
  </xsl:call-template>
  <xsl:text>    </xsl:text>
</xsl:template>
```

Output:

	A	B	C
1|	10.0000	3.5000	4.4400
2|	77.7777	8.0000-	1.0000
3|	444.0000	1.1234	7.7700
4|	3.1416	10.0000	9.0000
5|	8.0000	7.0000	666.0000
6|	5555.0000	4444444.0000-| 22.3300
7|	18.0000	36.5400	43.0000
8|	99999.0000	999999.0000	9999999.0000
9|	32.0000	64.0000	64.0001-

Formatting numbers using Arabic characters

Numeric characters from other languages can be used by setting the zero digit in
xsl:decimal-format to the zero of that language. This example uses the Unicode
character 0x660 (Arabic-Indic Digit Zero):

```
<xsl:stylesheet version="1.0" xmlns:xsl="http://www.w3.org/1999/XSL/Transform"
  xmlns:str="http://www.ora.com/XSLTCookbook/namespaces/strings">

<xsl:output method="text"  encoding="UTF-8"/>

<xsl:include href="../strings/str.dup.xslt"/>
```

```
<!-- This states that zero starts at character 0x660, which implies one is 0x661,
etc. -->
<xsl:decimal-format name="Arabic" zero-digit="&#x660;"/>

<xsl:template match="numbers">
  <xsl:for-each select="number">
      <xsl:call-template name="pad">
        <xsl:with-param name="string" select="format-number(.,'#,###.00')"/>
      </xsl:call-template> = <xsl:text/>
      <xsl:value-of select="format-number(.,'#,###.&#x660;&#x660;','Arabic')"/>
      <xsl:text>&#xa;</xsl:text>
  </xsl:for-each>
</xsl:template>

<xsl:template name="pad">
  <xsl:param name="string"/>
  <xsl:param name="width" select="16"/>
  <xsl:value-of select="$string"/>
  <xsl:call-template name="str:dup">
    <xsl:with-param name="input" select="' '"/>
    <xsl:with-param name="count" select="$width - string-length($string)"/>
  </xsl:call-template>
</xsl:template>

</xsl:stylesheet>
```

Here is the output of this code:

```
10.00           =    ١٠.٠٠
3.50            =    ٣.٥٠
4.44            =    ٤.٤٤
77.78           =    ٧٧.٧٨
-8.00           =    -٨.٠٠
1.00            =    ١.٠٠
444.00          =    ٤٤٤.٠٠
1.12            =    ١.١٢
7.77            =    ٧.٧٧
3.14            =    ٣.١٤
10.00           =    ١٠.٠٠
9.00            =    ٩.٠٠
8.00            =    ٨.٠٠
7.00            =    ٧.٠٠
666.00          =    ٦٦٦.٠٠
5,555.00        =    ٥ ٥٥٥.٠٠
-4,444,444.00   =    -٤ ٤٤٤ ٤٤٤.٠٠
22.33           =    ٢٢.٣٣
18.00           =    ١٨.٠٠
36.54           =    ٣٦.٥٤
43.00           =    ٤٣.٠٠
99,999.00       =    ٩٩ ٩٩٩.٠٠
999,999.00      =    ٩٩٩ ٩٩٩.٠٠
9,999,999.00    =    ٩ ٩٩٩ ٩٩٩.٠٠
32.00           =    ٣٢.٠٠
64.00           =    ٦٤.٠٠
-64.00          =    -٦٤.٠٠
```

2.2 Rounding Numbers to a Specified Precision

Problem

You want to round to a specific number of decimal places; however, XSLT's round, ceiling, and floor functions always map numbers to integer values.

Solution

Multiply, round, and divide using a power of ten that determines how many decimal digits are required. Assuming $pi = 3.1415926535897932:

```
<xsl:value-of select="round($pi * 10000) div 10000"/>
```

results in 3.1416. Similarily:

```
<xsl:value-of select="ceiling($pi * 10000) div 10000"/>
```

results in 3.1416, and:

```
<xsl:value-of select="floor($pi * 10000) div 10000"/>
```

results in 3.1415.

Rounding to a specific number of decimal places is also achieved using format-number( ):

```
<xsl:value-of select="format-number($pi,'#.####')"/>
```

This results in 3.1416. This will work even if more than one significant digit is in the whole part because format-number never uses a format specification as an indication to remove significant digits from the whole part:

```
<xsl:value-of select="format-number($pi * 100,'#.####')"/>
```

This results in 314.1593.

You can use format-number to get the effect of truncating rather than rounding by using one more formatting digit than required and then chopping of the last character:

```
<xsl:variable name="pi-to-5-sig" select="format-number($pi,'#.#####')"/>
<xsl:value-of select="substring($pi-to-5-sig,1,string-length($pi-to-5-sig) -1)"/>
```

This results in 3.1415.

Discussion

This multiply, round, and divide technique works well as long as the numbers involved remain within the representational limits of IEEE floating point. If you try to capture too many places after the decimal, then the rules of IEEE floating point will interfere with the expected result. For example, trying to pick up 16 decimal digits of pi will give you only 15:

```
<xsl:value-of select="round($pi * 10000000000000000) div 10000000000000000"/>
```

This results in 3.141592653589793, not 3.1415926535897932.

An alternative technique manipulates the number as a string and truncates:

```
<xsl:value-of select="concat(substring-before($pi,'.'),
                      '.',
                      substring(substring-after($pi,'.'),1,4))"/>
```

and results in 3.1415.

The effect of ceiling or round can be obtained by this technique at the cost additional complexity.

```
<xsl:variable name="whole" select="substring-before($pi,'.')"/>
<xsl:variable name="frac" select="substring-after($pi,'.')"/>
<xsl:value-of select="concat($whole,
                      '.',
                      substring($frac,1,3),
                  round(substring($frac,4,2) div 10))"/>
```

This results in 3.1416.

2.3   Converting from Roman Numerals to Numbers

Problem

You need to convert a Roman numeral to a number.

Solution

Roman numbers do not use a place value system; instead, the number is composed by adding or subtracting the fixed value of the specified Roman numeral characters. If the following character has a lower or equal value, you add; otherwise, you subtract:

```
<xsl:stylesheet version="1.0" xmlns:xsl="http://www.w3.org/1999/XSL/Transform"
    xmlns:math="http://www.ora.com/XSLTCookbook/math">

<math:romans>
  <math:roman value="1">i</math:roman>
  <math:roman value="1">I</math:roman>
  <math:roman value="5">v</math:roman>
  <math:roman value="5">V</math:roman>
  <math:roman value="10">x</math:roman>
  <math:roman value="10">X</math:roman>
  <math:roman value="50">l</math:roman>
  <math:roman value="50">L</math:roman>
  <math:roman value="100">c</math:roman>
  <math:roman value="100">C</math:roman>
```

```
      <math:roman value="500">d</math:roman>
      <math:roman value="500">D</math:roman>
      <math:roman value="1000">m</math:roman>
      <math:roman value="1000">M</math:roman>
  </math:romans>

<xsl:variable name="math:roman-nums" select="document('')/*/*/math:roman"/>

<xsl:template name="math:roman-to-number">
  <xsl:param name="roman"/>

  <xsl:variable name="valid-roman-chars">
    <xsl:value-of select="document('')/*/math:romans"/>
  </xsl:variable>

  <xsl:choose>
    <xsl:when test="translate($roman,$valid-roman-chars,'')">NaN</xsl:when>
    <xsl:otherwise>
      <xsl:call-template name="math:roman-to-number-impl">
        <xsl:with-param name="roman" select="$roman"/>
      </xsl:call-template>
    </xsl:otherwise>
  </xsl:choose>
</xsl:template>

<xsl:template name="math:roman-to-number-impl">
  <xsl:param name="roman"/>
  <xsl:param name="value" select="0"/>

  <xsl:variable name="len" select="string-length($roman)"/>

  <xsl:choose>
    <xsl:when test="not($len)">
      <xsl:value-of select="$value"/>
    </xsl:when>
    <xsl:when test="$len = 1">
      <xsl:value-of select="$value + $math:roman-nums[. = $roman]/@value"/>
    </xsl:when>
    <xsl:otherwise>
      <xsl:variable name="roman-num"
          select="$math:roman-nums[. = substring($roman, 1, 1)]"/>
      <xsl:choose>
        <xsl:when test="$roman-num/following-sibling::math:roman =
            substring($roman, 2, 1)">
          <xsl:call-template name="math:roman-to-number-impl">
            <xsl:with-param name="roman" select="substring($roman,2,$len - 1)"/>
            <xsl:with-param name="value" select="$value - $roman-num/@value"/>
          </xsl:call-template>
        </xsl:when>
        <xsl:otherwise>
          <xsl:call-template name="math:roman-to-number-impl">
```

```
            <xsl:with-param name="roman" select="substring($roman,2,$len - 1)"/>
            <xsl:with-param name="value" select="$value + $roman-num/@value"/>
        </xsl:call-template>
      </xsl:otherwise>
    </xsl:choose>
  </xsl:otherwise>
</xsl:choose>

</xsl:template>
```

Discussion

The xsl:number element provides a convenient way to convert numbers to Roman numerals; however, for converting from Roman numerals to numbers, you are on your own. The recursive template shown earlier is straightforward and much like that already found in Jeni Tennison's *XSLT and XPath on the Edge* (M&T Books, 2001).

There are two small caveats, but they should not cause trouble in most cases. The first is that the previous solution will not work with Roman numerals using mixed case (e.g., IiI). Such odd strings would hardly appear in reasonable data source, but this code will neither reject such input nor arrive at the "correct" value. Adding code to convert to one case allows the code to reject or correctly process these mixed Romans.

The second caveat relates to the fact that there is no standard Roman representation for numbers higher than 1,000. Saxon and Xalan keep stringing Ms together, but another processor might do something else.

If for some reason you object to storing data about Roman numerals in the stylesheet, then the following XPath decodes a Roman numeral:

```
<xsl:variable name="roman-value"
    select="($c = 'i' or $c = 'I') * 1 +
           ($c = 'v' or $c = 'V') * 5 +
           ($c = 'x' or $c = 'X') * 10 +
           ($c = 'l' or $c = 'L') * 50 +
           ($c = 'c' or $c = 'C') * 100 +
           ($c = 'd' or $c = 'D') * 500 +
           ($c = 'm' or $c = 'M') * 1000)"/>
```

2.4   Converting from One Base to Another

Problem

You need to convert strings representing numbers in some base to numbers in another base.

Solution

This example provides a general solution for converting from any base between 2 and 36 to any base in the same range. It uses two global variables to encode the value of all characters in a base 36 system as offsets into the string—one for uppercase encoding and the other for lowercase:

```
<xsl:variable name="math:base-lower"
    select="'0123456789abcdefghijklmnopqrstuvwxyz'"/>

<xsl:variable name="math:base-upper"
    select="'0123456789ABCDEFGHIJKLMNOPQRSTUVWXYZ'"/>

<xsl:template name="math:convert-base">
  <xsl:param name="number"/>
  <xsl:param name="from-base"/>
  <xsl:param name="to-base"/>

  <xsl:variable name="number-base10">
    <xsl:call-template name="math:convert-to-base-10">
      <xsl:with-param name="number" select="$number"/>
      <xsl:with-param name="from-base" select="$from-base"/>
    </xsl:call-template>
  </xsl:variable>
  <xsl:call-template name="math:convert-from-base-10">
    <xsl:with-param name="number" select="$number-base10"/>
    <xsl:with-param name="to-base" select="$to-base"/>
  </xsl:call-template>
</xsl:template>
```

This template reduces the general problem to two subproblems of converting to and from base 10. Performing base 10 conversions is easier because it is the native base of XPath numbers.

The template `math:convert-to-base-10` normalizes the input number to lowercase. Thus, for example, you treat ffff hex the same as FFFF hex, which is the normal convention. Two error checks are performed to make sure the base is in the range you can handle and that the number does not contain illegal characters inconsistent with the base. The trivial case of converting from base 10 to base 10 is also handled:

```
<xsl:template name="math:convert-to-base-10">
  <xsl:param name="number"/>
  <xsl:param name="from-base"/>

  <xsl:variable name="num"
          select="translate($number,$math:base-upper, $math:base-lower)"/>
  <xsl:variable name="valid-in-chars"
      select="substring($math:base-lower,1,$from-base)"/>

  <xsl:choose>
    <xsl:when test="$from-base &lt; 2 or $from-base > 36">NaN</xsl:when>
    <xsl:when test="not($num) or translate($num,$valid-in-chars,'')">NaN</xsl:when>
    <xsl:when test="$from-base = 10">
```

```
        <xsl:value-of select="$number"/>
      </xsl:when>
      <xsl:otherwise>
        <xsl:call-template name="math:convert-to-base-10-impl">
          <xsl:with-param name="number" select="$num"/>
          <xsl:with-param name="from-base" select="$from-base"/>
          <xsl:with-param name="from-chars" select="$valid-in-chars"/>
        </xsl:call-template>
      </xsl:otherwise>
    </xsl:choose>
  </xsl:template>
```

Once error checking is taken care of, you can defer the actual conversion to another recursive template that does the work. This template looks up the decimal value of each character as an offset into the string of characters you obtained from the caller. The recursion keeps multiplying the result by the base and adding in the value of the first character until you are left with a string of length 1:

```
<xsl:template name="math:convert-to-base-10-impl">
  <xsl:param name="number"/>
  <xsl:param name="from-base"/>
  <xsl:param name="from-chars"/>

  <xsl:param name="result" select="0"/>

  <xsl:variable name="value"
      select="string-length(substring-before($from-chars,substring($number,1,1)))"/>

  <xsl:variable name="total" select="$result * $from-base + $value"/>

  <xsl:choose>
    <xsl:when test="string-length($number) = 1">
      <xsl:value-of select="$total"/>
    </xsl:when>
    <xsl:otherwise>
      <xsl:call-template name="math:convert-to-base-10-impl">
        <xsl:with-param name="number" select="substring($number,2)"/>
        <xsl:with-param name="from-base" select="$from-base"/>
        <xsl:with-param name="from-chars" select="$from-chars"/>
        <xsl:with-param name="result" select="$total"/>
      </xsl:call-template>
    </xsl:otherwise>
  </xsl:choose>
</xsl:template>
```

The other half of the problem requires a conversion from base 10 to any base. Again, you separate error checking from the actual conversion:

```
<xsl:template name="math:convert-from-base-10">
  <xsl:param name="number"/>
  <xsl:param name="to-base"/>

  <xsl:choose>
    <xsl:when test="$to-base &lt; 2 or $to-base > 36">NaN</xsl:when>
```

```
      <xsl:when test="number($number) != number($number)">NaN</xsl:when>
      <xsl:when test="$to-base = 10">
        <xsl:value-of select="$number"/>
      </xsl:when>
      <xsl:otherwise>
        <xsl:call-template name="math:convert-from-base-10-impl">
          <xsl:with-param name="number" select="$number"/>
          <xsl:with-param name="to-base" select="$to-base"/>
        </xsl:call-template>
      </xsl:otherwise>
    </xsl:choose>
  </xsl:template>
```

The actual conversion is simply a matter of picking out each digit form the $math:
base-lower table based on the remainder (i.e., mod) obtained when dividing by the
$to-base. You recurse on the leftover integer portion, concatenating the digit onto
the front of the result. Recursion ends when the number is less than the base:

```
  <xsl:template name="math:convert-from-base-10-impl">
    <xsl:param name="number"/>
    <xsl:param name="to-base"/>
    <xsl:param name="result"/>

    <xsl:variable name="to-base-digit"
        select="substring($math:base-lower,$number mod $to-base + 1,1)"/>

    <xsl:choose>
      <xsl:when test="$number >= $to-base">
        <xsl:call-template name="math:convert-from-base-10-impl">
          <xsl:with-param name="number" select="floor($number div $to-base)"/>
          <xsl:with-param name="to-base" select="$to-base"/>
          <xsl:with-param name="result" select="concat($to-base-digit,$result)"/>
        </xsl:call-template>
      </xsl:when>
      <xsl:otherwise>
        <xsl:value-of select="concat($to-base-digit,$result)"/>
        </xsl:otherwise>
    </xsl:choose>
  </xsl:template>
```

Discussion

Base conversions are a common programming task and most developers already
know how to perform them. Many languages have built-in provisions for these conversions; XSLT does not. The fact that XPath and XSLT provide no means of getting
the integer value of a Unicode character makes these conversions more cumbersome. Hence, you most resort to playing tricks with strings that act like lookup
tables. These manipulations are inefficient, but reasonable for most conversion
needs.

The code assumes that bases higher than 10 will use the standard convention of assigning successive alphas to digits higher than 9. If you work with an unconventional encoding, then you will have to adjust the mapping strings accordingly. You can potentially extend this code beyond base 36 by adding the characters used to encode digits higher than Z.

2.5   Implementing Common Math Functions

Problem

You need to go beyond fifth-grade math even though XSLT 1.0 does not.

Solution

Pure XSLT implementations are provided for absolute value, square root, logarithms, power, and factorial.

Absolute value: math:abs(x)

The obvious but long-winded way to determine the absolute value of a number is shown here:

```
<xsl:template name="math:abs">
    <xsl:param name="x"/>

    <xsl:choose>
        <xsl:when test="$x &lt; 0">
            <xsl:value-of select="$x * -1"/>
        </xsl:when>
        <xsl:otherwise>
            <xsl:value-of select="$x"/>
        </xsl:otherwise>
    </xsl:choose>"

</xsl:template>
```

The short but obscure way relies on the fact that the true always converts to the number 1 and false to the number 0.

```
<xsl:template name="math:abs">
    <xsl:param name="x"/>
    <xsl:value-of select="(1 - 2 *($x &lt; 0)) * $x"/>
</xsl:template>
```

I prefer the latter because it is concise. Alternatively, you can use an extension function (see Chapter 12).

Square root: math:sqrt(x)

Nate Austin contributed a native XSLT sqrt to EXSLT that uses Newton's method:

```
<xsl:template name="math:sqrt">
    <!-- The number you want to find the square root of -->
    <xsl:param name="number" select="0"/>
    <!-- The current 'try'.  This is used internally. -->
    <xsl:param name="try" select="1"/>
    <!-- The current iteration, checked against maxiter to limit loop count -->
    <xsl:param name="iter" select="1"/>
    <!-- Set this up to ensure against infinite loops -->
    <xsl:param name="maxiter" select="20"/>
    <!-- This template was written by Nate Austin using Sir Isaac Newton's
     method of finding roots -->
    <xsl:choose>
      <xsl:when test="$try * $try = $number or $iter > $maxiter">
        <xsl:value-of select="$try"/>
      </xsl:when>
      <xsl:otherwise>
        <xsl:call-template name="math:sqrt">
         <xsl:with-param name="number" select="$number"/>
         <xsl:with-param name="try" select="$try -
                         (($try * $try - $number) div (2 * $try))"/>
         <xsl:with-param name="iter" select="$iter + 1"/>
         <xsl:with-param name="maxiter" select="$maxiter"/>
        </xsl:call-template>
      </xsl:otherwise>
    </xsl:choose>
</xsl:template>
```

Changing the initial value of try can improve performance significantly:

```
<xsl:template name="math:sqrt">
    <!-- The number you want to find the square root of -->
    <xsl:param name="number" select="0"/>
    <!-- The current 'try'.  This is used internally. -->
    <xsl:param name="try" select="($number &lt; 100) +
                       ($number >= 100 and $number &lt; 1000) * 10 +
                       ($number >= 1000 and $number &lt; 10000) * 31 +
                       ($number >= 10000) * 100"/>
    <!-- rest of code the same -->
</xsl:template>
```

This little trick (using Boolean-to-numeric conversion again) causes try to better approximate the square root on the first get go. On a test that computes all roots from 1 to 10,000, I achieved a 10% performance boost. More significantly, the change reduced the average error from 1×10^{-5} to 6×10^{-13}. This means you can reduce the number of iterations to get even more performance at the same average error rate. For example, I was able to reduce the iterations from 10 to 6 and achieve the same error rate of 10^{-5}, but at a 50% performance increase using the same test. If you need to compute square roots of number much greater than 10,000, you should keep the iterations at least 10 or add higher ranges to the try initialization.

Logarithms: math:log10(number), math:log(number), and math:logN(x,base)

If your XSLT processor supports EXSLT's math:log( ) (natural log), then implementing a logarithm to any other base is easy. In pseudocode:

```
<!-- A fundemetal rule of logarithms -->
math:logN(x,base) = math:log(x) div math:log(base)
```

Unfortunately, no XSLT processors are currently listed on EXSLT.org that implement math:log. Your next best bet is to implement an extension function in terms of Java's java.lang.Math.log class or JavaScript's Math.log. Finally, if you must avoid extensions, the following pure XSLT implementation computes log10 to a good degree of accuracy at an acceptable speed for most (sane) applications. Once you have log10(), then log() follows from the rule of logarithms:

```
<xsl:template name="math:log10">
    <xsl:param name="number" select="1"/>

    <xsl:param name="n" select="0"/> <!-- book keeping for whole part of
                          result -->

    <xsl:choose>
      <xsl:when test="$number &lt;= 0"> <!-- Logarithms are undefined for 0
                          and negative numbers. -->
        <xsl:value-of select="'NaN'"/>
      </xsl:when>
      <xsl:when test="$number &lt; 1">  <!-- Fractional numbers have
                          negative logs -->
        <xsl:call-template name="math:log10">
          <xsl:with-param name="number" select="$number * 10"/>
          <xsl:with-param name="n" select="$n - 1"/>
        </xsl:call-template>
      </xsl:when>
      <xsl:when test="$number > 10"> <!-- Numbers greater than 10 have logs
                          greater than 1 -->
        <xsl:call-template name="math:log10">
          <xsl:with-param name="number" select="$number div 10"/>
          <xsl:with-param name="n" select="$n + 1"/>
        </xsl:call-template>
      </xsl:when>
      <xsl:when test="$number = 10">
        <xsl:value-of select="$n + 1"/>
      </xsl:when>
      <xsl:otherwise>             <!-- We only need to know how to compute
                      for numbers in range [1,10) -->
        <xsl:call-template name="math:log10-util">
          <xsl:with-param name="number" select="$number"/>
          <xsl:with-param name="n" select="$n"/>
        </xsl:call-template>
      </xsl:otherwise>
    </xsl:choose>
</xsl:template>
```

```
<!-- Computes log (natural) of number-->
<xsl:template name="math:log">
    <xsl:param name="number" select="1"/>

    <xsl:variable name="log10-e" select="0.4342944819"/>
    <xsl:variable name="log10">
      <xsl:call-template name="math:log10">
        <xsl:with-param name="number" select="$number"/>
      </xsl:call-template>
    </xsl:variable>
    <xsl:value-of select="$log10 div $log10-e"/>
</xsl:template>

<!-- Computes log to base b of number-->
<xsl:template name="math:log-b">
    <xsl:param name="number" select="1"/>
    <xsl:param name="base" select="2"/>

    <xsl:variable name="log10-base">
      <xsl:call-template name="math:log10">
        <xsl:with-param name="number" select="$base"/>
      </xsl:call-template>
    </xsl:variable>

    <xsl:variable name="log10">
      <xsl:call-template name="math:log10">
        <xsl:with-param name="number" select="$number"/>
      </xsl:call-template>
    </xsl:variable>
    <xsl:value-of select="$log10 div $log10-base"/>
</xsl:template>

<!-- Computes log10 of numbers in the range [1,10) and
returns the result + n-->
<xsl:template name="math:log10-util">
    <xsl:param name="number"/>

    <xsl:param name="n"/>
    <xsl:param name="frac" select="0"/>
        <!-- book keeping variable for fractional part -->
    <xsl:param name="k" select="0"/>        <!-- iteration counter -->
    <xsl:param name="divisor" select="2"/>
        <!-- sucessive powers of 2 used to build up frac -->
    <xsl:param name="maxiter" select="38"/>
        <!-- Number of iterations. 38 is more than sufficient to get
          at least 10 dec place prec -->

    <xsl:variable name="x" select="$number * $number"/>

    <xsl:choose>
      <xsl:when test="$k >= $maxiter">
        <!-- Round to 10 decimal places -->
        <xsl:value-of select="$n + round($frac * 10000000000) div
            10000000000"/>
      </xsl:when>
```

```
    <xsl:when test="$x &lt; 10">
      <xsl:call-template name="math:log10-util">
        <xsl:with-param name="number" select="$x"/>
        <xsl:with-param name="n" select="$n"/>
        <xsl:with-param name="k" select="$k + 1"/>
        <xsl:with-param name="divisor" select="$divisor * 2"/>
        <xsl:with-param name="frac" select="$frac"/>
        <xsl:with-param name="maxiter" select="$maxiter"/>
      </xsl:call-template>
    </xsl:when>
    <xsl:otherwise>
      <xsl:call-template name="math:log10-util">
        <xsl:with-param name="number" select="$x div 10"/>
        <xsl:with-param name="n" select="$n"/>
        <xsl:with-param name="k" select="$k + 1"/>
        <xsl:with-param name="divisor" select="$divisor * 2"/>
        <xsl:with-param name="frac" select="$frac + (1 div $divisor)"/>
        <xsl:with-param name="maxiter" select="$maxiter"/>
      </xsl:call-template>
    </xsl:otherwise>
  </xsl:choose>
</xsl:template>
```

Math:log10's main purpose is to reduce the problem of computing log10(x) to the simpler problem of computing log10(x : 1 <= x < 10). This is done by observing that log10(x : x > 10) = log10(x div 10) + 1 and log10(x : x < 1) = log10(x * 10) - 1. Error checking is also performed because logarithms are not defined for zero or negative numbers.

The utility template, math:log10-util, does the hard part; it is a tail-recursive implementation of an iterative technique found in Knuth.[*] To keep the implementation tail recursive and greatly simplify the implementation, several bookkeeping parameters are defined:

n

> The whole part of the answer passed in by math:log10. This parameter is not strictly necessary because it could have held onto it until math:log10-util did its part. However, it eliminates the need to capture the result of math:log10-util in a variable.

frac

> The fractional part of the answer. This is what we are really after.

k

> An iteration counter that is incremented on each recursive call. The recursion terminates when $k > $maxiter.

---

[*] The math is beyond the scope of this book. See Knuth, D.E. *The Art of Computer Programming*, Vol. 1, p. 24 (Addison Wesley, 1973) for details.

divisor

> A number that is set to the next higher power of 2 on each recursive call (e.g., 2,4,8,16,...). The value 1 div $divisor is added to frac as you approximate the logarithm.

maxiter

> The number of iterations used to compute frac. The higher maxiter is, the greater the precision of the result (up to the limits of IEEE floating point). A parameter need not be used, but it opens the possibility of extending log10 to allow the caller to determine the required number of iterations and hence tweak speed versus accuracy.

Power: math:power(base,power)

At this time, EXSLT.org does not list any implementations that support math:power( ). However, as it is defined by EXSLT, power( ) is easy to implement in pure XSLT. Jeni Tennison provides the following implementation:

```
<xsl:template name="math:power">
    <xsl:param name="base"/>
    <xsl:param name="power"/>
    <xsl:choose>
      <xsl:when test="$power = 0">
        <xsl:value-of select="1"/>
      </xsl:when>
        <xsl:otherwise>
        <xsl:variable name="temp">
          <xsl:call-template name="math:power">
          <xsl:with-param name="base" select="$base"/>
          <xsl:with-param name="power" select="$power - 1"/>
          </xsl:call-template>
        </xsl:variable>
        <xsl:value-of select="$base * $temp"/>
      </xsl:otherwise>
    </xsl:choose>
</xsl:template>
```

For most applications, this code will do just fine; however, it is neither tail recursive nor the most algorithmically efficient implementation. The following implementation is tail recursive and reduces the number of multiplications from $O(\$power)$ to $O(log2(\$power))$. It also adds error handling, which prevents an infinite recursion if $power is NaN:

```
<xsl:template name="math:power">
    <xsl:param name="base"/>
    <xsl:param name="power"/>
    <xsl:param name="result" select="1"/>
    <xsl:choose>
      <xsl:when test="number($base) != $base or number($power) != $power">
        <xsl:value-of select="'NaN'"/>
      </xsl:when>
```

```
        <xsl:when test="$power = 0">
          <xsl:value-of select="$result"/>
        </xsl:when>
        <xsl:otherwise>
          <xsl:call-template name="math:power">
            <xsl:with-param name="base" select="$base * $base"/>
            <xsl:with-param name="power" select="floor($power div 2)"/>
            <xsl:with-param name="result"
                  select="$result * $base * ($power mod 2) +
                          $result * not($power mod 2)"/>
          </xsl:call-template>
        </xsl:otherwise>
      </xsl:choose>
    </xsl:template>
```

This section introduces a bookkeeping parameter, $result, to build up the final answer. It allows you to make the function tail recursive. On each recursive step, square the base and halve the power. Because you use floor( ), $result will reach 0 in ceiling(log2($power)) recursions. This accounts for the better performance. The tricky part is the computation of $result at each step.

Let's analyze this expression by looking at each side of the addition. The expression $result * $base * ($power mod 2) will be equal to $result * $base when $power is odd and 0 otherwise. Conversely, $result * not($power mod 2) will be equal to 0 when $power is odd and $result otherwise. If you were in C or Java you would write this expression as (power % 2) ? result * base : result. XPath 1.0 does not have a ?: operator, so you emulate it with this bit of XSLT hackery.[*] The net result is that this template ends up computing b_1 * base + b_2 * base^2 + b_3 * base^4 * b_4 * base^8 ..., where b_i is either 0 or 1. It should be fairly easy to see that this sum can add up to base^{power} for an arbitrary integer power by setting the b_is to appropriate values—whichis just what the expression $power mod 2 determines. If this concept is still unclear, then work out a few cases by hand to convince yourself that it works.[†]

The power function shown earlier only computes powers for positive integral powers. However, as any high-school algebra student can tell you, x^y is a real number for all real x and y, not just positive integers. It would be nice to have a generalized version of power( ) lying around in case you need it, so here it is. Not to be confused with power( ), this template is called power-f( ), where the f stands for floating point. If you prefer to have the most general version called power( ), then go right ahead and rename it in your own code. However, having the restricted version available as a separate function is still useful:

---

[*] XPath 2.0 will most likely have an equivalent construct. According to the 2.0 working draft, this example would look like if ($power mod 2) then $result * $base else $result.

[†] Despite the fact that formal proofs of algorithmic correctness are important, I find them tedious and boring, so you will not see any in this book. I prefer intuition and testing my code. Chapter 12 shows how the homoiconic nature (in which the program form is the same as the data form) of XSLT greatly simplifies testing. A real computer scientist would prove everything by induction and not need to test.

```
<xsl:template name="math:power-f">
      <xsl:param name="base"/>
      <xsl:param name="power"/>

      <xsl:choose>
        <xsl:when test="number($base) != $base or number($power) != $power">
          <xsl:value-of select="'NaN'"/>
        </xsl:when>
        <xsl:when test="$power &lt; 0">
          <xsl:variable name="result">
          <xsl:call-template name="math:power-f">
           <xsl:with-param name="base" select="$base"/>
           <xsl:with-param name="power" select="-1 * $power"/>
          </xsl:call-template>
          </xsl:variable>
          <xsl:value-of select="1 div $result"/>
        </xsl:when>
        <xsl:otherwise>
          <xsl:variable name="powerN" select="floor($power)"/>
          <xsl:variable name="resultN">
          <xsl:call-template name="math:power">
            <xsl:with-param name="base" select="$base"/>
            <xsl:with-param name="power" select="$powerN"/>
          </xsl:call-template>
          </xsl:variable>
          <xsl:choose>
           <xsl:when test="$power - $powerN">
             <xsl:variable name="resultF">
               <xsl:call-template name="math:power-frac">
                <xsl:with-param name="base" select="$base"/>
                <xsl:with-param name="power" select="$power - $powerN"/>
               </xsl:call-template>
             </xsl:variable>
             <xsl:value-of select="$resultN * $resultF"/>
           </xsl:when>
           <xsl:otherwise>
             <xsl:value-of select="$resultN"/>
            </xsl:otherwise>
          </xsl:choose>
        </xsl:otherwise>
      </xsl:choose>
</xsl:template>

<xsl:template name="math:power-frac">
      <xsl:param name="base"/>
      <xsl:param name="power"/>

      <xsl:param name="n" select="1"/>
      <xsl:param name="ln_base">
        <xsl:call-template name="math:log">
          <xsl:with-param name="number" select="$base"/>
        </xsl:call-template>
      </xsl:param>
```

```
            <xsl:param name="ln_base_n" select="$ln_base"/>
            <xsl:param name="power_n" select="$power"/>
            <xsl:param name="n_fact" select="$n"/>
            <xsl:param name="result" select="1"/>

            <xsl:choose>
              <xsl:when test="20 >= $n">
                <xsl:call-template name="math:power-frac">
                  <xsl:with-param name="base" select="$base"/>
                  <xsl:with-param name="power" select="$power"/>
                  <xsl:with-param name="n" select="$n + 1"/>
                  <xsl:with-param name="ln_base" select="$ln_base "/>
                  <xsl:with-param name="ln_base_n" select="$ln_base_n * $ln_base"/>
                  <xsl:with-param name="power_n" select="$power_n * $power"/>
                  <xsl:with-param name="n_fact" select="$n_fact * ($n+1)"/>
                  <xsl:with-param name="result" select="$result +
                                ($power_n * $ln_base_n) div $n_fact"/>
                </xsl:call-template>
              </xsl:when>
            <xsl:otherwise>
              <xsl:value-of select="round($result * 1000000000) div 1000000000"/>
            </xsl:otherwise>
          </xsl:choose>
        </xsl:template>
```

The `math:power-f` template does not do the meat of the calculation. Instead, it checks for errors and then computes the result in terms of the existing template, `math:power`, and a new template, `math:power-frac`. Template `math:power-f` takes advantage of the following two mathematical truths about powers:

- $base^{-y} = 1 / base^y$, which allows you to handle negative powers easily.
- $base^{(power1+power2)} = base^{power1} * base^{power2}$, which lets you reuse the accuracy and efficiency `math:power( )` for the whole part of $power and use a good approximation for the fractional part.

The template `math:power-frac` is a recursive implementation of the *Maclaurin* series for $base^{power}$, as shown in Figure 2-1.

$$\text{power [base, power]} := 1.0 + \sum_{i=1}^{n} \frac{\text{Log [base]}^i \text{ power}^i}{i!}$$

Figure 2-1. Maclaurin series for basepower

One way to implement the trigonometric functions is to create similar recursive implementations of their Maclaurin representation.

Factorial

Oddly, EXSLT has not defined a factorial function. Factorial is, of course, easy to implement:

```
<xsl:template name="math:fact">
    <xsl:param name="number" select="0"/>
    <xsl:param name="result" select="1"/>
    <xsl:choose>
      <xsl:when test="$number &lt; 0 or floor($number) != $number">
        <xsl:value-of select="'NaN'"/>
      </xsl:when>
      <xsl:when test="$number &lt; 2">
        <xsl:value-of select="$result"/>
      </xsl:when>
      <xsl:otherwise>
        <xsl:call-template name="math:fact">
         <xsl:with-param name="number" select="$number - 1"/>
         <xsl:with-param name="result" select="$number * $result"/>
        </xsl:call-template>
      </xsl:otherwise>
    </xsl:choose>
</xsl:template>
```

A useful generalization of factorial is a function that computes the product of all numbers in a range:

```
<xsl:template name="math:prod-range">
    <xsl:param name="start" select="1"/>
    <xsl:param name="end" select="1"/>
    <xsl:param name="result" select="1"/>
    <xsl:choose>
      <xsl:when test="$start > $end">
        <xsl:value-of select="$result"/>
      </xsl:when>
      <xsl:otherwise>
        <xsl:call-template name="math:prod-range">
          <xsl:with-param name="start" select="$start + 1"/>
          <xsl:with-param name="end" select="$end"/>
          <xsl:with-param name="result" select="$start * $result"/>
        </xsl:call-template>
      </xsl:otherwise>
    </xsl:choose>
</xsl:template>
```

Discussion

I would guess that at least 80% of your garden-variety XSLT applications never require math beyond the native capabilities of XPath 1.0. When the remaining 20% need to go beyond XPath 1.0, chances are high that one or more of the previous functions are necessary.

The biggest drawback of a pure XSLT 1.0 implementation is that the templates cannot be invoked as first-class functions from XPath expression. This makes doing math awkward and slightly more inefficient because you need to create artificial variables to capture the results of template calls as result-tree fragments. Internally, the XSLT processor has to convert these fragments back to numbers when you use them in subsequent calculations.

Another problem with XSLT implementations is that the public interface of these templates is polluted with bookkeeping parameters that obscure the nature of the function. The bookkeeping parameters are often necessary to make the implementation tail recursive and prevent unnecessary work. For example, the implementation of power-frac needs to compute the log of the base and have it available at all times. If ln_base were not a parameter, then log would be invoked on every recursive call, resulting in unacceptable performance.

EXSLT defines the extension elements func:function and func:result, which solve the first problem by allowing XSLT programmers to define first-class functions. If your XSLT 1.0 processor implements these extensions, you should consider using them if absolute W3C standard conformance is not a priority. The XSLT 2.0 working draft proposes xsl:function and xsl:result elements that are very similar to EXSLT's. Yeah!

The second problem would be alleviated if a future XSLT version had private parameters that can be used only in a recursive call.

Example 2-8 shows how power-frac might look if function, if-else, and private parameters became available.

Example 2-8. Nonstandard XSLT 1.0

```
<xsl:function name="math:power-frac">
    <xsl:param name="base"/>
    <xsl:param name="power"/>

    <xsl:private name="n" select="1"/>
    <xsl:private name="ln_base" select="math:log($base)"/>
    <xsl:private name="ln_base_n" select="$ln_base"/>
    <xsl:private name="power_n" select="$power"/>
    <xsl:private name="n_fact" select="$n"/>
    <xsl:private name="result" select="1"/>

    <xsl:result select="if (20 >= $n)
      then
        math:power-frac($base,$power,$n + 1,ln_base,
            $ln_base_n * $ln_base,$power_n * $power,
            $n_fact * ($n+1),
            $result + $power_n * $ln_base_n) div $n_fact)
      else
        round($result * 1000000000) div 1000000000"/>
</xsl:function>
```

2.6 Computing Sums and Products

Problem

You need to sum or multiply functions of numbers contained in a node set.

Solution

The abstract form of sum for processors that support tail-recursive optimization is as follows:

```
<xsl:template name="math:sum">
  <!-- Initialize nodes to empty node set -->
  <xsl:param name="nodes" select="/.."/>
  <xsl:param name="result" select="0"/>
  <xsl:choose>
    <xsl:when test="not($nodes)">
      <xsl:value-of select="$result"/>
    </xsl:when>
    <xsl:otherwise>
        <!-- call or apply template that will determine value of node
            unless the node is literally the value to be summed -->
      <xsl:variable name="value">
        <xsl:call-template name="some-function-of-a-node">
          <xsl:with-param name="node" select="$nodes[1]"/>
        </xsl:call-template>
      </xsl:variable>
        <!-- recurse to sum rest -->
      <xsl:call-template name="math:sum">
        <xsl:with-param name="nodes" select="$nodes[position() != 1]"/>
        <xsl:with-param name="result" select="$result + $value"/>
      </xsl:call-template>
    </xsl:otherwise>
  </xsl:choose>
</xsl:template>
```

Two techniques can handle a large number of nodes in the absence of tail-recursive optimization. The first is commonly called *divide and conquer*. The idea behind this technique is to reduce the amount of work by at least a factor of two on each recursive step:

```
<xsl:template name="math:sum-dvc">
  <xsl:param name="nodes" select="/.."/>
  <xsl:param name="result" select="0"/>
  <xsl:param name="dvc-threshold" select="100"/>
  <xsl:choose>
    <xsl:when test="count($nodes) &lt;= $dvc-threshold">
        <xsl:call-template name="math:sum">
          <xsl:with-param name="nodes" select="$nodes"/>
          <xsl:with-param name="result" select="$result"/>
        </xsl:call-template>
    </xsl:when>
```

```
      <xsl:otherwise>
        <xsl:variable name="half" select="floor(count($nodes) div 2)"/>
        <xsl:variable name="sum1">
          <xsl:call-template name="math:sum-dvc">
            <xsl:with-param name="nodes" select="$nodes[position() &lt;= $half]"/>
           <xsl:with-param name="result" select="$result"/>
            <xsl:with-param name="dvc-threshold" select="$dvc-threshold"/>
          </xsl:call-template>
        </xsl:variable>
        <xsl:call-template name="math:sum-dvc">
          <xsl:with-param name="nodes" select="$nodes[position() > $half]"/>
          <xsl:with-param name="result" select="$sum1"/>
          <xsl:with-param name="dvc-threshold" select="$dvc-threshold"/>
        </xsl:call-template>
      </xsl:otherwise>
    </xsl:choose>
  </xsl:template>
```

The second is called *batching*, which uses two recursive stages. The first stage divides the large problem into batches of reasonable size. The second stage processes each batch recursively.

```
<xsl:template name="math:sum-batcher">
  <xsl:param name="nodes" select="/.."/>
  <xsl:param name="result" select="0"/>
  <xsl:param name="batch-size" select="500"/>
  <xsl:choose>
    <xsl:when test="not($nodes)">
      <xsl:value-of select="$result"/>
    </xsl:when>
    <xsl:otherwise>
      <xsl:variable name="batch-sum">
        <xsl:call-template name="math:sum">
          <xsl:with-param name="nodes"
               select="$nodes[position() &lt; $batch-size]"/>
          <xsl:with-param name="result" select="$result"/>
        </xsl:call-template>
      </xsl:variable>
      <xsl:call-template name="math:sum-batcher">
        <xsl:with-param name="nodes" select="$nodes[position() >= $batch-size]"/>
        <xsl:with-param name="result" select="$batch-sum"/>
        <xsl:with-param name="batch-size" select="$batch-size"/>
      </xsl:call-template>
    </xsl:otherwise>
  </xsl:choose>
</xsl:template>
```

The solutions for product are similar:

```
<xsl:template name="math:product">
  <xsl:param name="nodes" select="/.."/>
  <xsl:param name="result" select="1"/>
  <xsl:choose>
    <xsl:when test="not($nodes)">
      <xsl:value-of select="$result"/>
    </xsl:when>
```

```
      <xsl:otherwise>
         <!-- call or apply template that will determine value of node unless the node
         is literally the value to be multiplied -->
        <xsl:variable name="value">
          <xsl:call-template name="some-function-of-a-node">
            <xsl:with-param name="node" select="$nodes[1]"/>
          </xsl:call-template>
        </xsl:variable>
        <xsl:call-template name="math:product">
          <xsl:with-param name="nodes" select="$nodes[position( ) != 1]"/>
          <xsl:with-param name="result" select="$result * $value"/>
        </xsl:call-template>
      </xsl:otherwise>
    </xsl:choose>
</xsl:template>

<xsl:template name="math:product-batcher">
  <xsl:param name="nodes" select="/.."/>
  <xsl:param name="result" select="1"/>
  <xsl:param name="batch-size" select="500"/>
  <xsl:choose>
    <xsl:when test="not($nodes)">
      <xsl:value-of select="$result"/>
    </xsl:when>
    <xsl:otherwise>
      <xsl:variable name="batch-product">
        <xsl:call-template name="math:product">
          <xsl:with-param name="nodes" select="$nodes[position( ) &lt; $batch-size]"/>
          <xsl:with-param name="result" select="$result"/>
        </xsl:call-template>
      </xsl:variable>
      <xsl:call-template name="math:product-batcher">
          <xsl:with-param name="nodes" select="$nodes[position( ) >= $batch-size]"/>
          <xsl:with-param name="result" select="$batch-product"/>
          <xsl:with-param name="batch-size" select="$batch-size"/>
      </xsl:call-template>
    </xsl:otherwise>
  </xsl:choose>
</xsl:template>

<xsl:template name="math:product-dvc">
  <xsl:param name="nodes" select="/.."/>
  <xsl:param name="result" select="1"/>
  <xsl:param name="dvc-threshold" select="100"/>
  <xsl:choose>
    <xsl:when test="count($nodes) &lt;= $dvc-threshold">
        <xsl:call-template name="math:product">
          <xsl:with-param name="nodes" select="$nodes"/>
          <xsl:with-param name="result" select="$result"/>
        </xsl:call-template>
    </xsl:when>
```

```
        <xsl:otherwise>
          <xsl:variable name="half" select="floor(count($nodes) div 2)"/>
          <xsl:variable name="product1">
            <xsl:call-template name="math:product-dvc">
              <xsl:with-param name="nodes" select="$nodes[position() &lt;= $half]"/>
              <xsl:with-param name="result" select="$result"/>
              <xsl:with-param name="dvc-threshold" select="$dvc-threshold"/>
            </xsl:call-template>
          </xsl:variable>
          <xsl:call-template name="math:product-dvc">
            <xsl:with-param name="nodes" select="$nodes[position() > $half]"/>
            <xsl:with-param name="result" select="$product1"/>
            <xsl:with-param name="dvc-threshold" select="$dvc-threshold"/>
          </xsl:call-template>
        </xsl:otherwise>
      </xsl:choose>
    </xsl:template>
```

Using the built-in XPath sum( ) function is the simplest way to perform simple sums. However, if you want to compute sums of the nodes' arbitrary function in a node-set, then you need either to:

- Use one of the recipes in this section.
- Compute the function of the nodes first, capturing the result in a variable as a result-tree fragment. Then use an extension function to convert the fragment to a node set that can be fed to sum. In XSLT 2.0, generalized sums will become trivial because of the banishment of result-tree fragments.

Discussion

Batching and divide and conquer are two techniques for managing recursion that are useful whenever you must process a potentially large set of nodes. Experimentation shows that even when using an XSLT processor that recognizes tail recursion, better performance results from these approaches.

Chapter 14 shows how to make a reusable batch and divide-and-conquer drivers.

See Also

Dimitre Novatchev and Slawomir Tyszko compare batching with divide and conquer at *http://www.vbxml.com/xsl/articles/recurse/*.

2.7   Finding Minimums and Maximums

Problem

You need to find the minimum (or maximum) numerical node (or nodes) in a node set.

Solution

The EXSLT functions that perform these operations are `math:min`, `math:max`, `math: lowest`, and `math:highest`. `min` and `max` find the value of the node with minimum and maximum numerical value, respectively. EXSLT defines `math:min` as follows:

> The minimum value is defined as follows. The node set passed as an argument is sorted in ascending order as it would be by *xsl:sort* with a data type of number. The minimum is the result of converting the string value of the first node in this sorted list to a number using the *number* function.

> If the node set is empty, or if the result of converting the string values of any of the nodes to a number is NaN, then NaN is returned.

`math:max` is defined similarly. EXSLT provides pure XSLT implementations that are literal implementations of this definition, as shown in Example 2-9.

Example 2-9. EXSLT min and max implement directly from the definition

```
<xsl:template name="math:min">
   <xsl:param name="nodes" select="/.." />
   <xsl:choose>
      <xsl:when test="not($nodes)">NaN</xsl:when>
      <xsl:otherwise>
         <xsl:for-each select="$nodes">
            <xsl:sort data-type="number" />
            <xsl:if test="position( ) = 1">
               <xsl:value-of select="number(.)" />
            </xsl:if>
         </xsl:for-each>
      </xsl:otherwise>
   </xsl:choose>
</xsl:template>

<xsl:template name="math:max">
   <xsl:param name="nodes" select="/.." />
   <xsl:choose>
      <xsl:when test="not($nodes)">NaN</xsl:when>
      <xsl:otherwise>
         <xsl:for-each select="$nodes">
            <xsl:sort data-type="number" order="descending" />
            <xsl:if test="position( ) = 1">
               <xsl:value-of select="number(.)" />
```

```
        </xsl:if>
      </xsl:for-each>
    </xsl:otherwise>
  </xsl:choose>
</xsl:template>
```

You may be scratching your head over the default value for the nodes parameter (select="/.."). This is simply an idiomatic way to initialize nodes to an empty node set (i.e., the parent of the root is empty by definition).

Although the definitions of math:min and math:max use xsl:sort, the implementations need not, so results that are more efficient are possible provided your XSLT processor supports tail recursion (see Example 2-10).

Example 2-10. min and max implemented with divide and conquer

```
<xsl:template name="math:max">
    <xsl:param name="nodes" select="/.."/>
    <xsl:param name="max"/>
  <xsl:variable name="count" select="count($nodes)"/>
  <xsl:variable name="aNode" select="$nodes[ceiling($count div 2)]"/>
  <xsl:choose>
    <xsl:when test="not($count)">
      <xsl:value-of select="number($max)"/>
    </xsl:when>
    <xsl:when test="number($aNode) != number($aNode)">
      <xsl:value-of select="number($aNode)"/>
    </xsl:when>
    <xsl:otherwise>
      <xsl:call-template name="math:max">
        <xsl:with-param name="nodes" select="$nodes[not(. &lt;= number($aNode))]"/>
        <xsl:with-param name="max">
          <xsl:choose>
            <xsl:when test="not($max) or $aNode > $max">
              <xsl:value-of select="$aNode"/>
            </xsl:when>
            <xsl:otherwise>
              <xsl:value-of select="$max"/>
            </xsl:otherwise>
          </xsl:choose>
        </xsl:with-param>
      </xsl:call-template>
    </xsl:otherwise>
  </xsl:choose>
</xsl:template>

<xsl:template name="math:min">
  <xsl:param name="nodes" select="/.."/>
  <xsl:param name="min"/>
  <xsl:variable name="count" select="count($nodes)"/>
  <xsl:variable name="aNode" select="$nodes[ceiling($count div 2)]"/>
  <xsl:choose>
```

```
    <xsl:when test="not($count)">
      <xsl:value-of select="number($min)"/>
    </xsl:when>
    <xsl:when test="number($aNode) != number($aNode)">
      <xsl:value-of select="number($aNode)"/>
    </xsl:when>
    <xsl:otherwise>
      <xsl:call-template name="math:min">
        <xsl:with-param name="nodes" select="$nodes[not(. >= number($aNode))]"/>
        <xsl:with-param name="min">
          <xsl:choose>
            <xsl:when test="not($min) or $aNode &lt; $min">
              <xsl:value-of select="$aNode"/>
            </xsl:when>
            <xsl:otherwise>
              <xsl:value-of select="$min"/>
            </xsl:otherwise>
          </xsl:choose>
        </xsl:with-param>
      </xsl:call-template>
    </xsl:otherwise>
  </xsl:choose>
</xsl:template>
```

Typically, the preceding implementations are faster than the version using `xsl:sort`. In some degenerate cases, they are likely to be slower. The reason is that efficiency hinges on removing half the nodes from consideration (on average) at each recursive step. One can imagine a scenario in which at each pass aNode is the minimum node (in the case of `math:max`) or the maximum remaining node (in the case of `math:min`). If this were to occur, each pass would remove only one node, resulting in poor performance. Luckily, data tends to come in two configurations: presorted and random. In both cases, these implementations should hold their own.

While you had to look out for non-numeric data explicitly, EXSLT's implementations let `xsl:sort` take care of this. The XSLT standard mandates that non-numeric data be placed up front by sort when `data-type='number'`.

Don't be tempted to write `not(number($var))` to test for NaN! I often catch myself doing this because it "sounds" correct. The number function does not test *for* a number; instead, it attempts to convert its argument *to* a number. This is not what you want—this test will conclude 0 is not a number due to the conversion of 0 to false. The correct test is `number($var) != number($var)`. This test works because NaN is never equal to NaN, but any number is always equal to itself. Do not be tempted to shorten this idiom to `number($var) != $var`. Doing so works most of the time, but if $var is an empty node set, it will fail. If you prefer, a more direct approach `string(number($var)) = 'NaN'` also works.

EXSLT defines `math:lowest` as follows.

> The `math:lowest` function returns the nodes in the node set whose value is the minimum value for the node set. The minimum value for the node set is the same as the value as calculated by *math:min*. A node has this minimum value if the result of converting its string value to a number as if by the *number* function is equal to the minimum value, where the equality comparison is defined as a numerical comparison using the = operator.
>
> If any of the nodes in the node set has a non-numeric value, the *math:min* function will return NaN. The definition numeric comparisons entails that NaN != NaN. Therefore if any of the nodes in the node set has a non-numeric value, `math:lowest` will return an empty node set.

The EXSLT implementation is literally based on this definition and might not be very efficient:

```
<xsl:template name="math:lowest">
    <xsl:param name="nodes" select="/.." />
    <xsl:if test="$nodes and not($nodes[number(.) != number(.)])">
        <xsl:variable name="min">
            <xsl:for-each select="$nodes">
                <xsl:sort data-type="number" />
                <xsl:if test="position() = 1">
                    <xsl:value-of select="number(.)" />
                </xsl:if>
            </xsl:for-each>
        </xsl:variable>
        <xsl:copy-of select="$nodes[. = $min]" />
    </xsl:if>
</xsl:template>
```

The `xsl:if` test scans all nodes to handle cases when a non-numeric is present. It then sorts to find the `min` and finally collects all nodes with that `min`. Example 2-11 reuses `math:min` to do the same without needing to sort.

Example 2-11. Lowest implemented by reusing math:min

```
<xsl:template name="math:lowest">
    <xsl:param name="nodes" select="/.."/>

    <xsl:variable name="min">
        <xsl:call-template name="math:min">
            <xsl:with-param name="nodes" select="$nodes"/>
        </xsl:call-template>
    </xsl:variable>
    <xsl:choose>
        <xsl:when test="number($min) = number($min)">
            <xsl:copy-of select="$nodes[. = $min]"/>
        </xsl:when>
    </xsl:choose>
</xsl:template>
```

Finally, you can implement math:lowest with only one pass over the nodes if you are willing to forego reuse of math:min (see Example 2-12).

Example 2-12. Lowest implemented without reuse of math:min

```
<xsl:template name="math:lowest">
  <xsl:param name="nodes" select="/.."/>
  <xsl:param name="lowest" select="/.."/>
  <xsl:variable name="index" select="ceiling(count($nodes) div 2)"/>
  <xsl:variable name="aNode" select="$nodes[$index]"/>
  <xsl:choose>
    <xsl:when test="not($index)">
      <xsl:copy-of select="$lowest"/>
    </xsl:when>
    <xsl:when test="number($aNode) != number($aNode)"/>
    <xsl:otherwise>
      <xsl:choose>
        <xsl:when test="not($lowest) or $aNode &lt; $lowest">
          <xsl:call-template name="math:lowest">
            <xsl:with-param name="nodes" select="$nodes[not(. >= $aNode)]"/>
            <xsl:with-param name="lowest" select="$nodes[. = $aNode]"/>
          </xsl:call-template>
        </xsl:when>
        <xsl:when test="$aNode = $lowest">
          <xsl:call-template name="math:lowest">
            <xsl:with-param name="nodes" select="$nodes[not(. >= $aNode)]"/>
            <xsl:with-param name="lowest" select="$lowest|$nodes[$index]"/>
          </xsl:call-template>
        </xsl:when>
        <xsl:otherwise>
          <xsl:call-template name="math:lowest">
            <xsl:with-param name="nodes" select="$nodes[not(. >= $aNode)]"/>
            <xsl:with-param name="lowest" select="$lowest"/>
          </xsl:call-template>
        </xsl:otherwise>
      </xsl:choose>
    </xsl:otherwise>
  </xsl:choose>
</xsl:template>
```

Interestingly, this implementation does worse, probably because of the additional copying that occurs. In performance tests on 10,000 data points using various distributions of data (sorted, reverse sorted, semirandom, and random), the math:min-based implementation beat the xsl:sort-based implementation by about 40% on average (often better). The recursive implementation that did not use math:min was 24% slower than the one that did.

The math:highest definition and implementations follow directly from inverting the relational logic of math:lowest, so I will not discuss them here.

Discussion

The minimum and maximum values of a node set can be determined by the simple XPath expressions `<xsl:value-of select="$nodes[not($nodes &lt; .)]"/>` and `<xsl:value-of select="$nodes[not($nodes > .)]"/>`. In English, the first says, "Select all nodes for which there is no node less than its value," and the second says, "Select all nodes for which there is no node greater than its value."

Although very simple, these expressions have $O(N^2)$ performance, where N is the number of nodes. Therefore, unless you are certain that the number of nodes is small, avoid this shortcut if you can. Occasionally, you are forced to use it because, for example, you have to find the min/max within the select attribute of `xsl:sort` or the use attribute of `xsl:key` (for which you cannot call a template).

In another XSLT publication, the following recursive implementation for finding minimums is described as more efficient than one using `xsl:sort`:

```
<xsl:template name="math:min">
  <xsl:param name="nodes" select="/.."/>
  <xsl:param name="min" select="number('NaN')"/>
  <xsl:choose>
    <xsl:when test="not($nodes)">
      <xsl:value-of select="number($min)"/>
    </xsl:when>
    <xsl:otherwise>
      <xsl:variable name="aNode" select="$nodes[1]"/>
      <xsl:call-template name="math:min">
        <xsl:with-param name="nodes" select="$nodes[position() > 1]"/>
        <xsl:with-param name="min">
          <xsl:choose>
            <xsl:when test="$aNode &lt; $min or string($min) = 'NaN'">
              <xsl:value-of select="$aNode"/>
            </xsl:when>
            <xsl:otherwise>
              <xsl:value-of select="$min"/>
            </xsl:otherwise>
          </xsl:choose>
        </xsl:with-param>
      </xsl:call-template>
    </xsl:otherwise>
  </xsl:choose>
</xsl:template>
```

This is simply not the case on any XSLT implementation I tested, and I can't imagine that it ever could be. The reason this is much more likely to be slow is because only one node is removed from consideration at each step. Even with tail recursion, there will be a lot of copying of nodes. It is easy to be fooled into thinking that this recursive solution is as efficient as the iterative-indexing solution you might come up with in C or Java. However, indexing is not the same as creating a brand-new node set with the first item removed, as is the case with `$nodes[position() > 1]`.

In many cases when you need to find the minimum of a data set, you end up also needing the maximum. It would be nice to have a function handy that gives two for the price of one. The following will do so for a slight increase in complexity:

```
<xsl:template name="math:min-max">
  <xsl:param name="nodes" select="/.."/>
  <xsl:param name="nodes-for-max" select="$nodes"/>
  <xsl:param name="min"/>
  <xsl:param name="max"/>
  <xsl:variable name="count1" select="count($nodes)"/>
  <xsl:variable name="aNode1" select="$nodes[ceiling($count1 div 2)]"/>
  <xsl:variable name="count2" select="count($nodes-for-max)"/>
  <xsl:variable name="aNode2" select="$nodes-for-max[ceiling($count2 div 2)]"/>
  <xsl:choose>
    <xsl:when test="not($count1) and not($count2)">
      <xsl:value-of select="concat(number($min),',',number($max))"/>
    </xsl:when>
    <xsl:when test="number($aNode1) != number($aNode1) and
              number($aNode2) != number($aNode2)">
      <xsl:value-of select="concat(number($aNode1),',',number($aNode2))"/>
    </xsl:when>
    <xsl:otherwise>
      <xsl:call-template name="math:min-max">
        <xsl:with-param name="nodes" select="$nodes[not(. >= number($aNode1))]"/>
        <xsl:with-param name="nodes-for-max"
          select="$nodes-for-max[not(. &lt;= number($aNode2))]"/>
        <xsl:with-param name="min">
          <xsl:choose>
            <xsl:when test="not($min) or $aNode1 &lt; $min">
              <xsl:value-of select="$aNode1"/>
            </xsl:when>
            <xsl:otherwise>
              <xsl:value-of select="$min"/>
            </xsl:otherwise>
          </xsl:choose>
        </xsl:with-param>
        <xsl:with-param name="max">
          <xsl:choose>
            <xsl:when test="not($max) or $aNode2 > $max">
              <xsl:value-of select="$aNode2"/>
            </xsl:when>
            <xsl:otherwise>
              <xsl:value-of select="$max"/>
            </xsl:otherwise>
          </xsl:choose>
        </xsl:with-param>
      </xsl:call-template>
    </xsl:otherwise>
  </xsl:choose>
</xsl:template>
```

Testing shows that this approach continues to outperform a sort-based solution.

When considering minima and maxima, only one special case was addressed: when the nodes are literally the numbers you must process. A more general problem involves finding the minimum or maximum of a function of the nodes in a node set. For example, consider the case in which you have a set of positive and negative numbers and you need the minimum of the square of their value. Although hacking the previous implementations to do the squaring is simple, a single reusable implementation is more desirable. Chapter 14 revisits this problem and describes several alternatives for creating generic solutions.

2.8   Computing Statistical Functions

Problem

You need to compute averages, variances, and standard deviations.

Solution

Three types of averages are used by statisticians: the mean (layperson's average), the median, and the mode.

The mean is trivial—simply sum using Recipe 2.6 and divide by the count.

The median is the number that falls in the middle of the set of numbers when they are sorted. If the count is even, then the mean of the two middle numbers is generally taken:

```
<xsl:template name="math:median">
  <xsl:param name="nodes" select="/.."/>
  <xsl:variable name="count" select="count($nodes)"/>
  <xsl:variable name="middle" select="ceiling($count div 2)"/>
  <xsl:variable name="even" select="not($count mod 2)"/>

  <xsl:variable name="m1">
    <xsl:for-each select="$nodes">
      <xsl:sort data-type="number"/>
      <xsl:if test="position( ) = $middle">
        <xsl:value-of select=". + ($even * ./following-sibling::*[1])"/>
      </xsl:if>
    </xsl:for-each>
  </xsl:variable>

  <!-- The median -->
  <xsl:value-of select="$m1 div ($even + 1)"/>
</xsl:template>
```

Handling the even case relies on the Boolean-to-number conversion trick used in several other examples in this book. If the number of nodes is odd, $m1 ends up being equal to the middle node, and you divide by 1 to get the answer. On the other hand, if the number of nodes is odd, $m1 ends up being the sum of the two middle nodes, and you divide by two to get the answer.

The mode is the most frequently occurring element(s) in a set of elements that need not be numbers. If identical nodes compare with equality on their string values, then the following solution does the trick:

```
<xsl:template name="math:mode">
  <xsl:param name="nodes" select="/.."/>
  <xsl:param name="max" select="0"/>
  <xsl:param name="mode" select="/.."/>

  <xsl:choose>
    <xsl:when test="not($nodes)">
      <xsl:copy-of select="$mode"/>
    </xsl:when>
    <xsl:otherwise>
      <xsl:variable name="first" select="$nodes[1]"/>
      <xsl:variable name="try" select="$nodes[. = $first]"/>
      <xsl:variable name="count" select="count($try)"/>
      <!-- Recurse with nodes not equal to first -->
      <xsl:call-template name="math:mode">
        <xsl:with-param name="nodes" select="$nodes[not(. = $first)]"/>
        <!-- If we have found a node that is more frequent then
          pass the count otherwise pass the old max count -->
        <xsl:with-param name="max"
          select="($count > $max) * $count + not($count > $max) * $max"/>
        <!-- Compute the new mode as ... -->
        <xsl:with-param name="mode">
          <xsl:choose>
            <!-- the first element in try if we found a new max -->
            <xsl:when test="$count > $max">
              <xsl:copy-of select="$try[1]"/>
            </xsl:when>
            <!-- the old mode union the first element in try if we
                found an equivalent count to current max -->
            <xsl:when test="$count = $max">
              <!-- Caution: you will need to convert $mode to a -->
              <!-- node set if you are using a version of XSLT -->
              <!-- that does not convert automatically -->
              <xsl:copy-of select="$mode | $try[1]"/>
            </xsl:when>
            <!-- othewise the old mode stays the same -->
            <xsl:otherwise>
              <xsl:copy-of select="$mode"/>
            </xsl:otherwise>
          </xsl:choose>
        </xsl:with-param>
      </xsl:call-template>
    </xsl:otherwise>
  </xsl:choose>
</xsl:template>
```

If not, then replace the comparisons with an appropriate test. For example, if equality is contingent on an attribute called age, the test would be `./@age = $first/@age`.

The variance and standard deviation are common statistical measures of dispersion or the spread in the values about the average. The easiest way to compute a variance is to obtain three values: sum = the sum of the numbers, sum-sq = the sum of each number squared, and count = the size of the set of numbers. The variance is then (sum-sq - sum² / count) / count - 1. You can compute them all in one shot with the following tail-recursive template:

```
<xsl:template name="math:variance">
  <xsl:param name="nodes" select="/.."/>
  <xsl:param name="sum" select="0"/>
  <xsl:param name="sum-sq" select="0"/>
  <xsl:param name="count" select="0"/>
  <xsl:choose>
    <xsl:when test="not($nodes)">
      <xsl:value-of select="($sum-sq - ($sum * $sum) div $count) div ($count - 1)"/>
    </xsl:when>
    <xsl:otherwise>
      <xsl:variable name="value" select="$nodes[1]"/>
      <xsl:call-template name="math:variance">
        <xsl:with-param name="nodes" select="$nodes[position() != 1]"/>
        <xsl:with-param name="sum" select="$sum + $value"/>
        <xsl:with-param name="sum-sq" select="$sum-sq + ($value * $value)"/>
        <xsl:with-param name="count" select="$count + 1"/>
      </xsl:call-template>
    </xsl:otherwise>
  </xsl:choose>
</xsl:template>
```

You may recognize this template as a variation of math:sum that was extended to compute the other two components that comprise the variance calculation. As such, an XSLT implementation without support for tail recursion runs into trouble on large sets. In that case, you must take an alternate piecewise strategy based on the standard definition of variance: $\sum(mean - x_i)^2 / (count - 1)$. First, compute the mean by using the divide-and-conquer or batch forms of sum and diving by the count. Then use a divide-and-conquer or batch template that computes the sum of the squares of the difference between the mean and each number. Finally, divide the result by count - 1.

Once you can compute the variance, the standard deviation follows as the square root of the variance. See Recipe 2.5 for square root.

Discussion

Statistical functions are common tools for analyzing numerical data, and these templates can be a useful addition to your toolkit. However, XSLT was never intended as a tool for statistical analysis. An alternate approach would use XSLT as a frontend for converting XML data to comma- or tab-delimited data and then import this data into a spreadsheet or statistics package.

2.9   Computing Combinatorial Functions

Problem

You need to compute the number of permutations or combinations of size r of a given set.

Solution

If you know the formula for permutations of size r is N! / r! and you know that the formula for combinations is N! / r! * (N-r)!, then you might disregard this example; this book already gave an example for factorial. However, since factorials get very big quickly, you need to be a little crafty to get the best bang for your calculating buck:

```
<xsl:template name="math:P">
    <xsl:param name="n" select="1"/>
    <xsl:param name="r" select="1"/>
     <xsl:choose>
       <xsl:when test="$n &lt; 0 or $r &lt; 0">NaN</xsl:when>
       <xsl:when test="$n = 0">0</xsl:when>
       <xsl:otherwise>
            <xsl:call-template name="prod-range">
            <xsl:with-param name="start" select="$r + 1"/>
            <xsl:with-param name="end" select="$n"/>
         </xsl:call-template>
       </xsl:otherwise>
     </xsl:choose>
</xsl:template>

<xsl:template name="math:C">
    <xsl:param name="n" select="1"/>
    <xsl:param name="r" select="1"/>
     <xsl:choose>
       <xsl:when test="$n &lt; 0 or $r &lt; 0">NaN</xsl:when>
       <xsl:when test="$n = 0">0</xsl:when>
       <xsl:otherwise>
         <xsl:variable name="min"
             select="($r &lt;= $n - $r) * $r +  ($r > $n - $r) * $n - $r"/>
         <xsl:variable name="max"
             select="($r >= $n - $r) * $r +  ($r &lt; $n - $r) * $n - $r"/>
         <xsl:variable name="numerator">
           <xsl:call-template name="prod-range">
                <xsl:with-param name="start" select="$max + 1"/>
                <xsl:with-param name="end" select="$n"/>
           </xsl:call-template>
         </xsl:variable>
         <xsl:variable name="denominator">
           <xsl:call-template name="math:fact">
             <xsl:with-param name="number" select="$min"/>
           </xsl:call-template>
         </xsl:variable>
```

```
            <xsl:value-of select="$numerator div $denominator"/>
         </xsl:otherwise>
      </xsl:choose>
   </xsl:template>
```

Discussion

The solutions are designed to reduce the number of multiplications; if you divide one factorial by a smaller factorial, then the smaller factorial effectively cancels out that many multiplications from the larger. Hence, it is better to implement such functions using prod-range (Recipe 2.5) rather than factorial. The combinatorial is slightly more complex because you want to cancel out the large of r and (n - r).

2.10   Testing Bits

Problem

You want to treat numbers as bit masks even though XSLT does not have integers or associated bitwise operators.

 When working with XML, don't go out of your way to encode information in bits. Use this solution only when you have no control over the encoding of the data.

Solution

The following solution works on 16-bit numbers, but can easily be extended up to 32:

```
<xsl:stylesheet xmlns:xsl="http://www.w3.org/1999/XSL/Transform"
    version="1.0" id="bittesting">

<!--powers of two-->
<xsl:variable name="bit15" select="32768"/>
<xsl:variable name="bit14" select="16384"/>
<xsl:variable name="bit13" select="8192"/>
<xsl:variable name="bit12" select="4096"/>
<xsl:variable name="bit11" select="2048"/>
<xsl:variable name="bit10" select="1024"/>
<xsl:variable name="bit9"  select="512"/>
<xsl:variable name="bit8"  select="256"/>
<xsl:variable name="bit7"  select="128"/>
<xsl:variable name="bit6"  select="64"/>
<xsl:variable name="bit5"  select="32"/>
<xsl:variable name="bit4"  select="16"/>
<xsl:variable name="bit3"  select="8"/>
<xsl:variable name="bit2"  select="4"/>
<xsl:variable name="bit1"  select="2"/>
<xsl:variable name="bit0"  select="1"/>
```

```
<xsl:template name="bitTest">
  <xsl:param name="num"/>
  <xsl:param name="bit" select="$bit0"/>
  <xsl:choose>
    <xsl:when test="( $num mod ( $bit * 2 ) ) -
                    ( $num mod ( $bit ) )">1</xsl:when>
    <xsl:otherwise>0</xsl:otherwise>
  </xsl:choose>
</xsl:template>

<xsl:template name="bitAnd">
  <xsl:param name="num1"/>
  <xsl:param name="num2"/>
  <xsl:param name="result" select="0"/>
  <xsl:param name="test" select="$bit15"/>

  <xsl:variable name="nextN1"
      select="($num1 >= $test) * ($num1 - $test) + not($num1 >= $test) * $num1"/>
  <xsl:variable name="nextN2"
      select="($num2 >= $test) * ($num2 - $test) + not($num2 >= $test) * $num2"/>

  <xsl:choose>
    <xsl:when test="$test &lt; 1">
      <xsl:value-of select="$result"/>
    </xsl:when>
    <xsl:when test="$num1 >= $test and $num2 >= $test">
      <xsl:call-template name="bitAnd">
        <xsl:with-param name="num1" select="$nextN1"/>
        <xsl:with-param name="num2" select="$nextN2"/>
        <xsl:with-param name="result" select="$result + $test"/>
        <xsl:with-param name="test" select="$test div 2"/>
      </xsl:call-template>
    </xsl:when>
    <xsl:otherwise>
      <xsl:call-template name="bitAnd">
        <xsl:with-param name="num1" select="$nextN1"/>
        <xsl:with-param name="num2" select="$nextN2"/>
        <xsl:with-param name="result" select="$result"/>
        <xsl:with-param name="test" select="$test div 2"/>
      </xsl:call-template>
    </xsl:otherwise>
  </xsl:choose>
</xsl:template>

<xsl:template name="bitOr">
  <xsl:param name="num1"/>
  <xsl:param name="num2"/>
  <xsl:param name="result" select="0"/>
  <xsl:param name="test" select="$bit15"/>

  <xsl:variable name="nextN1"
      select="($num1 >= $test) * ($num1 - $test) + not($num1 >= $test) * $num1"/>
  <xsl:variable name="nextN2"
      select="($num2 >= $test) * ($num2 - $test) + not($num2 >= $test) * $num2"/>
```

```
    <xsl:choose>
      <xsl:when test="$test &lt; 1">
        <xsl:value-of select="$result"/>
      </xsl:when>
      <xsl:when test="$num1 >= $test or $num2 >= $test">
        <xsl:call-template name="bitOr">
          <xsl:with-param name="num1" select="$nextN1"/>
          <xsl:with-param name="num2" select="$nextN2"/>
          <xsl:with-param name="result" select="$result + $test"/>
          <xsl:with-param name="test" select="$test div 2"/>
        </xsl:call-template>
      </xsl:when>
      <xsl:otherwise>
        <xsl:call-template name="bitOr">
          <xsl:with-param name="num1" select="$nextN1"/>
          <xsl:with-param name="num2" select="$nextN2"/>
          <xsl:with-param name="result" select="$result"/>
          <xsl:with-param name="test" select="$test div 2"/>
        </xsl:call-template>
      </xsl:otherwise>
    </xsl:choose>
</xsl:template>

<xsl:template name="bitXor">
  <xsl:param name="num1"/>
  <xsl:param name="num2"/>
  <xsl:param name="result" select="0"/>
  <xsl:param name="test" select="$bit15"/>

  <xsl:variable name="nextN1"
      select="($num1 >= $test) * ($num1 - $test) + not($num1 >= $test) * $num1"/>
  <xsl:variable name="nextN2"
      select="($num2 >= $test) * ($num2 - $test) + not($num2 >= $test) * $num2"/>

  <xsl:choose>
    <xsl:when test="$test &lt; 1">
      <xsl:value-of select="$result"/>
    </xsl:when>
    <xsl:when test="$num1 >= $test and not($num2 >= $test)
        or not($num1 >= $test) and $num2 >= $test">
      <xsl:call-template name="bitXor">
        <xsl:with-param name="num1" select="$nextN1"/>
        <xsl:with-param name="num2" select="$nextN2"/>
        <xsl:with-param name="result" select="$result + $test"/>
        <xsl:with-param name="test" select="$test div 2"/>
      </xsl:call-template>
    </xsl:when>
    <xsl:otherwise>
      <xsl:call-template name="bitXor">
        <xsl:with-param name="num1" select="$nextN1"/>
        <xsl:with-param name="num2" select="$nextN2"/>
        <xsl:with-param name="result" select="$result"/>
        <xsl:with-param name="test" select="$test div 2"/>
```

```
        </xsl:call-template>
      </xsl:otherwise>
    </xsl:choose>
</xsl:template>

<xsl:template name="bitNot">
  <xsl:param name="num"/>
  <xsl:param name="result" select="0"/>
  <xsl:param name="test" select="$bit15"/>

  <xsl:choose>
    <xsl:when test="$test &lt; 1">
      <xsl:value-of select="$result"/>
    </xsl:when>
    <xsl:when test="$num >= $test">
      <xsl:call-template name="bitNot">
        <xsl:with-param name="num" select="$num - $test"/>
        <xsl:with-param name="result" select="$result"/>
        <xsl:with-param name="test" select="$test div 2"/>
      </xsl:call-template>
    </xsl:when>
    <xsl:otherwise>
      <xsl:call-template name="bitNot">
        <xsl:with-param name="num" select="$num"/>
        <xsl:with-param name="result" select="$result + $test"/>
        <xsl:with-param name="test" select="$test div 2"/>
      </xsl:call-template>
    </xsl:otherwise>
  </xsl:choose>
</xsl:template>

</xsl:stylesheet>
```

Discussion

This solution for testing bits (bitTest template) based on modulo arithmetic was discussed at XML DevCon London in February 2001. We implemented the bitwise logical operations recursively using comparison and subtraction, but you could also use division and mod as shown in the following code:

```
<xsl:template name="bitAnd">
  <xsl:param name="num1"/>
  <xsl:param name="num2"/>
  <xsl:param name="result" select="0"/>
  <xsl:param name="pow2" select="$bit0"/>

  <xsl:choose>
    <xsl:when test="$num1 &lt; 1 or $num2 &lt; 1">
      <xsl:value-of select="$result"/>
    </xsl:when>
    <xsl:when test="$num1 mod 2 and $num2 mod 2">
      <xsl:call-template name="bitAnd">
```

```
          <xsl:with-param name="num1" select="floor($num1 div 2)"/>
          <xsl:with-param name="num2" select="floor($num2 div 2)"/>
          <xsl:with-param name="result" select="$result + $pow2"/>
          <xsl:with-param name="pow2" select="$pow2 * 2"/>
        </xsl:call-template>
      </xsl:when>
      <xsl:otherwise>
        <xsl:call-template name="bitAnd">
          <xsl:with-param name="num1" select="floor($num1 div 2)"/>
          <xsl:with-param name="num2" select="floor($num2 div 2)"/>
          <xsl:with-param name="result" select="$result"/>
          <xsl:with-param name="pow2" select="$pow2 * 2"/>
        </xsl:call-template>
      </xsl:otherwise>
    </xsl:choose>
</xsl:template>

<xsl:template name="bitOr">
  <xsl:param name="num1"/>
  <xsl:param name="num2"/>
  <xsl:param name="result" select="0"/>
  <xsl:param name="pow2" select="$bit0"/>

  <xsl:choose>
    <xsl:when test="$num1 &lt; 1 and $num2 &lt; 1">
      <xsl:value-of select="$result"/>
    </xsl:when>
    <xsl:when test="boolean($num1 mod 2) or boolean($num2 mod 2)">
      <xsl:call-template name="bitOr">
        <xsl:with-param name="num1" select="floor($num1 div 2)"/>
        <xsl:with-param name="num2" select="floor($num2 div 2)"/>
        <xsl:with-param name="result" select="$result + $pow2"/>
        <xsl:with-param name="pow2" select="$pow2 * 2"/>
      </xsl:call-template>
    </xsl:when>
    <xsl:otherwise>
      <xsl:call-template name="bitOr">
        <xsl:with-param name="num1" select="floor($num1 div 2)"/>
        <xsl:with-param name="num2" select="floor($num2 div 2)"/>
        <xsl:with-param name="result" select="$result"/>
        <xsl:with-param name="pow2" select="$pow2 * 2"/>
      </xsl:call-template>
    </xsl:otherwise>
  </xsl:choose>
</xsl:template>

<xsl:template name="bitXor">
  <xsl:param name="num1"/>
  <xsl:param name="num2"/>
  <xsl:param name="result" select="0"/>
  <xsl:param name="pow2" select="$bit0"/>
```

```
    <xsl:choose>
      <xsl:when test="$num1 &lt; 1 and $num2 &lt; 1">
        <xsl:value-of select="$result"/>
      </xsl:when>
      <xsl:when test="$num1 mod 2 + $num2 mod 2 = 1">
        <xsl:call-template name="bitXor">
          <xsl:with-param name="num1" select="floor($num1 div 2)"/>
          <xsl:with-param name="num2" select="floor($num2 div 2)"/>
          <xsl:with-param name="result" select="$result + $pow2"/>
          <xsl:with-param name="pow2" select="$pow2 * 2"/>
        </xsl:call-template>
      </xsl:when>
      <xsl:otherwise>
        <xsl:call-template name="bitXor">
          <xsl:with-param name="num1" select="floor($num1 div 2)"/>
          <xsl:with-param name="num2" select="floor($num2 div 2)"/>
          <xsl:with-param name="result" select="$result"/>
          <xsl:with-param name="pow2" select="$pow2 * 2"/>
        </xsl:call-template>
      </xsl:otherwise>
    </xsl:choose>
</xsl:template>
```

CHAPTER 3

Dates and Times

Does anyone really know what time it is?
Does anyone really care?
—Chicago

Native XSLT 1.0 does not know what time it is and does not seem to care. However, dates and times are a necessary aspect of everyday life. The need to manipulate them arises frequently in computing, especially in web development. Therefore, it is surprising and unfortunate that standard XSLT does not have any built-in date and time support.

The examples in this section can help compensate for XSLT's lack of support for dates and times. Unfortunately, one of the most crucial date and time capabilities cannot be implemented in XSLT—that is, getting the current date and time. For that, you need to call out to another language whose library supports interacting with the hardware's real-time clock. Both Java and JavaScript have this capability. If your application just needs to format dates and times that already exist in a document, then the routines here should cover most needs.

Data and time manipulation and conversion can be tricky, but it is almost purely an exercise in intricate integer arithmetic involving what are essentially base conversions in a mixed radix system. Working with non-Gregorian calendars and determining holidays also requires quite a bit of historical, religious, and cultural knowledge. Readers with no application for date and time routines may wish to skip this chapter because little by way of XSLT technique is unique to these algorithms. Those who are curious about the theory behind these calculations should definitely look at the papers sited in the "See Also" section.

I am grateful to Jason Diamond for graciously contributing many of the templates dealing with Gregorian time. The XSLT code for dealing with non-Gregorian calendars was adapted from Edward M. Reingold's public domain Lisp implementation. Some of the algorithms were adapted to better suit XSLT and build upon the existing foundation provided by Jason's code.

Do not be confused by the technique used to pass a date into most templates. It is designed for maximum convenience. You can pass in the date in two ways: by using a string formatted using ISO date-time rules and by using the individual parameters for the year, month, and day. The following example should clarify usage:

```
<xsl:call-template name="date:calculate-day-of-the-week">
    <xsl:with-param name="date-time" select="'2002-01-01T01:00:00'"/>
</xsl:call-template>

<xsl:call-template name="date:calculate-day-of-the-week">
    <xsl:with-param name="date" select="'2002-01-01'"/>
</xsl:call-template>

<xsl:call-template name="date:calculate-day-of-the-week">
    <xsl:with-param name="year" select="2002"/>
    <xsl:with-param name="month" select="01"/>
    <xsl:with-param name="day" select="01"/>
</xsl:call-template>
```

Each of the calls evaluates the day of the week for January 1, 2002. The first two variations are convenient when a date is already ISO formatted. The last variation is convenient when the components of the date are stored separately. You can also override parts of an ISO date string as follows:

```
<xsl:call-template name="date:calculate-day-of-the-week">
    <xsl:with-param name="date" select="'2002-01-01'"/>
    <xsl:with-parm name="day" select="25"/>
</xsl:call-template>
```

In all templates, unless otherwise stated, dates are Gregorian by default. This civil calendar system is used by most of the Western world.

See Also

Claus Tøndering's calendars FAQ *(http://www.pauahtun.org/CalendarFAQ/cal/ calendar24.pdf)* contains the illuminating theory behind many calculations in this chapter.

Jason Diamond's original XSLT implementation can be found at *http://xsltsl. sourceforge.net/date-time.html.*

Calendrical Calculations (*http://emr.cs.iit.edu/~reingold/calendar.ps*) by Nachum Dershowitz and Edward M. Reingold provides additional insight. Their paper discusses the non-Gregorian systems covered here.

I do not cover the Chinese or Indian calendars in this chapter because they are more complex. Information about the mathematics of the Chinese and Indian calendars can be found at *http://www.math.nus.edu.sg/aslaksen/calendar/chinese.shtml* and *http: //www.math.nus.edu.sg/aslaksen/calendar/indian.shtml*, respectively.

If for some reason you have an application for the Mayan, French Revolutionary, or Old Hindu calendars, then you should investigate Calendrical Calculations II (*http://emr.cs.iit.edu/~reingold/calendar2.ps*).

EXSLT.org has a date-time module that provides much of the same functionality as the Gregorian date-time templates implemented in this chapter. They also provide templates for working durations (differences between dates and times).

XForms (*http://www.w3.org/MarkUp/Forms/*) provides some date-time functionality. It uses XML Schema (ISO) lexical representations (with durations subdivided into dateTime and yearMonth flavors). The new functions are: now( ), days-from-date( ), seconds-from-dateTime( ), seconds( ), and months( ).

3.1 Calculating the Day of the Week

Problem

Given the year, month, and day, you want to determine the day of the week.

Solution

The following calculation does the trick and returns an integer in the range of 0–6, where 0=Sunday.

```
<xsl:template name="date:calculate-day-of-the-week">
  <xsl:param name="date-time"/>
  <xsl:param name="date" select="substring-before($date-time,'T')"/>
  <xsl:param name="year" select="substring-before($date,'-')"/>
  <xsl:param name="month"
        select="substring-before(substring-after($date,'-'),'-')"/>
  <xsl:param name="day" select="substring-after(substring-after($date,'-'),'-')"/>

  <xsl:variable name="a" select="floor((14 - $month) div 12)"/>
  <xsl:variable name="y" select="$year - $a"/>
  <xsl:variable name="m" select="$month + 12 * $a - 2"/>

  <xsl:value-of select="($day + $y + floor($y div 4) - floor($y div 100)
  + floor($y div 400) + floor((31 * $m) div 12)) mod 7"/>

</xsl:template>
```

Discussion

You will notice that these equations and those in other examples make judicious use of the XPath floor( ) function. This is the only way to emulate integer arithmetic in XSLT, since all numbers are represented in floating point internally. The reason why this calculation works has to do with intricacies of the Gregorian calendar that are not particularly relevant to XSLT. For example, the fact that 97 leap years occur every 400 years so that every year divisible by 4 is a leap year, except if it is divisible by 100 and not divisible by 400, explains the final calculation. For further information, see the sidebar "The Logic Behind the Math."

The Logic Behind the Math

Claus Tøndering was kind enough to clear up the mystery behind these calculations.

To get the formulas to work, first perform these calculations:

```
a = (14 - month) / 12
y = year - a
m = month + 12*a - 2
```

These calculations move the start of the year from January 1 to March 1. Since a=1 for January and February and 0 for all other months, 1 is subtracted from the year in these two months. Similarly, m becomes 1 for March, 2 for April, . . . , 10 for December, 11 for January, and 12 for February.

Once these three calculations are performed, you have a year that starts on March 1. This result gives two advantages. First, it means that the leap day is placed at the end of the year, which makes calculations simpler. Second, it means that the lengths of the months follow a simple pattern:

```
31 30 31 30 31 (March-July)
31 30 31 30 31 (August-December)
31 X (January-February)
```

This setup enables you to use the expression (31*m)/12 to calculate the weekday offset in each month.

3.2   Determining the Last Day of the Month

Problem

Given a month and a year, determine the last day of the month.

Solution

```
<xsl:template name="date:last-day-of-month">
    <xsl:param name="month"/>
    <xsl:param name="year"/>
    <xsl:choose>
      <xsl:when test="$month = 2 and
        not($year mod 4) and
        ($year mod 100 or not($year mod 400))">
        <xsl:value-of select="29"/>
        </xsl:when>
      <xsl:otherwise>
```

```
        <xsl:value-of
          select="substring('312831303130313130313031',
                    2 * $month - 1,2)"/>
      </xsl:otherwise>
    </xsl:choose>
  </xsl:template>
```

Discussion

This function has potential application for constructing pages of a calendar. It is simple enough to understand once you know the rules governing a leap year. This function was translated from Lisp, in which the number of days in each month was extracted from a list. I choose to use substring to accomplish the same task. You may prefer to place the logic in additional when elements. You might also store data about each month, including its length, in XML.

See Also

See Recipe 3.4 for ways to store calendar metadata in XML.

3.3   Getting Names for Days and Months

Problem

You want to convert from numerical values for days and months to symbolic values.

Solution

If internationalization is not important to your application, then the following simple code will do:

```
<xsl:template name="date:get-day-of-the-week-name">
  <xsl:param name="day-of-the-week"/>

  <xsl:choose>
    <xsl:when test="$day-of-the-week = 0">Sunday</xsl:when>
    <xsl:when test="$day-of-the-week = 1">Monday</xsl:when>
    <xsl:when test="$day-of-the-week = 2">Tuesday</xsl:when>
    <xsl:when test="$day-of-the-week = 3">Wednesday</xsl:when>
    <xsl:when test="$day-of-the-week = 4">Thursday</xsl:when>
    <xsl:when test="$day-of-the-week = 5">Friday</xsl:when>
    <xsl:when test="$day-of-the-week = 6">Saturday</xsl:when>
    <xsl:otherwise>
        error: <xsl:value-of select="$day-of-the-week"/>
      </xsl:otherwise>
  </xsl:choose>

</xsl:template>
```

```
<xsl:template name="date:get-day-of-the-week-abbreviation">
  <xsl:param name="day-of-the-week"/>

  <xsl:choose>
    <xsl:when test="$day-of-the-week = 0">Sun</xsl:when>
    <xsl:when test="$day-of-the-week = 1">Mon</xsl:when>
    <xsl:when test="$day-of-the-week = 2">Tue</xsl:when>
    <xsl:when test="$day-of-the-week = 3">Wed</xsl:when>
    <xsl:when test="$day-of-the-week = 4">Thu</xsl:when>
    <xsl:when test="$day-of-the-week = 5">Fri</xsl:when>
    <xsl:when test="$day-of-the-week = 6">Sat</xsl:when>
    <xsl:otherwise>
        error: <xsl:value-of select="$day-of-the-week"/>
      </xsl:otherwise>
  </xsl:choose>

</xsl:template>

<xsl:template name="date:get-month-name">
  <xsl:param name="month"/>

  <xsl:choose>
    <xsl:when test="$month = 1">January</xsl:when>
    <xsl:when test="$month = 2">February</xsl:when>
    <xsl:when test="$month = 3">March</xsl:when>
    <xsl:when test="$month = 4">April</xsl:when>
    <xsl:when test="$month = 5">May</xsl:when>
    <xsl:when test="$month = 6">June</xsl:when>
    <xsl:when test="$month = 7">July</xsl:when>
    <xsl:when test="$month = 8">August</xsl:when>
    <xsl:when test="$month = 9">September</xsl:when>
    <xsl:when test="$month = 10">October</xsl:when>
    <xsl:when test="$month = 11">November</xsl:when>
    <xsl:when test="$month = 12">December</xsl:when>
    <xsl:otherwise>error: <xsl:value-of select="$month"/></xsl:otherwise>
  </xsl:choose>

</xsl:template>

<xsl:template name="date:get-month-abbreviation">
  <xsl:param name="month"/>

  <xsl:choose>
    <xsl:when test="$month = 1">Jan</xsl:when>
    <xsl:when test="$month = 2">Feb</xsl:when>
    <xsl:when test="$month = 3">Mar</xsl:when>
    <xsl:when test="$month = 4">Apr</xsl:when>
    <xsl:when test="$month = 5">May</xsl:when>
    <xsl:when test="$month = 6">Jun</xsl:when>
    <xsl:when test="$month = 7">Jul</xsl:when>
    <xsl:when test="$month = 8">Aug</xsl:when>
    <xsl:when test="$month = 9">Sep</xsl:when>
    <xsl:when test="$month = 10">Oct</xsl:when>
    <xsl:when test="$month = 11">Nov</xsl:when>
    <xsl:when test="$month = 12">Dec</xsl:when>
```

```
        <xsl:otherwise>error: <xsl:value-of select="$month"/></xsl:otherwise>
      </xsl:choose>

   </xsl:template>
```

Discussion

These templates are just fine if your application will never be used outside of the English-speaking world. However, you might consider using a table-driven approach for added portability:

```
<xsl:stylesheet
   version="1.0"
   xmlns:xsl="http://www.w3.org/1999/XSL/Transform"
   xmlns:date="http://www.ora.com/XSLTCookbook/NS/dates">

<!-- United States : us -->
<date:month country="us" m="1"  name="January" abbrev="Jan" />
<date:month country="us" m="2"  name="February" abbrev="Feb"/>
<date:month country="us" m="3"  name="March" abbrev="Mar"/>
<date:month country="us" m="4"  name="April" abbrev="Apr"/>
<date:month country="us" m="5"  name="May" abbrev="May"/>
<date:month country="us" m="6"  name="June" abbrev="Jun"/>
<date:month country="us" m="7"  name="July" abbrev="Jul"/>
<date:month country="us" m="8"  name="August" abbrev="Aug"/>
<date:month country="us" m="9"  name="September" abbrev="Sep"/>
<date:month country="us" m="10" name="October" abbrev="Oct"/>
<date:month country="us" m="11" name="November" abbrev="Nov"/>
<date:month country="us" m="12" name="December" abbrev="Dec"/>

<!-- Germany : de -->
<date:month country="de" m="1"  name="Januar" abbrev="Jan"/>
<date:month country="de" m="2"name=";Februar" abbrev="Feb"/>
<date:month country="de" m="3"  name="März" abbrev="Mär"/>
<date:month country="de" m="4"  name="April" abbrev="Apr"/>
<date:month country="de" m="5"  name="Mai" abbrev="Mai"/>
<date:month country="de" m="6"  name="Juni" abbrev="Jun"/>
<date:month country="de" m="7"  name="Juli" abbrev="Jul"/>
<date:month country="de" m="8"  name="August" abbrev="Aug"/>
<date:month country="de" m="9"  name="September" abbrev="Sep"/>
<date:month country="de" m="10" name="Oktober" abbrev="Okt"/>
<date:month country="de" m="11" name="November" abbrev="Nov"/>
<date:month country="de" m="12" name="Dezember" abbrev="Dez"/>
<!-- You get the idea ... -->

<!-- Store element in variable for easy access -->
<xsl:variable name="date:months" select="document('')/*/date:month"/>

</xsl:stylesheet>

<xsl:stylesheet
   version="1.0"
   xmlns:xsl="http://www.w3.org/1999/XSL/Transform"
   xmlns:date="http://www.ora.com/XSLTCookbook/dates">
```

```
<xsl:include href="date-conversion.xsl"/>

<xsl:template name="date:get-month-name">
    <xsl:param name="month"/>
    <xsl:param name="country" select=" 'us' "/>

    <xsl:value-of select="$date:months[@country=$country and
        @m=$month]/@name"/>
</xsl:template>
```

3.4 Calculating Julian and Absolute Day Numbers from a Specified Date

Problem

You have a date and would like to know the corresponding Julian day number and/or Absolute day number.

Julian Day Versus Julian Dates

Do not make the mistake of confusing the Julian day with the Julian calendar. Joseph J. Scaliger has invented the Julian period so that every year could be associated with a positive number without having to worry about BC/AD. The period starts on January 1, 4713 BC (according to the Julian calendar) and lasts for 7980 years. Astronomers have used the Julian period to assign a unique number to every day since 1 January 4713 BC. This is the *Julian day*. As I write this chapter, the Julian day is 2,452,376. The curious can use the code in this section to determine the actual date. Another absolute numbering scheme used by N. Dershowitz and E. Reingold in their calendar algorithms begins on January 1, 1 AD. I refer to a number in their system as an *Absolute day number*. Absolute day 1 corresponds to Julian Day 1,721,426.

Solution

This template will give you the Julian day, given the year, month, and day:

```
<xsl:template name="date:calculate-julian-day">
    <xsl:param name="year"/>
    <xsl:param name="month"/>
    <xsl:param name="day"/>

    <xsl:variable name="a" select="floor((14 - $month) div 12)"/>
    <xsl:variable name="y" select="$year + 4800 - $a"/>
    <xsl:variable name="m" select="$month + 12 * $a - 3"/>

    <xsl:value-of select="$day + floor((153 * $m + 2) div 5) + $y * 365 +
```

```
        floor($y div 4) - floor($y div 100) + floor($y div 400) -
        32045"/>

    </xsl:template>
```

Once you have a way to calculate the Julian day number, it is easy to create a template for determining the number of days between any two dates:

```
<xsl:template name="date:date-difference">
    <xsl:param name="from-year"/>
    <xsl:param name="from-month"/>
    <xsl:param name="from-day"/>
    <xsl:param name="to-year"/>
    <xsl:param name="to-month"/>
    <xsl:param name="to-day"/>

    <xsl:variable name="jd1">
      <xsl:call-template name="date:calculate-julian-day">
       <xsl:with-param name="year" select="$from-year"/>
        <xsl:with-param name="month" select="$from-month"/>
        <xsl:with-param name="day" select="$from-day"/>
     </xsl:call-template>
    </xsl:variable>

    <xsl:variable name="jd2">
      <xsl:call-template name="date:calculate-julian-day">
       <xsl:with-param name="year" select="$to-year"/>
        <xsl:with-param name="month" select="$to-month"/>
        <xsl:with-param name="day" select="$to-day"/>
     </xsl:call-template>
    </xsl:variable>

    <xsl:value-of select="$jd1 - $jd2"/>
</xsl:template>
```

The following templates convert from a Julian day to a Gregorian date in the form YYYY/MM/DD. Use substring-before, substring-after, and translate to parse or convert to the conventions of a particular locale:

```
<xsl:template name="date:julian-day-to-julian-date">
    <xsl:param name="j-day"/>

    <xsl:call-template name="date:julian-or-gregorian-date-elem">
        <xsl:with param name="b" select="0"/>
        <xsl:with param name="c" select="$j-day + 32082"/>
    </xsl:call-template>

</xsl:template>

<xsl:template name="date:julian-day-to-gregorian-date">
    <xsl:param name="j-day"/>

    <xsl:variable name="a" select="$j-day + 32044"/>
    <xsl:variable name="b" select="floor((4 * $a + 3) div 146097)"/>
    <xsl:variable name="c" select="$a - 146097 * floor($b div 4)"/>
```

```
        <xsl:call-template name="date:julian-or-gregorian-date-elem">
            <xsl:with param name="b" select="$b"/>
            <xsl:with param name="c" select="$c"/>
        </xsl:call-template>


    </xsl:template>

    <!-- A utility that is used for both Gregorian and Julian calendars. -->
    <xsl:template name="date:julian-or-gregorian-date-elem">
        <xsl:param name="b"/>
        <xsl:param name="c"/>

        <xsl:variable name="d" select="floor((4 * $c + 3) div 1461)"/>
        <xsl:variable name="e" select="$c - floor((1461 * $d) div 4)"/>
        <xsl:variable name="m" select="floor((5 * $e + 2) div 153)"/>

        <xsl:variable name="day"
            select="$e - floor((153 * $m + 2) div 5) + 1"/>

        <xsl:variable name="month"
            select="$m + 3 - (12 * floor($m div 10))"/>

        <xsl:variable name="year"
            select="100 * $b + $d - 4800 + floor($m div 10)"/>

        <xsl:value-of select="concat($year,'/',$month,'/',$day)"/>

    </xsl:template>
```

You can easily convert between Julian days and Absolute days with the following templates:

```
    <xsl:template name="date:julian-day-to-absolute-day">
        <xsl:param name="j-day"/>
        <xsl:value-of select="$j-day - 1721425"/>
    </xsl:template>

    <xsl:template name="date:absolute-day-to-julian-day">
        <xsl:param name="abs-day"/>
        <xsl:value-of select="$abs-day + 1721425"/>
    </xsl:template>
```

You can then express Absolute day/Gregorian conversions in terms of the existing Julian day/Gregorian conversions:

```
    <xsl:template name="date:date-to-absolute-day">
        <xsl:param name="year"/>
        <xsl:param name="month"/>
        <xsl:param name="day"/>

        <xsl:call-template name="date:julian-day-to-absolute-day">
          <xsl:with-param name="j-day">
            <xsl:call-template name="date:date-to-julian-day">
              <xsl:with-param name="year" select="$year"/>
```

```
                <xsl:with-param name="month" select="$month"/>
                <xsl:with-param name="day" select="$day"/>
            </xsl:call template>
        </xsl:with-param>
    </xsl:call-template>
</xsl:template>

<xsl:template name="date:absolute-day-to-date">
    <xsl:param name="abs-day"/>

    <xsl:call-template name="date:julian-day-to-date">
        <xsl:with-param name="j-day">
            <xsl:call-template name="date:absolute-day-to-julian-day">
                <xsl:with-param name="abs-day" select="$abs-day"/>
            </xsl:call-template>
        </xsl:with-param>
    </xsl:call-template>
</xsl:template>
```

Discussion

The Julian day and Absolute day are useful because they greatly simplify other date algorithms. Other examples in this chapter reuse these conversions extensively. These numbering schemes act as a common currency for all the calendar systems in this chapter. Should you ever find yourself needing to convert a Hebrew date to a Muslim date, the sequence Muslim to Absolute to Hebrew will do the trick.

3.5 Calculating the Week Number for a Specified Date

Problem

You want to convert from a date to the number of the week with in the year.

Solution

The week number ranges from 1 to 53. Although most years have 52 weeks, years containing 53 Thursdays have 53.

The solution reuses the Julian day template:

```
<xsl:template name="date:calculate-week-number">
    <xsl:param name="year"/>
    <xsl:param name="month"/>
    <xsl:param name="day"/>

    <xsl:variable name="date:j-day">
        <xsl:call-template name="date:calculate-julian-day">
            <xsl:with-param name="year" select="$year"/>
            <xsl:with-param name="month" select="$month"/>
```

```
      <xsl:with-param name="day" select="$day"/>
    </xsl:call-template>
</xsl:variable>

<xsl:variable name="d4"
      select="($j-day + 31741 - ($j-day mod 7))
            mod 146097 mod 36524 mod 1461"/>

<xsl:variable name="L" select="floor($d4 div 1460)"/>

<xsl:variable name="d1" select="(($d4 - $L) mod 365) + $L"/>

<xsl:value-of select="floor($d1 div 7) + 1"/>

</xsl:template>
```

 This function assumes that Monday is the first day of the week. Most of the other functions in this chapter use the more popular convention in which weeks start on Sunday. See the ISO calendar recipes for an explanation of this idiosyncrasy.

Discussion

The week number is the number assigned to each week of the year. Week 1 of any year is the week that contains January 4 or, equivalently, the week that contains the first Thursday in January. A week that overlaps the end of one year and the beginning of the next is assigned to the year when most of the week's days lie. This will occur when the year starts on Thursday or Wednesday in a leap year. The U.S. does not currently use this numbering system.

See Also

See Recipe 3.7, "Working with the ISO Calendar," later in this chapter.

3.6 Working with the Julian Calendar

Problem

You need to work in the old Julian system of dates.

Solution

```
<xsl:template name="date:julian-date-to-julian-day">
    <xsl:param name="year"/>
    <xsl:param name="month"/>
    <xsl:param name="day"/>
```

```
<xsl:variable name="a" select="floor((14 - $month) div 12)"/>
<xsl:variable name="y" select="$year + 4800 - $a"/>
<xsl:variable name="m" select="$month + 12 * $a - 3"/>

<xsl:value-of
    select="$day + floor((153 * $m + 2) div 5) + 365 * $y
    + floor($y div 4) - 32083"/>

</xsl:template>
```

Once you have the Julian day, you can use other recipes in this chapter for date formatting, date math, or conversion to other calendar systems.

Discussion

The Julian system is rarely used in modern times. (One exception is the Russian Orthodox Church.) The Julian calendar was abandoned in favor of the Gregorian calendar due to its slightly inaccurate estimate of a year containing 365 1/4 days. The mean length is actually 365.2425 days, and over time, the seasons began to shift under the Julian system.

3.7 Working with the ISO Calendar

Problem

You need to work with dates in the International standard ISO-8601 calendar.[*]

Readers familiar with XML Schema should not confuse the ISO calendar with the ISO format for standard Gregorian dates (e.g., 2002-04-12 or 2002-04-12T09:26:00). Both the calendar and the formatting standard are covered in the 8601 standard. This recipe is concerned with the ISO calendar.

Solution

A basic facility you need to work with ISO dates (and, later, for determining certain holidays) is a function for finding the absolute day of the kth day on or before a specific absolute day. For example, the first Monday (k = 1) on or before January 4, 2004 (absolute day 731,584) is December 29, 2003 (absolute day 731,578):

```
<xsl:template name="date:k-day-on-or-before-abs-day">
    <xsl:param name="abs-day"/>
    <xsl:param name="k"/>
    <xsl:value-of select="$abs-day - (($abs-day - $k) mod 7)"/>
</xsl:template>
```

---

[*] ISO is the International Organization for Standardization (I guess they thought ISO rolled off the tongue better than IOS).

You can now convert ISO dates to absolute days, which is a simple matter of determining the number of absolute days in prior years and adding in the remaining days in the given ISO date:

```
<xsl:template name="date:iso-date-to-absolute-day">
    <xsl:param name="iso-week"/>
    <xsl:param name="iso-day"/>
    <xsl:param name="iso-year"/>

    <xsl:variable name="jan-4-of-year">
      <xsl:call-template name="date:date-to-absolute-day">
        <xsl:with-param name="year" select="$iso-year"/>
        <xsl:with-param name="month" select="1"/>
        <xsl:with-param name="day" select="4"/>
      </xsl:call-template>
    </xsl:variable>

    <xsl:variable name="days-in-prior-yrs">
      <xsl:call-template name="date:k-day-on-or-before-abs-day">
        <xsl:with-param name="abs-day" select="$jan-4-of-year"/>
        <xsl:with-param name="k" select="1"/>
      </xsl:call-template>
    </xsl:variable>

    <xsl:variable name="days-in-prior-weeks-this-yr"
        select="7 * ($iso-week - 1)"/>

    <xsl:variable name="prior-days-this-week"     select="$iso-day - 1"/>

    <xsl:value-of select="$days-in-prior-yrs +
        $days-in-prior-weeks-this-yr + $prior-days-this-week"/>
</xsl:template>
```

To convert from absolute days to an ISO date, the code will first try to establish the year by making a guess that it is the same as the Gregorian minus 3 days. This guess can be wrong only if the absolute day is actually on Jan 1 to Jan 3 of the following year. To correct for the possible off-by-one mistake, a comparison is made to Jan 1 of the following year using the iso-date-to-absolute-day code already on hand. Having firmly established the ISO year, the week and day follow by computing the offset from Jan 1 of that year. We return the ISO date formatted as *year-week-day*. This format is an ISO convention to prevent ISO dates from being confused with Gregorian dates:

```
<xsl:template name="date:absolute-day-to-iso-date">
    <xsl:param name="abs-day"/>

    <xsl:variable name="d">
      <xsl:call-template name="date:absolute-day-to-date">
        <xsl:with-param name="abs-day" select="$abs-day - 3"/>
      </xsl:call-template>
    </xsl:variable>
```

```
<xsl:variable name="approx" select="substring-before($d,'/')"/>

<xsl:variable name="iso-year">
  <xsl:variable name="a">
    <xsl:call-template name="date:iso-date-to-absolute-day">
     <xsl:with-param name="iso-week" select="1"/>
     <xsl:with-param name="iso-day" select="1"/>
     <xsl:with-param name="iso-year" select="$approx + 1"/>
    </xsl:call-template>
  </xsl:variable>
  <xsl:choose>
    <xsl:when test="$abs-day >= $a">
     <xsl:value-of select="$approx + 1"/>
    </xsl:when>
    <xsl:otherwise>
     <xsl:value-of select="$approx"/>
    </xsl:otherwise>
  </xsl:choose>
</xsl:variable>

<xsl:variable name="date:iso-week">
  <xsl:variable name="a">
    <xsl:call-template name="date:iso-date-to-absolute-day">
       <xsl:with-param name="iso-week" select="1"/>
       <xsl:with-param name="iso-day" select="1"/>
       <xsl:with-param name="iso-year" select="$iso-year"/>
    </xsl:call-template>
  </xsl:variable>
  <xsl:value-of select="1 + floor(($abs-day - $a) div 7)"/>
</xsl:variable>

<xsl:variable name="iso-day">
  <xsl:variable name="a" select="$abs-day mod 7"/>
    <xsl:choose>
      <xsl:when test="not($a)">
        <xsl:value-of select="7"/>
      </xsl:when>
      <xsl:otherwise>
            <xsl:value-of select="$a"/>
        </xsl:otherwise>
      </xsl:choose>
</xsl:variable>

<xsl:value-of select="concat($iso-year,'-W',$iso-week,'-',$iso-day)"/>

</xsl:template>
```

Discussion

In European commercial and industrial applications, reference to a week of a year is
often required. The ISO calendar specifies dates by using the Gregorian year, the week
number (1–53) within the year, and the ordinal day of the week (1–7, where ISO man-

dates the first day of the week is Monday). A week that overlaps successive years is assigned to the year with the most days in that week. According to this rule, the first week of the ISO calendar year can begin as late as January 4 and as early as December 29 of the previous year. Likewise, the last week of the ISO calendar year can end as early as December 28 and as late as January 3 of the following year. For example, in 2004, ISO week 1 will actually start on December 29, 2003!* To determine the start of the ISO week, then, you need to find the Monday on or before January 4.

See Also

You can see the ISO calendar in action at *http://personal.ecu.edu/mccartyr/isowdcal. html.*

3.8   Working with the Islamic Calendar

Problem

You need to work with dates in the Islamic system.

 It is difficult if not impossible to devise universally accepted algorithms for the Islamic calendar. This is because each month starts when the lunar crescent is first seen (by an actual human being) after a new moon. New moons can be calculated quite precisely, but the actual visibility of the crescent depends on factors such as weather and the location of the observer. It is therefore very difficult to compute accurately in advance when a new month will start. Furthermore, some Muslims depend on a local sighting of the moon, whereas others depend on a sighting by authorities somewhere in the Muslim world. Saudi Arabia is an exception, since they use astronomical calculation rather than visual sightings. The algorithms provided here can be off by a few days when computing Islamic dates far in advance.

Solution

The last day of an Islamic month can be estimated quite accurately by assigning 30 days to odd months and 29 days to even months, except during a leap year.

```
<xsl:template name="date:last-day-of-islamic-month">
    <xsl:param name="month"/>
    <xsl:param name="year"/>

    <xsl:variable name="islamic-leap-year"
        select="(11 * $year + 14) mod 30 &lt; 11"/>
```

---

* And you thought standards were supposed to simplify life!

```
  <xsl:choose>
    <xsl:when test="$month mod 2 or ($month = 12 and $islamic-leap-year)">
      <xsl:value-of select="30"/>
    </xsl:when>
    <xsl:otherwise>
      <xsl:value-of select="29"/>
    </xsl:otherwise>
  </xsl:choose>
</xsl:template>
```

The Islamic calendar began with the Hijra, Mohammed's emigration to Medina. For most Muslims, this date occurred on sunset of July 15, 622 AD (Julian calendar). This corresponds to absolute day 227,015, hence the offset of 227,014 in the otherwise straightforward calculation of the absolute day from the Islamic date:

```
<xsl:template name="date:islamic-date-to-absolute-day">
    <xsl:param name="year"/>
    <xsl:param name="month"/>
    <xsl:param name="day"/>

    <xsl:value-of select="$day + 29 * ($month - 1) + floor($month div 2) + 354
        * ($year - 1) + floor((11 * $year + 3) div 30) + 227014"/>
</xsl:template>
```

The absolute day to Islamic date conversion is different from the original Lisp code from which it was adapted. I use floating-point math to avoid a search technique employed in the Lisp implementation. The authors of the Lisp code desired to keep all calculations within 24-bit integer limits while retaining the greatest clarity. However, their techniques did not translate well to XSLT. Given that XSLT uses only floating-point math, it does not make sense to go through pains to avoid it. The numbers used stem from the average lunar month having 29.530555... days. The month number is approximated and then adjusted if it would result in a day with value less than 1. Once the year and month are established, the day can be computed as an offset from the first day of the year:

```
<xsl:template name="date:absolute-day-to-islamic-date">
    <xsl:param name="abs-day"/>


    <xsl:variable name="year"
        select="floor(($abs-day - 227014) div 354.36667) + 1"/>

    <xsl:variable name="month">
      <xsl:variable name="a"
          select="$abs-day - 227014 - floor((11 * $year + 3) div 30) -
                354 * ($year - 1)"/>
      <xsl:variable name="approx" select="floor($a div 29.53056)+1"/>
      <xsl:choose>
        <xsl:when test="(29 * ($approx - 1) + floor($approx div 2)) -
          $a &lt; 1">
          <xsl:value-of select="$approx - 1"/>
        </xsl:when>
```

```xsl
    <xsl:otherwise>
      <xsl:value-of select="$approx"/>
    </xsl:otherwise>
  </xsl:choose>
</xsl:variable>

<xsl:variable name="day">
  <xsl:variable name="a">
    <xsl:call-template name="date:islamic-date-to-absolute-day">
      <xsl:with-param name="year" select="$year"/>
      <xsl:with-param name="month" select="$month"/>
      <xsl:with-param name="day" select="1"/>
    </xsl:call-template>
  </xsl:variable>
  <xsl:value-of select="$abs-day - $a + 1"/>
</xsl:variable>

<xsl:value-of select="concat($year,'/',$month,'/',$day)"/>

</xsl:template>
```

Discussion

The Hijri or Islamic calendar is interesting because it is based on purely lunar cycles, and thus the Muslim months are not fixed with in the seasons. An Islamic year is approximately 354.36 days. The first year of the Islamic calendar is denoted 1 A.H. (After Hijra), Muhammad's flight from Mecca to Medina. The Islamic calendar has deep religious significance to devout Muslims and is almost always based on visual observations of the Moon. Approximate calendars can be computed in advance by using algorithms, but they should generally be used only for rough planning.

See Also

You can see the Muslim calendar in action at *http://www.sufisattari.com/calendar. html*.

Differences in convention among various Islamic counties are described at *http://www.math.nus.edu.sg/aslaksen/calendar/islamic.shtml*.

3.9   Working with the Hebrew Calendar

Problem

You need to work with dates in the Hebrew system.

Solution

You need to build up some basic utilities to work effectively with the Hebrew calendar. Hebrew years have 12 months in a regular year and 13 in a leap year. Leap years occur on the 3rd, 6th, 8th, 11th, 14th, 17th, and 19th years of the *Metonic cycle* (see the "Discussion" section). A concise means of making this determination is given by the relation $7y + 1 \bmod 19 < 7$. From this, you can easily devise a function to determine the last month of any Hebrew year:

```
<xsl:template name="date:last-month-of-hebrew-year">
    <xsl:param name="year"/>
    <xsl:choose>
        <xsl:when test="(7 * $year + 1) mod 19 &lt; 7">
            <xsl:value-of select="13"/>
        </xsl:when>
        <xsl:otherwise>
            <xsl:value-of select="12"/>
        </xsl:otherwise>
    </xsl:choose>
</xsl:template>
```

As a prerequisite to determining the number of days in any given month or year, you need to encapsulate the complex rules that determine when the Hebrew new year starts. See the paper by Dershowitz and Reingold for detailed explanation.

```
<-- Number of days ellased from the Sunday prior to the start of the Hebrew calender
to the mean conjunction of Tishri of Hebrew year. -->

<xsl:template name="date:hebrew-calendar-ellapsed-days">
    <xsl:param name="year"/>

    <xsl:variable name="hebrew-leap-year"
        select="(7 * $year + 1) mod 19 &lt; 7"/>
    <xsl:variable name="hebrew-leap-year-last-year"
        select="(7 * ($year - 1) + 1) mod 19 &lt; 7"/>

    <xsl:variable name="months-ellapsed"
        select="235 * floor(($year -1) div 19) +
            12 * (($year -1) mod 19) +
            floor((7 * (($year - 1) mod 19) + 1) div 19)"/>

    <xsl:variable name="parts-ellapsed"
        select="13753 * $months-ellapsed + 5604"/>

    <xsl:variable name="day" select="1 + 29 * $months-ellapsed +
                    floor($parts-ellapsed div 25920)"/>

    <xsl:variable name="parts" select="$parts-ellapsed mod 25920"/>

    <xsl:variable name="alternative-day">
      <xsl:choose>
        <xsl:when test="$parts >= 19440">
          <xsl:value-of select="$day + 1"/>
```

```
      </xsl:when>
      <xsl:when test="$day mod 7 = 2 and $parts >= 9924 and
              not($hebrew-leap-year)">
       <xsl:value-of select="$day + 1"/>
      </xsl:when>
      <xsl:when test="$day mod 7 = 1 and $parts >= 16789 and
              $hebrew-leap-year-last-year">
       <xsl:value-of select="$day + 1"/>
      </xsl:when>
      <xsl:otherwise>
       <xsl:value-of select="$day"/>
      </xsl:otherwise>
    </xsl:choose>
  </xsl:variable>

  <xsl:choose>
    <xsl:when test="$alternative-day mod 7 = 0">
      <xsl:value-of select="$alternative-day + 1"/>
    </xsl:when>
    <xsl:when test="$alternative-day mod 7 =3">
      <xsl:value-of select="$alternative-day + 1"/>
    </xsl:when>
    <xsl:when test="$alternative-day mod 7 = 5">
      <xsl:value-of select="$alternative-day + 1"/>
    </xsl:when>
    <xsl:otherwise>
      <xsl:value-of select="$alternative-day"/>
    </xsl:otherwise>
  </xsl:choose>

</xsl:template>
```

The number of days in a Hebrew year is calculated as the difference between the elapsed days in successive years:

```
<xsl:template name="date:days-in-hebrew-year">
    <xsl:param name="year"/>

    <xsl:variable name="e1">
      <xsl:call-template name="date:hebrew-calendar-ellapsed-days">
        <xsl:with-param name="year" select="$year + 1"/>
      </xsl:call-template>
    </xsl:variable>

    <xsl:variable name="e2">
      <xsl:call-template name="date:hebrew-calendar-ellapsed-days">
        <xsl:with-param name="year" select="$year"/>
      </xsl:call-template>
    </xsl:variable>

    <xsl:value-of select="$e1 - $e2"/>
</xsl:template>
```

Heshvan and Kislev are the eighth and nineth months of the Hebrew year and their number of days can vary. You need to know when Heshvan is long and Kislev is short, so you create two predicates.

```
<xsl:template name="date:long-heshvan">
    <xsl:param name="year"/>

    <xsl:variable name="days">
        <xsl:call-template name="date:days-in-hebrew-year">
            <xsl:with-param name="year" select="$year"/>
        </xsl:call-template>
    </xsl:variable>

    <xsl:if select="$days mod 10 = 5">
        <xsl:value-of select="true( )"/>
    </xsl:if>
</xsl:template>

<xsl:template name="date:short-kislev">
    <xsl:param name="year"/>

    <xsl:variable name="days">
        <xsl:call-template name="date:days-in-hebrew-year">
            <xsl:with-param name="year" select="$year"/>
        </xsl:call-template>
    </xsl:variable>

    <xsl:if select="$days mod 10 = 3">
        <xsl:value-of select="true( )"/>
    </xsl:if>
</xsl:template>
```

 If you write predicate templates in XSLT, you should code them to return true( ) (or alternatively, 'true') for true but '' (null string) for false. The problem here is that templates return trees, and any tree, even one whose only node contains false( ) or '', will evaluate to true. The advantage of a tree containing '' is that it can be effectively evaluated as a Boolean by using the string( ) conversion. This is one of the many awkward facts of XSLT.

Most of the machinery is now in place to tackle standard date-time functions provided in other recipes. The first standard function gives the last day in a month for a specified Hebrew month and year:

```
<xsl:template name="date:last-day-of-hebrew-month">
    <xsl:param name="month"/>
    <xsl:param name="year"/>

    <xsl:variable name="hebrew-leap-year"
        select="(7 * $year + 1) mod 19 &lt; 7"/>
```

```
<xsl:variable name="long-heshvan">
  <xsl:call-template name="date:long-heshvan">
    <xsl:with-param name="year" select="$year"/>
  </xsl:call-template>
</xsl:variable>

<xsl:variable name="short-kislev">
  <xsl:call-template name="date:short-kislev">
    <xsl:with-param name="year" select="$year"/>
  </xsl:call-template>
</xsl:variable>

<xsl:choose>
  <xsl:when test="$month=12 and $hebrew-leap-year">
    <xsl:value-of select="30"/>
  </xsl:when>
  <xsl:when test="$month=8 and string($long-heshvan)">
    <xsl:value-of select="30"/>
  </xsl:when>
  <xsl:when test="$month=9 and string($short-kislev)">
    <xsl:value-of select="29"/>
  </xsl:when>
  <xsl:when test="$month=13">
    <xsl:value-of select="29"/>
  </xsl:when>
  <xsl:when test="$month mod 2 = 0">
    <xsl:value-of select="29"/>
  </xsl:when>
  <xsl:otherwise>
    <xsl:value-of select="30"/>
  </xsl:otherwise>
</xsl:choose>
</xsl:template>
```

This recursive utility lets you sum the last days in a range of Hebrew months for a given year. It is used when converting a Hebrew date to an absolute year.

```
<xsl:template name="date:sum-last-day-in-hebrew-months">
    <xsl:param name="year"/>
    <xsl:param name="from-month"/>
    <xsl:param name="to-month"/>
    <xsl:param name="accum" select="0"/>

    <xsl:choose>
      <xsl:when test="$from-month &lt;= $to-month">
        <xsl:call-template name="date:sum-last-day-in-hebrew-months">
          <xsl:with-param name="year" select="$year"/>
          <xsl:with-param name="from-month" select="$from-month+1"/>
          <xsl:with-param name="to-month" select="$to-month"/>
          <xsl:with-param name="accum">
            <xsl:variable name="temp">
              <xsl:call-template name="date:last-day-of-hebrew-month">
                <xsl:with-param name="year" select="$year"/>
                <xsl:with-param name="month" select="$from-month"/>
```

```
            </xsl:call-template>
          </xsl:variable>
          <xsl:value-of select="$temp + $accum"/>
        </xsl:with-param>
      </xsl:call-template>
    </xsl:when>
    <xsl:otherwise>
      <xsl:value-of select="$accum"/>
    </xsl:otherwise>
  </xsl:choose>
</xsl:template>

<xsl:template name="date:hebrew-date-to-absolute-day">
    <xsl:param name="year"/>
    <xsl:param name="month"/>
    <xsl:param name="day"/>


    <xsl:variable name="prior-months-days">
      <xsl:choose>
        <xsl:when test="7 > $month"> <!-- before Tishri -->
          <xsl:variable name="last-month-of-year">
            <xsl:call-template name="date:last-month-of-hebrew-year">
              <xsl:with-param name="year" select="$year"/>
            </xsl:call-template>
          </xsl:variable>
          <!-- Add days before and after Nisan -->
          <xsl:variable name="days-before-nisan">
            <xsl:call-template name="date:sum-last-day-in-hebrew-months">
              <xsl:with-param name="year" select="$year"/>
              <xsl:with-param name="from-month" select="7"/>
              <xsl:with-param name="to-month"
               select="$last-month-of-year"/>
            </xsl:call-template>
          </xsl:variable>
          <xsl:call-template name="date:sum-last-day-in-hebrew-months">
            <xsl:with-param name="year" select="$year"/>
            <xsl:with-param name="from-month" select="1"/>
            <xsl:with-param name="to-month" select="$month - 1"/>
            <xsl:with-param name="accum" select="$days-before-nisan"/>
          </xsl:call-template>
        </xsl:when>
        <xsl:otherwise>
          <!-- days in prior months this year-->
          <xsl:call-template name="date:sum-last-day-in-hebrew-months">
            <xsl:with-param name="year" select="$year"/>
            <xsl:with-param name="from-month" select="7"/>
            <xsl:with-param name="to-month" select="$month - 1"/>
          </xsl:call-template>
        </xsl:otherwise>
      </xsl:choose>
    </xsl:variable>
```

```
    <xsl:variable name="days-in-prior-years">
      <xsl:call-template name="date:hebrew-calendar-ellapsed-days">
        <xsl:with-param name="year" select="$year"/>
      </xsl:call-template>
    </xsl:variable>

    <!--     1373429 days before absolute day 1 -->
    <xsl:value-of select="$day + $prior-months-days +
        $days-in-prior-years - 1373429"/>
</xsl:template>
```

Before implementing absolute-day-to-hebrew-date, you need two more recursive summation utilities that will help search for the actual year and month corresponding to an absolute day from approximations of the same year and month:

```
<xsl:template name="date:fixup-hebrew-year">
    <xsl:param name="start-year"/>
    <xsl:param name="abs-day"/>

    <xsl:param name="accum" select="0"/>

    <xsl:variable name="next">
      <xsl:call-template name="date:hebrew-date-to-absolute-day">
        <xsl:with-param name="month" select="7"/>
        <xsl:with-param name="day" select="1"/>
        <xsl:with-param name="year" select="$start-year + 1"/>
      </xsl:call-template>
    </xsl:variable>

    <xsl:choose>
      <xsl:when test="$abs-day >= $next">
        <xsl:call-template name="date:fixup-hebrew-year">
         <xsl:with-param name="start-year" select="$start-year+1"/>
         <xsl:with-param name="abs-day" select="$abs-day"/>
         <xsl:with-param name="accum" select="$accum + 1"/>
        </xsl:call-template>
      </xsl:when>
      <xsl:otherwise>
        <xsl:value-of select="$accum"/>
      </xsl:otherwise>
    </xsl:choose>
</xsl:template>

<xsl:template name="date:fixup-hebrew-month">
    <xsl:param name="year"/>
    <xsl:param name="start-month"/>
    <xsl:param name="abs-day"/>

    <xsl:param name="accum" select="0"/>

    <xsl:variable name="next">
      <xsl:call-template name="date:hebrew-date-to-absolute-day">
        <xsl:with-param name="month" select="$start-month"/>
        <xsl:with-param name="day">
```

```
          <xsl:call-template name="date:last-day-of-hebrew-month">
            <xsl:with-param name="month" select="$start-month"/>
            <xsl:with-param name="year" select="$year"/>
          </xsl:call-template>
        </xsl:with-param>
        <xsl:with-param name="year" select="$year"/>
      </xsl:call-template>
    </xsl:variable>

    <xsl:choose>
      <xsl:when test="$abs-day > $next">
        <xsl:call-template name="date:fixup-hebrew-month">
          <xsl:with-param name="year" select="$year"/>
          <xsl:with-param name="start-month" select="$start-month + 1"/>
          <xsl:with-param name="abs-day" select="$abs-day"/>
          <xsl:with-param name="accum" select="$accum + 1"/>
        </xsl:call-template>
      </xsl:when>
      <xsl:otherwise>
        <xsl:value-of select="$accum"/>
      </xsl:otherwise>
    </xsl:choose>
</xsl:template>

<xsl:template name="date:absolute-day-to-hebrew-date">
    <xsl:param name="abs-day"/>

    <xsl:variable name="year">
      <xsl:variable name="approx"
        select="floor(($abs-day + 1373429) div 366)"/>
      <xsl:variable name="fixup">
        <xsl:call-template name="date:fixup-hebrew-year">
          <xsl:with-param name="start-year" select="$approx"/>
          <xsl:with-param name="abs-day" select="$abs-day"/>
        </xsl:call-template>
      </xsl:variable>
      <xsl:value-of select="$approx + $fixup"/>
    </xsl:variable>

    <xsl:variable name="month">
      <xsl:variable name="first-day-of-year">
      <xsl:call-template name="date:hebrew-date-to-absolute-day">
        <xsl:with-param name="month" select="1"/>
        <xsl:with-param name="day" select="1"/>
        <xsl:with-param name="year" select="$year"/>
      </xsl:call-template>
    </xsl:variable>

    <xsl:variable name="approx">
      <xsl:choose>
        <xsl:when test="$abs-day &lt; $first-day-of-year">
          <xsl:value-of select="7"/>
        </xsl:when>
        <xsl:otherwise>
```

```
              <xsl:value-of select="1"/>
          </xsl:otherwise>
        </xsl:choose>
      </xsl:variable>

      <xsl:variable name="fixup">
        <xsl:call-template name="date:fixup-hebrew-month">
          <xsl:with-param name="year" select="$year"/>
          <xsl:with-param name="start-month" select="$approx"/>
          <xsl:with-param name="abs-day" select="$abs-day"/>
        </xsl:call-template>
      </xsl:variable>

      <xsl:value-of select="$approx + $fixup"/>
    </xsl:variable>

    <xsl:variable name="day">
      <xsl:variable name="days-to-first-of-month">
        <xsl:call-template name="date:hebrew-date-to-absolute-day">
          <xsl:with-param name="month" select="$month"/>
          <xsl:with-param name="day" select="1"/>
          <xsl:with-param name="year" select="$year"/>
        </xsl:call-template>
      </xsl:variable>

      <xsl:value-of select="$abs-day - ($days-to-first-of-month - 1)"/>
    </xsl:variable>

    <xsl:value-of select="concat($year,'-',$month,'-',$day)"/>

  </xsl:template>
```

In the previous example, you create three unique yet similar recursive templates that compute the sum of a function. Creating a generic utility that can sum an arbitrary function is highly desirable. Readers who are familiar with Lisp could probably guess that the original Lisp code from which this XSLT was derived used a Lisp macro to accomplish just that. Chapter 13 demonstrates how generic programming can be achieved in XSLT and how this recipe can be greatly simplified as a result.

Discussion

The Hebrew calendar is the most complex calendar covered in this chapter. Hence, the Hebrew date-time code is correspondingly complicated. The Hebrew calendar is intricate because its months are strictly lunar, yet it mandates that Passover must always occur in the spring. While most other calendars have a fixed number of months, the Hebrew calendar has 12 during a conventional year and 13 during a leap year.

3.10 Formatting Dates and Times

Problem

You want to format dates and times based on a format string.

Solution

These templates reuse many of the templates already presented in this chapter. The format-date-time uses a format string where %x is a formatting directive (see later) and all other text is output literally. The default format is the ISO date-time format for Gregorian dates:

```
<xsl:template name="date:format-date-time">
    <xsl:param name="year"/>
    <xsl:param name="month"/>
    <xsl:param name="day"/>
    <xsl:param name="hour"/>
    <xsl:param name="minute"/>
    <xsl:param name="second"/>
    <xsl:param name="time-zone"/>
    <xsl:param name="format" select="'%Y-%m-%dT%H:%M:%S%z'"/>

  <xsl:choose>
    <xsl:when test="contains($format, '%')">
     <xsl:value-of select="substring-before($format, '%')"/>
    </xsl:when>
    <xsl:otherwise>
     <xsl:value-of select="$format"/>
    </xsl:otherwise>
  </xsl:choose>

  <xsl:variable name="code"
                select="substring(substring-after($format, '%'), 1, 1)"/>
  <xsl:choose>

    <!-- Abbreviated weekday name -->
    <xsl:when test="$code='a'">
      <xsl:variable name="day-of-the-week">
        <xsl:call-template name="date:calculate-day-of-the-week">
          <xsl:with-param name="year" select="$year"/>
          <xsl:with-param name="month" select="$month"/>
          <xsl:with-param name="day" select="$day"/>
        </xsl:call-template>
      </xsl:variable>
      <xsl:call-template name="date:get-day-of-the-week-abbreviation">
        <xsl:with-param name="day-of-the-week"
          select="$day-of-the-week"/>
      </xsl:call-template>
    </xsl:when>
```

```
<!-- Full weekday name -->
<xsl:when test="$code='A'">
  <xsl:variable name="day-of-the-week">
    <xsl:call-template name="date:calculate-day-of-the-week">
      <xsl:with-param name="year" select="$year"/>
      <xsl:with-param name="month" select="$month"/>
      <xsl:with-param name="day" select="$day"/>
    </xsl:call-template>
  </xsl:variable>
  <xsl:call-template name="date:get-day-of-the-week-name">
    <xsl:with-param name="day-of-the-week"
                    select="$day-of-the-week"/>
  </xsl:call-template>
</xsl:when>

<!-- Abbreviated month name -->
<xsl:when test="$code='b'">
  <xsl:call-template name="date:get-month-abbreviation">
    <xsl:with-param name="month" select="$month"/>
  </xsl:call-template>
</xsl:when>

<!-- Full month name -->
<xsl:when test="$code='B'">
  <xsl:call-template name="date:get-month-name">
    <xsl:with-param name="month" select="$month"/>
  </xsl:call-template>
</xsl:when>

<!-- Date and time representation appropriate for locale -->
<xsl:when test="$code='c'">
  <xsl:text>[not implemented]</xsl:text>
</xsl:when>

<!-- Day of month as decimal number (01 - 31) -->
<xsl:when test="$code='d'">
  <xsl:value-of select="format-number($day,'00')"/>
</xsl:when>

<!-- Hour in 24-hour format (00 - 23) -->
<xsl:when test="$code='H'">
  <xsl:value-of select="format-number($hour,'00')"/>
</xsl:when>

<!-- Hour in 12-hour format (01 - 12) -->
<xsl:when test="$code='I'">
  <xsl:choose>
    <xsl:when test="$hour = 0">12</xsl:when>
    <xsl:when test="$hour &lt; 13">
      <xsl:value-of select="format-number($hour,'00')"/>
    </xsl:when>
    <xsl:otherwise>
      <xsl:value-of select="format-number($hour - 12,'00')"/>
```

```
      </xsl:otherwise>
    </xsl:choose>
  </xsl:when>

  <!-- Day of year as decimal number (001 - 366) -->
  <xsl:when test="$code='j'">
    <xsl:variable name="diff">
    <xsl:call-template name="date:date-difference">
      <xsl:with-param name="from-year" select="$year"/>
      <xsl:with-param name="from-month" select="1"/>
      <xsl:with-param name="form-day" select="1"/>
      <xsl:with-param name="to-year" select="$year"/>
      <xsl:with-param name="to-month" select="$month"/>
      <xsl:with-param name="to-day" select="$day"/>
    </xsl:call-template>
    </xsl:variable>
    <xsl:value-of select="format-number($diff + 1, '000')"/>
  </xsl:when>

  <!-- Month as decimal number (01 - 12) -->
  <xsl:when test="$code='m'">
    <xsl:value-of select="format-number($month,'00')"/>
  </xsl:when>

  <!-- Minute as decimal number (00 - 59) -->
  <xsl:when test="$code='M'">
    <xsl:value-of select="format-number($minute,'00')"/>
  </xsl:when>

  <!-- Current locale's A.M./P.M. indicator for 12-hour clock -->
  <xsl:when test="$code='p'">
    <xsl:choose>
      <xsl:when test="$hour &lt; 12">AM</xsl:when>
      <xsl:otherwise>PM</xsl:otherwise>
    </xsl:choose>
  </xsl:when>

  <!-- Second as decimal number (00 - 59) -->
  <xsl:when test="$code='S'">
    <xsl:value-of select="format-number($second,'00')"/>
  </xsl:when>

  <!-- Week of year as decimal number,
       with Sunday as first day of week (00 - 53) -->
  <xsl:when test="$code='U'">
    <!-- add 1 to day -->
    <xsl:call-template name="date:calculate-week-number">
      <xsl:with-param name="year" select="$year"/>
      <xsl:with-param name="month" select="$month"/>
      <xsl:with-param name="day" select="$day + 1"/>
    </xsl:call-template>
  </xsl:when>
```

```
<!-- Weekday as decimal number (0 - 6; Sunday is 0) -->
<xsl:when test="$code='w'">
  <xsl:call-template name="date:calculate-day-of-the-week">
    <xsl:with-param name="year" select="$year"/>
    <xsl:with-param name="month" select="$month"/>
    <xsl:with-param name="day" select="$day"/>
  </xsl:call-template>
</xsl:when>

<!-- Week of year as decimal number,
     with Monday as first day of week (00 - 53) -->
<xsl:when test="$code='W'">
  <xsl:call-template name="date:calculate-week-number">
    <xsl:with-param name="year" select="$year"/>
    <xsl:with-param name="month" select="$month"/>
    <xsl:with-param name="day" select="$day"/>
  </xsl:call-template>
</xsl:when>

<!-- Date representation for current locale -->
<xsl:when test="$code='x'">
  <xsl:text>[not implemented]</xsl:text>
</xsl:when>

<!-- Time representation for current locale -->
<xsl:when test="$code='X'">
  <xsl:text>[not implemented]</xsl:text>
</xsl:when>

<!-- Year without century, as decimal number (00 - 99) -->
<xsl:when test="$code='y'">
  <xsl:value-of select="format-number($year mod 100,'00')"/>
</xsl:when>

<!-- Year with century, as decimal number -->
<xsl:when test="$code='Y'">
    <xsl:value-of select="format-number($year,'0000')"/>
</xsl:when>

<!-- Time-zone name or abbreviation; -->
<!-- no characters if time zone is unknown -->
<xsl:when test="$code='z'">
  <xsl:value-of select="$time-zone"/>
</xsl:when>

<!-- Percent sign -->
<xsl:when test="$code='%'">
  <xsl:text>%</xsl:text>
</xsl:when>

</xsl:choose>
```

```
    <xsl:variable name="remainder"
                  select="substring(substring-after($format, '%'), 2)"/>

    <xsl:if test="$remainder">
      <xsl:call-template name="date:format-date-time">
        <xsl:with-param name="year" select="$year"/>
        <xsl:with-param name="month" select="$month"/>
        <xsl:with-param name="day" select="$day"/>
        <xsl:with-param name="hour" select="$hour"/>
        <xsl:with-param name="minute" select="$minute"/>
        <xsl:with-param name="second" select="$second"/>
        <xsl:with-param name="time-zone" select="$time-zone"/>
        <xsl:with-param name="format" select="$remainder"/>
      </xsl:call-template>
    </xsl:if>

</xsl:template>

<xsl:template name="date:format-julian-day">
    <xsl:param name="julian-day"/>
    <xsl:param name="format" select="'%Y-%m-%d'"/>

    <xsl:variable name="a" select="$julian-day + 32044"/>
    <xsl:variable name="b" select="floor((4 * $a + 3) div 146097)"/>
    <xsl:variable name="c" select="$a - floor(($b * 146097) div 4)"/>

    <xsl:variable name="d" select="floor((4 * $c + 3) div 1461)"/>
    <xsl:variable name="e" select="$c - floor((1461 * $d) div 4)"/>
    <xsl:variable name="m" select="floor((5 * $e + 2) div 153)"/>

    <xsl:variable name="day" select="$e - floor((153 * $m + 2) div 5) + 1"/>
    <xsl:variable name="month" select="$m + 3 - 12 * floor($m div 10)"/>
    <xsl:variable name="year" select="$b * 100 + $d - 4800 + floor($m div 10)"/>

    <xsl:call-template name="date:format-date-time">
      <xsl:with-param name="year" select="$year"/>
      <xsl:with-param name="month" select="$month"/>
      <xsl:with-param name="day" select="$day"/>
      <xsl:with-param name="format" select="$format"/>
    </xsl:call-template>

</xsl:template>
```

Discussion

This example was made possible by all the date work done in the prior examples.
The options requiring locale are not implemented, but could be implemented using
extension functions (see Chapter 12).

3.11 Determining Secular and Religious Holidays

Problem

You would like to know if a given date is a holiday.

Solution

The first type of holiday includes those that fall on the same day every year. For example, a function to determine the absolute day of American Independence for any year is simply:

```
<xsl:template name="date:independence-day">
    <xsl:param name="year"/>
    <xsl:call-template name="date:date-to-absolute-day">
        <xsl:with-param name="month" select="7"/>
        <xsl:with-param name="day" select="4"/>
        <xsl:with-param name="year" select="$year"/>
    </xsl:call-template>
</xsl:template>
```

The second type of holiday falls on the same day of the week relative to the start or end of a month. You can compute those days with the help of the following utility, which wraps the k-day-on-or-before-abs-day template contained in Recipe 3.7.

```
<xsl:template name="date:n-th-k-day">
    <!-- The n'th occurance of k in the given month -->
    <!-- Postive n counts from beginning of month; negative from end. -->
    <xsl:param name="n"/>

    <!-- k = the day of the week (0 = Sun) -->
    <xsl:param name="k"/>

    <xsl:param name="month"/>
    <xsl:param name="year"/>

    <xsl:choose>
      <xsl:when test="$n > 0">
        <xsl:variable name="k-day-on-or-before">
         <xsl:variable name="abs-day">
           <xsl:call-template name="date:date-to-absolute-day">
             <xsl:with-param name="month" select="$month"/>
             <xsl:with-param name="day" select="7"/>
             <xsl:with-param name="year" select="$year"/>
           </xsl:call-template>
         </xsl:variable>
         <xsl:call-template name="date:k-day-on-or-before-abs-day">
           <xsl:with-param name="abs-day" select="$abs-day"/>
           <xsl:with-param name="k" select="$k"/>
```

```
          </xsl:call-template>
        </xsl:variable>
        <xsl:value-of select="$k-day-on-or-before + 7 * ($n - 1)"/>
      </xsl:when>
      <xsl:otherwise>
        <xsl:variable name="k-day-on-or-before">
        <xsl:variable name="abs-day">
          <xsl:call-template name="date:date-to-absolute-day">
            <xsl:with-param name="month" select="$month"/>
            <xsl:with-param name="day">
             <xsl:call-template name="date:last-day-of-month">
               <xsl:with-param name="month" select="$month"/>
               <xsl:with-param name="year" select="$year"/>
             </xsl:call-template>
            </xsl:with-param>
            <xsl:with-param name="year" select="$year"/>
          </xsl:call-template>
        </xsl:variable>
        <xsl:call-template name="date:k-day-on-or-before-abs-day">
          <xsl:with-param name="abs-day" select="$abs-day"/>
          <xsl:with-param name="k" select="$k"/>
        </xsl:call-template>
        </xsl:variable>
        <xsl:value-of select="$k-day-on-or-before + 7 * ($n + 1)"/>
      </xsl:otherwise>
    </xsl:choose>
  </xsl:template>
```

This function assumes Gregorian dates. If you need to determine relative dates within other calendar systems, you need to write equivalent routines within those systems.

It is now easy to handle holidays like American Labor and Memorial days (the first Monday of September and the last Monday of May, respectively).

```
<xsl:template name="date:labor-day">
    <xsl:param name="year"/>
    <xsl:call-template name="date:n-th-k-day ">
        <xsl:with-param name="n" select="1"/>
        <xsl:with-param name="k" select="1"/>
        <xsl:with-param name="month" select="9"/>
        <xsl:with-param name="year" select="$year"/>
    </xsl:call-template>
</xsl:template>

<xsl:template name="date:memorial-day">
    <xsl:param name="year"/>
    <xsl:call-template name="date:n-th-k-day ">
        <xsl:with-param name="n" select="-1"/>
        <xsl:with-param name="k" select="1"/>
        <xsl:with-param name="month" select="5"/>
        <xsl:with-param name="year" select="$year"/>
    </xsl:call-template>
</xsl:template>
```

Although not a holiday, American daylight saving time can also be handled:

```
<xsl:template name="date:day-light-savings-start">
    <xsl:param name="year"/>
    <xsl:call-template name="date:n-th-k-day ">
        <xsl:with-param name="n" select="1"/>
        <xsl:with-param name="k" select="0"/>
        <xsl:with-param name="month" select="4"/>
        <xsl:with-param name="year" select="$year"/>
    </xsl:call-template>
</xsl:template>

<xsl:template name="date:day-light-savings-end">
    <xsl:param name="year"/>
    <xsl:call-template name="date:n-th-k-day ">
        <xsl:with-param name="n" select="-1"/>
        <xsl:with-param name="k" select="0"/>
        <xsl:with-param name="month" select="10"/>
        <xsl:with-param name="year" select="$year"/>
    </xsl:call-template>
</xsl:template>
```

Discussion

Covering every secular and religious holiday in each country and year is impossible. However, you can classify most holidays into two types: those that fall on the same day every year (e.g., U.S. Independence Day) in their respective calendars and those that are on a particular day of the week relative to the start or end of a month (e.g., U.S. Labor Day). Religious holidays are often simple within their native calendrical system, but can be more difficult to determine within another system. For example, Eastern Orthodox Christmas always falls on December 25 of the *Julian* calendar. Thus, in a Gregorian year, Eastern Orthodox Christmas can fall in the beginning, the end, or not appear at all. Since we cannot cover every religious holiday in every faith, please explore the references mentioned in this chapter's introduction.

CHAPTER 4
Selecting and Traversing

I choose a block of marble and chop off
whatever I don't need.
—Francois-Auguste Rodin

I have [traversed] the length and breadth of this country
and talked with the best people, and I can assure you that
data processing is a fad that won't last out the year.
—The editor in charge of business books
for a major publishing company, 1957

Doing anything remotely interesting in XSLT involves two related operations: determining which elements to visit (selecting) and determining in what order you want to visit them (traversing). Selecting is largely in the domain of XPath, a separate specification but one intimately related to XSLT. Traversing is a function of built-in control structures of XSLT and how you organize your templates to harness them.

XSLT veterans are unlikely to find much revelation in this particular chapter. Nevertheless, it is important for two reasons. First, the ideas presented in these recipes distinguish XSLT from other programming languages and therefore tend to be things that trip up novices on their first attempts to master XSLT. Second, the examples covered in this section are the primitive building blocks of many more complex recipes covered in later chapters. Virtually everything one does in XSLT involves application of selection and traversal. By analogy to cooking, knowing how to make a good brown stock is a prerequisite to making a sauce espagnole!* This chapter is comprised of examples of the "brown stock" variety and should be mastered before proceeding to more advanced applications of XSLT.

---

* Sauce espagnole is highly concentrated brown stock with tomatoes bound with roux and reduced. The brown stock is made from veal and beef shanks. Sauce espagnole is necessary for making demi-glace, the "mother sauce" for many other brown sauces. When it comes to "reuse," the chefs have the software developers beat!

Although this chapter presents some primitive examples, it is not an XPath or XSLT tutorial. The reader should know the basics. I assume you are familiar with the syntax of XPath and that you know the meaning of common XPath expressions. I also assume you know what the default XSLT processing rules are and how XSLT determines what templates should be processed next. If you feel you need some help in these areas, I would recommend either Michael Kay's *XSLT Programmer's Reference* (Wrox Press, 2001) or Doug Tidwell's *XSLT* (O'Reilly, 2002).

Several examples in this section use computer-science terminology commonly associated with algorithms involving tree-data structures. The uninitiated may wonder what trees have to do with XML. The answer is that XML can be viewed as a language for specifying trees and XSLT as a language that processes these trees. In fact, it is possible to make an XSLT processor process non-XML input by making the processor think it is a tree by using a SAX driver. Michael Kay demonstrates this technique in *Professional XSLT* (Wrox, 2001), as does Eric M. Burke in *Java and XSLT* (O'Reilly, 2001). In any case, the important concept that motivates the examples in this chapter is that thinking in terms of trees allows one to discover several useful XML processing techniques.

The examples provided in the chapter draw heavily on the following two test documents. To avoid repeating them in each recipe, I list them in Examples 4-1 and 4-2.

Example 4-1. SalesBySalesPerson.xml

```
<?xml version="1.0" encoding="UTF-8"?>
<salesBySalesperson>
  <salesperson name="John Adams" seniority="1">
    <product sku="10000" totalSales="10000.00"/>
    <product sku="20000" totalSales="50000.00"/>
    <product sku="25000" totalSales="920000.00"/>
  </salesperson>
  <salesperson name="Wendy Long" seniority="5">
    <product sku="10000" totalSales="990000.00"/>
    <product sku="20000" totalSales="150000.00"/>
    <product sku="30000" totalSales="5500.00"/>
  </salesperson>
  <salesperson name="Willie B. Aggressive" seniority="10">
    <product sku="10000" totalSales="1110000.00"/>
    <product sku="20000" totalSales="150000.00"/>
    <product sku="25000" totalSales="2920000.00"/>
    <product sku="30000" totalSales="115500.00"/>
    <product sku="70000" totalSales="10000.00"/>
  </salesperson>
  <salesperson name="Arty Outtolunch" seniority="10"/>
</salesBySalesperson>
```

Example 4-2. orgchart.xml

```
<?xml version="1.0" encoding="UTF-8"?>
<employee name="Jil Michel" sex="female">
    <employee name="Nancy Pratt" sex="female">
```

Example 4-2. orgchart.xml (continued)

```
            <employee name="Phill McKraken" sex="male"/>
            <employee name="Ima Little" sex="female">
                <employee name="Betsy Ross" sex="female"/>
            </employee>
        </employee>
        <employee name="Jane Doe" sex="female">
            <employee name="Walter H. Potter" sex="male"/>
            <employee name="Wendy B.K. McDonald" sex="female">
                <employee name="Craig F. Frye" sex="male"/>
                <employee name="Hardy Hamburg" sex="male"/>
                <employee name="Rich Shaker" sex="male"/>
            </employee>
        </employee>
        <employee name="Mike Rosenbaum" sex="male">
            <employee name="Cindy Post-Kellog" sex="female">
                <employee name="Allen Bran" sex="male"/>
                <employee name="Frank N. Berry" sex="male"/>
                <employee name="Jack Apple" sex="male"/>
            </employee>
            <employee name="Oscar A. Winner" sex="male">
                <employee name="Jack Nickolas" sex="male">
                    <employee name="R.P. McMurphy" sex="male"/>
                </employee>
                <employee name="Tom Hanks" sex="male">
                    <employee name="Forest Gump" sex="male"/>
                    <employee name="Andrew Beckett" sex="male"/>
                </employee>
                <employee name="Susan Sarandon" sex="female">
                    <employee name="Helen Prejean" sex="female"/>
                </employee>
            </employee>
        </employee>
    </employee>
</employee>
```

4.1 Optimizing Node Selections

Problem

You want to improve the efficiency of your stylesheet when selecting and traversing nodes from a large XML document.

Solution

You can optimize XSLT in many ways and, when applicable, each example in this book addresses performance issues. This particular example explains several strategies for minimizing the number of elements your stylesheet will process when selecting and traversing a document.

Avoid unnecessary reliance on default processing rules

If you know exactly what you want to process and where it is located in a documents structure, you are better off going directly to the relevant nodes. Consider the following complex Microsoft Visio XML document, shown in Example 4-3, and two stylesheets for extracting shapes shown in Examples 4-4 to 4-5.

Example 4-3. A partial Visio XML document

```xml
<VisioDocument xmlns="urn:schemas-microsoft-com:office:visio">
    <DocumentProperties>
        <!--elements elided -->
    <DocumentSettings TopPage="0" DefaultTextStyle="26" DefaultLineStyle="26"
        DefaultFillStyle="26" DefaultGuideStyle="4">
        <!--elements elided -->
    </DocumentSettings>
    <Colors>
        <!--elements elided -->
    </Colors>
    <PrintSetup>
        <!--elements elided -->
    </PrintSetup>
    <Fonts>
        <!--elements elided -->
    </Fonts>
    <StyleSheets>
        <!--elements elided -->
    </StyleSheets>
    <DocumentSheet NameU="TheDoc" LineStyle="0" FillStyle="0" TextStyle="0">
        <!--elements elided -->
    </DocumentSheet>
    <Masters>
        <!--elements elided -->
    </Masters>
    <Pages>
        <Page ID="0" NameU="Page-1" ViewScale="1" ViewCenterX="1.484375"
            ViewCenterY="2.2552083333333">
        <!--elements elided -->
        <Shapes>
            <Shape ID="1" NameU="Square" Type="Shape" Master="0">
              <!--elements elided -->
            </Shape>
            <Shape ID="2" Type="Shape" Master="0">
              <!--elements elided -->
            </Shape>
        </Shapes>
        </Page>
    </Pages>
    <!--elements elided -->
</VisioDocument>
```

Example 4-4. A stylesheet that relies on default rules

```
<xsl:stylesheet version="1.0" xmlns:xsl="http://www.w3.org/1999/XSL/Transform"
    xmlns:vxd="urn:schemas-microsoft-com:office:visio">

<xsl:output method="text" />

<xsl:strip-space elements="*"/>

<xsl:template match="vxd:Shape">
    <xsl:value-of select="@ID"/>-<xsl:value-of
                        select="@NameU"/><xsl:text>&#xa;</xsl:text>
</xsl:template>

<xsl:template match="text()"/>

</xsl:stylesheet>
```

Example 4-5. A stylesheet that bypassesdefault rules

```
<xsl:stylesheet version="1.0" xmlns:xsl="http://www.w3.org/1999/XSL/Transform"
    xmlns:vxd="urn:schemas-microsoft-com:office:visio">

<xsl:output method="text" />

<xsl:strip-space elements="*"/>

<xsl:template match="/">
    <xsl:apply-templates
        select="vxd:VisioDocument/vxd:Pages/vxd:Page/vxd:Shapes/vxd:Shape"/>
</xsl:template>

<xsl:template match="vxd:Shape">
    <xsl:value-of select="@ID"/>-<xsl:value-of
    select="@NameU"/><xsl:text>&#xa;</xsl:text>
</xsl:template>

<xsl:template match="text()"/>

</xsl:stylesheet>
```

By selecting only the elements of interest (e.g., Shapes), the second stylesheet avoids processing the entire document.

Avoid using the descendant, descendant-or-self, preceding, or following axes when they aren't necessary

On very large documents, you will see a noticeable performance improvement if you prefer explicit XPath expressions to expressions that select nodes at an arbitrary location in the tree. Descendant, descendant-or-self, preceding, or following axes fall into the latter category.

Preferable:

```
<xsl:template match="/">
    <xsl:apply-templates
        select="vxd:VisioDocument/vxd:Pages/vxd:Page/vxd:Shapes/vxd:Shape"/>
</xsl:template>
```

Potential performance problem:

```
<xsl:template match="/">
    <xsl:apply-templates select="//vxd:Shape"/>
</xsl:template>
```

However, many XSLT gurus overstate the performance penalty of these axes. If you actually measure performance on small- to medium-sized documents (50,000 elements or less) on a wide variety of processor implementations, you will see little performance penalty. So if you need the flexibility or convenience that these relative paths give, do not hesitate to use them until performance actually becomes a factor. On the other hand, if you have no foreknowledge of the size of document your stylesheet may be asked to process, you would be wise to err on the conservative side.

Prefer "selecting" and "matching" over "filtering"

If you need to process nodes that meet a particular criterion, then try to select the nodes rather than filtering them with <xsl:if> or <xsl:choose>. For example, consider the following three XSLT fragments in Examples 4-6 through 4-8 that search for a person element named "John Smith" and display his age.

Example 4-6. Processing a specific person by filtering

```
<xsl:stylesheet version="1.0" xmlns:xsl="http://www.w3.org/1999/XSL/Transform">
    <xsl:output method="text" />

    <xsl:template match="/">
        <xsl:apply-templates select="people"/>
    </xsl:template>

    <xsl:template match="people">
        <xsl:for-each select="person">
            <xsl:if test="@name='John Smith' ">
                <xsl:value-of select="@age"/>
            </xsl:if>
        </xsl:for-each>
    </xsl:template>
</xsl:stylesheet>
```

Example 4-7. Processing a specific person by matching

```
<xsl:stylesheet version="1.0" xmlns:xsl="http://www.w3.org/1999/XSL/Transform">

    <xsl:output method="text" />

    <xsl:template match="/">
```

Example 4-7. Processing a specific person by matching (continued)

```
        <xsl:apply-templates select="people/person"/>
    </xsl:template>

    <xsl:template match="person[@name='John Smith']">
        <xsl:value-of select="@age"/>
    </xsl:template>

    <xsl:template match="person"/>
</xsl:stylesheet>
```

Example 4-8. Processing a specific person by selecting

```
<xsl:stylesheet version="1.0" xmlns:xsl="http://www.w3.org/1999/XSL/Transform">

    <xsl:output method="text" />

    <xsl:template match="/">
        <xsl:apply-templates select="people"/>
    </xsl:template>

    <xsl:template match="people">
        <xsl:for-each select="person[@name='John Smith']">
            <xsl:value-of select="@age"/>
        </xsl:for-each>
    </xsl:template>
</xsl:stylesheet>
```

Testing these stylesheets on a 100,000-element document using Saxon showed the selecting method to be 30% faster than the matching method and 44% faster than the filtering method. However, with Xalan and XT, the results were much closer, but the selecting method still had a slight advantage. Oddly, filtering was slightly faster (12%) than matching when using Xalan.

Cache frequently used node sets in variables

Stylesheets often refer to the same set of nodes. Rather than selecting those nodes repeatedly, it might make sense to store them in a variable. I say "might" because your mileage will vary depending on how much work needs to be done to access those nodes and how frequently you refer to them. One must also consider the memory overhead of caching nodes in this way. In fact, some processors may not cache a variable's data unless the variable is referenced multiple times.

One case where a variable is clearly necessary is when the result was obtained from an expensive process such as a sort, as in the following:

```
<xsl:variable name="products">
  <xsl:for-each select="//product">
    <xsl:sort select="@sku"/>
    <xsl:copy-of select="."/>
  </xsl:for-each>
</xsl:variable>
```

Examples 4-9 through 4-11 show a variables with *no* effect:

Example 4-9. Loading an external lookup table inline

```
<xsl:stylesheet version="1.0" xmlns:xsl="http://www.w3.org/1999/XSL/Transform"
    xmlns:us="http://www.ora.com/XSLTCookbook/nampespaces/us">

    <xsl:strip-space elements="*"/>

    <xsl:output method="text" />

    <xsl:template match="person">
        <xsl:value-of select="@name"/>
        <xsl:text>&#xa;</xsl:text>
        <xsl:apply-templates/>
    </xsl:template>

    <xsl:template match="address">
        <xsl:variable name="state" select="@state"/>
        <xsl:value-of select="@line1"/>
        <xsl:text>&#xa;</xsl:text>
        <xsl:if test="@line2">
        <xsl:value-of select="@line2"/>
        <xsl:text>&#xa;</xsl:text>
        </xsl:if>
        <xsl:value-of select="@city"/>
        <xsl:text>, </xsl:text>
        <xsl:value-of select="document('states.xml')
        /*/us:state[@abbrev=$state]/@name"/>
        <xsl:text> </xsl:text>
        <xsl:value-of select="@zip"/><xsl:text>&#xa;&#xa;</xsl:text>
    </xsl:template>

    <xsl:template match="text( )"/>

</xsl:stylesheet>
```

Example 4-10. Loading an external lookup table into a variable

```
<xsl:stylesheet version="1.0" xmlns:xsl="http://www.w3.org/1999/XSL/Transform"
    xmlns:us="http://www.ora.com/XSLTCookbook/nampespaces/us">

    <xsl:strip-space elements="*"/>

    <xsl:output method="text" />

    <xsl:variable name="states" select="document('states.xml')/*/us:state"/>

    <xsl:template match="person">
        <xsl:value-of select="@name"/>
        <xsl:text>&#xa;</xsl:text>
        <xsl:apply-templates/>
    </xsl:template>
```

```
<xsl:template match="address">
    <xsl:variable name="state" select="@state"/>
    <xsl:value-of select="@line1"/>
    <xsl:text>&#xa;</xsl:text>
    <xsl:if test="@line2">
    <xsl:value-of select="@line2"/>
    <xsl:text>&#xa;</xsl:text>
    </xsl:if>
    <xsl:value-of select="@city"/>
    <xsl:text>, </xsl:text>
    <xsl:value-of select="$states[@abbrev=$state]/@name"/>
    <xsl:text> </xsl:text>
    <xsl:value-of select="@zip"/><xsl:text>&#xa;&#xa;</xsl:text>
</xsl:template>

<xsl:template match="text( )"/>
```

Example 4-11. A partial listing of states.xml

```
<?xml version="1.0" encoding="UTF-8"?>
<us:states xmlns:us="http://www.ora.com/XSLTCookbook/nampespaces/us">
    <us:state name="ALABAMA" abbrev="AL"/>
    <us:state name="ALASKA" abbrev="AK"/>
    <us:state name="AMERICAN SAMOA" abbrev="AS"/>
    <us:state name="ARIZONA" abbrev="AZ"/>
    <us:state name="ARKANSAS" abbrev="AR"/>
    <us:state name="CALIFORNIA" abbrev="CA"/>
    <us:state name="COLORADO" abbrev="CO"/>
    <us:state name="CONNECTICUT" abbrev="CT"/>
    <!--- elided -->
    <us:state name="WEST VIRGINIA" abbrev="WV"/>
    <us:state name="WISCONSIN" abbrev="WI"/>
    <us:state name="WYOMING" abbrev="WY"/>
</us:states>
```

You might expect that the second template is faster because it loads *states.xml* only once. However, for an XSLT processor to conform to the no-side-effect rule, it must load the document just once in either case; therefore, the variable provides at most an aesthetic improvement.

Use xsl:key if nodes are frequently selected by static criteria

Using a variable to cache nodes is fine when the set of nodes is constant. However, if you make repeated access to nodes selected by some criteria, you should establish an index. XSLT uses the xsl:key element in conjunction with the key( ) function to establish an index. This solution is not guaranteed by the XSLT standard to result in a performance boost, but on most implementations, it has the desired effect if used wisely. Here "wisely" means that the cost of building the index is outweighed by the frequency in which it is used. If your stylesheet uses the key only once or twice, then do not expect to see any noticeable improvement, and you may actually experience degradation.

Using a key significantly improves the following modification to the address stylesheet when it is used to process a document with many people elements:

```
<xsl:stylesheet version="1.0" xmlns:xsl="http://www.w3.org/1999/XSL/Transform"
        xmlns:us="http://www.ora.com/XSLTCoobook/nampespaces/us">

    <xsl:strip-space elements="*"/>

    <xsl:output method="text" />

    <xsl:key name="state" match="us:state" use="@abbrev"/>

    <xsl:template match="person">
        <xsl:value-of select="@name"/>
        <xsl:text>&#xa;</xsl:text>
        <xsl:apply-templates/>
    </xsl:template>

    <xsl:template match="address">
        <xsl:variable name="state" select="@state"/>
        <xsl:value-of select="@line1"/>
        <xsl:text>&#xa;</xsl:text>
        <xsl:if test="@line2">
        <xsl:value-of select="@line2"/>
        <xsl:text>&#xa;</xsl:text>
        </xsl:if>
        <xsl:value-of select="@city"/>
        <xsl:text>, </xsl:text>
        <!-- We use for-each to change context to the states.xml doc
        because key( ) only locates elements in the same document as the
        context node -->
        <xsl:for-each select="document('states.xml')">
            <xsl:value-of select="key('state',$state)/@name"/>
        </xsl:for-each>
        <xsl:text> </xsl:text>
        <xsl:value-of select="@zip"/><xsl:text>&#xa;&#xa;</xsl:text>
    </xsl:template>

    <xsl:template match="text( )"/>
```

Discussion

Avoid unnecessarily reliance on default processing rules

As many of you know, XSLT has built-in processing rules that are invoked when XSLT is called on to process a node but no template in the stylesheet matches the node. Two rules are relevant here:

- If no template rule matches the root (/) in the current calling mode, <xsl:apply-templates/> is automatically invoked to process the children of the root in the current calling mode.

- If no template rule matches an element in the current calling mode, `<xsl:apply-templates/>` is automatically invoked to process the children of the element in the current calling mode.

These rules are useful since they effectively cause XSLT to descend the document tree until it finds something useful to do. Relying on these rules is a good practice if you want to create robust stylesheets that are insensitive to certain changes in the document structure. However, when you process documents whose structure is unlikely to change, it is best to eliminate unnecessary processing by selecting relevant nodes as early as possible.

Prefer "selecting" and "matching" over "filtering"

This recommendation is arguably the weakest of the four from a pure optimization standpoint. As XSLT processors become smarter, the performance difference between these styles is likely to grow smaller. Aesthetics, maintainability, and clarity are better drivers than performance for preferring one form over another.

Cache frequently used node sets in variables

Although judicious use of variables can result in performance improvements, you should not obsess over their use for this reason. Rather, use variables when they help clarify the code or make it easier to maintain. In two situations, variables are mandatory simply because of the nature of XSLT. Michael Kay calls them *context-sensitive* and *temporary-tree* variables. Context-sensitive variables arise in nested for-each loops when the inner loop must refer to the current context of the outer loop. In Example 4-12, the code fragment is borrowed from Example 4-14 in Recipe 4.2, $product1 is a necessary context-sensitive variable, while $product2 simply helps clarify the code.

Example 4-12. A context-sensitive variable

```
<xsl:template name="process-products">
    <xsl:param name="products"/>
    <xsl:for-each select="$products">
      <xsl:variable name="product1" select="."/>
      <xsl:for-each select="$products">
        <xsl:variable name="product2" select="."/>
        <-- Don't analyze the product against itself -->
        <xsl:if test="generate-id($product1) != generate-id($product2)">
          <xsl:call-template name="show-products-sold-in-common">
            <xsl:with-param name="product1" select="$product1"/>
            <xsl:with-param name="product2" select="$product2"/>
          </xsl:call-template>
        </xsl:if>
      </xsl:for-each>
    </xsl:for-each>
</xsl:template>
```

Temporary-tree variables arise when you want to store the result of XSLT code in a variable. This scenario arises most often when capturing the value returned by the call to a template (see Example 4-13).

Example 4-13. Storing a temporary tree

```
<xsl:varaible name="result-tree">
    <xsl:call-template name="compute-something"/>
</xsl:varaible>
```

 XSLT 2.0 (and 1.1 for the processors that support it) allow such variables to be processed as node sets, which is very convenient if you want to do anything significant with them. XSLT 1.0 calls them *result-tree fragments*, and you cannot do much more than output them without first applying a nonstandard extension node-set( ) function. With 20/20 hindsight, result-tree fragments are the classic example of a really bad idea. However, when XSLT 1.0 was developed, it was unclear how it would be used and whether technical problems would prevent the creation of temporary node trees.

Use xsl:key if nodes will be selected by static criteria frequently

Of all the optimization methods keys, those of xsl:key are the most likely to give you the biggest bang for the buck if used properly. Of course, nothing in the XSLT standard says that keys must result in the creation of an index, but any decent implementation will create one. Saxon and Xalan are two processors that show significant gain from the key facility.

4.2   Determining if Two Nodes Are the Same

Problem

You need to determine if two separate references to a node are the same node.

Solution

If the compared nodes are element nodes with a unique attribute of type ID, then comparison is most conveniently made by comparing these attributes. If this is not the case, then use generate-id, as in:

```
<xsl:if test="generate-id($node1) = generate-id($node2)">
```

Here we assume $node1 and $node2 are node sets containing a single node.

An interesting generalization of this test checks if all the nodes in one node-set are the same as all the nodes in another. For this task, generate-id is not useful because it only generates an ID for the first node in document order. Instead, you need to take advantage the XPath union operator's (|) ability to determine node equality.

```
<xsl:if test="count($ns1|$ns2) = count($ns1) and
                 count($ns1) = count($ns2)">
```

In other words, if two node sets have the same number of nodes, and the number of nodes resulting from the union of both node sets is the same as the number of nodes in one of those two original node sets, then they must be the same sets. If they are not, then the union must contain at least one more node than either individual set.

If you only care if $ns2 is either equal to or a subset of $ns1, then you can simply write:

```
<xsl:if test="count($ns1|$ns2) = count($ns1)">
```

On the other hand, if you want to test that $ns2 is a *proper* subset of $ns1, then you need to write:[*]

```
<xsl:if test="count($ns1|$ns2) = count($ns1) and count($ns1) > count(ns2)">
```

From these examples, you should also conclude that the alternative to using generate-id( ) to test equality in the single node instance is to write:

```
<xsl:if test="count($ns1|$ns2) = 1">
```

Discussion

You can apply these techniques to make sophisticated queries against a document. For example, consider the stylesheet shown in Example 4-14 that analyzes *SalesBySalesPerson.xml* to find products sold by common sets of salespeople. Its output is listed in Example 4-15.

Example 4-14. products-sold-in-common.xslt

```
<xsl:stylesheet version="1.0" xmlns:xsl="http://www.w3.org/1999/XSL/Transform">

<xsl:output method="text"/>

<!-- Extract the unique set of products -->
<xsl:template match="/">
    <xsl:call-template name="process-products">
        <xsl:with-param name="products"
        select="/*/salesperson/product[not(@sku=preceding::product/@sku)]"/>
    </xsl:call-template>
</xsl:template>

<!-- Process all pairs of products -->
<xsl:template name="process-products">
    <xsl:param name="products"/>
    <xsl:for-each select="$products">
      <xsl:variable name="product1" select="."/>
      <xsl:for-each select="$products">
```

---

[*] Recall that a proper subset does not include the entire set as a subset.

Example 4-14. products-sold-in-common.xslt (continued)

```
            <xsl:variable name="product2" select="."/>
            <-- Don't analyze the product against itself -->
            <xsl:if test="generate-id($product1) != generate-id($product2)">
              <xsl:call-template name="show-products-sold-in-common">
                <xsl:with-param name="product1" select="$product1"/>
                <xsl:with-param name="product2" select="$product2"/>
              </xsl:call-template>
            </xsl:if>
        </xsl:for-each>
    </xsl:for-each>
</xsl:template>

<!-- Determine if two products have salespeople in common. -->
<xsl:template name="show-products-sold-in-common">
    <xsl:param name="product1"/>
    <xsl:param name="product2"/>
    <xsl:variable name="who-sold-p1"
        select="//salesperson[product/@sku = $product1/@sku]"/>
    <xsl:variable name="who-sold-p2"
        select="//salesperson[product/@sku = $product2/@sku]"/>

    <!-- If those who sold product2 is a subset of those who sold product1
         then they have these products have common salespeople -->
    <xsl:if test="count($who-sold-p1|$who-sold-p2) = count($who-sold-p1)">
      <xsl:text>All the salespeople who sold product </xsl:text>
      <xsl:value-of select="$product2/@sku"/>
      <xsl:text> also sold product </xsl:text>
      <xsl:value-of select="$product1/@sku"/>
      <!-- If the counts of both sets are also equal then the two sets are
           actually the same. -->
      <xsl:if test="count($who-sold-p1) = count($who-sold-p2)">
        <xsl:text> and visa versa</xsl:text>
      </xsl:if>
      <xsl:text>.&#xa;</xsl:text>
    </xsl:if>
</xsl:template>

</xsl:stylesheet>
```

Example 4-15. Output

```
All the salespeople who sold product 20000 also sold product 10000 and visa versa.
All the salespeople who sold product 25000 also sold product 10000.
All the salespeople who sold product 30000 also sold product 10000.
All the salespeople who sold product 70000 also sold product 10000.
All the salespeople who sold product 10000 also sold product 20000 and visa versa.
All the salespeople who sold product 25000 also sold product 20000.
All the salespeople who sold product 30000 also sold product 20000.
All the salespeople who sold product 70000 also sold product 20000.
All the salespeople who sold product 70000 also sold product 25000.
All the salespeople who sold product 70000 also sold product 30000.
```

To stay focused on node-identity testing, this example did not present the most efficient solution to this task. The following solution is preferable in this specific case:

```
<xsl:template name="process-products">
  <xsl:param name="products"/>
  <xsl:for-each select="$products">
     <xsl:variable name="product1" select="."/>
     <xsl:variable name="pos" select="position()"/>
     <xsl:for-each select="$products[position() > $pos]">
      <xsl:variable name="product2" select="."/>
      <xsl:call-template name="show-products-sold-in-common">
          <xsl:with-param name="product1" select="$product1"/>
          <xsl:with-param name="product2" select="$product2"/>
      </xsl:call-template>
     </xsl:for-each>
  </xsl:for-each>
</xsl:template>
```

Notice how the solution avoids generate-id( ) by relying on the uniqueness of position within a single node set. However, if there were two independent node sets rather than one, you wouldn't necessarily rely on position as an indicator of identity.

In addition, tests like:

```
<xsl:variable name="who-sold-p1"
              select="//salesperson[product/@sku = $product1/@sku]"/>
```

might be done more efficiently with a key, as was suggested in Recipe 4.1:

```
<xsl:key name="sp_key" match="salesperson" use="product/@sku"/>
```

```
<xsl:variable name="who-sold-p1"  select="key('sp_key',$product1/@sku)"/>
```

See Also

Testing node equality has important applications in grouping problems. See Chapter 5 for examples of grouping.

4.3   Ignoring Duplicate Elements

Problem

You want to select all nodes that are unique in a given context based on uniqueness criteria.

Solution

Selecting unique nodes is a common application of the preceding and preceding-sibling axes. If the elements you select are not all siblings, then use preceding. The following code produces a unique list of products from *SalesBySalesperson.xml*:

```
<xsl:stylesheet version="1.0" xmlns:xsl="http://www.w3.org/1999/XSL/Transform">
    <xsl:output method="xml" version="1.0" encoding="UTF-8" indent="yes"/>

<xsl:template match="/">
<products>
    <xsl:for-each select="//product[not(@sku=preceding::product/@sku)]">
        <xsl:copy-of select="."/>
    </xsl:for-each>
</products>
</xsl:template>

</xsl:stylesheet>
```
If the elements are all siblings then use preceding-sibling.
```
<products>
    <product sku="10000" totalSales="10000.00"/>
    <product sku="10000" totalSales="990000.00"/>
    <product sku="10000" totalSales="1110000.00"/>
    <product sku="20000" totalSales="50000.00"/>
    <product sku="20000" totalSales="150000.00"/>
    <product sku="20000" totalSales="150000.00"/>
    <product sku="25000" totalSales="920000.00"/>
    <product sku="25000" totalSales="2920000.00"/>
    <product sku="30000" totalSales="5500.00"/>
    <product sku="30000" totalSales="115500.00"/>
    <product sku="70000" totalSales="10000.00"/>
</products>

<xsl:stylesheet version="1.0" xmlns:xsl="http://www.w3.org/1999/XSL/Transform">
    <xsl:output method="xml" version="1.0" encoding="UTF-8" indent="yes"/>

<xsl:template match="/">
<products>
    <xsl:for-each select="product[not(@sku=preceding-sibling::product/@sku)]">
        <xsl:copy-of select="."/>
    </xsl:for-each>
</products>
</xsl:template>

</xsl:stylesheet>
```

To avoid preceding, which can be inefficient, travel up to the ancestors that *are* siblings, and then use preceding-sibling and travel down to the nodes you want to test:

```
<xsl:for-each select="//product[not(@sku=../preceding-sibling::*/product/@sku)]">
    <xsl:copy-of select="."/>
</xsl:for-each>
```

If you are certain that the elements are sorted so that duplicate nodes are adjacent (as in the earlier products), then you only have to consider the immediately preceding sibling:

```
<xsl:for-each
    select="/salesperson/product[not(@name=preceding-sibling::product[1]/@name]">
    <!-- do something with each uniquiely named product -->
</xsl:for-each>
```

Discussion

In XSLT Version 2.0 (or Version 1.0 in conjunction with the node-set( ) extension function), you can also do the following:

```
<xsl:stylesheet version="1.1" xmlns:xsl="http://www.w3.org/1999/XSL/Transform">
    <xsl:output method="xml" version="1.0" encoding="UTF-8" indent="yes"/>

<xsl:template match="/">

<xsl:variable name="products">
    <xsl:for-each select="//product">
        <xsl:sort select="@sku"/>
        <xsl:copy-of select="."/>
    </xsl:for-each>
</xsl:variable>

<products>
    <xsl:for-each select="$products/product">
        <xsl:variable name="pos" select="position( )"/>
        <xsl:if test="$pos = 1 or
        not(@sku = $products/preceding-sibling::product[1]/@sku">
            <xsl:copy-of select="."/>
        </xsl:if>
    </xsl:for-each>
</products>

</xsl:template>
```

However, I have never found this technique to be faster than using the preceding axis. This technique does have an advantage in situations where the duplicate testing is not trivial. For example, consider a case where duplicates are determined by the concatenation of two attributes.

```
<xsl:stylesheet version="1.1" xmlns:xsl="http://www.w3.org/1999/XSL/Transform">
    <xsl:output method="xml" version="1.0" encoding="UTF-8" indent="yes"/>

<xsl:template match="/">

<xsl:variable name="people">
    <xsl:for-each select="//person">
        <xsl:sort select="concat(@lastname,@firstname)"/>
        <xsl:copy-of select="."/>
    </xsl:for-each>
</xsl:variable>

<products>
    <xsl:for-each select="$people/person">
        <xsl:variable name="pos" select="position( )"/>
        <xsl:if test="$pos = 1 or
            concat(@lastname,@firstname) !=
                    concat(people/person[$pos - 1]/@lastname,
                        people/person[$pos - 1]/@firstname)">
```

```
            <xsl:copy-of select="."/>
        </xsl:if>
    </xsl:for-each>
</products>

</xsl:template>
```

When you attempt to remove duplicates, the following examples *do not* work:

```
<xsl:template match="/">
<products>
    <xsl:for-each select="//product[not(@sku=preceding::product[1]/@sku)]">
        <xsl:sort select="@sku"/>
        <xsl:copy-of select="."/>
    </xsl:for-each>
</products>
</xsl:template>
```

Do not sort to avoid considering all but the immediately preceding element. The axis is relative to the node's original order in the document. The same situation applies when using preceding-sibling. The following code is also sure to fail:

```
<xsl:template match="/">

<xsl:variable name="products">
    <xsl:for-each select="//product">
    <!-- sort removed from here -->
        <xsl:copy-of select="."/>
    </xsl:for-each>
</xsl:variable>

<products>
    <xsl:for-each select="$products/product">
        <xsl:sort select="@sku"/>
        <xsl:variable name="pos" select="position()"/>
        <xsl:if test="$pos = 1 or
                @sku != $products/product[$pos - 1]/@sku">
            <xsl:copy-of select="."/>
        </xsl:if>
    </xsl:for-each>
</products>
</xsl:template>
```

This code fails because position( ) returns the position after sorting, but the contents of $products has not been sorted; instead, an inaccessible copy of it was.

See Also

The XSLT FAQ (*http://www.dpawson.co.uk/xsl/sect2/N2696.html*) describes a solution that uses keys and describes solutions to related problems.

4.4   Selecting All but a Specific Element

Problem

You want to select all elements in a specific context, except the ones you choose to exclude.

Solution

The best way to select all but a specific element is to say:

```
<xsl:apply-templates select="*[not(self::element-to-ignore)]"/>
```

or, if iterating, say:

```
<xsl:for-each select="*[not(self::element-to-ignore)]">
...
</xsl:for-each>
```

Discussion

When XSLT newbies first need to select all but a specific element, they will probably think of the following construct first:

```
<xsl:apply-templates select="*[name() != 'element-to-ignore']"/>
```

This code works in many cases, but it could cause trouble when the document uses namespaces. Recall that name() returns the node's QName: the namespace prefix concatenated to the local part of the name. However, in any given XML document, nothing forces the author to use a specific prefix:

```
<!--This will fail if the author decided to use SALES:product instead of
sales:product -->
<xsl:apply-templates select="*[name() != 'sales:product']"/>
```

Alternatively, you could use local-name(). However, this prefix would ignore elements from all namespaces that have that particular local name, which might not be what you want.

This recommendation applies only in the case of elements, not attributes. If you need to select all but a specific attribute, use local-name(). The self axis, when applied to a name, refers only to elements. In other words, use <xsl:copy-of select=@*[local-name() != 'ignored-attribute']/> and not <xsl:copy-of select=@*[not(self:: ignored-attribute)]/>.

Finally, just in case of confusion, selecting all but a single element is different from selecting all but a single *instance* of element. The latter is used in an example discussed earlier in this chapter:

```
<xsl:apply-templates select="*[generate-id() != generate-id($node-to-ignore)]"/>
```

See Also

Jeni Tennison's book, *XSLT and XPath on the Edge* (M&T Books, 2001), details when and when not to use name( ) and local-name( ).

4.5   Performing a Preorder Traversal

Problem

You want to recursively process an element first and then process its child elements.

Solution

Solutions to this recipe have the following general form:

```
<xsl:template match="node( )">
    <!-- Do something with current node -->

    <!--Process children -->
    <xsl:apply-templates/>
</xsl:template>
```

Discussion

The term *preorder* is computer-science jargon for traversing a tree so you visit the root and recursively visit the children of the root in preorder. This process is arguably the most common means of processing XML. Of this idiom's many applications, this chapter will consider two. As you review recipes in later sections, you will see this mode of traversal arise frequently.

Consider an organization chart (Example 4-2) encoded in a simplistic fashion so that an employee element *B* is a child of another employee element *A* if *B* reports to *A*. Example 4-16 employs a preorder traversal to explain who manages whom. Example 4-17 shows the output.

Example 4-16. Stylesheet

```
<?xml version="1.0" encoding="UTF-8"?>
<xsl:stylesheet version="1.0" xmlns:xsl="http://www.w3.org/1999/XSL/Transform">

<xsl:output method="text"/>
<xsl:strip-space elements="*"/>

<xsl:template match="/employee" priority="10">
    <xsl:value-of select="@name"/><xsl:text> is the head of the company. </xsl:text>
    <xsl:call-template name="HeShe"/><xsl:text> manages </xsl:text>
    <xsl:call-template name="manages"/>
    <xsl:apply-templates/>
</xsl:template>
```

Example 4-16. Stylesheet (continued)

```
<xsl:template match="employee[employee]">
     <xsl:value-of select="@name"/><xsl:text> is a manager. </xsl:text>
     <xsl:call-template name="HeShe"/> <xsl:text> manages </xsl:text>
     <xsl:call-template name="manages"/>
     <xsl:apply-templates/>
</xsl:template>

<xsl:template match="employee">
     <xsl:value-of select="@name"/><xsl:text> has no worries. </xsl:text>
     <xsl:text>&#xa;&#xa;</xsl:text>
</xsl:template>

<xsl:template name="HeShe">
    <xsl:choose>
        <xsl:when test="@sex = 'male' ">
             <xsl:text>He</xsl:text>
        </xsl:when>
        <xsl:otherwise>
             <xsl:text>She</xsl:text>
        </xsl:otherwise>
    </xsl:choose>
</xsl:template>

<xsl:template name="manages">
    <xsl:for-each select="*">
        <xsl:choose>
          <xsl:when test="position() != last() and last() > 2">
            <xsl:value-of select="@name"/><xsl:text>, </xsl:text>
          </xsl:when>
          <xsl:when test="position() = last() and last() > 1">
            <xsl:text> and </xsl:text><xsl:value-of
                        select="@name"/><xsl:text>. </xsl:text>
          </xsl:when>
          <xsl:when test="last() = 1">
            <xsl:value-of select="@name"/><xsl:text>. </xsl:text>
          </xsl:when>
          <xsl:otherwise>
            <xsl:value-of select="@name"/>
          </xsl:otherwise>
        </xsl:choose>
    </xsl:for-each>
    <xsl:text>&#xa;&#xa;</xsl:text>
</xsl:template>
</xsl:stylesheet>
```

Example 4-17. Output

Jil Michel is the head of the company. She manages Nancy Pratt, Jane Doe, and Mike
Rosenbaum.

Nancy Pratt is a manager. She manages Phill McKraken and Ima Little.

Example 4-17. Output (continued)

Phill McKraken has no worries.

Ima Little is a manager. She manages Betsy Ross.

Betsy Ross has no worries.

Jane Doe is a manager. She manages Walter H. Potter and Wendy B.K. McDonald.

Walter H. Potter has no worries.

Wendy B.K. McDonald is a manager. She manages Craig F. Frye, Hardy Hamburg, and Rich Shaker.

Craig F. Frye has no worries.

Hardy Hamburg has no worries.

Rich Shaker has no worries.

Mike Rosenbaum is a manager. He manages Cindy Post-Kellog and Oscar A. Winner.

Cindy Post-Kellog is a manager. She manages Allen Bran, Frank N. Berry, and Jack Apple.

Allen Bran has no worries.

Frank N. Berry has no worries.

Jack Apple has no worries.

Oscar A. Winner is a manager. He manages Jack Nickolas, Tom Hanks, and Susan Sarandon.

Jack Nickolas is a manager. He manages R.P. McMurphy.

R.P. McMurphy has no worries.

Tom Hanks is a manager. He manages Forest Gump and Andrew Beckett.

Forest Gump has no worries.

Andrew Beckett has no worries.

Susan Sarandon is a manager. She manages Helen Prejean.

Helen Prejean has no worries.

A more serious application of preorder traversal is the conversion of an expression tree to prefix notation. Given the MathML content fragment in Examples 4-18 and 4-19, you can create a transformation to a Lisp-like syntax. Example 4-20 shows the output.

Example 4-18. MathML fragment representing x2+4x+4 = 0

```
<apply>
    <eq/>
    <apply>
        <plus/>
        <apply>
            <power/>
            <ci>x</ci>
            <cn>2</cn>
        </apply>
        <apply>
            <times/>
            <cn>4</cn>
            <ci>x</ci>
        </apply>
        <cn>4</cn>
    </apply>
    <cn>0</cn>
</apply>
```

Example 4-19. Stylesheet to convert MathML fragment to prefix notation

```
<?xml version="1.0" encoding="UTF-8"?><xsl:stylesheet version="1.0"
    xmlns:xsl="http://www.w3.org/1999/XSL/Transform">
    <xsl:output method="text"/>
    <xsl:strip-space elements="*"/>

    <xsl:template match="apply">
        <xsl:value-of select="local-name(*[1])"/>
        <xsl:text>(</xsl:text>
        <xsl:apply-templates/>
        <xsl:text>)</xsl:text>
        <xsl:if test="following-sibling::*">,</xsl:if>
    </xsl:template>

    <xsl:template match="ci|cn">
        <xsl:value-of select="."/>
        <xsl:if test="following-sibling::*">,</xsl:if>
    </xsl:template>
</xsl:stylesheet>
```

Example 4-20. Output

```
eq(plus(power(x,2),times(4,x),4),0)
```

The MathML converter is not the purest example of a preorder traversal, largely because MathML encodes mathematical expressions unconventionally. This is largely an instance of the preorder idiom because the code processes the apply element first (and outputs the name of its first child element) and then processes its child elements recursively (via `<xsl:apply-templates/>`). The code following apply-templates balances the parentheses, inserts commas where necessary, and involves no further traversal.

4.6   Performing a Postorder Traversal

Problem

You want to recursively process the children of an element first and then the element itself.

Solution

Solutions to this recipe have the following general form:

```
<xsl:template match="node( )">
     <!--Process children -->
     <xsl:apply-templates/>

     <!-- Do something with current node -->

</xsl:template>
```

Discussion

The term *postorder* is computer-science jargon for traversing a tree so that you recursively visit the children of the root in postorder and then visit the root. This algorithm produces a stylesheet that processes the outermost leaf nodes and works its way up to the document root.

You can apply a postorder traversal to the organizational chart (*orgchart.xml*) to produce an explanation of who reports to whom, starting from the bottom, as shown in Example 4-21. Example 4-22 shows the output.

Example 4-21. Stylesheet

```
<xsl:stylesheet version="1.0" xmlns:xsl="http://www.w3.org/1999/XSL/Transform">

<xsl:output method="text"/>
<xsl:strip-space elements="*"/>

<xsl:template match="/employee" priority="10">
    <xsl:apply-templates/>
    <xsl:value-of select="@name"/><xsl:text> is the head of the company. </xsl:text>
    <xsl:call-template name="reportsTo"/>
    <xsl:call-template name="HimHer"/> <xsl:text>. </xsl:text>
    <xsl:text>&#xa;&#xa;</xsl:text>
</xsl:template>

<xsl:template match="employee[employee]">
    <xsl:apply-templates/>
    <xsl:value-of select="@name"/><xsl:text> is a manager. </xsl:text>
    <xsl:call-template name="reportsTo"/>
    <xsl:call-template name="HimHer"/> <xsl:text>. </xsl:text>
    <xsl:text>&#xa;&#xa;</xsl:text>
```

Example 4-21. Stylesheet (continued)

```
</xsl:template>

<xsl:template match="employee">
    <xsl:text>Nobody reports to </xsl:text>
    <xsl:value-of select="@name"/><xsl:text>. &#xa;</xsl:text>
</xsl:template>

<xsl:template name="HimHer">
    <xsl:choose>
      <xsl:when test="@sex = 'male' ">
        <xsl:text>him</xsl:text>
      </xsl:when>
      <xsl:otherwise>
        <xsl:text>her</xsl:text>
      </xsl:otherwise>
    </xsl:choose>
</xsl:template>

<xsl:template name="reportsTo">
    <xsl:for-each select="*">
      <xsl:choose>
        <xsl:when test="position( ) &lt; last( ) - 1 and last( ) > 2">
         <xsl:value-of select="@name"/><xsl:text>, </xsl:text>
        </xsl:when>
        <xsl:when test="position( ) = last( ) - 1  and last( ) > 1">
         <xsl:value-of select="@name"/><xsl:text> and </xsl:text>
        </xsl:when>
        <xsl:when test="position( ) = last( ) and last( ) = 1">
         <xsl:value-of select="@name"/><xsl:text> reports to </xsl:text>
        </xsl:when>
        <xsl:when test="position( ) = last( )">
         <xsl:value-of select="@name"/><xsl:text> report to </xsl:text>
        </xsl:when>
        <xsl:otherwise>
         <xsl:value-of select="@name"/>
        </xsl:otherwise>
      </xsl:choose>
    </xsl:for-each>
</xsl:template>

</xsl:stylesheet>
```

Example 4-22. Output

```
Nobody reports to Phill McKraken.
Nobody reports to Betsy Ross.
Ima Little is a manager. Betsy Ross reports to her.

Nancy Pratt is a manager. Phill McKraken and Ima Little report to her.

Nobody reports to Walter H. Potter.
Nobody reports to Craig F. Frye.
```

Example 4-22. Output (continued)

Nobody reports to Hardy Hamburg.
Nobody reports to Rich Shaker.
Wendy B.K. McDonald is a manager. Craig F. Frye, Hardy Hamburg and Rich Shaker report to her.

Jane Doe is a manager. Walter H. Potter and Wendy B.K. McDonald report to her.

Nobody reports to Allen Bran.
Nobody reports to Frank N. Berry.
Nobody reports to Jack Apple.
Cindy Post-Kellog is a manager. Allen Bran, Frank N. Berry and Jack Apple report to her.

Nobody reports to R.P. McMurphy.
Jack Nickolas is a manager. R.P. McMurphy reports to him.

Nobody reports to Forest Gump.
Nobody reports to Andrew Beckett.
Tom Hanks is a manager. Forest Gump and Andrew Beckett report to him.

Nobody reports to Helen Prejean.
Susan Sarandon is a manager. Helen Prejean reports to her.

Oscar A. Winner is a manager. Jack Nickolas, Tom Hanks and Susan Sarandon report to him.

Mike Rosenbaum is a manager. Cindy Post-Kellog and Oscar A. Winner report to him.

Jil Michel is the head of the company. Nancy Pratt, Jane Doe and Mike Rosenbaum report to her.

4.7   Performing an In-Order Traversal

Problem

You have an XML document or fragment that represents an expression to be processed in-order.

Solution

An in-order traversal is most applicable to a binary tree. The general form of the algorithm in this case follows:

```
<xsl:template match="node( )">
    <!--Process left subtree -->
    <xsl:apply-templates select="*[1]"/>

    <!-- Do something with current node -->

    <!--Process right subtree -->
    <xsl:apply-templates select="*[2]"/>
</xsl:template>
```

However, in-order traversal can extend to n-ary trees with the following algorithm:

```
<xsl:template match="node()">
    <xsl:variable name="current-node" select="."/>
    <!--Process left subtree -->
    <xsl:apply-templates select="*[1]"/>

    <!-- Do something with $current-node -->

    <!-- Apply recursively to middle children
    <xsl:for-each select="*[position() > 1 and position() &lt; last()]">

        <!-- Process "left" subtree -->
        <xsl:apply-templates select="."/>

        <!--Do something with $current-node -->

    </xsl:for-each>

    <!--Process right subtree -->
    <xsl:apply-templates select="*[last()]"/>

</xsl:template>
```

The rational behind this algorithm can be better understood by considering Figure 4-1, which shows the binary equivalent of an n-ary tree. The generalized n-ary in-order traversal produces the same result as the binary in-order traversal on the binary equivalent tree.

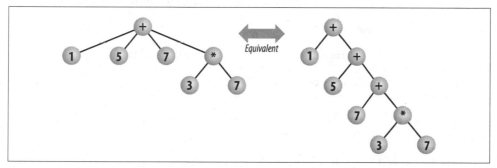

Figure 4-1. N-ary to binary tree equivalent

Discussion

This form of traversal has a much narrower range of applicability then other traversal examples in this chapter. One notable application, shown in Examples 4-23 and 4-24, is as a component of a stylesheet that converts MathML markup to C or Java-style infix expressions. Example 4-25 shows the output.

Example 4-23. Input MathML fragment

```
<apply>
    <eq/>
    <apply>
        <plus/>
        <apply>
            <minus/>
            <ci>y</ci>
            <cn>2</cn>
        </apply>
        <apply>
            <times/>
            <cn>4</cn>
            <apply>
                <plus/>
                <ci>x</ci>
                <cn>1</cn>
            </apply>
        </apply>
        <cn>8</cn>
    </apply>
    <cn>0</cn>
</apply>
```

Example 4-24. In-order traversal of MathML fragment to produce a C expression

```
<?xml version="1.0" encoding="UTF-8"?>
<xsl:stylesheet version="1.0" xmlns:xsl="http://www.w3.org/1999/XSL/Transform"
                              xmlns:C="http://www.ora.com/XSLTCookbook/nampespaces/C">
    <xsl:output method="text"/>
    <xsl:strip-space elements="*"/>

    <!-- Table to convert from MathML operation names to C operators -->
    <C:operator mathML="plus" c="+" precedence="2"/>
    <C:operator mathML="minus" c="-" precedence="2"/>
    <C:operator mathML="times" c="*" precedence="3"/>
    <C:operator mathML="div" c="/" precedence="3"/>
    <C:operator mathML="mod" c="%" precedence="3"/>
    <C:operator mathML="eq" c="==" precedence="1"/>

    <!-- load operation conversion table into a variable -->
    <xsl:variable name="ops" select="document('')/*/C:operator"/>

    <xsl:template match="apply">
        <xsl:param name="parent-precedence" select="0"/>

        <!-- Map mathML operation to operator name and precedence -->
        <xsl:variable name="mathML-opName" select="local-name(*[1])"/>
        <xsl:variable name="c-opName"
            select="$ops[@mathML=$mathML-opName]/@c"/>
        <xsl:variable name="c-opPrecedence"
            select="$ops[@mathML=$mathML-opName]/@precedence"/>
```

Example 4-24. In-order traversal of MathML fragment to produce a C expression (continued)

```
        <!-- Parenthises required if if the precedence of the containing
         expression is greater than current sub-expression -->
        <xsl:if test="$parent-precedence > $c-opPrecedence">
        <xsl:text>(</xsl:text>
        </xsl:if>

        <!-- Recursively process the left sub-tree which is at
             position 2 in MathML apply element-->
        <xsl:apply-templates select="*[2]">
            <xsl:with-param name="parent-precedence"
                 select="$c-opPrecedence"/>
        </xsl:apply-templates>

        <!-- Process the current node (i.e. the operator at
             position 1 in MathML apply element -->
        <xsl:value-of select="concat(' ',$c-opName,' ')"/>

        <!-- Recursively process middle children -->
        <xsl:for-each select="*[position()>2 and
                              position() &lt; last()]">
            <xsl:apply-templates select=".">
                <xsl:with-param name="parent-precedence"
                     select="$c-opPrecedence"/>
            </xsl:apply-templates>
            <xsl:value-of select="concat(' ',$c-opName,' ')"/>
        </xsl:for-each>

        <!-- Recursively process right subtree-->
        <xsl:apply-templates select="*[last()]">
            <xsl:with-param name="parent-precedence"
                     select="$c-opPrecedence"/>
        </xsl:apply-templates>

        <!-- Parenthises required if if the precedence of the containing
             expression is greater than current sub-expression -->
        <xsl:if test="$parent-precedence > $c-opPrecedence">
            <xsl:text>)</xsl:text>
        </xsl:if>

    </xsl:template>

    <xsl:template match="ci|cn">
        <xsl:value-of select="."/>
    </xsl:template>

</xsl:stylesheet>
```

Example 4-25. Output

```
y - 2 + 4 * (x + 1) + 8 == 0
```

Obviously, this stylesheet is not a full-fledged MathML-to-C translator. However, Chapter 9 discusses this problem more thoroughly.

4.8   Performing a Level-Order Traversal

Problem

You want to order elements by increasing level (tree depth). In other words, you want to traverse the tree breadth first.

Solution

This form of traversal is tailor-made for using xsl:for-each along with xsl:sort:

```
<xsl:for-each select="//*">
    <xsl:sort select="count(ancestor::*)" data-type="number"/>
    <!-- process the current element -->
</xsl:for-each>
```

This recursive solution is longer and less obvious:

```
<xsl:template match="/*">
    <xsl:call-template name="level-order"/>
</xsl:template>

<xsl:template name="level-order">
<xsl:param name="max-level" select="10"/>
<xsl:param name="current-level" select="1"/>

<xsl:choose>
    <xsl:when test="$current-depth &lt;= $max-level">
        <!-- process the current level -->
        <xsl:call-template name="level-order-aux">
            <xsl:with-param name="level"
                        select="$current-level"/>
            <xsl:with-param name="actual-level"
                        select="$current-level"/>
        </xsl:call-template>
        <!-- process the next level -->
        <xsl:call-template name="level-order">
            <xsl:with-param name="current-level"
                        select="$current-level + 1"/>
        </xsl:call-template>
    </xsl:when>
</xsl:choose>

</xsl:template>

<xsl:template name="level-order-aux">
    <xsl:param name="level" select="1"/>
    <xsl:param name="actual-level" select="1"/>
    <xsl:choose>
```

```
        <xsl:when test="$level = 1">
            <!-- Process the current element here -->
            <!-- $actual-level is the number of the current level -->
        </xsl:when>
        <xsl:otherwise>
            <!-- Recursively descend to the next level on
                 all children -->
            <xsl:for-each select="*">
                <xsl:call-template name="level-order-aux">
                    <xsl:with-param name="level"
                        select="$level - 1"/>
                    <xsl:with-param name="actual-level"
                        select="$actual-level"/>
                </xsl:call-template>
            </xsl:for-each>
        </xsl:otherwise>
    </xsl:choose>
</xsl:template>
```

This solution requires that you either set an arbitrary bound for the maximum depth of the tree or compute the max depth. One way of doing so is by finding the node that has no children and more ancestors than any other node without children:

```
<xsl:param name="max-level">
    <xsl:for-each select="//*[not(*)]">
        <xsl:sort select="count(ancestor::*)" data-type="number" order="descending" />
        <xsl:if test="position() = 1">
            <xsl:value-of select="count(ancestor::*) + 1" />
        </xsl:if>
    </xsl:for-each>
</xsl:param>
```

Discussion

Arguably, the need to traverse an XML document by level does not arise often. Grouping nodes by depth or distance from the root does not fit into XSLT's natural control flow, which is organized to express traversals that descend the document tree. This is apparent by the fact that that you had to use xsl:sort to coerce the stylesheet to process nodes by their depth or, equivalently, the number of ancestors. The complexity of the recursive solution provides further evidence of this unnatural process.

Still, this form of traversal is sometimes handy. For example, you can use it to process an organizational chart that lists employees by their distance form the top spot, as shown in Example 4-26. The output is shown in Example 4-27.

Example 4-26. Level-order traversal of orgrchart.xml using sort

```
<?xml version="1.0" encoding="UTF-8"?>
<xsl:stylesheet version="1.0" xmlns:xsl="http://www.w3.org/1999/XSL/Transform">
    <xsl:output method="text"/>
```

```
<xsl:template match="/">
  <xsl:for-each select="//employee">
    <xsl:sort select="count(ancestor::*)" order="ascending"/>
    <xsl:variable name="level" select="count(ancestor::*)"/>
    <xsl:choose>
      <xsl:when test="$level = 0">
        <xsl:value-of select="@name"/>
        <xsl:text> is the head honcho.&#xA;</xsl:text>
      </xsl:when>
      <xsl:otherwise>
        <xsl:value-of select="@name"/>
      <xsl:text> has </xsl:text>
      <xsl:value-of select="$level"/>
      <xsl:text> boss(es) to knock off.&#xA;</xsl:text>
    </xsl:otherwise>
    </xsl:choose>
  </xsl:for-each>
</xsl:template>

</xsl:stylesheet>
```

Example 4-27. Output

```
Jil Michel is the head honcho.
Nancy Pratt has 1 boss(es) to knock off.
Jane Doe has 1 boss(es) to knock off.
Mike Rosenbaum has 1 boss(es) to knock off.
Phill McKraken has 2 boss(es) to knock off.
Ima Little has 2 boss(es) to knock off.
Walter H. Potter has 2 boss(es) to knock off.
Wendy B.K. McDonald has 2 boss(es) to knock off.
Cindy Post-Kellog has 2 boss(es) to knock off.
Oscar A. Winner has 2 boss(es) to knock off.
Betsy Ross has 3 boss(es) to knock off.
Craig F. Frye has 3 boss(es) to knock off.
Hardy Hamburg has 3 boss(es) to knock off.
Rich Shaker has 3 boss(es) to knock off.
Allen Bran has 3 boss(es) to knock off.
Frank N. Berry has 3 boss(es) to knock off.
Jack Apple has 3 boss(es) to knock off.
Jack Nickolas has 3 boss(es) to knock off.
Tom Hanks has 3 boss(es) to knock off.
Susan Sarandon has 3 boss(es) to knock off.
R.P. McMurphy has 4 boss(es) to knock off.
Forest Gump has 4 boss(es) to knock off.
Andrew Beckett has 4 boss(es) to knock off.
Helen Prejean has 4 boss(es) to knock off.
```

One advantage of the recursive variation is that it is easy to tell when you transition from one level to the next. You could use this information to better format your output, as shown in Examples 4-28 and 4-29.

Example 4-28. Level-order traversal of orgrchart.xml using recursion

```
<?xml version="1.0" encoding="UTF-8"?>
<xsl:stylesheet version="1.0" xmlns:xsl="http://www.w3.org/1999/XSL/Transform">

<xsl:output method="text" version="1.0" encoding="UTF-8"/>

<xsl:strip-space elements="*"/>

<xsl:template match="/employee">
    <xsl:call-template name="level-order"/>
</xsl:template>

<xsl:template name="level-order">
<xsl:param name="max-depth" select="10"/>
<xsl:param name="current-depth" select="0"/>

<xsl:choose>
  <xsl:when test="$current-depth &lt;= $max-depth">
    <xsl:variable name="text">
      <xsl:call-template name="level-order-aux">
         <xsl:with-param name="level" select="$current-depth"/>
         <xsl:with-param name="actual-level" select="$current-depth"/>
      </xsl:call-template>
    </xsl:variable>
    <xsl:if test="normalize-space($text)">
      <xsl:value-of select="$text"/>
      <xsl:text>&#xa;</xsl:text>
      <xsl:call-template name="level-order">
        <xsl:with-param name="current-depth" select="$current-depth + 1"/>
        </xsl:call-template>
    </xsl:if>
  </xsl:when>
</xsl:choose>

</xsl:template>

<xsl:template name="level-order-aux">
  <xsl:param name="level" select="0"/>
  <xsl:param name="actual-level" select="0"/>
  <xsl:choose>
    <xsl:when test="$level = 0">
      <xsl:choose>
        <xsl:when test="$actual-level = 0">
        <xsl:value-of select="@name"/>
        <xsl:text> is the head honcho.&#xA;</xsl:text>
      </xsl:when>
      <xsl:otherwise>
        <xsl:value-of select="@name"/>
        <xsl:text> has </xsl:text>
        <xsl:value-of select="$actual-level"/>
        <xsl:text> boss(es) to knock off.&#xA;</xsl:text>
      </xsl:otherwise>
      </xsl:choose>
    </xsl:when>
```

```
    <xsl:otherwise>
      <xsl:for-each select="employee">
        <xsl:call-template name="level-order-aux">
          <xsl:with-param name="level" select="$level - 1"/>
          <xsl:with-param name="actual-level" select="$actual-level"/>
        </xsl:call-template>
      </xsl:for-each>
    </xsl:otherwise>
  </xsl:choose>
</xsl:template>

</xsl:stylesheet>
```

Example 4-29. Output

```
Jil Michel is the head honcho.

Nancy Pratt has 1 boss(es) to knock off.
Jane Doe has 1 boss(es) to knock off.
Mike Rosenbaum has 1 boss(es) to knock off.

Phill McKraken has 2 boss(es) to knock off.
Ima Little has 2 boss(es) to knock off.
Walter H. Potter has 2 boss(es) to knock off.
Wendy B.K. McDonald has 2 boss(es) to knock off.
Cindy Post-Kellog has 2 boss(es) to knock off.
Oscar A. Winner has 2 boss(es) to knock off.

Betsy Ross has 3 boss(es) to knock off.
Craig F. Frye has 3 boss(es) to knock off.
Hardy Hamburg has 3 boss(es) to knock off.
Rich Shaker has 3 boss(es) to knock off.
Allen Bran has 3 boss(es) to knock off.
Frank N. Berry has 3 boss(es) to knock off.
Jack Apple has 3 boss(es) to knock off.
Jack Nickolas has 3 boss(es) to knock off.
Tom Hanks has 3 boss(es) to knock off.
Susan Sarandon has 3 boss(es) to knock off.

R.P. McMurphy has 4 boss(es) to knock off.
Forest Gump has 4 boss(es) to knock off.
Andrew Beckett has 4 boss(es) to knock off.
Helen Prejean has 4 boss(es) to knock off.
```

If, for some reason, you wished to have random access to nodes at any specific level, you could define a key as follows:

```
<xsl:key name="level" match="employee" use="count(ancestor::*)"/>

<xsl:template match="/">
    <xsl:for-each select="key('level',3)">
        <!-- do something with the nodes on level 3 -->
```

```
        </xsl:for-each>
    </xsl:template>
```

You can also make the match more specific or use a predicate with the key function:

```
<xsl:key name="level" match="//employee" use="count(ancestor::*)"/>
```

```
<xsl:template match="/">
    <xsl:for-each select="key('level',3)[@sex='female']">
        <!-- do something with the female employees on level 3 -->
    </xsl:for-each>
</xsl:template>
```

The use of the XSLT's key facility is not mandatory because you can always write select="//*[count(ancestors::*)=3]" when you need access to level-3 elements; however, performance will suffer if your stylesheet repeatedly evaluates such an expression. In fact, if your stylesheet has a well-defined structure, you'd be much better off explicitly navigating to the desired level, e.g., select="/employee/employee/employee", although this navigation can become quite unwieldy.

4.9   Processing Nodes by Position

Problem

You want to process nodes in a sequence that is a function of their position in a document or node set.

Solution

Use xsl:sort with the select set to the position() or last() functions. The most trivial application of this example processes nodes in reverse document order:

```
<xsl:apply-templates>
    <xsl:sort select="position()" order="descending" data-type="number"/>
</xsl:apply-templates>
```

or:

```
<xsl:for-each select="*">
    <xsl:sort select="position()" order="descending" data-type="number"/>
    <!-- ... -->
</xsl:for-each>
```

Another common version of this example traverses a node set as if it were a matrix of a specified number of columns. Here, you process all nodes in the first column, then the second, and then the third:

```
<xsl:for-each select="*">
    <xsl:sort select="(position() - 1)  mod 3" />
    <!-- ... -->
</xsl:for-each>
```

Or, perhaps more cleanly with:

```
<xsl:for-each select="*[position( ) mod 3 = 1]">
    <xsl:apply-templates
        select=". | following-sibling::*[position( ) &lt; 3]" />
</xsl:for-each>
```

Sometimes you need to use position( ) to separate the first node in a node set from the remaining nodes. Doing so lets you perform complex aggregation operations on a document using recursion. I call this example *recursive-aggregation*. The abstract form of this example follows:

```
<xsl:template name="aggregation">
    <xsl:param name="node-set"/>
    <xsl:choose>
      <xsl:when test="$node-set">
        <!--We compute some function of the first element that produces
        a value that we want to aggregate. The function may depend on
        the type of the element (i.e. it can be polymorphic)-->
        <xsl:variable name="first">
         <xsl:apply-templates select="$node-set[1]" mode="calc"/>
        </xsl:variable>
        <!--We recursivly process the remaining nodes using position( ) -->
        <xsl:variable name="rest">
         <xsl:call-template name="aggregation">
           <xsl:with-param name="node-set"
             select="$node-set[position( )!=1]"/>
           </xsl:call-template>
        </xsl:variable>
        <!-- We perform some aggragation operation. This might not require
           a call to a template. For example, this might be
           $first + $rest           or
           $first * $rest           or
           concat($first,$rest)     etc. -->
        <xsl:call-template name="aggregate-func">
         <xsl:with-param name="a" select="$first"/>
         <xsl:with-param name="b" select="$rest"/>
        </xsl:call-template>
      </xsl:when>
      <!-- Here IDENTITY-VALUE should be replaced with the identity
           under the aggragate-func. For example, 0 is the identity
           for addition, 1 is the identity for subtarction, "" is the
           identity for concatentation, etc. -->
      <xsl:otherwise>IDENTITY-VALUE</xsl:otherwise>
    </xsl:choose>
</xsl:template>
```

Discussion

XSLT's natural tendency is to process nodes in document order. This is equivalent to saying that nodes are processed in order of their position. Thus, the following two XSLT fragments are equivalent (the sort is redundant):

```
<xsl:for-each select="*">
    <xsl:sort select="position( )"/>
    <!-- ... -->
</xsl:for-each>

<xsl:for-each select="*">
    <!-- ... -->
</xsl:for-each>
```

You can format our organizations chart into a two-column report using a variation of this idea, shown in Examples 4-30 and 4-31.

Example 4-30. 2-columns-orgchat.xslt stylesheet

```
<?xml version="1.0" encoding="UTF-8"?>
<xsl:stylesheet version="1.0" xmlns:xsl="http://www.w3.org/1999/XSL/Transform">

<xsl:output method="text" />
<xsl:strip-space elements="*"/>

<xsl:template match="employee[employee]">
<xsl:value-of select="@name"/>
<xsl:text>&#xA;</xsl:text>
<xsl:call-template name="dup">
    <xsl:with-param name="input" select=" '-' " />
    <xsl:with-param name="count" select="80"/>
</xsl:call-template>
<xsl:text>&#xA;</xsl:text>
<xsl:for-each select="employee[(position( ) - 1) mod 2 = 0]">
    <xsl:value-of select="@name"/>
    <xsl:call-template name="dup">
        <xsl:with-param name="input" select=" ' ' "/>
        <xsl:with-param name="count" select="40 - string-length(@name)"/>
    </xsl:call-template>
    <xsl:value-of select="following-sibling::*[1]/@name"/>
    <xsl:text>&#xA;</xsl:text>
</xsl:for-each>
<xsl:text>&#xA;</xsl:text>
<xsl:apply-templates/>
</xsl:template>

<xsl:template name="dup">
<xsl:param name="input"/>
<xsl:param name="count" select="1"/>
<xsl:choose>
    <xsl:when test="not($count) or not($input)"/>
    <xsl:when test="$count = 1">
        <xsl:value-of select="$input"/>
    </xsl:when>
    <xsl:otherwise>
        <xsl:if test="$count mod 2">
            <xsl:value-of select="$input"/>
        </xsl:if>
        <xsl:call-template name="dup">
```

Example 4-30. 2-columns-orgchat.xslt stylesheet (continued)

```
            <xsl:with-param name="input"
                    select="concat($input,$input)"/>
            <xsl:with-param name="count"
                    select="floor($count div 2)"/>
        </xsl:call-template>
    </xsl:otherwise>
</xsl:choose>
</xsl:template>

</xsl:stylesheet>
```

Example 4-31. Output

```
Jil Michel
-------------------------------------------------------------
Nancy Pratt                 Jane Doe
Mike Rosenbaum

Nancy Pratt
-------------------------------------------------------------
Phill McKraken              Ima Little

Ima Little
-------------------------------------------------------------
Betsy Ross

Jane Doe
-------------------------------------------------------------
Walter H. Potter           Wendy B.K. McDonald

Wendy B.K. McDonald
-------------------------------------------------------------
Craig F. Frye              Hardy Hamburg
Rich Shaker

Mike Rosenbaum
-------------------------------------------------------------
Cindy Post-Kellog          Oscar A. Winner

Cindy Post-Kellog
-------------------------------------------------------------
Allen Bran                 Frank N. Berry
Jack Apple

Oscar A. Winner
-------------------------------------------------------------
Jack Nickolas              Tom Hanks
Susan Sarandon

Jack Nickolas
-------------------------------------------------------------
R.P. McMurphy
```

Example 4-31. Output (continued)

Tom Hanks

Forest Gump   Andrew Beckett

Susan Sarandon

Helen Prejean

One example of recursive-aggregation is a stylesheet that computes the total commission paid to salespeople whose commission is a function of their total sales over all products, shown in Examples 4-32 and 4-33.

Example 4-32. Total-commission.xslt stylesheet

```
<xsl:stylesheet version="1.0" xmlns:xsl="http://www.w3.org/1999/XSL/Transform">
    <xsl:output method="text"/>

<xsl:template match="salesBySalesperson">
    <xsl:text>Total commision = </xsl:text>
    <xsl:call-template name="total-commision">
        <xsl:with-param name="salespeople" select="*"/>
    </xsl:call-template>
</xsl:template>

<!-- By default salespeople get 2% commsison and no base salary -->
<xsl:template match="salesperson" mode="commision">
    <xsl:value-of select="0.02 * sum(product/@totalSales)"/>
</xsl:template>

<!-- salespeople with seniority > 4 get $10000.00 base + 0.5% commsison -->
<xsl:template match="salesperson[@seniority > 4]" mode="commision" priority="1">
    <xsl:value-of select="10000.00 + 0.05 * sum(product/@totalSales)"/>
</xsl:template>

<!-- salespeople with seniority > 8 get (seniority * $2000.00) base + 0.8% commsison -->
<xsl:template match="salesperson[@seniority > 8]" mode="commision" priority="2">
    <xsl:value-of select="@seniority * 2000.00 + 0.08 *
        sum(product/@totalSales)"/>
</xsl:template>

<xsl:template name="total-commision">
    <xsl:param name="salespeople"/>
    <xsl:choose>
      <xsl:when test="$salespeople">
        <xsl:variable name="first">
         <xsl:apply-templates select="$salespeople[1]" mode="commision"/>
        </xsl:variable>
        <xsl:variable name="rest">
         <xsl:call-template name="total-commision">
           <xsl:with-param name="salespeople"
             select="$salespeople[position( )!=1]"/>
```

Example 4-32. Total-commission.xslt stylesheet (continued)

```
            </xsl:call-template>
          </xsl:variable>
          <xsl:value-of select="$first + $rest"/>
        </xsl:when>
        <xsl:otherwise>0</xsl:otherwise>
      </xsl:choose>
</xsl:template>

</xsl:stylesheet>
```

Example 4-33. Output

```
Total commision = 471315
```

See Also

Michael Kay has a nice example of recursive-aggregation on page 535 of *XSLT Programmers Reference* (Wrox Press, 2001). He uses this example to compute the total area of various shapes in which the formula for area varies by the type of shape.

Jeni Tennison also provides examples of recursive-aggregation and alternative ways to perform similar types of processing in *XSLT and XPath on the Edge* (M&T Books, 2001).

CHAPTER 5

XML to Text

Text processing has made it possible to right-justify any idea,
even one which cannot be justified on any other grounds.

—J. Finegan

In the age of the Internet, formats such as HTML, XHTML, XML, and PDF clearly dominate the application of XSL and XSLT on the output side. However, plain old text will never become obsolete because it is the lowest common denominator in both human- and machine-readable formats. XML is often converted to text for import into another application that does not know how to read XML or does not interpret it the way you prefer. Text output is also used when the result will be sent to a terminal or post-processed in, for example, a Unix pipeline.

Many examples in this section focus on XSLT techniques that create generic XML-to-text converters. Here, generic means that the transformation can be customized easily to work on many different XML inputs or produce a variety of outputs, or both. The techniques employed in these examples have application beyond the specifics of a given recipe and often beyond the domain of text processing. In particular, you may want to look at Recipes 5.2 through 5.5, even if they do not address a present need.

Of all the output formats supported by xsl:output, text is the one for which managing whitespace is the most crucial. For this reason, this chapter addresses the issue separately in Recipe 5.1. Developers inexperienced in XML and XSLT are often vexed by what seems fickle treatment of whitespace. However, once you understand the rules and techniques for exploiting the rules, it is easier to create output that is formatted correctly.

Source-code generation from XML is arguably in the domain of XML-to-text transformation. However, code generation involves issues that transcend mere transformation and formatting. Chapter 10 will deal with code generation as a subject unto itself.

5.1 Dealing with Whitespace

Problem

You need to convert XML into formatted text, but whitespace issues are ruining the results.

Solution

Consider the following annotated XML sample. The symbols ↵ (newline), → (tab), and ☐ (space) mark whitespace-only text nodes that are often overlooked but subject to being copied to the output:

```
<review>↵
→<author>↵
→→ <name>Sal Mangano</name>↵
→→<email>smangano@somewhere.com</email>↵
→</author>↵
<title>XSLT Cookbook</title>↵
<reviewer>↵
→→<name>☐<annonymous/>☐</name>↵
→→<email>smangano@somewhere.com</email>↵
→→<comment>↵
Totally awesome. <b>Worth every cent!</b>☐<i>Must buy because I ↵
know the author peronally and he can sure use the money.</i>↵
→→</comment>↵
→</reviewer>↵
</review>↵
```

Too much whitespace

1. Use `xsl:strip-space` to get rid of whitespace-only nodes.

    This top-level element with a single attribute, `elements`, is assigned a whitespace-separated list of element names that you want stripped of extra whitespace. Here, extra whitespace means whitespace-only text nodes. This means, for example, that the whitespace separating words in the previous `comment` element are significant because they are not whitespace only. On the other hand, the whitespace designated by the special symbols are whitespace only.

    A common idiom uses `<xsl:strip-space elements="*"/>` to strip whitespace by default and `xsl:preserve-space` (see later) to override specific elements.

2. Use `normalize-space` to get rid of extra whitespace.

    A common mistake is to assume that `xsl:strip-space` takes care of "extra" whitespace like that used to align text in the previous `comment` element. This is not the case. The parser always considers significant whitespace inside an element's text that is mixed with nonwhitespace. To remove this extra space, use `normalize-space`, as in `<xsl:value-of select="normalize-space(comment)"/>`.

3. Use `translate` to get rid of all whitespace.

   Another common mistake is to assume `normalize-space` strips all whitespace. This is not the case. Instead, it strips only leading and trailing whitespace and converts multiple internal whitespace characters to single spaces. If you need to strip all whitespace, use `translate(`*something*`,'&#x20;&#xa;&#xd; &#x9;', '')`.

4. Use an empty `xsl:text` element to prevent terminating whitespace in the stylesheet from being considered relevant.

   `xsl:text` is normally considered a way to preserve whitespace. However, a strategically placed empty `xsl:text` element can prevent trailing whitespace in the stylesheet from being interpreted as significant.

Consider the results of the two modes in the following document and stylesheet, shown in Examples 5-1 to 5-3.

Example 5-1. Input

```
<numbers>
  <number>10</number>
  <number>3.5</number>
  <number>4.44</number>
  <number>77.7777</number>
</numbers>
```

Example 5-2. Processing numbers with and without an empty xsl:text element

```
<xsl:stylesheet version="1.0" xmlns:xsl="http://www.w3.org/1999/XSL/Transform">

<xsl:output method="text"/>
<xsl:strip-space elements="*"/>

<xsl:template match="numbers">
Without empty text element:
<xsl:apply-templates mode="without"/>
With empty text element:
<xsl:apply-templates mode="with"/>
</xsl:template>

<xsl:template match="number" mode="without">
  <xsl:value-of select="."/>,
</xsl:template>

<xsl:template match="number" mode="with">
  <xsl:value-of select="."/>,<xsl:text/>
</xsl:template>

</xsl:stylesheet>
```

Example 5-3. Output

```
Without empty text element:
10,
3.5,
```

Example 5-3. Output (continued)

```
4.44,
77.7777,

With empty text element:
10,3.5,4.44,77.7777,
```

Note that there is nothing magical about xsl:text when it is used this way. It works just as well if you replace <xsl:text/> with <xsl:if test="0"/> (but don't do so unless you enjoy confusing others). The effect is the placement of an element node between the comma and the trailing newline, which creates a whitespace-only node that will be ignored.

Too little whitespace

1. Use xsl:preserve-space to override xsl:strip-space for specific elements.

   There is not much point in using xsl:preserve-space unless you also use xsl:strip-space. This is because the default behavior preserves space in the input document and documents loaded with the document( ) function.

    Remember, MSXML strips whitespace-only text nodes by default. In this case, you can use xsl:preserve-space to counteract this nonconformance.

2. Use xsl:text to precisely specify text-output spacing.

   All whitespace inside an xsl:text element is preserved. This preservation allows precise control over whitespace placement. Sometimes you can use xsl:text to simply introduce line breaks:

   ```
   <xsl:stylesheet version="1.0" xmlns:xsl="http://www.w3.org/1999/XSL/Transform">

   <xsl:output method="text"/>
   <xsl:strip-space elements="*"/>

   <xsl:template match="number">
     <xsl:value-of select="."/>
     <xsl:text>&#xa;</xsl:text>
   </xsl:template>
   </xsl:stylesheet>
   ```

   However, the problem with outputting newline characters directly is that some platforms (e.g., Microsoft's) expect a line break to be represented as carriage-return plus newline. However, since XML parsers are required to convert carriage return plus newline into a single newline, there is no way to create a platform-independent stylesheet. Fortunately, most Windows-based editors and the Windows command prompt handle single newlines correctly. The one exception is the notepad editor that comes free with Windows.

3. Use nonbreaking space characters.

   XSLT does not treat character &#A0; (nonbreaking space) as normal whitespace. In particular, `xsl:strip-space` and `normalize-space( )` both ignore this character. If you need to strip whitespace most of the time but have specific instances when it should remain in place, you might try to use this character in the XML input. Nonbreaking space is particularly useful for HTML output, but may be of lesser value in other contexts (depending on how the renderer handles it).

Discussion

The solution section lists techniques for managing whitespace. However, knowing the XSLT rules that underlie the techniques is also useful.

The most important rules to know applies to *both* the stylesheet and input document(s):

1. A text node is never stripped unless it contains only whitespace characters (#x20, #x9, #xD, or #xA).

   Although they are not all that common, you should also understand the effect of `xml:space` attributes in both the stylesheet and the input document(s).

2. If a text-node's ancestor element has an `xml:space` attribute with a value of `preserve`, and no closer ancestor element has `xml:space` with a value of `default`, then whitespace-only text nodes are not stripped.

   The chapter now looks at the rules for stylesheets and source documents separately. For stylesheets, your options are simple.

3. The only stylesheet elements for which whitespace-only nodes are preserved by default are `xsl:text`. Here, "by default" means unless otherwise specified using `xml:space="preserve"` as stated earlier in Step 2,. See Examples 5-4 and 5-5.

Example 5-4. Stylesheet demonstrating the effect of xsl:text and xml:space=preserve

```
<xsl:stylesheet version="1.0" xmlns:xsl="http://www.w3.org/1999/XSL/Transform">

<xsl:output method="text"/>

<xsl:strip-space elements="*"/>

<xsl:template match="numbers">
Without xml:space="preserve":
<xsl:apply-templates mode="without-preserve"/>
With xml:space="preserve":
<xsl:apply-templates mode="with-preserve"/>
</xsl:template>
```

```
<xsl:template match="number" mode="without-preserve">
  <xsl:value-of select="."/><xsl:text> </xsl:text>
</xsl:template>

<xsl:template match="number" mode="with-preserve" xml:space="preserve">
  <xsl:value-of select="."/><xsl:text> </xsl:text>
</xsl:template>

</xsl:stylesheet>
```

Example 5-5. Output

```
Without xml:space="preserve":
10 3.5 4.44 77.7777
With xml:space="preserve":

  10

  3.5

  4.44

  77.7777
```

The only whitespace introduced by the first number match is the single space contained in the xsl:text element. However, when you use xml:space="preserve" in the second number match template, you pick up all the whitespace contained in the element including the two line breaks (the first is after the <xsl:template ...> and the second is after the </xsl:text>).

For source documents, the rules are as follows:

- Initially, the list of elements in which whitespace is preserved includes all elements in the document.

- If an element matches a NameTest in an xsl:strip-space element, then it is removed from the list of whitespace-preserving element names.

- If an element name matches a NameTest in an xsl:preserve-space element, then it is added to the list of whitespace-preserving element names.

A NameTest is either a simple name (e.g., doc) or a name with a namespace prefix (e.g., my:doc), wildcard (e.g., *), or a wildcard with a namespace prefix (e.g., my:*). The default priority and import precedence rules apply when conflicts exist between xml:strip-space and xml:preserve-space:

```
<xsl:stylesheet version="1.0" xmlns:xsl="http://www.w3.org/1999/XSL/Transform"
xmlns:my="http://www.ora.com/XSLTCookbook/ns/my">

<!-- Strip whitespace in all elements -->
<xsl:strip-space="*"/>
```

```
<!-- except those in the "my" namespace -->
<xsl:preserve-space="my:*"/>

<!-- and those named foo -->
<xsl:preserve-space="foo"/>
```

See Also

One of the most complete discussions of whitespace handling is in Michael Kay's *XSLT Programmer's Reference* (Wrox, 2001). The book also includes good coverage of the import precedence rules.

5.2   Exporting XML to Delimited Data

Problem

You need to convert some XML into data suitable for importing into another application such as a spreadsheet.

Solution

Many applications import delimited data. The most common format is called Comma Separated Values (CSV). Many spreadsheets and databases can handle CSV and other forms of delimited data. Mapping XML to delimited data can be simple or complex, depending on the difficulty of the mapping. This section starts with simple cases and progresses toward more complicated scenarios.

Create a CSV file from flat attribute-encoded elements

In this scenario, you have a flat XML file with elements mapping to rows and attributes mapping to columns.

This problem is trivial for any given XML file of the appropriate format. For example, the following stylesheet shown in Examples 5-6 through 5-8 outputs a CSV based on the input *people.xml*.

Example 5-6. people.xml

```
<?xml version="1.0" encoding="UTF-8"?>

<people>
  <person name="Al Zehtooney" age="33" sex="m" smoker="no"/>
  <person name="Brad York" age="38" sex="m" smoker="yes"/>
  <person name="Charles Xavier" age="32" sex="m" smoker="no"/>
  <person name="David Willimas" age="33" sex="m" smoker="no"/>
  <person name="Edward Ulster" age="33" sex="m" smoker="yes"/>
  <person name="Frank Townsend" age="35" sex="m" smoker="no"/>
  <person name="Greg Sutter" age="40" sex="m" smoker="no"/>
```

Example 5-6. people.xml (continued)

```
  <person name="Harry Rogers" age="37" sex="m" smoker="no"/>
  <person name="John Quincy" age="43" sex="m" smoker="yes"/>
  <person name="Kent Peterson" age="31" sex="m" smoker="no"/>
  <person name="Larry Newell" age="23" sex="m" smoker="no"/>
  <person name="Max Milton" age="22" sex="m" smoker="no"/>
  <person name="Norman Lamagna" age="30" sex="m" smoker="no"/>
  <person name="Ollie Kensinton" age="44" sex="m" smoker="no"/>
  <person name="John Frank" age="24" sex="m" smoker="no"/>
  <person name="Mary Williams" age="33" sex="f" smoker="no"/>
  <person name="Jane Frank" age="38" sex="f" smoker="yes"/>
  <person name="Jo Peterson" age="32" sex="f" smoker="no"/>
  <person name="Angie Frost" age="33" sex="f" smoker="no"/>
  <person name="Betty Bates" age="33" sex="f" smoker="no"/>
  <person name="Connie Date" age="35" sex="f" smoker="no"/>
  <person name="Donna Finster" age="20" sex="f" smoker="no"/>
  <person name="Esther Gates" age="37" sex="f" smoker="no"/>
  <person name="Fanny Hill" age="33" sex="f" smoker="yes"/>
  <person name="Geta Iota" age="27" sex="f" smoker="no"/>
  <person name="Hillary Johnson" age="22" sex="f" smoker="no"/>
  <person name="Ingrid Kent" age="21" sex="f" smoker="no"/>
  <person name="Jill Larson" age="20" sex="f" smoker="no"/>
  <person name="Kim Mulrooney" age="41" sex="f" smoker="no"/>
  <person name="Lisa Nevins" age="21" sex="f" smoker="no"/>
</people>
```

Example 5-7. A simple but input-specific CSV transform

```
<xsl:stylesheet version="1.0" xmlns:xsl="http://www.w3.org/1999/XSL/Transform">
    <xsl:output method="text"/>
    <xsl:strip-space elements="*"/>

    <xsl:template match="person">
      <xsl:value-of select="@name"/>,<xsl:text/>
      <xsl:value-of select="@age"/>,<xsl:text/>
      <xsl:value-of select="@sex"/>,<xsl:text/>
      <xsl:value-of select="@smoker"/>
      <xsl:text>&#xa;</xsl:text>
    </xsl:template>

</xsl:stylesheet>
```

Example 5-8. Output

```
Al Zehtooney,33,m,no
Brad York,38,m,yes
Charles Xavier,32,m,no
David Willimas,33,m,no
Edward Ulster,33,m,yes
Frank Townsend,35,m,no
Greg Sutter,40,m,no
...
```

Although the solution is simple, it would be nice to create a generic stylesheet that can be customized easily for this class of conversion. Examples 5-9 and 5-10 show a generic solution and how it might be used in the case of *people.xml*.

Example 5-9. generic-attr-to-csv.xslt

```
<xsl:stylesheet version="1.0" xmlns:xsl="http://www.w3.org/1999/XSL/Transform"
 xmlns:csv="http://www.ora.com/XSLTCookbook/namespaces/csv">

<xsl:param name="delimiter" select=" ',' "/>

<xsl:output method="text" />

<xsl:strip-space elements="*"/>

<xsl:template match="/">
  <xsl:for-each select="$columns">
    <xsl:value-of select="@name"/>
    <xsl:value-of select="$delimiter"/>
  </xsl:for-each>
  <xsl:text>&#xa;</xsl:text>
  <xsl:apply-templates/>
</xsl:template>

<xsl:template match="/*/*">
  <xsl:variable name="row" select="."/>

  <xsl:for-each select="$columns">
    <xsl:apply-templates select="$row/@*[local-name(.)=current()/@attr]"
    mode="csv:map-value"/>
    <xsl:if test="position() != last()">
    <xsl:value-of select="$delimiter"/>
    </xsl:if>
  </xsl:for-each>

  <xsl:text>&#xa;</xsl:text>

</xsl:template>

<xsl:template match="@*" mode="map-value">
  <xsl:value-of select="."/>
</xsl:template>

</xsl:stylesheet>
```

Example 5-10. Using the generic solution to process people.xml

```
<xsl:stylesheet version="1.0" xmlns:xsl="http://www.w3.org/1999/XSL/Transform"
 xmlns:csv="http://www.ora.com/XSLTCookbook/namespaces/csv">

<xsl:import href="generic-attr-to-csv.xslt"/>

<!--Defines the mapping from attributes to columns -->
<xsl:variable name="columns" select="document('')/*/csv:column"/>
```

```
<csv:column name="Name" attr="name"/>
<csv:column name="Age" attr="age"/>
<csv:column name="Gender" attr="sex"/>
<csv:column name="Smoker" attr="smoker"/>

<!-- Handle custom attribute mappings -->

<xsl:template match="@sex" mode="csv:map-value">
  <xsl:choose>
    <xsl:when test=".='m'">male</xsl:when>
    <xsl:when test=".='f'">female</xsl:when>
    <xsl:otherwise>error</xsl:otherwise>
  </xsl:choose>
</xsl:template>

</xsl:stylesheet>
```

This solution is table driven. The *generic-attr-to-csv.xslt* stylesheet uses a variable containing `csv:column` elements that are defined in the importing spreadsheet. The importing spreadsheet needs only to arrange the `csv:column` elements in the order in which the resulting columns should appear in the output. The `csv:column` elements define the mapping between a named column and an attribute name in the input XML. Optionally, the importing stylesheet can translate the values of certain attributes by providing a template that matches the specified attribute using the mode `csv:map-value`. Here you use such a template to translate the abbreviated `@sex` values in *people.xml*. Any common sets of mapping in use can be placed in a third stylesheet and imported as well. The nice thing about this solution is that it is easy for someone with only very limited XSLT knowledge to define a new CSV mapping. As an added benefit, the generic stylesheet defines a top-level parameter that can change the default delimiting character from a comma to something else.

Create a CSV file from flat element-encoded data

In this scenario, you have a flat XML file with elements mapping to rows and children mapping to columns.

This problem is similar to the previous one, except you have XML that uses elements rather than attributes to encode the columns. You can also provide a generic solution here, as shown in Examples 5-11 to 5-14.

Example 5-11. People using elements

```
<people>
  <person>
    <name>Al Zehtooney</name>
    <age>33</age>
    <sex>m</sex>
    <smoker>no</smoker>
  </person>
```

Example 5-11. People using elements (continued)

```
<person>
  <name>Brad York</name>
  <age>38</age>
  <sex>m</sex>
  <smoker>yes</smoker>
</person>
<person>
  <name>Charles Xavier</name>
  <age>32</age>
  <sex>m</sex>
  <smoker>no</smoker>
</person>
<person>
  <name>David Willimas</name>
  <age>33</age>
  <sex>m</sex>
  <smoker>no</smoker>
</person>
...
</people>
```

Example 5-12. generic-elem-to-csv.xslt

```
<xsl:stylesheet version="1.0" xmlns:xsl="http://www.w3.org/1999/XSL/Transform"
    xmlns:csv="http://www.ora.com/XSLTCookbook/namespaces/csv">

<xsl:param name="delimiter" select=" ',' " />

<xsl:output method="text" />

<xsl:strip-space elements="*"/>

<xsl:template match="/">
  <xsl:for-each select="$columns">
    <xsl:value-of select="@name"/>
   <xsl:if test="position( ) != last( )">
      <xsl:value-of select="$delimiter"/>
    </xsl:if>
  </xsl:for-each>
  <xsl:text>&#xa;</xsl:text>
  <xsl:apply-templates/>
</xsl:template>

<xsl:template match="/*/*">
  <xsl:variable name="row" select="."/>

  <xsl:for-each select="$columns">
    <xsl:apply-templates
        select="$row/*[local-name(.)=current( )/@elem]"mode="csv:map-value"/>
    <xsl:if test="position( ) != last( )">
    <xsl:value-of select="$delimiter"/>
    </xsl:if>
  </xsl:for-each>
```

Example 5-12. generic-elem-to-csv.xslt (continued)

```
  <xsl:text>&#xa;</xsl:text>

</xsl:template>

<xsl:template match="node()" mode="map-value">
  <xsl:value-of select="."/>
</xsl:template>
```

Example 5-13. people-elem-to-csv.xslt

```
<xsl:stylesheet version="1.0" xmlns:xsl="http://www.w3.org/1999/XSL/Transform"
    xmlns:csv="http://www.ora.com/XSLTCookbook/namespaces/csv">

<xsl:import href="generic-elem-to-csv.xslt"/>

<!--Defines the mapping from attributes to columns -->
<xsl:variable name="columns" select="document('')/*/csv:column"/>

<csv:column name="Name" elem="name"/>
<csv:column name="Age" elem="age"/>
<csv:column name="Gender" elem="sex"/>
<csv:column name="Smoker" elem="smoker"/>

</xsl:stylesheet>
```

Example 5-14. Output

```
Name,Age,Gender,Smoker
Al Zehtooney,33,m,no
Brad York,38,m,yes
Charles Xavier,32,m,no
David Willimas,33,m,no
...
```

Handle more complex mappings

In this scenario, you must deal with an arbitrary mapping of both attributes and elements to rows and columns. Here the document order does not map as nicely onto row or column order. In addition, the mapping may be sparse, in the sense that many empty values must be generated in the CSV data.

Consider, for example, the following XML representing an expense report of a soon-to-be-fired employee:

```
<ExpenseReport statementNum="123">
  <Employee>
    <Name>Salvatore Mangano</Name>
    <SSN>999-99-9999</SSN>
    <Dept>XSLT Hacking</Dept>
    <EmpNo>1</EmpNo>
    <Position>Cook</Position>
    <Mangager>Big Boss O'Reilly</Mangager>
  </Employee>
```

```
<PayPeriod>
  <From>1/1/02</From>
  <To>1/31/02</To>
</PayPeriod>
<Expenses>
  <Expense>
    <Date>12/20/01</Date>
    <Account>12345</Account>
    <Desc>Goofing off instead of going to confrence.</Desc>
    <Lodging>500.00</Lodging>
    <Transport>50.00</Transport>
    <Fuel>0</Fuel>
    <Meals>300.00</Meals>
    <Phone>100</Phone>
    <Entertainment>1000.00</Entertainment>
    <Other>300.00</Other>
  </Expense>
  <Expense>
    <Date>12/20/01</Date>
    <Account>12345</Account>
    <Desc>On the beach</Desc>
    <Lodging>500.00</Lodging>
    <Transport>50.00</Transport>
    <Fuel>0</Fuel>
    <Meals>200.00</Meals>
    <Phone>20</Phone>
    <Entertainment>300.00</Entertainment>
    <Other>100.00</Other>
  </Expense>
</Expenses>
</ExpenseReport>
```

Now imagine that you need to import this XML into a spreadsheet so that when appropriate spreadsheet styles are applied, the result looks like Figure 5-1.

To place the data correctly in all cells so that styling is the only further processing necessary, the following comma-delimited file must be produced:

```
,,,,,,,,,,,,Statement No.,123,

,,,,,,,,,,,,Expense Statement,


,,,Employee,,,,,,,,,Pay Period,

,,,Name,Salvatore Mangano,,Emp #,1,,,,,From,1/1/02,
,,,SSN,999-99-9999,,Position,Cook,
,,,Department,XSLT Hacking,,,,,,,,To,1/31/02,

,,,Date,Account,Description,Lodging,Transport,Fuel,Meals,Phone,Entertainment,Other,To
tal,

,,,12/20/01,12345,Goofing off instead of going to confrence.,500.00,50.00,0,300.
00,100,1000.00,300.00,
```

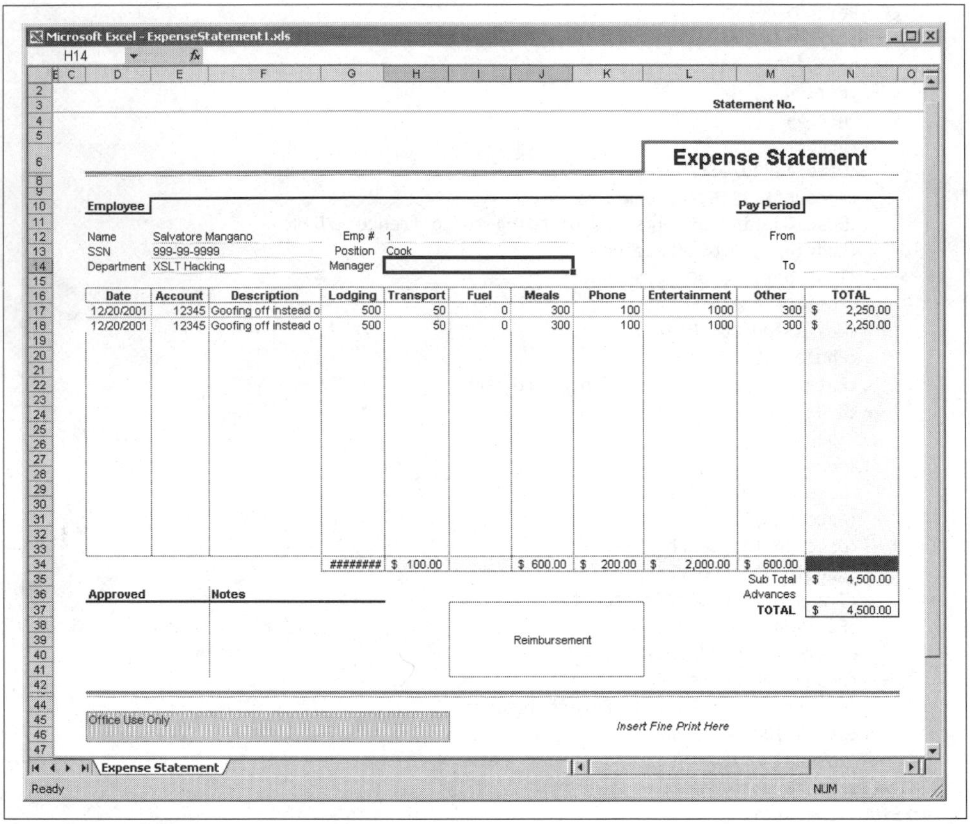

Figure 5-1. Expense report spreadsheet

```
,,,12/20/01,12345,On the beach,500.00,50.00,0,200.00,20,300.00,100.00,Sub Total,
,,,Approved,,Notes,,,,,,,Advances,
,,,,,,,,,,,,,Total,
```

As you can see, mapping from XML to delimited data lacks the uniformity that made the previous examples simple to implement. This is not to say that a stylesheet cannot be created to do the required mapping. However, if you attack the problem directly, we will probably end up with an ad-hoc and complex stylesheet.

When confronted with complex transformations, see if the problem could be simplified by first transforming the source document to an intermediate form, and then transform the intermediate form to the desired result. In other words, try to break complex transformation problems into two or more less-complicated problems.

Thinking along these lines, you'll see that the problem of mapping the XML to the spreadsheet is really a problem of assigning XML content to cells in the spreadsheet. You can therefore invent an intermediate form consisting of *cell elements*. For example, a cell element that places the value "foo" in cell A1 would be <cell col="A"

`row="1" value="foo"/>`. Your goal is to create a stylesheet that maps each significant element in the source onto a cell element. Because you no longer have to worry about ordering, mapping is simple:

```
<xsl:template match="ExpenseReport">
    <c:cell col="M" row="3" value="Statement No."/>
    <c:cell col="N" row="3" value="{@statementNum}"/>
    <c:cell col="L" row="6" value="Expense Statement"/>
    <xsl:apply-templates/>
    <xsl:variable name="offset" select="count(Expenses/Expense)+18"/>
    <c:cell col="M" row="{$offset}" value="Sub Total"/>
    <c:cell col="D" row="{$offset + 1}" value="Approved"/>
    <c:cell col="F" row="{$offset + 1}" value="Notes"/>
    <c:cell col="M" row="{$offset + 1}" value="Advances"/>
    <c:cell col="M" row="{$offset + 2}" value="Total"/>
</xsl:template>

<xsl:template match="Employee">
  <c:cell col="D" row="10" value="Employee"/>
  <xsl:apply-templates/>
</xsl:template>

<xsl:template match="Employee/Name">
  <c:cell col="D" row="12" value="Name"/>
  <c:cell col="E" row="12" value="{.}"/>
</xsl:template>

<xsl:template match="Employee/SSN">
  <c:cell col="D" row="13" value="SSN"/>
  <c:cell col="E" row="13" value="{.}"/>
</xsl:template>

<xsl:template match="Employee/Dept">
  <c:cell col="D" row="14" value="Department"/>
  <c:cell col="E" row="14" value="{.}"/>
</xsl:template>

<xsl:template match="Employee/EmpNo">
  <c:cell col="G" row="12" value="Emp #"/>
  <c:cell col="H" row="12" value="{.}"/>
</xsl:template>

<xsl:template match="Employee/Position">
  <c:cell col="G" row="13" value="Position"/>
  <c:cell col="H" row="13" value="{.}"/>
</xsl:template>

<xsl:template match="Employee/Manager">
  <c:cell col="G" row="14" value="Manager"/>
  <c:cell col="H" row="14" value="{.}"/>
</xsl:template>
```

```
<xsl:template match="PayPeriod">
  <c:cell col="M" row="10" value="Pay Period"/>
  <xsl:apply-templates/>
</xsl:template>

<xsl:template match="PayPeriod/From">
  <c:cell col="M" row="12" value="From"/>
  <c:cell col="N" row="12" value="{.}"/>
</xsl:template>

<xsl:template match="PayPeriod/To">
  <c:cell col="M" row="14" value="To"/>
  <c:cell col="N" row="14" value="{.}"/>
</xsl:template>

<xsl:template match="Expenses">
  <c:cell col="D" row="16" value="Date"/>
  <c:cell col="E" row="16" value="Account"/>
  <c:cell col="F" row="16" value="Description"/>
  <c:cell col="G" row="16" value="Lodging"/>
  <c:cell col="H" row="16" value="Transport"/>
  <c:cell col="I" row="16" value="Fuel"/>
  <c:cell col="J" row="16" value="Meals"/>
  <c:cell col="K" row="16" value="Phone"/>
  <c:cell col="L" row="16" value="Entertainment"/>
  <c:cell col="M" row="16" value="Other"/>
  <c:cell col="N" row="16" value="Total"/>
  <xsl:apply-templates/>
</xsl:template>

<xsl:template match="Expenses/Expense">
  <xsl:apply-templates>
    <xsl:with-param name="row" select="position( )+16"/>
  </xsl:apply-templates>
</xsl:template>

<xsl:template match="Expense/Date">
  <xsl:param name="row"/>
  <c:cell col="D" row="{$row}" value="{.}"/>
</xsl:template>

<xsl:template match="Expense/Account">
  <xsl:param name="row"/>
  <c:cell col="E" row="{$row}" value="{.}"/>
</xsl:template>

<xsl:template match="Expense/Desc">
  <xsl:param name="row"/>
  <c:cell col="F" row="{$row}" value="{.}"/>
</xsl:template>
```

```
<xsl:template match="Expense/Lodging">
  <xsl:param name="row"/>
  <c:cell col="G" row="{$row}" value="{.}"/>
</xsl:template>

<xsl:template match="Expense/Transport">
  <xsl:param name="row"/>
  <c:cell col="H" row="{$row}" value="{.}"/>
</xsl:template>

<xsl:template match="Expense/Fuel">
  <xsl:param name="row"/>
  <c:cell col="I" row="{$row}" value="{.}"/>
</xsl:template>

<xsl:template match="Expense/Meals">
  <xsl:param name="row"/>
  <c:cell col="J" row="{$row}" value="{.}"/>
</xsl:template>

<xsl:template match="Expense/Phone">
  <xsl:param name="row"/>
  <c:cell col="K" row="{$row}" value="{.}"/>
</xsl:template>

<xsl:template match="Expense/Entertainment">
  <xsl:param name="row"/>
  <c:cell col="L" row="{$row}" value="{.}"/>
</xsl:template>

<xsl:template match="Expense/Other">
  <xsl:param name="row"/>
  <c:cell col="M" row="{$row}" value="{.}"/>
</xsl:template>
```

One major advantage of using an attribute to encode a cell's value is that it lets you use attribute-value templates, thus creating a very concise translation scheme. Two types of mappings occur in this stylesheet. The first type is absolute. For example, you want the employee name to map to cell E12. The second type is relative; you want each expense item to map relative to row 16, based on its position in the source document.

When you apply this stylesheet to the source document, you get the following output:

```
<c:cells xmlns:c="http://www.ora.com/XSLTCookbook/namespaces/cells" >
  <c:cell col="M" row="3" value="Statement No."/>
  <c:cell col="N" row="3" value="123"/>
  <c:cell col="L" row="6" value="Expense Statement"/>
  <c:cell col="D" row="10" value="Employee"/>
  <c:cell col="D" row="12" value="Name"/>
  <c:cell col="E" row="12" value="Salvatore Mangano"/>
  <c:cell col="D" row="13" value="SSN"/>
```

```
<c:cell col="E" row="13" value="999-99-9999"/>
<c:cell col="D" row="14" value="Department"/>
<c:cell col="E" row="14" value="XSLT Hacking"/>
<c:cell col="G" row="12" value="Emp #"/>
<c:cell col="H" row="12" value="1"/>
<c:cell col="G" row="13" value="Position"/>
<c:cell col="H" row="13" value="Cook"/>
<c:cell col="G" row="14" value="Manager"/>
<c:cell col="H" row="14" value="Big Boss O'Reilly"/>
<c:cell col="M" row="10" value="Pay Period"/>
<c:cell col="M" row="12" value="From"/>
<c:cell col="N" row="12" value="1/1/02"/>
<c:cell col="M" row="14" value="To"/>
<c:cell col="N" row="14" value="1/31/02"/>
<c:cell col="D" row="16" value="Date"/>
<c:cell col="E" row="16" value="Account"/>
<c:cell col="F" row="16" value="Description"/>
<c:cell col="G" row="16" value="Lodging"/>
<c:cell col="H" row="16" value="Transport"/>
<c:cell col="I" row="16" value="Fuel"/>
<c:cell col="J" row="16" value="Meals"/>
<c:cell col="K" row="16" value="Phone"/>
<c:cell col="L" row="16" value="Entertainment"/>
<c:cell col="M" row="16" value="Other"/>
<c:cell col="N" row="16" value="Total"/>
<c:cell col="D" row="18" value="12/20/01"/>
<c:cell col="E" row="18" value="12345"/>
<c:cell col="F" row="18" value="Goofing off instead of going to confrence."/>
<c:cell col="G" row="18" value="500.00"/>
<c:cell col="H" row="18" value="50.00"/>
<c:cell col="I" row="18" value="0"/>
<c:cell col="J" row="18" value="300.00"/>
<c:cell col="K" row="18" value="100"/>
<c:cell col="L" row="18" value="1000.00"/>
<c:cell col="M" row="18" value="300.00"/>
<c:cell col="D" row="20" value="12/20/01"/>
<c:cell col="E" row="20" value="12345"/>
<c:cell col="F" row="20" value="On the beach"/>
<c:cell col="G" row="20" value="500.00"/>
<c:cell col="H" row="20" value="50.00"/>
<c:cell col="I" row="20" value="0"/>
<c:cell col="J" row="20" value="200.00"/>
<c:cell col="K" row="20" value="20"/>
<c:cell col="L" row="20" value="300.00"/>
<c:cell col="M" row="20" value="100.00"/>
<c:cell col="M" row="20" value="Sub Total"/>
<c:cell col="D" row="21" value="Approved"/>
<c:cell col="F" row="21" value="Notes"/>
<c:cell col="M" row="21" value="Advances"/>
<c:cell col="M" row="22" value="Total"/>
</c:cells>
```

Of course, this is not the final result you are after. However, it is not to0 difficult to see that by sorting these cells first by @row and then by @col makes mapping the cells into a comma-delimited form simple. In fact, if you are willing to use the EXSLT node-set extension, you can obtain your result with a single pass. Also notice that the cell-to-comma delimited mapping is completely generic, so you can reuse it in the future for other complex XML-to-comma-delimited mappings. See Examples 5-15 and 5-16.

Example 5-15. Generic cells-to-comma-delimited.xslt

```
<xsl:stylesheet version="1.0"
    xmlns:xsl="http://www.w3.org/1999/XSL/Transform"
    xmlns:c="http://www.ora.com/XSLTCookbook/namespaces/cells"
    xmlns:exsl="http://exslt.org/common" extension-element-prefixes="exsl">

<xsl:output method="text"/>

<!-- Used to map column letters to numbers -->
<xsl:variable name="columns" select=" '_ABCDEFGHIJKLMNOPQRSTUVWXYZ' "/>

<xsl:template match="/">

   <!-- Capture cells in a variable -->
   <xsl:variable name="cells">
     <xsl:apply-templates/>
   </xsl:variable>

   <!-- Sort into row-column order -->
   <xsl:variable name="cells-sorted">
     <xsl:for-each select="exsl:node-set($cells)/c:cell">
        <xsl:sort select="@row" data-type="number"/>
        <xsl:sort select="@col" data-type="text"/>
        <xsl:copy-of select="."/>
     </xsl:for-each>
   </xsl:variable>

   <xsl:apply-templates select="exsl:node-set($cells-sorted)/c:cell"/>

</xsl:template>

<xsl:template match="c:cell">
  <xsl:choose>
     <!-- Detect a row change -->
    <xsl:when test="preceding-sibling::c:cell[1]/@row != @row">
       <!-- Compute how many rows to skip, if any -->
      <xsl:variable name="skip-rows">
        <xsl:choose>
          <xsl:when test="preceding-sibling::c:cell[1]/@row">
            <xsl:value-of
             select="@row - preceding-sibling::c:cell[1]/@row"/>
          </xsl:when>
          <xsl:otherwise>
```

Example 5-15. Generic cells-to-comma-delimited.xslt (continued)

```
                <xsl:value-of select="@row - 1"/>
              </xsl:otherwise>
            </xsl:choose>
          </xsl:variable>
          <xsl:call-template name="skip-rows">
            <xsl:with-param name="skip" select="$skip-rows"/>
          </xsl:call-template>

          <xsl:variable name="current-col"
                select="string-length(substring-before($columns,@col))"/>
          <xsl:call-template name="skip-cols">
            <xsl:with-param name="skip" select="$current-col - 1"/>
          </xsl:call-template>
          <xsl:value-of select="@value"/>,<xsl:text/>
        </xsl:when>

        <xsl:otherwise>
            <!-- Compute how many cols to skip, if any -->
            <xsl:variable name="skip-cols">
              <xsl:variable name="current-col"
                  select="string-length(substring-before($columns,@col))"/>

              <xsl:choose>
                <xsl:when test="preceding-sibling::c:cell[1]/@col">
                  <xsl:variable name="prev-col"
                    select="string-length(substring-before($columns,
                            preceding-sibling::c:cell[1]/@col))"/>
                  <xsl:value-of select="$current-col - $prev-col - 1"/>
                </xsl:when>
                <xsl:otherwise>
                  <xsl:value-of select="$current-col - 1"/>
                </xsl:otherwise>
              </xsl:choose>
            </xsl:variable>

            <xsl:call-template name="skip-cols">
              <xsl:with-param name="skip" select="$skip-cols"/>
            </xsl:call-template>
            <!--Output the value of the cell and a comma -->
            <xsl:value-of select="@value"/>,<xsl:text/>
        </xsl:otherwise>
      </xsl:choose>
  </xsl:template>

<!-- Used to insert empty lines for non contiguous rows -->
<xsl:template name="skip-rows">
  <xsl:param name="skip"/>
  <xsl:choose>
    <xsl:when test="$skip > 0">
      <xsl:text>&#xa;</xsl:text>
      <xsl:call-template name="skip-rows">
        <xsl:with-param name="skip" select="$skip - 1"/>
```

Example 5-15. Generic cells-to-comma-delimited.xslt (continued)

```
      </xsl:call-template>
    </xsl:when>
    <xsl:otherwise/>
  </xsl:choose>
</xsl:template>

<!-- Used to insert extra commas for non contiguous cols -->
<xsl:template name="skip-cols">
  <xsl:param name="skip"/>
  <xsl:choose>
    <xsl:when test="$skip > 0">
      <xsl:text>,</xsl:text>
      <xsl:call-template name="skip-cols">
        <xsl:with-param name="skip" select="$skip - 1"/>
      </xsl:call-template>
    </xsl:when>
    <xsl:otherwise/>
  </xsl:choose>
</xsl:template>

</xsl:stylesheet>
```

Example 5-16. Applications-specific expense-to-delimited.xslt

```
<xsl:stylesheet version="1.0" xmlns:xsl="http://www.w3.org/1999/XSL/Transform"
  xmlns:c="http://www.ora.com/XSLTCookbook/namespaces/cells"
  xmlns:exsl="http://exslt.org/common" extension-element-prefixes="exsl">

  <xsl:include href="cells-to-comma-delimited.xslt"/>

  <xsl:template match="ExpenseReport">
    <c:cell col="M" row="3" value="Statement No."/>
    <c:cell col="N" row="3" value="{@statementNum}"/>
    <c:cell col="L" row="6" value="Expense Statement"/>
    <xsl:apply-templates/>
    <xsl:variable name="offset" select="count(Expenses/Expense)+18"/>
    <c:cell col="M" row="{$offset}" value="Sub Total"/>
    <c:cell col="D" row="{$offset + 1}" value="Approved"/>
    <c:cell col="F" row="{$offset + 1}" value="Notes"/>
    <c:cell col="M" row="{$offset + 1}" value="Advances"/>
    <c:cell col="M" row="{$offset + 2}" value="Total"/>
  </xsl:template>

  <xsl:template match="Employee">
    <c:cell col="D" row="10" value="Employee"/>
    <xsl:apply-templates/>
  </xsl:template>

  <xsl:template match="Employee/Name">
    <c:cell col="D" row="12" value="Name"/>
    <c:cell col="E" row="12" value="{.}"/>
  </xsl:template>
```

```
<!-- ... -->
<!-- Remainder elided, same as original stylesheet above -->
<!-- ... -->

</xsl:stylesheet>
```

The reusable *cells-to-comma-delimited.xslt* captures the cells produced by the application-specific stylesheet into a variable and sorts. It then transforms those cells into comma-delimited output. This is done by considering each cell relative to its predecessor in sorted order. If the predecessor is on a different row, then one or more newlines must be output. On the other hand, if the predecessor is on a nonadjacent column, then one or more extra commas must be output. You must also handle the case when the first row or column within a row is not the first row or column in the spreadsheet. Once these details are handled, you only need to output the value of the cell followed by a comma.

Discussion

Most XML-to-delimited transformations you are likely to encounter are fairly simple for someone well-versed in XSLT. The value of the previous examples is that they demonstrate that problems can be separated into two parts: a reusable part that requires XSLT expertise and an application-specific part that does not require much XSLT knowledge once its conventions are understood.

The true value of this technique is that it allows individuals who are less skilled in XSLT to do useful work. For example, suppose you had to convert a large base of XML to comma-delimited data and it needed to be done yesterday. Showing someone how to reuse these generic solutions would be much easier than teaching them enough XSLT to come up with custom scripts.

5.3   Creating a Columnar Report

Problem

You want to format data into columns for presentation.

Solution

There are two general kinds of XML-to-columnar mappings. The first maps different elements or attributes into separate columns. The second maps elements based on their relative position.

Before tackling these variations, you need a generic template that will help justify output text into a fixed-width column. You can build such a routine, shown in Example 5-17, on top of the str:dup template you created in Recipe 1.5.

Example 5-17. Generic text-justification template—text.justify.xslt

```
<xsl:stylesheet version="1.0" xmlns:xsl="http://www.w3.org/1999/XSL/Transform"
  xmlns:str="http://www.ora.com/XSLTCookbook/namespaces/strings"
  xmlns:text="http://www.ora.com/XSLTCookbook/namespaces/text"
  extension-element-prefixes="text">

<xsl:include href="../strings/str.dup.xslt"/>

<xsl:template name="text:justify">
  <xsl:param name="value" />
  <xsl:param name="width" select="10"/>
  <xsl:param name="align" select=" 'left' "/>

  <!-- Truncate if too long -->
  <xsl:variable name="output" select="substring($value,1,$width)"/>

  <xsl:choose>
    <xsl:when test="$align = 'left'">
      <xsl:value-of select="$output"/>
      <xsl:call-template name="str:dup">
        <xsl:with-param name="input" select=" ' ' "/>
        <xsl:with-param name="count"
          select="$width - string-length($output)"/>
      </xsl:call-template>
    </xsl:when>
    <xsl:when test="$align = 'right'">
      <xsl:call-template name="str:dup">
        <xsl:with-param name="input" select=" ' ' "/>
        <xsl:with-param name="count"
                select="$width - string-length($output)"/>
      </xsl:call-template>
      <xsl:value-of select="$output"/>
    </xsl:when>
    <xsl:when test="$align = 'center'">
      <xsl:call-template name="str:dup">
        <xsl:with-param name="input" select=" ' ' "/>
        <xsl:with-param name="count"
          select="floor(($width - string-length($output)) div 2)"/>
      </xsl:call-template>
      <xsl:value-of select="$output"/>
      <xsl:call-template name="str:dup">
        <xsl:with-param name="input" select=" ' ' "/>
        <xsl:with-param name="count"
          select="ceiling(($width - string-length($output)) div 2)"/>
      </xsl:call-template>
    </xsl:when>
    <xsl:otherwise>INVALID ALIGN</xsl:otherwise>
  </xsl:choose>
</xsl:template>

</xsl:stylesheet>
```

Given this template, producing a columnar report is simply a matter of deciding the order and column layouts for the data. Examples 5-18 and 5-19 do this for the person attributes in *people.xml*. A similar solution could be used for element encoding used in *people-elem.xml*.

Example 5-18. people-to-columns.xslt

```
<xsl:stylesheet version="1.0" xmlns:xsl="http://www.w3.org/1999/XSL/Transform"
  xmlns:str="http://www.ora.com/XSLTCookbook/namespaces/strings"
  xmlns:text="http://www.ora.com/XSLTCookbook/namespaces/text">

<xsl:include href="text.justify.xslt"/>

<xsl:output method="text" />

<xsl:strip-space elements="*"/>

<xsl:template match="people">
Name                 Age    Sex   Smoker
--------------------|------|-----|---------
<xsl:apply-templates/>
</xsl:template>

<xsl:template match="person">

  <xsl:call-template name="text:justify">
    <xsl:with-param name="value" select="@name"/>
    <xsl:with-param name="width" select="20"/>
  </xsl:call-template>
 <xsl:text>|</xsl:text>
  <xsl:call-template name="text:justify">
    <xsl:with-param name="value" select="@age"/>
    <xsl:with-param name="width" select="6"/>
    <xsl:with-param name="align" select=" 'right' "/>
  </xsl:call-template>
 <xsl:text>|</xsl:text>
  <xsl:call-template name="text:justify">
    <xsl:with-param name="value" select="@sex"/>
    <xsl:with-param name="width" select="6"/>
    <xsl:with-param name="align" select=" 'center' "/>
  </xsl:call-template>
 <xsl:text>|</xsl:text>
  <xsl:call-template name="text:justify">
    <xsl:with-param name="value" select="@smoker"/>
    <xsl:with-param name="width" select="9"/>
    <xsl:with-param name="align" select=" 'center' "/>
  </xsl:call-template>
  <xsl:text>
</xsl:text>
</xsl:template>

</xsl:stylesheet>
```

Example 5-19. Output

```
Name                   Age   Sex   Smoker
--------------------|------|-----|---------
Al Zehtooney        |  33|  m  |   no
Brad York           |  38|  m  |   yes
Charles Xavier      |  32|  m  |   no
David Willimas      |  33|  m  |   no
Edward Ulster       |  33|  m  |   yes
Frank Townsend      |  35|  m  |   no
Greg Sutter         |  40|  m  |   no
Harry Rogers        |  37|  m  |   no
John Quincy         |  43|  m  |   yes
Kent Peterson       |  31|  m  |   no
Larry Newell        |  23|  m  |   no
Max Milton          |  22|  m  |   no
Norman Lamagna      |  30|  m  |   no
Ollie Kensinton     |  44|  m  |   no
John Frank          |  24|  m  |   no
Mary Williams       |  33|  f  |   no
Jane Frank          |  38|  f  |   yes
Jo Peterson         |  32|  f  |   no
Angie Frost         |  33|  f  |   no
Betty Bates         |  33|  f  |   no
Connie Date         |  35|  f  |   no
Donna Finster       |  20|  f  |   no
Esther Gates        |  37|  f  |   no
Fanny Hill          |  33|  f  |   yes
Geta Iota           |  27|  f  |   no
Hillary Johnson     |  22|  f  |   no
Ingrid Kent         |  21|  f  |   no
Jill Larson         |  20|  f  |   no
Kim Mulrooney       |  41|  f  |   no
Lisa Nevins         |  21|  f  |   no
```

To transform data based on its position in the document, you must take a slightly different approach. First, decide how many columns you will have. You can use a parameter that specifies the number of columns and allow the number of rows to follow based on the number of elements, or you can specify the number of rows and let the columns vary. Second, decide how the position of the element will map onto the columns. The two most common mappings are row major and column major. In row major, the first element maps to the first column, the second element maps to the second column, and so on until you run out of columns—in which case, you begin a new row. In column major, the first (N div num-columns) elements go into the first column, then the next (N div num-columns) elements go into the second column, and so on. You can think of this concept more simply in terms of a transposition of rows to columns.

You can create two templates that output columns in each order, as shown in Example 5-20.

Example 5-20. text.matrix.xslt

```
<xsl:stylesheet version="1.0" xmlns:xsl="http://www.w3.org/1999/XSL/Transform"
  xmlns:text="http://www.ora.com/XSLTCookbook/namespaces/text"
  extension-element-prefixes="text">

  <xsl:output method="text"/>

  <xsl:include href="text.justify.xslt"/>

  <xsl:template name="text:row-major">
    <xsl:param name="nodes" select="/.."/>
    <xsl:param name="num-cols" select="2"/>
    <xsl:param name="width" select="10"/>
    <xsl:param name="align" select=" 'left' "/>
    <xsl:param name="gutter" select=" ' ' "/>

    <xsl:if test="$nodes">
        <xsl:call-template name="text:row">
          <xsl:with-param name="nodes"
              select="$nodes[position( ) &lt;= $num-cols]"/>
          <xsl:with-param name="width" select="$width"/>
          <xsl:with-param name="align" select="$align"/>
          <xsl:with-param name="gutter" select="$gutter"/>
        </xsl:call-template>
        <!-- process remaining rows -->
        <xsl:call-template name="text:row-major">
          <xsl:with-param name="nodes"
              select="$nodes[position( ) > $num-cols]"/>
          <xsl:with-param name="num-cols" select="$num-cols"/>
          <xsl:with-param name="width" select="$width"/>
          <xsl:with-param name="align" select="$align"/>
          <xsl:with-param name="gutter" select="$gutter"/>
        </xsl:call-template>
    </xsl:if>
  </xsl:template>

  <xsl:template name="text:col-major">
    <xsl:param name="nodes" select="/.."/>
    <xsl:param name="num-cols" select="2"/>
    <xsl:param name="width" select="10"/>
    <xsl:param name="align" select=" 'left' "/>
    <xsl:param name="gutter" select=" ' ' "/>

    <xsl:if test="$nodes">
        <xsl:call-template name="text:row">
          <xsl:with-param name="nodes"
              select="$nodes[(position( ) - 1) mod
                        ceiling(last( ) div $num-cols) = 0]"/>
          <xsl:with-param name="width" select="$width"/>
          <xsl:with-param name="align" select="$align"/>
          <xsl:with-param name="gutter" select="$gutter"/>
        </xsl:call-template>
```

Example 5-20. text.matrix.xslt (continued)

```
    <!-- process remaining rows -->
    <xsl:call-template name="text:col-major">
      <xsl:with-param name="nodes"
            select="$nodes[(position() - 1) mod
                        ceiling(last() div $num-cols) != 0]"/>
      <xsl:with-param name="num-cols" select="$num-cols"/>
      <xsl:with-param name="width" select="$width"/>
      <xsl:with-param name="align" select="$align"/>
      <xsl:with-param name="gutter" select="$gutter"/>
    </xsl:call-template>
  </xsl:if>

</xsl:template>

<xsl:template name="text:row">
  <xsl:param name="nodes" select="/.."/>
  <xsl:param name="width" select="10"/>
  <xsl:param name="align" select=" 'left' "/>
  <xsl:param name="gutter" select=" ' ' "/>


  <xsl:for-each select="$nodes">
    <xsl:call-template name="text:justify">
      <xsl:with-param name="value" select="."/>
      <xsl:with-param name="width" select="$width"/>
      <xsl:with-param name="align" select="$align"/>
    </xsl:call-template>
    <xsl:value-of select="$gutter"/>
  </xsl:for-each>

  <xsl:text>&#xa;</xsl:text>

</xsl:template>

</xsl:stylesheet>
```

We can use these templates as shown in Examples 5-21 to 5-23.

Example 5-21. Input

```
<numbers>
  <number>10</number>
  <number>3.5</number>
  <number>4.44</number>
  <number>77.7777</number>
  <number>-8</number>
  <number>1</number>
  <number>444</number>
  <number>1.1234</number>
  <number>7.77</number>
  <number>3.1415927</number>
  <number>10</number>
```

Example 5-21. Input (continued)

```
  <number>9</number>
  <number>8</number>
  <number>7</number>
  <number>666</number>
  <number>5555</number>
  <number>-4444444</number>
  <number>22.33</number>
  <number>18</number>
  <number>36.54</number>
  <number>43</number>
  <number>99999</number>
  <number>999999</number>
  <number>9999999</number>
  <number>32</number>
  <number>64</number>
  <number>-64.0001</number>
</numbers>
```

Example 5-22. Stylesheet

```
<xsl:stylesheet version="1.0" xmlns:xsl="http://www.w3.org/1999/XSL/Transform"
  xmlns:text="http://www.ora.com/XSLTCookbook/namespaces/text">

<xsl:output method="text" />

<xsl:include href="text.matrix.xslt"/>

<xsl:template match="numbers">
Five columns of numbers in row major order:
<xsl:text/>
  <xsl:call-template name="text:row-major">
    <xsl:with-param name="nodes" select="number"/>
    <xsl:with-param name="align" select=" 'right' "/>
    <xsl:with-param name="num-cols" select="5"/>
    <xsl:with-param name="gutter" select=" ' | ' "/>
  </xsl:call-template>

Five columns of numbers in column major order:
<xsl:text/>
  <xsl:call-template name="text:col-major">
    <xsl:with-param name="nodes" select="number"/>
    <xsl:with-param name="align" select=" 'right' "/>
    <xsl:with-param name="num-cols" select="5"/>
    <xsl:with-param name="gutter" select=" ' | ' "/>
  </xsl:call-template>

</xsl:template>

</xsl:stylesheet>
```

Example 5-23. Output

```
Five columns of numbers in row major order:
        10 |       3.5 |      4.44 |   77.7777 |        -8 |
         1 |       444 |    1.1234 |      7.77 | 3.1415927 |
        10 |         9 |         8 |         7 |       666 |
      5555 |  -4444444 |     22.33 |        18 |     36.54 |
        43 |     99999 |    999999 |   9999999 |        32 |
        64 |  -64.0001 |

Five columns of numbers in column major order:
        10 |       444 |         8 |        18 |        32 |
       3.5 |    1.1234 |         7 |     36.54 |        64 |
      4.44 |      7.77 |       666 |        43 |  -64.0001 |
   77.7777 | 3.1415927 |      5555 |     99999 |
        -8 |        10 |  -4444444 |    999999 |
         1 |         9 |     22.33 |   9999999 |
```

Discussion

The problem of transforming element- or attribute-encoded data into columns is structurally similar to the delimited problem discussed in Recipe 5.2. The main difference is that in the delimited case, you prepare data for machine processing and in the present case, you prepare the data for human processing. In some ways, humans are more finicky then machines, especially when it comes to alignment and other visual aids that facilitate easy comprehension. You could apply the same data-driven generic approach used in the delimited example but you would have to provide more information about each column to ensure proper formatting. Examples 5-24 to 5-26 show the attribute-based solution.

Example 5-24. generic-attr-to-columns.xslt

```xml
<xsl:stylesheet version="1.0" xmlns:xsl="http://www.w3.org/1999/XSL/Transform"
  xmlns:str="http://www.ora.com/XSLTCookbook/namespaces/strings"
  xmlns:text="http://www.ora.com/XSLTCookbook/namespaces/text">

<xsl:include href="text.justify.xslt"/>

<xsl:param name="gutter" select=" ' ' "/>

<xsl:output method="text"/>

<xsl:strip-space elements="*"/>

<xsl:variable name="columns" select="/.."/>

<xsl:template match="/">
  <xsl:for-each select="$columns">
    <xsl:call-template name="text:justify" >
      <xsl:with-param name="value" select="@name"/>
      <xsl:with-param name="width" select="@width"/>
      <xsl:with-param name="align" select=" 'left' "/>
```

Example 5-24. generic-attr-to-columns.xslt (continued)

```
      </xsl:call-template>
      <xsl:value-of select="$gutter"/>
    </xsl:for-each>
    <xsl:text>&#xa;</xsl:text>
    <xsl:for-each select="$columns">
      <xsl:call-template name="str:dup">
        <xsl:with-param name="input" select=" '-' "/>
        <xsl:with-param name="count" select="@width"/>
      </xsl:call-template>
      <xsl:call-template name="str:dup">
        <xsl:with-param name="input" select=" '-' "/>
        <xsl:with-param name="count" select="string-length($gutter)"/>
      </xsl:call-template>
    </xsl:for-each>
    <xsl:text>&#xa;</xsl:text>
    <xsl:apply-templates/>
</xsl:template>

<xsl:template match="/*/*">
  <xsl:variable name="row" select="."/>

  <xsl:for-each select="$columns">
    <xsl:variable name="value">
      <xsl:apply-templates
      select="$row/@*[local-name(.)=current( )/@attr]" mode="text:map-col-value"/>
    </xsl:variable>
    <xsl:call-template name="text:justify" >
      <xsl:with-param name="value" select="$value"/>
      <xsl:with-param name="width" select="@width"/>
      <xsl:with-param name="align" select="@align"/>
    </xsl:call-template>
    <xsl:value-of select="$gutter"/>
  </xsl:for-each>

  <xsl:text>&#xa;</xsl:text>

</xsl:template>

<xsl:template match="@*" mode="text:map-col-value">
  <xsl:value-of select="."/>
</xsl:template>
```

Example 5-25. people-to-cols-using-generic.xslt

```
<xsl:stylesheet version="1.0" xmlns:xsl="http://www.w3.org/1999/XSL/Transform"
  xmlns:str="http://www.ora.com/XSLTCookbook/namespaces/strings"
  xmlns:text="http://www.ora.com/XSLTCookbook/namespaces/text">

<xsl:import href="generic-attr-to-columns.xslt"/>

<!--Defines the mapping from attributes to columns -->
<xsl:variable name="columns" select="document('')/*/text:column"/>
```

Example 5-25. people-to-cols-using-generic.xslt (continued)

```
<text:column name="Name" width="20" align="left" attr="name"/>
<text:column name="Age" width="6" align="right" attr="age"/>
<text:column name="Gender" width="6" align="left" attr="sex"/>
<text:column name="Smoker" width="6" align="left" attr="smoker"/>

<!-- Handle custom attribute mappings -->

<xsl:template match="@sex" mode="text:map-col-value">
  <xsl:choose>
    <xsl:when test=".='m'">male</xsl:when>
    <xsl:when test=".='f'">female</xsl:when>
    <xsl:otherwise>error</xsl:otherwise>
  </xsl:choose>
</xsl:template>

</xsl:stylesheet>
```

Example 5-26. Output (with gutter param = " | ")

```
Name                 | Age   | Gender | Smoker |
-----------------------------------------------
Al Zehtooney         |    33 | male   | no     |
Brad York            |    38 | male   | yes    |
Charles Xavier       |    32 | male   | no     |
David Willimas       |    33 | male   | no     |
Edward Ulster        |    33 | male   | yes    |
Frank Townsend       |    35 | male   | no     |
Greg Sutter          |    40 | male   | no     |
Harry Rogers         |    37 | male   | no     |
John Quincy          |    43 | male   | yes    |
Kent Peterson        |    31 | male   | no     |
Larry Newell         |    23 | male   | no     |
Max Milton           |    22 | male   | no     |
Norman Lamagna       |    30 | male   | no     |
Ollie Kensinton      |    44 | male   | no     |
John Frank           |    24 | male   | no     |
Mary Williams        |    33 | female | no     |
Jane Frank           |    38 | female | yes    |
Jo Peterson          |    32 | female | no     |
Angie Frost          |    33 | female | no     |
Betty Bates          |    33 | female | no     |
Connie Date          |    35 | female | no     |
Donna Finster        |    20 | female | no     |
Esther Gates         |    37 | female | no     |
Fanny Hill           |    33 | female | yes    |
Geta Iota            |    27 | female | no     |
Hillary Johnson      |    22 | female | no     |
Ingrid Kent          |    21 | female | no     |
Jill Larson          |    20 | female | no     |
Kim Mulrooney        |    41 | female | no     |
Lisa Nevins          |    21 | female | no     |
```

5.4 Displaying a Hierarchy

Problem

You want to create text output that is indented or annotated to reflect the hierarchal nature of the original XML.

Solution

The most obvious hierarchical representation uses indentation to mimic the hierarchical structure of the source XML. You can create a generic stylesheet, shown in Examples 5-27 and 5-28, which makes reasonable choices for mapping the information in the input document to a hierarchical output.

Example 5-27. text.hierarchy.xslt

```
<xsl:stylesheet version="1.0" xmlns:xsl="http://www.w3.org/1999/XSL/Transform"
  xmlns:str="http://www.ora.com/XSLTCookbook/namespaces/strings">

<xsl:include href="../strings/str.dup.xslt"/>
<xsl:include href="../strings/str.replace.xslt"/>

<xsl:output method="text"/>

<!--Levels indented with two spaces by default -->
<xsl:param name="indent" select=" '  ' "/>

<xsl:template match="*">
  <xsl:param  name="level" select="count(./ancestor::*)"/>

  <!-- Indent this element -->
  <xsl:call-template name="str:dup" >
    <xsl:with-param name="input" select="$indent"/>
    <xsl:with-param name="count" select="$level"/>
  </xsl:call-template>

  <!--Process the element name. Default will output local-name -->
  <xsl:apply-templates select="." mode="name">
    <xsl:with-param name="level" select="$level"/>
  </xsl:apply-templates>

  <!--Signal the start of processing of attributes.
      Default will output '(' -->
  <xsl:apply-templates select="." mode="begin-attributes">
    <xsl:with-param name="level" select="$level"/>
  </xsl:apply-templates>

  <!--Process attributes.
      Default will output name="value". -->
  <xsl:apply-templates select="@*">
    <xsl:with-param name="element" select="."/>
```

Example 5-27. text.hierarchy.xslt (continued)

```
      <xsl:with-param name="level" select="$level"/>
  </xsl:apply-templates>

  <!--Signal the end of processing of attributes.
      Default will output ')' -->
  <xsl:apply-templates select="." mode="end-attributes">
    <xsl:with-param name="level" select="$level"/>
  </xsl:apply-templates>

  <!-- Process the elements value. -->
  <!-- Default will format the value of a leaf element -->
  <!-- so it is indented at next line -->
  <xsl:apply-templates select="." mode="value">
    <xsl:with-param name="level" select="$level"/>
  </xsl:apply-templates>

  <xsl:apply-templates select="." mode="line-break">
    <xsl:with-param name="level" select="$level"/>
  </xsl:apply-templates>

  <!-- Process children -->
  <xsl:apply-templates select="*">
    <xsl:with-param name="level" select="$level + 1"/>
  </xsl:apply-templates>

</xsl:template>

<!--Default handling of element names. -->
<xsl:template match="*"     mode="name">[<xsl:value-of
                                  select="local-name(.)"/></xsl:template>

<!--Default handling of start of attributes. -->
<xsl:template match="*" mode="begin-attributes">
  <xsl:if test="@*"><xsl:text> </xsl:text></xsl:if>
</xsl:template>

<!--Default handling of attributes. -->
<xsl:template match="@*">
  <xsl:value-of select="local-name(.)"/>="<xsl:value-of select="."/>"<xsl:text/>
  <xsl:if test="position() != last()">
    <xsl:text> </xsl:text>
  </xsl:if>
</xsl:template>

<!--Default handling of end of attributes. -->
<xsl:template match="*" mode="end-attributes">]</xsl:template>

<!--Default handling of element values. -->
<xsl:template match="*" mode="value">
  <xsl:param name="level"/>

  <!-- Only output value for leaves -->
```

Example 5-27. text.hierarchy.xslt (continued)

```
  <xsl:if test="not(*)">
    <xsl:variable name="indent-str">
      <xsl:call-template name="str:dup" >
        <xsl:with-param name="input" select="$indent"/>
        <xsl:with-param name="count" select="$level"/>
      </xsl:call-template>
    </xsl:variable>

    <xsl:text>&#xa;</xsl:text>

    <xsl:value-of select="$indent-str"/>

    <xsl:call-template name="str:replace">
      <xsl:with-param name="input" select="."/>
      <xsl:with-param name="search-string" select=" '&#xa;' "/>
      <xsl:with-param name="replace-string"
                      select="concat('&#xa;',$indent-str)"/>
    </xsl:call-template>
  </xsl:if>
</xsl:template>

<xsl:template match="*" mode="line-break">
  <xsl:text>&#xa;</xsl:text>
</xsl:template>

</xsl:stylesheet>
```

Example 5-28. Output when used to process ExpenseReport.xml

```
[ExpenseReport statementNum="123"]
  [Employee]
    [Name]
    Salvatore Mangano
    [SSN]
    999-99-9999
    [Dept]
    XSLT Hacking
    [EmpNo]
    1
    [Position]
    Cook
    [Manager]
    Big Boss O'Reilly
  [PayPeriod]
    [From]
    1/1/02
    [To]
    1/31/02
  [Expenses]
    [Expense]
      [Date]
      12/20/01
```

Example 5-28. Output when used to process ExpenseReport.xml (continued)

```
  [Account]
  12345
  [Desc]
  Goofing off instead of going to confrence.
  [Lodging]
  500.00
  [Transport]
  50.00
  [Fuel]
  0
  [Meals]
  300.00
  [Phone]
  100
  [Entertainment]
  1000.00
  [Other]
  300.00
[Expense]
  [Date]
  12/20/01
  [Account]
  12345
  [Desc]
  On the beach
  [Lodging]
  500.00
  [Transport]
  50.00
  [Fuel]
  0
  [Meals]
  200.00
  [Phone]
  20
  [Entertainment]
  300.00
  [Other]
  100.00
```

Discussion

You might object to the particular choices made by this stylesheet for mapping the information items in the source document to a hierarchical layout. That objection is OK because the stylesheet was designed to be customized. For example, you might prefer the results obtained with the customizations shown in Examples 5-29 and 5-30.

Example 5-29. Customized Expense Report stylesheet

```
<xsl:stylesheet version="1.0" xmlns:xsl="http://www.w3.org/1999/XSL/Transform">

<xsl:import href="text.hierarchy.xslt"/>

<!--Ignore attributes -->
<xsl:template match="@*"/>
<xsl:template match="*" mode="begin-attributes"/>
<xsl:template match="*" mode="end-attributes"/>

<xsl:template match="*"     mode="name">
  <!--Display element loacl name-->
  <xsl:value-of select="local-name(.)"/>
  <!--Follow by a colon+space if a leaf -->
  <xsl:if test="not(*)">: </xsl:if>
</xsl:template>

<xsl:template match="*" mode="value">
  <xsl:if test="not(*)">
    <xsl:value-of select="."/>
  </xsl:if>
</xsl:template>

</xsl:stylesheet>
```

Example 5-30. Output with overridden formatting

```
ExpenseReport
  Employee
    Name: Salvatore Mangano
    SSN: 999-99-9999
    Dept: XSLT Hacking
    EmpNo: 1
    Position: Cook
    Manager: Big Boss O'Reilly
  PayPeriod
    From: 1/1/02
    To: 1/31/02
  Expenses
    Expense
      Date: 12/20/01
      Account: 12345
      Desc: Goofing off instead of going to confrence.
      Lodging: 500.00
      Transport: 50.00
      Fuel: 0
      Meals: 300.00
      Phone: 100
      Entertainment: 1000.00
      Other: 300.00
    Expense
      Date: 12/20/01
```

Example 5-30. Output with overridden formatting (continued)

```
Account: 12345
Desc: On the beach
Lodging: 500.00
Transport: 50.00
Fuel: 0
Meals: 200.00
Phone: 20
Entertainment: 300.00
Other: 100.00
```

Or perhaps you like the format in Examples 5-31 and 5-32, inspired by Jeni Tennison.

Example 5-31. tree-control.xslt

```
<xsl:stylesheet version="1.0" xmlns:xsl="http://www.w3.org/1999/XSL/Transform">

<xsl:import href="text.hierarchy.xslt"/>

<!--Ignore attributes -->
<xsl:template match="@*"/>
<xsl:template match="*" mode="begin-attributes"/>
<xsl:template match="*" mode="end-attributes"/>

<xsl:template match="*"      mode="name">
  <!--Display element loacl name-->
  <xsl:text>[</xsl:text>
  <xsl:value-of select="local-name(.)"/>
  <!--Follow by a colon+space if a leaf -->
  <xsl:text>] </xsl:text>
</xsl:template>

<xsl:template match="*" mode="value">
  <xsl:if test="not(*)">
    <xsl:value-of select="."/>
  </xsl:if>
</xsl:template>

<xsl:template match="*" mode="indent">
  <xsl:for-each select="ancestor::*">
    <xsl:choose>
      <xsl:when test="following-sibling::*"> | </xsl:when>
      <xsl:otherwise><xsl:text>    </xsl:text></xsl:otherwise>
    </xsl:choose>
  </xsl:for-each>
  <xsl:choose>
    <xsl:when test="*"> o-</xsl:when>
    <xsl:when test="following-sibling::*"> +-</xsl:when>
    <xsl:otherwise> `-</xsl:otherwise>
  </xsl:choose>
</xsl:template>
```

Example 5-31. tree-control.xslt (continued)

```
<xsl:template match="*" mode="line-break">
  <xsl:text>&#xa;</xsl:text>
</xsl:template>

</xsl:stylesheet>
```

Example 5-32. Output with tree-control-like formatting

```
o-[ExpenseReport]
    o-[Employee]
    | +-[Name] Salvatore Mangano
    | +-[SSN] 999-99-9999
    | +-[Dept] XSLT Hacking
    | +-[EmpNo] 1
    | +-[Position] Cook
    | `-[Manager] Big Boss O'Reilly
    o-[PayPeriod]
    | +-[From] 1/1/02
    | `-[To] 1/31/02
    o-[Expenses]
        o-[Expense]
        | +-[Date] 12/20/01
        | +-[Account] 12345
        | +-[Desc] Goofing off instead of going to confrence.
        | +-[Lodging] 500.00
        | +-[Transport] 50.00
        | +-[Fuel] 0
        | +-[Meals] 300.00
        | +-[Phone] 100
        | +-[Entertainment] 1000.00
        | `-[Other] 300.00
        o-[Expense]
            +-[Date] 12/20/01
            +-[Account] 12345
            +-[Desc] On the beach
            +-[Lodging] 500.00
            +-[Transport] 50.00
            +-[Fuel] 0
            +-[Meals] 200.00
            +-[Phone] 20
            +-[Entertainment] 300.00
            `-[Other] 100.00
```

You can take this concept even further by creating a stylesheet that imports *tree-control.xslt* and takes a global parameter containing a list of element names that should be collapsed. Collapsed levels are indicated by an x prefix. See Examples 5-33 and 5-34.

Example 5-33. Stylesheet creating collapsed levels

```
<xsl:stylesheet version="1.0" xmlns:xsl="http://www.w3.org/1999/XSL/Transform">

<xsl:import href="tree-control.xslt"/>

<xsl:param name="collapse"/>
<xsl:variable name="collapse-test" select="concat(' ',$collapse,' ')"/>

<xsl:template match="*"     mode="name">
    <xsl:if test="not(ancestor::*[contains($collapse-test,
                              concat(' ',local-name(.),' '))])">
      <xsl:apply-imports/>
    </xsl:if>
</xsl:template>

<xsl:template match="*" mode="value">
    <xsl:if test="not(ancestor::*[contains($collapse-test,
                              concat(' ',local-name(.),' '))])">
      <xsl:apply-imports/>
    </xsl:if>
</xsl:template>

<xsl:template match="*" mode="line-break">
    <xsl:if test="not(ancestor::*[contains($collapse-test,
                              concat(' ',local-name(.),' '))])">
      <xsl:apply-imports/>
    </xsl:if>
</xsl:template>

<xsl:template match="*" mode="indent">
  <xsl:choose>
    <xsl:when test="self::*[contains($collapse-test,
                                  concat(' ',local-name(.),' '))]">
      <xsl:for-each select="ancestor::*">
        <xsl:text>   </xsl:text>
      </xsl:for-each>
      <xsl:text> x-</xsl:text>
    </xsl:when>
    <xsl:when test="ancestor::*[contains($collapse-test,
                            concat(' ',local-name(.),' '))]"/>
    <xsl:otherwise>
      <xsl:apply-imports/>
    </xsl:otherwise>
  </xsl:choose>
</xsl:template>

</xsl:stylesheet>
```

Example 5-34. Output with $collapse="Employee PayPeriod"

```
o-[ExpenseReport]
    x-[Employee]
    x-[PayPeriod]
    o-[Expenses]
        o-[Expense]
        |   +-[Date] 12/20/01
        |   +-[Account] 12345
        |   +-[Desc] Goofing off instead of going to confrence.
        |   +-[Lodging] 500.00
        |   +-[Transport] 50.00
        |   +-[Fuel] 0
        |   +-[Meals] 300.00
        |   +-[Phone] 100
        |   +-[Entertainment] 1000.00
        |   `-[Other] 300.00
        o-[Expense]
            +-[Date] 12/20/01
            +-[Account] 12345
            +-[Desc] On the beach
            +-[Lodging] 500.00
            +-[Transport] 50.00
            +-[Fuel] 0
            +-[Meals] 200.00
            +-[Phone] 20
            +-[Entertainment] 300.00
            `-[Other] 100.00
```

There is literally no end to the variety of custom tree formats you can create from overrides to the basic stylesheet. In object-oriented circles, this technique is called the *template-method pattern*. It involves building the skeleton of an algorithm and allowing subclasses to redefine certain steps without changing the algorithm's structure. In the case of XSLT, importing stylesheets take the place of subclasses. The power of this example does not stem from the fact that creating tree-like rendering is difficult; it is not. Instead, the power lies in the ability to reuse the example's structure while considering only the aspects you want to change.

5.5 Numbering Textual Output

Problem

You want to create sequentially numbered output.

Solution

Since output can be numbered in many ways, this example presents a series of increasingly complex examples that address the most common (and a few uncommon) numbering needs.

Number siblings sequentially

This category is the simplest form of numbering. For example, you can produce a numbered list of people using the stylesheet in Examples 5-35 and 5-36.

Example 5-35. Stylesheet

```
<xsl:stylesheet version="1.0" xmlns:xsl="http://www.w3.org/1999/XSL/Transform">
  <xsl:output method="text"/>

  <xsl:template match="person">
    <xsl:number count="*" format="1. "/>
    <xsl:value-of select="@name"/>
  </xsl:template>

</xsl:stylesheet>
```

Example 5-36. Output

```
1. Al Zehtooney
2. Brad York
3. Charles Xavier
4. David Willimas
5. Edward Ulster
6. Frank Townsend
7. Greg Sutter
8. Harry Rogers
9. John Quincy
10. Kent Peterson
...
```

You can use the justify template discussed in Recipe 5.3 if you want right-justified numbers.

Start from a number other than one

xsl:number does not provide a standard facility for starting from or incrementing by a number other than one, but you can handle this task with a little math. Examples 5-37 and 5-38 start from ten and increment by five, just to be different.

Example 5-37. Stylesheet using nonsequential numbering

```
<xsl:stylesheet version="1.0" xmlns:xsl="http://www.w3.org/1999/XSL/Transform">
  <xsl:output method="text"/>
  <xsl:strip-space elements="*"/>

  <xsl:template match="person">
    <xsl:variable name="num">
      <xsl:number count="*"/>
    </xsl:variable>
    <xsl:number value="($num - 1) * 5 + 10" format="1. "/>
    <xsl:value-of select="@name"/>
    <xsl:text>&#xa;</xsl:text>
```

Example 5-37. Stylesheet using nonsequential numbering (continued)

```
  </xsl:template>

</xsl:stylesheet>
```

Example 5-38. Output

```
10. Al Zehtooney
15. Brad York
20. Charles Xavier
25. David Willimas
30. Edward Ulster
35. Frank Townsend
40. Greg Sutter
45. Harry Rogers
50. John Quincy
55. Kent Peterson
...
```

This scenario works even if you want the final output to use a non-numerical format. For example, Examples 5-39 and 5-40 use the same technique to start numbering at L.

Example 5-39. Stylesheet for numbering from L

```
<xsl:stylesheet version="1.0" xmlns:xsl="http://www.w3.org/1999/XSL/Transform">
  <xsl:output method="text"/>
  <xsl:strip-space elements="*"/>

  <xsl:template match="person">
    <xsl:variable name="num">
      <xsl:number count="*"/>
    </xsl:variable>
    <xsl:number value="$num + 11" format="A. "/>
    <xsl:value-of select="@name"/>
    <xsl:text>&#xa;</xsl:text>
  </xsl:template>

</xsl:stylesheet>
```

Example 5-40. People numbered successively from letter L

```
L. Al Zehtooney
M. Brad York
N. Charles Xavier
O. David Willimas
P. Edward Ulster
Q. Frank Townsend
R. Greg Sutter
S. Harry Rogers
T. John Quincy
U. Kent Peterson
...
```

Number elements globally

Sometimes you want to number elements sequentially without regard to their context. The most common example involves a document that contains footnote elements. The footnotes can appear at any level in the document's structure, yet they should be numbered sequentially. However, to continue the theme of your example, here is a document that divides people into various groups and subgroups:

```
<people>
  <group>
    <person name="Al Zehtooney" age="33" sex="m" smoker="no"/>
    <person name="Brad York" age="38" sex="m" smoker="yes"/>
    <person name="Charles Xavier" age="32" sex="m" smoker="no"/>
    <person name="David Willimas" age="33" sex="m" smoker="no"/>
    <person name="Edward Ulster" age="33" sex="m" smoker="yes"/>
    <person name="Frank Townsend" age="35" sex="m" smoker="no"/>
  </group>
  <group>
    <person name="Greg Sutter" age="40" sex="m" smoker="no"/>
    <person name="Harry Rogers" age="37" sex="m" smoker="no"/>
    <group>
      <person name="John Quincy" age="43" sex="m" smoker="yes"/>
      <person name="Kent Peterson" age="31" sex="m" smoker="no"/>
      <person name="Larry Newell" age="23" sex="m" smoker="no"/>
      <group>
        <person name="Max Milton" age="22" sex="m" smoker="no"/>
        <person name="Norman Lamagna" age="30" sex="m" smoker="no"/>
        <person name="Ollie Kensinton" age="44" sex="m" smoker="no"/>
      </group>
      <person name="John Frank" age="24" sex="m" smoker="no"/>
    </group>
  </group>
  <group>
    <person name="Mary Williams" age="33" sex="f" smoker="no"/>
    <person name="Jane Frank" age="38" sex="f" smoker="yes"/>
    <person name="Jo Peterson" age="32" sex="f" smoker="no"/>
    <person name="Angie Frost" age="33" sex="f" smoker="no"/>
    <person name="Betty Bates" age="33" sex="f" smoker="no"/>
    <person name="Connie Date" age="35" sex="f" smoker="no"/>
    <person name="Donna Finster" age="20" sex="f" smoker="no"/>
  </group>
  <group>
    <person name="Esther Gates" age="37" sex="f" smoker="no"/>
    <person name="Fanny Hill" age="33" sex="f" smoker="yes"/>
    <person name="Geta Iota" age="27" sex="f" smoker="no"/>
    <person name="Hillary Johnson" age="22" sex="f" smoker="no"/>
    <person name="Ingrid Kent" age="21" sex="f" smoker="no"/>
    <person name="Jill Larson" age="20" sex="f" smoker="no"/>
    <person name="Kim Mulrooney" age="41" sex="f" smoker="no"/>
    <person name="Lisa Nevins" age="21" sex="f" smoker="no"/>
  </group>
  </group>
</people>
```

The only necessary change is to use the `xsl:number` attribute `level="any"`. This attribute instructs the XSLT processor to consider all preceding occurrences of the person element when determining numbering. See Examples 5-41 and 5-42.

Example 5-41. Stylesheet for level="any"

```
<xsl:stylesheet version="1.0" xmlns:xsl="http://www.w3.org/1999/XSL/Transform">
  <xsl:output method="text"/>
  <xsl:strip-space elements="*"/>

  <xsl:template match="person">
    <xsl:number count="person" level="any" format="1. "/>
    <xsl:value-of select="@name"/>
    <xsl:text>&#xa;</xsl:text>
  </xsl:template>

</xsl:stylesheet>
```

Example 5-42. Output with level="any"

1. Al Zehtooney
2. Brad York
3. Charles Xavier
4. David Willimas
5. Edward Ulster
6. Frank Townsend
7. Greg Sutter
8. Harry Rogers
9. John Quincy
10. Kent Peterson
11. Larry Newell
12. Max Milton
13. Norman Lamagna
14. Ollie Kensinton
15. John Frank
16. Mary Williams
17. Jane Frank
18. Jo Peterson
19. Angie Frost
20. Betty Bates
21. Connie Date
22. Donna Finster
23. Esther Gates
24. Fanny Hill
25. Geta Iota
26. Hillary Johnson
27. Ingrid Kent
28. Jill Larson
29. Kim Mulrooney
30. Lisa Nevins

Number elements globally within a subcontext

Sometimes you want to restrict global numbering to a specific context. For example, suppose you want to number people within their top-level group and ignore subgroups:

```
<xsl:stylesheet version="1.0" xmlns:xsl="http://www.w3.org/1999/XSL/Transform">
  <xsl:output method="text"/>
  <xsl:strip-space elements="*"/>

  <xsl:template match="people/group">
    <xsl:text>Group </xsl:text>
    <xsl:number count="group"/>
    <xsl:text>&#xa;</xsl:text>
    <xsl:apply-templates/>
    <xsl:text>&#xa;</xsl:text>
  </xsl:template>

  <xsl:template match="person">
    <xsl:number count="person" level="any" from="people/group" format="1. "/>
    <xsl:value-of select="@name"/>
    <xsl:text>&#xa;</xsl:text>
  </xsl:template>

</xsl:stylesheet>

Group 1
1. Al Zehtooney
2. Brad York
3. Charles Xavier
4. David Willimas
5. Edward Ulster
6. Frank Townsend

Group 2
1. Greg Sutter
2. Harry Rogers
3. John Quincy
4. Kent Peterson
5. Larry Newell
6. Max Milton
7. Norman Lamagna
8. Ollie Kensinton
9. John Frank
10. Mary Williams
11. Jane Frank
12. Jo Peterson
13. Angie Frost
14. Betty Bates
15. Connie Date
16. Donna Finster
17. Esther Gates
18. Fanny Hill
19. Geta Iota
```

```
20. Hillary Johnson
21. Ingrid Kent
22. Jill Larson
23. Kim Mulrooney
24. Lisa Nevins
```

Number hierarchically

In formal and legal documents, items are often numbered based on both their sequence and level within a hierarchy. As shown in Examples 5-43 to 5-45, xsl:number supports this via attribute level="multiple".

Example 5-43. Hierarchical numbering based on group and person

```
<xsl:stylesheet version="1.0" xmlns:xsl="http://www.w3.org/1999/XSL/Transform">
  <xsl:output method="text"/>
  <xsl:strip-space elements="*"/>

  <xsl:template match="people/group">
    <xsl:text>Group </xsl:text>
    <xsl:number count="group"/>
    <xsl:text>&#xa;</xsl:text>
    <xsl:apply-templates/>
    <xsl:text>&#xa;</xsl:text>
  </xsl:template>

  <xsl:template match="person">
    <xsl:number count="group | person" level="multiple" format="1.1.1 "/>
    <xsl:value-of select="@name"/>
    <xsl:text>&#xa;</xsl:text>
  </xsl:template>

</xsl:stylesheet>
```

The numbering achieved by the stylesheet in Example 5-45 is somewhat odd, but it effectively illustrates the effect of attribute count when it is used with level = "multiple". The count attribute is simply a specification for determining what ancestor elements should be included when composing a hierarchical number. The stylesheet assigned numbers to people based on group or person elements. Bard York is assigned 1.2 because he is in Group 1 and is the second person in the group. Likewise, Max Milton is assigned 2.3.4.1 because he is in Group 2 when considering only top-level groups; he is in Group 3 when considering *both* top- and second-level groups; he is in Group 4 when considering all top-, second-, and third-level groups; and he is the first person within his own group:

```
Group 1
1.1 Al Zehtooney
1.2 Brad York
1.3 Charles Xavier
1.4 David Willimas
1.5 Edward Ulster
1.6 Frank Townsend
```

```
Group 2
2.1 Greg Sutter
2.2 Harry Rogers
2.3.1 John Quincy
2.3.2 Kent Peterson
2.3.3 Larry Newell
2.3.4.1 Max Milton
2.3.4.2 Norman Lamagna
2.3.4.3 Ollie Kensinton
2.3.5 John Frank
2.4.1 Mary Williams
2.4.2 Jane Frank
2.4.3 Jo Peterson
2.4.4 Angie Frost
2.4.5 Betty Bates
2.4.6 Connie Date
2.4.7 Donna Finster
2.5.1 Esther Gates
2.5.2 Fanny Hill
2.5.3 Geta Iota
2.5.4 Hillary Johnson
2.5.5 Ingrid Kent
2.5.6 Jill Larson
2.5.7 Kim Mulrooney
2.5.8 Lisa Nevins
```

In typical applications, you expect a numbering scheme in which the number at any level is *relative* to the number at the next higher level. You can achieve this relationship by using multiple and adjacent xsl:number elements, as shown in Examples 5-44 and 5-45.

Example 5-44. Stylesheet for creating muliple ordered levels

```
<xsl:stylesheet version="1.0" xmlns:xsl="http://www.w3.org/1999/XSL/Transform">
 <xsl:output method="text"/>
 <xsl:strip-space elements="*"/>

 <xsl:template match="group">
   <xsl:text>Group </xsl:text>
   <xsl:number count="group" level="multiple"/>
   <xsl:text>&#xa;</xsl:text>
   <xsl:apply-templates/>
 </xsl:template>

 <xsl:template match="person">
   <xsl:number count="group" level="multiple" format="1.1.1."/>
   <xsl:number count="person" level="single" format="1 "/>
   <xsl:value-of select="@name"/>
   <xsl:text>&#xa;</xsl:text>
 </xsl:template>

</xsl:stylesheet>
```

Example 5-45. Output

```
Group 1
1.1 Al Zehtooney
1.2 Brad York
1.3 Charles Xavier
1.4 David Willimas
1.5 Edward Ulster
1.6 Frank Townsend
Group 2
2.1 Greg Sutter
2.2 Harry Rogers
Group 2.1
2.1.1 John Quincy
2.1.2 Kent Peterson
2.1.3 Larry Newell
Group 2.1.1
2.1.1.1 Max Milton
2.1.1.2 Norman Lamagna
2.1.1.3 Ollie Kensinton
2.1.4 John Frank
Group 2.2
2.2.1 Mary Williams
2.2.2 Jane Frank
2.2.3 Jo Peterson
2.2.4 Angie Frost
2.2.5 Betty Bates
2.2.6 Connie Date
2.2.7 Donna Finster
Group 2.3
2.3.1 Esther Gates
2.3.2 Fanny Hill
2.3.3 Geta Iota
2.3.4 Hillary Johnson
2.3.5 Ingrid Kent
2.3.6 Jill Larson
2.3.7 Kim Mulrooney
2.3.8 Lisa Nevins
```

Discussion

Almost any numbering scheme is realizable by using one or more xsl:number elements with the appropriate attribute settings. However, extensive use of xsl:number (especially with level="multiple") can slow down your stylesheets. With very deeply nested hierarchical numbers, you can achieve a performance boost by passing the parent-level numbering down to the children via a parameter. Notice how you can achieve a hierarchal numbering in this fashion without using xsl:number at all:

```
<xsl:stylesheet version="1.0" xmlns:xsl="http://www.w3.org/1999/XSL/Transform">
  <xsl:output method="text"/>
  <xsl:strip-space elements="*"/>
```

```
<xsl:template match="group">
  <xsl:param name="parent-level" select=" '' "/>

  <xsl:variable name="number" select="concat($parent-level,position())"/>

  <xsl:text>Group </xsl:text>
  <xsl:value-of select="$number"/>
  <xsl:text>&#xa;</xsl:text>

  <xsl:apply-templates>
    <xsl:with-param name="parent-level" select="concat($number,'.')"/>
  </xsl:apply-templates>

</xsl:template>

<xsl:template match="person">
  <xsl:param name="parent-level" select=" '' "/>

  <xsl:variable name="number">
    <xsl:value-of select="concat($parent-level,position(),' ')"/>
  </xsl:variable>

  <xsl:value-of select="$number"/>
  <xsl:value-of select="@name"/>
  <xsl:text>&#xa;</xsl:text>
</xsl:template>

</xsl:stylesheet>
```

This use of position is less convenient when the numbering scheme requires letters for roman numerals.

5.6 Wrapping Text to a Specified Width and Alignment

Problem

You want to format multilined text within an XML document into a fixed-width-aligned format, insuring that lines wrap at word boundaries.

Solution

Here is a solution that handles both wrapping and alignment by reusing the text:justify template constructed in Recipe 5.3. For added flexibility, you can allow the alignment width to be specified separately from wrapping width, but default to it when unspecified:

```
<xsl:stylesheet version="1.0"
  xmlns:xsl="http://www.w3.org/1999/XSL/Transform" id="text.wrap"
  xmlns:str="http://www.ora.com/XSLTCookbook/namespaces/strings"
```

```
        xmlns:text="http://www.ora.com/XSLTCookbook/namespaces/text"
        exclude-result-prefixes="text">

  <xsl:include href="../strings/str.find-last.xslt"/>
  <xsl:include href="text.justify.xslt"/>

  <xsl:template match="node( ) | @*" mode="text:wrap" name="text:wrap">
    <xsl:param name="input" select="normalize-space( )"/>
    <xsl:param name="width" select="70"/>
    <xsl:param name="align-width" select="$width"/>
    <xsl:param name="align" select=" 'left' "/>

    <xsl:if test="$input">
      <xsl:variable name="line">
        <xsl:choose>
          <xsl:when test="string-length($input) > $width">
            <xsl:call-template name="str:substring-before-last">
              <xsl:with-param name="input"
                select="substring($input,1,$width)"/>
              <xsl:with-param name="substr" select=" ' ' "/>
            </xsl:call-template>
          </xsl:when>
          <xsl:otherwise>
            <xsl:value-of select="$input"/>
          </xsl:otherwise>
        </xsl:choose>
      </xsl:variable>

      <xsl:if test="$line">
        <xsl:call-template name="text:justify">
          <xsl:with-param name="value" select="$line"/>
          <xsl:with-param name="width" select="$align-width"/>
          <xsl:with-param name="align" select="$align"/>
        </xsl:call-template>
        <xsl:text>&#xa;</xsl:text>
      </xsl:if>

      <xsl:call-template name="text:wrap">
        <xsl:with-param name="input"
            select="substring($input, string-length($line) + 2)"/>
        <xsl:with-param name="width" select="$width"/>
        <xsl:with-param name="align-width" select="$align-width"/>
        <xsl:with-param name="align" select="$align"/>
      </xsl:call-template>
    </xsl:if>

  </xsl:template>
```

The solution reuses the str:substring-before-last template created in Recipe 1.4.
The basic idea is to extract a line containing up to $width characters, extracting less if
the line would not end in a space. The rest of the input is then processed recursively.
The tricky part is to make sure that if a word with $width characters is encountered,
you allow it to be split.

The following example shows how you can use this recipe to wrap and center some sample. It uses different alignment and wrapping widths to demonstrate the effect of these parameters:

```
<xsl:stylesheet version="1.0" xmlns:xsl="http://www.w3.org/1999/XSL/Transform"
  xmlns:text="http://www.ora.com/XSLTCookbook/namespaces/text">

<xsl:include href="text.wrap.xslt"/>

<xsl:strip-space elements="*"/>
<xsl:output method="text"/>

<xsl:template match="p">
  <xsl:apply-templates select="." mode="text:wrap">
    <xsl:with-param name="width" select="40"/>
      <xsl:with-param name="align" select=" 'center' "/>
    <xsl:with-param name="align-width" select="60"/>
  </xsl:apply-templates>
  <xsl:text>&#xa;</xsl:text>
</xsl:template>

</xsl:stylesheet>
```

Input:

```
<doc>
  <p>In the age of the internet, formats such HTML, XHTML and PDF clearly dominate
the application of XSL and XSLT. However, plain old text will never become obsolete
because it is the lowest common denominator in both human and machine-readable
formats.  XML is often converted to text to be imported into another application that
does not know how to read XML or does not interpret it the way you would prefer. Text
output is also used when the result will be sent to a terminal or post processed in a
Unix pipeline.</p>
  <p>Many recipes in this section place stress on XSLT techniques that create very
generic XML to text converters. Here generic means that the transformation can easily
be customized to work on many different XML inputs or produce a variety of outputs or
both. The techniques employed in these recipes have application beyond specifics of a
given recipe and often beyond the domain of text processing. In particular, you may
want to look at recipes 5.2 through 5.5 even if they do not address a present need.
  </p>
</doc>
```

Output:

```
        In the age of the internet, formats
            such HTML, XHTML and PDF clearly
          dominate the application of XSL and
            XSLT. However, plain old text will
         never become obsolete because it is the
         lowest common denominator in both human
           and machine-readable formats. XML is
          often converted to text to be imported
          into another application that does not
             know how to read XML or does not
            interpret it the way you would prefer.
```

```
         Text output is also used when the
        result will be sent to a terminal or
         post processed in a Unix pipeline.

        Many recipes in this section place
        stress on XSLT techniques that create
         very generic XML to text converters.
            Here generic means that the
        transformation can easily be customized
        to work on many different XML inputs or
         produce a variety of outputs or both.
          The techniques employed in these
            recipes have application beyond
         specifics of a given recipe and often
         beyond the domain of text processing.
          In particular, you may want to look at
        recipes 5.2 through 5.5 even if they do
             not address a present need.
```

Discussion

In many text-conversion scenarios, the final output device cannot handle text of arbitrary line length. Most devices (such as terminals) wrap the text that overflows its horizontal display area. This wrapping results in a sloppy-looking output. This example allows you to deal with fixed-width formatting more intelligently.

See Also

A similar text-wrapping template can be found in Jeni Tennison's *XSLT and XPath on the Edge* (M&T, 2001). However, this solution adds alignment capabilities and handles the case in which words are longer than the desired width.

CHAPTER 6

XML to XML

> *To change and to change for the better are*
> *two different things.*
> —German proverb

One of the beauties of XML is that if you don't like something, you can change it. Since it is impossible to please everyone, transforming XML to XML is extremely common. However, you will not transform XML only to improve the structure of a poorly designed schema. Sometimes you need to merge disparate XML documents into a single document. At other times you want to break up a large document into smaller subdocuments. You might also wish to preprocess a document to filter out only the relevant information, without changing its structure, before sending it off for further processing.

A simple but important tool in many XML-to-XML transformations is the *identity transform*. This tool is a stylesheet that copies an input document to an output document without changing it. This task may seem better suited to the operating systems copy operation, but as the following examples demonstrate, this simple stylesheet can be imported into other stylesheets to yield very common types of transformations with little added coding effort.

Example 6-1 shows the identity stylesheet. I actually prefer calling this stylesheet the copying stylesheet, and I call the techniques that utilize it the *overriding copy idiom*.

Example 6-1. copy.xslt

```
<xsl:stylesheet version="1.0" xmlns:xsl="http://www.w3.org/1999/XSL/Transform">

<xsl:template match="node() | @*">
  <xsl:copy>
    <xsl:apply-templates select="@* | node()"/>
  </xsl:copy>
</xsl:template>

</xsl:stylesheet>
```

6.1   Converting Attributes to Elements

Problem

You have a document that encodes information with attributes, and you would like to use child elements instead.

Solution

This problem is tailor-made for what the introduction to this chapter calls the *overriding copy idiom*. This example transforms attributes to elements globally:

```
<xsl:stylesheet version="1.0" xmlns:xsl="http://www.w3.org/1999/XSL/Transform">

<xsl:import href="copy.xslt"/>

<xsl:output method="xml" version="1.0" encoding="UTF-8" indent="yes"/>

<xsl:template match="@*">
  <xsl:element name="{local-name(.)}" namespace="{namespace-uri(..)}">
    <xsl:value-of select="."/>
  </xsl:element>
</xsl:template>

</xsl:stylesheet>
```

The stylesheet works by overriding the copy behavior for attributes. It replaces the behavior with a template that converts an attribute into an element (of the same name) whose value is the attribute's value. It also assumes that this new element should be in the same namespace as the attribute's parent. If you prefer not to make assumptions, then use the following code:

```
<xsl:template match="@*">
  <xsl:variable name="namespace">
    <xsl:choose>
      <!--Use namespsace of attribute, if there is one -->
      <xsl:when test="namespace-uri()">
        <xsl:value-of select="namespace-uri()" />
      </xsl:when>
      <!--Otherwise use parents namespace -->
      <xsl:otherwise>
        <xsl:value-of select="namespace-uri(..)" />
      </xsl:otherwise>
    </xsl:choose>
  </xsl:variable>
  <xsl:element name="{name()}" namespace="{$namespace}">
    <xsl:value-of select="." />
  </xsl:element>
</xsl:template>
```

You'll often want to be selective when transforming attributes to elements (see Examples 6-2 to 6-4).

Example 6-2. Input

```
<people which="MeAndMyFriends">
  <person firstname="Sal" lastname="Mangano" age="38" height="5.75"/>
  <person firstname="Mike" lastname="Palmieri" age="28" height="5.10"/>
  <person firstname="Vito" lastname="Palmieri" age="38" height="6.0"/>
  <person firstname="Vinny" lastname="Mari" age="37" height="5.8"/>
</people>
```

Example 6-3. A stylesheet that transforms person attributes only

```
<xsl:stylesheet version="1.0" xmlns:xsl="http://www.w3.org/1999/XSL/Transform">

<xsl:import href="copy.xslt"/>

<xsl:output method="xml" version="1.0" encoding="UTF-8" indent="yes"/>

<xsl:template match="person/@*">
  <xsl:element name="{local-name(.)}" namespace="{namespace-uri(..)}">
    <xsl:value-of select="."/>
  </xsl:element>
</xsl:template>

</xsl:stylesheet>
```

Example 6-4. Output

```
<people which="MeAndMyFriends">

  <person>
    <firstname>Sal</firstname>
    <lastname>Mangano</lastname>
    <age>38</age>
    <height>5.75</height>
  </person>

  <person>
    <firstname>Mike</firstname>
    <lastname>Palmieri</lastname>
    <age>28</age>
    <height>5.10</height>
  </person>

  <person>
    <firstname>Vito</firstname>
    <lastname>Palmieri</lastname>
    <age>38</age>
    <height>6.0</height>
  </person>

  <person>
    <firstname>Vinny</firstname>
    <lastname>Mari</lastname>
    <age>37</age>
    <height>5.8</height>
```

Example 6-4. Output (continued)

```
    </person>

</people>
```

Discussion

This section and Recipe 6.2 address the problems that arise when a document designer makes a poor choice between encoding information in attributes versus elements. The attribute-versus-element decision is one of the most controversial aspects of document design.* These examples are helpful because they allow you to correct your own or others' (perceived) mistakes.

6.2   Converting Elements to Attributes

Problem

You have a document that encodes information using child elements, and you would like to use attributes instead.

Solution

As with Recipe 6.1, you can use the overriding copy idiom. However, when transforming elements to attributes, you must selectively determine where the transformation will be applied. This is because the idea of transforming all elements to attributes is nonsensical. The following stylesheet reverses the attribute-to-element transformation we performed in Recipe 6.1:

```
<xsl:stylesheet version="1.0" xmlns:xsl="http://www.w3.org/1999/XSL/Transform">

<xsl:import href="copy.xslt"/>

<xsl:output method="xml" version="1.0" encoding="UTF-8"/>

<xsl:template match="person">
  <xsl:copy>
    <xsl:for-each select="*">
      <xsl:attribute name="{local-name(.)}">
        <xsl:value-of select="."/>
      </xsl:attribute>
    </xsl:for-each>
  </xsl:copy>
</xsl:template>

</xsl:stylesheet>
```

---

* The only other stylistic issue I have seen software developers get more passionate about is where to put the curly braces in C-like programming languages (e.g., C++ and Java).

Discussion

Converting from elements to attributes is not always as straightforward as transforming in the opposite direction. If the elements being converted to attributes have attributes themselves, you must decide what will become of them. In the preceding solution, they would be lost. Another alternative would be to promote them to the new parent:

```
<xsl:stylesheet version="1.0" xmlns:xsl="http://www.w3.org/1999/XSL/Transform">

<xsl:import href="copy.xslt"/>

<xsl:output method="xml" version="1.0" encoding="UTF-8"/>

<xsl:template match="person">
  <xsl:copy>
    <xsl:for-each select="*">
      <xsl:attribute name="{local-name(.)}">
        <xsl:value-of select="."/>
      </xsl:attribute>
      <xsl:copy-of select="@*"/>
    </xsl:for-each>
  </xsl:copy>
</xsl:template>

</xsl:stylesheet>
```

However, this works only if all the attributes names in question are unique. If this is not the case, you will have to rename attributes, perhaps as follows:

```
<xsl:stylesheet version="1.0" xmlns:xsl="http://www.w3.org/1999/XSL/Transform">

<xsl:import href="copy.xslt"/>

<xsl:output method="xml" version="1.0" encoding="UTF-8"/>

<xsl:template match="person">
  <xsl:copy>
    <xsl:for-each select="*">
      <xsl:attribute name="{local-name(.)}">
        <xsl:value-of select="."/>
      </xsl:attribute>
      <xsl:variable name="elem-name" select="local-name(.)"/>
      <xsl:for-each select="@*">
        <xsl:attribute name="{concat($elem-name,'-',local-name(.))}">
          <xsl:value-of select="."/>
        </xsl:attribute>
      </xsl:for-each>
    </xsl:for-each>
  </xsl:copy>
</xsl:template>

</xsl:stylesheet>
```

Another complication arises if the siblings elements do not have unique names, because in this case, they would clash upon becoming attributes. Another possible strategy is to create an attribute from an element only if the element does not have attributes or element children of its own, does not repeat in its parent element, and has parents without attributes:

```
<xsl:stylesheet version="1.0" xmlns:xsl="http://www.w3.org/1999/XSL/Transform">

<xsl:import href="copy.xslt"/>

<xsl:output method="xml" indent="yes" version="1.0" encoding="UTF-8"/>

<!-- Match elements that are parents -->
<xsl:template match="*[*]">
  <xsl:choose>
    <!-- Only convert children if this element has no attributes -->
    <!-- of its own -->
    <xsl:when test="not(@*)">
      <xsl:copy>
        <!-- Convert children to attributes if the child has -->
        <!-- no children or attributes and has a unique name -->
        <!-- amoung its siblings -->
        <xsl:for-each select="*">
          <xsl:choose>
            <xsl:when test="not(*) and not(@*) and
                            not(preceding-sibling::*[name( ) =
                                                    name(current( ))])
                            and
                            not(following-sibling::*[name( ) =
                                                    name(current( ))])">
              <xsl:attribute name="{local-name(.)}">
                <xsl:value-of select="."/>
              </xsl:attribute>
            </xsl:when>
            <xsl:otherwise>
              <xsl:apply-templates select="."/>
            </xsl:otherwise>
          </xsl:choose>
        </xsl:for-each>
      </xsl:copy>
    </xsl:when>
    <xsl:otherwise>
      <xsl:copy>
        <xsl:apply-templates/>
      </xsl:copy>
    </xsl:otherwise>
  </xsl:choose>
</xsl:template>

</xsl:stylesheet>
```

6.3 Renaming Elements or Attributes

Problem

You need to rename or re-namespace elements or attributes in an XML document.

Solution

If you need to rename a small number of attributes or elements, use a straightforward version of the overriding copy idiom, as shown in Example 6-5.

Example 6-5. Rename person to individual

```
<xsl:stylesheet version="1.0" xmlns:xsl="http://www.w3.org/1999/XSL/Transform">

<xsl:import href="copy.xslt"/>

<xsl:output method="xml" version="1.0" encoding="UTF-8"/>

<xsl:template match="person">
  <individual>
    <xsl:apply-templates/>
  </individual>
</xsl:template>

</xsl:stylesheet>
```

Or, alternatively, use `xsl:element`:

```
...
<xsl:template match="person">
  <xsl:element name="individual">
    <xsl:apply-templates/>
  </xsl:element>
</xsl:template>
...
```

Renaming attributes is just as straightforward:

```
<xsl:stylesheet version="1.0" xmlns:xsl="http://www.w3.org/1999/XSL/Transform">

<xsl:import href="copy.xslt"/>

<xsl:output method="xml" version="1.0" encoding="UTF-8"/>

<xsl:template match="@lastname">
  <xsl:attribute name="surname">
    <xsl:value-of select="."/>
  </xsl:attribute>
</xsl:template>

</xsl:stylesheet>
```

Sometimes you need to re-namespace rather than rename, as shown in Example 6-6.

Example 6-6. A document using the namespace foo

```
<foo:someElement xmlns:foo="http://www.ora.com/XMLCookbook/namespaces/foo">
  <foo:aChild>
    <foo:aGrandChild/>
    <foo:aGrandChild>
    </foo:aGrandChild>
  </foo:aChild>
</foo:someElement>
```

For each element in the foo namespace, create a new element in the bar namespace, as shown in Examples 6-7 and 6-8.

Example 6-7. A stylesheet that maps foo to bar

```
<xsl:stylesheet version="1.0"
 xmlns:xsl="http://www.w3.org/1999/XSL/Transform"
 xmlns:foo="http://www.ora.com/XMLCookbook/namespaces/foo"
 xmlns:bar="http://www.ora.com/XMLCookbook/namespaces/bar">

<xsl:import href="copy.xslt"/>

<xsl:output method="xml" version="1.0" encoding="UTF-8" indent="yes"/>

<xsl:strip-space elements="*"/>

<xsl:template match="foo:*">
  <xsl:element name="bar:{local-name( )}">
    <xsl:apply-templates/>
  </xsl:element>
</xsl:template>

</xsl:stylesheet>
```

Example 6-8. Output

```
<bar:someElement xmlns:bar="http://www.ora.com/XMLCookbook/namespaces/bar">
   <bar:aChild>
      <bar:aGrandChild/>
      <bar:aGrandChild/>
   </bar:aChild>
</bar:someElement>
```

Discussion

Naming is an important skill that few software practitioners (including yours truly) have mastered.* Hence, you should know how to rename things when you don't get the names quite right on the first get go.

---

* As evidence of my naming ineptitude, my son actually spent two whole days in this world without a name. My wife and I simply could not think of a good one that we both liked. To our credit, we both understood the importance of picking a good name and we hope Leonardo will agree when he is old enough to know the difference.

If many elements or attributes need renaming, then you may want to use a generic table-driven approach, as shown in Examples 6-9 to 6-11.

Example 6-9. A generic table-driven rename stylesheet

```
<xsl:stylesheet version="1.0" xmlns:xsl="http://www.w3.org/1999/XSL/Transform"
 xmlns:ren="http://www.ora.com/namespaces/rename">

<xsl:import href="copy.xslt"/>

<!--Override in importing stylesheet -->
<xsl:variable name="lookup"  select="/.."/>

<xsl:output method="xml" version="1.0" encoding="UTF-8" indent="yes"/>

<xsl:template match="*">
  <xsl:choose>
    <xsl:when test="$lookup/ren:element[@from=name(current())]">
      <xsl:element
          name="{$lookup/ren:element[@from=local-name(current())]/@to}">
        <xsl:apply-templates select="@*"/>
        <xsl:apply-templates/>
      </xsl:element>
    </xsl:when>
    <xsl:otherwise>
      <xsl:apply-imports/>
    </xsl:otherwise>
  </xsl:choose>
</xsl:template>

<xsl:template match="@*">
  <xsl:choose>
    <xsl:when test="$lookup/ren:attribute[@from=name(current())]">
      <xsl:attribute name="{$lookup/ren:attribute[@from=name(current())]/@to}">
        <xsl:value-of select="."/>
      </xsl:attribute>
    </xsl:when>
    <xsl:otherwise>
      <xsl:apply-imports/>
    </xsl:otherwise>
  </xsl:choose>
</xsl:template>

</xsl:stylesheet>
```

Example 6-10. Using the table driven stylesheet

```
<xsl:stylesheet version="1.0"
 xmlns:xsl="http://www.w3.org/1999/XSL/Transform"
 xmlns:ren="http://www.ora.com/namespaces/rename">

<xsl:import href="TableDrivenRename.xslt"/>

<!-- Load the lookup table. We define it locally but it can also
```

Example 6-10. Using the table driven stylesheet (continued)

```
 come from an external file -->
<xsl:variable name="lookup"  select="document('')/*[ren:*]"/>

<!-- Define the renaming rules -->
<ren:element from="person" to="individual"/>
<ren:attribute from="firstname" to="givenname"/>
<ren:attribute from="lastname" to="surname"/>
<ren:attribute from="age" to="yearsOld"/>

</xsl:stylesheet>
```

Example 6-11. Output

```
<?xml version="1.0" encoding="UTF-8"?>
<people which="MeAndMyFriends">

   <individual givenname="Sal" surname="Mangano" yearsOld="38" height="5.75"/>

   <individual givenname="Mike" surname="Palmieri" yearsOld="28" height="5.10"/>

   <individual givenname="Vito" surname="Palmieri" yearsOld="38" height="6.0"/>

   <individual givenname="Vinny" surname="Mari" yearsOld="37" height="5.8"/>

</people>
```

You can still use this approach if some elements or attributes need context-sensitive handling. For example, consider the following document fragment:

```
<clubs>
  <club name="The 500 Club">
    <members>
       <member name="Joe Smith">
         <position name="president"/>
       </member>
       <member name="Jill McFonald">
          <position name="treasurer"/>
       </member>
       <!-- ... -->
    <members>
  </club>
  <!-- ... -->
<clubs>
```

Suppose you want to change attribute @name to attribute @title, but only for position elements. If you use the table-driven approach, all elements containing a name attribute will be changed. The solution is to create a template that overrides the default behavior for all elements except position:

```
<xsl:stylesheet version="1.0"
  xmlns:xsl="http://www.w3.org/1999/XSL/Transform"
  xmlns:ren="http://www.ora.com/namespaces/rename">
```

```
<xsl:import href="TableDrivenRename.xslt"/>

<!-- Load the lookup table. We define it locally but it can also
 come from an external file -->
<xsl:variable name="lookup" select="document('')/*[ren:*]"/>

<!-- Define the renaming rules -->
<ren:attribute from="name" to="title"/>

<!--OVEVRIDE: Simply copy all names that are not attributes of position element -->
<xsl:template match="@name[not(../../position)]">
    <xsl:copy/>
</xsl:template>

</xsl:stylesheet>
```

When re-namespacing using copy, the old namespace may stubbornly refuse to go away even when it is not needed. Consider the foo document again with an additional element from a doc namespace:

```
<foo:someElement xmlns:foo="http://www.ora.com/XMLCookbook/namespaces/foo" xmlns:
doc="http://www.ora.com/XMLCookbook/namespaces/doc">
  <foo:aChild>
    <foo:aGrandChild/>
    <foo:aGrandChild>
      <doc:doc>This documentation should not be removed or altered in any way.
      </doc:doc>
    </foo:aGrandChild>
  </foo:aChild>
</foo:someElement>
```

If you apply the re-namespacing stylesheet to this document, the foo namespace is carried along with the doc element:

```
<bar:someElement xmlns:bar="http://www.ora.com/XMLCookbook/namespaces/bar">
  <bar:aChild>
    <bar:aGrandChild/>
    <bar:aGrandChild>
      <doc:doc xmlns:doc="http://www.ora.com/XMLCookbook/namespaces/doc"
          xmlns:foo="http://www.ora.com/XMLCookbook/namespaces/foo">
        This documentation should not be removed or altered in any way.
      </doc:doc>
    </bar:aGrandChild>
  </bar:aChild>
</bar:someElement>
```

This is because the doc element is processed by xsl:copy. Both xsl:copy and xsl:copy-of always copy all namespaces associated with an element. Since the doc element is enclosed in elements from the foo namespace, it has a foo namespace node, even though it is not directly visible in the input. To avoid copying this unwanted namespace, use xsl:element to make sure that elements are recreated, not recopied:

```
<xsl:stylesheet version="1.0" xmlns:xsl="http://www.w3.org/1999/XSL/Transform"
 xmlns:foo="http://www.ora.com/XMLCookbook/namespaces/foo"
 xmlns:bar="http://www.ora.com/XMLCookbook/namespaces/bar">

<xsl:import href="copy.xslt"/>

<xsl:output method="xml" version="1.0" encoding="UTF-8" indent="yes"/>

<xsl:strip-space elements="*"/>

<!-- For all elements create a new element with the same
name and namespace
-->
<xsl:template match="*">
  <xsl:element name="{name( )}" namespace="{namespace-uri( )}">
    <xsl:apply-templates/>
  </xsl:element>
</xsl:template>

<xsl:template match="foo:*">
  <xsl:element name="bar:{local-name( )}">
    <xsl:apply-templates/>
  </xsl:element>
</xsl:template>

</xsl:stylesheet>
```

You can even use this technique to strip all namespaces from a document:

```
<xsl:stylesheet version="1.0" xmlns:xsl="http://www.w3.org/1999/XSL/Transform">
<xsl:import href="copy.xslt"/>

<xsl:output method="xml" version="1.0" encoding="UTF-8" indent="yes"/>

<xsl:strip-space elements="*"/>

<xsl:template match="*">
  <xsl:element name="{local-name( )}">
    <xsl:apply-templates/>
  </xsl:element>
</xsl:template>

</xsl:stylesheet>
```

6.4   Merging Documents with Identical Schema

Problem

You have two or more identically structured documents and you would like to merge
them into a single document.

Solution

If the content of the documents is distinct or you are not concerned about duplicates, then the solution is simple:

```
<xsl:stylesheet version="1.0" xmlns:xsl="http://www.w3.org/1999/XSL/Transform">

<xsl:output method="xml" indent="yes"/>

<xsl:param name="doc2"/>

<xsl:template match="/*">
  <xsl:copy>
    <xsl:copy-of select="* | document($doc2)/*/*"/>
  </xsl:copy>
</xsl:template>

</xsl:stylesheet>
```

If duplicates exist among input documents but you want the output document to contain unique entries, you can use techniques discussed in Recipe 4.3 for removing duplicates. Consider the following two documents in Examples 6-12 and 6-13.

Example 6-12. Document 1

```
<people which="MeAndMyFriends">
    <person firstname="Sal" lastname="Mangano" age="38" height="5.75"/>
    <person firstname="Mike" lastname="Palmieri" age="28" height="5.10"/>
    <person firstname="Vito" lastname="Palmieri" age="38" height="6.0"/>
    <person firstname="Vinny" lastname="Mari" age="37" height="5.8"/>
</people>
```

Example 6-13. Document 2

```
<people which="MeAndMyCoWorkers">
    <person firstname="Sal" lastname="Mangano" age="38" height="5.75"/>
    <person firstname="Al" lastname="Zehtooney" age="33" height="5.3"/>
    <person firstname="Brad" lastname="York" age="38" height="6.0"/>
    <person firstname="Charles" lastname="Xavier" age="32" height="5.8"/>
</people>
```

This stylesheet merges and removes the duplicate element using xsl:sort and the exsl:node-set extensions:

```
<xsl:stylesheet version="1.0"
    xmlns:xsl="http://www.w3.org/1999/XSL/Transform">

<xsl:output method="xml" version="1.0" encoding="UTF-8" indent="yes"/>

<xsl:param name="doc2"/>
<!-- Here we introduce a 'key' attribute to make removing duplicates -->
<!-- easier -->
<xsl:variable name="all">
  <xsl:for-each select="/*/person | document($doc2)/*/person">
```

```
        <xsl:sort select="concat(@lastname,@firstname)"/>
        <person key="{concat(@lastname, @firstname)}">
          <xsl:copy-of select="@* | node( )" />
        </person>  </xsl:for-each>
</xsl:variable>

<xsl:template match="/">

<people>
    <xsl:for-each
        select="exsl:node-set($all)/person[not(@key =
                        preceding-sibling::person[1]/@key)]">
          <xsl:copy-of select="."/>
      </xsl:for-each>
</people>

</xsl:template>
```

Removing duplicates this way has three drawbacks. First, it alters the order of the elements, which might be undesirable. Second, it requires the use of node-set or XSLT 1.1 or higher. Third, it is not generic in the sense that you must rewrite the entire stylesheet for every situation when you want a nonduplicating merge.

One way to address these problems uses xsl:key:

```
<!-- Stylesheet: merge-simple-using-key.xslt -->
<!-- Import this stylesheet into another that defines the key -->

<xsl:stylesheet version="1.0" xmlns:xsl="http://www.w3.org/1999/XSL/Transform"
 xmlns:merge="http:www.ora.com/XSLTCookbook/mnamespaces/merge">

<xsl:param name="doc2"/>

<xsl:template match="/*">
  <!--Copy the outter most element of the source document -->
  <xsl:copy>
    <!-- For each child in the source, detemine if it should be
    copied to the destination based on its existence in the other document.
    -->
    <xsl:for-each select="*">

      <!-- Call a template which determines a unique key value for this
          element. It must be defined in the including stylesheet.
      -->
      <xsl:variable name="key-value">
        <xsl:call-template name="merge:key-value"/>
      </xsl:variable>

      <xsl:variable name="element" select="."/>
      <!--This for-each is simply to change context
          to the second document
      -->
      <xsl:for-each select="document($doc2)/*">
        <!-- Use key as a mechanism for testing the precence
```

```
              of the element in the second document. The
              key should be defined by the including stylesheet
          -->
          <xsl:if test="not(key('merge:key', $key-value))">
            <xsl:copy-of select="$element"/>
          </xsl:if>
        </xsl:for-each>

      </xsl:for-each>

      <!--Copy all elements in the second document -->
      <xsl:copy-of select="document($doc2)/*/*"/>

    </xsl:copy>
  </xsl:template>

</xsl:stylesheet>
```

The following stylesheet imports the previous one and defines the key and a template to retrieve the key's value:

```
<!-- This stylesheet defines uniqueness of elements in terms of a key. -->
<xsl:stylesheet version="1.0"
 xmlns:xsl="http://www.w3.org/1999/XSL/Transform"
 xmlns:merge="http:www.ora.com/XSLTCookbook/mnamespaces/merge">

<xsl:include href="merge-simple-using-key.xslt"/>

<!--A person is uniquely defined by the concatenation of
    last and first names -->
<xsl:key name="merge:key" match="person"
        use="concat(@lastname,@firstname)"/>

<xsl:output method="xml" indent="yes"/>

<!-- This template retrieves the key value for an element -->
<xsl:template name="merge:key-value">
  <xsl:value-of select="concat(@lastname,@firstname)"/>
</xsl:template>

</xsl:stylesheet>
```

A second way to merge and remove duplicates uses value-based set operations that are discussed in Recipe 7.2. This books presents the solution, but refers the reader to that recipe for more information. Examples 6-14 and 6-15 include more stylesheets.

Example 6-14. A reusable stylesheet that implements the merge in terms of a union

```
<xsl:stylesheet version="1.0" xmlns:xsl="http://www.w3.org/1999/XSL/Transform"
  xmlns:vset="http:/www.ora.com/XSLTCookbook/namespaces/vset">

<xsl:import href="../query/vset.ops.xslt"/>

<xsl:output method="xml" indent="yes"/>
```

```
<xsl:param name="doc2"/>

<xsl:template match="/*">
  <xsl:copy>
    <xsl:call-template name="vset:union">
      <xsl:with-param name="nodes1" select="*"/>
      <xsl:with-param name="nodes2" select="document($doc2)/*/*"/>
    </xsl:call-template>
  </xsl:copy>
</xsl:template>

</xsl:stylesheet>
```

Example 6-15. A stylesheet defining what element equality means

```
<xsl:stylesheet version="1.0" xmlns:xsl="http://www.w3.org/1999/XSL/Transform"
  xmlns:vset="http:/www.ora.com/XSLTCookbook/namespaces/vset">

<xsl:import href="merge-using-vset-union.xslt"/>

<xsl:template match="person" mode="vset:element-equality">
  <xsl:param name="other"/>
  <xsl:if test="concat(@lastname,@firstname) =
                concat($other/@lastname,$other/@firstname)">
    <xsl:value-of select="true( )"/>
  </xsl:if>
</xsl:template>

</xsl:stylesheet>
```

The vset:union-based solution involves less new code than the key-based solution; however, for large documents, the xsl:key-based solution is likely to be faster.

Discussion

Merging documents is often necessary when separate individuals or processes produce parts of the document. Merging is also necessary when reconstituting a very large document that was split up to be processed in parallel or because it was too cumbersome to handle as a whole.

The examples in this section address the simple case when just two documents are merged. If an arbitrary number of documents are merged, a mechanism is required to pass a list of documents into the stylesheet. One technique uses a parameter containing all filenames separated by spaces and employs a simple tokenizer (Recipe 1.9) to extract the names. Another technique passes all the filenames in the source document, as shown in Examples 6-16 and 6-17.

Example 6-16. XML-containing documents to be merged

```
<mergeDocs>
  <doc path="people1.xml"/>
  <doc path="people2.xml"/>
  <doc path="people3.xml"/>
  <doc path="people4.xml"/>
</mergeDocs>
```

Example 6-17. A stylesheet for merging the documents (assumes no duplicates are in the content)

```
<xsl:stylesheet version="1.0" xmlns:xsl="http://www.w3.org/1999/XSL/Transform">

<xsl:output method="xml" indent="yes"/>

<xsl:variable name="docs" select="/*/doc"/>

<xsl:template match="mergeDocs">
    <xsl:apply-templates select="doc[1]"/>
</xsl:template>

<!--Match the first doc to create the top most element -->
<xsl:template match="doc">
  <xsl:variable name="path" select="@path"/>
  <xsl:for-each select="document($path)/*">
    <xsl:copy>
       <!-- Merge children of doc 1 -->
       <xsl:copy-of select="@* | *"/>
       <!--Loop over remaining docs to merge their children -->
       <xsl:for-each select="$docs[position( ) > 1]">
           <xsl:copy-of select="document(@path)/*/*"/>
       </xsl:for-each>
    </xsl:copy>
  </xsl:for-each>
</xsl:template>

</xsl:stylesheet>
```

6.5   Merging Documents with Unlike Schema

Problem

You have two or more dissimilar documents, and you would like to merge them into a single document.

Solution

The process of merging dissimilar data can vary from application to application. Therefore, this chapter cannot present a single generic solution. Instead, it antici-pates common ways for two dissimilar documents to be brought together and pro-vides solutions for each case.

Incorporate one document as a subpart of a parent document

Incorporating a document as a subpart is the most trivial interpretation of this type of merge. The basic idea is to use xsl:copy-of to copy one document or document part into the appropriate part of a second document. The following example merges two documents into a container document that uses element names in the container as indications of what files to merge:

```
<MyNoteBook>
  <friends>
  </friends>
  <coworkers>
  </coworkers>
  <projects>
    <project>Replalce mapML with XSLT engine using Xalan C++</project>
    <project>Figure out the meaning of life.</project>
    <project>Figure out where the dryer is hinding all those missing socks</project>
  </projects>
</MyNoteBook>

<xsl:stylesheet version="1.0" xmlns:xsl="http://www.w3.org/1999/XSL/Transform">

  <xsl:import href="copy.xslt"/>

  <xsl:output method="xml" version="1.0" encoding="UTF-8" indent="yes"/>
  <xsl:strip-space elements="*"/>

  <xsl:template match="friends | coworkers">
    <xsl:copy>
      <xsl:variable name="file" select="concat(local-name( ),'.xml')"/>
      <xsl:copy-of select="document($file)/*/*"/>
    </xsl:copy>
  </xsl:template>
...
</xsl:stylesheet>

<?xml version="1.0" encoding="UTF-8"?>
<MyNoteBook>
  <friends>
    <person firstname="Sal" lastname="Mangano" age="38" height="5.75"/>
    <person firstname="Mike" lastname="Palmieri" age="28" height="5.10"/>
    <person firstname="Vito" lastname="Palmieri" age="38" height="6.0"/>
    <person firstname="Vinny" lastname="Mari" age="37" height="5.8"/>
  </friends>
  <coworkers>
    <person firstname="Sal" lastname="Mangano" age="38" height="5.75"/>
    <person firstname="Al" lastname="Zehtooney" age="33" height="5.3"/>
    <person firstname="Brad" lastname="York" age="38" height="6.0"/>
    <person firstname="Charles" lastname="Xavier" age="32" height="5.8"/>
  </coworkers>
```

```
    <projects>
        <project>Replalce mapML with XSLT engine using Xalan C++</project>
        <project>Figure out the meaning of life.</project>
        <project>Figure out where the dryer is hinding all those missing socks
        </project>
    </projects>
</MyNoteBook>
```

An interesting variation of this case is a document that signals the inline inclusion of another document. The W3C defines a standard way of doing this, called *XInclude* (*http://www.w3.org/TR/xinclude/*). You can implement a general-purpose XInclude processor in XSLT by extending *copy.xslt*:

```
<xsl:stylesheet version="1.0" xmlns:xsl="http://www.w3.org/1999/XSL/Transform">

<xsl:import href="copy.xslt"/>

<xsl:output method="xml" indent="yes"/>
<xsl:strip-space elements="*"/>

<xsl:template match="xi:include" xmlns:xi="http://www.w3.org/2001/XInclude">
  <xsl:for-each select="document(@href)">
    <xsl:apply-templates/>
  </xsl:for-each>
</xsl:template>

</xsl:stylesheet>
```

The xsl:for-each only changes the context to the included document. Then use xsl:apply-templates to continue copying the included document's content.

Weave two documents together

A variation of simple inclusion combines elements that are children of common parent element types. Consider two biologists who have collected information about animals separately. As a first step to building a unified animal database, they may decide to weave the data together at a point of structural commonality.

Biologist1 has this file:

```
<animals>
  <mammals>
    <animal common="chimpanzee" species="Pan troglodytes" order="Primates"/>
    <animal common="human" species="Homo Sapien" family="Primates"/>
  </mammals>
  <reptiles>
    <animal common="boa constrictor" species="Boa constrictor" order="Squamata"/>
    <animal common="gecko" species="Gekko gecko" order="Squamata"/>
  </reptiles>
```

```
    <birds>
      <animal common="sea gull" species="Larus occidentalis" order="Charadriiformes"/>
      <animal common="Black-Backed Woodpecker" species="Picoides arcticus"
      order="Piciformes"/>
    </birds>
  </animals>
```

Biologist2 has this file:

```
<animals>
  <mammals>
    <animal common="hippo" species="Hippopotamus amphibius"
    family=" Hippopotamidae"/>
    <animal common="arabian camel" species="Camelus dromedarius" family="Camelidae"/>
  </mammals>
  <insects>
    <animal common="Lady Bug" species="Adalia bipunctata" family="Coccinellidae"/>
    <animal common="Dung Bettle" species=" Onthophagus australis"
    family="Scarabaeidae"/>
  </insects>
  <amphibians>
    <animal common="Green Sea Turtle" species="Chelonia mydas" family="Cheloniidae"/>
    <animal common="Green Tree Frog" species=" Hyla cinerea" family="Hylidae "/>
  </amphibians>
</animals>
```

The files have similar but not identical schema. Both files contain the class
Mammalia, but differ in the other organizational levels. At the animal level, one biol-
ogist recorded information about the animal's order, while the other recorded data
about the animal's family. The following stylesheet weaves the documents together
at the animal's class level (the second level in document structure):

```
<xsl:stylesheet version="1.0" xmlns:xsl="http://www.w3.org/1999/XSL/Transform">

<xsl:output method="xml" version="1.0" encoding="UTF-8" indent="yes"/>
<xsl:strip-space elements="*"/>

  <xsl:param name="doc2file"/>

  <xsl:variable name="doc2"        select="document($doc2file)"/>
  <xsl:variable name="thisDocsClasses" select="/*/*"/>

<xsl:template match="/*">
  <xsl:copy>
    <!-- Merge common sections between source doc and doc2. Also includes
         sections unique to source doc. -->
    <xsl:for-each select="*">
      <xsl:copy>
        <xsl:copy-of select="*"/>
        <xsl:copy-of select="$doc2/*/*[name( ) = name(current( ))]/*"/>
      </xsl:copy>
    </xsl:for-each>
```

```
<!-- Merge sections unique to doc2 -->
<xsl:for-each select="$doc2/*/*">
  <xsl:if test="not($thisDocsClasses[name() = name(current())])">
    <xsl:copy-of select="."/>
  </xsl:if>
</xsl:for-each>
    </xsl:copy>
  </xsl:template>

</xsl:stylesheet>
```

Application of the stylesheet results in a document that can be further normalized by hand or through another automated method:

```
<animals>
  <mammals>
    <animal common="chimpanzee" species="Pan troglodytes" order="Primates"/>
    <animal common="human" species="Homo Sapien" order="Primates"/>
    <animal common="hippo" species="Hippopotamus amphibius"
    family=" Hippopotamidae"/>
    <animal common="arabian camel" species="Camelus dromedarius"
    family="Camelidae"/>
  </mammals>
  <reptiles>
    <animal common="boa constrictor" species="Boa constrictor" order="Squamata"/>
    <animal common="gecko" species="Gekko gecko" order="Squamata"/>
  </reptiles>
  <birds>
    <animal common="sea gull" species="Larus occidentalis"
    order="Charadriiformes"/>
    <animal common="Black-Backed Woodpecker" species="Picoides arcticus"
    order="Piciformes"/>
  </birds>
  <insects>
    <animal common="Lady Bug" species="Adalia bipunctata" family="Coccinellidae"/>
    <animal common="Dung Bettle" species=" Onthophagus australis"
    family="Scarabaeidae"/>
  </insects>
  <amphibians>
    <animal common="Green Sea Turtle" species="Chelonia mydas"
    family="Cheloniidae"/>
    <animal common="Green Tree Frog" species=" Hyla cinerea" family="Hylidae "/>
  </amphibians>
</animals>
```

Join elements from two documents to make new elements

A less-trivial merge occurs when one document is juxtaposed with another document or made children of its elements, based on the elements' matching characteristic. For example, consider the following merge of documents containing different information about people:

```
<xsl:stylesheet version="1.0" xmlns:xsl="http://www.w3.org/1999/XSL/Transform">

  <xsl:import href="copy.xslt"/>

  <xsl:output method="xml" version="1.0" encoding="UTF-8" indent="yes"/>

  <xsl:param name="doc2file"/>

  <xsl:variable name="doc2" select="document($doc2file)"/>

  <xsl:template match="person">
    <xsl:copy>
      <xsl:for-each select="@*">
        <xsl:element name="{local-name()}">
          <xsl:value-of select="."/>
        </xsl:element>
      </xsl:for-each>
      <xsl:variable name="matching-person"
          select="$doc2/*/person[@name=concat(current()/@firstname,' ',
                                              current()/@lastname)]"/>
      <xsl:element name="smoker">
        <xsl:value-of select="$matching-person/@smoker"/>
      </xsl:element>
      <xsl:element name="sex">
        <xsl:value-of select="$matching-person/@sex"/>
      </xsl:element>
    </xsl:copy>
  </xsl:template>

</xsl:stylesheet>
```

This stylesheet performs two tasks. It converts attribute-encoded information in the input stylesheets to elements and merges information from $doc2 that is not present in the source document.

Discussion

Merging XML with disparate schema is less well-defined then merging documents of identical schema. This chapter discusses three interpretations of merging, but other, more complicated types could exist. One possibility is that a merge could bring documents together so that inclusion, weaving, and joining all play a part in the final result. As such, it would be difficult to create a single, generic, XSLT-based merge utility that solves everyone's particular merge problems. However, the examples in this section provide a useful head start in crafting more ambitious types of merges.

See Also

The examples in this section focused on merging elements in a one-to-one relationship. Recipe 7.5 shows how to join information in disparate XML from the perspective of database queries. These techniques are also applicable to merging in a one-to-many relationship.

6.6   Splitting Documents

Problem

You want to partition elements from a single document into subdocuments.

Solution

For XSLT 1.0, you must rely on a widely available but nonstandard extension that allows multiple output documents.[*] The solution determines the level in the document structure to serialize and determines the name of the resulting file. The following stylesheet splits the *salesBySalesPerson.xml* from Chapter 4 into separate files for each salesperson. The stylesheet works in Saxon. Saxon allows use of the XSLT 1.1 xsl:document element when the stylesheet version is set to 1.1.[†] If you prefer not to use Version 1.1, then you can use the saxon:output extension:

```
<xsl:stylesheet version="1.1" xmlns:xsl="http://www.w3.org/1999/XSL/Transform">

<xsl:include href="copy.xslt"/>

<xsl:output method="xml" version="1.0" encoding="UTF-8" indent="yes"/>
<xsl:strip-space elements="*"/>

<xsl:template match="salesperson">
  <xsl:variable name="outFile"
  select="concat('salesperson.',translate(@name,' ','_'),'.xml')"/>
  <!-- Non-standard saxon xsl:document! -->
  <xsl:document href="{$outFile}">
      <xsl:copy>
              <xsl:copy-of select="@*"/>
          <xsl:apply-templates/>
      </xsl:copy>
  </xsl:document>
</xsl:template>

<xsl:template match="salesBySalesperson">
  <xsl:apply-templates/>
</xsl:template>

</xsl:stylesheet>
```

Discussion

Although the previous stylesheet is specific to Saxon, the technique works with most XSLT 1.0 processors with only minor changes. Saxon also has the saxon:output extension element (xmlns:saxon = "http://icl.com/saxon"). Xalan uses xalan:redirect (xmlns:xalan = "http://xml.apache.org/xalan").

---

[*] In XSLT 2.0, this facility is available and uses a new element called xsl:result-document.

[†] XSLT 1.1 is no longer an official version. It was abandoned in favor of XSLT 2.0.

An interesting variation of splitting also produces an output file that xincludes the generated subfiles:

```
<xsl:stylesheet version="1.1" xmlns:xsl="http://www.w3.org/1999/XSL/Transform">

<xsl:import href="copy.xslt"/>

<xsl:output method="xml" version="1.0" encoding="UTF-8" indent="yes"/>
<xsl:strip-space elements="*"/>

<xsl:template match="salesperson">
  <xsl:variable name="outFile"
      select="concat('salesperson.',translate(@name,' ','_'),'.xml')"/>
  <xsl:document href="{$outFile}">
      <xsl:copy>
              <xsl:copy-of select="@*"/>
            <xsl:apply-templates/>
      </xsl:copy>
  </xsl:document>

  <xi:include href="{$outFile}"
                      xmlns:xi="http://www.w3.org/2001/XInclude"/>

</xsl:template>

</xsl:stylesheet>
```

If you worry that your XSLT processor might someday recognize XInclude and mistakenly try to include the same file that was just output, you can replace the xi:include literal result element with xsl:element:

```
<xsl:element name="xi:include"
        xmlns:xi="http://www.w3.org/2001/XInclude">
  <xsl:attribute name="href">
    <xsl:value-of select="$outFile"/>
  </xsl:attribute>
</xsl:element>
```

See Also

Recipe 12.1 contains more examples that use multiple output document extensions.

6.7   Flattening an XML Hierarchy

Problem

You have a document with elements organized in a more deeply nested fashion than you would prefer. You want to flatten the tree.

Solution

If your goal is simply to flatten without regard to the information encoded by the deeper structure, then you need to apply an overriding copy. The overriding template must match the elements you wish to discard and apply templates without copying.

Consider the following input, which segregates people into two categories—salaried and union:

```
<people>
  <union>
    <person>
      <firstname>Warren</firstname>
      <lastname>Rosenbaum</lastname>
      <age>37</age>
      <height>5.75</height>
    </person>
    <person>
      <firstname>Dror</firstname>
      <lastname>Seagull</lastname>
      <age>28</age>
      <height>5.10</height>
    </person>
    <person>
      <firstname>Mike</firstname>
      <lastname>Heavyman</lastname>
      <age>45</age>
      <height>6.0</height>
    </person>
    <person>
      <firstname>Theresa</firstname>
      <lastname>Archul</lastname>
      <age>37</age>
      <height>5.5</height>
    </person>
  </union>
  <salaried>
    <person>
      <firstname>Sal</firstname>
      <lastname>Mangano</lastname>
      <age>37</age>
      <height>5.75</height>
    </person>
    <person>
      <firstname>Jane</firstname>
      <lastname>Smith</lastname>
      <age>28</age>
      <height>5.10</height>
    </person>
    <person>
      <firstname>Rick</firstname>
      <lastname>Winters</lastname>
```

```
      <age>45</age>
      <height>6.0</height>
   </person>
   <person>
      <firstname>James</firstname>
      <lastname>O'Riely</lastname>
      <age>33</age>
      <height>5.5</height>
   </person>
  </salaried>
</people>
```

This stylesheet simply discards the extra structure:

```
<xsl:stylesheet version="1.0" xmlns:xsl="http://www.w3.org/1999/XSL/Transform">

  <xsl:import href="copy.xslt"/>

  <xsl:output method="xml" version="1.0" encoding="UTF-8"/>

  <xsl:template match="people">
    <xsl:copy>
      <!--discard parents of person elements -->
      <xsl:apply-templates select="*/person" />
    </xsl:copy>
  </xsl:template>

</xsl:stylesheet>
```

Discussion

Having additional structure in a document is generally good because it usually makes the document easier to process with XSLT. However, too much structure bloats the document and makes it harder for people to understand. Humans generally prefer to infer relationships by spatial text organization rather than with extra syntactic baggage.

The following example shows that the extra structure is not superfluous, but encodes additional information. If you want to retain information about the structure while flattening, then you should probably create an attribute or child element to capture the information.

This stylesheet creates an attribute:

```
<xsl:stylesheet version="1.0" xmlns:xsl="http://www.w3.org/1999/XSL/Transform">

  <xsl:import href="copy.xslt"/>

  <xsl:output method="xml" version="1.0" encoding="UTF-8"
  omit-xml-declaration="yes"/>
```

```
<!--discard parents of person elements -->
<xsl:template match="*[person]">
      <xsl:apply-templates/>
</xsl:template>

<xsl:template match="person">
  <xsl:copy>
    <xsl:apply-templates select="@*"/>
    <xsl:attribute name="class">
      <xsl:value-of select="local-name(..)"/>
    </xsl:attribute>
    <xsl:apply-templates/>
  </xsl:copy>
</xsl:template>

</xsl:stylesheet>
```

This variation creates an element:

```
<xsl:stylesheet version="1.0" xmlns:xsl="http://www.w3.org/1999/XSL/Transform">

    <xsl:import href="copy.xslt"/>

    <xsl:strip-space elements="*"/>

    <xsl:output method="xml" version="1.0" encoding="UTF-8" indent="yes" />

    <!--discard parents of person elements -->
    <xsl:template match="*[person]">
          <xsl:apply-templates/>
    </xsl:template>

<xsl:template match="person">
  <xsl:copy>
    <xsl:copy-of select="@*"/>
    <xsl:element name="class">
      <xsl:value-of select="local-name(..)"/>
    </xsl:element>
    <xsl:apply-templates/>
  </xsl:copy>
</xsl:template>

</xsl:stylesheet>
```

You can use xsl:strip-space and indent="yes" on the xsl:output element so the output will not contain a whitespace gap, as shown here:

```
<people>
...
    <person>
      <class>union</class>
      <firstname>Warren</firstname>
      <lastname>Rosenbaum</lastname>
      <age>37</age>
      <height>5.75</height>
    </person>
```

```
    <person>
      <class>salaried</class>
      <firstname>Sal</firstname>
      <lastname>Mangano</lastname>
      <age>37</age>
      <height>5.75</height>
    </person>
  ...
  </people>
```

6.8   Deepening an XML Hierarchy

Problem

You have a poorly designed document that can use extra structure.[*]

Solution

This is the opposite problem from that solved in Recipe 6.7. Here you need to add additional structure to a document, possibly to organize its elements by some additional criteria.

Add structure based on existing data

This type of deepening transformation example undoes the flattening transformation performed in Recipe 6.7:

```
<xsl:stylesheet version="1.0" xmlns:xsl="http://www.w3.org/1999/XSL/Transform">

  <xsl:import href="copy.xslt"/>

  <xsl:output method="xml" version="1.0" encoding="UTF-8" indent="yes"/>
  <xsl:strip-space elements="*"/>

  <xsl:template match="people">
    <union>
      <xsl:apply-templates select="person[@class = 'union']" />
    </union>
    <salaried>
      <xsl:apply-templates select="person[@class = 'salaried']" />
    </salaried>
  </xsl:template>

</xsl:stylesheet>
```

---

[*] It may be well-designed from a particular set of goals, but those goals aren't yours.

Add structure to correct a poorly designed document

In a misguided effort to streamline XML, some people attempt to encode information by inserting sibling elements rather than parent elements.* For example, suppose someone distinguished between union and salaried employees in the following way:

```
<people>
  <class name="union"/>
  <person>
    <firstname>Warren</firstname>
    <lastname>Rosenbaum</lastname>
    <age>37</age>
    <height>5.75</height>
  </person>
  ...
  <person>
    <firstname>Theresa</firstname>
    <lastname>Archul</lastname>
    <age>37</age>
    <height>5.5</height>
  </person>
  <class name="salaried"/>
  <person>
    <firstname>Sal</firstname>
    <lastname>Mangano</lastname>
    <age>37</age>
    <height>5.75</height>
  </person>
  ...
  <person>
    <firstname>James</firstname>
    <lastname>O'Riely</lastname>
    <age>33</age>
    <height>5.5</height>
  </person>
</people>
```

Notice that the elements signifying union and salaried class elements are now empty. The intent is that all following-siblings of a class element belong to that class until another class element is encountered or there are no more siblings. This type of encoding is easy to grasp, but more difficult for an XSLT program to process. To correct this representation, you need to create a stylesheet that computes the set difference between all person elements following the first occurrence of a class element and the person elements following the next occurrence of a class element. XSLT 1.0 does not have an explicit set difference function. You can get essentially the same effect and be more efficient by considering all elements following a class element whose position is less than the position of elements following the next class element:

---

* To be fair, not every occurrence of this technique is misguided. Design is a navigation between competing tradeoffs.

```
<xsl:stylesheet version="1.0" xmlns:xsl="http://www.w3.org/1999/XSL/Transform">

  <xsl:import href="copy.xslt"/>

  <xsl:output method="xml" version="1.0" encoding="UTF-8" indent="yes"/>
  <xsl:strip-space elements="*"/>

  <!-- The total number of people -->
  <xsl:variable name="num-people" select="count(/*/person)"/>

  <xsl:template match="class">
    <!--The last position we want to consider. -->
    <xsl:variable name="pos"
            select="$num-people -
               count(following-sibling::class/following-sibling::person)"/>
    <xsl:element name="{@name}">
      <!-- Copy people that follow this class but whose  position is
           less than or equal to $pos.-->
      <xsl:copy-of
              select="following-sibling::person[position( ) &lt;= $pos]"/>
    </xsl:element>
  </xsl:template>

  <!-- Ignore person elements. They were coppied above. -->
  <xsl:template match="person"/>

</xsl:stylesheet>
```

More subtly, a key can be used as follows:

```
<xsl:key name="people" match="person"
        use="preceding-sibling::class[1]/@name" />

<xsl:template match="people">
  <people>
    <xsl:apply-templates select="class" />
  </people>
</xsl:template>

<xsl:template match="class">
  <xsl:element name="{@name}">
    <xsl:copy-of select="key('people', @name)" />
  </xsl:element>
</xsl:template>
```

A step-by-step approach is another alternative:

```
<xsl:template match="people">
  <people>
    <xsl:apply-templates select="class[1]" />
  </people>
</xsl:template>

<xsl:template match="class">
  <xsl:element name="{@name}">
```

```
      <xsl:apply-templates select="following-sibling::*[1][self::person]" />
    </xsl:element>
    <xsl:apply-templates select="following-sibling::class[1]" />
  </xsl:template>

  <xsl:template match="person">
    <xsl:copy-of select="." />
    <xsl:apply-templates select="following-sibling::*[1][self::person]" />
  </xsl:template>
```

Discussion

Add structure based on existing data

When you added structure based on existing data, you explicitly referred to the criteria that formed the categories of interest (e.g., union and salaried). It would be better if the stylesheet figured these categories out by itself. This makes the stylesheet more generic at the cost of added complexity:

```
<xsl:stylesheet version="1.0" xmlns:xsl="http://www.w3.org/1999/XSL/Transform">

  <xsl:import href="copy.xslt"/>

  <xsl:output method="xml" version="1.0" encoding="UTF-8" indent="yes"/>
  <xsl:strip-space elements="*"/>

  <!-- build a unique list of all classes -->
  <xsl:variable name="classes"
          select="/*/*/@class[not(. = ../preceding-sibling::*/@class)]"/>
  <xsl:template match="/*">
    <!-- For each class create an element named after that
         class that contains elements of that class -->
    <xsl:for-each select="$classes">
      <xsl:variable name="class-name" select="."/>
      <xsl:element name="{$class-name}">
        <xsl:for-each select="/*/*[@class=$class-name]">
          <xsl:copy>
            <xsl:apply-templates/>
          </xsl:copy>
        </xsl:for-each>
      </xsl:element>
    </xsl:for-each>
  </xsl:template>

</xsl:stylesheet>
```

Although not 100% generic, this stylesheet avoids making assumptions about what kinds of classes exist in the document. The only application-specific information in this stylesheet is the fact that the categories are encoded in an attribute @class and that the attribute occurs in elements that are two levels down from the root.

Add structure to correct a poorly designed document

The solution can be implemented explicitly in terms of set difference. This solution is elegant, but impractical for large documents with many categories. The trick used here for computing set difference is explained in Recipe 7.1:

```
<xsl:stylesheet version="1.0" xmlns:xsl="http://www.w3.org/1999/XSL/Transform">

  <xsl:import href="copy.xslt"/>

  <xsl:output method="xml" version="1.0" encoding="UTF-8" indent="yes"/>
  <xsl:strip-space elements="*"/>

  <xsl:template match="class">
    <!--All people following this class element -->
    <xsl:variable name="nodes1" select="following-sibling::person"/>
    <!--All people following the next class element -->
    <xsl:variable name="nodes2"
          select="following-sibling::class/following-sibling::person"/>
    <xsl:element name="{@name}">
      <xsl:copy-of select="$nodes1[count(. | $nodes2) != count($nodes2)]"/>
    </xsl:element>
  </xsl:template>

  <xsl:template match="person"/>

</xsl:stylesheet>
```

6.9   Reorganizing an XML Hierarchy

Problem

You need to reorganize the information in an XML document to make some implicit information explicit and some explicit information implicit.

Solution

Again, consider the *SalesBySalesPerson.xml* document from Chapter 4:

```
<salesBySalesperson>
  <salesperson name="John Adams" seniority="1">
    <product sku="10000" totalSales="10000.00"/>
    <product sku="20000" totalSales="50000.00"/>
    <product sku="25000" totalSales="920000.00"/>
  </salesperson>
  <salesperson name="Wendy Long" seniority="5">
    <product sku="10000" totalSales="990000.00"/>
    <product sku="20000" totalSales="150000.00"/>
    <product sku="30000" totalSales="5500.00"/>
  </salesperson>
```

```
      <salesperson name="Willie B. Aggressive" seniority="10">
        <product sku="10000" totalSales="1110000.00"/>
        <product sku="20000" totalSales="150000.00"/>
        <product sku="25000" totalSales="2920000.00"/>
        <product sku="30000" totalSales="115500.00"/>
        <product sku="70000" totalSales="10000.00"/>
      </salesperson>
      <salesperson name="Arty Outtolunch" seniority="10"/>
    </salesBySalesperson>
```

Which products were sold by which salesperson and how much income the salesperson created for each sold product is explicit. The total income generated by each product is implicit, as are the names of all salespeople who sold any given product.

Therefore, to reorganize this document, you would need to convert to a view that shows sales by product. The following stylesheet accomplishes this transformation:

```
<xsl:stylesheet version="1.0" xmlns:xsl="http://www.w3.org/1999/XSL/Transform">

<xsl:output method="xml" version="1.0" encoding="UTF-8" indent="yes"/>

<xsl:key name="sales_key" match="salesperson" use="product/@sku"/>

<xsl:variable name="products" select="//product"/>
<xsl:variable name="unique-products"
    select="$products[not(@sku = preceding::product/@sku)]"/>

<xsl:template match="/">
  <salesByProduct>
    <xsl:for-each select="$unique-products">
      <xsl:variable name="sku" select="@sku"/>
      <xsl:copy>
        <xsl:copy-of select="$sku"/>
        <xsl:attribute name="totalSales">
          <xsl:value-of select="sum($products[@sku=$sku]/@totalSales)"/>
        </xsl:attribute>
        <xsl:for-each select="key('sales_key',$sku)">
          <xsl:copy>
            <xsl:copy-of select="@*"/>
            <xsl:attribute name="sold">
              <xsl:value-of select="product[@sku=$sku]/@totalSales"/>
            </xsl:attribute>
          </xsl:copy>
        </xsl:for-each>
      </xsl:copy>
    </xsl:for-each>
  </salesByProduct>
</xsl:template>

</xsl:stylesheet>
```

The resulting output is shown here:

```
<salesByProduct>
    <product sku="10000" totalSales="2110000">
        <salesperson name="John Adams" seniority="1" sold="10000.00"/>
        <salesperson name="Wendy Long" seniority="5" sold="990000.00"/>
        <salesperson name="Willie B. Aggressive" seniority="10" sold="1110000.00"/>
    </product>
    <product sku="20000" totalSales="350000">
        <salesperson name="John Adams" seniority="1" sold="50000.00"/>
        <salesperson name="Wendy Long" seniority="5" sold="150000.00"/>
        <salesperson name="Willie B. Aggressive" seniority="10" sold="150000.00"/>
    </product>
    <product sku="25000" totalSales="3840000">
        <salesperson name="John Adams" seniority="1" sold="920000.00"/>
        <salesperson name="Willie B. Aggressive" seniority="10" sold="2920000.00"/>
    </product>
    <product sku="30000" totalSales="121000">
        <salesperson name="Wendy Long" seniority="5" sold="5500.00"/>
        <salesperson name="Willie B. Aggressive" seniority="10" sold="115500.00"/>
    </product>
    <product sku="70000" totalSales="10000">
        <salesperson name="Willie B. Aggressive" seniority="10" sold="10000.00"/>
    </product>
</salesByProduct>$
```

An alternative solution is based on the Muenchian Method named after Steve Muench. This method uses an xsl:key to facilitate the extraction of unique products. The expression $products[count(.|key('product_key', @sku)[1]) = 1] selects the first product in the particular group, where the grouping is by sku:

```
<xsl:stylesheet version="1.0" xmlns:xsl="http://www.w3.org/1999/XSL/Transform">

<xsl:output method="xml" version="1.0" encoding="UTF-8" indent="yes"/>

<xsl:variable name="doc" select="/"/>

<xsl:key name="product_key" match="product" use="@sku"/>
<xsl:key name="sales_key" match="salesperson" use="product/@sku"/>

<xsl:variable name="products" select="//product"/>

<xsl:template match="/">
  <salesByProduct>
    <xsl:for-each select="$products[count(.|key('product_key',@sku)[1])
                          = 1]">
      <xsl:variable name="sku" select="@sku"/>
      <xsl:copy>
        <xsl:copy-of select="$sku"/>
        <xsl:attribute name="totalSales">
          <xsl:value-of select="sum(key('product_key',$sku)/@totalSales)"/>
        </xsl:attribute>
```

```
        <xsl:for-each select="key('sales_key',$sku)">
          <xsl:copy>
            <xsl:copy-of select="@*"/>
            <xsl:attribute name="sold">
              <xsl:value-of select="product[@sku=$sku]/@totalSales"/>
            </xsl:attribute>
          </xsl:copy>
        </xsl:for-each>
      </xsl:copy>
    </xsl:for-each>
  </salesByProduct>
</xsl:template>

</xsl:stylesheet>
```

Discussion

The solution presents a very application-specific example. This scenario cannot be helped. Presenting a generic reorganizing stylesheet is difficult, if not impossible, because these types of reorganizations vary based on the nature of the particular transformed document.

However, some common idioms are likely to appear in these sorts of reorganizations.

First, since you reorganize the document tree completely, it is unlikely that a solution will rely primarily on matching and applying templates. These sorts of stylesheets are much more likely to use an iterative style. In other words, the solutions will probably rely heavily on xsl:for-each.

Second, recipes in this class almost always initialize global variables that contain elements extracted from deep within the XML structure. In addition, you will probably need to determine a unique subset of these elements. See Recipe 4.3 for a complete discussion of the techniques available for constructing unique sets of elements.

Third, reorganization often involves reaggregating data by using sums, products, or other more complex aggregations. Chapters 2 and 14 discuss advanced techniques for computing these aggregations.

CHAPTER 7

Querying XML

```
<xsl:template name="child-query">
<xsl:with-param name="parent" select=" 'Daddy' "/>
<xsl:value-of select="concat('But, why',$parent,'?')"/>
<xsl:apply-templates select="reasonable_response"/>
<xsl:call-template name="child-query">
<xsl:with-param name="parent" select="$parent"/>
</xsl:call-template>
</xsl:template>
```
—Parents not recognizing tail recursion
  may risk blowing their stack

This chapter covers recipes for using XSLT as an XML query language. Querying XML means extracting information from one or more XML documents to answer questions about facts and relationships occurring in and among these documents. By analogy, querying an XML document involves asking the same types of questions of XML using XSLT that one might ask of a relational database using SQL.

The "official" query language for XML promulgated by the W3C is not XSLT, but XQuery (*http://www.w3.org/TR/xquery/*). XSLT and XQuery have many similarities, but also some striking differences. For example, XSLT and XQuery both rely on XPath. However, an XSLT script is always in XML syntax, while an XQuery script has both a human-friendly and XML syntax (*http://www.w3.org/TR/xqueryx*).

When the idea for an XML query language distinct from XSLT was proposed, it was controversial. Many members of the XML community thought there would be too much overlap between the two. Indeed, any query formulated in XQuery could also be implemented in XSLT. In many cases, the XSLT solution is as concise as the XQuery solution. The advantage of XQuery is that it is generally easier to understand than the equivalent XSLT. Indeed, XQuery should present a much smaller learning curve to those already versed in SQL. Obviously, comprehension is also a function of what you are used to, so these comparisons are not absolute.

Explaining XQuery in detail or providing a detailed comparison between it and XSLT is beyond the scope of this chapter. Instead, this chapter provides query examples for those who have already invested time into XSLT and do not wish to learn yet another XML-related language.

It would be impossible to create examples that exhausted all types of queries you might want to run on XML data. Instead, this chapter takes a two-pronged approach. First, it presents primitive and generally applicable query examples. These examples are building blocks that can be adapted to solve more complex query problems. Second, it presents a recipe that shows solutions to most XML query-use cases presented in the W3C document *XML Query Use Cases* (*http://www.w3.org/TR/xmlquery-use-cases*). In many cases, you can find a solution to a use-case instance that is similar enough to the particular query problem you face. It then becomes a simple matter of adapting the solution to the particulars of your XML data.

7.1 Performing Set Operations on Node Sets

Problem

You need to find the union, intersection, set difference, or symmetrical set difference between two node sets. You may also need to test equality and subset relationships between two node sets.

Solution

The union is trivial because XPath supports it directly:

```
<xsl:copy-of select="$node-set1 | $node-set2"/>
```

The intersection of two node sets requires a more convoluted expression:

```
<xsl:copy-of select="$node-set1[count(. | $node-set2) = count($node-set2)]"/>
```

This means all elements in node-set1 that are also in node-set2 by virtue of the fact that forming the union with node-set2 and some specified element in node-set1 leaves the same set of elements.

Set difference (those elements that are in the first set but not the second) follows:

```
<xsl:copy-of select="$node-set1[count(. | $node-set2) != count($node-set2)]"/>
```

This means all elements in node-set1 that are not also in node-set2 by virtue of the fact that forming the union with node-set2 and some specified element in node-set1 produces a set with more elements.

An example of symmetrical set difference (the elements are in one set but not the other) follows:

```
<xsl:copy-of select="$node-set1[count(. | $node-set2) != count($node-set2)] |
    $node-set2[count(. | $node-set1) != count($node-set1)] "/>
```

The symmetrical set difference is simply the union of the differences taken both ways.

To test if node-set1 is equal to node-set2:

```
<xsl:if test="count($ns1|$ns2) = count($ns1) and
              count($ns1) = count($ns2)">
```

Two sets are equal if their union produces a set with the same number of elements as are contained in both sets individually.

To test if node-set1 is a subset of node-set2:

```
<xsl:if test="count($node-set1|$node-set2) = count($node-set1)">
```

To test if node-set1 is a proper subset of node-set2:

```
<xsl:if test="count($ns1|$ns2) = count($ns1) and count($ns1) > count(ns2)">
```

Discussion

You may wonder what set operations have to do with XML queries. Set operations are ways of finding commonalities and differences between sets of elements extracted from a document. Many basic questions one can ask of data have to do with common and distinguishing traits.

For example, imagine extracting person elements from *people.xml* as follows:

```
<xsl:variable name="males" select="//person[@sex='m']"/>
<xsl:variable name="females" select="//person[@sex='f']"/>
<xsl:variable name="smokers" select="//person[@smoker='yes']"/>
<xsl:variable name="non-smokers" select="//person[@smoker='no']"/>
```

Now if you were issuing life insurance, you might consider charging each of the following sets of people different rates:

```
<!-- Male smokers -->
<xsl:variable name="super-risk"
    select="$males[count(. | $smokers) = count($smokers)]"/>
<!-- Female smokers -->
<xsl:variable name="high-risk"
    select="$females[count(. | $smokers) = count($smokers)]"/>
<!-- Male non-smokers -->
<xsl:variable name="moderate-risk"
    select="$males[count(. | $non-smokers) = count($non-smokers)]"/>
<!-- Female non-smokers -->
<xsl:variable name="low-risk"
    select="$females[count(. | $non-smokers) = count($non-smokers)]"/>
```

You probably noticed that the same answers could have been acquired more directly by using logic rather than set theory:

```
<!-- Male smokers -->
<xsl:variable name="super-risk"
    select="//person[@sex='m' and @smoker='y']"/>
<!-- Female smokers -->
```

```
<xsl:variable name="high-risk"
    select="//person[@sex='f' and @smoker='y']"/>
<!-- Male non-smokers -->
<xsl:variable name="moderate-risk"
    select="//person[@sex='m' and @smoker='n']"/>
<!-- Female non-smokers -->
<xsl:variable name="low-risk"
    select="//person[@sex='f' and @smoker='n']"/>
```

Better still, if you already had the set of males and females extracted, it would be more efficient to say:

```
<!-- Male smokers -->
<xsl:variable name="super-risk"
    select="$males[@smoker='y']"/>
<!-- Female smokers -->
<xsl:variable name="high-risk"
    select="$females[@smoker='y']"/>
<!-- Male non-smokers -->
<xsl:variable name="moderate-risk"
    select="$males[@smoker='n']"/>
<!-- Female non-smokers -->
<xsl:variable name="low-risk"
    select="$females[@smoker='n']"/>
```

These observations do not invalidate the utility of the set approach. Notice that the set operations work without knowledge of what the sets themselves contain. Set operations work at a higher level of abstraction. Imagine that you have a complex XML document and are interested in the following four sets:

```
<!-- All elements that have elements c1 or c2  as children-->
<xsl:variable name="set1" select="//*[c1 or c2]"/>
<!-- All elements that have elements c3 and c4  as children-->
<xsl:variable name="set2" select="//*[c3 and c4]"/>
<!-- All elements whose parent has attribute a1-->
<xsl:variable name="set3" select="//*[../@a1]"/>
<!-- All elements whose parent has attribute a2-->
<xsl:variable name="set4" select="//*[../@a2]"/>
```

In the original example, it was obvious that the sets of males and females (and smokers and nonsmokers) are disjoint. Here you have no such knowledge. The sets may be completely disjointed, completely overlap, or share only some elements. There are only two ways to find out what is in common between, say, set1 and set3. The first is to take their intersection; the second is to traverse the entire document again using the logical and of their predicates. In this case, the intersection is clearly the way to go.

EXSLT defines a set module that includes functions performing the set operations discussed here. The EXSLT uses an interesting technique to return the result of its set operations. Instead of returning the result directly, it applies templates to the result in a mode particular to the type of set operation. For example, after EXSLT set:intersection computes the intersection, it invokes <xsl:apply-templates

mode="set:intersection"/> on the result. A default template exists in EXSLT with this mode, and it will return a copy of the result as a node-tree fragment. This indirect means of returning the result allows users importing the EXSLT set module to override the default to process it further. This technique is useful but limited. It is useful because it potentially eliminates the need to use the node-set extension function to convert the result back into a node set. It is limited because there can be at most one such overriding template per matching pattern in the user stylesheet for each operation. However, you may want to do very different post-processing tasks with the result of intersections invoked from different places in the same stylesheet.

 Do not be alarmed if you do not grasp the subtleties of EXSLT's technique discussed here. Chapter 14 will discuss in more detail these and other techniques for making XSLT code reusable.

See Also

You can find an explanation of the EXSLT set operations at *http://www.exslt.org/set/index.html*.

7.2 Performing Set Operations on Node Sets Using Value Semantics

Problem

You need to find the union, intersection, set difference, or symmetrical set difference between elements in two node sets; however, in your problem, *equality* is not defined as *node-set identity*. In other words, *equality* is a function of a node's value.

Solution

The need for this solution may arise when working with multiple documents. Consider two documents with the same DTD but content that may not contain duplicate element values. XSLT elements coming from distinct documents are distinct even if they contain elements with the same namespace, attribute, and text values. See Examples 7-1 to 7-4.

Example 7-1. people1.xslt

```
<people>
  <person name="Brad York" age="38" sex="m" smoker="yes"/>
  <person name="Charles Xavier" age="32" sex="m" smoker="no"/>
  <person name="David Willimas" age="33" sex="m" smoker="no"/>
</people>
```

Example 7-2. people2.xslt

```
<people>
  <person name="Al Zehtooney" age="33" sex="m" smoker="no"/>
  <person name="Brad York" age="38" sex="m" smoker="yes"/>
  <person name="Charles Xavier" age="32" sex="m" smoker="no"/>
</people>
```

Example 7-3. Failed attempt to use XSLT union to select unique people

```
<xsl:template match="/">
  <people>
    <xsl:copy-of select="//person | document('people2.xml')//person"/>
  </people>
</xsl:template>
```

Example 7-4. Output when run with people1.xml as input

```
<people>
  <person name="Brad York" age="38" sex="m" smoker="yes"/>
  <person name="Charles Xavier" age="32" sex="m" smoker="no"/>
  <person name="David Willimas" age="33" sex="m" smoker="no"/>
  <person name="Al Zehtooney" age="33" sex="m" smoker="no"/>
  <person name="Brad York" age="38" sex="m" smoker="yes"/>
  <person name="Charles Xavier" age="32" sex="m" smoker="no"/>
</people>
```

Relying on node identity can also break down in single document cases when you want equality of nodes to be a function of their text or attribute values.

The following stylesheet provides a reusable implementation of union, intersection, and set difference based on value semantics. The idea is that a stylesheet importing this one will override the template whose mode=" vset:element-equality". This allows the importing stylesheet to define whatever equality semantics make sense for the given input:

```
<xsl:stylesheet version="1.0" xmlns:xsl="http://www.w3.org/1999/XSL/Transform"
  xmlns:vset="http://www.ora.com/XSLTCookbook/namespaces/vset">

<xsl:output method="xml" version="1.0" encoding="UTF-8" indent="yes"/>

<!-- The default implementation of element equality. Override in the importing
stylesheet as neccessary. -->
<xsl:template match="node() | @*" mode="vset:element-equality">
  <xsl:param name="other"/>
  <xsl:if test=". = $other">
    <xsl:value-of select="true()"/>
  </xsl:if>
</xsl:template>

<!-- The default set membership test uses element equality. You will rarely need to
override this in the importing stylesheet. -->
<xsl:template match="node() | @*" mode="vset:member-of">
  <xsl:param name="elem"/>
```

```
    <xsl:variable name="member-of">
      <xsl:for-each select=".">
        <xsl:apply-templates select="." mode="vset:element-equality">
          <xsl:with-param name="other" select="$elem"/>
        </xsl:apply-templates>
      </xsl:for-each>
    </xsl:variable>
    <xsl:value-of select="string($member-of)"/>
</xsl:template>


<!-- Compute the union of two sets using "by value" equality. -->
<xsl:template name="vset:union">
  <xsl:param name="nodes1" select="/.." />
  <xsl:param name="nodes2" select="/.." />
  <!-- for internal use -->
  <xsl:param name="nodes" select="$nodes1 | $nodes2" />
  <xsl:param name="union" select="/.." />
  <xsl:choose>
    <xsl:when test="$nodes">
      <xsl:variable name="test">
        <xsl:apply-templates select="$union" mode="vset:member-of">
          <xsl:with-param name="elem" select="$nodes[1]" />
        </xsl:apply-templates>
      </xsl:variable>
      <xsl:call-template name="vset:union">
        <xsl:with-param name="nodes" select="$nodes[position( ) > 1]" />
        <xsl:with-param name="union"
                        select="$union | $nodes[1][not(string($test))]" />
      </xsl:call-template>
    </xsl:when>
    <xsl:otherwise>
      <xsl:apply-templates select="$union" mode="vset:union" />
    </xsl:otherwise>
  </xsl:choose>
</xsl:template>


<!-- Return a copy of union by default. Override in importing stylesheet  to recieve
reults as a "callback"-->
<xsl:template match="/ | node( ) | @*" mode="vset:union">
  <xsl:copy-of select="."/>
</xsl:template>


<!-- Compute the intersection of two sets using "by value" equality. -->
<xsl:template name="vset:intersection">
  <xsl:param name="nodes1" select="/.."/>
  <xsl:param name="nodes2" select="/.."/>
  <!-- For internal use -->
  <xsl:param name="intersect" select="/.."/>

  <xsl:choose>
    <xsl:when test="not($nodes1)">
      <xsl:apply-templates select="$intersect" mode="vset:intersection"/>
    </xsl:when>
    <xsl:when test="not($nodes2)">
```

```
          <xsl:apply-templates select="$intersect" mode="vset:intersection"/>
      </xsl:when>
      <xsl:otherwise>
        <xsl:variable name="test1">
          <xsl:apply-templates select="$nodes2" mode="vset:member-of">
            <xsl:with-param name="elem" select="$nodes1[1]"/>
          </xsl:apply-templates>
        </xsl:variable>
        <xsl:variable name="test2">
          <xsl:apply-templates select="$intersect" mode="vset:member-of">
            <xsl:with-param name="elem" select="$nodes1[1]"/>
          </xsl:apply-templates>
        </xsl:variable>
        <xsl:choose>
          <xsl:when test="string($test1) and not(string($test2))">
            <xsl:call-template name="vset:intersection">
              <xsl:with-param name="nodes1"
                      select="$nodes1[position() > 1]"/>
              <xsl:with-param name="nodes2" select="$nodes2"/>
              <xsl:with-param name="intersect"
                      select="$intersect | $nodes1[1]"/>
            </xsl:call-template>
          </xsl:when>
          <xsl:otherwise>
            <xsl:call-template name="vset:intersection">
              <xsl:with-param name="nodes1"
                      select="$nodes1[position() > 1]"/>
              <xsl:with-param name="nodes2" select="$nodes2"/>
              <xsl:with-param name="intersect" select="$intersect"/>
            </xsl:call-template>
          </xsl:otherwise>
        </xsl:choose>
      </xsl:otherwise>
    </xsl:choose>
</xsl:template>

<!-- Return a copy of intersection by default. Override in importing stylesheet to
recieve results as a "callback"-->
<xsl:template match="/ | node() | @*" mode="vset:intersection">
  <xsl:copy-of select="."/>
</xsl:template>

<!-- Compute the differnce between two sets (node1 - nodes2) using "by value"
equality. -->
<xsl:template name="vset:difference">
  <xsl:param name="nodes1" select="/.."/>
  <xsl:param name="nodes2" select="/.."/>
  <!-- For internal use -->
  <xsl:param name="difference" select="/.."/>

  <xsl:choose>
    <xsl:when test="not($nodes1)">
      <xsl:apply-templates select="$difference" mode="vset:difference"/>
    </xsl:when>
```

```
<xsl:when test="not($nodes2)">
  <xsl:apply-templates select="$nodes1" mode="vset:difference"/>
</xsl:when>
<xsl:otherwise>
  <xsl:variable name="test1">
    <xsl:apply-templates select="$nodes2" mode="vset:member-of">
      <xsl:with-param name="elem" select="$nodes1[1]"/>
    </xsl:apply-templates>
  </xsl:variable>
  <xsl:variable name="test2">
    <xsl:apply-templates select="$difference" mode="vset:member-of">
      <xsl:with-param name="elem" select="$nodes1[1]"/>
    </xsl:apply-templates>
  </xsl:variable>
  <xsl:choose>
    <xsl:when test="string($test1) or string($test2)">
      <xsl:call-template name="vset:difference">
        <xsl:with-param name="nodes1"
                select="$nodes1[position( ) > 1]"/>
        <xsl:with-param name="nodes2" select="$nodes2"/>
        <xsl:with-param name="difference" select="$difference"/>
      </xsl:call-template>
    </xsl:when>
    <xsl:otherwise>
      <xsl:call-template name="vset:difference">
        <xsl:with-param name="nodes1"
                select="$nodes1[position( ) > 1]"/>
        <xsl:with-param name="nodes2" select="$nodes2"/>
        <xsl:with-param name="difference"
                select="$difference | $nodes1[1]"/>
      </xsl:call-template>
    </xsl:otherwise>
  </xsl:choose>
</xsl:otherwise>
</xsl:choose>
</xsl:template>

<!-- Return a copy of difference by default. Override in importing stylesheet to
recieve results as a "callback"-->
<xsl:template match="/ | node( ) | @*" mode="vset:difference">
  <xsl:copy-of select="."/>
</xsl:template>
```

These recursive templates are implemented in terms of the following definitions:

Union(nodes1,nodes2)

> The union includes everything in nodes2 plus everything in nodes1 not already a member of nodes2.

Intersection(nodes1,nodes2)

> The intersection includes everything in nodes1 that is also a member of nodes2.

Difference(nodes1,nodes2)

> The difference includes everything in nodes1 that is not also a member of nodes2.

In all cases, membership defaults to equality of string values, but the importing stylesheet can override this default.

Given these value-oriented set operations, you can achieve the desired effect on *people1.xml* and *people2.xml* using the following stylesheet:

```
<xsl:stylesheet version="1.0" xmlns:xsl="http://www.w3.org/1999/XSL/Transform"
 xmlns:vset="http://www.ora.com/XSLTCookbook/namespaces/vset">

<xsl:import href="set.ops.xslt"/>

<xsl:output method="xml" version="1.0" encoding="UTF-8" indent="yes"/>

<xsl:template match="/">
  <people>
    <xsl:call-template name="vset:union">
      <xsl:with-param name="nodes1" select="//person"/>
      <xsl:with-param name="nodes2" select="document('people2.xml')//person"/>
    </xsl:call-template>
  </people>
</xsl:template>

<!--Define person equality as having the same name -->
<xsl:template match="person" mode="vset:element-equality">
  <xsl:param name="other"/>
  <xsl:if test="@name = $other/@name">
    <xsl:value-of select="true( )"/>
  </xsl:if>
</xsl:template>

</xsl:stylesheet>
```

Discussion

You might think that equality is a cut-and-dried issue; two things are either equal or they're not. However, in programming (as in politics), equality is in the eye of the beholder. In a typical document, an element is associated with a uniquely identifiable object. For example, a paragraph element, `<p>...</p>`, is distinct from another paragraph element somewhere else in the document, even if they have the same content. Hence, set operations based on the unique identity of elements are the norm. However, when considering XSLT operations crossing multiple documents or acting on elements that result from applying `xsl:copy`, we need to carefully consider what we want equality to be.

Here are some query examples in which value set semantics are required:

1. You have two documents from different namespaces. Examples 7-5 to 7-8 help you find all the element (local) names these documents have in common and those that are unique to each namespace.

Example 7-5. doc1.xml

```
<doc xmlns:doc1="doc1" xmlns="doc1">
  <chapter number="1">
    <section number="1">
      <p>
        Once upon a time...
      </p>
    </section>
  </chapter>
  <chapter number="2">
    <note to="editor">I am still waiting for my $100000 advance.</note>
    <section number="1">
      <p>
        ... and they lived happily ever after.
      </p>
    </section>
  </chapter>
</doc>
```

Example 7-6. doc2.xml

```
<doc xmlns:doc1="doc2" xmlns="doc2">
  <chapter number="1">
    <section number="1">
      <sub>
        <p>
          Once upon a time...
          <ref type="footnote" number="1"/>
        </p>
      </sub>
      <fig>Figure1</fig>
    </section>
    <footnote number="1">
      Hey diddle diddle.
    </footnote>
  </chapter>
  <chapter number="2">
    <section number="1">
      <p>
        ... and they lived happily ever after.
      </p>
    </section>
  </chapter>
</doc>
```

Example 7-7. unique-element-names.xslt

```
<xsl:stylesheet version="1.0" xmlns:xsl="http://www.w3.org/1999/XSL/Transform"
  xmlns:doc1="doc1" xmlns:doc2="doc2"
  xmlns:vset="http:/www.ora.com/XSLTCookbook/namespaces/vset"
  extension-element-prefixes="vset">

  <xsl:import href="set.ops.xslt"/>
```

Example 7-7. unique-element-names.xslt (continued)

```
<xsl:output method="text" />

<xsl:template match="/">
  <xsl:text>&#xa;The elements in common are: </xsl:text>
  <xsl:call-template name="vset:intersection">
    <xsl:with-param name="nodes1" select="//*"/>
    <xsl:with-param name="nodes2" select="document('doc2.xml')//*"/>
  </xsl:call-template>

  <xsl:text>&#xa;The elements only in doc1 are: </xsl:text>
  <xsl:call-template name="vset:difference">
    <xsl:with-param name="nodes1" select="//*"/>
    <xsl:with-param name="nodes2" select="document('doc2.xml')//*"/>
  </xsl:call-template>

  <xsl:text>&#xa;The elements only in doc2 are: </xsl:text>
  <xsl:call-template name="vset:difference">
    <xsl:with-param name="nodes1" select="document('doc2.xml')//*"/>
    <xsl:with-param name="nodes2" select="//*"/>
  </xsl:call-template>
  <xsl:text>&#xa;</xsl:text>

</xsl:template>

<xsl:template match="*" mode="vset:intersection">
  <xsl:value-of select="local-name(.)"/>
  <xsl:if test="position() != last()">
    <xsl:text>, </xsl:text>
  </xsl:if>
</xsl:template>

<xsl:template match="*" mode="vset:difference">
  <xsl:value-of select="local-name(.)"/>
  <xsl:if test="position() != last()">
    <xsl:text>, </xsl:text>
  </xsl:if>
</xsl:template>

<xsl:template match="doc1:* | doc2:*" mode="vset:element-equality">
 <xsl:param name="other"/>
  <xsl:if test="local-name(.) = local-name($other)">
    <xsl:value-of select="true()"/>
  </xsl:if>
</xsl:template>

</xsl:stylesheet>
```

Example 7-8. Output

```
The elements in common are: doc, chapter, section, p
The elements only in doc1 are: note
The elements only in doc2 are: sub, ref, fig, footnote
```

2. A Visio XML document consists of master shapes, master-shape instances, and user-defined shapes with no corresponding master. You would like to extract the data for all unique shapes. For purpose of this query, two shapes are equal if either of the following are true:

a. They both have master attributes, @Master, and these attribute values are equal.

b. At least one lacks a master attribute, but their geometry elements, Geom, are equal. Geometry elements are equal if all attributes of all descendants of Geom are equal.

Otherwise, they are not equal.

This query can be implemented by taking the intersection of the set all shapes with itself under the rules of equality stated earlier.* You can also use the vset:union template with the nodes parameter:

```
<xsl:stylesheet version="1.0" xmlns:xsl="http://www.w3.org/1999/XSL/Transform"
  xmlns:vxd="urn:schemas-microsoft-com:office:visio"
  xmlns:vset="http:/www.ora.com/XSLTCookbook/namespaces/vset"
  extension-element-prefixes="vset">

<xsl:import href="set.ops.xslt"/>

<xsl:output method="xml" version="1.0" encoding="UTF-8" indent="yes"/>

<xsl:template match="/">
<UniqueShapes>
    <xsl:call-template name="vset:intersection">
      <xsl:with-param name="nodes1" select="//vxd:Pages/*/*/vxd:Shape"/>
      <xsl:with-param name="nodes2" select="//vxd:Pages/*/*/vxd:Shape"/>
    </xsl:call-template>
  </UniqueShapes>
</xsl:template>

<xsl:template match="vxd:Shape" mode="vset:intersection">
  <xsl:copy-of select="." />
</xsl:template>

<xsl:template match="vxd:Shape" mode="vset:element-equality">
  <xsl:param name="other"/>
  <xsl:choose>
    <xsl:when test="@Master and $other/@Master and @Master = $other/@Master">
      <xsl:value-of select="true()"/>
    </xsl:when>
    <xsl:when test="not(@Master) or not($other/@Master)">
      <xsl:variable name="geom1">
```

---

* A mathematician will tell you that the intersection of a set with itself will always yield the same set. This is true for proper sets (with no duplicates). However, here you are using an application-specific notion of equality, and the node sets typically will not be proper sets under that equality test. However, the value-set operations always produce proper sets, so this technique is a way of removing duplicates.

```
          <xsl:for-each select="vxd:Geom//*/@*">
            <xsl:sort select="name( )"/>
            <xsl:value-of select="."/>
          </xsl:for-each>
        </xsl:variable>
        <xsl:variable name="geom2">
          <xsl:for-each select="$other/vxd:Geom//*/@*">
            <xsl:sort select="name( )"/>
            <xsl:value-of select="."/>
          </xsl:for-each>
        </xsl:variable>
        <xsl:if test="$geom1 = $geom2">
          <xsl:value-of select="true( )"/>
        </xsl:if>
      </xsl:when>
    </xsl:choose>
  </xsl:template>


</xsl:stylesheet>
```

7.3   Determining Set Equality by Value

Problem

You need to determine if the nodes in one node set are equal (by value) to the nodes in another node set (ignoring order).

Solution

This problem is slightly more subtle than it appears on the surface. Consider an obvious solution that works in many cases:

```
<xsl:template name="vset:equal-text-values">
  <xsl:param name="nodes1" select="/.."/>
  <xsl:param name="nodes2" select="/.."/>
  <xsl:choose>
   <!--Empty node-sets have equal values -->
    <xsl:when test="not($nodes1) and not($nodes2)">
      <xsl:value-of select="true( )"/>
      </xsl:when>
    <!--Node sets of unequal sizes can not have equal values -->
    <xsl:when test="count($nodes1) != count($nodes2)"/>
    <!--If an element of nodes1 is present in nodes2 then the node sets
      have equal values if the node sets without the common element have equal
      values -->
    <xsl:when test="$nodes1[1] = $nodes2">
      <xsl:call-template name="vset:equal-text-values">
          <xsl:with-param name="nodes1" select="$nodes1[position( )>1]"/>
          <xsl:with-param name="nodes2"
                          select="$nodes2[not(. = $nodes1[1])]"/>
```

```
        </xsl:call-template>
      </xsl:when>
      <xsl:otherwise/>
    </xsl:choose>
  </xsl:template>
```

We have chosen a name for this equality test to emphasize the context in which it should be applied. That is when value equality indicate string-value equality. Clearly, this template will not give the correct result if equality is based on attributes or criteria that are more complex. However, this template has a more subtle problem. It tacitly assumes that the compared node sets are proper sets (i.e., they contain no duplicates) under string-value equality. In some circumstances, this may not be the case. Consider the following XML that represents the individuals who borrowed books from a library:

```
<?xml version="1.0" encoding="UTF-8"?>
<library>
  <book>
    <name>High performance Java programming.</name>
    <borrowers>
      <borrower>James Straub</borower>
    </borrowers>
  </book>
  <book>
    <name>Exceptional C++</name>
    <borrowers>
      <borrower>Steven Levitt</borower>
    </borrowers>
  </book>
  <book>
    <name>Design Patterns</name>
    <borrowers>
      <borrower>Steven Levitt</borower>
      <borrower>James Straub</borower>
      <borrower>Steven Levitt</borower>
    </borrowers>
  </book>
  <book>
    <name>The C++ Programming Language</name>
    <borrowers>
      <borrower>James Straub</borower>
      <borrower>James Straub</borower>
      <borrower>Steven Levitt</borower>
    </borrowers>
  </book>
</library>
```

If an individual's name appears more than once, it simply means he borrowed the book more than once. Now, if you wrote a query to determine all books borrowed by the same people, most would agree that *Design Patterns* and *The C++ Programming Language* qualify as two such books. However, if you used vset:equal-text-values in the implementation of that query, you would not get this result because it assumes that sets do not contain duplicates. You can alter vset:equal-text-values to tolerate duplicates with the following changes:

```
<xsl:template name="vset:equal-text-values-ignore-dups">
  <xsl:param name="nodes1" select="/.."/>
  <xsl:param name="nodes2" select="/.."/>
  <xsl:choose>
   <!--Empty node-sets have equal values -->
    <xsl:when test="not($nodes1) and not($nodes2)">
      <xsl:value-of select="true( )"/>
      </xsl:when>
    <!--If an element of nodes1 is present in nodes2 then the node sets
     have equal values if the node sets without the common element have equal
     values -->
    <!--delete this line
          <xsl:when test="count($nodes1) != count($nodes2)"/> -->
    <xsl:when test="$nodes1[1] = $nodes2">
      <xsl:call-template name="vset:equal-text-values">
        <xsl:with-param name="nodes1"
                          select="$nodes1[not(. = $nodes1[1])]"/>
        <xsl:with-param name="nodes2"
              select="$nodes2[not(. = $nodes1[1])]"/>      </xsl:call-template>
    </xsl:when>
    <xsl:otherwise/>
  </xsl:choose>
</xsl:template>
```

Notice that we have commented out the test for unequal sizes because that test is not valid in the presence of duplicates. For example, one set might have three occurrences of an element with string value foo, while the other has a single element foo. These sets should be equal when duplicates are ignored. You also must do more than remove just the first element on the recursive step; you should remove all elements with the same value as the first element, just as you do for the second set. This will ensure that duplicates are fully accounted for on each recursive pass. These changes make all equality tests based on text value come out correct, but at the cost of doing additional work on sets that are obviously unequal.

These equality tests are not as general as the value-set operations produced in Recipe 7.2 because they presume that the only notion of equality you care about is text-value equality. You can generalize them by reusing the same technique you used for testing membership based on a test of element equality that can be overridden by an importing stylesheet:

```
<xsl:template name="vset:equal">
  <xsl:param name="nodes1" select="/.."/>
  <xsl:param name="nodes2" select="/.."/>
  <xsl:if test="count($nodes1) = count($nodes2)">
    <xsl:call-template name="vset:equal-impl">
      <xsl:with-param name="nodes1" select="$nodes1"/>
      <xsl:with-param name="nodes2" select="$nodes2"/>
    </xsl:call-template>
  </xsl:if>
</xsl:template>
```

```
<!-- Once we know the sets have the same number of elements -->
<!-- we only need to test that every member of the first set is -->
<!-- a member of the second -->
<xsl:template name="vset:equal-impl">
  <xsl:param name="nodes1" select="/.."/>
  <xsl:param name="nodes2" select="/.."/>
  <xsl:choose>
    <xsl:when test="not($nodes1)">
      <xsl:value-of select="true( )"/>
    </xsl:when>
    <xsl:otherwise>
      <xsl:variable name="test">
        <xsl:apply-templates select="$nodes2" mode="vset:member-of">
          <xsl:with-param name="elem" select="$nodes1[1]"/>
        </xsl:apply-templates>
      </xsl:variable>
      <xsl:if test="string($test)">
        <xsl:call-template name="vset:equal-impl">
          <xsl:with-param name="nodes1" select="$nodes1[position( ) > 1]"/>
          <xsl:with-param name="nodes2" select="$nodes2"/>
        </xsl:call-template>
      </xsl:if>
    </xsl:otherwise>
  </xsl:choose>
</xsl:template>
```

If you want generalized equality that works in the presence of duplicates, then you must apply a more brute-force approach that makes two passes over the sets:

```
<xsl:template name="vset:equal-ignore-dups">
  <xsl:param name="nodes1" select="/.."/>
  <xsl:param name="nodes2" select="/.."/>

  <xsl:variable name="mismatch1">
    <xsl:for-each select="$nodes1">
      <xsl:variable name="test-elem">
        <xsl:apply-templates select="$nodes2" mode="vset:member-of">
          <xsl:with-param name="elem" select="."/>
        </xsl:apply-templates>
      </xsl:variable>
      <xsl:if test="not(string($test-elem))">
        <xsl:value-of select=" 'false' "/>
      </xsl:if>
    </xsl:for-each>
  </xsl:variable>
  <xsl:if test="not($mismatch1)">
    <xsl:variable name="mismatch2">
      <xsl:for-each select="$nodes2">
        <xsl:variable name="test-elem">
          <xsl:apply-templates select="$nodes1" mode="vset:member-of">
            <xsl:with-param name="elem" select="."/>
          </xsl:apply-templates>
        </xsl:variable>
      </xsl:for-each>
    </xsl:variable>
```

```
      <xsl:if test="not(string($test-elem))">
        <xsl:value-of select=" 'false' "/>
      </xsl:if>
    </xsl:for-each>
  </xsl:variable>
  <xsl:if test="not($mismatch2)">
    <xsl:value-of select="true( )"/>
  </xsl:if>
    </xsl:if>
  </xsl:template>
```

This template works by iterating over the first set and looking for elements that are not a member of the second. If no such element is found, the variable $mismatch1 will be null. In that case, it must repeat the test in the other direction by iterating over the second set.

Discussion

The need to test set equality comes up often in queries. Consider the following tasks:

- Find all books having the same authors.
- Find all suppliers who stock the same set of parts.
- Find all families with same-age children.

Whenever you encounter a one-to-many relationship and you are interested in elements that have the same set of associated elements, the need to test set equality will arise.

7.4   Performing Structure-Preserving Queries

Problem

You need to query an XML document so that the response has a structure that is identical to the original.

Solution

Structure-preserving queries filter out irrelevant information while preserving most of the document structure. The degree by which the output structure resembles the structure of the input is the metric that determines the applicability of this example. The more similar it is, the more this example applies.

The example has two components—one reusable and the other custom. The reusable component is a stylesheet that copies all nodes to the output (identity transform). We used this stylesheet, shown in Example 7-9, extensively in Chapter 6.

Example 7-9. copy.xslt

```
<xsl:stylesheet version="1.0" xmlns:xsl="http://www.w3.org/1999/XSL/Transform">

<xsl:template match="/ | node( ) | @*">
  <xsl:copy>
    <xsl:apply-templates select="@*"/>
    <xsl:apply-templates/>
  </xsl:copy>
</xsl:template>

</xsl:stylesheet>
```

The custom component is a stylesheet that imports *copy.xslt* and creates rules to override its default behavior. For example, the following stylesheet results in output identical to *people.xml*, but with only female smokers:

```
<?xml version="1.0" encoding="UTF-8"?>
<xsl:stylesheet version="1.0" xmlns:xsl="http://www.w3.org/1999/XSL/Transform">

    <xsl:import href="copy.xslt"/>

    <!-- Collapse space left by removing person elements -->
    <xsl:strip-space elements="people"/>

    <xsl:output method="xml" version="1.0" encoding="UTF-8" indent="yes"/>

    <xsl:template match="person[@sex = 'f' and @smoker='yes']">
      <!-- Apply default behavior, which is to copy -->
      <xsl:apply-imports/>
    </xsl:template>

    <!-- Ignore other people -->
    <xsl:template match="person"/>

</xsl:stylesheet>
```

Alternatively, a single template can match the things that you want to exclude and do nothing with them:

```
<xsl:template match="person[@sex != 'f' or @smoker != 'yes']" />
```

Discussion

This example is extremely useful because it lets you preserve the structure of an XML document without necessarily knowing what its structure is. You only need to know what elements should be filtered out and that you create templates that do so.

This example is applicable in contexts that most people would not describe as queries. For example, suppose you wanted to clone an XML document, but remove all attributes named sex and replace them with an attribute called gender:

```xsl
<xsl:stylesheet version="1.0" xmlns:xsl="http://www.w3.org/1999/XSL/Transform">

    <xsl:import href="copy.xslt"/>

    <xsl:output method="xml" version="1.0" encoding="UTF-8" indent="yes"/>

    <xsl:template match="@sex">
      <xsl:attribute name="gender">
         <xsl:value-of select="."/>
      </xsl:attribute>
    </xsl:template>

</xsl:stylesheet>
```

The beauty of this example is that it works on any XML document, regardless of its schema. If the document has elements with an attribute named sex, they will become gender:

Can you guess what the following variation does?*

```xsl
<xsl:stylesheet version="1.0" xmlns:xsl="http://www.w3.org/1999/XSL/Transform">

    <xsl:import href="copy.xslt"/>

    <xsl:output method="xml" version="1.0" encoding="UTF-8" indent="yes"/>

    <xsl:template match="@sex">
      <xsl:attribute name="gender">
         <xsl:value-of select="."/>
      </xsl:attribute>
    <xsl:apply-imports/>
    </xsl:template>

</xsl:stylesheet>
```

7.5   Joins

Problem

You want to relate elements in a document to other elements in the same or different document.

Solution

A *join* is the process of considering all pairs of element as being related (i.e., a Cartesian product) and keeping only those pairs that meet the join relationship (usually equality).

---

* It outputs both gender and sex attributes, but you knew that already!

To demonstrate, I have adapted the supplier parts database found in Date's *An Intro-duction to Database Systems* (Addison Wesley, 1986) to XML:

```
<database>
  <suppliers>
    <supplier id="S1" name="Smith" status="20" city="London"/>
    <supplier id="S2" name="Jones" status="10" city="Paris"/>
    <supplier id="S3" name="Blake" status="30" city="Paris"/>
    <supplier id="S4" name="Clark" status="20" city="London"/>
    <supplier id="S5" name="Adams" status="30" city="Athens"/>
  </suppliers>
  <parts>
    <part id="P1" name="Nut" color="Red" weight="12" city="London"/>
    <part id="P2" name="Bult" color="Green" weight="17" city="Paris"/>
    <part id="P3" name="Screw" color="Blue" weight="17" city="Rome"/>
    <part id="P4" name="Screw" color="Red" weight="14" city="London"/>
    <part id="P5" name="Cam" color="Blue" weight="12" city="Paris"/>
    <part id="P6" name="Cog" color="Red" weight="19" city="London"/>
  </parts>
  <inventory>
    <invrec sid="S1" pid="P1" qty="300"/>
    <invrec sid="S1" pid="P2" qty="200"/>
    <invrec sid="S1" pid="P3" qty="400"/>
    <invrec sid="S1" pid="P4" qty="200"/>
    <invrec sid="S1" pid="P5" qty="100"/>
    <invrec sid="S1" pid="P6" qty="100"/>
    <invrec sid="S2" pid="P1" qty="300"/>
    <invrec sid="S2" pid="P2" qty="400"/>
    <invrec sid="S3" pid="P2" qty="200"/>
    <invrec sid="S4" pid="P2" qty="200"/>
    <invrec sid="S4" pid="P4" qty="300"/>
    <invrec sid="S4" pid="P5" qty="400"/>
  </inventory>
</database>
```

The join to be performed will answer the question, "Which suppliers and parts are in the same city (co-located)?"

You can use two basic techniques to approach this problem in XSLT. The first uses nested for-each loops:

```
<xsl:template match="/">
  <result>
    <xsl:for-each select="database/suppliers/*">
      <xsl:variable name="supplier" select="."/>
      <xsl:for-each select="/database/parts/*[@city=current()/@city]">
      <colocated>
        <xsl:copy-of select="$supplier"/>
        <xsl:copy-of select="."/>
      </colocated>
      </xsl:for-each>
    </xsl:for-each>
  </result>
</xsl:template>
```

The second approach uses apply-templates:

```
<xsl:template match="/">
  <result>
    <xsl:apply-templates select="database/suppliers/supplier" />
  </result>
</xsl:template>

<xsl:template match="supplier">
  <xsl:apply-templates select="/database/parts/part[@city = current( )/@city]">
    <xsl:with-param name="supplier" select="." />
  </xsl:apply-templates>
</xsl:template>

<xsl:template match="part">
  <xsl:param name="supplier" select="/.." />
  <colocated>
    <xsl:copy-of select="$supplier" />
    <xsl:copy-of select="." />
  </colocated>
</xsl:template>
```

If one of the sets of elements to be joined has a large number of members, then consider using xsl:key to improve performance:

```
<xsl:key name="part-city" match="part" use="@city"/>

<xsl:template match="/">
  <result>
    <xsl:for-each select="database/suppliers/*">
      <xsl:variable name="supplier" select="."/>
      <xsl:for-each select="key('part-city',$supplier/@city)">
      <colocated>
        <xsl:copy-of select="$supplier"/>
        <xsl:copy-of select="."/>
      </colocated>
      </xsl:for-each>
    </xsl:for-each>
  </result>
</xsl:template>
```

Each stylesheet produces the same result:

```
<result>
  <colocated>
      <supplier id="S1" name="Smith" status="20" city="London"/>
      <part id="P1" name="Nut" color="Red" weight="12" city="London"/>
  </colocated>
  <colocated>
      <supplier id="S1" name="Smith" status="20" city="London"/>
      <part id="P4" name="Screw" color="Red" weight="14" city="London"/>
  </colocated>
  <colocated>
      <supplier id="S1" name="Smith" status="20" city="London"/>
      <part id="P6" name="Cog" color="Red" weight="19" city="London"/>
  </colocated>
```

```
  <colocated>
     <supplier id="S2" name="Jones" status="10" city="Paris"/>
     <part id="P2" name="Bult" color="Green" weight="17" city="Paris"/>
  </colocated>
  <colocated>
     <supplier id="S2" name="Jones" status="10" city="Paris"/>
     <part id="P5" name="Cam" color="Blue" weight="12" city="Paris"/>
  </colocated>
  <colocated>
     <supplier id="S3" name="Blake" status="30" city="Paris"/>
     <part id="P2" name="Bult" color="Green" weight="17" city="Paris"/>
  </colocated>
  <colocated>
     <supplier id="S3" name="Blake" status="30" city="Paris"/>
     <part id="P5" name="Cam" color="Blue" weight="12" city="Paris"/>
  </colocated>
  <colocated>
     <supplier id="S4" name="Clark" status="20" city="London"/>
     <part id="P1" name="Nut" color="Red" weight="12" city="London"/>
  </colocated>
  <colocated>
     <supplier id="S4" name="Clark" status="20" city="London"/>
     <part id="P4" name="Screw" color="Red" weight="14" city="London"/>
  </colocated>
  <colocated>
     <supplier id="S4" name="Clark" status="20" city="London"/>
     <part id="P6" name="Cog" color="Red" weight="19" city="London"/>
  </colocated>
</result>
```

Discussion

The join you performed is called an *equi-join* because the elements are related by equality. More generally, joins can be formed using other relations. For example, consider the query, "Select all combinations of supplier and part information for which the supplier city follows the part city in alphabetical order."

It would be nice if you could simply write the following stylesheet, but XSLT 1.0 does not define relational operations on string types:

```
<xsl:template match="/">
  <result>
    <xsl:for-each select="database/suppliers/*">
      <xsl:variable name="supplier" select="."/>
      <!-- This does not work! -->
      <xsl:for-each select="/database/parts/*[current( )/@city > @city]">
      <colocated>
        <xsl:copy-of select="$supplier"/>
        <xsl:copy-of select="."/>
      </colocated>
      </xsl:for-each>
    </xsl:for-each>
  </result>
</xsl:template>
```

Instead, you must create a table using xsl:sort that can map city names onto integers that reflect the ordering. Here you rely on Saxon's ability to treat variables containing result-tree fragments as node sets when the version is set to 1.1. However, you can also use the node-set function of your particular XSLT 1.0 processor or use an XSLT 2.0 processor:

```
<xsl:stylesheet version="1.1" xmlns:xsl="http://www.w3.org/1999/XSL/Transform">
    <xsl:output method="xml" version="1.0" encoding="UTF-8" indent="yes"/>

<xsl:variable name="unique-cities"
    select="//@city[not(. = ../preceding::*/@city)]"/>

<xsl:variable name="city-ordering">
  <xsl:for-each select="$unique-cities">
    <xsl:sort select="."/>
    <city name="{.}" order="{position()}"/>
  </xsl:for-each>
</xsl:variable>

<xsl:template match="/">
  <result>
    <xsl:for-each select="database/suppliers/*">
      <xsl:variable name="s" select="."/>
      <xsl:for-each select="/database/parts/*">
        <xsl:variable name="p" select="."/>
        <xsl:if
          test="$city-ordering/*[@name = $s/@city]/@order &gt;
                $city-ordering/*[@name = $p/@city]/@order">
          <supplier-city-follows-part-city>
            <xsl:copy-of select="$s"/>
            <xsl:copy-of select="$p"/>
          </supplier-city-follows-part-city>
        </xsl:if>
      </xsl:for-each>
    </xsl:for-each>
  </result>
</xsl:template>

</xsl:stylesheet>
```

This query results in the following output:

```
<result>
  <supplier-city-follows-part-city>
    <supplier id="S2" name="Jones" status="10" city="Paris"/>
    <part id="P1" name="Nut" color="Red" weight="12" city="London"/>
  </supplier-city-follows-part-city>
  <supplier-city-follows-part-city>
    <supplier id="S2" name="Jones" status="10" city="Paris"/>
    <part id="P4" name="Screw" color="Red" weight="14" city="London"/>
  </supplier-city-follows-part-city>
  <supplier-city-follows-part-city>
    <supplier id="S2" name="Jones" status="10" city="Paris"/>
    <part id="P6" name="Cog" color="Red" weight="19" city="London"/>
  </supplier-city-follows-part-city>
```

```
<supplier-city-follows-part-city>
    <supplier id="S3" name="Blake" status="30" city="Paris"/>
    <part id="P1" name="Nut" color="Red" weight="12" city="London"/>
</supplier-city-follows-part-city>
<supplier-city-follows-part-city>
    <supplier id="S3" name="Blake" status="30" city="Paris"/>
    <part id="P4" name="Screw" color="Red" weight="14" city="London"/>
</supplier-city-follows-part-city>
<supplier-city-follows-part-city>
    <supplier id="S3" name="Blake" status="30" city="Paris"/>
    <part id="P6" name="Cog" color="Red" weight="19" city="London"/>
</supplier-city-follows-part-city>
</result>
```

7.6   Implementing the W3C XML Query-Use Cases in XSLT

Problem

You need to perform a query operation similar to one of the use cases in *http://www. w3.org/TR/2001/WD-xmlquery-use-cases-20011220*, but you want to use XSLT rather than XQuery (*http://www.w3.org/TR/xquery/*).

Solution

The following examples are XSLT solutions to most of the XML query-use cases presented in the W3C document. The descriptions of each use case are taken almost verbatim from the W3C document.

1. Use case "XMP": experiences and exemplars

   This use case contains several example queries that illustrate requirements gathered by the W3C from the database and document communities. The data use by these queries follows in Examples 7-10 to 7-13.

Example 7-10. bib.xml

```
<bib>
    <book year="1994">
        <title>TCP/IP Illustrated</title>
        <author><last>Stevens</last><first>W.</first></author>
        <publisher>Addison-Wesley</publisher>
        <price> 65.95</price>
    </book>

    <book year="1992">
        <title>Advanced Programming in the Unix environment</title>
        <author><last>Stevens</last><first>W.</first></author>
        <publisher>Addison-Wesley</publisher>
        <price>65.95</price>
```

Example 7-10. bib.xml (continued)

```
    </book>

    <book year="2000">
        <title>Data on the Web</title>
        <author><last>Abiteboul</last><first>Serge</first></author>
        <author><last>Buneman</last><first>Peter</first></author>
        <author><last>Suciu</last><first>Dan</first></author>
        <publisher>Morgan Kaufmann Publishers</publisher>
        <price> 39.95</price>
    </book>

    <book year="1999">
        <title>The Economics of Technology and Content for Digital TV</title>
        <editor>
                <last>Gerbarg</last><first>Darcy</first>
                 <affiliation>CITI</affiliation>
        </editor>
            <publisher>Kluwer Academic Publishers</publisher>
        <price>129.95</price>
    </book>

</bib>
```

Example 7-11. reviews.xml

```
reviews>
    <entry>
        <title>Data on the Web</title>
        <price>34.95</price>
        <review>
                A very good discussion of semi-structured database
                systems and XML.
        </review>
    </entry>
    <entry>
        <title>Advanced Programming in the Unix environment</title>
        <price>65.95</price>
        <review>
                A clear and detailed discussion of UNIX programming.
        </review>
    </entry>
    <entry>
        <title>TCP/IP Illustrated</title>
        <price>65.95</price>
        <review>
                One of the best books on TCP/IP.
        </review>
    </entry>
</reviews>
```

Example 7-12. books.xml

```
<chapter>
    <title>Data Model</title>
    <section>
        <title>Syntax For Data Model</title>
    </section>
    <section>
        <title>XML</title>
        <section>
            <title>Basic Syntax</title>
        </section>
        <section>
            <title>XML and Semistructured Data</title>
        </section>
    </section>
</chapter>
```

Example 7-13. prices.xml

```
<prices>
    <book>
        <title>Advanced Programming in the Unix environment</title>
        <source>www.amazon.com</source>
        <price>65.95</price>
    </book>
    <book>
        <title>Advanced Programming in the Unix environment </title>
        <source>www.bn.com</source>
        <price>65.95</price>
    </book>
    <book>
        <title> TCP/IP Illustrated </title>
        <source>www.amazon.com</source>
        <price>65.95</price>
    </book>
    <book>
        <title> TCP/IP Illustrated </title>
        <source>www.bn.com</source>
        <price>65.95</price>
    </book>
    <book>
        <title>Data on the Web</title>
        <source>www.amazon.com</source>
        <price>34.95</price>
    </book>
    <book>
        <title>Data on the Web</title>
        <source>www.bn.com</source>
        <price>39.95</price>
    </book>
</prices>
```

Question 1. List books in *bib.xml* published by Addison-Wesley after 1991, including their year and title:

```
<xsl:stylesheet version="1.0"
xmlns:xsl="http://www.w3.org/1999/XSL/Transform">

<xsl:import href="copy.xslt"/>

<xsl:template match="book[publisher = 'Addison-Wesley' and @year > 1991]">
  <xsl:copy-of select="."/>
</xsl:template>

<xsl:template match="book"/>

</xsl:stylesheet>
```

Question 2. Create a flat list of all the title-author pairs from *bib.xml*, with each pair enclosed in a "result" element:

```
<xsl:template match="/">
<results>
  <xsl:apply-templates select="bib/book/author"/>
</results>
</xsl:template>

<xsl:template match="author">
  <result>
    <xsl:copy-of select="preceding-sibling::title"/>
    <xsl:copy-of select="."/>
  </result>
</xsl:template>
```

Question 3. For each book in *bib.xml*, list the title and authors, grouped inside a "result" element:

```
<xsl:template match="bib">
  <results>
    <xsl:for-each select="book">
    <result>
      <xsl:copy-of select="title"/>
      <xsl:copy-of select="author"/>
    </result>
    </xsl:for-each>
  </results>
</xsl:template>
```

Question 4. For each author in *bib.xml*, list the author's name and the titles of all books by that author, grouped inside a "result" element:

```
<xsl:template match="/">
<results>
  <xsl:for-each select="//author[not(.=preceding::author)]">
    <result>
      <xsl:copy-of select="."/>
      <xsl:for-each select="/bib/book[author=current()]">
        <xsl:copy-of select="title"/>
```

```
        </xsl:for-each>
      </result>
    </xsl:for-each>
  </results>
```

Question 5. For each book found on both *http://www.bn.com* (*bib.xml*) and *http: //www.amazon.com* (*reviews.xml*), list the title of the book and its price from each source:

```
<xsl:variable name="bn" select="document('bib.xml')"/>
<xsl:variable name="amazon" select="document('reviews.xml')"/>

<!--Solution 1 -->
<xsl:template match="/">
  <books-with-prices>
  <xsl:for-each select="$bn//book[title = $amazon//entry/title]">
    <book-with-prices>
      <xsl:copy-of select="title"/>
      <price-amazon><xsl:value-of
      select="$amazon//entry[title=current( )/title]/price"/></price-amazon>
      <price-bn><xsl:value-of select="price"/></price-bn>
    </book-with-prices>
  </xsl:for-each>
  </books-with-prices>
</xsl:template>

<!--Solution 2-->
<xsl:template match="/">
  <books-with-prices>
  <xsl:for-each select="$bn//book">
    <xsl:variable name="bn-book" select="."/>
    <xsl:for-each select="$amazon//entry[title=$bn-book/title]">
      <book-with-prices>
        <xsl:copy-of select="title"/>
        <price-amazon><xsl:value-of select="price"/></price-amazon>
        <price-bn><xsl:value-of select="$bn-book/price"/></price-bn>
      </book-with-prices>
    </xsl:for-each>
  </xsl:for-each>
  </books-with-prices>
</xsl:template>
```

Question 6. For each book that has at least one author, list the title and first two authors, as well as an empty "et-al" element if the book has additional authors:

```
<xsl:template match="bib">
  <xsl:copy>
    <xsl:for-each select="book[author]">
      <xsl:copy>
        <xsl:copy-of select="title"/>
        <xsl:copy-of select="author[position( ) &lt;= 2]"/>
        <xsl:if test="author[3]">
        <et-al/>
```

```
                </xsl:if>
            </xsl:copy>
        </xsl:for-each>
    </xsl:copy>
</xsl:template>
```

Question 7. List the titles and years of all books published by Addison-Wesley after 1991, in alphabetic order:

```
<xsl:template match="bib">
  <xsl:copy>
    <xsl:for-each select="book[publisher = 'Addison-Wesley'
          and @year > 1991]">
    <xsl:sort select="title"/>
    <xsl:copy>
      <xsl:copy-of select="@year"/>
      <xsl:copy-of select="title"/>
    </xsl:copy>
    </xsl:for-each>
  </xsl:copy>
</xsl:template>
```

Question 8. In the document *books.xml*, find all section or chapter titles that contain the word "XML", regardless of the nesting level:

```
<xsl:template match="/">
<results>
  <xsl:copy-of select="(//chapter/title |
  //section/title)[contains(.,'XML')]"/>
</results>
</xsl:template>
```

Question 9. In the document *prices.xml*, find the minimum price for each book in the form of a "minprice" element with the book title as its title attribute:

```
<xsl:include href="../math/math.min.xslt"/>

<xsl:template match="/">
<results>
  <xsl:for-each select="//book/title[not(. = ./preceding::title)]">
    <xsl:variable name="min-price">
      <xsl:call-template name="math:min">
        <xsl:with-param name="nodes" select="//book[title =
                                    current( )]/price"/>
      </xsl:call-template>
    </xsl:variable>
    <minprice title="{.}">
      <price><xsl:value-of select="$min-price"/></prices>
    </minprice>
  </xsl:for-each>
</results>
</xsl:template>
```

Question 10. For each book with an author, return the book with its title and authors. For each book with an editor, return a reference with the book title and the editor's affiliation:

```
<xsl:template match="bib">
<xsl:copy>
  <xsl:for-each select="book[author]">
    <xsl:copy>
      <xsl:copy-of select="title"/>
      <xsl:copy-of select="author"/>
    </xsl:copy>
  </xsl:for-each>

  <xsl:for-each select="book[editor]">
    <reference>
      <xsl:copy-of select="title"/>
      <org><xsl:value-of select="editor/affiliation"/></org>
    </reference>
  </xsl:for-each>
  </xsl:copy>
</xsl:template>
```

Question 11. Find pairs of books that have different titles but the same set of authors (possibly in a different order):

```
<xsl:include href="query.equal-values.xslt"/>

<xsl:template match="bib">
  <xsl:copy>
    <xsl:for-each select="book[author]">
      <xsl:variable name="book1" select="."/>
      <xsl:for-each select="./following-sibling::book[author]">
        <xsl:variable name="same-authors">
          <xsl:call-template name="query:equal-values">
            <xsl:with-param name="nodes1" select="$book1/author"/>
            <xsl:with-param name="nodes2" select="author"/>
          </xsl:call-template>
        </xsl:variable>
        <xsl:if test="string($same-authors)">
          <book-pair>
            <xsl:copy-of select="$book1/title"/>
            <xsl:copy-of select="title"/>
          </book-pair>
        </xsl:if>
      </xsl:for-each>
    </xsl:for-each>
  </xsl:copy>
</xsl:template>
```

2. Use case "TREE": queries that preserve hierarchy.

   Some XML document types have a very flexible structure in which text is mixed with elements and many elements are optional. These document-types show a wide variation in structure from one document to another. In these types of documents, the ways in which elements are ordered and nested are usually quite important. An XML query language should have the ability to extract elements from documents while preserving their original hierarchy. This use-case illustrates this requirement by means of a flexible document type named Book.

The DTD and XML data used by these queries follows in Examples 7-14 to 7-15.

Example 7-14. book.dtd

```
<!ELEMENT book (title, author+, section+)>
  <!ELEMENT title (#PCDATA)>
  <!ELEMENT author (#PCDATA)>
  <!ELEMENT section (title, (p | figure | section)* )>
  <!ATTLIST section
      id         ID    #IMPLIED
      difficulty CDATA #IMPLIED>
  <!ELEMENT p (#PCDATA)>
  <!ELEMENT figure (title, image)>
  <!ATTLIST figure
      width    CDATA   #REQUIRED
      height   CDATA   #REQUIRED >
  <!ELEMENT image EMPTY>
  <!ATTLIST image
      source   CDATA   #REQUIRED >
```

Example 7-15. book.xml

```
<?xml version="1.0" encoding="UTF-8"?>
<!DOCTYPE book SYSTEM "book.dtd">
<book>
  <title>Data on the Web</title>
  <author>Serge Abiteboul</author>
  <author>Peter Buneman</author>
  <author>Dan Suciu</author>
  <section id="intro" difficulty="easy" >
    <title>Introduction</title>
    <p>Text ... </p>
    <section>
      <title>Audience</title>
      <p>Text ... </p>
    </section>
    <section>
      <title>Web Data and the Two Cultures</title>
      <p>Text ... </p>
      <figure height="400" width="400">
        <title>Traditional client/server architecture</title>
        <image source="csarch.gif"/>
      </figure>
      <p>Text ... </p>
    </section>
  </section>
  <section id="syntax" difficulty="medium" >
    <title>A Syntax For Data</title>
    <p>Text ... </p>
    <figure height="200" width="500">
      <title>Graph representations of structures</title>
      <image source="graphs.gif"/>
    </figure>
    <p>Text ... </p>
```

Example 7-15. book.xml (continued)

```
    <section>
      <title>Base Types</title>
      <p>Text ... </p>
    </section>
    <section>
      <title>Representing Relational Databases</title>
      <p>Text ... </p>
      <figure height="250" width="400">
        <title>Examples of Relations</title>
        <image source="relations.gif"/>
      </figure>
    </section>
    <section>
      <title>Representing Object Databases</title>
      <p>Text ... </p>
    </section>
  </section>
</book>
```

Question 1. Prepare a (nested) table of contents for *Book1*, listing all the sections and their titles. Preserve the original attributes of each <section> element, if any exist:

```
<xsl:template match="book">
  <toc>
    <xsl:apply-templates/>
  </toc>
</xsl:template>

<!-- Copy element of toc -->
<xsl:template match="section | section/title | section/title/text()">
  <xsl:copy>
    <xsl:copy-of select="@*"/>
      <xsl:apply-templates/>
  </xsl:copy>
</xsl:template>

<!-- Supress other elements -->
<xsl:template match="* | text()"/>
```

Question 2. Prepare a (flat) figure list for *Book1*, listing all figures and their titles. Preserve the original attributes of each <figure> element, if any exist:

```
<xsl:template match="book">
  <figlist>
    <xsl:for-each select=".//figure">
      <xsl:copy>
        <xsl:copy-of select="@*"/>
        <xsl:copy-of select="title"/>
      </xsl:copy>
    </xsl:for-each>
  </figlist>
</xsl:template>
```

Question 3. How many sections are in *Book1*, and how many figures?

```
<xsl:template match="/">
  <section-count><xsl:value-of select="count(//section)"/></section-count>
  <figure-count><xsl:value-of select="count(//figure)"/></figure-count>
</xsl:template>
```

Question 4. How many top-level sections are in *Book1*?

```
<xsl:template match="book">
  <top_section_count>
    <xsl:value-of select="count(section)"/>
  </top_section_count>
</xsl:template>
```

Question 5. Make a flat list of the section elements in *Book1*. In place of its original attributes, each section element should have two attributes, containing the title of the section and the number of figures immediately contained in the section:

```
<xsl:template match="book">
<section_list>
  <xsl:for-each select=".//section">
    <section title="{title}" figcount="{count(figure)}"/>
  </xsl:for-each>
</section_list>
</xsl:template>
```

Question 6. Make a nested list of the section elements in *Book1*, preserving their original attributes and hierarchy. Inside each section element, include the title of the section and an element that includes the number of figures immediately contained in the section. See Examples 7-16 and 7-17.

Example 7-16. The solution as I would interpret the English requirements

```
<xsl:template match="book">
<toc>
  <xsl:apply-templates select="section"/>
</toc>
</xsl:template>

<xsl:template match="section">
  <xsl:copy>
    <xsl:copy-of select="@*"/>
    <xsl:copy-of select="title"/>
    <figcount><xsl:value-of select="count(figure)"/></figcount>
    <xsl:apply-templates select="section"/>
  </xsl:copy>
</xsl:template>
```

Example 7-17. What the W3C use case wants based on a sample result and XQuery

```
<xsl:template match="book">
<toc>
  <xsl:for-each select="//section">
    <xsl:sort select="count(ancestor::section)"/>
    <xsl:apply-templates select="."/>
```

```
    </xsl:for-each>
  </toc>
</xsl:template>

<xsl:template match="section">
  <xsl:copy>
    <xsl:copy-of select="@*"/>
    <xsl:copy-of select="title"/>
    <figcount><xsl:value-of select="count(figure)"/></figcount>
    <xsl:apply-templates select="section"/>
  </xsl:copy>
</xsl:template>
```

3. Use case "SEQ": queries based on sequence.

   This use case illustrates queries based on the sequence in which elements appear in a document. Although sequence is not significant in most traditional database systems or object systems, it can be important in structured documents. This use case presents a series of queries based on a medical report:

```
            <!DOCTYPE report [
              <!ELEMENT report (section*)>
              <!ELEMENT section (section.title, section.content)>
              <!ELEMENT section.title (#PCDATA )>
              <!ELEMENT section.content  (#PCDATA | anesthesia | prep
                                          | incision | action | observation )*>
              <!ELEMENT anesthesia (#PCDATA)>
              <!ELEMENT prep ( (#PCDATA | action)* )>
              <!ELEMENT incision ( (#PCDATA | geography | instrument)* )>
              <!ELEMENT action ( (#PCDATA | instrument )* )>
              <!ELEMENT observation (#PCDATA)>
              <!ELEMENT geography (#PCDATA)>
              <!ELEMENT instrument (#PCDATA)>
            ]>
            <report>
              <section>
                <section.title>Procedure</section.title>
                 <section.content>
                  The patient was taken to the operating room where she was placed
                  in supine position and
                  <anesthesia>induced under general anesthesia.</anesthesia>
                  <prep>
                    <action>A Foley catheter was placed to decompress the bladder</action>
                    and the abdomen was then prepped and draped in sterile fashion.
                  </prep>
                  <incision>
                    A curvilinear incision was made
                    <geography>in the midline immediately infraumbilical</geography>
                    and the subcutaneous tissue was divided
                    <instrument>using electrocautery.</instrument>
                  </incision>
                  The fascia was identified and
                  <action>#2 0 Maxon stay sutures were placed on each side of the midline.
                  </action>
```

```
    <incision>
      The fascia was divided using
      <instrument>electrocautery</instrument>
      and the peritoneum was entered.
    </incision>
    <observation>The small bowel was identified.</observation>
    and
    <action>
      the
      <instrument>Hasson trocar</instrument>
      was placed under direct visualization.
    </action>
    <action>
      The
      <instrument>trocar</instrument>
      was secured to the fascia using the stay sutures.
    </action>
    </section.content>
  </section>
</report>
```

Question 1. In the Procedure section of *Report1*, what instruments were used in the second incision?

```
<xsl:template match="section[section.title = 'Procedure']">
<xsl:copy-of select="(.//incision)[2]/instrument"/>
</xsl:template>
```

Question 2. In the Procedure section of *Report1*, what are the first two instruments to be used?

```
<xsl:template match="section[section.title = 'Procedure']">
<xsl:copy-of select="(.//instrument)[position() &lt;= 2]"/>
</xsl:template>
```

Question 3. In *Report1*, what instruments were used in the first two actions after the second incision?

```
<xsl:template match="report">
<!-- i2 = Second incision in the entire report -->
<xsl:variable name="i2" select="(.//incision)[2]"/>
<!-- Of all the actions following i2
     get the instruments used in the first two -->
<xsl:copy-of
     select="($i2/following::action)[position() &lt;= 2]/instrument"/>
</xsl:template>
```

Question 4. In *Report1*, find "Procedure" sections for which no anesthesia element occurs before the first incision:

```
<xsl:template match="section[section.title = 'Procedure']">
  <xsl:variable name="i1" select="(.//incision)[1]"/>
  <xsl:if test=".//anesthesia[preceding::incision = $i1]">
    <xsl:copy-of select="current()"/>
  </xsl:if>
</xsl:template>
```

If the result is not empty then a major lawsuit is soon to follow!

Question 5. In *Report1*, what happened between the first and second incision?

```
<xsl:template match="report">
<critical_sequence>
  <!-- i1 = First incision in the entire report -->
  <xsl:variable name="i1" select="(.//incision)[1]"/>
  <!-- i2 = Second incision in the entire report -->
  <xsl:variable name="i2" select="(.//incision)[2]"/>
  <!-- copy all sibling nodes following i1
       that don't have a preceding element i2 and are not themeseves i2 -->
  <xsl:for-each select="$i1/following-sibling::node()
                 [not(./preceding::incision = $i2) and not(. = $i2)]">
    <xsl:copy-of select="."/>
  </xsl:for-each>
</critical_sequence>
</xsl:template>
```

 In Questions 4 and 5, I assume that the string values of incision elements are unique. This is true in the sample data, but may not be true in the most general case. To be precise, you should apply Recipe 4.2. For example, in Question 4, the test should be:

```
test=".//anesthesia[
count(./preceding::incision | $i1) =
count(./preceding::incision)]"
```

4. Use case "R": access to relational data.

One important use of an XML query language is the access of data stored in relational databases. This use case describes one possible way in which this access might be accomplished. A relational database system might present a view in which each table (relation) takes the form of an XML document. One way to represent a database table as an XML document is to allow the document element to represent the table itself and each row (tuple) inside the table to be represented by a nested element. Inside the tuple-elements, each column is in turn represented by a nested element. Columns that allow null values are represented by optional elements, and a missing element denotes a null value.

For example, consider a relational database used by an online auction. The auction maintains a USERS table containing information on registered users, each identified by a unique user ID that can either offer items for sale or bid on items. An ITEMS table lists items currently or recently for sale, with the user ID of the user who offered each item. A BIDS table contains all bids on record, keyed by the user ID of the bidder and the number of the item to which the bid applies.

Due to the large number of queries in this use case, you will only implement a subset. Implementing the others is a nice exercise if you wish to strengthen your XSLT skills. See Examples 7-18 to 7-20.

Example 7-18. users.xml

```
<users>
  <user_tuple>
    <userid>U01</userid>
    <name>Tom Jones</name>
    <rating>B</rating>
  </user_tuple>
  <user_tuple>
    <userid>U02</userid>
    <name>Mary Doe</name>
    <rating>A</rating>
  </user_tuple>
  <user_tuple>
    <userid>U03</userid>
    <name>Dee Linquent</name>
    <rating>D</rating>
  </user_tuple>
  <user_tuple>
    <userid>U04</userid>
    <name>Roger Smith</name>
    <rating>C</rating>
  </user_tuple>
  <user_tuple>
    <userid>U05</userid>
    <name>Jack Sprat</name>
    <rating>B</rating>
  </user_tuple>
  <user_tuple>
    <userid>U06</userid>
    <name>Rip Van Winkle</name>
    <rating>B</rating>
  </user_tuple>
</users>
```

Example 7-19. items.xml

```
<items>
  <item_tuple>
    <itemno>1001</itemno>
    <description>Red Bicycle</description>
    <offered_by>U01</offered_by>
    <start_date>99-01-05</start_date>
    <end_date>99-01-20</end_date>
    <reserve_price>40</reserve_price>
  </item_tuple>
  <item_tuple>
    <itemno>1002</itemno>
    <description>Motorcycle</description>
    <offered_by>U02</offered_by>
    <start_date>99-02-11</start_date>
    <end_date>99-03-15</end_date>
    <reserve_price>500</reserve_price>
  </item_tuple>
```

Example 7-19. items.xml (continued)

```
<item_tuple>
  <itemno>1003</itemno>
  <description>Old Bicycle</description>
  <offered_by>U02</offered_by>
  <start_date>99-01-10</start_date>
  <end_date>99-02-20</end_date>
  <reserve_price>25</reserve_price>
</item_tuple>
<item_tuple>
  <itemno>1004</itemno>
  <description>Tricycle</description>
  <offered_by>U01</offered_by>
  <start_date>99-02-25</start_date>
  <end_date>99-03-08</end_date>
  <reserve_price>15</reserve_price>
</item_tuple>
<item_tuple>
  <itemno>1005</itemno>
  <description>Tennis Racket</description>
  <offered_by>U03</offered_by>
  <start_date>99-03-19</start_date>
  <end_date>99-04-30</end_date>
  <reserve_price>20</reserve_price>
</item_tuple>
<item_tuple>
  <itemno>1006</itemno>
  <description>Helicopter</description>
  <offered_by>U03</offered_by>
  <start_date>99-05-05</start_date>
  <end_date>99-05-25</end_date>
  <reserve_price>50000</reserve_price>
</item_tuple>
<item_tuple>
  <itemno>1007</itemno>
  <description>Racing Bicycle</description>
  <offered_by>U04</offered_by>
  <start_date>99-01-20</start_date>
  <end_date>99-02-20</end_date>
  <reserve_price>200</reserve_price>
</item_tuple>
<item_tuple>
  <itemno>1008</itemno>
  <description>Broken Bicycle</description>
  <offered_by>U01</offered_by>
  <start_date>99-02-05</start_date>
  <end_date>99-03-06</end_date>
  <reserve_price>25</reserve_price>
</item_tuple>
</items>
```

Example 7-20. bids.xml

```
<bids>
  <bid_tuple>
    <userid>U02</userid>
    <itemno>1001</itemno>
    <bid> 35</bid>
    <bid_date>99-01-07 </bid_date>
  </bid_tuple>
  <bid_tuple>
    <userid>U04</userid>
    <itemno>1001</itemno>
    <bid>40</bid>
    <bid_date>99-01-08</bid_date>
  </bid_tuple>
  <bid_tuple>
    <userid>U02</userid>
    <itemno>1001 </itemno>
    <bid>45</bid>
    <bid_date>99-01-11</bid_date>
  </bid_tuple>
  <bid_tuple>
    <userid>U04</userid>
    <itemno>1001</itemno>
    <bid>50</bid>
    <bid_date>99-01-13</bid_date>
  </bid_tuple>
  <bid_tuple>
    <userid>U02</userid>
    <itemno>1001</itemno>
    <bid>55</bid>
    <bid_date>99-01-15</bid_date>
  </bid_tuple>
  <bid_tuple>
    <userid>U01</userid>
    <itemno>1002</itemno>
    <bid>400</bid>
    <bid_date>99-02-14</bid_date>
  </bid_tuple>
  <bid_tuple>
    <userid>U02</userid>
    <itemno>1002</itemno>
    <bid>600</bid>
    <bid_date>99-02-16</bid_date>
  </bid_tuple>
  <bid_tuple>
    <userid>U03</userid>
    <itemno>1002</itemno>
    <bid>800</bid>
    <bid_date>99-02-17</bid_date>
  </bid_tuple>
  <bid_tuple>
    <userid>U04</userid>
    <itemno>1002</itemno>
```

Example 7-20. bids.xml (continued)

```
        <bid>1000</bid>
        <bid_date>99-02-25</bid_date>
    </bid_tuple>
    <bid_tuple>
        <userid>U02</userid>
        <itemno>1002</itemno>
        <bid>1200</bid>
        <bid_date>99-03-02</bid_date>
    </bid_tuple>
    <bid_tuple>
        <userid>U04</userid>
        <itemno>1003</itemno>
        <bid>15</bid>
        <bid_date>99-01-22</bid_date>
    </bid_tuple>
    <bid_tuple>
        <userid>U05</userid>
        <itemno>1003</itemno>
        <bid>20</bid>
        <bid_date>99-02-03</bid_date>
    </bid_tuple>
    <bid_tuple>
        <userid>U01</userid>
        <itemno>1004</itemno>
        <bid>40</bid>
        <bid_date>99-03-05</bid_date>
    </bid_tuple>
    <bid_tuple>
        <userid>U03</userid>
        <itemno>1007</itemno>
        <bid>175</bid>
        <bid_date>99-01-25</bid_date>
    </bid_tuple>
    <bid_tuple>
        <userid>U05</userid>
        <itemno>1007</itemno>
        <bid>200</bid>
        <bid_date>99-02-08</bid_date>
    </bid_tuple>
    <bid_tuple>
        <userid>U04</userid>
        <itemno>1007</itemno>
        <bid>225</bid>
        <bid_date>99-02-12</bid_date>
    </bid_tuple>
</bids>
```

Question 1. List the item number and description of all bicycles that currently have an auction in progress, ordered by item number:

```
<xsl:include href="../date/date.date-time.xslt"/>

<!-- To make the result come out like the W3C example -->
<xsl:param name="today" select="'1999-01-21'"/>

<xsl:template match="items">

  <xsl:variable name="today-abs">
    <xsl:call-template name="date:date-to-absolute-day">
      <xsl:with-param name="date" select="$today"/>
    </xsl:call-template>
  </xsl:variable>

<result>
  <xsl:for-each select="item_tuple">
    <xsl:sort select="itemno" data-type="number"/>

    <xsl:variable name="start-abs">
      <xsl:call-template name="date:date-to-absolute-day">
        <xsl:with-param name="date" select="start_date"/>
      </xsl:call-template>
    </xsl:variable>

    <xsl:variable name="end-abs">
      <xsl:call-template name="date:date-to-absolute-day">
        <xsl:with-param name="date" select="end_date"/>
      </xsl:call-template>
    </xsl:variable>

    <xsl:if test="$start-abs &lt;= $today-abs and $end-abs >=
        $today-abs and contains(description, 'Bicycle')">
      <xsl:copy>
        <xsl:copy-of select="itemno"/>
        <xsl:copy-of select="description"/>
      </xsl:copy>
    </xsl:if>

  </xsl:for-each>
</result>
</xsl:template>
```

Question 2. For all bicycles, list the item number, description, and highest bid (if any), ordered by item number:

```
<xsl:include href="../math/math.max.xslt"/>

<xsl:template match="items">

<result>
  <xsl:for-each select="item_tuple[contains(description,'Bicycle')]">
    <xsl:sort select="itemno" data-type="number"/>

  <xsl:variable name="bids"
    select="document('bids.xml')//bid_tuple[itemno=current()/itemno]/bid"/>
```

```
        <xsl:variable name="high-bid">
          <xsl:call-template name="math:max">
            <xsl:with-param name="nodes" select="$bids"/>
          </xsl:call-template>
        </xsl:variable>

        <xsl:copy>
          <xsl:copy-of select="itemno"/>
          <xsl:copy-of select="description"/>
          <high_bid><xsl:if test="$bids"><xsl:value-of
                select="$high-bid"/></xsl:if></high_bid>
        </xsl:copy>

      </xsl:for-each>
    </result>
  </xsl:template>
```

Question 3. Find cases when a user with a rating worse (alphabetically, greater) than "C" offers an item with a reserve price of more than 1,000:

```
<!-- Not strictly nec. but spec does not define ratings system so we derive
it dynamically! -->
<xsl:variable name="ratings">
  <xsl:for-each select="document('users.xml')//user_tuple/rating">
    <xsl:sort select="." data-type="text"/>
    <xsl:if test="not(. = ./preceding::rating)">
      <xsl:value-of select="."/>
    </xsl:if>
  </xsl:for-each>
</xsl:variable>

<xsl:template match="items">
<result>
  <xsl:for-each select="item_tuple[reserve_price > 1000]">

  <xsl:variable name="user" select="document('users.xml')//user_tuple[userid
  = current()/offered_by]"/>

  <xsl:if test="string-length(substring-before($ratings,$user/rating)) >
  string-length(substring-before($ratings,'C'))">
    <warning>
      <xsl:copy-of select="$user/name"/>
      <xsl:copy-of select="$user/rating"/>
      <xsl:copy-of select="description"/>
      <xsl:copy-of select="reserve_price"/>
    </warning>
  </xsl:if>
  </xsl:for-each>
</result>
</xsl:template>
```

Question 4. List item numbers and descriptions of items that have no bids:

```
<xsl:template match="items">
<result>
  <xsl:for-each select="item_tuple">

  <xsl:if test="not(document('bids.xml')//bid_tuple[itemno =
  current( )/itemno])">
    <no_bid_item>
      <xsl:copy-of select="itemno"/>
      <xsl:copy-of select="description"/>
    </no_bid_item>
  </xsl:if>

  </xsl:for-each>
</result>
</xsl:template>
```

5. Use case "SGML": Standard Generalized Markup Language.

   The example document and queries in this use case were first created for a 1992 conference on Standard Generalized Markup Language (SGML). For your use, the Document Type Definition (DTD) and example document are translated from SGML to XML.

   This chapter does not implement these queries because they are not significantly different from queries in other use cases.

6. Use case "TEXT": full-text search.

   This use case is based on company profiles and a set of news documents that contain data for PR, mergers, and acquisitions. Given a company, the use case illustrates several different queries for searching text in news documents and different ways of providing query results by matching the information from the company profile and news content.

   In this use case, searches for company names are interpreted as word-based. The words in a company name may be in any case and separated by any kind of whitespace.

   All queries can be expressed in XSLT 1.0. However, doing so can result in the need for a lot of text-search machinery. For example, the most difficult queries require a mechanism for testing the existence of any member of a set of text values in another string. Furthermore, many queries require testing of text subunits, such as sentence boundaries.

   Based on techniques covered in Chapter 1, it should be clear that these problems have solutions in XSLT. However, if you will do a lot text querying in XSLT, you will need a generic library of text-search utilities. Developing generic libraries is the focus of Chapter 14, which will revisit some of the most complex full-text queries. For now, you will solve two of the most straightforward text-search problems in the W3C document. This chapter lists the others to give a sense of why these queries can be challenging for XSLT 1.0. The difficult parts are emphasized.

Question 1. Find all news items in which the name "Foobar Corporation" appears in the title:

```
<xsl:template match="news">
<result>
  <xsl:copy-of select="news_item/title[contains(., 'Foobar Corporation')]"/>
</result>
</xsl:template>
```

Question 2. For each news item that is relevant to the Gorilla Corporation, create an "item summary" element. The content of the item summary is the title, date, and first paragraph of the news item, separated by periods. A news item is relevant if the name of the company is mentioned anywhere within the content of the news item:

```
<xsl:template match="news">
<result>
  <xsl:for-each select="news_item[contains(content,'Gorilla Corporation')]">
    <item_summary>
      <xsl:value-of select="normalize-space(title)"/>. <xsl:text/>
      <xsl:value-of select="normalize-space(date)"/>. <xsl:text/>
      <xsl:value-of select="normalize-space(content/par[1])"/>
    </item_summary>
  </xsl:for-each>
</result>
</xsl:template>
```

7. Use case "PARTS": recursive parts explosion

This use case illustrates how a recursive query might can construct a hierarchical document of arbitrary depth from flat structures stored in a database.

This use case is based on a "parts explosion" database that contains information about how parts are used in other parts.

The input to the use case is a "flat" document in which each different part is represented by a <part> element with partid and name attributes. Each part may or may not be part of a larger part; if so, the partid of the larger part is contained in a partof attribute. This input document might be derived from a relational database in which each part is represented by a table row with partid as primary key and partof as a foreign key referencing partid.

The challenge of this use case is to write a query that converts the "flat" representation of the parts explosion, based on foreign keys, into a hierarchical representation in which part containment is represented by the document structure.

The input data set uses the following DTD:

```
<!DOCTYPE partlist [
    <!ELEMENT partlist (part*)>
    <!ELEMENT part EMPTY>
    <!ATTLIST part
        partid CDATA  #REQUIRED
        partof CDATA  #IMPLIED
        name   CDATA  #REQUIRED>
]>
```

Although the `partid` and `partof` attributes could have been of type ID and IDREF, respectively, in this schema they are treated as character data, possibly materialized in a straightforward way from a relational database. Each `partof` attribute matches exactly one `partid`. Parts having no `partof` attribute are not contained in any other part.

The output data conforms to the following DTD:

```
<!DOCTYPE parttree [
    <!ELEMENT parttree (part*)>
    <!ELEMENT part (part*)>
    <!ATTLIST part
          partid  CDATA  #REQUIRED
          name    CDATA  #REQUIRED>
]>
```

Sample data conforming to that DTD might look like this:

```
<?xml version="1.0" encoding="ISO-8859-1"?>
<partlist>
  <part partid="0" name="car"/>
  <part partid="1" partof="0" name="engine"/>
  <part partid="2" partof="0" name="door"/>
  <part partid="3" partof="1" name="piston"/>
  <part partid="4" partof="2" name="window"/>
  <part partid="5" partof="2" name="lock"/>
  <part partid="10" name="skateboard"/>
  <part partid="11" partof="10" name="board"/>
  <part partid="12" partof="10" name="wheel"/>
  <part partid="20" name="canoe"/>
</partlist>
```

Question 1. Convert the sample document from "partlist" to "parttree" format (see the DTD section for definitions). In the result document, part containment is represented by containment of one <part> element inside another. Each part that is not part of any other part should appear as a separate top-level element in the output document:

```
<xsl:template match="partlist">
  <parttree>
     <!-- Start with the part that is not part of anything -->
     <xsl:apply-templates select="part[not(@partof)]"/>
  </parttree>
</xsl:template>

<xsl:template match="part">
  <part partid="{@partid}" name="{@name}">
     <xsl:apply-templates select="../part[@partof = current()/@partid]"/>
  </part>
</xsl:template>
```

It turns out that this sort of transformation is easier to code and understand in XSLT than in XQuery. For comparison, here is the XQuery solution offered by the W3C paper:

```
define function one_level (element $p) returns element
{
    <part partid="{ $p/@partid }"
        name="{ $p/@name }" >
        {
            for $s in document("partlist.xml")//part
            where $s/@partof = $p/@partid
            return one_level($s)
        }
    </part>
}

<parttree>
  {
    for $p in document("partlist.xml")//part[empty(@partof)]
    return one_level($p)
  }
</parttree>
```

Even without a detailed understanding of XQuery, you should be able to see that the XQuery solution is needed to explicitly implement the recursion while XSLT's apply-templates and pattern matching allow a more declarative solution. Granted, the difference is not that dramatic, but I find XSLT more elegant for this type of problem.

8. Use case "REF": queries based on references.[*]

References are an important aspect of XML. This use case describes a database in which references play a significant role and contains several representative queries that exploit these references.

Suppose that the file *census.xml* contains an element for each person recorded in a recent census. For each person element, the person's name, job, and spouse (if any) are recorded as attributes. The spouse attribute is an IDREF-type attribute that matches the spouse element's ID-type name attribute.

The parent-child relationship among persons is recorded by containment in the element hierarchy. In other words, the element that represents a child is contained within the element that represents the child's father or mother. Due to deaths, divorces, and remarriages, a child might be recorded under either its father or mother (but not both). In this exercise, the term "children of X" includes "children of the spouse of X." For example, if Joe and Martha are spouses, Joe's element contains an element Sam, and Martha's element contains an element Dave, then both Joe's and Martha's children are considered to be Sam and Daveve. Each person in the census has zero, one, or two parents.

---

[*] These use cases were dropped from the latest version of the W3C document.

This use case is based on an input document named *census.xml*, with the following DTD:

```
<!DOCTYPE census [
  <!ELEMENT census (person*)>
  <!ELEMENT person (person*)>
  <!ATTLIST person
        name    ID      #REQUIRED
        spouse  IDREF   #IMPLIED
        job     CDATA   #IMPLIED >
]>
```

The following census data describes two friendly families that have several inter-marriages:

```
<census>
  <person name="Bill" job="Teacher">
    <person name="Joe" job="Painter" spouse="Martha">
      <person name="Sam" job="Nurse">
        <person name="Fred" job="Senator" spouse="Jane">
        </person>
      </person>
      <person name="Karen" job="Doctor" spouse="Steve">
      </person>
    </person>
    <person name="Mary" job="Pilot">
      <person name="Susan" job="Pilot" spouse="Dave">
      </person>
    </person>
  </person>
  <person name="Frank" job="Writer">
    <person name="Martha" job="Programmer" spouse="Joe">
      <person name="Dave" job="Athlete" spouse="Susan">
      </person>
    </person>
    <person name="John" job="Artist">
      <person name="Helen" job="Athlete">
      </person>
      <person name="Steve" job="Accountant" spouse="Karen">
        <person name="Jane" job="Doctor" spouse="Fred">
        </person>
      </person>
    </person>
  </person>
</census>
```

Question 1. Find Martha's spouse:

```
<xsl:strip-space elements="*"/>

<xsl:template match="person[@spouse='Martha']">
  <xsl:copy>
    <xsl:copy-of select="@*"/>
  </xsl:copy>
</xsl:template>
```

Question 2. Find parents of athletes:

```
<xsl:template match="census">
  <xsl:variable name="everyone"  select="//person"/>
  <result>
     <!-- For each person with children -->
    <xsl:for-each select="$everyone[person]">
      <xsl:variable name="spouse"
          select="$everyone[@spouse=current( )/@name]"/>
      <xsl:if test="./person/@job = 'Athlete' or
                    $spouse/person/@job = 'Athlete'">
        <xsl:copy>
           <xsl:copy-of select="@*"/>
        </xsl:copy>
      </xsl:if>
    </xsl:for-each>
  </result>
</xsl:template>
```

Question 3. Find people who have the same job as one of their parents.

Try it yourself.

Question 4. List names of parents and children who have the same job, and list their jobs:

```
<xsl:template match="census">
  <xsl:variable name="everyone"  select="//person"/>
  <result>
     <!-- For each person with children -->
    <xsl:for-each select="$everyone[person]">

      <xsl:variable name="spouse"
          select="$everyone[@spouse=current( )/@name]"/>

      <xsl:apply-templates select="person[@job = current( )/@job]">
        <xsl:with-param name="parent" select="@name"/>
      </xsl:apply-templates>

      <xsl:apply-templates select="person[@job = $spouse/@job]">
        <xsl:with-param name="parent" select="$spouse/@name"/>
      </xsl:apply-templates>

    </xsl:for-each>
  </result>
</xsl:template>

<xsl:template match="person">
  <xsl:param name="parent"/>
  <match parent="{$parent}"  child="{@name}" job="{@job}"/>
</xsl:template>
```

Question 5. List name-pairs of grandparents and grandchildren:

```
<xsl:template match="census">
  <xsl:variable name="everyone"  select="//person"/>
  <result>
    <!-- For each grandchild -->
```

```
      <xsl:for-each select="$everyone[../../../person]">
          <!-- Get the grandparent1 (guaranteed to exist by for each -->
          <grandparent name="{../../@name}" grandchild="{@name}"/>
          <!-- Get the grandparent2 is grandparent1's  spouse if listed -->
          <xsl:if test="../../@spouse">
            <grandparent name="{../../@spouse}" grandchild="{@name}"/>
          </xsl:if>
          <!-- Get the names of this person's parent's spouse
             (i.e. their mother or father as the case may be) -->
          <xsl:variable name="spouse-of-parent" select="../@spouse"/>
          <!-- Get parents of spouse-of-parent, if present -->
          <xsl:variable name="gp3"
            select="$everyone[person/@name=$spouse-of-parent]"/>
          <xsl:if test="$gp3">
            <grandparent name="{$gp3/@name}" grandchild="{@name}"/>
            <xsl:if test="$gp3/@spouse">
              <grandparent name="{$gp3/@spouse}" grandchild="{@name}"/>
            </xsl:if>
          </xsl:if>
        </xsl:for-each>
      </result>
    </xsl:template>
```

Question 6. Find people with no children:

```
<xsl:strip-space elements="*"/>
<xsl:template match="census">
  <xsl:variable name="everyone"  select="//person"/>
  <result>
    <xsl:for-each select="$everyone[not(./person)]">
      <xsl:variable name="spouse"
      select="$everyone[@name = current( )/@spouse]"/>
      <xsl:if test="not ($spouse) or not($spouse/person)">
        <xsl:copy-of select="."/>
      </xsl:if>
    </xsl:for-each>
  </result>
</xsl:template>
```

Question 7. List the names of all Joe's descendants. Show each descendant as an element with the descendant's name as content and his or her marital status and number of children as attributes. Sort the descendants in descending order by number of children and secondarily in alphabetical order by name:

```
<xsl:variable name="everyone" select="//person"/>

<xsl:template match="census">
  <result>
    <xsl:apply-templates select="//person[@name='Joe']"/>
  </result>
</xsl:template>

<xsl:template match="person">
```

```
<xsl:variable name="all-desc">
  <xsl:call-template name="descendants">
    <xsl:with-param name="nodes" select="."/>
  </xsl:call-template>
</xsl:variable>

<xsl:for-each select="exsl:node-set($all-desc)/*">
  <xsl:sort select="count(./* | $everyone[@name = current( )/@spouse]/*)"
  order="descending" data-type="number"/>
  <xsl:sort select="@name"/>
  <xsl:variable name="mstatus"
        select="normalize-space(
              substring('No Yes',boolean(@spouse)* 3+1,3))"/>
  <person married="{$mstatus}"
        nkids="{count(./* | $everyone[@name = current( )/@spouse]/*)}">
        <xsl:value-of select="@name"/>
    </person>
  </xsl:for-each>
</xsl:template>

<xsl:template name="descendants">
  <xsl:param name="nodes"/>
  <xsl:param name="descendants" select="/.."/>

  <xsl:choose>
    <xsl:when test="not($nodes)">
      <xsl:copy-of select="$descendants"/>
    </xsl:when>
    <xsl:otherwise>
      <xsl:call-template name="descendants">
        <xsl:with-param name="nodes" select="$nodes[position( ) > 1] |
          $nodes[1]/person | id($nodes[1]/@spouse)/person"/>
        <xsl:with-param name="descendants" select="$descendants |
          $nodes[1]/person | id($nodes[1]/@spouse)/person"/>
      </xsl:call-template>
    </xsl:otherwise>
  </xsl:choose>

</xsl:template>
```

This example accomplishes the query, but it isn't pretty! The complications come from the need to collect all descendants into a node set so they can be sorted. This forces the use of the node-set extension function. It also means that the id( ) function will not help find the spouse because it only works relative to the node's document. However, the nodes are copies of the original nodes and thus do not have the same document. This situation forces you to go after the spouse elements in a much more cumbersome way by searching for a variable containing all person elements. Contrast this solution to the following XQuery solution:

```
define function descrip (element $e) returns element
{
    let $kids := $e/* union $e/@spouse=>person/*
    let $mstatus :=  if ($e[@spouse]) then "Yes" else "No"
    return
        <person married={ $mstatus } nkids={ count($kids) }>{ $e/@name/text(
) }</person>
}

define function descendants (element $e)
{
    if (empty($e/* union $e/@spouse=>person/*))
    then $e
    else $e union descendants($e/* union $e/@spouse=>person/*)
}

descrip(descendants(//person[@name = "Joe"])) sortby(@nkids descending, .)
```

Discussion

Unlike most other examples in this book, this one is a smorgasbord of prepared
meals. Querying XML can mean so many things that are difficult to come up with.
The W3C did a decent job classifying the kinds of queries that come up in various
domains. The demonstration of these query solutions in XSLT should provide a
sound base for approaching many types of query problems.

Due to space considerations, this chapter did not include the XQuery solutions to
the previous problems. Nevertheless, contrasting the two approaches is instructive,
so I encourage the reader to examine the W3C Query Use Case document.

Providing individual commentary on each query implemented earlier would be
impractical. However, most readers with basic XSLT skills should have little trouble
deciphering the solution. Many solutions shown have alternate solutions in XSLT.
Some of the alternatives may actually be better than the ones in this chapter. My
solutions were heavily influenced by the XQuery solution presented in the original
W3C document. However, I also tried to vary the XSLT constructs used, sometimes
favoring an iterative style (xsl:for-each) and other times using the declarative style
provided by patterns and xsl:apply-templates.

CHAPTER 8

XML to HTML

*That was a surprise to me—that people
were prepared to painstakingly write HTML.*
—Tim Berners-Lee

If I had to hazard a guess, I would say that at least 60% of the HTML delivered over the Internet today is at least partially generated. This is not because HTML is painstakingly hard to write, as Tim Berners-Lee states in the opening quotation (it is, but now we have fancy HTML editors), but because dynamically generated HTML allows you to do so much more.

There are many open and proprietary technologies for delivering HTML content from data stored in other forms. However, when the data is in XML, XSLT is one of the most important tools of which web authors should be aware.

You can use XSLT to generate HTML in three basic ways.

First, XSLT can transform XML into HTML and statically store the generated HTML on a web server or hard drive for delivery to a browser. This is also a good way to test such transformations.

Second, you can use XSLT as a server-side scripting solution in which XML extracted from flat files or databases is dynamically transformed by the web server as requested by the client browser. This solution is necessary when the underlying data changes frequently. However, sometimes a hybrid solution is used in which HTML is constructed on demand, but then cached on the server to avoid the need for subsequent transformations as long as the underlying data does not change.

Third, you can use XSLT as a client-side stylesheet, provided the browser supports XSLT processing. At this time, only the latest versions of Microsoft Internet Explorer (Version 6.0) and Netscape Navigator (6.1) have support for XSLT right out of the box. Older versions of IE require installation of MSXML 3.0 in replacement mode. In addition, XSmiles (*http://www.x-smiles.org/*) and the Antenna House XSL Formatter (*http://www.antennahouse.com/*) perform client-side XSLT processing and display the result. X-Smiles can handle all sorts of results, including SVG and XSL-FO, although the HTML handling is not perfect. The Antenna House XSL Formatter handles XSL-FO. As the state of the world changes rapidly in this area, you should check the latest online documentation of your favorite browser or browser add-in.

8.1 Using XSLT as a Styling Language

Problem

You want the browser to dynamically stylize an XML document into HTML.

Solution

Here is an example for publishing a snippet of a DocBook document in HTML using an XSLT stylesheet. The document source is a portion of this chapter:

```
<?xml version="1.0" encoding="utf-8"?>
<?xml-stylesheet type="application/xml" href="chapter.xsl"?>
<chapter label="8">
  <chapterinfo>
    <author>
      <surname>Mangano</surname>
      <firstname>Sal</firstname>
    </author>
    <copyright>
      <year>2002</year>
      <holder>O'Reilly</holder>
    </copyright>
  </chapterinfo>
  <title>XML to HTML</title>
  <epigraph>
    <para>That was a surprise to me - that people were prepared to painstakingly
write HTML</para>
    <attribution>Tim Berners-Lee</attribution>
  </epigraph>
  <sect1>
    <title>Using XSLT as a Styling Language</title>
    <sect2>
      <title>Problem</title>
      <para>You want to use XSLT to stylize a XML document for dissemination via
HTML.</para>
    </sect2>
    <sect2>
      <title>Solution</title>
      <para>Here we show an example for publishing a snippet of a DocBook document in
HTML using a XSLT stylesheet. The document source is a portion of this chapter.</
para>
    </sect2>
    <sect2>
      <title>Discussion</title>
```

```
    <para>DocBook is an example of a document centric DTD that enables you to
author and store document content in a presentation-neutral form that captures the
logical structure of the content. The beauty of authoring documents (especially
technical ones) in a this form is that one can use XSLT to transform a single content
specification into multiple delivery vehicles such as HTML, PDF, Microsoft Help files
and Unix man pages. Although we present this recipe in terms of DocBook, the
techniques are applicable to other public domain document schema or documents of your
own creation. </para>
    </sect2>
  </sect1>
</chapter>
```

Notice that the second line of this document includes a processing instruction, xml-stylesheet. This instructs the browser to apply the following stylesheet to the XML and render the stylesheet's output rather than the actual XML. (Remember, this instruction works only in the most recent browser versions):

```
<?xml version="1.0" encoding="UTF-8"?>
<xsl:stylesheet version="1.0" xmlns:xsl="http://www.w3.org/1999/XSL/Transform">
  <xsl:output method="html"/>

  <xsl:template match="/">
    <html>
      <head>
        <xsl:apply-templates mode="head"/>
      </head>
      <!-- You may want to use styles in a CSS style element rather -->
      <!-- than hardcoding as I do here -->
      <body style="margin-left:100;margin-right:100;margin-top:50;margin-bottom:50">
        <xsl:apply-templates/>
        <xsl:apply-templates select="chapter/chapterinfo/*" mode="copyright"/>
      </body>
    </html>

  </xsl:template>

  <!-- Head -->

  <xsl:template match="chapter" mode="head">
    <xsl:apply-templates select="chapterinfo" mode="head" />
    <xsl:apply-templates select="title" mode="head" />
  </xsl:template>


  <xsl:template match="chapter/title" mode="head">
      <title><xsl:value-of select="."/></title>
  </xsl:template>

  <xsl:template match="author" mode="head">
      <meta name="author" content="{concat(firstname,' ', surname)}"/>
  </xsl:template>
```

```xsl
    <xsl:template match="copyright" mode="head">
        <meta name="copyright" content="{concat(holder,' ',year)}"/>
    </xsl:template>

    <xsl:template match="text()" mode="head"/>

<!-- Body -->

    <xsl:template match="chapter">
      <div align="right" style="font-size : 48pt; font-family: Times serif; font-weight
: bold; padding-bottom:10; color:red" ><xsl:value-of select="@label"/></div>
      <xsl:apply-templates/>
    </xsl:template>

    <xsl:template match="chapter/title">
      <div align="right" style="font-size : 24pt; font-family: Times serif; padding-
bottom:150; color:red"><xsl:value-of select="."/></div>
    </xsl:template>

    <xsl:template match="epigraph/para">
      <div align="right" style="font-size : 10pt; font-family: Times serif; font-style
: italic; padding-top:4; padding-bottom:4"><xsl:value-of select="."/></div>
    </xsl:template>

    <xsl:template match="epigraph/attribution">
      <div align="right" style="font-size : 10pt; font-family: Times serif; padding-
top:4; padding-bottom:4"><xsl:value-of select="."/></div>
    </xsl:template>


    <xsl:template match="sect1">
      <h1 style="font-size : 18pt; font-family: Times serif; font-weight : bold">
        <xsl:value-of select="title"/>
      </h1>
      <xsl:apply-templates/>
    </xsl:template>

    <xsl:template match="sect2">
      <h2 style="font-size : 14pt; font-family: Times serif; font-weight : bold">
      <xsl:value-of select="title"/>
      </h2>
        <xsl:apply-templates/>
    </xsl:template>

    <xsl:template match="para">
      <p style="font-size : 12pt; font-family: Times serif">
        <xsl:value-of select="."/>
      </p>
    </xsl:template>

    <xsl:template match="text()"/>
```

```
<xsl:template match="copyright" mode="copyright">
  <div style="font-size : 10pt; font-family: Times serif; padding-top : 100">
    <xsl:text>Copyright </xsl:text>
    <xsl:value-of select="holder"/>
    <xsl:text> </xsl:text>
    <xsl:value-of select="year"/>
    <xsl:text>. All rights reserved.</xsl:text>
  </div>
</xsl:template>

<xsl:template match="*" mode="copyright"/>

</xsl:stylesheet>
```

Ultimately, the browser sees the following HTML:

```
<html>
  <head>
    <meta name="author" content="Sal Mangano">
    <meta name="copyright" content="O'Reilly 2002">
    <title>XML to HTML</title>
  </head>
  <body style="margin-left:100;margin-right:100;margin-top:50;margin-bottom:50">
    <div align="right" style="font-size : 48pt; font-family: Times serif; font-
weight : bold; padding-bottom:10; color:red">8</div>
    <div align="right" style="font-size : 24pt; font-family: Times serif; padding-
bottom:150; color:red">XML to HTML</div>
    <div align="right" style="font-size : 10pt; font-family: Times serif; font-
style : italic; padding-top:4; padding-bottom:4">That was a surprise to me - that
people were prepared to painstakingly write HTML</div>
    <div align="right" style="font-size : 10pt; font-family: Times serif; padding-
top:4; padding-bottom:4">Tim Berners-Lee</div>
    <h1 style="font-size : 18pt; font-family: Times serif; font-weight : bold">
Using XSLT as a Styling Language</h1>
    <h2 style="font-size : 14pt; font-family: Times serif; font-weight : bold">
Problem</h2>
    <p style="font-size : 12pt; font-family: Times serif">You want to use XSLT to
stylize a XML document for dissemination via HTML.</p>
    <h2 style="font-size : 14pt; font-family: Times serif; font-weight : bold">
Solution</h2>
    <p style="font-size : 12pt; font-family: Times serif">Here we show an example
for publishing a snippet of a DocBook document in HTML using a XSLT stylesheet. The
document source
        is a portion of this chapter.
    </p>
    <h2 style="font-size : 14pt; font-family: Times serif; font-weight : bold">
Discussion</h2>
    <p style="font-size : 12pt; font-family: Times serif">DocBook is an example of
a document centric DTD that enables you to author and store document content in a
presentation-neutral
        form that captures the logical structure of the content. The beauty of
authoring documents (especially technical ones) in
        a this form is that one can use XSLT to transform a single content
specification into multiple delivery vehicles such as HTML,
```

```
        PDF, Microsoft Help files and Unix man pages. Although we present this
    recipe in terms of DocBook, the techniques are applicable
            to other public domain document schema or documents of your own creation.
        </p>
        <div style="font-size : 10pt; font-family: Times serif; padding-top : 100">
    Copyright O'Reilly 2002. All rights reserved.</div>
        </body>
    </html>
```

Discussion

DocBook is a document-centric DTD that enables you to author and store document content in a presentation-neutral form that captures the content's logical structure. The beauty of authoring documents (especially technical ones) in this form is that you can use XSLT to transform a single content specification into multiple delivery vehicles such as HTML, PDF, Microsoft Help files, and Unix manpages. Although the book presents this example in terms of DocBook, the techniques apply to other public-domain document schema(s) of your own creation.

Since you only used a subset of the DocBook DTD, creating a simple monolithic stylesheet was convenient. However, an industrial-strength solution would modularize the handling of many DocBook elements by using separate stylesheets and moded templates.

See Also

The best source for information about DocBook is *http://www.docbook.org/*. Norman Walsh has developed a set of open source stylesheets to convert DocBook into various publishing formats. These stylesheets are located at *http://docbook.sourceforge. net/projects/xsl/*.

Recipe 14.1 demonstrates several techniques for creating more modular and extensible stylesheets.

8.2   Creating Hyperlinked Documents

Problem

You want to convert XML into hyperlinked HTML content.

Solution

A typical course of action when converting XML into HTML is to make two or more passes over the XML to create menu or index pages and content pages. The menu pages contain links to the content pages. The following solution generates an index and summary pages for *SalesBySalesPerson.xml* (see Chapter 2):

```
<xsl:stylesheet version="1.0"
 xmlns:xsl="http://www.w3.org/1999/XSL/Transform"
 xmlns:saxon="http://icl.com/saxon"
 extension-element-prefixes="saxon">

<xsl:output method="html"/>

<xsl:template match="/">
  <xsl:apply-templates select="*" mode="index"/>
  <xsl:apply-templates select="*" mode="content"/>
</xsl:template>

<!-- ============================================================ -->
<!--                 Create index.html  (mode = "index")          -->
<!-- ============================================================ -->
<xsl:template match="salesBySalesperson" mode="index">
  <saxon:output href="index.html">
    <html>
     <head>
       <title>Sales By Salesperson Index</title>
     </head>

     <body bgcolor="#FFFFFF" text="#000000">
      <h1>Sales By Salesperson</h1>
      <xsl:apply-templates mode="index"/>
     </body>
    </html>
  </saxon:output>
</xsl:template>

<xsl:template match="salesperson" mode="index">
  <h2>
    <a href="{concat(@name,'.html')}">
      <xsl:value-of select="@name"/>
    </a>
  </h2>
</xsl:template>

<!-- ============================================================ -->
<!--                 Create @name.html  (mode = "content")        -->
<!-- ============================================================ -->

<xsl:template match="salesperson" mode="content">
  <saxon:output href="{@name}.html">
    <html>
     <head>
       <title><xsl:value-of select="@name"/> Sales</title>
     </head>

     <body bgcolor="#FFFFFF" text="#000000">
      <h1><xsl:value-of select="@name"/> Sales</h1>
```

```
          <ol>
              <xsl:apply-templates mode="content"/>
          </ol>
        </body>
      </html>
    </saxon:output>
  </xsl:template>

  <xsl:template match="product" mode="content">
      <li><xsl:value-of select="@sku"/>      $<xsl:value-
  of select="@totalSales"/></li>
  </xsl:template>

</xsl:stylesheet>
```

Notice how the modes separate the transformation of XML elements into index content versus the information content of each salesperson's HTML page. Modes are used commonly in HTML transformations because they allow data to be mapped onto presentation in multiple ways within a single stylesheet.

As designed, this stylesheet is limited to batch processing. You can parameterize it to control which document gets created. This parameter also removes the need for the nonstandard saxon:output extension:

```
<xsl:stylesheet version="1.0"
 xmlns:xsl="http://www.w3.org/1999/XSL/Transform">

<xsl:output method="html"/>
<!--Used to specify which document to output-->
<!--INDEX : creates the index document -->
<!--Sales Person's name : creates the page for that salesperson -->
<xsl:param name="which" select="'INDEX'"/>

<xsl:template match="/">
  <xsl:choose>
    <xsl:when test="$which='INDEX'">
      <xsl:apply-templates select="*" mode="index"/>
    </xsl:when>
    <xsl:otherwise>
      <xsl:apply-templates select="*/salesperson[@name = $which]"
                           mode="content"/>
    </xsl:otherwise>
  </xsl:choose>
</xsl:template>

<!-- ============================================================ -->
<!--              Create index.html  (mode = "index")          -->
<!-- ============================================================ -->
<xsl:template match="salesBySalesperson" mode="index">
  <!-- Removed saxon:output. The rest is the same. -->
</xsl:template>

<!-- ... -->
```

```
<xsl:template match="salesperson" mode="content">
  <!-- Removed saxon:output. The rest is the same. -->
</xsl:template>

<!-- ... -->

</xsl:stylesheet>
```

This technique would be slightly more robust if each salesperson used an ID rather than her name as the parameter.

Discussion

The solution does not create fancy content, but it does illustrate the basic mechanics of producing linked HTML content. To produce all web pages with a single stylesheet, you were forced to use a nonstandard XSLT 1.0 element (saxon:output). Similar extensions are available in most processors.

The stylesheet produces relative links, which is what you want most of the time. However, when you need absolute links, rather than hardcoding a URL, you might consider incorporating a top-level parameter that can be set to the URL:

```
<xsl:stylesheet version="1.1" xmlns:xsl="http://www.w3.org/1999/XSL/Transform">

<xsl:output method="html"/>

<xsl:param name="URL" select="http://www.mycompany.com/"/>

<!-- elided ... -->

<xsl:template match="salesperson" mode="index">
  <h2>
    <a href="{$URL}{@name}.html'">
      <xsl:value-of select="@name"/>
    </a>
  </h2>
</xsl:template>
```

See Also

See Recipe 6.6 for more information on producing multiple output documents.

The content produced by these transformations is not very user friendly. Recipes 8.3 and 8.4 show how to improve the result's aesthetics.

8.3   Creating HTML Tables

Problem

You want to map XML content onto HTML tables.

Solution

Tables are often created in two stages. First, the top-level table markup is generated, and then templates are applied to create rows and fields. The solution is a modification of part of the stylesheet produced in Recipe 8.2. The changed portion is highlighted:

```
<xsl:stylesheet version="1.1" xmlns:xsl="http://www.w3.org/1999/XSL/Transform">

<xsl:output method="html"/>

<xsl:param name="URL"/>

<xsl:template match="/">
  <xsl:apply-templates select="*" mode="index"/>
  <xsl:apply-templates select="*" mode="content"/>
</xsl:template>

<!-- ============================================================ -->
<!--              Create index.html  (mode = "index")             -->
<!-- ============================================================ -->
<xsl:template match="salesBySalesperson" mode="index">
  <!-- Non-standard saxon xsl:document! -->
  <xsl:document href="index.html">
    <html>
     <head>
      <title>Sales by Salesperson</title>
     </head>

     <body bgcolor="#FFFFFF" text="#000000">
      <h1>Sales By Salesperson</h1>
      <xsl:apply-templates mode="index"/>
     </body>
    </html>
  </xsl:document>
</xsl:template>

<xsl:template match="salesperson" mode="index">
  <h2>
    <a href="{concat($URL,@name,'.html')}">
      <xsl:value-of select="@name"/>
    </a>
  </h2>
</xsl:template>

<!-- ============================================================ -->
<!--              Create @name.html  (mode = "content")           -->
<!-- ============================================================ -->
<xsl:template match="salesperson" mode="content">
  <xsl:document href="{concat(@name,'.html')}">
    <html>
     <head>
```

```
        <title><xsl:value select="@name"/></title>
      </head>

      <body bgcolor="#FFFFFF" text="#000000">
       <h1><xsl:value-of select="@name"/> Sales</h1>
       <table border="1" cellpadding="3">
         <tbody >
           <tr>
             <th>SKU</th>
             <th>Sales (in US $)</th>
           </tr>
           <xsl:apply-templates mode="content"/>
         </tbody>
       </table>
       <h2><a href="{concat($URL,'index.html')}">Home</a></h2>
      </body>
    </html>
   </xsl:document>
  </xsl:template>

  <xsl:template match="product" mode="content">
     <tr>
       <td><xsl:value-of select="@sku"/></td>
       <td><xsl:value-of select="@totalSales"/></td>
     </tr>

  </xsl:template>

  </xsl:stylesheet>
```

Discussion

When creating tables, you often need to group data based on specific criteria. The difficulty of a grouping problem is related to whether the input data is already grouped and whether the grouping criteria are close- or open-ended. For example, imagine that you need to group sales data by region:

```
<sales>
  <product sku="10000" sales="90000.00" region="NE"/>
  <product sku="10000" sales="10000.00" region="NW"/>
  <product sku="10000" sales="55000.00" region="SE"/>
  <product sku="10000" sales="32000.00" region="SW"/>
  <product sku="10000" sales="95000.00" region="NC"/>
  <product sku="10000" sales="88000.00" region="SC"/>
  <product sku="20000" sales="77000.00" region="NE"/>
  <product sku="20000" sales="11100.00" region="NW"/>
  <product sku="20000" sales="33210.00" region="SE"/>
  <product sku="20000" sales="78000.00" region="SW"/>
  <product sku="20000" sales="105000.00" region="NC"/>
  <product sku="20000" sales="12300.00" region="SC"/>
  <product sku="30000" sales="1000.00" region="NE"/>
  <product sku="30000" sales="5100.00" region="NW"/>
  <product sku="30000" sales="3210.00" region="SE"/>
```

```
      <product sku="30000" sales="8000.00" region="SW"/>
      <product sku="30000" sales="5000.00" region="NC"/>
      <product sku="30000" sales="11300.00" region="SC"/>
    </sales>
```

Here, you know in advance that there are six regions. You could solve the grouping problem by explicit selection:

```
<xsl:stylesheet version="1.0" xmlns:xsl="http://www.w3.org/1999/XSL/Transform">
  <xsl:output method="html"/>

<xsl:template match="sales">
  <html>
    <head>
      <title>Sales by Region</title>
    </head>
    <body>
      <h1>Sales by Region</h1>
      <table border="1" cellpadding="3">
        <tbody>
          <tr>
            <th>SKU</th>
            <th>Sales</th>
          </tr>
          <xsl:call-template name="group-region">
            <xsl:with-param name="region" select=" 'NE' "/>
            <xsl:with-param name="title" select="'North East Sales'"/>
          </xsl:call-template>
          <xsl:call-template name="group-region">
            <xsl:with-param name="region" select=" 'NW' "/>
            <xsl:with-param name="title" select="'North West Sales'"/>
          </xsl:call-template>
          <xsl:call-template name="group-region">
            <xsl:with-param name="region" select=" 'NC' "/>
            <xsl:with-param name="title" select="'North Central Sales'"/>
          </xsl:call-template>
          <xsl:call-template name="group-region">
            <xsl:with-param name="region" select=" 'SE' "/>
            <xsl:with-param name="title" select="'South East Sales'"/>
          </xsl:call-template>
          <xsl:call-template name="group-region">
            <xsl:with-param name="region" select=" 'SC' "/>
            <xsl:with-param name="title" select="'South Central Sales'"/>
          </xsl:call-template>
          <xsl:call-template name="group-region">
            <xsl:with-param name="region" select=" 'SW' "/>
            <xsl:with-param name="title" select="'South West Sales'"/>
          </xsl:call-template>
        </tbody>
      </table>
    </body>
  </html>
</xsl:template>
```

```
<xsl:template name="group-region">
    <xsl:param name="region"/>
    <xsl:param name="title"/>
    <xsl:variable name="products" select="product[@region = $region]" />
    <tr>
      <th colspan="2"><xsl:value-of select="$title" /></th>
    </tr>
    <xsl:apply-templates select="$products"/>
    <tr style="font-weight:bold">
      <td >Total</td>
      <td align="right">
        <xsl:value-of
             select="format-number(sum($products/@sales), '#.00')"/>
      </td>
     </tr>
  </xsl:template>

  <xsl:template match="product">
    <tr>
      <td><xsl:value-of select="@sku"/></td>
      <td align="right"><xsl:value-of select="@sales"/></td>
    </tr>
  </xsl:template>

</xsl:stylesheet>
```

If you find the hardcoding of group names objectionable, use a table-driven approach:

```
<xsl:stylesheet version="1.0" xmlns:xsl="http://www.w3.org/1999/XSL/Transform" xmlns:
sales="sales">

  <sales:region code="NE" name="North East"/>
  <sales:region code="NC" name="North Central"/>
  <sales:region code="NW" name="North West"/>
  <sales:region code="SE" name="South East"/>
  <sales:region code="SC" name="South Central"/>
  <sales:region code="SW" name="South West"/>

 <xsl:variable name="products" select="/sales/product"/>

 <xsl:output method="html"/>

 <xsl:template match="sales">
   <html>
     <head>
       <title>Sales by Region</title>
     </head>
     <body>
       <h1>Sales by Region</h1>
       <table border="1" cellpadding="3">
         <tbody>
           <tr>
```

```
                  <th>SKU</th>
                  <th>Sales</th>
                </tr>
                <xsl:for-each select="document('')/*/sales:region">
                  <tr >
                    <th colspan="2"><xsl:value-of select="@name"/> Sales</th>
                  </tr>
                  <xsl:call-template name="group-region">
                    <xsl:with-param name="region" select="@code"/>
                  </xsl:call-template>
                </xsl:for-each>
              </tbody>
            </table>
          </body>
        </html>
      </xsl:template>

      <xsl:template name="group-region">
        <xsl:param name="region"/>
          <xsl:apply-templates select="$products[@region=$region]"/>
          <tr style="font-weight:bold">
            <td >Total</td>
            <td align="right"><xsl:value-of
            select="format-number(sum($products[@region=$region]/@sales),'#.00')"/>
            </td>
          </tr>
      </xsl:template>


      <xsl:template match="product">
        <tr>
          <td><xsl:value-of select="@sku"/></td>
          <td align="right"><xsl:value-of select="@sales"/></td>
        </tr>
      </xsl:template>

    </xsl:stylesheet>
```

Of course, many grouping problems are not this easy. Imagine that you are design-
ing a stylesheet to be used by many companies or divisions within a large company
that each had their own conventions for naming sales regions. You can tackle this
problem in several ways, but one of the most efficient is called the Muenchian grouping technique (named after Steve Muench of Oracle who invented it):

```
    <xsl:stylesheet version="1.0" xmlns:xsl="http://www.w3.org/1999/XSL/Transform"
        xmlns:sales="sales">

    <xsl:output method="html"/>

    <xsl:key name="region-key" match="product" use="@region"/>

    <xsl:template match="sales">
      <html>
```

```
      <head>
        <title>Sales by Region</title>
      </head>
      <body>
        <h1>Sales by Region</h1>
        <table border="1" cellpadding="3">
          <tbody>
            <tr>
              <th>SKU</th>
              <th>Sales</th>
            </tr>
            <xsl:variable name="unique-regions"
                select="/sales
                        /product[generate-id(.) =
                                 generate-id(key('region-key',@region))]
                        /@region"/>
            <xsl:for-each select="$unique-regions">
              <tr >
                <th colspan="2"><xsl:value-of select="."/> Sales</th>
              </tr>
              <xsl:call-template name="group-region">
                <xsl:with-param name="region" select="."/>
              </xsl:call-template>
            </xsl:for-each>
          </tbody>
        </table>
      </body>
    </html>
  </xsl:template>

  <xsl:template name="group-region">
    <xsl:param name="region"/>
      <xsl:apply-templates select="key('region-key', @region)"/>
      <tr style="font-weight:bold">
        <td >Total</td>
        <td align="right"><xsl:value-of
        select="format-number(sum(key('region-key', @region)/@sales),'#.00')"/>
        </td>
      </tr>
  </xsl:template>

  <xsl:template match="product">
    <tr>
      <td><xsl:value-of select="@sku"/></td>
      <td align="right"><xsl:value-of select="@sales"/></td>
    </tr>
  </xsl:template>

</xsl:stylesheet>
```

Structurally, the solution is similar to the table-driven method. The main difference is in how you determine the unique set of groups. In the table-driven case, the unique sales regions are literally encoded in sales:region elements. The Muenchian technique uses a key to define the grouping value. You know that the expression `key('region-key',@region)` returns a node set of all products whose region is `@region`. You also know that `generate-id`, when presented with a node-set, returns a unique ID for the first element in the node set. Thus, the expression `[generate-id(.) = generate-id( key( 'region-key', @region))]` will be true only for the first node within each group, in this case allowing you to obtain all unique regions that make up the group. Having this key also makes other parts of the stylesheet that refer to product by region more efficient.

8.4 Creating Frames

Problem

You want to generate HTML that organizes content by using HTML frames.

Solution

As in Recipe 8.2, you will use modes to make multiple passes over the XML. First, create the frameset container document. To do so, you use two frames. The smaller left frame holds the names of the salespeople as hyperlinks for activating content in the mainframe. The main frame contains the sales figures for the salesperson selected by the user. This example provides a default main frame that is displayed when the page first comes up:

```
<xsl:stylesheet version="1.1" xmlns:xsl="http://www.w3.org/1999/XSL/Transform">

<xsl:output method="html"/>

<xsl:param name="URL"/>

<xsl:template match="/">
  <xsl:apply-templates select="*" mode="frameset"/>
  <xsl:apply-templates select="*" mode="salespeople_frame"/>
  <xsl:apply-templates select="*" mode="sales_frames"/>
</xsl:template>

<!-- ============================================================ -->
<!--              Create frameset container (mode ="frameset")    -->
<!-- ============================================================ -->
<xsl:template match="salesBySalesperson" mode="frameset">
  <!-- Non-standard saxon xsl:document! -->
  <xsl:document href="index.html">
    <html>
     <head>
      <title>Salesperson Frameset</title>
     </head>
     <frameset rows="100%" cols="25%, 75%" border="0">
       <frame name="salespeople" src="salespeople_frame.html" noresize=""/>
       <frame name="mainFrame" src="default_sales.html" noresize=""/>
     </frameset>
```

```
      <body bgcolor="#FFFFFF" text="#000000">
      </body>
     </html>
   </xsl:document>
</xsl:template>


<!-- =========================================================== -->
<!-- Create salespeople_frame.html  (mode = "salespeople_frame")    -->
<!-- =========================================================== -->
<xsl:template match="salesBySalesperson" mode="salespeople_frame">
   <!-- Non-standard xsl: saxon:document! -->
   <xsl:document href="salespeople_frame.html">
     <html>
      <head>
        <title>Salespeople</title>
      </head>
      <body bgcolor="#FFFFFF" text="#000000">
        <table>
         <tbody>
           <xsl:apply-templates mode="index"/>
         </tbody>
        </table>
      </body>
     </html>
   </xsl:document>
</xsl:template>

<xsl:template match="salesperson" mode="index">
   <tr>
     <td>
      <a href="{concat(@name,'.html')}"
          target="mainFrame"><xsl:value-of select="@name"/></a>
     </td>
   </tr>
</xsl:template>


<!-- =========================================================== -->
<!--                  Create @name.html  (mode = "content")        -->
<!-- =========================================================== -->

<xsl:template match="salesperson" mode="sales_frames">

   <xsl:document href="default_sales.html">
     <html>
      <head>
        <title>Default</title>
      </head>

      <body bgcolor="#FFFFFF" text="#000000">
      <h1><center>Sales By Salesperson</center></h1>
       <br/>
      Click on a salesperson on the left to load his or her sales figures.
```

```
            </body>
          </html>
        </xsl:document>

        <xsl:document href="{concat(@name,'.html')}">
          <html>
            <head>
              <title><xsl:value-of select="@name"/></title>
            </head>

            <body bgcolor="#FFFFFF" text="#000000">
            <h1><center>Sales By Salesperson</center></h1>
             <h2><xsl:value-of select="@name"/></h2>
             <table border="1" cellpadding="3">
               <tbody >
                 <tr>
                   <th>SKU</th>
                   <th>Sales (in US $)</th>
                 </tr>
                 <xsl:apply-templates mode="content"/>
               </tbody>
             </table>
            </body>
          </html>
        </xsl:document>
      </xsl:template>

      <xsl:template match="product" mode="content">
         <tr>
           <td><xsl:value-of select="@sku"/></td>
           <td align="right"><xsl:value-of select="@totalSales"/></td>
         </tr>

      </xsl:template>

      </xsl:stylesheet>
```

Discussion

Frames are useful for splitting a page into logical sections; however, using frames with visible or resizable borders is somewhat passé. Your stylesheet cannot be used for client-side transformation because it outputs many separate HTML files—one for the frameset, one for the left frame that lists salespeople, and a separate page for each salesperson.

The solution demonstrates an example that is dynamic and open-ended in terms of the number of separate pages that might be generated from a single XML file. However, cases in which frames can be used with client-side XSLT processing are more straightforward. Simply create a page containing a frameset where the frames hold separate XML documents, each with their own transformation:

```
<html>
  <head>
    <title>Frameset</title>
  </head>
  <frameset rows="100%" cols="25%, 75%" border="0">
    <frame name="leftFrame" src="left.xml" noresize="">
    <frame name="mainFrame" src="main.xml" noresize="">
  </frameset>
  <body bgcolor="#FFFFFF" text="#000000"></body>
</html>
```

You must reference different XML documents for each frame because there can be only one xml-stylesheet processing instruction per file. However, you can still keep the content in one stylesheet by using an xinclude link and an XSLT template to process it.

left.xml looks like this:

```
<?xml version="1.0" encoding="UTF-8"?>
<?xml-stylesheet type="application/xml" href="left.xsl"?>
<xi:include href="salesBySalesperson.xml"
            xmlns:xi="http://www.w3.org/2001/XInclude"/>
```

main.xml is similar:

```
<?xml version="1.0" encoding="UTF-8"?>
<?xml-stylesheet type="application/xml" href="main.xsl"?>
<xi:include href="salesBySalesperson.xml"
            xmlns:xi="http://www.w3.org/2001/XInclude"/>
```

left.xsl and *main.xsl* contain a template that processes the xinclude element by using the document function:

```
<!-- left.xsl -->
<?xml version="1.0" encoding="UTF-8"?>
<xsl:stylesheet version="1.0" xmlns:xsl="http://www.w3.org/1999/XSL/Transform">

<xsl:output method="html"/>

<xsl:template match="xi:include" xmlns:xi="http://www.w3.org/2001/XInclude">
  <xsl:for-each select="document(@href,.)">
    <xsl:apply-templates/>
  </xsl:for-each>
</xsl:template>

<xsl:template match="salesBySalesperson">
  <html>
   <head>
    <title>Salespeople</title>
   </head>
   <body bgcolor="#FFFFFF" text="#000000">
     <table>
      <tbody>
        <xsl:apply-templates/>
```

```
        </tbody>
      </table>
     </body>
    </html>
</xsl:template>

<xsl:template match="salesperson">
  <tr>
    <td>
      <a href="{concat('main.xml#',@name)}" target="mainFrame">
      <xsl:value-of select="@name"/></a>
    </td>
  </tr>
</xsl:template>

</xsl:stylesheet>

<!-- main.xsl -->
<xsl:stylesheet version="1.0" xmlns:xsl="http://www.w3.org/1999/XSL/Transform">
  <xsl:output method="html"/>

<xsl:template match="xi:include" xmlns:xi="http://www.w3.org/2001/XInclude">
  <xsl:for-each select="document(@href)">
    <xsl:apply-templates/>
  </xsl:for-each>
</xsl:template>

<xsl:template match="salesBySalesperson">
    <html>
     <head>
      <title>Sales By Salesperson</title>
     </head>

     <body bgcolor="#FFFFFF" text="#000000">
     <xsl:apply-templates/>
     </body>
    </html>
</xsl:template>

<xsl:template match="salesperson">
    <h1><a name="{@name}"><center>Sales By Salesperson</center></a></h1>
     <h2><xsl:value-of select="@name"/></h2>
     <table border="1" cellpadding="3">
       <tbody >
         <tr>
           <th>SKU</th>
           <th>Sales (in US $)</th>
         </tr>
         <xsl:apply-templates />
       </tbody>
     </table>
     <div style="padding-top:1000"/>
</xsl:template>
```

```xsl
<xsl:template match="product">
    <tr>
       <td><xsl:value-of select="@sku"/></td>
       <td align="right"><xsl:value-of select="@totalSales"/></td>
    </tr>

</xsl:template>

</xsl:stylesheet>
```

In the *main.xsl* stylesheet, you generate named anchors for each salesperson and separate them by a large amount of whitespace by using `<div style="padding-top:1000"/>`. In *left.xsl*, you generate links to the anchors. This generation crudely emulates behavior of the "Solution" section's multipage example.

See Also

Jeni Tennison's *XSLT and XPath on the Edge* (M&T, 2001) includes a detailed discussion of client-side XSLT processing with frames that shows how JavaScripting can create more sophisticated results.

8.5   Creating Data-Driven Stylesheets

Problem

You want to generate HTML that is styled based on data content.

Solution

XSLT attribute sets provide a nice vehicle for encapsulating the complexity of data-driven stylization. Consider how XML describes an investment portfolio:

```
<portfolio>
  <investment>
    <symbol>IBM</symbol>
    <current>72.70</current>
    <paid>65.00</paid>
    <qty>1000</qty>
  </investment>
  <investment>
    <symbol>JMAR</symbol>
    <current>1.90</current>
    <paid>5.10</paid>
    <qty>5000</qty>
  </investment>
  <investment>
    <symbol>DELL</symbol>
    <current>24.50</current>
    <paid>18.00</paid>
```

```
      <qty>100000</qty>
    </investment>
    <investment>
      <symbol>P</symbol>
      <current>57.33</current>
      <paid>63</paid>
      <qty>100</qty>
    </investment>
  </portfolio>
```

You should display this portfolio in a table with a column showing the gain in black or the loss in red:

```
<xsl:stylesheet version="1.0" xmlns:xsl="http://www.w3.org/1999/XSL/Transform">

  <xsl:output method="html"/>

  <xsl:attribute-set name="gain-loss-font">
    <xsl:attribute name="color">
      <xsl:choose>
        <xsl:when test="(current - paid) * qty >= 0">black</xsl:when>
        <xsl:otherwise>red</xsl:otherwise>
      </xsl:choose>
    </xsl:attribute>
  </xsl:attribute-set>

<xsl:template match="portfolio">
    <html>
     <head>
      <title>My Portfolio</title>
     </head>

     <body bgcolor="#FFFFFF" text="#000000">
      <h1>Portfolio</h1>
      <table border="1" cellpadding="2">
        <tbody>
          <tr>
            <th>Symbol</th>
            <th>Current</th>
            <th>Paid</th>
            <th>Qty</th>
            <th>Gain/Loss</th>
          </tr>
          <xsl:apply-templates/>
        </tbody>
      </table>
     </body>
    </html>
</xsl:template>

<xsl:template match="investment">
  <tr>
    <td><xsl:value-of select="symbol"/></td>
    <td><xsl:value-of select="current"/></td>
```

```
        <td><xsl:value-of select="paid"/></td>
        <td><xsl:value-of select="qty"/></td>
        <td>
         <font xsl:use-attribute-sets="gain-loss-font">
          <xsl:value-of
            select="format-number((current - paid) * qty, '#,##0.00')"/>
         </font>
        </td>
      </tr>
    </xsl:template>

  </xsl:stylesheet>
```

If you are not concerned with backward compatibility to older browsers, this example can be made cleaner by using the HTML 4.0 style attribute instead of the font element:

```
    <xsl:attribute-set name="gain-loss-color">
      <xsl:attribute name="style">color:<xsl:text/>
        <xsl:choose>
          <xsl:when test="(current - paid) * qty >= 0">black</xsl:when>
          <xsl:otherwise>red</xsl:otherwise>
        </xsl:choose>
      </xsl:attribute>
    </xsl:attribute-set>

    ...

    <xsl:template match="investment">
      <tr>
        <td><xsl:value-of select="symbol"/></td>
        <td><xsl:value-of select="current"/></td>
        <td><xsl:value-of select="paid"/></td>
        <td><xsl:value-of select="qty"/></td>
        <td xsl:use-attribute-sets="gain-loss-color">
          <xsl:value-of
                select="format-number((current - paid) * qty, '#,##0.00')"/>
        </td>
      </tr>
    </xsl:template>
```

Discussion

As is usually the case with XSLT, you can approach this problem in many ways. You might consider embedding the style logic directly into the table-generation logic:

```
    <xsl:template match="investment">
      <tr>
        <td><xsl:value-of select="symbol"/></td>
        <td><xsl:value-of select="current"/></td>
        <td><xsl:value-of select="paid"/></td>
        <td><xsl:value-of select="qty"/></td>
        <td>
```

```
      <font>
        <xsl:attribute name="color">
          <xsl:choose>
            <xsl:when test="(current - paid) * qty >= 0">black</xsl:when>
            <xsl:otherwise>red</xsl:otherwise>
          </xsl:choose>
        </xsl:attribute>
        <xsl:value-of
          select="format-number((current - paid) * qty, '#,##0.00')"/>
      </font>
    </td>
  </tr>
</xsl:template>
```

Although placing the color determination logic inline might help you figure out what is happening, it complicates the table-creation logic. A more complex example might compute style attributes for many elements. Mixing the structural building aspect of the stylesheet with the stylization aspect will make each aspect harder to understand and modify.

Nevertheless, you can argue that the hardcoding element references in attributes sets detract from their reusability. However, you can usually remedy this problem by simply moving the logic of the attribute determination outside of the attribute set by using templates and modes. Consider a portfolio with varied investments whose profitability is calculated in different ways:

```
<portfolio>

  <stock>
    <symbol>IBM</symbol>
    <current>72.70</current>
    <paid>65.00</paid>
    <qty>1000</qty>
  </stock>

  <stock>
    <symbol>JMAR</symbol>
    <current>1.90</current>
    <paid>5.10</paid>
    <qty>5000</qty>
  </stock>

  <stock>
    <symbol>DELL</symbol>
    <current>24.50</current>
    <paid>18.00</paid>
    <qty>100000</qty>
  </stock>
```

```
<stock>
  <symbol>P</symbol>
  <current>57.33</current>
  <paid>63.00</paid>
  <qty>100</qty>
</stock>

<property>
  <address>123 Main St. Anytown NY</address>
  <paid>100000</paid>
  <appriasal>250000</appriasal>
</property>

<property>
  <address>13 Skunks Misery Dr. Stinksville NJ</address>
  <paid>200000</paid>
  <appriasal>50000</appriasal>
</property>

</portfolio>
```

You can avoid having to define two attribute sets that perform the same function by pushing the logic into templates:

```
<xsl:stylesheet version="1.0" xmlns:xsl="http://www.w3.org/1999/XSL/Transform">

  <xsl:output method="html"/>

  <xsl:attribute-set name="gain-loss-font">
    <xsl:attribute name="color">
      <xsl:apply-templates select="." mode="gain-loss-font-color"/>
    </xsl:attribute>
  </xsl:attribute-set>

<xsl:template match="stock" mode="gain-loss-font-color">
    <xsl:choose>
      <xsl:when test="(current - paid) * qty >= 0">black</xsl:when>
      <xsl:otherwise>red</xsl:otherwise>
    </xsl:choose>
</xsl:template>

<xsl:template match="property" mode="gain-loss-font-color">
    <xsl:choose>
      <xsl:when test="appriasal - paid  >= 0">black</xsl:when>
      <xsl:otherwise>red</xsl:otherwise>
    </xsl:choose>
</xsl:template>

...

</xsl:stylesheet>
```

You might be uncomfortable incorporating any purely stylistic attributes such as colors, fonts, and the like into your XSLT transformation. Perhaps it is not your job—but the job of a company style czar—to decide how to render gains and losses. In this case, you can simply classify the elements and defer stylizing decisions to a separately defined stylesheet:

```
<xsl:stylesheet version="1.0" xmlns:xsl="http://www.w3.org/1999/XSL/Transform">

  <xsl:output method="html"/>

  <xsl:attribute-set name="gain-loss">
    <xsl:attribute name="class">
      <xsl:apply-templates select="." mode="gain-loss"/>
    </xsl:attribute>
  </xsl:attribute-set>

<xsl:template match="stock" mode="gain-loss">
    <xsl:choose>
      <xsl:when test="(current - paid) * qty >= 0">gain</xsl:when>
      <xsl:otherwise>loss</xsl:otherwise>
    </xsl:choose>
</xsl:template>

<xsl:template match="property" mode="gain-loss">
    <xsl:choose>
      <xsl:when test="appriasal - paid  >= 0">gain</xsl:when>
      <xsl:otherwise>loss</xsl:otherwise>
    </xsl:choose>
</xsl:template>

<xsl:template match="portfolio">
    <html>
     <head>
      <title>My Portfolio</title>
      <link rel="stylesheet" type="text/css" href="portfolio.css"/>
     </head>

     ...

</xsl:template>

<xsl:template match="stock">
  <tr>
    <td><xsl:value-of select="symbol"/></td>
    <td align="right"><xsl:value-of select="current"/></td>
    <td align="right"><xsl:value-of select="paid"/></td>
    <td align="right"><xsl:value-of select="qty"/></td>
    <td align="right" xsl:use-attribute-sets="gain-loss">
      <xsl:value-of
            select="format-number((current - paid) * qty, '#,##0.00')"/>
    </td>
  </tr>
</xsl:template>
```

```
<xsl:template match="property">
  <tr>
    <td><xsl:value-of select="address"/></td>
    <td align="right"><xsl:value-of select="paid"/></td>
    <td align="right"><xsl:value-of select="appriasal"/></td>
    <td align="right" xsl:use-attribute-sets="gain-loss">
      <xsl:value-of
              select="format-number(appriasal - paid, '#,##0.00')"/>
    </td>
  </tr>
</xsl:template>

</xsl:stylesheet>
```

The style czar can then decide how to render <td class="gain"> and <td class="loss"> by using *portfolio.css*, as shown in Example 8-1.

Example 8-1. portfolio.css

```
td.gain
{
    color:black;
}

td.loss
{
    color:red;
    font-weight:700;
}
```

8.6   Creating a Self-Contained HTML Transformation

Problem

You want to package XML data, as well as a stylesheet for converting it to HTML, into a single file.

Solution

This recipe assumes you have a browser that supports client-side XSLT transformations (IE 6.0, IE 5.x + MSXML 3.0, Netscape Navigator 6.0, etc.):

```
<?xml version="1.0" encoding="UTF-8"?>

<?xml-stylesheet type="application/xml" href="selfcontained.xsl"?>

<xsl:stylesheet version="1.0" xmlns:xsl="http://www.w3.org/1999/XSL/Transform"
 xmlns:pf="http://www.ora.com/XSLTCookbook/namespaces/portfolio">
```

```
<portfolio xmlns="http://www.ora.com/XSLTCookbook/namespaces/portfolio">
  <investment>
    <symbol>IBM</symbol>
    <current>72.70</current>
    <paid>65.00</paid>
    <qty>1000</qty>
  </investment>
  <investment>
    <symbol>JMAR</symbol>
    <current>1.90</current>
    <paid>5.10</paid>
    <qty>5000</qty>
  </investment>
  <investment>
    <symbol>DELL</symbol>
    <current>24.50</current>
    <paid>18.00</paid>
    <qty>100000</qty>
  </investment>
  <investment>
    <symbol>P</symbol>
    <current>57.33</current>
    <paid>63</paid>
    <qty>100</qty>
  </investment>
</portfolio>

<xsl:output method="html" />

  <xsl:attribute-set name="gain-loss-font">
    <xsl:attribute name="color">
      <xsl:choose>
        <xsl:when test="(pf:current - pf:paid) * pf:qty >= 0">black</xsl:when>
        <xsl:otherwise>red</xsl:otherwise>
      </xsl:choose>
    </xsl:attribute>
  </xsl:attribute-set>

<xsl:template match="xsl:stylesheet">
  <xsl:apply-templates select="pf:portfolio"/>
</xsl:template>

<xsl:template match="pf:portfolio">
    <html>
     <head>
      <title>My Portfolio</title>
     </head>

     <body bgcolor="#FFFFFF" text="#000000">
      <h1>Portfolio</h1>
      <table border="1" cellpadding="2">
        <tbody>
          <tr>
            <th>Symbol</th>
```

```
                  <th>Current</th>
                  <th>Paid</th>
                  <th>Qty</th>
                  <th>Gain/Loss</th>
                </tr>
                <xsl:apply-templates/>
              </tbody>
          </table>
        </body>
      </html>
  </xsl:template>

  <xsl:template match="pf:investment">
    <tr>
      <td><xsl:value-of select="pf:symbol"/></td>
      <td><xsl:value-of select="pf:current"/></td>
      <td><xsl:value-of select="pf:paid"/></td>
      <td><xsl:value-of select="pf:qty"/></td>
      <td><font xsl:use-attribute-sets="gain-loss-font"><xsl:value-of select="format-
number((pf:current - pf:paid) * pf:qty, '#,##0.00')"/></font></td>
    </tr>
  </xsl:template>


  </xsl:stylesheet>
```

Two elements in this stylesheet make it work.

The first is the `xml-stylesheet` processing instruction, which tells the browser that the stylesheet associated with the document it loads is the very same document. You can refer to the same document as its stylesheet with `href=""` rather than specifying the name of the file, which is helpful if you ever rename it.

The second is the template that matches the `xsl:stylesheet` element and redirects stylesheet processing to the embedded XML data. In this case, the elements are in the *http://www.ora.com/XSLTCookbook/namespaces/portfolio* namespace.

Discussion

This recipe is somewhat of a trick to impress your friends. Intermixing content and styling, in some ways, goes against the spirit of the technology. However, delivering just a single file can be convenient, so you should not feel guilty about using this recipe if it suits your needs.

The official way to achieve these results is to embed the stylesheet in the document rather than vice versa. See *http://www.w3.org/TR/xslt#section-Embedding-Stylesheets* for more details. However, IE does not yet support embedded stylesheets, so this trick gets around the problem.

You can deliver content in this form without necessarily developing the content directly in this form. The following stylesheet merges a stylesheet and an XML file into the self-contained format. The only two criteria are that the XML must be in a namespace and the stylesheet should not begin processing at the root node (/):

```
<!-- generate-selfcontained.xslt -->
<xsl:stylesheet version="1.0" xmlns:xsl="http://www.w3.org/1999/XSL/Transform"
    xmlns:xso="dummy">

<!-- Reuse the identity transform -->
<xsl:import href="../util/copy.xslt"/>

<!-- This stylesheet will be generating styleshhet content
     so use xso as alias for xsl -->
<xsl:namespace-alias stylesheet-prefix="xso" result-prefix="xsl"/>

<xsl:output method="xml" version="1.0" encoding="UTF-8" indent="yes"/>

<xsl:strip-space elements="*"/>
<!--Not a good idea to strip space from text nodes -->
<xsl:preserve-space elements="xsl:text"/>

<!--The name of the file containing xml data -->
<xsl:param name="datafile"/>
<!-- The name of the resulting output file -->
<xsl:param name="outfile"/>

<xsl:template match="/">
  <!-- Insert the processing instruction to tell the browser that
       $outfile is the stylesheet -->
  <xsl:processing-instruction name="xml-stylesheet">
   <xsl:text>type="application/xml" href="</xsl:text>
   <xsl:value-of select="$outfile"/>"<xsl:text/>
  </xsl:processing-instruction>

 <xsl:apply-templates/>

</xsl:template>

<xsl:template match="xsl:stylesheet">

  <xsl:copy>
    <xsl:copy-of select="@*"/>

    <xsl:apply-templates/>

     <!-- Generate the xslt that tells the
    <xso:template match="xsl:stylesheet">
      <xso:apply-templates select="{name(document($datafile)/*)}"/>
    </xso:template>
```

```
<!-- Insert the data -->
<xsl:copy-of select="document($datafile)"/>

  </xsl:copy>

</xsl:template>

</xsl:stylesheet>
```

You can use this stylesheet to transform another stylesheet and its data into a self-contained HTML transformation. The source should be the stylesheet, and the $datafile is provided as a parameter. You need an additional parameter, $outfile, to allow correct generation of the xml-stylesheet processing instruction.

Using Saxon, the generation might be invoked as:

```
saxon -o self-contained.xsl pf-portfolio.xslt generate-selfcontained.xslt
        datafile="pf-portfolio.xml" outfile="self-contained.xsl"
```

Where *self-contained.xsl* is the name of the resulting stylesheet and *pf-portfolio.xslt* is the stylesheet being merged with *pf-portfolio.xml*.

8.7   Populating a Form

Problem

You want to merge XML data into a predesigned form before delivering it to the client.

Solution

Provided you use XHTML or otherwise create well-formed HTML, you can use XSLT to merge an HTML document with data in an XML document. Here we will merge data in an XML document with a boilerplate HTML form. For example, imagine that your company's web designer created a form used when online customers are ready to complete a purchase. The form needs to add sales tax, based on the state selected by the customers, when entering their billing addresses. Since the states your company must collect tax for and the tax rates themselves can change, hardcoding these rates into the form would not be a good idea. Instead, you could have the server merge the tax data into the form dynamically by using XSLT.

The sales tax data might be stored (or extracted from a database) like this:

```
<salesTax>
  <state>
    <name>AL</name>
    <tax>4</tax>
  </state>
  <state>
```

```
    <name>AK</name>
    <tax>0</tax>
  </state>
  <state>
    <name>AZ</name>
    <tax>5.6</tax>
  </state>

...

  <state>
    <name>WY</name>
    <tax>4</tax>
  </state>
</salesTax>
```

The boilerplate HTML form might look like this:

```
<html>
  <head>
    <title>Check Out</title>
    <script type="text/javascript" language="JavaScript">
    <!--
    /* Initialize tax for default state */
    setTax(document.customerInfo.billState)

    /*Recompute tax when state changes */
      function setTax(field)
        {
        var value = new String(field.value)
        var commaPos = value.indexOf(",")
        var taxObj = document.customerInfo.tax
        var tax = value.substr(commaPos + 1)
        var subtotalObj = document.customerInfo.subtotal
        taxObj.value = tax
        document.customerInfo.total.value =
            parseFloat(subtotalObj.value) +
            (parseFloat(subtotalObj.value) * parseFloat(tax) / 100.00)
      }
    -->
    </script>
  </head>

<body bgcolor="#FFFFFF" text="#000000">
<h1>Check Out</h1>
<form name="customerInfo" method="post" action="">
  <table width="70%" border="0" cellspacing="3" cellpadding="3">
    <tr>
      <td width="7%"> </td>
      <td width="32%">
        <div align="center"><b>Shipping Address</b></div>
      </td>
      <td width="20%"> </td>
      <td width="7%"> </td>
      <td width="34%">
```

```
        <div align="center"><b>Billing Address</b></div>
      </td>
    </tr>
    <tr>
      <td width="7%">Name</td>
      <td width="32%">
        <input type="text" name="shipName" maxlength="40" size="50" border="0"
        align="absmiddle"/>
      </td>
      <td width="20%"> </td>
      <td width="7%">Name</td>
      <td width="34%">
        <input type="text" name="billName" maxlength="40" size="50" border="0"
        align="absmiddle"/>
      </td>
    </tr>
    <tr>
      <td width="7%">Address</td>
      <td width="32%">
        <input type="text" name="shipAddr" maxlength="40" size="50" border="0"
        align="absmiddle"/>
      </td>
      <td width="20%"> </td>
      <td width="7%">Address</td>
      <td width="34%">
        <input type="text" name="billAddr" maxlength="40" size="50" border="0"
        align="absmiddle"/>
      </td>
    </tr>
    <tr>
      <td width="7%">City</td>
      <td width="32%">
        <input type="text" name="shipCity" maxlength="40" size="50" border="0"
        align="absmiddle"/>
      </td>
      <td width="20%"> </td>
      <td width="7%">City</td>
      <td width="34%">
        <input type="text" name="billCity" maxlength="40" size="50" border="0"
        align="absmiddle"/>
      </td>
    </tr>
    <tr>
      <td width="7%">State</td>
      <td width="32%">
        <select name="shipState" size="1" align="absmiddle">
        </select>
      </td>
      <td width="20%"> </td>
      <td width="7%">State</td>
      <td width="34%">
        <select name="billState" size="1" align="absmiddle" onChange="setTax(this)">
```

```
          </select>
        </td>
      </tr>
      <tr>
        <td width="7%">Zip</td>
        <td width="32%">
          <input type="text" name="shipZip" maxlength="10" size="15" border="0"
          align="absmiddle"/>
        </td>
        <td width="20%"> </td>
        <td width="7%">Zip</td>
        <td width="34%">
          <input type="text" name="billZip" maxlength="10" size="15" border="0"
          align="absmiddle"/>
        </td>
      </tr>
      <tr>
        <td width="7%"> </td>
        <td width="32%"> </td>
        <td width="20%"> </td>
        <td width="7%"> </td>
        <td width="34%"> </td>
      </tr>
      <tr>
        <td width="7%"> </td>
        <td width="32%"> </td>
        <td width="20%"> </td>
        <td width="7%">Subtotal</td>
        <td width="34%">
          <input type="text" name="subtotal" readonly="1" value="100.00"/>
        </td>
      </tr>
      <tr>
        <td width="7%"> </td>
        <td width="32%"> </td>
        <td width="20%"> </td>
        <td width="7%">Tax</td>
        <td width="34%">
          <input type="text" name="tax" readonly="1"/>
        </td>
      </tr>
      <tr>
        <td width="7%"> </td>
        <td width="32%"> </td>
        <td width="20%"> </td>
        <td width="7%">Total</td>
        <td width="34%">
          <input type="text" name="total" readonly="1"/>
        </td>
      </tr>
    </table>
</form>
</body>
</html>
```

The transformation is a merge where the default action is to copy the contents from the boilerplate HTML to the output (see Recipe 6.5). When select elements are encountered for the bill-to and ship-to states, the state data is inserted as option elements. To keep the example relatively simple, I encoded the state name and tax rate into the option element's value attribute, but you might want to use a JavaScript-based lookup

```
<xsl:stylesheet version="1.0" xmlns:xsl="http://www.w3.org/1999/XSL/Transform">

  <xsl:import href="../util/copy.xslt"/>

  <xsl:output method="html"/>

  <xsl:template match="html">
    <xsl:copy>
      <xsl:apply-templates/>
    </xsl:copy>
  </xsl:template>

  <xsl:template match="select[@name='shipState' or @name='billState']">
    <xsl:copy>
      <xsl:copy-of select="@*"/>
      <xsl:for-each select="document('salesTax.xml')/salesTax/state">
        <option value="{name}',',{tax}">
          <xsl:value-of select="name"/>
        </option>
      </xsl:for-each>
    </xsl:copy>
  </xsl:template>

</xsl:stylesheet>
```

Discussion

Clearly technologies other than XSLT (ASP and JSP come to mind) might be better suited for the particular example covered in this solution. However, two aspects of the example might lead you to favor an XSLT-based solution.

First, notice that the boilerplate HTML contains standard HTML; there is no embedded server-side or client-side scripting. There is a bit of client-side scripting, but that could be inserted by the XSLT transformation. The author of the boilerplate HTML needs to know nothing about the technology or methodology that will be used to populate the form when it is loaded from the server. In fact, the web page author need not have any programming skills whatsoever. Likewise, the programmer of the transformation need not have any HTML or graphic design skills.* Between them,

---

* This sentence pretty much describes me.

they merely need to agree on content and naming conventions. Thus, a transformation-based solution to dynamic content provides true separation of concerns that is lacking in other techniques.

Second, a transformational approach can do far more than simply inject content; it can also subtract and rearrange existing content without polluting the HTML with foreign gobbledygook.

See Also

Time and space did not permit me to cover XForms in this book, but readers interested in this topic should definitely investigate this new technology (*http://www.w3.org/MarkUp/Forms/*). The W3C describes XForms as follows:

> The current design of Web forms doesn't separate the purpose from the presentation of a form. XForms, in contrast, are comprised of separate sections that describe what the form does, and how the form looks. This allows for flexible presentation options, including classic XHTML forms, to be attached to an XML form definition.
>
> Key Goals of XForms:
>
> • Support for handheld, television, and desktop browsers, plus printers and scanners
>
> • Richer user interface to meet the needs of business, consumer and device control applications
>
> • Decoupled data, logic and presentation
>
> • Improved internationalization
>
> • Support for structured form data
>
> • Advanced forms logic
>
> • Multiple forms per page, and pages per form
>
> • Suspend and Resume support
>
> • Seamless integration with other XML tag sets

CHAPTER 9

XML to SVG

You can find pictures anywhere. It's simply a matter
of noticing things and organizing them.
—Elliott Erwitt

Scalable Vector Graphics (SVG) is a vector graphics format encoded in XML that has
the potential to revolutionize the way graphical content is delivered over the Internet. One of the most compelling reasons for encoding graphics as XML is that it
allows graphical rendering of data to occur as a transformation. Hence, XSLT, which
has no inherent graphics abilities, is capable of complex graphical results because it
allows the SVG engine embedded in a browser to do most of the work.

Although this chapter assumes that the reader is already familiar with SVG, it covers
a few techniques you will use often.

One of the first things you need to know about a graphics system is how its coordinate system is arranged. After years of algebra, trigonometry, and calculus, many
technical readers find the Cartesian coordinate system the most natural. In this system, the x-coordinates increase in value from left to right, and the y-coordinates
increase in value from the bottom of the graph to the top. Alas, SVG does not use a
Cartesian system. Instead, it reverses the y-axis so that the coordinate 0,0 is in the
upper-left corner and y-coordinates increase as you move downward. For many types
of applications, the coordinate system is irrelevant. However, for situations involving the graphical display of data, the Cartesian system is better because it leads to
display orientations that most people find intuitive. SVG has a powerful facility that
lets you transform the coordinate system to the needs of your application. This is
done via translations, rotations, and scaling of the coordinate system that can apply
to individual lines and shapes or to graphical-element groupings. In particular, you
can choose to work in a Cartesian coordinate system simply by specifying the following transformation:

```
<g transform="translate(0,{$height}) scale(1,-1)">
    <!—All contents in cartesion coordinates -->
</g>
```

Here, $height is the height of the entire SVG graphic or the max y-coordinate in the group.

When plotting data in a graph, you can translate and scale the coordinate system to the range of the data so data values can be used as coordinate values:

```
<svg:g transform="scale(1,{$height div $max})">
    <!--All contents in cartesion coordinates -->
</g>
```

In this example, you scale the y-coordinate based on $height (the height of the SVG graphic) and $max (the maximum data value that will be plotted).

Converting to Cartesian coordinates and rescaling is convenient for plotting data, but it is problematic when you want to position text within the transformed coordinate system. The text is rendered upside down due to the Cartesian mapping and distorted due to the scaling. Hence, you must apply an offsetting transformation to the text:

```
<svg:text x="{$someXPos}"
          y="{$someYPos}"
          transform="translate({$someXPos},{$someYPos})
                    scale(1,{-$max div $height})
                    translate({-$someXPos},{-$someYPos})">
Some Text
</svg:text>
```

Such transformations make my head spin, but are sometimes the easiest way to achieve a desired result.

9.1   Transforming an Existing Boilerplate SVG

Problem

You want to display data graphically by populating a pre-existing SVG image with data.

Solution

Imagine that you need to display data in a bar graph. You can imagine creating an XSLT transformation that constructs the SVG representation of the bar graph from scratch (see Recipe 9.2). However, for those uncomfortable with graphical manipulation, this task may seem too daunting. In some cases, though, the data you need to plot is fixed in the number of data points. In this case, you can create the SVG graphic in a drawing program as a boilerplate template that will be instantiated with actual data using XSLT. Doing so greatly simplifies the task.

Consider the following bar-graph template:

```
<svg width="650" height="500">
    <g id="axis" transform="translate(0 500) scale(1 -1)">
        <line id="axis-y" x1="30" y1="20" x2="30" y2="450"
            style="fill:none;stroke:rgb(0,0,0);stroke-width:2"/>
        <line id="axis-x" x1="30" y1="20" x2="460" y2="20"
            style="fill:none;stroke:rgb(0,0,0);stroke-width:2"/>
    </g>
    <g id="bars" transform="translate(30 479) scale(1 -430)">
        <rect x="30" y="0" width="50" height="0.25"
            style="fill:rgb(255,0,0);stroke:rgb(0,0,0);stroke-width:0"/>
        <rect x="100" y="0" width="50" height="0.5"
            style="fill:rgb(0,255,0);stroke:rgb(0,0,0);stroke-width:0"/>
        <rect x="170" y="0" width="50" height="0.75"
            style="fill:rgb(255,255,0);stroke:rgb(0,0,0);stroke-width:0"/>
        <rect x="240" y="0" width="50" height="0.9"
            style="fill:rgb(0,255,255);stroke:rgb(0,0,0);stroke-width:0"/>
        <rect x="310" y="0" width="50" height="1"
            style="fill:rgb(0,0,255);stroke:rgb(0,0,0);stroke-width:0"/>
    </g>
    <g id="scale" transform="translate(29 60)">
        <text id="scale1" x="0px" y="320px"
            style="text-anchor:end;fill:rgb(0,0,0);font-size:10;font-family:
            Arial">0.25</text>
        <text id="scale2" x="0px" y="215px"
            style="text-anchor:end;fill:rgb(0,0,0);font-size:10;font-family:
            Arial">0.50</text>
        <text id="scale3" x="0px" y="107.5px"
            style="text-anchor:end;fill:rgb(0,0,0);font-size:10;font-family:
            Arial">0.75</text>
        <text id="scale4" x="0px" y="0px" style="text-anchor:end;fill:
            rgb(0,0,0);font-size:10;font-family:Arial">1.00</text>
    </g>
    <g id="key">
        <rect id="key1" x="430" y="80" width="25" height="15"
            style="fill:rgb(255,0,0);stroke:rgb(0,0,0);stroke-width:1"/>
        <rect id="key2" x="430" y="100" width="25" height="15"
            style="fill:rgb(0,255,0);stroke:rgb(0,0,0);stroke-width:1"/>
        <rect id="key3" x="430" y="120" width="25" height="15"
            style="fill:rgb(255,255,0);stroke:rgb(0,0,0);stroke-width:1"/>
        <rect id="key5" x="430" y="140" width="25" height="15"
            style="fill:rgb(0,255,255);stroke:rgb(0,0,0);stroke-width:1"/>
        <rect id="key4" x="430" y="160" width="25" height="15"
            style="fill:rgb(0,0,255);stroke:rgb(0,0,0);stroke-width:1"/>
        <text id="key1-text" x="465px" y="92px"
            style="fill:rgb(0,0,0);font-size:18;font-family:Arial">key1</text>
        <text id="key2-text" x="465px" y="112px"
            style="fill:rgb(0,0,0);font-size:18;font-family:Arial">key2</text>
        <text id="key3-text" x="465px" y="132px"
            style="fill:rgb(0,0,0);font-size:18;font-family:Arial">key3</text>
        <text id="key4-text" x="465px" y="152px"
            style="fill:rgb(0,0,0);font-size:18;font-family:Arial">key4</text>
```

```
        <text id="key5-text" x="465px" y="172px"
                style="fill:rgb(0,0,0);font-size:18;font-family:Arial">key5</text>
    </g>
    <g id="title">
        <text x="325px" y="20px" style="text-anchor:middle;fill:rgb(0,0,0);font-
size:24;font-family:Arial">Title</text>
    </g>
</svg>
```

When rendered, the template looks like Figure 9-1.

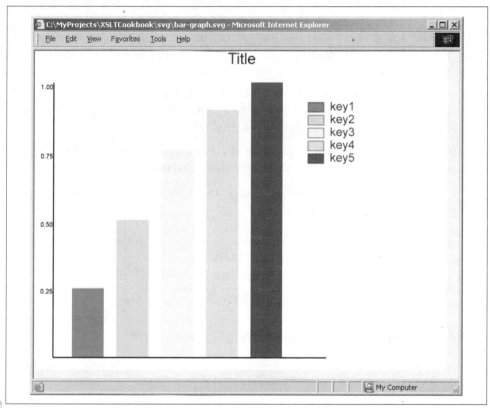

Figure 9-1. An SVG bar-graph template

This SVG was created using the following guidelines:

First, you knew that you needed to plot five data values, so you created five bars. You placed the bars in an SVG group with id="bars". You then did something very important: you transformed the coordinate system of the bars so that the bar height represents the value you want to plot. Specifically, you used transform="translate(30 479) scale(1 -430)". translate moves the origin of the bars to the origin of the axes. transform flips and scales the y-axis so that the height="1" creates a bar of the maximum height. The negative value does the flipping, and 430 does the scaling (430 comes from the length of the y-axis). The scale(1,-1) value within the transform attribute is simply a placeholder that works for the dummy data in the SVG graph. Your stylesheet will replace it with an appropriate value when processing the actual data.

Second, you created a dummy key within a SVG group with id="key". You made sure the elements in the key were ordered to match the bar order. Your transformation will rely on this ordering to fill in the graph correctly.

Third, you created four appropriately spaced text elements that represent the scale on the y-axis within a group with id="scale". You gave each text node an ID with a numeric suffix that represents the number of quarters its position represents. For example, the text element 0.50 has id="scale2" because it is at 2/4 (or 1/2) of the scale. Your stylesheet will use the number when it remaps the scale to values appropriate to the actual data.

Fourth, you created a dummy title text element, also within a group. This text is positioned and anchored to the center of the graphic. This means that it will remain centered when you replace its text with an actual title.

The fact that each major component of the SVG bar graph is in a group simplifies the stylesheet you create so it can load the graph with real data.

The data you load into the bar graph is sales data for your company's five top-selling products:

```
<product-sales description="Top 5 Product Sales (in $1000)">
  <product name="Widget">
    <sales multiple="1000" currency="USD">70</sales>
  </product>
  <product name="Foo Bar">
    <sales multiple="1000" currency="USD">880</sales>
  </product>
  <product name="Grunt Master 9000">
    <sales multiple="1000" currency="USD">1000</sales>
  </product>
  <product name="Spam Slicer">
    <sales multiple="1000" currency="USD">532</sales>
  </product>
  <product name="Wonder Bar">
    <sales multiple="1000" currency="USD">100</sales>
  </product>
</product-sales>
```

The stylesheet merges boilerplate SVG with this data file to create a plot of the actual data:

```
<xsl:stylesheet version="1.0" xmlns:xsl="http://www.w3.org/1999/XSL/Transform"
  xmlns:math="http://www.exslt.org/math"
  exclude-result-prefixes="math">

<!-- By default, copy the SVG to the output -->
<xsl:import href="../util/copy.xslt"/>
```

```
<!-- We need max to find the maximum data value. -->
<!-- We use the max for scaling purposes -->
<xsl:include href="../math/math.max.xslt"/>

<!-- The data file names is pased as a paramter -->
<xsl:param name="data-file"/>

<!--We define the output type  be an SVG file and reference the SVG DTD -->
<xsl:output method="xml" version="1.0" encoding="UTF-8" indent="yes"
  doctype-public="-//W3C//DTD SVG 1.0/EN"
  doctype-system="http://www.w3.org/TR/2001/REC-SVG-20010904/DTD/svg10.dtd"/>

<!-- We load all the data values into a node set variable for -->
<!-- easy access -->
<xsl:variable name="bar-values" select="document($data-file)/*/*/sales"/>

<!-- We load all the data names of each bar into a node set variable for easy access
-->
<xsl:variable name="bar-names" select="document($data-file)/*/*/@name"/>

<!--We find the max data value -->
<xsl:variable name="max-data">
  <xsl:call-template name="math:max">
    <xsl:with-param name="nodes" select="$bar-values"/>
  </xsl:call-template>
</xsl:variable>

<!-- For purely aethetic reason we scale the graph so the maxium value -->
<!-- that can be plotted is 10% greater than the true data maximum. -->
<xsl:variable name="max-bar" select="$max-data + $max-data div 10"/>

<!-- Since we gave each component of the graph a named group, -->
<!-- we can easily structure the stylesheet to match each -->
<!-- group and perform the appropriate transformation. -->

<!-- We copy the scale group and replace the text values with values -->
<!-- that refelect the range of our data. We use the numeric part -->
<!-- of each id to create the correct multiple of 0.25 -->

<xsl:template match="g[@id='scale']">
  <xsl:copy>
    <xsl:copy-of select="@*"/>
    <xsl:for-each select="text">
      <xsl:copy>
      <xsl:copy-of select="@*"/>
            <xsl:variable name="factor"
            select="substring-after(@id,'scale') * 0.25"/>
            <xsl:value-of select="$factor * $max-bar"/>
        </xsl:copy>
    </xsl:for-each>
  </xsl:copy>
</xsl:template>

<!--For the key component we simply replace the text values -->
```

```
<xsl:template match="g[@id='key']">
  <xsl:copy>
    <xsl:copy-of select="@*"/>
    <xsl:apply-templates select="rect"/>
    <xsl:for-each select="text">
    <xsl:variable name="pos" select="position()"/>
    <xsl:copy>
      <xsl:copy-of select="@*"/>
      <xsl:value-of select="$bar-names[$pos]"/>
    </xsl:copy>
    </xsl:for-each>
  </xsl:copy>
</xsl:template>

<!--We replace the title with a description extracted from the data.  -->
<!--We might also have allowed the title to be passed in as a parameter-->
<xsl:template match="g[@id='title']">
  <xsl:copy>
    <xsl:copy-of select="@*"/>
    <xsl:for-each select="text">
      <xsl:copy>
        <xsl:copy-of select="@*"/>
        <xsl:value-of select="document($data-file)/*/@description"/>
      </xsl:copy>
    </xsl:for-each>
  </xsl:copy>
</xsl:template>

<!-- The bars are created by -->
<!-- 1) replacing the transform attribute with one that scales based on the value of
$max-bar -->
<!-- 2) Loads the data value into the height of the bar -->
<xsl:template match="g[@id='bars']">
<xsl:copy>
  <xsl:copy-of select="@id"/>
  <xsl:attribute name="transform">
    <xsl:value-of select="concat('translate(60 479) scale(1 ',
    -430 div $max-bar,')')"/>
  </xsl:attribute>
  <xsl:for-each select="rect">
    <xsl:variable name="pos" select="position()"/>
    <xsl:copy>
      <xsl:copy-of select="@*"/>
      <xsl:attribute name="height">
        <xsl:value-of select="$bar-values[$pos]"/>
      </xsl:attribute>
    </xsl:copy>
  </xsl:for-each>
</xsl:copy>
</xsl:template>

</xsl:stylesheet>
```

When you apply this stylesheet to the template SVG, the result is the bar graph shown in Figure 9-2.

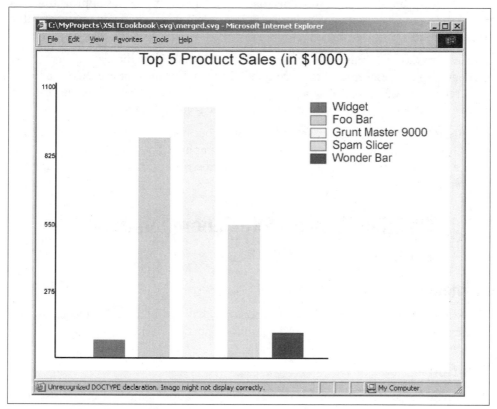

Figure 9-2. An SVG bar graph generated using XSLT

Discussion

Creating SVG directly from data can involve a great deal of mathematical manipulation, trial and error, and frustration, especially if graphics manipulation is not your cup of tea. This recipe provides a way around the problem by using SVG that was laid out visually rather than programmatically. Furthermore, the transformation facilities of SVG were exploited to simplify data to graphical mapping.

Of course, this recipe has some obvious limitations.

First, you must know beforehand the number of data points you need to plot. A more general bar-graph builder would compute and distribute the bars automatically based on runtime inspection of the data. You can partially get around this problem by creating a SVG template with, say, ten bars, and remove the ones you don't need at runtime. This workaround would detract from the presentation's aesthetics because obvious gaps would emerge if only two data elements were mapped into a template originally laid out for ten.

Second, although you can create graphics that are more sophisticated than this simple example, the technique is limited to linear mappings of magnitude to graphical display. For example, it is not obvious that you could easily use this approach with a pie chart; changing the area of a pie slice is not simply a matter of adjusting the value of a single attribute.

A third limitation of this approach stems from the fact that the data source, SVG template, and stylesheet tend to be coupled. Thus, each time you use this technique, you create a new SVG template and stylesheet. Over time, this situation can result in more effort than if you simply built a more generic solution in the first place.

Despite its limitations, this example is valuable because it provides a good starting point for someone just learning to exploit SVG graphics. Specifically, it lets you rely on the facilities of the SVG editor for aligning, distributing, and proportioning the graphics.

9.2 Creating Reusable SVG Generation Utilities for Graphs and Charts

Problem

You want to create a library of SVG generators that can be mixed and matched in applications involving graphical presentation of data.

Solution

If you plan to do a significant amount of SVG generation using XSLT, it is useful to develop a library of templates that generate graphical components that can be mixed and matched. This section shows several components that can graph data.

Axis generation

This example creates a general set of templates for generating graduated x- and y-axes:

```
<!-- Draw a graduated X-Axis -->
<xsl:template name="svgu:xAxis">
    <xsl:param name="min"
               select="0"/>   <!-- Min x coordinate -->
    <xsl:param name="max"
               select="100"/> <!-- Max x coordinate -->
    <xsl:param name="offsetX"
               select="0"/>   <!-- X offset of axis placement -->
    <xsl:param name="offsetY"
               select="0"/>   <!-- Y offset of axis placement -->
    <xsl:param name="width"
               select="500"/> <!-- Width of the physical
                                             plotting area -->
```

```
<xsl:param name="height"
           select="500"/> <!-- Height of the physical plotting area -->
<xsl:param name="majorTicks"
           select="10"/>       <!-- Number of major axis divisions -->
<xsl:param name="majorBottomExtent"
           select="4"/>         <!-- Length of the major tick mark from
                                     axis downward -->
<xsl:param name="majorTopExtent"
           select="$majorBottomExtent"/> <!-- Length of the major tick
                                            mark from axis upward -->
<xsl:param name="labelMajor"
           select="true( )"/> <!-- Label the major tick marks if
                                   true -->
<xsl:param name="minorTicks"
           select="4"/>         <!-- Number of minor axis divisions per
                                     major division-->
<xsl:param name="minorBottomExtent"
           select="2"/>         <!-- Length of the minor tick mark from
                                     axis downward -->
<xsl:param name="minorTopExtent"
           select="$minorBottomExtent"/> <!-- Length of the minor tick
                                            mark from axis upward -->
<xsl:param name="context"/>    <!-- A user defined context indicator for
                                    formatting template calls. -->

<!-- Compute the range and scaling factors -->
<xsl:variable name="range" select="$max - $min"/>
<xsl:variable name="scale" select="$width div $range"/>

<!-- Establish a Cartesian coordinate system with correct offset -->
<!-- and scaling                                                 -->
<svg:g transform="translate({$offsetX},{$offsetY+$height})
            scale({$scale},-1) translate({$min},0)">
  <!-- Draw a line for the axis -->
  <svg:line x1="{$min}" y1="0" x2="{$max}"  y2="0">
    <xsl:attribute name="style">
     <!-- Call a template that can be overridden to -->
     <!-- determine the axis style -->
      <xsl:call-template name="xAxisStyle">
        <xsl:with-param name="context" select="$context"/>
      </xsl:call-template>
    </xsl:attribute>
  </svg:line>

  <!-- Draw the tick marks and labels -->
  <xsl:call-template name="svgu:ticks">
    <xsl:with-param name="xMajor1" select="$min"/>
    <xsl:with-param name="yMajor1" select="$majorTopExtent"/>
    <xsl:with-param name="xMajor2" select="$min"/>
    <xsl:with-param name="yMajor2" select="-$majorBottomExtent"/>
    <xsl:with-param name="labelMajor" select="$labelMajor"/>
    <xsl:with-param name="freq" select="$minorTicks"/>
    <xsl:with-param name="xMinor1" select="$min"/>
    <xsl:with-param name="yMinor1" select="$minorTopExtent"/>
```

```
      <xsl:with-param name="xMinor2" select="$min"/>
      <xsl:with-param name="yMinor2" select="-$minorBottomExtent"/>
      <xsl:with-param name="nTicks"
                      select="$majorTicks * $minorTicks + 1"/>
      <xsl:with-param name="xIncr"
          select="($max - $min) div ($majorTicks * $minorTicks)"/>
      <xsl:with-param name="scale" select="1 div $scale"/>
    </xsl:call-template>
  </svg:g>

</xsl:template>

<xsl:template name="svgu:yAxis">
  <xsl:param name="min"
             select="0"/>    <!-- Min x coordinate -->
  <xsl:param name="max"
             select="100"/> <!-- Max x coordinate -->
  <xsl:param name="offsetX"
             select="0"/>    <!-- X offset of axis placement -->
  <xsl:param name="offsetY"
             select="0"/>    <!-- Y offset of axis placement -->
  <xsl:param name="width"
             select="500"/> <!-- Width of the physical
                                          plotting area -->
  <xsl:param name="height"
             select="500"/> <!-- Height of the physical plotting area -->
  <xsl:param name="majorTicks"
             select="10"/>     <!-- Number of major axis divisions -->
  <xsl:param name="majorLeftExtent"
             select="4"/>      <!-- Length of the major tick mark from
                                          axis downward -->
  <xsl:param name="majorRightExtent"
             select="$majorBottomExtent"/> <!-- Length of the major tick
                                          mark from axis upward -->
  <xsl:param name="labelMajor"
             select="true()"/> <!-- Label the major tick marks if
                                          true -->
  <xsl:param name="minorTicks"
             select="4"/>      <!-- Number of minor axis divisions per
                                          major division-->
  <xsl:param name="minorLeftExtent"
             select="2"/>      <!-- Length of the minor tick mark from
                                          axis right -->
  <xsl:param name="minorRightExtent"
             select="$minorBottomExtent"/> <!-- Length of the minor tick
                                          mark from axis left -->
  <xsl:param name="context"/>   <!-- A user defined context indicator for
                                          formatting template calls -->

  <xsl:param name="majorLeftExtent"
             select="4"/>
  <xsl:param name="majorRightExtent"
             select="$majorLeftExtent"/>
  <xsl:param name="minorLeftExtent"
             select="2"/>
```

```
    <xsl:param name="minorRightExtent"
               select="$minorLeftExtent"/>

    <!-- Compute the range and scaling factors -->
    <xsl:variable name="range" select="$max - $min"/>
    <xsl:variable name="scale" select="$height div $range"/>


    <!-- Establish a Cartesian coordinate system with correct offset -->
    <!-- and scaling                                                  -->
    <svg:g transform="translate({$offsetX},{$offsetY+$height})
                scale(1,{-$scale}) translate(0,{-$min})">
      <svg:line x1="0" y1="{$min}" x2="0"  y2="{$max}">
        <xsl:attribute name="style">
          <xsl:call-template name="yAxisStyle">
            <xsl:with-param name="context" select="$context"/>
          </xsl:call-template>
        </xsl:attribute>
      </svg:line>

      <xsl:call-template name="svgu:ticks">
        <xsl:with-param name="xMajor1" select="-$majorLeftExtent"/>
        <xsl:with-param name="yMajor1" select="$min"/>
        <xsl:with-param name="xMajor2" select="$majorRightExtent"/>
        <xsl:with-param name="yMajor2" select="$min"/>
        <xsl:with-param name="labelMajor" select="$labelMajor"/>
        <xsl:with-param name="freq" select="$minorTicks"/>
        <xsl:with-param name="xMinor1" select="-$minorLeftExtent"/>
        <xsl:with-param name="yMinor1" select="$min"/>
        <xsl:with-param name="xMinor2" select="$minorRightExtent"/>
        <xsl:with-param name="yMinor2" select="$min"/>
        <xsl:with-param name="nTicks"
                        select="$majorTicks * $minorTicks + 1"/>
        <xsl:with-param name="yIncr"
              select="($max - $min) div ($majorTicks * $minorTicks)"/>
        <xsl:with-param name="scale" select="1 div $scale"/>
      </xsl:call-template>
    </svg:g>

</xsl:template>

<!--Recursive utility for drawing tick marks and labels -->
<xsl:template name="svgu:ticks">
  <xsl:param name="xMajor1" />
  <xsl:param name="yMajor1" />
  <xsl:param name="xMajor2" />
  <xsl:param name="yMajor2" />
  <xsl:param name="labelMajor"/>
  <xsl:param name="freq" />
  <xsl:param name="xMinor1" />
  <xsl:param name="yMinor1" />
  <xsl:param name="xMinor2" />
  <xsl:param name="yMinor2" />
  <xsl:param name="nTicks" select="0"/>
  <xsl:param name="xIncr" select="0"/>
```

```
<xsl:param name="yIncr" select="0"/>
<xsl:param name="i" select="0"/>
<xsl:param name="scale"/>
<xsl:param name="context"/>

<xsl:if test="$i &lt; $nTicks">
  <xsl:choose>
    <!-- Time to draw a major tick -->
    <xsl:when test="$i mod $freq = 0">
      <svg:line x1="{$xMajor1}" y1="{$yMajor1}"
             x2="{$xMajor2}" y2="{$yMajor2}">
      </svg:line>
      <xsl:if test="$labelMajor">
        <xsl:choose>
```

This part of the code renders the tick marks along the x- and y-axes. This example hardcodes the format string to avoid yet another parameter, but you might consider using a parameter or passing the value to another template for formatting:

```
            <!-- Ticking along x-axis -->
            <xsl:when test="$xIncr > 0">
              <!-- Tick label must compensate for distorted coordinate
                   system -->
              <svg:text x="{$xMajor1}" y="{$yMajor2}"
                    transform="translate({$xMajor1},{$yMajor2})
                              scale({$scale},-1)
                              translate({-$xMajor1},{-$yMajor2})">
                  <xsl:attribute name="style">
                    <xsl:call-template name="xAxisLabelStyle">
                      <xsl:with-param name="context"
                                      select="$context"/>
                    </xsl:call-template>
                  </xsl:attribute>
                <!-- Perhaps label format should be parameter -->
                <xsl:value-of select="format-number($xMajor1,'#0.0')"/>
              </svg:text>
            </xsl:when>
            <!-- Ticking along y-axis -->
            <xsl:otherwise>
              <svg:text x="{$xMajor1}" y="{$yMajor1}"
                    transform="translate({$xMajor1},{$yMajor1})
                    scale(1,{-$scale})
                    translate({-$xMajor1},{-$yMajor1})">
                <xsl:attribute name="style">
                  <xsl:call-template name="yAxisLabelStyle">
                    <xsl:with-param name="context" select="$context"/>
                  </xsl:call-template>
                </xsl:attribute>
                <xsl:value-of select="format-number($yMajor1,'#0.0')"/>
              </svg:text>
            </xsl:otherwise>
          </xsl:choose>
        </xsl:if>
      </xsl:when>
      <!-- Time to draw a minor tick -->
```

```
      <xsl:otherwise>
        <svg:line x1="{$xMinor1}" y1="{$yMinor1}"
              x2="{$xMinor2}" y2="{$yMinor2}">
        </svg:line>
      </xsl:otherwise>
    </xsl:choose>

    <!-- Recursive call for next tick -->
    <xsl:call-template name="svgu:ticks">
      <xsl:with-param name="xMajor1" select="$xMajor1 + $xIncr"/>
      <xsl:with-param name="yMajor1" select="$yMajor1 + $yIncr"/>
      <xsl:with-param name="xMajor2" select="$xMajor2 + $xIncr"/>
      <xsl:with-param name="yMajor2" select="$yMajor2 + $yIncr"/>
      <xsl:with-param name="labelMajor" select="$labelMajor"/>
      <xsl:with-param name="freq" select="$freq"/>
      <xsl:with-param name="xMinor1" select="$xMinor1 + $xIncr"/>
      <xsl:with-param name="yMinor1" select="$yMinor1 + $yIncr"/>
      <xsl:with-param name="xMinor2" select="$xMinor2 + $xIncr"/>
      <xsl:with-param name="yMinor2" select="$yMinor2 + $yIncr"/>
      <xsl:with-param name="nTicks" select="$nTicks"/>
      <xsl:with-param name="xIncr" select="$xIncr"/>
      <xsl:with-param name="yIncr" select="$yIncr"/>
      <xsl:with-param name="i" select="$i + 1"/>
      <xsl:with-param name="scale" select="$scale"/>
      <xsl:with-param name="context" select="$context"/>
    </xsl:call-template>
  </xsl:if>

</xsl:template>


<!-- Override this template to change x-axis style -->
<xsl:template name="xAxisStyle">
  <xsl:param name="context"/>
    <xsl:text>stroke-width:0.5;stroke:black</xsl:text>
</xsl:template>


<!-- Override this template to change y-axis style -->
<xsl:template name="yAxisStyle">
  <xsl:param name="context"/>
    <xsl:text>stroke-width:0.5;stroke:black</xsl:text>
</xsl:template>


<!-- Override this template to change x-axis label style -->
<xsl:template name="xAxisLabelStyle">
  <xsl:param name="context"/>
  <xsl:text>text-anchor:middle; font-size:8;
          baseline-shift:-110%</xsl:text>
</xsl:template>


<!-- Override this template to change y-axis label style -->
<xsl:template name="yAxisLabelStyle">
  <xsl:param name="context"/>
  <xsl:text>text-anchor:end;font-size:8;baseline-shift:-50%</xsl:text>
</xsl:template>
```

This XSLT script produces x- and y-axes with major and minor tick marks and labels:

```
<xsl:stylesheet version="1.0"
  xmlns:xsl="http://www.w3.org/1999/XSL/Transform"
  xmlns:svg="http://www.w3.org/2000/svg"
  xmlns:svgu="http://www.ora.com/XSLTCookbook/ns/svg-utils"
  xmlns:test="http://www.ora.com/XSLTCookbook/ns/test"
  exclude-result-prefixes="svgu test">

<xsl:import href="svg-utils.xslt"/>

<xsl:output method="xml" version="1.0" encoding="UTF-8" indent="yes"
  doctype-public="-//W3C//DTD SVG 1.0/EN"
  doctype-system="http://www.w3.org/TR/2001/REC-SVG-20010904/DTD/svg10.dtd"/>

<xsl:variable name="width" select="300"/>
<xsl:variable name="height" select="300"/>
<xsl:variable name="pwidth" select="$width * 0.8"/>
<xsl:variable name="pheight" select="$height * 0.8"/>
<xsl:variable name="offsetX" select="($width - $pwidth) div 2"/>
<xsl:variable name="offsetY" select="($height - $pheight) div 2"/>

<xsl:template match="/">


  <svg:svg width="{$width}" height="{$height}">

    <xsl:call-template name="svgu:xAxis">
      <xsl:with-param name="min" select="0"/>
      <xsl:with-param name="max" select="10"/>
      <xsl:with-param name="offsetX" select="$offsetX"/>
      <xsl:with-param name="offsetY" select="$offsetY"/>
      <xsl:with-param name="width" select="$pwidth"/>
      <xsl:with-param name="height" select="$pheight"/>
    </xsl:call-template>

    <xsl:call-template name="svgu:yAxis">
      <xsl:with-param name="min" select="0"/>
      <xsl:with-param name="max" select="10"/>
      <xsl:with-param name="offsetX" select="$offsetX"/>
      <xsl:with-param name="offsetY" select="$offsetY"/>
      <xsl:with-param name="width" select="$pwidth"/>
      <xsl:with-param name="height" select="$pheight"/>
    </xsl:call-template>

  </svg:svg>

</xsl:template>

</xsl:stylesheet>
```

This template gives the axes shown in Figure 9-3.

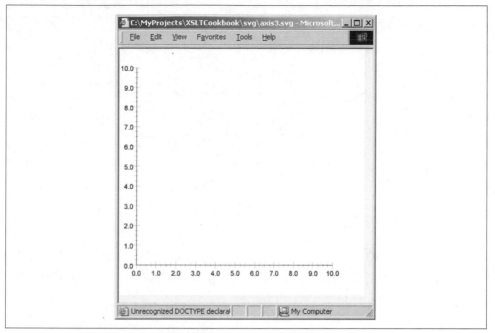

Figure 9-3. A reusable set of SVG axes

By extending the major ticks across the full width and height, you can create a grid, shown in Figure 9-4.

```
<xsl:call-template name="svgu:xAxis">
  <xsl:with-param name="min" select="0"/>
  <xsl:with-param name="max" select="10"/>
  <xsl:with-param name="offsetX" select="$offsetX"/>
  <xsl:with-param name="offsetY" select="$offsetY"/>
  <xsl:with-param name="width" select="$pwidth"/>
  <xsl:with-param name="height" select="$pheight"/>
  <xsl:with-param name="majorTopExtent" select="$pheight"/>
</xsl:call-template>

<xsl:call-template name="svgu:yAxis">
  <xsl:with-param name="min" select="0"/>
  <xsl:with-param name="max" select="10"/>
  <xsl:with-param name="offsetX" select="$offsetX"/>
  <xsl:with-param name="offsetY" select="$offsetY"/>
  <xsl:with-param name="width" select="$pwidth"/>
  <xsl:with-param name="height" select="$pheight"/>
  <xsl:with-param name="majorRightExtent" select="$pwidth"/>
</xsl:call-template>
```

By also extending the minor ticks across the full width and height, you can create a finer grid, shown in Figure 9-5.

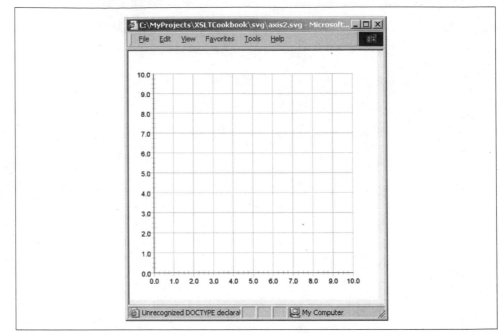

Figure 9-4. A reusable SVG grid

```
<xsl:call-template name="svgu:xAxis">
  <xsl:with-param name="min" select="0"/>
  <xsl:with-param name="max" select="10"/>
  <xsl:with-param name="offsetX" select="$offsetX"/>
  <xsl:with-param name="offsetY" select="$offsetY"/>
  <xsl:with-param name="width" select="$pwidth"/>
  <xsl:with-param name="height" select="$pheight"/>
  <xsl:with-param name="majorTopExtent" select="$pheight"/>
  <xsl:with-param name="minorTopExtent" select="$pheight"/>
</xsl:call-template>

<xsl:call-template name="svgu:yAxis">
  <xsl:with-param name="min" select="0"/>
  <xsl:with-param name="max" select="10"/>
  <xsl:with-param name="offsetX" select="$offsetX"/>
  <xsl:with-param name="offsetY" select="$offsetY"/>
  <xsl:with-param name="width" select="$pwidth"/>
  <xsl:with-param name="height" select="$pheight"/>
  <xsl:with-param name="majorRightExtent" select="$pwidth"/>
  <xsl:with-param name="minorRightExtent" select="$pwidth"/>
</xsl:call-template>
```

You can create a four-quadrant plot, shown in Figure 9-6, by shifting the axis and adjusting the extents for the grid:

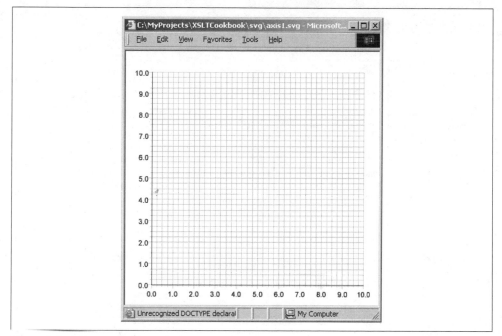

Figure 9-5. A finer reusable grid

```
<xsl:call-template name="svgu:xAxis">
  <xsl:with-param name="min" select="-5"/>
  <xsl:with-param name="max" select="5"/>
  <xsl:with-param name="offsetX" select="0"/>
  <xsl:with-param name="offsetY" select="-$pheight div 2"/>
  <xsl:with-param name="width" select="$pwidth"/>
  <xsl:with-param name="height" select="$pheight"/>
  <xsl:with-param name="majorTopExtent" select="$pwidth div 2"/>
  <xsl:with-param name="majorBottomExtent" select="$pwidth div 2"/>
</xsl:call-template>

<xsl:call-template name="svgu:yAxis">
  <xsl:with-param name="min" select="-5"/>
  <xsl:with-param name="max" select="5"/>
  <xsl:with-param name="offsetX" select="-$pwidth div 2"/>
  <xsl:with-param name="offsetY" select="0"/>
  <xsl:with-param name="width" select="$pwidth"/>
  <xsl:with-param name="height" select="$pheight"/>
  <xsl:with-param name="majorRightExtent" select="$pwidth div 2"/>
  <xsl:with-param name="majorLeftExtent" select="$pwidth div 2"/>
</xsl:call-template>
```

By default this code will align the labels to the ends of the grid lines; however, you can force the labels back to the axes by overriding two templates, producing the results shown in Figure 9-7.

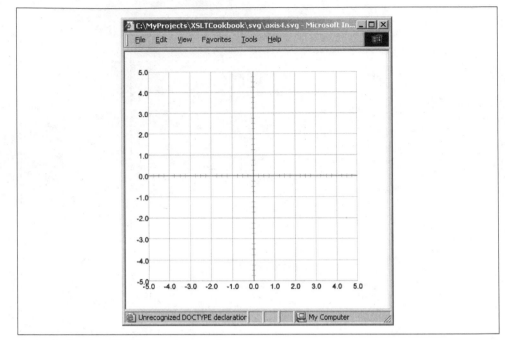

Figure 9-6. A reusable four-quadrant grid

```
<xsl:template name="xAxisLabelYOffset">
  <xsl:value-of select="-$pheight div 2"/>
</xsl:template>

<xsl:template name="yAxisLabelXOffset">
  <xsl:value-of select="$pwidth div 2"/>
</xsl:template>
```

Bar generation

Another common way to plot data is in a bar chart. Bar charts are useful for comparisons. Create a utility that produces a bar for each data value passed to it. The width and color of the bars can be customized easily. The next example allows the bars to be oriented in various directions by using a rotation transformation on the coordinate system. Although this feature is useful, you have to compensate for how rotation affects text and the apparent order of the data values:

```
<xsl:template name="svgu:bars">
<xsl:param name="data" select="/.."/>  <!-- data to chart -->
<xsl:param name="width" select="500"/>
<xsl:param name="height" select="500"/>
<xsl:param name="orientation" select="0"/>
<xsl:param name="barWidth" select="5"/>
<xsl:param name="offsetX" select="0"/>
<xsl:param name="offsetY" select="0"/>
<xsl:param name="boundingBox" select="false()"/>
```

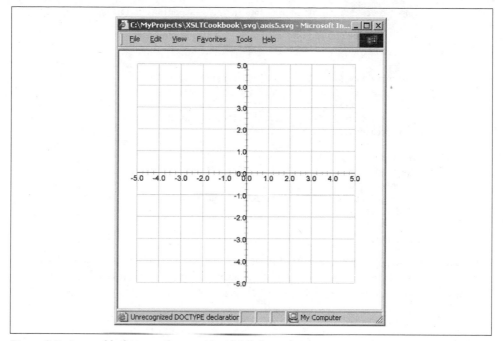

Figure 9-7. A reusable four-quadrant grid with labels on the axes

```
<xsl:param name="barLabel" select="false()"/>
<xsl:param name="max">
 <xsl:call-template name="emath:max">
   <xsl:with-param name="nodes" select="$data"/>
 </xsl:call-template>
</xsl:param>
<xsl:param name="context"/>

<xsl:variable name="numBars" select="count($data)"/>
 <xsl:variable name="spacing" select="$width div ($numBars + 1)"/>

<xsl:if test="$boundingBox">
 <svg:g transform="translate({$offsetX},{$offsetY})
               translate({$width div 2},{$height div 2})
               rotate({$orientation - 180})
               translate({-$width div 2},{-$height div 2})">
   <svg:rect x="0" y="0"
    height="{$height}" width="{$width}"
    style="stroke: black;
           stroke-width:0.5;stroke-opacity:0.5;fill:none"/>
 </svg:g>
</xsl:if>
<!-- We change the data order to compenstate for rotation -->
<!-- See sort below -->
 <xsl:variable name="data-order">
   <xsl:choose>
```

```
      <xsl:when test="$orientation mod 360 >= 180">ascending</xsl:when>
      <xsl:otherwise>descending</xsl:otherwise>
    </xsl:choose>
</xsl:variable>

<svg:g transform="translate({$offsetX},{$offsetY})
            translate({$width div 2},{$height div 2})
            rotate({$orientation - 180})
            translate({-$width div 2},{-$height div 2})
            scale(1,{$height div $max})">

  <xsl:for-each select="$data">
    <!-- We use a sort on position to traverse the data in reverse -->
    <!-- when necessary. -->
    <xsl:sort select="position()" data-type="number"
        order="{$data-order}"/>

    <xsl:variable name="pos" select="position()"/>
```

This example uses lines for the bars. Color and stroke width can be altered by over-riding the BarStyle template. You might consider using rectangles, which give you the option of altering the border style:

```
      <svg:line x1="{$spacing * $pos}"
          y1="0"
          x2="{$spacing * $pos}"
          y2="{current()}" id="{$context}_bar_{$pos}">
        <xsl:attribute name="style">
          <xsl:value-of     select="concat('stroke-width: ',$barWidth,'; ')"/>
          <xsl:call-template name="svgu:barStyle">
            <xsl:with-param name="pos" select="$pos"/>
            <xsl:with-param name="context" select="$context"/>
          </xsl:call-template>
        </xsl:attribute>
      </svg:line>

      <!-- If user requests bar labels we position a text value of the -->
      <!-- of the data point above the bar. The complex serries of     -->
      <!-- transformations is used to make the text display correctly  -->
      <!-- despite the rotations and scalings to the coordinate system -->
      <xsl:if test="$barLabel">
        <svg:text x="{$spacing * $pos}"
            y="{current() * ($height div $max)}"
            transform="scale(1,{$max div $height})
                    translate(0,10)
                    translate({$spacing * $pos},{current() *
                        ($height div $max)})
                    rotate({180 - $orientation})
                    translate({-$spacing * $pos},
                     {-current() * ($height div $max)})"
            id="{$context}_barLabel_{$pos}">
          <xsl:attribute name="style">
            <xsl:call-template name="svgu:barLabelStyle">
              <xsl:with-param name="pos" select="$pos"/>
              <xsl:with-param name="context" select="$context"/>
```

```
                    </xsl:call-template>
                </xsl:attribute>
            <xsl:value-of select="."/>
          </svg:text>
        </xsl:if>
      </xsl:for-each>
    </svg:g>

  </xsl:template>

  <xsl:template name="svgu:barStyle">
    <xsl:param name="pos"/>
    <xsl:param name="context"/>
    <xsl:variable name="colors" select="document('')/*/svgu:color"/>
     <xsl:value-of
          select="concat('stroke: ',$colors[($pos - 1 ) mod count($colors)
                  + 1])"/>
  </xsl:template>

  <xsl:template name="svgu:barLabelStyle">
    <xsl:param name="pos"/>
    <xsl:param name="context"/>
    <xsl:value-of select=" 'text-anchor: middle' "/>
  </xsl:template>
```

The following stylesheet plots data by using bars. The results are shown in
Figure 9-8.

```
<xsl:stylesheet version="1.0"
  xmlns:xsl="http://www.w3.org/1999/XSL/Transform"
  xmlns:svg="http://www.w3.org/2000/svg"
  xmlns:svgu="http://www.ora.com/XSLTCookbook/ns/svg-utils"
  xmlns:test="http://www.ora.com/XSLTCookbook/ns/test"
  exclude-result-prefixes="svgu">

<xsl:import href="svg-utils.xslt"/>

<xsl:output method="xml" version="1.0" encoding="UTF-8" indent="yes"
  doctype-public="-//W3C//DTD SVG 1.0/EN"
  doctype-system="http://www.w3.org/TR/2001/REC-SVG-20010904/DTD/svg10.dtd"/>

<test:data>1.0</test:data>
<test:data>2.0</test:data>
<test:data>3.0</test:data>
<test:data>4.0</test:data>
<test:data>5.0</test:data>
<test:data>13.0</test:data>
<test:data>2.7</test:data>
<test:data>13.9</test:data>
<test:data>22.0</test:data>
<test:data>8.5</test:data>

<xsl:template match="/">
```

```
<svg:svg width="400" height="400">

  <xsl:call-template name="svgu:bars">
    <xsl:with-param name="data" select="document('')/*/test:data"/>
    <xsl:with-param name="width" select=" '300' "/>
    <xsl:with-param name="height" select=" '350' "/>
    <xsl:with-param name="orientation" select=" '0' "/>
    <xsl:with-param name="offsetX" select=" '50' "/>
    <xsl:with-param name="offsetY" select=" '25' "/>
    <xsl:with-param name="boundingBox" select="1"/>
    <xsl:with-param name="barLabel" select="1"/>
    <xsl:with-param name="max" select="25"/>
  </xsl:call-template>

</svg:svg>

</xsl:template>

 <xsl:template name="svgu:barLabelStyle">
   <xsl:param name="pos"/>
   <xsl:param name="context"/>
   <xsl:text>text-anchor: middle; font-size: 8</xsl:text>
 </xsl:template>

</xsl:stylesheet>
```

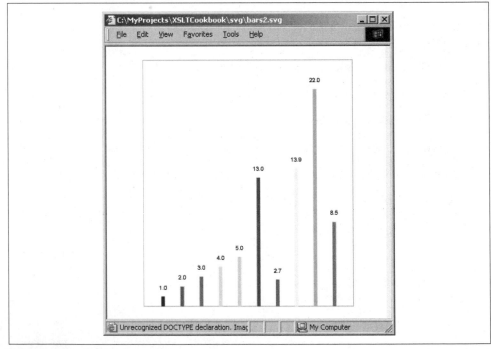

Figure 9-8. A generated bar graph

This variation rotates the display to create a horizontal bar chart, as shown in Figure 9-9. The code does not attempt to constrain the angle of orientation, even though only multiples of 90 degrees are likely values.*

```
<xsl:call-template name="svgu:bars">
  <xsl:with-param name="data" select="document('')/*/test:data"/>
  <xsl:with-param name="width" select=" '300' "/>
  <xsl:with-param name="height" select=" '350' "/>
  <xsl:with-param name="orientation" select=" '90' "/>
  <xsl:with-param name="offsetX" select=" '50' "/>
  <xsl:with-param name="offsetY" select=" '25' "/>
  <xsl:with-param name="boundingBox" select="1"/>
  <xsl:with-param name="barLabel" select="1"/>
  <xsl:with-param name="max" select="25"/>
</xsl:call-template>
```

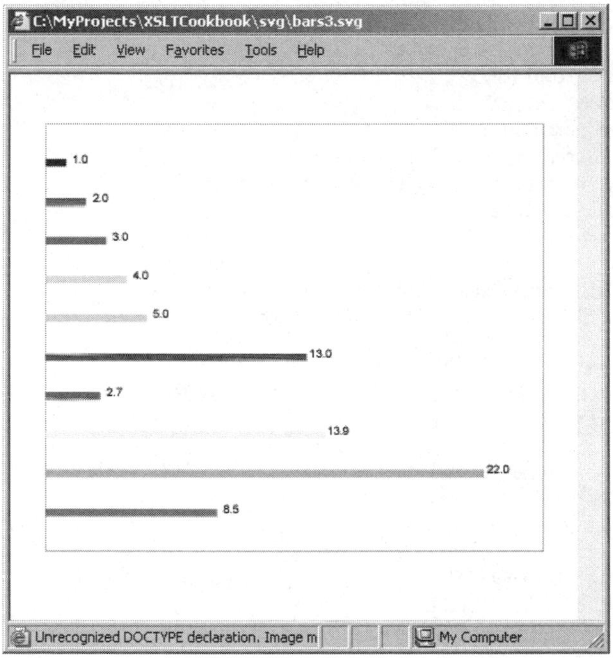

Figure 9-9. A rotated bar graph

---

* If you want to annoy an anal-retentive boss, you can generate a bar chart with an orientation of 72 degrees. Better still, plot the data using an orientation of 1 degree and get your colleagues to swear it looks perfectly straight to them!

XY plots

Axes and grids are useless unless you can actually plot some data in them. One common way to plot data is with an XY plot in which one value is shown as a function of another. You can create a utility that handles one set of data points at a time and use it several times to plot different data sets on the same graph:

```
<xsl:template name="svgu:xyPlot">
  <xsl:param name="dataX" select="/.."/> <!-- x values -->
  <xsl:param name="dataY" select="/.."/>
  <xsl:param name="offsetX" select="0"/>
  <xsl:param name="offsetY" select="0"/>
  <xsl:param name="width" select="500"/>
  <xsl:param name="height" select="500"/>
  <xsl:param name="boundingBox" select="false()"/>
  <xsl:param name="context"/>
  <xsl:param name="maxX">
   <xsl:call-template name="emath:max">
     <xsl:with-param name="nodes" select="$dataX"/>
   </xsl:call-template>
  </xsl:param>
  <xsl:param name="maxY">
   <xsl:call-template name="emath:max">
     <xsl:with-param name="nodes" select="$dataY"/>
   </xsl:call-template>
  </xsl:param>

  <xsl:variable name="scaleX" select="$width div $maxX"/>
  <xsl:variable name="scaleY" select="$height div $maxY"/>
```

This section uses a Java extension function for simplicity, but you could also implement max in XPath by using select="($scaleX > $scaleY) * $scaleX + not($scaleX > $scaleY) * $scaleY)":

```
  <xsl:variable name="scale" select="Math:max($scaleX,$scaleY)"/>

  <xsl:if test="$boundingBox">
    <svg:g transform="translate({$offsetX},{$offsetY})">
    <svg:rect x="0" y="0" height="{$height}" width="{$width}"
              style="stroke: black;stroke-width:0.5;
                     stroke-opacity:0.5;fill:none"/>
  </svg:g>
  </xsl:if>
```

I draw the curve using simple line segments, but a Bézier curve command could result in a smoother effect at the expense of greater code complexity. Since this book covers XSLT rather than SVG, you'll have to settle for simplicity. The trick to using cubic Bézier curves might be to plot three points at a time using the center point as the control point, but I have not tested this idea. An intuitive visualization of Bézier curves is available at *http://home.earthlink.net/~edwardsrg/Adobe/bezier.html*:

```
    <svg:path transform="translate({$offsetX},{$height + $offsetY})
                         scale({$scaleX},{-$scaleY})">
      <xsl:attribute name="d">
        <xsl:for-each select="$dataX">
          <xsl:variable name="pos" select="position( )"/>
          <xsl:variable name="x" select="current( ) "/>
          <xsl:variable name="y" select="$dataY[$pos]"/>
          <xsl:choose>
            <xsl:when test="$pos = 1">
              <xsl:text>M </xsl:text>
            </xsl:when>
            <xsl:otherwise> L </xsl:otherwise>
          </xsl:choose>
          <xsl:value-of select="$x"/>,<xsl:value-of select="$y"/>
        </xsl:for-each>
      </xsl:attribute>
      <xsl:attribute name="style">
        <xsl:call-template name="svgu:xyPlotStyle">
          <xsl:with-param name="scale" select="$scale"/>
          <xsl:with-param name="context" select="$context"/>
        </xsl:call-template>
      </xsl:attribute>
    </svg:path>
  </xsl:template>

  <xsl:template name="svgu:xyPlotStyle">
    <xsl:param name="context"/>
    <xsl:param name="scale"/>
    <xsl:value-of select="concat('fill: none; stroke: black; stroke-width:',1 div
        $scale,'; ')"/>
  </xsl:template>
```

This XSLT script exercises the XY plot template, producing the results shown in
Figure 9-10. For simplicity, I embed the data within the actual stylesheet. In practice, you would extract the data from another XML document:

```
<xsl:stylesheet version="1.0"
  xmlns:xsl="http://www.w3.org/1999/XSL/Transform"
  xmlns:svg="http://www.w3.org/2000/svg"
  xmlns:svgu="http://www.ora.com/XSLTCookbook/ns/svg-utils"
  xmlns:test="http://www.ora.com/XSLTCookbook/ns/test"
  exclude-result-prefixes="svgu test">

<xsl:import href="svg-utils.xslt"/>

<xsl:output method="xml" version="1.0" encoding="UTF-8" indent="yes"
  doctype-public="-//W3C//DTD SVG 1.0//EN"
  doctype-system="http://www.w3.org/TR/2001/REC-SVG-20010904/DTD/svg10.dtd"/>

<test:xdata>0</test:xdata>
<test:xdata>5</test:xdata>
<test:xdata>10</test:xdata>
<test:xdata>15</test:xdata>
<test:xdata>20</test:xdata>
```

```
<test:xdata>25</test:xdata>
<test:xdata>30</test:xdata>
<!-- Rest of x data elided ... -->

<test:ydata>0</test:ydata>
<test:ydata>0.087155743</test:ydata>
<test:ydata>0.173648178</test:ydata>
<test:ydata>0.258819045</test:ydata>
<test:ydata>0.342020143</test:ydata>
<test:ydata>0.422618262</test:ydata>
<test:ydata>0.5</test:ydata>
<!-- Rest of y data elided ... -->

<xsl:variable name="w" select="400"/>
<xsl:variable name="h" select="300"/>
<xsl:variable name="pwidth" select="$w * 0.8"/>
<xsl:variable name="pheight" select="$h * 0.8"/>
<xsl:variable name="offsetX" select="($w - $pwidth) div 2"/>
<xsl:variable name="offsetY" select="($h - $pheight) div 2"/>


<xsl:template match="/">

<svg:svg width="{$w}" height="{$h}">

  <xsl:call-template name="svgu:xyPlot">
    <xsl:with-param name="dataX" select="document('')/*/test:xdata"/>
    <xsl:with-param name="dataY" select="document('')/*/test:ydata"/>
    <xsl:with-param name="offsetX" select="$offsetX"/>
    <xsl:with-param name="offsetY" select="$offsetY"/>
    <xsl:with-param name="width" select="$pwidth"/>
    <xsl:with-param name="height" select="$pheight"/>
    <!--
    <xsl:with-param name="minY" select="-1"/>
    <xsl:with-param name="maxY" select="1"/>
    -->
  </xsl:call-template>

  <xsl:call-template name="svgu:xAxis">
    <xsl:with-param name="min" select="0"/>
    <xsl:with-param name="max" select="360"/>
    <xsl:with-param name="offsetX" select="$offsetX"/>
    <xsl:with-param name="offsetY" select="-$pheight div 2 + $offsetY"/>
    <xsl:with-param name="width" select="$pwidth"/>
    <xsl:with-param name="height" select="$pheight"/>
    <xsl:with-param name="majorTicks" select="6"/>
      <!-- Number of major axis divisions -->
    <xsl:with-param name="minorTicks" select="4"/>
      <!-- Number of major axis divisions -->
  </xsl:call-template>

  <xsl:call-template name="svgu:yAxis">
    <xsl:with-param name="min" select="-1"/>
    <xsl:with-param name="max" select="1"/>
    <xsl:with-param name="offsetX" select="$offsetX"/>
```

```
          <xsl:with-param name="offsetY" select="$offsetY"/>
          <xsl:with-param name="width" select="$pwidth"/>
          <xsl:with-param name="height" select="$pheight"/>
        </xsl:call-template>

    </svg:svg>

  </xsl:template>

</xsl:stylesheet>
```

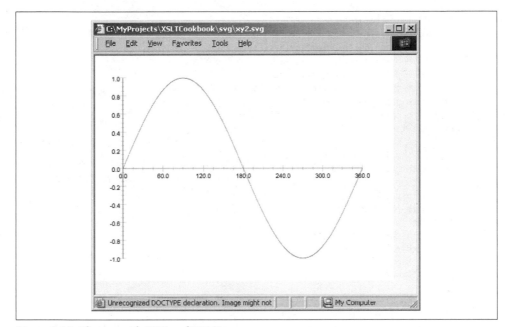

Figure 9-10. Plotting with SVG and XSLT

The following code, whose results are shown in Figure 9-11, demonstrates how to plot multiple data sets and customize the line style by overriding a template:

```
<xsl:stylesheet version="1.0"
  xmlns:xsl="http://www.w3.org/1999/XSL/Transform"
  xmlns:svg="http://www.w3.org/2000/svg"
  xmlns:svgu="http://www.ora.com/XSLTCookbook/ns/svg-utils"
  xmlns:test="http://www.ora.com/XSLTCookbook/ns/test"
  exclude-result-prefixes="svgu test">

<xsl:import href="svg-utils.xslt"/>

<xsl:output method="xml" version="1.0" encoding="UTF-8" indent="yes"
  doctype-public="-//W3C//DTD SVG 1.0//EN"
  doctype-system="http://www.w3.org/TR/2001/REC-SVG-20010904/DTD/svg10.dtd"/>

<!-- Data values elided ... -->
```

```
<xsl:variable name="w" select="400"/>
<xsl:variable name="h" select="300"/>
<xsl:variable name="pwidth" select="$w * 0.8"/>
<xsl:variable name="pheight" select="$h * 0.8"/>
<xsl:variable name="offsetX" select="($w - $pwidth) div 2"/>
<xsl:variable name="offsetY" select="($h - $pheight) div 2"/>

<xsl:template match="/">

<svg:svg width="{$w}" height="{$h}">

  <xsl:call-template name="svgu:xyPlot">
    <xsl:with-param name="dataX" select="document('')/*/test:xdata"/>
    <xsl:with-param name="dataY" select="document('')/*/test:ydata"/>
    <xsl:with-param name="offsetX" select="$offsetX"/>
    <xsl:with-param name="offsetY" select="$offsetY"/>
    <xsl:with-param name="width" select="$pwidth"/>
    <xsl:with-param name="height" select="$pheight"/>
    <xsl:with-param name="maxY" select="40"/>
  </xsl:call-template>

  <xsl:call-template name="svgu:xyPlot">
    <xsl:with-param name="dataX" select="document('')/*/test:xdata"/>
    <xsl:with-param name="dataY" select="document('')/*/test:y2data"/>
    <xsl:with-param name="offsetX" select="$offsetX"/>
    <xsl:with-param name="offsetY" select="$offsetY"/>
    <xsl:with-param name="width" select="$pwidth"/>
    <xsl:with-param name="height" select="$pheight"/>
    <xsl:with-param name="maxY" select="40"/>
    <xsl:with-param name="context" select="2"/>
  </xsl:call-template>

  <xsl:call-template name="svgu:xAxis">
    <xsl:with-param name="min" select="0"/>
    <xsl:with-param name="max" select="6"/>
    <xsl:with-param name="offsetX" select="$offsetX"/>
    <xsl:with-param name="offsetY" select="$offsetY"/>
    <xsl:with-param name="width" select="$pwidth"/>
    <xsl:with-param name="height" select="$pheight"/>
    <xsl:with-param name="majorTopExtent" select="$pheight"/>
    <xsl:with-param name="minorTopExtent" select="$pheight"/>
  </xsl:call-template>

  <xsl:call-template name="svgu:yAxis">
    <xsl:with-param name="min" select="0"/>
    <xsl:with-param name="max" select="40"/>
    <xsl:with-param name="offsetX" select="$offsetX"/>
    <xsl:with-param name="offsetY" select="$offsetY"/>
    <xsl:with-param name="width" select="$pwidth"/>
    <xsl:with-param name="height" select="$pheight"/>
    <xsl:with-param name="majorRightExtent" select="$pwidth"/>
    <xsl:with-param name="minorRightExtent" select="$pwidth"/>
  </xsl:call-template>
```

```
    </svg:svg>

</xsl:template>

<!-- Custom style uses context to figure out what line is being drawn -->
<xsl:template name="svgu:xyPlotStyle">
    <xsl:param name="context"/>
    <xsl:param name="scale"/>
    <xsl:choose>
     <xsl:when test="$context = 2">
      <xsl:value-of select="concat('fill: none; stroke: red;
        stroke-width:',16 div $scale,'; ')"/>
     </xsl:when>
     <xsl:otherwise>
      <xsl:value-of select="concat('fill: none; stroke: black;
        stroke-width:',1 div $scale,'; ')"/>
     </xsl:otherwise>
    </xsl:choose>
</xsl:template>

</xsl:stylesheet>
```

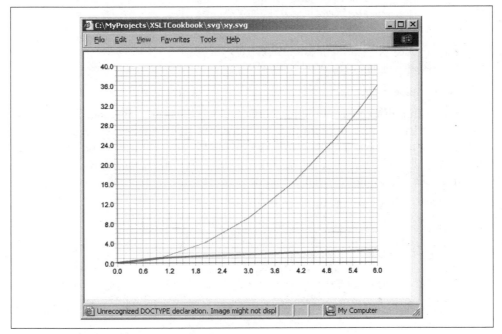

Figure 9-11. Multiple plots generated with XSLT

Pie-slice generation

Pie charts provide another common way to compare data. You can create a utility for generating these charts. The key to creating a pie chart is having a means to create the slices of the pie, which invariably involves trigonometry. Since XSLT does not come with trigonometric functions, you will use a Java-based extension. Of course, this immediately limits the portability of our stylesheet. If portability is a must, you could implement sine and cosine functions in XSLT (see Recipe 2.5 for guidance.) Otherwise, include the following code in stylesheets that require Java math extensions. Details vary from processor to processor, so see Chapter 12 for more detailed information. This example works for Saxon:

```
<xsl:stylesheet
  <!-- v. 1.1 is defunct but works in Saxon to enable the -->
  <!-- xsl:script feature. -->
  version="1.1"
  xmlns:xsl="http://www.w3.org/1999/XSL/Transform"
  xmlns:svg="http://www.w3.org/2000/svg"
  xmlns:svgu="http://www.ora.com/XSLTCookbook/ns/svg-utils"
  xmlns:emath="http://www.exslt.org/math"
  xmlns:Math="java:java.lang.Math" extension-element-prefixes="Math"
        exclude-result-prefixes="svgu">

  <xsl:script implements-prefix="Math"
                    xmlns:Math="java:java.lang.Math"
                    language="java"
                    src="java:java.lang.Math"/>

  <!-- We use some XSLT stuff already developed in chatper 2 -->
  <xsl:include href="../math/math.max.xslt"/>
  <xsl:include href="../math/math.min.xslt"/>
  ...
</xsl:stylesheet>
```

The routine that does most of the mathematical work is svgu:pieSlice. This routine was adapted from a Perl program in *SVG Essentials* by J. David Eisenberg (O'Reilly, 2002). The trigonometry is beyond the scope of this book, but essentially, the routine lets you draw arcs (based on rotations around a center coordinate) to compensate for SVG's less-intuitive specification of arcs:

```
<xsl:variable name="svgu:pi" select="3.1415927"/>

<xsl:template name="svgu:pieSlice">
  <xsl:param name="cx" select="100"/>  <!-- Center x -->
  <xsl:param name="cy" select="100"/>  <!-- Center y -->
  <xsl:param name="r" select="50"/>    <!-- Radius -->
  <xsl:param name="theta" select="0"/> <!-- Beginning angle in degrees-->
  <xsl:param name="delta" select="90"/>  <!-- Arc extent in degrees -->
  <xsl:param name="phi" select="0"/>  <!-- x-axis rotation angle -->
  <xsl:param name="style" select=" 'fill: red;' "/>
  <xsl:param name="num"/>
  <xsl:param name="context"/>

  <!--Convert angles to radians -->
  <xsl:variable name="theta1"
                    select="$theta * $svgu:pi div 180"/>
  <xsl:variable name="theta2"
                    select="($delta + $theta) * $svgu:pi div 180"/>
```

```
<xsl:variable name="phi_r" select="$phi * $svgu:pi div 180"/>

<!--Figure out begin and end coordinates -->
<xsl:variable name="x0"
    select="$cx + Math:cos($phi_r) * $r * Math:cos($theta1) +
                    Math:sin(-$phi_r) * $r * Math:sin($theta1)"/>
<xsl:variable name="y0"
    select="$cy + Math:sin($phi_r) * $r * Math:cos($theta1) +
                    Math:cos($phi_r) * $r * Math:sin($theta1)"/>

<xsl:variable name="x1"
    select="$cx + Math:cos($phi_r) * $r * Math:cos($theta2) +
                    Math:sin(-$phi_r) * $r * Math:sin($theta2)"/>
<xsl:variable name="y1"
    select="$cy + Math:sin($phi_r) * $r * Math:cos($theta2) +
                    Math:cos($phi_r) * $r * Math:sin($theta2)"/>

<xsl:variable name="large-arc" select="($delta > 180) * 1"/>
<xsl:variable name="sweep" select="($delta > 0) * 1"/>

<svg:path style="{$style} id="{$context}_pieSlice_{$num}">
  <xsl:attribute name="d">
    <xsl:value-of select="concat('M ', $x0,' ',$y0,
                            ' A ', $r,' ',$r,',',
                            $phi,',',
                            $large-arc,',',
                            $sweep,',',
                            $x1,' ',$y1,
                            ' L ',$cx,' ',$cy,
                            ' L ', $x0,' ',$y0)"/>

  </xsl:attribute>
  </svg:path>
</xsl:template>

<xsl:template name="svgu:pieSliceLabel">
  <xsl:param name="label" />           <!-- Label -->
  <xsl:param name="cx" select="100"/>  <!-- Center x -->
  <xsl:param name="cy" select="100"/>  <!-- Center y -->
  <xsl:param name="r" select="50"/>    <!-- Radius -->
  <xsl:param name="theta" select="0"/> <!-- Beginning angle in degrees-->
  <xsl:param name="delta" select="90"/>  <!-- Arc extent in degrees -->
  <xsl:param name="style" select=" 'font-size: 18;' "/>
  <xsl:param name="num"/>
  <xsl:param name="context"/>

  <!--Convert angles to radians -->
  <xsl:variable name="theta2" select="(($delta + $theta) mod 360 + 360) mod 360"/>
<!-- normalize angles -->
  <xsl:variable name="theta2_r" select="$theta2 * $svgu:pi div 180"/>
  <xsl:variable name="x"    select="$cx + $r * Math:cos($theta2_r)"/>
  <xsl:variable name="y"    select="$cy + $r * Math:sin($theta2_r)"/>
```

```
<!-- Compute the point to anchor text based on position -->
<!-- around the pie. This create a more or less uniform spacing -->
<xsl:variable name="anchor">
  <xsl:choose>
    <xsl:when test="contains($style,'text-anchor')"></xsl:when>
    <xsl:when test="$theta2 >= 0 and $theta2 &lt;= 45">start</xsl:when>
    <xsl:when test="$theta2 > 45 and
                    $theta2 &lt;= 135">middle</xsl:when>
    <xsl:when test="$theta2 > 135 and $theta2 &lt;= 225">end</xsl:when>
    <xsl:when test="$theta2 > 225 and
                    $theta2 &lt;= 315">middle</xsl:when>
    <xsl:otherwise>start</xsl:otherwise>
  </xsl:choose>
</xsl:variable>

<svg:text x="{$x}" y="{$y}"
     style="text-anchor:{$anchor};{$style}"
     id="{$context}_pieSliceLabel_{$num}">
  <xsl:value-of select="$label"/>
</svg:text>
</xsl:template>

<xsl:template name="svgu:pie">
  <xsl:param name="data" select="/.."/> <!-- Data to chart -->
  <xsl:param name="cx" select="100"/>  <!-- Center x -->
  <xsl:param name="cy" select="100"/>  <!-- Center y -->
  <xsl:param name="r" select="50"/>    <!-- Radius -->
  <xsl:param name="theta" select="-90"/> <!-- Beginning angle for first
                                              slice in degrees-->
  <xsl:param name="context"/>          <!-- User data to identify this
                                            invocation -->

  <xsl:call-template name="svgu:pieImpl">
    <xsl:with-param name="data" select="$data"/>
    <xsl:with-param name="cx" select="$cx"/>
    <xsl:with-param name="cy" select="$cy"/>
    <xsl:with-param name="r" select="$r"/>
    <xsl:with-param name="theta" select="$theta"/>
    <xsl:with-param name="sum" select="sum($data)"/>
    <xsl:with-param name="context" select="$context"/>
  </xsl:call-template>

</xsl:template>

<!-- Recursive implementation -->
<xsl:template name="svgu:pieImpl">
  <xsl:param name="data" />
  <xsl:param name="cx" />
  <xsl:param name="cy" />
  <xsl:param name="r" />
  <xsl:param name="theta"/>
  <xsl:param name="sum"/>
  <xsl:param name="context"/>
  <xsl:param name="i" select="1"/>
```

```
    <xsl:if test="count($data) >= $i">
      <xsl:variable name="delta" select="($data[$i] * 360) div $sum"/>

      <!-- Draw slice of pie -->
      <xsl:call-template name="svgu:pieSlice">
        <xsl:with-param name="cx" select="$cx"/>
        <xsl:with-param name="cy" select="$cy"/>
        <xsl:with-param name="r" select="$r"/>
        <xsl:with-param name="theta" select="$theta"/>
        <xsl:with-param name="delta" select="$delta"/>
        <xsl:with-param name="style">
          <xsl:call-template name="svgu:pieSliceStyle">
            <xsl:with-param name="i" select="$i"/>
            <xsl:with-param name="context" select="$context"/>
          </xsl:call-template>
        </xsl:with-param>
        <xsl:with-param name="num" select="$i"/>
        <xsl:with-param name="context" select="$context"/>
      </xsl:call-template>

      <!-- Recursive call for next slice -->
      <xsl:call-template name="svgu:pieImpl">
        <xsl:with-param name="data" select="$data"/>
        <xsl:with-param name="cx" select="$cx"/>
        <xsl:with-param name="cy" select="$cy"/>
        <xsl:with-param name="r" select="$r"/>
        <xsl:with-param name="theta" select="$theta + $delta"/>
        <xsl:with-param name="sum" select="$sum"/>
        <xsl:with-param name="context" select="$context"/>
        <xsl:with-param name="i" select="$i + 1"/>
      </xsl:call-template>
    </xsl:if>

</xsl:template>

<!-- Arranges the lables around the chart for each slice -->
<xsl:template name="svgu:pieLabels">
  <xsl:param name="data" select="/.."/>   <!-- Data for slices -->
  <xsl:param name="labels" select="$data"/>   <!-- Node set of labels to
                                 chart. Defaults to data -->
  <xsl:param name="cx" select="100"/>     <!-- Center x -->
  <xsl:param name="cy" select="100"/>     <!-- Center y -->
  <xsl:param name="r" select="50"/>       <!-- Radius -->
  <xsl:param name="theta" select="-90"/> <!-- Beginning angle for first
                                         slice in degrees-->
  <xsl:param name="context"/>             <!-- User data to identify this
                                         invocation -->

  <xsl:call-template name="svgu:pieLabelsImpl">
    <xsl:with-param name="data" select="$data"/>
    <xsl:with-param name="labels" select="$labels"/>
    <xsl:with-param name="cx" select="$cx"/>
    <xsl:with-param name="cy" select="$cy"/>
    <xsl:with-param name="r" select="$r"/>
```

```
      <xsl:with-param name="theta" select="$theta"/>
      <xsl:with-param name="sum" select="sum($data)"/>
      <xsl:with-param name="context" select="$context"/>
    </xsl:call-template>

</xsl:template>

<xsl:template name="svgu:pieLabelsImpl">
  <xsl:param name="data" />
  <xsl:param name="labels"/>
  <xsl:param name="cx" />
  <xsl:param name="cy" />
  <xsl:param name="r" />
  <xsl:param name="theta"/>
  <xsl:param name="sum"/>
  <xsl:param name="context"/>
  <xsl:param name="i" select="1"/>

  <xsl:if test="count($data) >= $i">
    <xsl:variable name="delta" select="($data[$i] * 360) div $sum"/>

    <!-- Draw slice of pie -->
    <xsl:call-template name="svgu:pieSliceLabel">
      <xsl:with-param name="label" select="$labels[$i]"/>
      <xsl:with-param name="cx" select="$cx"/>
      <xsl:with-param name="cy" select="$cy"/>
      <xsl:with-param name="r" select="$r"/>
      <xsl:with-param name="theta" select="$theta"/>
      <xsl:with-param name="delta" select="$delta div 2"/>
      <xsl:with-param name="style">
        <xsl:call-template name="svgu:pieSliceLabelStyle">
          <xsl:with-param name="i" select="$i"/>
          <xsl:with-param name="value" select="$data[$i]"/>
          <xsl:with-param name="label" select="$labels[$i]"/>
          <xsl:with-param name="context" select="$context"/>
        </xsl:call-template>
      </xsl:with-param>
      <xsl:with-param name="num" select="$i"/>
      <xsl:with-param name="context" select="$context"/>
    </xsl:call-template>

    <!-- Recursive call for next slice label -->
    <xsl:call-template name="svgu:pieLabelsImpl">
      <xsl:with-param name="data" select="$data"/>
      <xsl:with-param name="labels" select="$labels"/>
      <xsl:with-param name="cx" select="$cx"/>
      <xsl:with-param name="cy" select="$cy"/>
      <xsl:with-param name="r" select="$r"/>
      <xsl:with-param name="theta" select="$theta + $delta"/>
      <xsl:with-param name="sum" select="$sum"/>
      <xsl:with-param name="context" select="$context"/>
      <xsl:with-param name="i" select="$i + 1"/>
    </xsl:call-template>
  </xsl:if>
```

```
  </xsl:template>

  <!-- Override to alter a slice's style -->
  <xsl:template name="svgu:pieSliceStyle">
    <xsl:param name="i"/>
    <xsl:param name="context"/>
    <xsl:variable name="colors" select="document('')/*/svgu:color"/>
    <xsl:value-of select="concat('stroke:black;
                                  stroke-width:0.5;
                                  fill: ',$colors[($i - 1 ) mod
                                          count($colors) + 1])"/>
  </xsl:template>

  <!-- Override to alter a slice label's style -->
  <xsl:template name="svgu:pieSliceLabelStyle">
    <xsl:param name="i"/>
    <xsl:param name="value"/>
    <xsl:param name="label" />
    <xsl:param name="context"/>
    <xsl:text>font-size: 16;</xsl:text>
  </xsl:template>
```

The following stylesheet creates a pie chart, as shown in Figure 9-12, from sample data:

```
<xsl:stylesheet version="1.0"
  xmlns:xsl="http://www.w3.org/1999/XSL/Transform"
  xmlns:svg="http://www.w3.org/2000/svg"
  xmlns:svgu="http://www.ora.com/XSLTCookbook/ns/svg-utils"
  xmlns:test="http://www.ora.com/XSLTCookbook/ns/test"
  exclude-result-prefixes="svgu test">

<xsl:include href="svg-utils.xslt"/>

<xsl:output method="xml" version="1.0" encoding="UTF-8" indent="yes"
  doctype-public="-//W3C//DTD SVG 1.0/EN"
  doctype-system="http://www.w3.org/TR/2001/REC-SVG-20010904/DTD/svg10.dtd"/>

<test:data>1.0</test:data>
<test:data>2.0</test:data>
<test:data>3.0</test:data>
<test:data>4.0</test:data>
<test:data>5.0</test:data>
<test:data>13.0</test:data>

<xsl:template match="/">

<svg:svg width="500" height="500">

  <xsl:call-template name="svgu:pie">
    <xsl:with-param name="data" select="document('')/*/test:data"/>
    <xsl:with-param name="cx" select="250"/>
    <xsl:with-param name="cy" select="250"/>
    <xsl:with-param name="r" select="100"/>
```

```
      <xsl:with-param name="theta" select="-90"/>
    </xsl:call-template>

    <xsl:call-template name="svgu:pieLabels">
      <xsl:with-param name="data" select="document('')/*/test:data"/>
      <xsl:with-param name="cx" select="250"/>
      <xsl:with-param name="cy" select="250"/>
      <xsl:with-param name="r" select="125"/>
      <xsl:with-param name="theta" select="-90"/>
    </xsl:call-template>

  </svg:svg>

  </xsl:template>
```

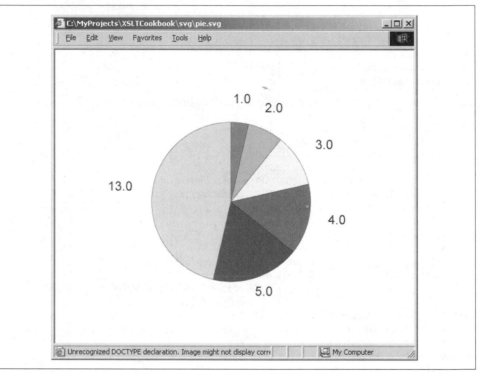

Figure 9-12. A generated pie chart

Open-Hi-Lo-Close plots

Open-Hi-Lo-Close plots are commonly used to plot securities data, but can be used in other applications (for example, to show min, max, mean, and median). The data is passed into this template as four different node sets representing each series. Only the high and low sets are required. The template also handles series with missing data points:

```
<xsl:template name="svgu:openHiLoClose">
  <xsl:param name="openData" select="/.."/>
  <xsl:param name="hiData" select="/.."/>
  <xsl:param name="loData" select="/.."/>
  <xsl:param name="closeData" select="/.."/>
  <xsl:param name="width" select=" '500' "/>
  <xsl:param name="height" select=" '500' "/>
  <xsl:param name="offsetX" select="0"/>
  <xsl:param name="offsetY" select="0"/>
  <xsl:param name="openCloseExtent" select="8"/>
  <xsl:param name="max">
   <xsl:call-template name="emath:max">
     <xsl:with-param name="nodes" select="$hiData"/>
   </xsl:call-template>
  </xsl:param>
  <xsl:param name="min">
   <xsl:call-template name="emath:min">
     <xsl:with-param name="nodes" select="$loData"/>
   </xsl:call-template>
  </xsl:param>
  <xsl:param name="context"/>

  <xsl:variable name="hiCount" select="count($hiData)"/>
  <xsl:variable name="loCount" select="count($loData)"/>
  <xsl:variable name="openCount" select="count($openData)"/>
  <xsl:variable name="closeCount" select="count($closeData)"/>

  <xsl:variable name="numBars" select="Math:min($hiCount, $loCount)"/>

  <xsl:variable name="spacing" select="$width div ($numBars + 1)"/>

  <xsl:variable name="range" select="$max - $min"/>
  <xsl:variable name="scale" select="$height div $range"/>

  <svg:g transform="translate({$offsetX},{$offsetY+$height})
                    scale(1,{-$scale})
                    translate(0,{-$min})">

    <xsl:for-each select="$hiData">
      <xsl:variable name="pos" select="position()"/>

      <!--draw hi-lo line -->
      <svg:line x1="{$spacing * $pos}"
            y1="{$loData[$pos]}"
            x2="{$spacing * $pos}"
            y2="{current()}"id="{$context}_highLow_{$pos}">
        <xsl:attribute name="style">
          <xsl:call-template name="svgu:hiLoBarStyle">
            <xsl:with-param name="pos" select="$pos"/>
            <xsl:with-param name="context" select="$context"/>
          </xsl:call-template>
        </xsl:attribute>
      </svg:line>
```

```
        <!--draw open mark if opening data present -->
        <xsl:if test="$openCount >= $pos">
          <svg:line x1="{$spacing * $pos - $openCloseExtent}"
                    y1="{$openData[$pos]}"
                    x2="{$spacing * $pos}"
                    y2="{$openData[$pos]}"
                    id="{$context}_open_{$pos}">
            <xsl:attribute name="style">
              <xsl:call-template name="svgu:openCloseBarStyle">
                <xsl:with-param name="pos" select="$pos"/>
                <xsl:with-param name="scale" select="$scale"/>
                <xsl:with-param name="context" select="$context"/>
              </xsl:call-template>
            </xsl:attribute>
          </svg:line>
        </xsl:if>

        <!--draw close mark if closing data present -->
        <xsl:if test="$closeCount >= $pos">
          <svg:line x1="{$spacing * $pos}"
                    y1="{$closeData[$pos]}"
                    x2="{$spacing * $pos +  $openCloseExtent}"
                    y2="{$closeData[$pos]}"
                    id="{$context}_close_{$pos}">
            <xsl:attribute name="style">
              <xsl:call-template name="svgu:openCloseBarStyle">
                <xsl:with-param name="pos" select="$pos"/>
                <xsl:with-param name="scale" select="$scale"/>
                <xsl:with-param name="context" select="$context"/>
              </xsl:call-template>
            </xsl:attribute>
          </svg:line>
        </xsl:if>

      </xsl:for-each>
    </svg:g>

  </xsl:template>

  <xsl:template name="svgu:hiLoBarStyle">
    <xsl:param name="pos"/>
    <xsl:param name="context"/>
    <xsl:text>stroke: black; stroke-width: 1 </xsl:text>
  </xsl:template>

  <xsl:template name="svgu:openCloseBarStyle">
    <xsl:param name="pos"/>
    <xsl:param name="scale"/>
    <xsl:param name="context"/>
    <xsl:text>stroke: black; stroke-width: </xsl:text><xsl:value-of select="2 div
$scale"/>
  </xsl:template>

</xsl:stylesheet>
```

You can use this routine to plot stock data, as shown in Figure 9-13:

```
<xsl:stylesheet version="1.0"
  xmlns:xsl="http://www.w3.org/1999/XSL/Transform"
  xmlns:svg="http://www.w3.org/2000/svg"
  xmlns:svgu="http://www.ora.com/XSLTCookbook/ns/svg-utils"
  exclude-result-prefixes="svgu">

<xsl:include href="svg-utils.xslt"/>

<xsl:output method="xml" version="1.0" encoding="UTF-8" indent="yes"
  doctype-public="-//W3C//DTD SVG 1.0/EN"
  doctype-system="http://www.w3.org/TR/2001/REC-SVG-20010904/DTD/svg10.dtd"/>

<xsl:template match="/">

<svg:svg width="600" height="400">

  <xsl:call-template name="svgu:openHiLoClose">
    <xsl:with-param name="openData" select="*/row/open"/>
    <xsl:with-param name="hiData" select="*/row/high"/>
    <xsl:with-param name="loData" select="*/row/low"/>
    <xsl:with-param name="closeData" select="*/row/close"/>
    <xsl:with-param name="min" select="30"/>
    <xsl:with-param name="max" select="80"/>
    <xsl:with-param name="width" select="600"/>
    <xsl:with-param name="height" select="350"/>
    <xsl:with-param name="offsetX" select="20"/>
    <xsl:with-param name="offsetY" select="20"/>
    <xsl:with-param name="boundingBox" select="1"/>
  </xsl:call-template>

  <xsl:call-template name="svgu:yAxis">
    <xsl:with-param name="min" select="30"/>
    <xsl:with-param name="max" select="80"/>
    <xsl:with-param name="offsetX" select="20"/>
    <xsl:with-param name="offsetY" select="20"/>
    <xsl:with-param name="width" select="600"/>
    <xsl:with-param name="height" select="350"/>
  </xsl:call-template>

</svg:svg>

</xsl:template>

</xsl:stylesheet>
```

Discussion

XML-to-SVG transformations are not usually trivial. Graphical layout of data requires careful planning, even to get the relatively modest results obtained by these examples. Approaching every XML-to-SVG transformation anew would be fool-hardy—a toolbox of reusable utilities is essential. I have concentrated on utilities for

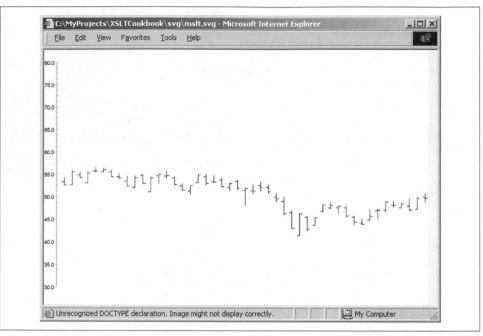

Figure 9-13. An Open-Hi-Lo-Close plot generated with XSLT

charting, but you can certainly come up with utilities for other domains. The technique used to design these utilities breaks the construction of a graphic into component parts and creates templates that construct those parts in a way that allows mixing and matching. A key consideration in employing this technique is to make sure that each template can accept enough information to scale its coordinate system in a way that is compatible with graphics created by independent templates. For example, most of these templates contain $min and $max parameters, even when reasonable values can be computed from the input data. This situation lets the caller override the defaults to consider the range of data appearing in the graph as a whole.

One design decision made in these templates was to allow style information to be obtained via calls to default templates that can be overridden by an importing stylesheet. In many cases, this information could have been supplied by additional parameters. This callback-driven approach was selected because it provides a flexible way to stylize as a function of the plotted data. For example, consider how the pie slice or bars can vary as a function of the data point being plotted at any instant:

```
<xsl:template name="svgu:pieSliceStyle">
  <xsl:param name="i"/>
  <xsl:param name="context"/>
  <xsl:variable name="colors" select="document('')/*/svgu:color"/>
  <xsl:value-of select="concat('stroke:black;
                                stroke-width:0.5;
                                fill: ',$colors[($i - 1 ) mod
                                      count($colors) + 1])"/>
</xsl:template>
```

You might even consider passing additional parameters to such functions from the main template. One obvious addition would pass the actual data point so that, for example, the actual data magnitude can drive the choice of color. One limitation of this technique is that any given stylesheet can only override a template one time. This section compensates for the limitation by using a user-specified context parameter. This parameter allows overridden templates to alter their behavior based on the context. The context plays double duty; you can use it as a basis for generating identifiers for an SVG Element's id attribute. This is useful if you want to interact with the generated SVG (see Recipe 9.4).

The final example creates a complex chart that utilizes Open-High-Low-Close bars for stock data, a bar chart for volume, an XY-plot for volume-moving average, and two y-axes for the price and volume scales. The results are shown in Figure 9-14.

```
<xsl:stylesheet version="1.0"
  xmlns:xsl="http://www.w3.org/1999/XSL/Transform"
  xmlns:svg="http://www.w3.org/2000/svg"
  xmlns:svgu="http://www.ora.com/XSLTCookbook/ns/svg-utils"
  xmlns:emath="http://www.exslt.org/math"
  exclude-result-prefixes="svgu">

<xsl:include href="svg-utils.xslt"/>

<xsl:output method="xml" version="1.0" encoding="UTF-8" indent="yes"
  doctype-public="-//W3C//DTD SVG 1.0//EN"
  doctype-system="http://www.w3.org/TR/2001/REC-SVG-20010904/DTD/svg10.dtd"/>

<xsl:variable name="width" select="600"/>
<xsl:variable name="height" select="500"/>
<xsl:variable name="pwidth" select="$width * 0.8"/>
<xsl:variable name="pheight" select="$height * 0.8"/>
<xsl:variable name="offsetX" select="($width - $pwidth) div 2"/>
<xsl:variable name="offsetY" select="10"/>

<xsl:variable name="dataMin">
  <xsl:call-template name="emath:min">
    <xsl:with-param name="nodes" select="//Low"/>
  </xsl:call-template>
</xsl:variable>

<xsl:variable name="dataMax">
  <xsl:call-template name="emath:max">
    <xsl:with-param name="nodes" select="//High"/>
  </xsl:call-template>
</xsl:variable>

<xsl:variable name="min" select="$dataMin * 0.9"/>
<xsl:variable name="max" select="$dataMax * 1.1"/>

<xsl:template match="/">
```

```
<svg:svg width="{$width}" height="{$height}">

<svg:text x="{$width div 2}" y="{2 * $offsetY}"
    style="text-anchor:middle; font-size:24">MSFT Stock Chart</svg:text>
<svg:text x="{$width div 2}" y="{4 * $offsetY}"
    style="text-anchor:middle; font-size:12">05/23/2002 to 08/16/2002</svg:text>
<!-- PRICE -->

  <xsl:call-template name="svgu:openHiLoClose">
    <xsl:with-param name="openData" select="*/row/Open"/>
    <xsl:with-param name="hiData" select="*/row/High"/>
    <xsl:with-param name="loData" select="*/row/Low"/>
    <xsl:with-param name="closeData" select="*/row/Close"/>
    <xsl:with-param name="min" select="$min"/>
    <xsl:with-param name="max" select="$max"/>
    <xsl:with-param name="width" select="$pwidth"/>
    <xsl:with-param name="height" select="$pheight"/>
    <xsl:with-param name="offsetX" select="$offsetX"/>
    <xsl:with-param name="offsetY" select="$offsetY"/>
    <xsl:with-param name="boundingBox" select="1"/>
  </xsl:call-template>

  <xsl:call-template name="svgu:yAxis">
    <xsl:with-param name="offsetX" select="$offsetX"/>
    <xsl:with-param name="offsetY" select="$offsetY"/>
    <xsl:with-param name="width" select="$pwidth"/>
    <xsl:with-param name="height" select="$pheight"/>
    <xsl:with-param name="min" select="$min"/>
    <xsl:with-param name="max" select="$max"/>
    <xsl:with-param name="context" select=" 'price' "/>
  </xsl:call-template>

<!-- VOLUME -->
<xsl:variable name="vheight" select="100"/>

<xsl:call-template name="svgu:bars">
  <xsl:with-param name="data" select="*/row/Volume"/>
  <xsl:with-param name="width" select="$pwidth"/>
  <xsl:with-param name="height" select="$vheight"/>
  <xsl:with-param name="orientation" select="0"/>
  <xsl:with-param name="offsetX" select="$offsetX"/>
  <xsl:with-param name="offsetY" select="$pheight - $offsetY"/>
  <xsl:with-param name="barLabel" select="false( )"/>
  <xsl:with-param name="min" select="0"/>
  <xsl:with-param name="max" select="1500000"/>
</xsl:call-template>

<!-- This is to make the line plot start on first bar and end on last bar -->
<xsl:variable name="spacing" select="$pwidth div count(*/row/High) + 1"/>

<xsl:call-template name="svgu:xyPlot">
  <xsl:with-param name="dataY" select="*/row/Vol10MA"/>
  <xsl:with-param name="width" select="$pwidth - 2 * $spacing"/>
  <xsl:with-param name="height" select="$vheight"/>
```

```
      <xsl:with-param name="offsetX" select="$offsetX + $spacing"/>
      <xsl:with-param name="offsetY" select="$pheight - $offsetY"/>
      <xsl:with-param name="minY" select="0"/>
      <xsl:with-param name="maxY" select="1500000"/>
   </xsl:call-template>

   <xsl:call-template name="svgu:yAxis">
      <xsl:with-param name="offsetX" select="$width - $offsetX"/>
      <xsl:with-param name="offsetY" select="$height - $vheight - $offsetY"/>
      <xsl:with-param name="width" select="$pwidth"/>
      <xsl:with-param name="height" select="$vheight"/>
      <xsl:with-param name="min" select="0"/>
      <xsl:with-param name="max" select="1500000"/>
      <xsl:with-param name="context" select=" 'volume' "/>
   </xsl:call-template>

 </svg:svg>

</xsl:template>

<xsl:template name="svgu:barStyle">
   <xsl:text>stroke: black; stroke-wdth: 0.15</xsl:text>
</xsl:template>

<xsl:template name="svgu:xyPlotStyle">
  <xsl:param name="context"/>
  <xsl:param name="scale"/>
  <xsl:value-of select="concat('fill: none; stroke: black; stroke-width:',4 div
      $scale,'; ')"/>
</xsl:template>

   <xsl:template name="yAxisLabelStyle">
     <xsl:param name="context"/>
     <xsl:choose>
      <xsl:when test="$context = 'price'">
       <xsl:text>text-anchor:end;font-size:8;baseline-shift:-50%</xsl:text>
      </xsl:when>
      <xsl:otherwise>
       <xsl:text>text-anchor:start;font-size:8;baseline-shift:-50%</xsl:text>
      </xsl:otherwise>
     </xsl:choose>
   </xsl:template>

   <!-- Shift the volume labels away from the tick marks -->
   <xsl:template name="yAxisLabelXOffset">
     <xsl:param name="context"/>
     <xsl:if test="$context = 'volume'">
       <xsl:value-of select="6"/>
     </xsl:if>
   </xsl:template>

</xsl:stylesheet>
```

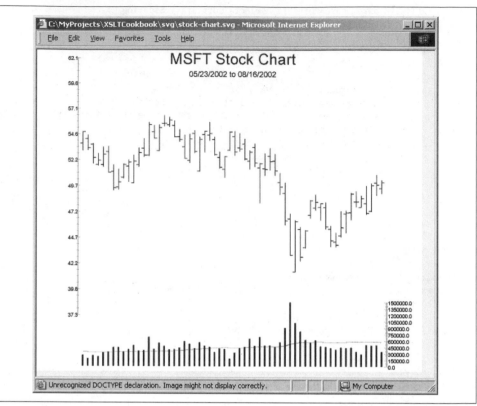

Figure 9-14. A complex combination of graphs

9.3   Creating a Tree Diagram

Problem

You want to show the hierarchical structure of your data as a tree.

Solution

This section presents two different algorithms for rendering a tree. Neither is the most sophisticated algorithm available, but both give reasonable results.

If all the trees you needed to render were balanced, then rendering a tree would be easy because you would need to divide the available horizontal space by the number of nodes at each level and the vertical space by the number of levels.[*] Unfortunately, real-world trees are not as symmetrical. You need an algorithm that considers the breadth of each branch.

---

[*] Actually, you need to divide by the number of nodes + 1, lest you have a so-called "fencepost" error.

The first technique makes only one pass over the tree. However, to accomplish this, it needs to embed foreign bookkeeping attributes into the resulting SVG. This example places these attributes in a namespace to ensure they will not conflict with SVG-specific attributes:

```
<?xml version="1.0" encoding="UTF-8"?>
<xsl:stylesheet
  <!-- v. 1.1 is defunct but works in Saxon to enable the -->
  <!-- xsl:script feature. -->
  version="1.1"
  xmlns:emath="http://www.exslt.org/math"
  xmlns:xsl="http://www.w3.org/1999/XSL/Transform"
  xmlns:tree="http://www.ora.com/XSLTCookbook/ns/tree"
  xmlns:Math="java:java.lang.Math"
  extension-element-prefixes="Math"
  exclude-result-prefixes="Math emath">

  <xsl:script implements-prefix="Math"
              xmlns:Math="java:java.lang.Math"
              language="java"
              src="java:java.lang.Math"/>

  <xsl:include href="../math/math.max.xslt"/>

  <xsl:output method="xml" version="1.0" encoding="UTF-8" indent="yes"
    doctype-public="-//W3C//DTD SVG 1.0//EN"
    doctype-system="http://www.w3.org/TR/2001/REC-SVG-20010904/DTD/svg10.dtd"/>

  <!-- These parameters control the proportions of the tree -->
  <!-- and its nodes -->
  <xsl:variable name="width" select="500"/>
  <xsl:variable name="height" select="500"/>
  <xsl:variable name="nodeWidth" select="2"/>
  <xsl:variable name="nodeHeight" select="1"/>
  <xsl:variable name="horzSpace" select="0.5"/>
  <xsl:variable name="vertSpace" select="1"/>

  <xsl:template match="/">

  <svg width="{$width}" height="{$height}">

    <!-- Capture the subtree of this node in a variable -->
    <xsl:variable name="subTree">
      <xsl:apply-templates/>
    </xsl:variable>

    <!--maxPos is the max of the furthest X or Y coordinate used in -->
    <!--rendering a node -->
    <xsl:variable name="maxPos"
                  select="Math:max(number($subTree/g/@tree:MAXX),
                          number($subTree/g/@tree:MAXY))"/>
    <xsl:variable name="maxDim" select="Math:max($width,$height)"/>
```

```
<!--We scale the tree so all nodes will fit in the -->
<!--coordinate system -->
<g transform="scale({$maxDim div ($maxPos + 1)})">

<!-- Use exsl:node-set($subTree) -->
<!-- if your XSLT processor is version 1.0 -->
  <xsl:copy-of select="$subTree/g/*"/>
</g>

</svg>
</xsl:template>

<!-- This matches all non-leaf nodes -->
<xsl:template match="*[*]">

  <xsl:variable name="subTree">
      <xsl:apply-templates/>
  </xsl:variable>

  <!-- Position this node horizontally based on the average -->
  <!-- position of its children -->
  <xsl:variable name="thisX"
                      select="sum($subTree/*/@tree:THISX)
                                   div count($subTree/*)"/>

  <xsl:variable name="maxX" select="$subTree/*[last()]/@tree:MAXX"/>

  <!-- Position this node vertically based on its level -->
  <xsl:variable name="thisY"
        select="($vertSpace + $nodeHeight) * count(ancestor-or-self::*)"/>

  <xsl:variable name="maxY">
    <xsl:call-template name="emath:max">
      <!-- Use exsl:node-set($subTree) if your XSLT processor -->
      <!-- is version 1.0 -->
      <xsl:with-param name="nodes" select="$subTree/*/@tree:MAXY"/>
    </xsl:call-template>
  </xsl:variable>

  <!-- We place the parent and its children and the connectors -->
  <!-- in a group -->
  <!-- We also add bookkeeping attributes to the group as a means of -->
  <!--passing information up the tree -->
  <g tree:THISX="{$thisX}" tree:MAXX="{$maxX}" tree:MAXY="{$maxY}">
    <rect x="{$thisX - $nodeWidth}"
            y="{$thisY - $nodeHeight}"
            width="{$nodeWidth}"
            height="{$nodeHeight}"
            style="fill: none; stroke: black; stroke-width:0.1"/>

    <!--Draw connecting line between current node and its children -->
    <xsl:call-template name="drawConnections">
        <xsl:with-param name="xParent" select="$thisX - $nodeWidth"/>
        <xsl:with-param name="yParent" select="$thisY - $nodeHeight"/>
```

```
            <xsl:with-param name="widthParent" select="$nodeWidth"/>
            <xsl:with-param name="heightParent" select="$nodeHeight"/>
            <xsl:with-param name="children" select="$subTree/g/rect"/>
    </xsl:call-template>

    <!--Copy the SVG of the sub tree -->
    <xsl:copy-of select="$subTree"/>
  </g>

</xsl:template>

<!-- This matches all leaf nodes -->
<xsl:template match="*">

  <!-- Position leaf nodes horizontally based on the number of -->
  <!-- preceding leaf nodes -->
  <xsl:variable name="maxX"
      select="($horzSpace + $nodeWidth) *
              (count(preceding::*[not(child::*)] ) + 1) "/>
```

You can use count(ancestor-or-self::*) to get the level each time. However, you
might consider adding a parameter to pass the level down the tree rather than recom-
puting each time:

```
  <!-- Position this node vertically based on its level -->
  <xsl:variable name="maxY"
      select="($vertSpace + $nodeHeight) * count(ancestor-or-self::*) "/>

  <g tree:THISX="{$maxX}" tree:MAXX="{$maxX}" tree:MAXY="{$maxY}">
    <rect x="{$maxX - $nodeWidth}"
          y="{$maxY - $nodeHeight}"
          width="{$nodeWidth}"
          height="{$nodeHeight}"
          style="fill: none; stroke: black; stroke-width:0.1;"/>
  </g>

</xsl:template>

<!-- Override in importing stylesheet if you want -->
<!-- straight or some custom type of connection -->
<xsl:template name="drawConnections">
  <xsl:param name="xParent"/>
  <xsl:param name="yParent"/>
  <xsl:param name="widthParent"/>
  <xsl:param name="heightParent"/>
  <xsl:param name="children"/>
  <xsl:call-template name="drawSquareConnections">
    <xsl:with-param name="xParent" select="$xParent"/>
    <xsl:with-param name="yParent" select="$yParent"/>
    <xsl:with-param name="widthParent" select="$widthParent"/>
    <xsl:with-param name="heightParent" select="$heightParent"/>
    <xsl:with-param name="children" select="$children"/>
  </xsl:call-template>
</xsl:template>
```

```
<!-- Straight connections take the shortest path from center -->
<!-- of parent bottom to center of child top -->
<xsl:template name="drawStraightConnections">
  <xsl:param name="xParent"/>
  <xsl:param name="yParent"/>
  <xsl:param name="widthParent"/>
  <xsl:param name="heightParent"/>
  <xsl:param name="children"/>
  <xsl:for-each select="$children">
    <line x1="{$xParent + $widthParent div 2}"
          y1="{$yParent + $heightParent}"
          x2="{@x + $nodeWidth div 2}"
          y2="{@y}"
          style="stroke: black; stroke-width:0.1;"/>
  </xsl:for-each>
</xsl:template>

<!-- Square connections take the shortest path using only horizontal -->
<!-- and vertical lines from center of parent bottom to center of -->
<!-- child top -->
<xsl:template name="drawSquareConnections">
  <xsl:param name="xParent"/>
  <xsl:param name="yParent"/>
  <xsl:param name="widthParent"/>
  <xsl:param name="heightParent"/>
  <xsl:param name="children"/>

  <xsl:variable name="midY"
      select="($children[1]/@y + ($yParent + $heightParent)) div 2"/>

  <!--vertical parent line -->
  <line x1="{$xParent + $widthParent div 2}"
        y1="{$yParent + $heightParent}"
        x2="{$xParent + $widthParent div 2}"
        y2="{$midY}"
        style="stroke: black; stroke-width:0.1;"/>

  <!--central horizontal line -->
  <line x1="{$children[1]/@x + $children[1]/@width div 2}"
        y1="{$midY}"
        x2="{$children[last()]/@x + $children[1]/@width div 2}"
        y2="{$midY}"
        style="stroke: black; stroke-width:0.1;"/>

  <!--vertical child lines -->
  <xsl:for-each select="$children">
    <line x1="{@x + $nodeWidth div 2}"
          y1="{$midY}"
          x2="{@x + $nodeWidth div 2}"
          y2="{@y}"
          style="stroke: black; stroke-width:0.1;"/>
  </xsl:for-each>
```

```
    </xsl:template>

</xsl:stylesheet>
```

This stylesheet renders the structure of any XML document as a tree. Figure 9-15 shows the result against a simple XML input file.

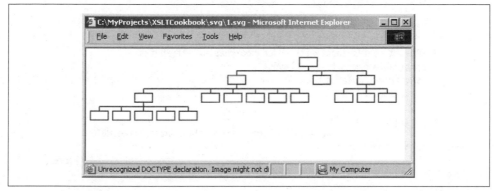

Figure 9-15. An XML document structure turned into SVG

The first algorithm yields trees whose parent nodes' horizontal position is a function of the average position of its children. This causes the root node to be placed off center for unbalanced trees. The following algorithm is a slight improvement because it fixes the skewing problem and does not pollute the SVG with foreign attributes. However, it makes two passes over the input tree:

```
<?xml version="1.0" encoding="UTF-8"?>
<xsl:stylesheet version="1.1"
                        xmlns:emath="http://www.exslt.org/math"
                        xmlns:xsl="http://www.w3.org/1999/XSL/Transform"
                        xmlns:tree="http://www.ora.com/XSLTCookbook/ns/tree"
                        xmlns:Math="java:java.lang.Math"
                        extension-element-prefixes="Math"
                        exclude-result-prefixes="Math emath">

    <xsl:script implements-prefix="Math"
                    xmlns:Math="java:java.lang.Math"
                      language="java"
                      src="java:java.lang.Math"/>

    <xsl:include href="../math/math.max.xslt"/>

    <xsl:output method="xml" version="1.0"
                      encoding="UTF-8"
                      indent="yes"
                      doctype-public="-//W3C//DTD SVG 1.0/EN"
                      doctype-system="http://www.w3.org/TR/2001/REC-SVG-20010904/DTD/
svg10.dtd"/>
```

```
<xsl:variable name="width" select="500"/>
<xsl:variable name="height" select="500"/>
<xsl:variable name="nodeWidth" select="2"/>
<xsl:variable name="nodeHeight" select="1"/>
<xsl:variable name="horzSpace" select="0.5"/>
<xsl:variable name="vertSpace" select="1"/>
<xsl:variable name="strokeWidth" select="0.1"/>

<xsl:template match="/">

  <!--Pass 1 copies input with added bookkeeping attributes -->
  <xsl:variable name="treeWithLayout">
    <xsl:apply-templates mode="layout"/>
  </xsl:variable>

  <xsl:variable name="maxPos"
                     select="Math:max($treeWithLayout/*/@tree:WEIGHT *
($nodeWidth + $horzSpace),
                                                    $treeWithLayout/*/@tree:
MAXDEPTH * ($nodeHeight + $vertSpace))"/>

  <xsl:variable name="maxDim" select="Math:max($width,$height)"/>

  <xsl:variable name="scale" select="$maxDim div ($maxPos + 1)"/>

  <!--Pass 2 creates SVG -->
  <svg height="{$height}" width="{$width}">
    <g transform="scale({$scale})">
      <xsl:apply-templates select="$treeWithLayout/*" mode="draw">
        <xsl:with-param name="x" select="0"/>
        <xsl:with-param name="y" select="0"/>
        <xsl:with-param name="width" select="$width div $scale"/>
        <xsl:with-param name="height" select="$height div $scale"/>
      </xsl:apply-templates>
    </g>
  </svg>
</xsl:template>

<!--Layout nodes with children -->
<xsl:template match="node( )[*]" mode="layout">
  <xsl:variable name="subTree">
    <xsl:apply-templates mode="layout"/>
  </xsl:variable>

  <!--Non-leaf nodes are assigned the sum of their child weights -->
  <xsl:variable name="thisWeight"
                     select="sum($subTree/*/@tree:WEIGHT)"/>

  <xsl:variable name="maxDepth">
    <xsl:call-template name="emath:max">
      <xsl:with-param name="nodes"
                                select="$subTree/*/@tree:MAXDEPTH"/>
    </xsl:call-template>
  </xsl:variable>
```

```
  <xsl:copy>
    <xsl:copy-of select="@*"/>
    <xsl:attribute name="tree:WEIGHT">
      <xsl:value-of select="$thisWeight"/>
    </xsl:attribute>
    <xsl:attribute name="tree:MAXDEPTH">
      <xsl:value-of select="$maxDepth"/>
    </xsl:attribute>
    <xsl:copy-of select="$subTree"/>
  </xsl:copy>

</xsl:template>

<!--Layout leaf nodes -->
<xsl:template match="*" mode="layout">
  <xsl:variable name="depth" select="count(ancestor-or-self::*) "/>
  <xsl:copy>
    <xsl:copy-of select="@*"/>
    <!--Leaf nodes are assigned weight 1 -->
    <xsl:attribute name="tree:WEIGHT">
      <xsl:value-of select="1"/>
    </xsl:attribute>
    <xsl:attribute name="tree:MAXDEPTH">
      <xsl:value-of select="$depth"/>
    </xsl:attribute>
  </xsl:copy>
</xsl:template>

<!--Draw non-leaf nodes -->
<xsl:template match="node( )[*]" mode="draw">
  <xsl:param name="x"/>
  <xsl:param name="y"/>
  <xsl:param name="width"/>
  <xsl:variable name="thisX"
                  select="$x + $width div 2 - ($nodeWidth+$horzSpace) div 2"/>
  <xsl:variable name="subTree">
    <xsl:call-template name="drawSubtree">
      <xsl:with-param name="nodes" select="*"/>
      <xsl:with-param name="weight" select="@tree:WEIGHT"/>
      <xsl:with-param name="x" select="$x"/>
      <xsl:with-param name="y" select="$y + $nodeHeight + $vertSpace"/>
      <xsl:with-param name="width" select="$width"/>
    </xsl:call-template>
  </xsl:variable>
  <g>

    <rect x="{$thisX}"
            y="{$y}"
            width="{$nodeWidth}"
            height="{$nodeHeight}"
            style="fill: none; stroke: black; stroke-width:{$strokeWidth};"/>

    <xsl:call-template name="drawConnections">
      <xsl:with-param name="xParent" select="$thisX"/>
```

```
            <xsl:with-param name="yParent" select="$y"/>
            <xsl:with-param name="widthParent" select="$nodeWidth"/>
            <xsl:with-param name="heightParent" select="$nodeHeight"/>
            <xsl:with-param name="children" select="$subTree/g/rect"/>
        </xsl:call-template>

        <xsl:copy-of select="$subTree"/>

    </g>

</xsl:template>


<!--Draw leaf nodes -->
<xsl:template match="*" mode="draw">
  <xsl:param name="x"/>
  <xsl:param name="y"/>
  <xsl:param name="width"/>
  <xsl:variable name="thisX"
                   select="$x + $width div 2 - ($nodeWidth+$horzSpace) div 2"/>
  <g>
    <rect x="{$thisX}"
             y="{$y}"
             width="{$nodeWidth}"
             height="{$nodeHeight}"
             style="fill: none; stroke: black; stroke-width:{$strokeWidth};"/>
  </g>
</xsl:template>

<!-- Recursive routine for drawing subtree -->
<!-- Allocates horz space based on weight given to node -->
<xsl:template name="drawSubtree">
  <xsl:param name="nodes" select="/.."/>
  <xsl:param name="weight"/>
  <xsl:param name="x"/>
  <xsl:param name="y"/>
  <xsl:param name="width"/>

  <xsl:if test="$nodes">
    <xsl:variable name="node" select="$nodes[1]"/>
    <xsl:variable name="ratio" select="$node/@tree:WEIGHT div $weight"/>

    <!--Draw node and its children in sub partition of space-->
    <!--based on current x and width allocation -->
    <xsl:apply-templates select="$node" mode="draw">
      <xsl:with-param name="x" select="$x"/>
      <xsl:with-param name="y" select="$y"/>
      <xsl:with-param name="width" select="$width * $ratio"/>
    </xsl:apply-templates>

    <!-- Process remaining nodes -->
    <xsl:call-template name="drawSubtree">
      <xsl:with-param name="nodes" select="$nodes[position( ) > 1]"/>
      <xsl:with-param name="weight" select="$weight"/>
```

```
            <xsl:with-param name="x" select="$x + $width * $ratio"/>
            <xsl:with-param name="y" select="$y"/>
            <xsl:with-param name="width" select="$width"/>
        </xsl:call-template>
    </xsl:if>

  </xsl:template>

  <!-- Elided code for connctions. Same as previous stylesheet -->

</xsl:stylesheet>
```

Figure 9-16 shows the same input XML rendered with this new algorithm.

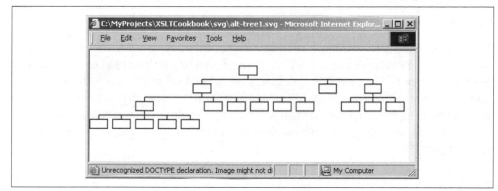

Figure 9-16. A more balanced version of the XML document structure turned into SVG

Discussion

The previous recipes are incomplete because they render only the tree's skeleton and not any of its content. An obvious extension would add text to the nodes to make them identifiable. This extension can be tricky because SVG doesn't scale text automatically, and it becomes especially difficult if the width of the boxes change based on the amount of text they contain. See Recipe 12.3 for a Java-extension function that can help solve SVG text-layout problems.

You chose to map all nodes in the input document to nodes in the SVG tree. In a real-life problem, you would probably filter out irrelevant nodes by using match patterns more specific than match="node( )[*]" and match="*".

If the tree structure of your data is not modeled literally by the hierarchical structure of the XML, then you need to preprocess the input to create such a structure. For example, this would be the case if the parent-child structure were encoded as pointers and targets stored in attributes.

The stylesheets have code that support two types of connections. The examples use square connections. Straight connections, shown in Figure 9-17, can be obtained by overriding drawConnections to call drawStraightConnections.

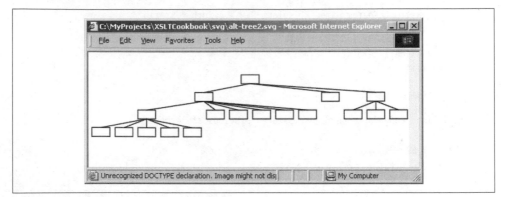

Figure 9-17. An XML document structure turned into SVG by using straight connections

These stylesheets present two portability issues. First, they use a Java extension to access the Java Math:max function. This function can be implemented easily in XSLT. However, since SVG-generating stylesheets often need other types of extension functions, the problem may be unavoidable. The other portability issue is that they assume support for XSLT 1.1 or higher where the result-tree fragments can be properly treated as node sets. You may wish to use your XSLT processor's nodes set converter instead.

See Also

To learn more about sophisticated algorithms for drawing trees and more general graphs, consult *Graph Drawing: Algorithms for the Visualization of Graphs* by Giuseppe Di Battista, Peter Eades, Roberto Tamassia, and Ionnis G. Tollis (Prentice Hall, 1999). Be forewarned that the book is heavy on the mathematical side; it is not an algorithms pseudocode cookbook.

9.4 Creating Interactive SVG-Enabled Web Pages

Problem

You want to embed SVG in HTML to create an interactive user experience.

Solution

This solution is based on an adaptation of code presented in Didier Martin's XML.com article *Integration by Parts: XSLT, XLink and SVG (http://www.xml.com/lpt/a/2000/03/22/style/index.html)*. The stylesheet embeds an SVG graphic in an HTML page along with information obtained from an XML document. JavaScript is added to allow the user to interact with the graphic. This particular example is a prototype of an online real-estate application in which users can interact with a layout diagram of a house.

The input XML contains information about the house. Each room is associated with an id that links the data in the room to a <g> element in the SVG diagram with the same identifier:

```
<?xml version="1.0" encoding="UTF-8"?>
<?xml-stylesheet type="text/xsl" href="HouseLayout.xsl"?>
<House>
  <Location>
    <Address>1234 Main St. </Address>
    <City>Pleasantville </City>
    <State>NJ</State>
  </Location>
  <Layout figure="HouseLayout.svg">
    <Room id="bedroom1">
      <Name>Bedroom</Name>
      <Length>10</Length>
      <Width>10</Width>
      <Windows>2</Windows>
      <Misc>View of junk yard</Misc>
    </Room>
    <Room id="bedroom2">
      <Name>Bedroom</Name>
      <Length>10</Length>
      <Width>10</Width>
      <Windows>1</Windows>
      <Misc>Elvis slept here</Misc>
    </Room>
    <Room id="masterBedroom">
      <Name>Master Bedroom</Name>
      <Length>18</Length>
      <Width>10</Width>
      <Windows>3</Windows>
      <Misc>Walk in Closet</Misc>
    </Room>
    <Room id="masterBath">
      <Name>Master Bath</Name>
      <Length>5</Length>
      <Width>5</Width>
      <Windows>1</Windows>
      <Misc>Full Bath w/ bidet</Misc>
    </Room>
    <Room id="kitchen">
      <Name>Kitchen</Name>
      <Length>20</Length>
      <Width>18</Width>
      <Windows>2</Windows>
      <Misc>New Cabinets</Misc>
    </Room>
    <Room id="livingRoom">
      <Name>Living Room</Name>
```

```
      <Length>18</Length>
      <Width>18</Width>
      <Windows>2</Windows>
      <Misc>View of Rose Garden</Misc>
    </Room>
    <Room id="bath1">
      <Name>Bathroom</Name>
      <Length>6</Length>
      <Width>5</Width>
      <Windows>1</Windows>
      <Misc>Heart Shapped Tub</Misc>
    </Room>
  </Layout>
</House>
```

The stylesheet embeds the SVG file, converts the XML data into a table, and adds canned JavaScript that makes the page interactive, as shown in Figure 9-18.

```
<xsl:stylesheet xmlns:xsl="http://www.w3.org/1999/XSL/Transform"
        xmlns:xlink="http://www.w3.org/1999/xlink"
        version="1.0">
<xsl:output method="html" version="4"/>

<xsl:template match="/">
<html>
<head>
<title><xsl:value-of select="concat(*/*/Address,*/*/City,*/*/State)"/></title>
<script><![CDATA[

var item_selected = null;

// When the mouse pointer triggers the mouse over event
// This function is called.
// We are using both the SVGDOM and the XML DOM
// to access the document's tree nodes.
// More particularly, this function change elements
// identified by the id attribute.
// Note that to change a style attribute with the SVG DOM does not
// require to know in advance the value of the style attribute.
// In contrast, with the XML DOM you need to know the full content
// of the style attribute.
function on_mouse_over (ID)
{
    if (ID == item_selected)
        return true;

    var obj_name = ID ;

    // Change the SVG element's style
    // ------------------------------
    // 1 - get the SVGDOM document element from the Adobe SVG viewer
    // 2 - Then, get the element included in the SVG document and which is
    // referred by the id identifier.
    // 3 - Finally, Get the style attribute from the SVG DOM element node.
```

```
    // the getStyle function is particular to the SVG DOM.
    // the get style function returns a style object.
    // We change the 'fill' style attribute with the returned
    // style object. Note that in contrast to the XML DOM
    // we do not need to know in advance the content of the
    // style attribute's value to change one of the CSS attribute.
    var svgdoc = document.figure.getSVGDocument();
    var svgobj = svgdoc.getElementById(obj_name);
    if (svgobj != null)
    {
        var svgStyle = svgobj.getStyle();
        svgStyle.setProperty ('fill', 'yellow');
    }

    // Here is what we should have if the target browser
    // would fully support the XML DOM
    // --------------------------------------------------
    // Get the element inluded in this HTML document (see in the body
    // section) and which is referred by the identifier.
    ///Change the element's style attribute using the
    // XML DOM. Please note that in contrast to the SVG DOM
    // function, the whole style attribute's value is changed and
    // not the value of a single contained CSS attribute.
    // DOES NOT WORK...
    var svgdesc - document.getElementById(obj_name);
    if (svgdesc != null)
        svgdesc.setAttribute("style", "background-color:yellow; cursor:hand");

    // Here is what we do for the IE 5 DHTML DOM
    // ------------------------------------------
    var DHTMLobj = document.all.item(obj_name)
    if (DHTMLobj != null)
        DHTMLobj.style.backgroundColor = "yellow";
    return true;
}

// When the mouse ponter triggers the mouse over event
// This function is called.
// We are using both the SVGDOM and the XML DOM
// to access the document's tree nodes.
// More particularly, this function change elements
// identified by the id attribute.
// Note that to change a style attribute with the SVG DOM does not
// require to know in advance the value of the style attribute.
// In contrast, with the XML DOM you need to know the full content
// of the style attribute.
function on_mouse_out (ID)
{
    if (ID == item_selected)
        return true;

    var obj_name = ID ;

    // Change the SVG element's style
```

```
    // --------------------------------
    // 1 - get the SVGDOM document element from the Adobe SVG viewer
    // 2 - Then, get the element included in the SVG document and which is
    // referred by the identifier.
    // 3 - Finally, Get the style attribute from the SVG DOM element node.
    // the getStyle function is particular to the SVG DOM.
    // the get style function returns a style object.
    // We change the 'fill' style attribute with the returned
    // style object. Note that in contrast to the XML DOM
    // we do not need to know in advance the content of the
    // style attribute's value to change one of the CSS attribute.
    var svgdoc = document.figure.getSVGDocument();
    var svgobj = svgdoc.getElementById(obj_name);
    if (svgobj != null)
    {
        var svgStyle = svgobj.getStyle();
        svgStyle.setProperty ('fill', 'white');
        svgStyle.setProperty ('stroke', 'white');
    }

    // Here is what we should have if the target browser
    // would fully support the XML DOM
    // ----------------------------------------------------
    // Get the element inluded in this HTML document (see in the body
    // section) and which is referred by the identifier.
    ///Change the element's style attribute using the
    // XML DOM. Please note that in contrast to the SVG DOM
    // function, the whole style attribute's value is changed and
    // not the value of a single contained CSS attribute.
    // DOES NOT WORK...
    var svgdesc = document.getElementById(obj_name);
    if (svgdesc != null)
        svgdesc.setAttribute("style", "background-color:white;");

    // Here is what we for the IE 5 DHTML DOM
    // -------------------------------------
    var DHTMLobj = document.all.item(obj_name)
    if (DHTMLobj != null)
        DHTMLobj.style.backgroundColor = "white";

    return true;
}

function on_mouse_click(ID)
{
    var obj_name = ID ;

    // reset the color of the previously selected room
    if (item_selected)
    {
        var svgdoc = document.figure.getSVGDocument();
        var svgobj = svgdoc.getElementById(obj_name);
        if (svgobj != null)
```

```
            {
                var svgStyle = svgobj.getStyle( );
                svgStyle.setProperty ('fill', 'white');
            }
            var DHTMLobj = document.all.item(obj_name)
            if (DHTMLobj != null)
            {
                DHTMLobj.style.backgroundColor = "white";
                DHTMLobj.style.fontWeight   = "normal";
            }
        }
        // Now select the new room
        if (item_selected != ID)
        {
            var svgdoc = document.figure.getSVGDocument( );
            var svgobj = svgdoc.getElementById(obj_name);
            if (svgobj != null)
            {
                var svgStyle = svgobj.getStyle( );
                svgStyle.setProperty ('fill', '#C0C0C0');
            }
            var DHTMLobj = document.all.item(obj_name)
            if (DHTMLobj != null)
            {
                DHTMLobj.style.backgroundColor = "#C0C0C0";
                DHTMLobj.style.fontWeight   = "bolder";
            }
            item_selected = ID;
        }
        else
            item_selected = null;


        return true;
}
]]></script>
</head>

<body>
    <xsl:apply-templates/>
</body>
</html>
</xsl:template>

<xsl:template match="Layout">
    <div align="center">
        <embed name="figure" width="540" height="540" type="image/svg"
        pluginspage="http://www.adobe.com/svg/viewer/install/">
        <xsl:attribute name="src"><xsl:value-of select="@figure"/></xsl:attribute>
        </embed>
    </div>
    <table border="0" cellpadding="1" cellspacing="0" width="100%" bgcolor="black">
    <tr>
        <table border="0" cellpadding="5" cellspacing="0" width="100%"
```

```
                bgcolor="white">
                    <tr style="background-color:#990033; color:white;">
                        <td>Room</td>
                        <td align="right">Length</td>
                        <td align="right">Width</td>
                        <td align="right">Windows</td>
                        <td>Miscelaneous</td>
                    </tr>
                    <xsl:apply-templates/>
                </table>
            </tr>
    </table>
</xsl:template>

<xsl:template match="Room">
    <tr id="{@id}" style="'background-color:white;'"
        onmouseover="on_mouse_over('{@id}')"
        onmouseout="on_mouse_out('{@id}')"
        onclick="on_mouse_click('{@id}')">
      <td><xsl:value-of select="Name"/></td>
      <td align="right"><xsl:value-of select="Length"/></td>
      <td align="right"><xsl:value-of select="Width"/></td>
      <td align="right"><xsl:value-of select="Windows"/></td>
      <td><xsl:value-of select="Misc"/></td>
    </tr>
</xsl:template>

<xsl:template match="text( )"/>

</xsl:stylesheet>
```

Discussion

Prior examples focused on generating SVG from XML, while this one focuses on integrating SVG into a larger application based on other web technologies. This recipe only touches on the potential of such applications. SVG contains facilities for animation and dynamic content that, when coupled with XSLT's transformation capabilities, can lead to some impressive results. Consider the following stylesheet that is based on the graph-drawing primitives of Recipe 9.2, but allows the user to interact with the graph:

```
<?xml version="1.0" encoding="UTF-8"?>
<xsl:stylesheet version="1.0"
  xmlns:svg="http://www.w3.org/2000/svg"
  xmlns:xsl="http://www.w3.org/1999/XSL/Transform"
  xmlns:svgu="http://www.ora.com/XSLTCookbook/ns/svg-utils"
  xmlns:test="http://www.ora.com/XSLTCookbook/ns/test"
  exclude-result-prefixes="svgu test">

<xsl:import href="svg-utils.xslt"/>

<xsl:output method="html"/>
```

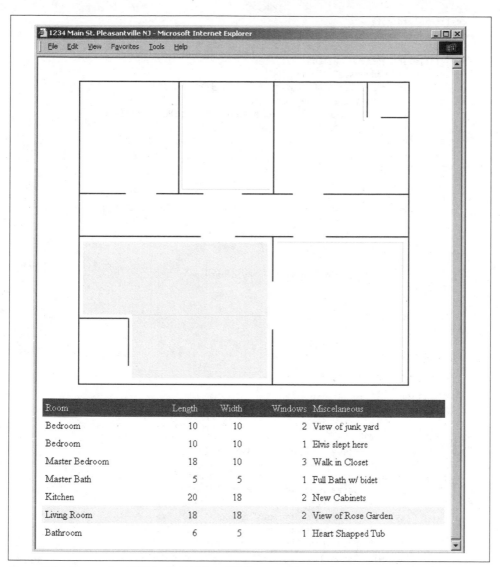

Figure 9-18. Interactive SVG generated from XML

```
<test:data>1.0</test:data>
<test:data>2.0</test:data>
<test:data>3.0</test:data>
<test:data>4.0</test:data>
<test:data>5.0</test:data>
<test:data>13.0</test:data>
<test:data>2.7</test:data>
<test:data>13.9</test:data>
<test:data>22.0</test:data>
<test:data>8.5</test:data>
```

```
<xsl:template match="/">
<html>
  <head>
    <title>Interactive Bar Chart</title>
    <object id="AdobeSVG"
      classid="clsid:78156a80-c6a1-4bbf-8e6a-3cd390eeb4e2"/>
    <xsl:processing-instruction name="import">
      <xsl:text>namespace="svg" implementation="#AdobeSVG"</xsl:text>
    </xsl:processing-instruction>
<script><![CDATA[

function on_change (ID,VALUE)
{
    //Get the svg doc
     var svgDocument = document.all.item('figure').getSVGDocument( );

    //The bars id is prefixed with the context value + _bar_ + ID
    var barName = "interact_bar_" + ID ;

    var barObj = svgDocument.getElementById(barName);
    if (barObj != null)
    {
      barObj.setAttribute('y2', VALUE);
    }

    return true;
}

]]></script>
  </head>
  <body>
    <div align="center">
      <svg:svg width="400" height="400" id="figure">
        <xsl:call-template name="svgu:bars">
          <xsl:with-param name="data" select="document('')/*/test:data"/>
          <xsl:with-param name="width" select=" '300' "/>
          <xsl:with-param name="height" select=" '350' "/>
          <xsl:with-param name="offsetX" select=" '50' "/>
          <xsl:with-param name="offsetY" select=" '25' "/>
          <xsl:with-param name="boundingBox" select="1"/>
          <xsl:with-param name="max" select="25"/>
          <xsl:with-param name="context" select=" 'interact' "/>
        </xsl:call-template>
      </svg:svg>
    </div>
    <table border="1" cellspacing="1" cellpadding="1">
      <tbody>
        <xsl:for-each select="document('')/*/test:data">
          <xsl:variable name="pos" select="position( )"/>
          <xsl:variable name="last" select="last( )"/>
          <tr>
            <td>Bar <xsl:value-of select="$pos"/></td>
            <td>
              <input type="text">
```

```
                  <xsl:attribute name="value">
                    <xsl:value-of select="."/>
                  </xsl:attribute>
                  <xsl:attribute name="onchange">
                    <xsl:text>on_change(</xsl:text>
                    <!-- Bars oriented upward are rotated so the ids need
                    <!-- to be reversed. See svgu:bars implementation -->
                    <!-- for clarification. -->
                    <xsl:value-of select="$last - $pos + 1"/>
                    <xsl:text>, this.value)</xsl:text>
                  </xsl:attribute>
                </input>
              </td>
            </tr>
          </xsl:for-each>
        </tbody>
      </table>
    </body>
  </html>
  </xsl:template>

  </xsl:stylesheet>
```

This stylesheet results is a web page that allows you to change data while the height of the bars responds in kind. This stylesheet also demonstrates the technique for inlining SVG content in HTML. Unfortunately, it works only with IE 5.5 or higher browsers and assumes that you use the Adobe SVG plug-in.[*]

See Also

Didier Martin's XML.com article *Integration by Parts: XSLT, XLink and SVG* (*http://www.xml.com/lpt/a/2000/03/22/style/index.html*) contains a more compelling example involving interaction with a CAD diagram of a complex part.

J. David Eisenberg's *SVG Essentials* (O'Reilly, 2002) contains detailed information about SVG animation and scripting.

---

[*] This, of course, is the configuration used by a large segment of the modern world.

CHAPTER 10

Code Generation

Good programmers write good code.
Great programmers write programs to generate it.
—Unknown

Automation is the holy grail of software development. In fact, much of the progress in software development is driven by the notion of code generation from some higher-level specification. After all, isn't that what assemblers and compilers do? However, in another form of code generation, the target language is not executable machine code, but a high-level language such as Java or C++. Why would you want to generate code in this way, and what does XML have to do with it?

When you write programs, you essentially encode many kinds of knowledge into a very specific syntax that is optimized for one particular development life-cycle phase. It is difficult to leverage the work done in coding to other important development tasks because programming languages are difficult to parse and much of the interesting information is encoded in ad-hoc comments. Representing application knowledge in XML provides the opportunity for much greater leverage. From XML specifications, you can generate application code, test programs, documentation, and possibly even test data. This is not to say that XML gives you this for free. As with all software-development tasks, a great deal of planning and infrastructure building is required to reap the benefits.

This chapter is different from most other chapters in this book because most examples are components of a solution within the context of a particular application. The reason for this structure is two-fold.

First, it is unlikely that you would encode information in XML to generate code just because XML is cool. In most cases, a larger problem must be solved in which XML can be further leveraged. The examples in this section will make more sense if they are presented in the context of a larger problem.

Second, the particular problem is common in large-scale application development, so readers might find it interesting in its own right. However, even if this is not the case, the larger problem will not take away from the application of the concepts to other development tasks.

So what is this large problem?

Imagine a complex client-server application. *Complex* means that it consists of many types of server and client processes. These processes communicate via messages using message-oriented middleware (either pointing to point, publish/subscribe, or both). IBM MQSeries, Microsoft Message Queuing (MSMQ), BEA Systems Tuxedo, and TIBCO Rendezvous are just a few of the many products in this space. In this example, the particular middleware product is not particularly relevant. What is relevant is that all significant work performed by the system is triggered by the receipt of a message and the subsequent response involving one or more messages.* The message may contain XML (SOAP), non-XML text, or binary data. Chapter 12 covers SOAP in the context of WSDL. This chapter is primarily interested in server-to-server communication in which XML is used less often.

What is particularly daunting about such complex systems is that you cannot simply understand them by viewing the source code of any one particular type of process. You must begin by first understanding the conversations or *inter-process messaging protocols* spoken by these processes. This chapter goes even further and states that, at a first level of approximation, the details of each individual process are irrelevant. You can simply treat each process as a black box. Then, rather than understand the hundreds of thousands of lines of code that make up the entire system, you can start by understanding the smaller set of messages that these processes exchange.

Thus the question becomes, how do you go about understanding the interprocess language of a complex application? Can you go to a single place to get this information? Sadly, this is often not the case. I find that you can rarely find an up-to-date and complete specification of an application's messaging protocols. You can usually find pieces of the puzzle in various shared header files and other pieces in design documents developed over the system's life cycle, but rarely will you find a one-stop source for such vital information. And in many cases, the only truly reliable method of obtaining such information is to reverse-engineer it from the applications' source code, which is exactly what I claimed you should not have to do!

Okay, so what does this problem have to do with XML, XSLT, and, in particular, code generation? You can describe the solution to this problem in terms of the need for a documentation that describes in complete detail an application's interprocess messaging structure. What kind of document should this be? Maybe the developers should maintain an MS Word document describing all the messages or, better still, a messaging web site that can be browsed and searched. Or, maybe (and you should have guessed the answer already) the information should be kept in XML! Perhaps

---

* Obviously, user input and output is also relevant. However, you can think of I/O in terms of messages. These user I/O messages are normally sent and received over different channels, though, not interprocess messages.

you should generate the web site from this XML. While you're at it, maybe you should generate some of the code needed by the applications that processes these messages. This is, in fact, exactly what you shall do in this chapter. I call the set of XML files an *interprocess message repository*. Many recipes in this chapter demonstrate how to generate code using this repository.

Before moving to the actual recipes, this chapter presents the repository's design in terms of its schema. It uses W3C XSD Schema for this purpose but only shows an intuitive graphical view for those unfamiliar with XML schema.

Figure 10-1 was produced using Altova's XML Spy 4.0 (*http://www.xmlspy.com*). The icons with three dots (...) represent an ordered sequence. The icon that looks like a multiway switch represents a choice.

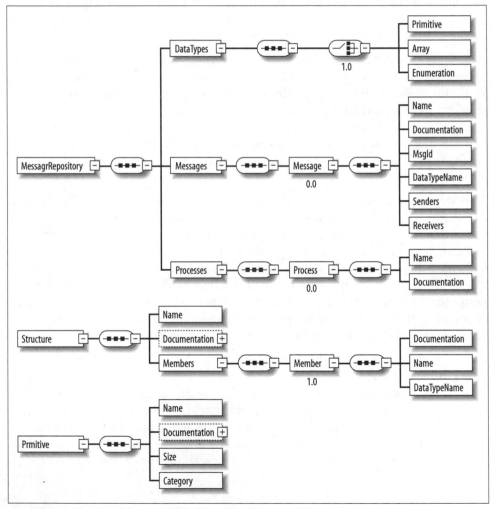

Figure 10-1. Graphical representation of XSD schema for repository

Although this schema is sufficient to illustrate interesting code-generation recipes, it is probably inadequate for an industrial-strength message repository. Additional data might be stored in a message repository, as shown in the following list:

- Symbolic constants used in array and string sizes, as well as enumerated values
- Information about more complex data representations, such as unions and type-name aliases (C typedefs)
- Information about message protocols (complex sequences of messages exchanged by sets of processes to achieve a specific functionality)
- Historical information such as authors, last changed by, change dates, etc.
- Delivery and transport information related to publishers and subscribers or queue names

As sample repository data, imagine a simple client-server application that submits orders and cancelations for common stock. The repository for such an application might look like this:

```xml
<MessageRepository xmlns:xsi="http://www.w3.org/2001/XMLSchema-instance" xsi:
noNamespaceSchemaLocation="C:\MyProjects\XSLT Cookbook\code gen\MessageRepository.
xsd">
  <DataTypes>
    <Primitive>
      <Name>Real</Name>
      <Size>8</Size>
      <Category>real</Category>
    </Primitive>
    <Primitive>
      <Name>Integer</Name>
      <Size>4</Size>
      <Category>signed integer</Category>
    </Primitive>
    <Primitive>
      <Name>StkSymbol</Name>
      <Size>10</Size>
      <Category>string</Category>
    </Primitive>
    <Primitive>
      <Name>Message</Name>
      <Size>100</Size>
      <Category>string</Category>
    </Primitive>
    <Primitive>
      <Name>Shares</Name>
      <Size>4</Size>
      <Category>signed integer</Category>
    </Primitive>
    <Enumeration>
      <Name>BuyOrSell</Name>
      <Enumerators>
        <Enumerator>
          <Name>BUY</Name>
```

```
      <Value>0</Value>
    </Enumerator>
    <Enumerator>
      <Name>SELL</Name>
      <Value>1</Value>
    </Enumerator>
  </Enumerators>
</Enumeration>
<Enumeration>
  <Name>OrderType</Name>
  <Enumerators>
    <Enumerator>
      <Name>MARKET</Name>
      <Value>0</Value>
    </Enumerator>
    <Enumerator>
      <Name>LIMIT</Name>
      <Value>1</Value>
    </Enumerator>
  </Enumerators>
</Enumeration>
<Structure>
  <Name>TestData</Name>
  <Members>
    <Member>
      <Name>order</Name>
      <DataTypeName>AddStockOrderData</DataTypeName>
    </Member>
    <Member>
      <Name>cancel</Name>
      <DataTypeName>CancelStockOrderData</DataTypeName>
    </Member>
  </Members>
</Structure>
<Structure>
  <Name>AddStockOrderData</Name>
  <Documentation>A request to add a new order.</Documentation>
  <Members>
    <Member>
      <Name>symbol</Name>
      <DataTypeName>StkSymbol</DataTypeName>
    </Member>
    <Member>
      <Name>quantity</Name>
      <DataTypeName>Shares</DataTypeName>
    </Member>
    <Member>
      <Name>side</Name>
      <DataTypeName>BuyOrSell</DataTypeName>
    </Member>
    <Member>
      <Name>type</Name>
      <DataTypeName>OrderType</DataTypeName>
    </Member>
```

```
    <Member>
      <Name>price</Name>
      <DataTypeName>Real</DataTypeName>
    </Member>
  </Members>
</Structure>
<Structure>
  <Name>AddStockOrderAckData</Name>
  <Documentation>A positive acknowledgment that order was added successfully.
  </Documentation>
  <Members>
    <Member>
      <Name>orderId</Name>
      <DataTypeName>Integer</DataTypeName>
    </Member>
  </Members>
</Structure>
<Structure>
  <Name>AddStockOrderNackData</Name>
  <Documentation>An negative acknowledgment that order add was unsuccessful.
  </Documentation>
  <Members>
    <Member>
      <Name>reason</Name>
      <DataTypeName>Message</DataTypeName>
    </Member>
  </Members>
</Structure>
<Structure>
  <Name>CancelStockOrderData</Name>
  <Documentation>A request to cancel all or part of an order</Documentation>
  <Members>
    <Member>
      <Name>orderId</Name>
      <DataTypeName>Integer</DataTypeName>
    </Member>
    <Member>
      <Name>quantity</Name>
      <DataTypeName>Shares</DataTypeName>
    </Member>
  </Members>
</Structure>
<Structure>
  <Name>CancelStockOrderAckData</Name>
  <Documentation>A positive acknowledgment that order was canceled successfully.
  </Documentation>
  <Members>
    <Member>
      <Name>orderId</Name>
      <DataTypeName>Integer</DataTypeName>
    </Member>
    <Member>
      <Name>quantityRemaining</Name>
      <DataTypeName>Shares</DataTypeName>
```

```
        </Member>
      </Members>
    </Structure>
    <Structure>
      <Name>CancelStockOrderNackData</Name>
      <Documentation>An negative acknowledgment that the order cancel was
      unsuccessful.</Documentation>
      <Members>
        <Member>
          <Name>orderId</Name>
          <DataTypeName>Integer</DataTypeName>
        </Member>
        <Member>
          <Name>reason</Name>
          <DataTypeName>Message</DataTypeName>
        </Member>
      </Members>
    </Structure>
  </DataTypes>
  <Messages>
    <Message>
      <Name>ADD_STOCK_ORDER</Name>
      <MsgId>1</MsgId>
      <DataTypeName>AddStockOrderData</DataTypeName>
      <Senders>
        <ProcessRef>StockClient</ProcessRef>
      </Senders>
      <Receivers>
        <ProcessRef>StockServer</ProcessRef>
      </Receivers>
    </Message>
    <Message>
      <Name>ADD_STOCK_ORDER_ACK</Name>
      <MsgId>2</MsgId>
      <DataTypeName>AddStockOrderAckData</DataTypeName>
      <Senders>
        <ProcessRef>StockServer</ProcessRef>
      </Senders>
      <Receivers>
        <ProcessRef>StockClient</ProcessRef>
      </Receivers>
    </Message>
    <Message>
      <Name>ADD_STOCK_ORDER_NACK</Name>
      <MsgId>3</MsgId>
      <DataTypeName>AddStockOrderNackData</DataTypeName>
      <Senders>
        <ProcessRef>StockServer</ProcessRef>
      </Senders>
      <Receivers>
        <ProcessRef>StockClient</ProcessRef>
      </Receivers>
    </Message>
    <Message>
```

```xml
      <Name>CANCEL_STOCK_ORDER</Name>
      <MsgId>4</MsgId>
      <DataTypeName>CancelStockOrderData</DataTypeName>
      <Senders>
         <ProcessRef>StockClient</ProcessRef>
      </Senders>
      <Receivers>
         <ProcessRef>StockServer</ProcessRef>
      </Receivers>
    </Message>
    <Message>
      <Name>CANCEL_STOCK_ORDER_ACK</Name>
      <MsgId>5</MsgId>
      <DataTypeName>CancelStockOrderAckData</DataTypeName>
      <Senders>
         <ProcessRef>StockServer</ProcessRef>
      </Senders>
      <Receivers>
         <ProcessRef>StockClient</ProcessRef>
      </Receivers>
    </Message>
    <Message>
      <Name>CANCEL_STOCK_ORDER_NACK</Name>
      <MsgId>6</MsgId>
      <DataTypeName>CancelStockOrderNackData</DataTypeName>
      <Senders>
         <ProcessRef>StockServer</ProcessRef>
      </Senders>
      <Receivers>
         <ProcessRef>StockClient</ProcessRef>
      </Receivers>
    </Message>
    <Message>
      <Name>TEST</Name>
      <MsgId>7</MsgId>
      <DataTypeName>TestData</DataTypeName>
      <Senders>
         <ProcessRef>StockServer</ProcessRef>
      </Senders>
      <Receivers>
         <ProcessRef>StockClient</ProcessRef>
      </Receivers>
    </Message>
  </Messages>
  <Processes>
    <Process>
      <Name>StockClient</Name>
    </Process>
    <Process>
      <Name>StockServer</Name>
    </Process>
  </Processes>
</MessageRepository>
```

This repository describes the messages that are sent between a client (called StockClient) and a server (called StockServer) as the application performs its various duties. Readers familiar with WSDL will see a similarity; however, WSDL is specific to web-service specifications and is most often used in the context of SOAP services, even though the WSDL specification is technically protocol-neutral (*http://www.w3. org/TR/wsdl*). Note that WSDL is a W3C note, not a recommendation. The official Web Services Description Working Group (*http://www.w3.org/2002/ws/desc/*) is working on what will eventually be a W3C-sanctioned standard.

The last two examples in this chapter are independent of the messaging problem. The first focuses on generating C++ code from Unified Modeling Language (UML) models exported from a UML modeling tool via XML Metadata Interchange (XMI). The second discusses using XSLT to generate XSLT.

Before proceeding with the actual examples, I apologize for using C++ for most of the examples. I did this only because it is the language with which I am most familiar; it is the language for which I have actually written generators; and the conceptual framework is transferable to other languages, even if the literal XSLT is not.*

10.1 Generating Constant Definitions

Problem

You want to generate a source file containing all message names as constants equivalent to their message IDs.

Solution

You can construct a single transformation that uses C++ as the default target but is easily customized for C, C#, or Java:

```
<?xml version="1.0" encoding="UTF-8"?>
<xsl:stylesheet version="1.0" xmlns:xsl="http://www.w3.org/1999/XSL/Transform">

  <xsl:output method="text"/>
  <xsl:strip-space elements="*"/>

  <!--The name of the output source code file. -->
  <xsl:param name="file" select=" 'MESSAGE_IDS.h' "/>

  <!-- The default behavior is to generate C++ style constants -->
  <xsl:variable name="constants-type" select=" 'const int' "/>
```

---

* I am tempted to add, only half in jest, that C++ is such a horrendously complex language that its developers are the most motivated to generate rather than code it!

```
<!-- The default C++ assigment operator -->
<xsl:variable name="assignment" select=" ' = ' "/>

<!-- The default C++ statement terminator -->
<xsl:variable name="terminator" select=" ';' "/>


<!--Transform repository into a sequence of message constant
    definitions -->
<xsl:template match="MessageRepository">
  <xsl:call-template name="constants-start"/>
  <xsl:apply-templates select="Messages/Message"/>
  <xsl:call-template name="constants-end"/>
</xsl:template>

<!--Each meesage becomes a comment and an constant definition -->
<xsl:template match="Message">
  <xsl:apply-templates select="." mode="doc" />
  <xsl:apply-templates select="." mode="constant" />
</xsl:template>

<!-- C++ header files start with an inclusion guard -->
<xsl:template name="constants-start">
  <xsl:variable name="guard" select="translate($file,'.','_')"/>
  <xsl:text>#ifndef </xsl:text>
  <xsl:value-of select="$guard"/>
  <xsl:text>&#xa;</xsl:text>
  <xsl:text>#define </xsl:text>
  <xsl:value-of select="$guard"/>
  <xsl:text>&#xa;&#xa;&#xa;</xsl:text>
</xsl:template>

<!-- C++ header files end with the closure of the top level inclusion
     guard -->
<xsl:template name="constants-end">
  <xsl:variable name="guard" select="translate($file,'.','_')"/>
  <xsl:text>&#xa;&#xa;&#xa;#endif /* </xsl:text>
  <xsl:value-of select="$guard"/>
  <xsl:text> */&#xa;</xsl:text>
</xsl:template>

<!-- Each constant definition is preceeded by a cooment describing the
     associated message -->
<xsl:template match="Message" mode="doc">
/*
 * Purpose:      <xsl:call-template name="format-comment">
                    <xsl:with-param name="text" select="Documentation"/>
                  </xsl:call-template>
 * Data Format: <xsl:value-of select="DataTypeName"/>
 * From:        <xsl:apply-templates select="Senders" mode="doc"/>
 * To:          <xsl:apply-templates select="Receivers" mode="doc"/>
 */
</xsl:template>
```

```
<!-- Used in the generation of message documentation. Lists sender or
     receiver processes -->
<xsl:template match="Senders|Receivers" mode="doc">
  <xsl:for-each select="ProcessRef">
    <xsl:value-of select="."/>
    <xsl:if test="position( ) != last( )">
     <xsl:text>, </xsl:text>
    </xsl:if>
  </xsl:for-each>
</xsl:template>

<!-- This utility wraps comments at 40 characters wide -->
<xsl:template name="format-comment">
  <xsl:param name="text"/>
  <xsl:choose>
    <xsl:when test="string-length($text)&lt;40">
      <xsl:value-of select="$text"/>
    </xsl:when>
    <xsl:otherwise>
      <xsl:value-of select="substring($text,1,39)"/>
      <xsl:text>*&#xa;</xsl:text>
      <xsl:call-template name="format-comment">
        <xsl:with-param name="text" select="substring($text,40)"/>
      </xsl:call-template>
    </xsl:otherwise>
  </xsl:choose>
</xsl:template>

<!-- Each message name becomes a constant whose value is the message
     id -->
<xsl:template match="Message" mode="constant">
  <xsl:value-of select="$constants-type"/><xsl:text> </xsl:text>
  <xsl:value-of select="Name"/>
  <xsl:value-of select="$assignment"/>
  <xsl:value-of select="MsgId"/>
  <xsl:value-of select="$terminator"/>
  <xsl:text>&#xa;</xsl:text>
</xsl:template>

<!-- Ignore text nodes not explicitly handled by above templates -->
<xsl:template match="text( )"/>

</xsl:stylesheet>
```

When run against your repository, this transform generates the following code:

```
#ifndef MESSAGE_IDS_h
#define MESSAGE_IDS_h


/*
 * Purpose:     Add a new order.
 * Data Format: AddStockOrderData
 * From:        StockClient
 * To:          StockServer
```

```
    */
    const int ADD_STOCK_ORDER_ID = 1;

    /*
     * Purpose:      Acknowledge the order has been added.
     * Data Format: AddStockOrderAckData
     * From:         StockServer
     * To:           StockClient
     */
    const int ADD_STOCK_ORDER_ACK_ID = 2;

    /*
     * Purpose:      Error adding the order. Perhaps it violates
     *               a rule.
     * Data Format: AddStockOrderNackData
     * From:         StockServer
     * To:           StockClient
     */
    const int ADD_STOCK_ORDER_NACK_ID = 3;

//Etc ...

#endif /* MESSAGE_IDS_h */
```

Discussion

To make the code-generation transformation customizable for several languages, I use a stylesheet that is more complex than necessary for any single language. Still, this chapter did not generalize it completely. For example, the commenting conventions assume the language is in the C ancestry. The content of the comments also may not suit your particular style or taste. However, as you create your own code-generation templates, you should apply these customization techniques:

1. Encode language-specific constructs in top-level parameters or variables so they can be overridden by importing stylesheets or (if you use parameters) by passing in parameter values when the stylesheet is run.

2. Break the various generated components into separate templates that can be overridden individually by importing stylesheets.

Having designed the transformation in this way allows C-style #define constants to be generated with only minor changes:

```
<?xml version="1.0" encoding="UTF-8"?>
<xsl:stylesheet version="1.0" xmlns:xsl="http://www.w3.org/1999/XSL/Transform">

    <xsl:import href="msgIds.xslt"/>

    <xsl:variable name="constants-type" select=" '#define ' "/>
    <xsl:variable name="assignment" select=" '   ' "/>
    <xsl:variable name="terminator" select=" '' "/>

</xsl:stylesheet>
```

Java requires everything to live inside a class, but you can accommodate that too:

```
<xsl:stylesheet version="1.0" xmlns:xsl="http://www.w3.org/1999/XSL/Transform">

<xsl:import href="msgIds.xslt"/>

 <xsl:variable name="constants-type" select=" 'public static final int' "/>

  <xsl:template name="constants-start">
  <xsl:text>final public class MESSAGE_IDS &#xa;</xsl:text>
  <xsl:text>{&#xa;</xsl:text>
  </xsl:template>

  <xsl:template name="constants-end">
  <xsl:text>&#xa;&#xa;}&#xa;</xsl:text>
  </xsl:template>

</xsl:stylesheet>
```

10.2   Generating Switching Code

Problem

You want to generate the switching code that will route incoming messages to their message handlers.

Solution

The message repository stores information about which processes receive which messages. Therefore, given a process name, you can generate a message switch that routes inbound messages to handlers:

```
<?xml version="1.0" encoding="UTF-8"?>
<xsl:stylesheet version="1.0" xmlns:xsl="http://www.w3.org/1999/XSL/Transform">

  <xsl:output method="text"/>

  <xsl:param name="process" select=" '*' "/>

  <xsl:variable name="message-dir" select=" 'messages' "/>
  <xsl:variable name="directory-sep" select=" '/' "/>
  <xsl:variable name="include-ext" select=" '.h' "/>


  <xsl:template match="MessageRepository">
    <!-- Generate source file preliminaries -->
    <xsl:call-template name="file-start"/>

    <!-- Generate includes for messages this process recives -->
    <xsl:apply-templates select="Messages/
                                 Message[Receivers/
```

```
                                        ProcessRef = $process or
                                        $process = '*']"
                        mode="includes"/>

  <!-- Generate message switch preliminaries -->
  <xsl:call-template name="switch-start"/>

  <!-- Generate switch body -->
  <xsl:apply-templates select="Messages/
                                Message[Receivers/
                                        ProcessRef = $process or
                                        $process = '*']"
                        mode="switch"/>

  <!-- Generate switch end -->
  <xsl:call-template name="switch-end"/>

  <!-- Generate file end -->
  <xsl:call-template name="file-end"/>
</xsl:template>

<!-- Generate an include for each message -->
<xsl:template match="Message" mode="includes">
  <xsl:text>#include &lt;</xsl:text>
  <xsl:value-of select="$message-dir"/>
  <xsl:value-of select="$directory-sep"/>
  <xsl:value-of select="Name"/>
  <xsl:value-of select="$include-ext"/>
  <xsl:text>&gt;&#xa;</xsl:text>
</xsl:template>

<!-- Generate handler case for each message type -->
<xsl:template match="Message" mode="switch">
  case <xsl:value-of select="Name"/>_ID:
    <xsl:call-template name="case-action"/>
</xsl:template>

<!-- Generate the message handler action -->
<xsl:template name="case-action">
    return <xsl:value-of select="Name"/>(*static_cast&lt;const <xsl:value-of
    select="DataTypeName"/>*&gt;(msg.getData( ))).process( ) ;
</xsl:template>

<!-- Do nothing by default. Users will override if necessary -->
<xsl:template name="file-start"/>
<xsl:template name="file-end"/>

<!-- Generate satrt of switch statement -->
<xsl:template name="switch-start">
#include &lt;transport/Message.h&gt;
#include &lt;transport/MESSAGE_IDS.h&gt;

<xsl:text>&#xa;&#xa;</xsl:text>
<xsl:call-template name="process-function"/>
```

```
{
  switch (msg.getId( ))
  {
  </xsl:template>

  <xsl:template name="switch-end">
    return false ;
  }
}
  </xsl:template>

  <!-- Generate signiture for message processing entry point -->
  <xsl:template name="process-function">
bool processMessage(const Message&amp; msg)
  </xsl:template>


  </xsl:stylesheet>
```

When applied to your test repository, this example produces the following switch-ing code:

```
#include <messages/ADD_STOCK_ORDER.h>
#include <messages/CANCEL_STOCK_ORDER.h>

#include <transport/Message.h>
#include <transport/MESSAGE_IDS.h>

bool processMessage(const Message& msg)

{
  switch (msg.getId( ))
  {

    case ADD_STOCK_ORDER_ID:

      return ADD_STOCK_ORDER(*static_cast<const
      AddStockOrderData*>(msg.getData( ))).process( ) ;

    case CANCEL_STOCK_ORDER_ID:

      return CANCEL_STOCK_ORDER(*static_cast<const
      CancelStockOrderData*>(msg.getData( ))).process( ) ;

    return false ;
  }
}
```

Discussion

Applications that process messages always have some form of message switch. The structure of these switches can vary somewhat, but they typically must check for some message identifier and route the message to a handler. The identifier can take the form of an integer (as in your case) or a string. In some cases, multipart identifiers consist of a message type and subtype. On the processing side, the handler can take the form of a simple function or an object that is instantiated to process the message. It is important to make even simple code generators modular so that they can be resued in more than one context. At a company where I once worked, a group decided to create a very interesting Perl-based facility that generated C++ code from an XSD schema. It was of sufficient usefulness that other groups wanted to use it. Unfortunately, the developers thought only in terms of their particular needs, and their otherwise impressive solution was not reusable. Writing even basic code generators is a formidable task, and you should try to make them as general as is practical so others will not have to relive your pain.

The particular solution shown provides several hooks for customizing what appears at the start of the generated file, the start of the switching code, the end of the switching code, and the end of the file. This flexibility allows Recipe 10.5 to reuse this generator. Still, it could use further improvement. For example, this generator assumes that a C switch statement performs message switching. However, some applications may use an if-else style switch, especially if the message IDs are strings. Others may use a table lookup from the message ID to a function pointer.

Can a single generator be made general enough to handle all these possibilities? Maybe, but the result will probably be extremely complex. A better approach would create generation components that could be reused in more complex generation scenarios. Here is what a generic C-switch statement generator might look like:

```
<?xml version="1.0" encoding="UTF-8"?>
<!DOCTYPE xslt [
  <!--Used to control code intenting -->
  <!ENTITY INDENT "    ">
  <!ENTITY INDENT2 "&INDENT;&INDENT;">
]>
<xsl:stylesheet version="1.0" xmlns:xsl="http://www.w3.org/1999/XSL/Transform">

  <xsl:template name="gen-C-Switch">
    <xsl:param name="variable"/>
    <xsl:param name="cases" select="/.."/>
    <xsl:param name="actions" select="/.."/>
    <xsl:param name="default"/>
    <xsl:param name="baseIndent" select="'&INDENT;'"/>
    <xsl:param name="genBreak" select="true()"/>

    <xsl:value-of select="$baseIndent"/>
    <xsl:text>switch (</xsl:text>
    <xsl:value-of select="$variable"/>
    <xsl:text>)&#xa;</xsl:text>
    <xsl:value-of select="$baseIndent"/>
    <xsl:text>{&#xa;</xsl:text>
```

```
<xsl:for-each select="$cases">
  <xsl:variable name="pos" select="position( )"/>

  <xsl:value-of select="$baseIndent"/>
  <xsl:text>&INDENT;case </xsl:text>
  <xsl:value-of select="."/>
  <xsl:text>:&#xa;</xsl:text>
  <xsl:call-template name="gen-C-Switch-caseBody">
    <xsl:with-param name="case" select="."/>
    <xsl:with-param name="action" select="$actions[$pos]"/>
    <xsl:with-param name="baseIndent"
                              select="concat('&INDENT2;',$baseIndent)"/>
  </xsl:call-template>
  <xsl:if test="$genBreak">
    <xsl:value-of select="$baseIndent"/>
    <xsl:text>&INDENT2;break;</xsl:text>
  </xsl:if>
  <xsl:text>&#xa;</xsl:text>
</xsl:for-each>

<xsl:if test="$default">
  <xsl:value-of select="$baseIndent"/>
  <xsl:text>&INDENT;default:</xsl:text>
  <xsl:text>:&#xa;</xsl:text>
  <xsl:call-template name="gen-C-Switch-default-caseBody">
    <xsl:with-param name="action" select="$default"/>
    <xsl:with-param name="baseIndent"
         select="concat('&INDENT2;',$baseIndent)"/>
  </xsl:call-template>
  <xsl:text>&#xa;</xsl:text>
</xsl:if>
<xsl:value-of select="$baseIndent"/>
<xsl:text>}&#xa;</xsl:text>
</xsl:template>


<!-- This generates a null statement by default. -->
<!-- Override to generate code for the case -->
<xsl:template name="gen-C-Switch-caseBody">
  <xsl:param name="case"/>
  <xsl:param name="action"/>
  <xsl:param name="baseIndent"/>

  <xsl:value-of select="$baseIndent"/>
  <xsl:text>;</xsl:text>
</xsl:template>

<!-- This invokes the regular case body generator. -->
<!-- Overide to do something special for the default case. -->
<xsl:template name="gen-C-Switch-default-caseBody">
  <xsl:param name="action"/>
  <xsl:param name="baseIndent"/>
```

```
    <xsl:call-template name="gen-C-Switch-caseBody">
      <xsl:with-param name="action" select="$action"/>
      <xsl:with-param name="baseIndent" select="$baseIndent"/>
    </xsl:call-template>
  </xsl:template>

</xsl:stylesheet>
```

Chapter 14 demonstrates techniques that make generators like this even more generic.

10.3   Generating Message-Handling Stub Code

Problem

You want to generate the skeleton of your message handlers.

Solution

The following stylesheet creates a simple skeleton that takes a process name and generates stub code:

```
<?xml version="1.0" encoding="UTF-8"?>
<xsl:stylesheet version="1.1" xmlns:xsl="http://www.w3.org/1999/XSL/Transform">

  <xsl:output method="text"/>

  <!-- Specifies which process to generate handlers for -->
  <xsl:param name="process"/>
  <!-- Specifies which message to generate handlers for. A special value of %ALL%
       signifies all messages -->
  <xsl:param name="message" select=" '%ALL%' "/>


  <!-- The directory where -->
  <xsl:variable name="message-dir" select=" 'messages' "/>
  <xsl:variable name="directory-sep" select=" '/' "/>
  <xsl:variable name="include-ext" select=" '.h' "/>


  <xsl:template match="MessageRepository">
    <xsl:choose>
      <xsl:when test="$message='%ALL%'"  >
          <xsl:apply-templates
              select="Messages/Message[Receivers/ProcessRef = $process]"/>
      </xsl:when>
      <xsl:otherwise>
        <xsl:apply-templates
            select="Messages/Message[Receivers/ProcessRef = $process and
                                      Name=$message]"/>
      </xsl:otherwise>
    </xsl:choose>
```

```
    </xsl:template>

    <xsl:template match="Message"      >
    <xsl:document href="{concat(Name,'.h')}">
      <xsl:call-template name="makeHeader"/>
    </xsl:document>
    <xsl:document href="{concat(Name,'.cpp')}">
      <xsl:call-template name="makeSource"/>
    </xsl:document>
    </xsl:template>

  <xsl:template name="makeHeader">
#ifndef <xsl:value-of select="Name"/>_h
#define <xsl:value-of select="Name"/>_h

#include &lt;transport/MessageHandler.h&gt;

//Forward Declarations
class <xsl:value-of select="DataTypeName"/> ;
/*!TODO:  Insert addition forward declarations here.*/

class <xsl:value-of select="Name"/> : public MessageHandler
{
public:
    <xsl:value-of select="Name"/>(const <xsl:value-of
        select="DataTypeName"/>&amp; data) ;
    bool process( ) ;
private:

    const <xsl:value-of select="DataTypeName"/>&amp; m_Data ;
} ;

#endif
  </xsl:template>

  <xsl:template name="makeSource">
#include &lt;messages/<xsl:value-of select="Name"/>.h&gt;

/*!TODO:  Insert addition includes here.*/

<xsl:value-of select="Name"/>::<xsl:value-of select="Name"/>(const
    <xsl:value-of select="DataTypeName"/>&amp; data)
  : m_Data(data)
{
}

bool <xsl:value-of select="Name"/>::process( )
{
  /*!TODO:  Insert message handler code here. */
  return true;
}
  </xsl:template>

</xsl:stylesheet>
```

This stylesheet generates a header and a source file for each message it processes, as shown in Examples 10-1 and 10-2.

Example 10-1. AddStockOrder.h

```
#ifndef ADD_STOCK_ORDER_h
#define ADD_STOCK_ORDER_h

#include <transport/MessageHandler.h>

//Forward Declarations
class AddStockOrderData ;
/*!TODO:  Insert addition forward declarations here.*/

class ADD_STOCK_ORDER : public MessageHandler
{
public:
    ADD_STOCK_ORDER(const AddStockOrderData& data) ;
    bool process() ;
private:

    const AddStockOrderData& m_Data ;
} ;

#endif
```

Example 10-2. AddStockOrder.cpp

```
#include <messages/ADD_STOCK_ORDER.h>

/*!TODO:  Insert addition includes here.*/

ADD_STOCK_ORDER::ADD_STOCK_ORDER(const AddStockOrderData& data)
  : m_Data(data)
{
}

bool ADD_STOCK_ORDER::process()
{
  /*!TODO:  Insert message handler code here. */
  return true;
}
```

Discussion

Much of what developers do is repetitive in structure but unique in substance. In other words, we write a lot of boilerplate code that gets specialized based on the particular context. Performing any sort of repetitive work leads to boredom; boredom leads to distraction; and distraction results in bugs. Generating the repetitive parts of your code lets you concentrate on the important parts.

Tools that generate code with TODO sections are often called wizards. This message handler wizard is a very basic example of this genre. Some commercially available wizards generate the structure of entire applications. It is not clear whether XSLT can scale to create wizards of that magnitude. However, for simple kinds of stub generators for which the input is XML, XSLT is preferable to other languages, including Perl. Many Perl fanatics disagree with this statement because they view XML processing as just another form of text processing (and we all know Perl is the undisputed king of text-processing languages). However, a strong argument can be made that XML processing is not text processing, but the processing of trees that contain text nodes. As such, XSLT facilities transform trees more nimbly than Perl does. Nevertheless, Perl and XSLT can team up to create a best-of-both-worlds approach, as shown in Chapter 12. Chapter 12 also presents an extension to XSLT that removes the verbosity that gets in the way of pure XSLT-based generators.

10.4   Generating Data Wrappers

Problem

You want to create classes that wrap the data contained in each message with a type-safe interface.

Solution

The solution works in two modes. If a message name is provided in a parameter, then it generates a wrapper only for that message data. Otherwise, if no message is specified, it generates wrappers for all messages:

```
<xsl:stylesheet version="1.1" xmlns:xsl="http://www.w3.org/1999/XSL/Transform">

  <xsl:output method="text"/>
  <xsl:strip-space elements="*"/>

  <!--The message to generate data for. '*' for all -->
  <xsl:param name="message" select=" '*' "/>
  <!--The directory to generate code -->
  <xsl:param name="generationDir" select=" 'src/' "/>
  <!--The C++ header extension to use -->
  <xsl:param name="headerExt" select=" '.h' "/>
  <!--The C++ source extension to use -->
  <xsl:param name="sourceExt" select=" '.C' "/>

  <!--Key to locate data types by name -->
  <xsl:key name="dataTypes" match="Structure" use="Name" />
  <xsl:key name="dataTypes" match="Primitive" use="Name" />
  <xsl:key name="dataTypes" match="Array" use="Name" />
  <xsl:key name="dataTypes" match="Enumeration" use="Name" />
```

```
<!-- Top level template determines which messages to process -->
<xsl:template match="/">
  <xsl:choose>
      <xsl:when test="$message = '*'">
        <xsl:apply-templates select="*/Messages/*"/>
      </xsl:when>
      <xsl:when test="*/Messages/Message[Name=$message]">
        <xsl:apply-templates select="*/Messages/Message[Name=$message]"/>
      </xsl:when>
      <xsl:otherwise>
        <xsl:message terminate="yes">No such message name
        [<xsl:value-of select="$message"/>]</xsl:message>
      </xsl:otherwise>
    </xsl:choose>
  </xsl:template>


<!-- If the messages data type is contained in the repository then gnerate data
wrapper header and source file for it -->
<xsl:template match="Message">
  <xsl:choose>
    <xsl:when test="key('dataTypes',DataTypeName)">
      <xsl:apply-templates select="key('dataTypes',DataTypeName)" mode="header"/>
      <xsl:apply-templates select="key('dataTypes',DataTypeName)" mode="source"/>
    </xsl:when>
    <xsl:otherwise>
            <xsl:message>Message name [<xsl:value-of select="Name"/>] uses data
            [<xsl:value-of select="DataTypeName"/>] that is not defined in the
            repository.</xsl:message>
    </xsl:otherwise>
  </xsl:choose>
</xsl:template>


<!-- We only generate headers if a messages data type is a Stucture.
The only other typical message data type is XML. We don't generate wrappers for XML
payloads.-->
<xsl:template match="Structure" mode="header">
<xsl:document href="{concat($generationDir,Name,$headerExt)}">
#include &lt;primitives/primitives.h&gt;

class <xsl:value-of select="Name"/>
{
public:<xsl:text>&#xa;&#xa;</xsl:text>
  <xsl:for-each select="Members/Member">
    <xsl:text>     </xsl:text>
    <xsl:apply-templates select="key('dataTypes',DataTypeName)" mode="returnType"/>
    get_<xsl:value-of select="Name"/>() const ;<xsl:text/>
    <xsl:text>&#xa;</xsl:text>
  </xsl:for-each>
<xsl:text>&#xa;</xsl:text>
private:<xsl:text>&#xa;&#xa;</xsl:text>
  <xsl:for-each select="Members/Member">
    <xsl:text>     </xsl:text>
    <xsl:apply-templates select="key('dataTypes',DataTypeName)" mode="data"/>  m_
<xsl:value-of select="Name"/> ;<xsl:text/>
```

```xsl
    <xsl:text>&#xa;</xsl:text>
  </xsl:for-each>
} ;
</xsl:document>
</xsl:template>

<!-- We only generate source if a messages data type is a Stucture. -->
<!-- The only other typical message data type is XML. We don't        -->
<!-- generate wrappers for XML payloads.                              -->
<xsl:template match="Structure" mode="source">
<xsl:document href="{concat($generationDir,Name,$sourceExt)}">
#include "<xsl:value-of select="Name"/><xsl:value-of select="$headerExt"/>"

<xsl:text/>

  <xsl:for-each select="Members/Member">
    <xsl:apply-templates select="key('dataTypes',DataTypeName)" mode="returnType"/>
    <xsl:text>   </xsl:text>
    <xsl:value-of select="../../Name"/>::get_<xsl:value-of select="Name"/>() const
    <xsl:text>&#xa;</xsl:text>
    <xsl:text>{&#xa;</xsl:text>
    <xsl:text>      return m_</xsl:text><xsl:value-of select="Name"/>
    <xsl:text>;&#xa;</xsl:text>
    <xsl:text>}&#xa;&#xa;</xsl:text>
  </xsl:for-each>

</xsl:document>
</xsl:template>

<!-- We assume members that are themselves structures are -->
<!-- returned by reference. -->
<xsl:template match="Structure" mode="returnType">
const <xsl:value-of select="Name"/>&amp;<xsl:text/>
</xsl:template>

<!-- We map primitives that can be represented by native C++ types to those native
types. -->
<!-- Otherwise we assume the primitive is externally defined. -->
<xsl:template match="Primitive" mode="returnType">
  <xsl:choose>
    <xsl:when test="Name='Integer' ">int</xsl:when>
    <xsl:when test="Name='Real' ">double</xsl:when>
    <xsl:otherwise><xsl:value-of select="Name"/></xsl:otherwise>
  </xsl:choose>
</xsl:template>

<xsl:template match="*" mode="returnType">
<xsl:value-of select="Name"/>
</xsl:template>

<xsl:template match="Primitive" mode="data">
  <xsl:choose>
    <xsl:when test="Name='Integer' ">int</xsl:when>
    <xsl:when test="Name='Real' ">double</xsl:when>
```

```
        <xsl:otherwise><xsl:value-of select="Name"/></xsl:otherwise>
    </xsl:choose>
</xsl:template>

<xsl:template match="*" mode="data">
<xsl:value-of select="Name"/>
</xsl:template>

</xsl:stylesheet>
```

This generator produces only a get interface, but you can easily extend it to generate set functions or other types of functions. Here is a sample generated header file:

```
#include <primitives/primitives.h>

class AddStockOrderData
{
public:

    StkSymbol get_symbol() const ;
    Shares get_quantity() const ;
    BuyOrSell get_side() const ;
    OrderType get_type() const ;
    double get_price() const ;


    private:

    StkSymbol  m_symbol ;
    Shares  m_quantity ;
    BuyOrSell° m_side ;
    OrderType  m_type ;
    double  m_price ;

} ;
```

Here is a sample *cpp* file:

```
#include "AddStockOrderData.h"

StkSymbol  AddStockOrderData::get_symbol() const
{
    return m_symbol;
}

Shares  AddStockOrderData::get_quantity() const
{
    return m_quantity;
}

BuyOrSell  AddStockOrderData::get_side() const
{
    return m_side;
}
```

```
OrderType  AddStockOrderData::get_type( ) const
{
    return m_type;
}

double  AddStockOrderData::get_price( ) const
{
    return m_price;
}
```

Discussion

This section uses the term *wrapper* to denote a class that provides an object-oriented interface to data that is otherwise just a plain old C struct. I once worked on a project that hand-coded all our message wrappers. Although the work was tedious, the result was well worth the effort. Consider a message that contains prices, quantities, and dates. An integer type might encode both of these higher-level types. You could easily make a mistake and substitute one for the other with out the compiler noticing. Wrappers provide a way to put a skin around your message data that converts low-level representations to class-based primitives such as Price, Qty, and Date. An autogenerated wrapper provides this benefit with less effort.

A message repository and XSLT-based generator allow you to automate the task of producing wrappers. In practice, wrappers sometimes contain some smarts, and you might need to store additional metadata in the repository to get corresponding code generation smarts. One common case occurs when message data contains arrays. Often another field is present that states how many items are actually stored in the array. If you hand-coded a wrapper function to add an item to this array, it would need to reference this field to find the next empty locations and increment it after adding the new data. You could generate such code only if the repository associated the array size field with the array field.

10.5   Generating Pretty Printers

Problem

You need tools to help debug your application. In particular, you want the ability to render binary messages in human-readable form.

Solution

When developing messaging applications, developers often hand-code pretty printers because they make debugging these applications considerably easier. However, this kind of code can be generated if you have a message repository. This solution shows how to reuse the message switch generator from Recipe 10.2:

```xml
<?xml version="1.0" encoding="UTF-8"?>
<!DOCTYPE xslt [
  <!--Used to control code intenting -->
  <!ENTITY INDENT "    ">
  <!ENTITY INDENT2 "&INDENT;&INDENT;">
  <!ENTITY LS "&lt;&lt;">
]>
<xsl:stylesheet version="1.1" xmlns:xsl="http://www.w3.org/1999/XSL/Transform">

<!-- This pretty-printer generator needs a message switch so we -->
<!-- reuse the one we already wrote. -->
<xsl:import href="messageSwitch.xslt"/>

  <!--The directory to generate code -->
  <xsl:param name="generationDir" select=" 'src/' "/>
  <!--The C++ header file name -->
  <xsl:param name="prettyPrintHeader" select=" 'prettyPrint.h' "/>
  <!--The C++ source file name -->
  <xsl:param name="prettyPrintSource" select=" 'prettyPrint.C' "/>

  <!--Key to locate data types by name -->
  <xsl:key name="dataTypes" match="Structure" use="Name" />
  <xsl:key name="dataTypes" match="Primitive" use="Name" />
  <xsl:key name="dataTypes" match="Array" use="Name" />
  <xsl:key name="dataTypes" match="Enumeration" use="Name" />

  <xsl:template match="MessageRepository">
    <xsl:document href="{concat($generationDir,$prettyPrintHeader)}">
      <xsl:text>void prettyPrintMessage</xsl:text>
      <xsl:text>(ostream&amp; stream, const Message&amp; msg);&#xa;</xsl:text>
      <xsl:apply-templates select="DataTypes/Structure" mode="declare"/>
    </xsl:document>

    <xsl:document href="{concat($generationDir,$prettyPrintSource)}">
      <xsl:apply-imports/>
      <xsl:apply-templates select="DataTypes/Structure" mode="printers"/>
    </xsl:document>

  </xsl:template>

<!--Override the message processing function name from -->
<!-- messageSwitch.xslt to customize the function -->
<!-- signiture to take a stream -->
<xsl:template name="process-function">
<xsl:text>void prettyPrintMessage</xsl:text>
<xsl:text>(ostream&amp; stream, const Message&amp; msg)</xsl:text>
</xsl:template>

<!--Override case action from messageSwitch.xslt to generate -->
<!-- call to prettyPrinter for message data -->
<xsl:template name="case-action">
 <xsl:text>    prettyPrint(stream, *static_cast&lt;const </xsl:text>
 <xsl:value-of select="DataTypeName"/>
 <xsl:text>*&gt;(msg.getData())) ;</xsl:text>
```

```
        break;</xsl:text>
</xsl:template>

<!--Generate declarations for each message data type -->
<xsl:template match="Structure" mode="declare">
<!--Forward declare the message data class -->
<xsl:text>class </xsl:text>
<xsl:value-of select="Name"/>
<xsl:text> ;&#xa;</xsl:text>
<!--Forward declare the message prettyPrint function -->
<xsl:text>ostream prettyPrint(ostream &amp; stream, const </xsl:text>
<xsl:value-of select="Name"/>
<xsl:text>&amp; data);&#xa;</xsl:text>
</xsl:template>

<!--Generate the body of  a pretty-printer -->
<xsl:template match="Structure" mode="printers">
<xsl:text>ostream prettyPrint(ostream &amp; stream, const </xsl:text>
<xsl:value-of select="Name"/>
<xsl:text>&amp; data)&#xa;</xsl:text>
<xsl:text>{&#xa;</xsl:text>
<xsl:text>&INDENT;stream &#xa;</xsl:text>
<xsl:text>&INDENT2;&LS; "</xsl:text>
<xsl:value-of select="Name"/>
<xsl:text>" &LS;  endl  &LS; "{"  &LS; endl &#xa;</xsl:text>
  <xsl:for-each select="Members/Member">
      <xsl:text>&INDENT2;&LS; "</xsl:text>
      <xsl:value-of select="Name"/>: " &LS; <xsl:text/>
      <xsl:apply-templates
                  select="key('dataTypes',DataTypeName)" mode="print">
        <xsl:with-param name="name" select="Name"/>
      </xsl:apply-templates>
      <xsl:text>&#xa;</xsl:text>
  </xsl:for-each>
  <xsl:text>&INDENT2;&LS; "}"  &LS; endl ; &#xa;</xsl:text>
  <xsl:text>&INDENT;return stream ;&#xa;</xsl:text>
  <xsl:text>}&#xa;&#xa;</xsl:text>
</xsl:template>

<!--Nested structures invoke the pretty-printer for that structure -->
<xsl:template match="Structure" mode="print">
  <xsl:param name="name"/>
  <xsl:text>prettyPrint(stream, data.get_</xsl:text>
  <xsl:value-of select="$name"/><xsl:text>())</xsl:text>
</xsl:template>

<!--We assume there is a get function for each -->
<!-- primitive component of the message -->
<xsl:template match="*" mode="print">
  <xsl:param name="name"/>
  <xsl:text>data.get_</xsl:text>
  <xsl:value-of select="$name"/>() &lt;&lt; endl<xsl:text/>
</xsl:template>

</xsl:stylesheet>
```

The following source file is generated. We omit the header since it contains only declarations:

```cpp
#include <messages/ADD_STOCK_ORDER.h>
#include <messages/ADD_STOCK_ORDER_ACK.h>
#include <messages/ADD_STOCK_ORDER_NACK.h>
#include <messages/CANCEL_STOCK_ORDER.h>
#include <messages/CANCEL_STOCK_ORDER_ACK.h>
#include <messages/CANCEL_STOCK_ORDER_NACK.h>
#include <messages/TEST.h>

#include <transport/Message.h>
#include <transport/MESSAGE_IDS.h>



void prettyPrintMessage(ostream& stream, const Message& msg)
{
  switch (msg.getId())
  {

    case ADD_STOCK_ORDER_ID:
        prettyPrint(stream, *static_cast<const
        AddStockOrderData*>(msg.getData())) ;
        break;
    case ADD_STOCK_ORDER_ACK_ID:
        prettyPrint(stream, *static_cast<const
        AddStockOrderAckData*>(msg.getData())) ;
        break;
    case ADD_STOCK_ORDER_NACK_ID:
        prettyPrint(stream, *static_cast<const
        AddStockOrderNackData*>(msg.getData())) ;
        break;
    case CANCEL_STOCK_ORDER_ID:
        prettyPrint(stream, *static_cast<const
        CancelStockOrderData*>(msg.getData())) ;
        break;
    case CANCEL_STOCK_ORDER_ACK_ID:
        prettyPrint(stream, *static_cast<const
        CancelStockOrderAckData*>(msg.getData())) ;
        break;
    case CANCEL_STOCK_ORDER_NACK_ID:
        prettyPrint(stream, *static_cast<const
        CancelStockOrderNackData*>(msg.getData())) ;
        break;
    case TEST_ID:
        prettyPrint(stream, *static_cast<const TestData*>(msg.getData())) ;
        break;
    return false ;
  }
}
  ostream prettyPrint(ostream & stream, const TestData& data)
```

```
{
    stream
        << "TestData" << endl  << "{"  << endl
        << "order: " << prettyPrint(stream, data.get_order())
        << "cancel: " << prettyPrint(stream, data.get_cancel())
        << "}"  << endl ;
    return stream ;
}

ostream prettyPrint(ostream & stream, const AddStockOrderData& data)
{
    stream
        << "AddStockOrderData" <<  endl  << "{"  << endl
        << "symbol: " << data.get_symbol() << endl
        << "quantity: " << data.get_quantity() << endl
        << "side: " << data.get_side() << endl
        << "type: " << data.get_type() << endl
        << "price: " << data.get_price() << endl
        << "}"  << endl ;
    return stream ;
}


ostream prettyPrint(ostream & stream, const AddStockOrderAckData& data)
{
    stream
        << "AddStockOrderAckData" <<  endl  << "{"  << endl
        << "orderId: " << data.get_orderId() << endl
        << "}"  << endl ;
    return stream ;
}

ostream prettyPrint(ostream & stream, const AddStockOrderNackData& data)
{
    stream
        << "AddStockOrderNackData" <<  endl  << "{"  << endl
        << "reason: " << data.get_reason() << endl
        << "}"  << endl ;
    return stream ;
}

ostream prettyPrint(ostream & stream, const CancelStockOrderData& data)
{
    stream
        << "CancelStockOrderData" <<  endl  << "{"  << endl
        << "orderId: " << data.get_orderId() << endl
        << "quantity: " << data.get_quantity() << endl
        << "}"  << endl ;
    return stream ;
}

ostream prettyPrint(ostream & stream, const CancelStockOrderAckData& data)
{
    stream
```

```
        << "CancelStockOrderAckData" <<  endl  << "{"  << endl
        << "orderId: " << data.get_orderId() << endl
        << "quantityRemaining: " << data.get_quantityRemaining() << endl
        << "}"  << endl ;
    return stream ;
}

ostream prettyPrint(ostream & stream, const CancelStockOrderNackData& data)
{
    stream
        << "CancelStockOrderNackData" <<  endl  << "{"  << endl
        << "orderId: " << data.get_orderId() << endl
        << "reason: " << data.get_reason() << endl
        << "}"  << endl ;
    return stream ;
}
```

Discussion

This code-generation recipe attacks the pretty-printing problem head on by literally generating the pretty-print code for each message. Following this example is simple, and the results are effective. However, you could approach the problem more generally, and in the process create a more useful code generator.

Specifically, you can break the pretty-printing process into two stages. One stage is the process of parsing a monolithic message into its constituent parts. The other is the process of taking those parts and formatting them into human-readable text.

Looking at the problem in this way changes the solution from the generation of a single-purpose set of functions (a pretty printer) to the generation of a more generic message parser. Such parsers are usually event driven. Readers familiar with the Simple API for XML (SAX) will recognize this style of processing. The stylesheet used to generate a message parser is a variation of the pretty-print generator. Instead of sending message components to a stream, it sends parse events to a handler:

```
<?xml version="1.0" encoding="UTF-8"?>
<!DOCTYPE xslt [
  <!--Used to control code intenting -->
  <!ENTITY INDENT "    ">
  <!ENTITY INDENT2 "&INDENT;&INDENT;">
  <!ENTITY LS "&lt;&lt;">
]>
<xsl:stylesheet version="1.1" xmlns:xsl="http://www.w3.org/1999/XSL/Transform">

<!-- This mesage parse generator needs a message switch so we -->
<!-- reuse the one we already wrote. -->
<xsl:import href="messageSwitch.xslt"/>

  <!--The directory to generate code -->
  <xsl:param name="generationDir" select=" 'src/' "/>
  <!--The C++ header file name -->
  <xsl:param name="msgParseHeader" select=" 'msgParse.h' "/>
```

```xslt
<!--The C++ source file name -->
<xsl:param name="msgParseSource" select=" 'msgParse.C' "/>

<!--Key to locate data types by name -->
<xsl:key name="dataTypes" match="Structure" use="Name" />
<xsl:key name="dataTypes" match="Primitive" use="Name" />
<xsl:key name="dataTypes" match="Array" use="Name" />
<xsl:key name="dataTypes" match="Enumeration" use="Name" />

<xsl:template match="MessageRepository">
  <xsl:document href="{concat($generationDir,$msgParseHeader)}">
    <xsl:text>void parseMessage</xsl:text>
     <xsl:text>(MessageHandler&amp; handler, const Message&amp; msg);&#xa;
     </xsl:text>
     <xsl:apply-templates select="DataTypes/Structure" mode="declare"/>
  </xsl:document>

  <xsl:document href="{concat($generationDir,$msgParseSource)}">
    <xsl:apply-imports/>
    <xsl:apply-templates select="DataTypes/Structure" mode="parsers"/>
  </xsl:document>

</xsl:template>

<!--Override the message processing function name from -->
<!-- messageSwitch.xslt to customize the function signiture -->
<!-- to take a handler -->
<xsl:template name="process-function">
<xsl:text>void parseMessage</xsl:text>
<xsl:text>(MessageHandler&amp; handler, const Message&amp; msg)</xsl:text>
</xsl:template>

<!--Override case action from messageSwitch.xslt to generate -->
<!-- call to parse for message data -->
<xsl:template name="case-action">
 <xsl:text>    parse(handler, *static_cast&lt;const </xsl:text>
 <xsl:value-of select="DataTypeName"/>
 <xsl:text>*&gt;(msg.getData())) ;
        break;</xsl:text>
</xsl:template>

<!--Generate declarations for each message data type -->
<xsl:template match="Structure" mode="declare">
<!--Forward declare the message data class -->
<xsl:text>class </xsl:text>
<xsl:value-of select="Name"/>
<xsl:text> ;&#xa;</xsl:text>
<!--Forward declare the message parse function -->
<xsl:text>void parse(MessageHandler &amp; handler, const </xsl:text>
<xsl:value-of select="Name"/>
<xsl:text>&amp; data);&#xa;</xsl:text>
</xsl:template>
```

```
<!--Generate the body of a parser -->
<xsl:template match="Structure" mode="parsers">
<xsl:text>void parse(MessageHandler &amp; handler, const </xsl:text>
<xsl:value-of select="Name"/>
<xsl:text>&amp; data)&#xa;</xsl:text>
<xsl:text>{&#xa;</xsl:text>
<xsl:text>&INDENT;handler.beginStruct("</xsl:text>
<xsl:value-of select="Name"/>
<xsl:text>") ;&#xa;</xsl:text>
  <xsl:for-each select="Members/Member">
      <xsl:apply-templates
          select="key('dataTypes',DataTypeName)" mode="parse">
        <xsl:with-param name="name" select="Name"/>
      </xsl:apply-templates>
  </xsl:for-each>
<xsl:text>&INDENT;handler.endStruct("</xsl:text>
<xsl:value-of select="Name"/>
<xsl:text>") ;&#xa;</xsl:text>
  <xsl:text>}&#xa;&#xa;</xsl:text>
</xsl:template>

<!--Nested structures invoke the parser for that structure -->
<xsl:template match="Structure" mode="parse">
  <xsl:param name="name"/>
  <xsl:text>&INDENT;parse(handler, data.get_</xsl:text>
  <xsl:value-of select="$name"/><xsl:text>());&#xa;</xsl:text>
</xsl:template>

<!--We assume there is a get function for each -->
<!-- primitive component of the message -->
<xsl:template match="*" mode="parse">
  <xsl:param name="name"/>
  <xsl:text>&INDENT;handler.field("</xsl:text>
  <xsl:value-of select="$name"/>","<xsl:text/>
  <xsl:value-of select="Name"/>",<xsl:text/>
  <xsl:text>data.get_</xsl:text>
  <xsl:value-of select="$name"/>()<xsl:text/>
  <xsl:text>);&#xa;</xsl:text>
</xsl:template>

</xsl:stylesheet>
```

It produces parse functions that look like the following code:

```
void parse(MessageHandler & handler, const AddStockOrderData& data)
{
    handler.beginStruct("AddStockOrderData") ;
    handler.field("symbol","StkSymbol",data.get_symbol());
    handler.field("quantity","Shares",data.get_quantity());
    handler.field("side","BuyOrSell",data.get_side());
    handler.field("type","OrderType",data.get_type());
    handler.field("price","Real",data.get_price());
    handler.endStruct("AddStockOrderData") ;
}
```

10.6   Generating a Test Data-Entry Web Client

Problem

You want to test a process in isolation by entering information in a form and having the information converted into a message that is sent to a process.

Solution

This example generates a test data-entry tool's client side. It takes the shape of an HTML-based form that can be used to enter the fields that make up a message. It specifies that the form data be handled by a CGI that is generated in Recipe 10.7:

```
<xsl:stylesheet version="1.0" xmlns:xsl="http://www.w3.org/1999/XSL/Transform">
<xsl:output method="html" />

<xsl:param name="message"/>

<!--Key to locate data types by name -->
<xsl:key name="dataTypes" match="Structure" use="Name" />
<xsl:key name="dataTypes" match="Primitive" use="Name" />
<xsl:key name="dataTypes" match="Array" use="Name" />
<xsl:key name="dataTypes" match="Enumeration" use="Name" />

<xsl:template match="/">
  <html>
    <head>
      <title><xsl:value-of select="$message"/> Entry</title>
    </head>
    <body bgcolor="#FFFFFF" text="#000000">
      <h1><xsl:value-of select="$message"/> Entry</h1>
      <form name="{concat($message,'Form')}" method="post"
      action="{concat('/cgi-bin/',$message,'Process.pl')}">
        <xsl:apply-templates select="*/Messages/Message[Name=$message]"/>
        <br/><center><input type="submit" name="Submit" value="Submit"/></center>
      </form>
    </body>
  </html>
</xsl:template>

<xsl:template match="Message">
  <xsl:apply-templates select="key('dataTypes',DataTypeName)">
    <xsl:with-param name="field" select="Name"/>
  </xsl:apply-templates>
</xsl:template>

<xsl:template match="Structure">
  <xsl:param name="field"/>
  <table width="100%" border="0" cellspacing="1" cellpadding="1">
    <tbody>
      <xsl:for-each select="Members/Member">
```

```
    <tr>
      <td valign="top"><xsl:value-of select="Name"/></td>
      <td>
        <xsl:apply-templates select="key('dataTypes',DataTypeName)">
          <xsl:with-param name="field"
                  select="concat($field,'_',Name)"/>
        </xsl:apply-templates>
      </td>
    </tr>
   </xsl:for-each>
   </tbody>
  </table>
 </xsl:template>

<xsl:template match="*">
  <xsl:param name="field"/>
  <input type="text" name="{$field}" size="30"/>
</xsl:template>

</xsl:stylesheet>
```

Discussion

Generating the UI in HTML is one of the easiest ways to autogenerate a test-data frontend; however, it is not the only way. You might also want to generate a text-based frontend that prompts and reads input from stdin. If you feel ambitious, you might generate a GUI frontend. One advantage of not using HTML is that you can combine the functionality of this example and Recipe 10.7 into a single application. However, do not be surprised if such a generator is more complex then the generators produced in these examples; the HTML-CGI approach builds on a substantial existing infrastructure present in the browser and web server.

An important extension to this recipe would generate validation code in JavaScript or VBScript. Again, the quality of this validation code depends on what type of metadata is kept in the repository. You might want to extend the repository to store minimum and maximum values and/or regular expressions for use in data validation.

10.7 Generating Test-Entry Web CGI

Problem

You want to test a process in isolation by processing text data received from a form and converting that data into a physical message that can be sent to the process under test.

Solution

This server generator goes along with the client generator created in Recipe 10.6. This section shows only a piece of the solution, but the discussion gives further detail.

The generated server is a C++ CGI program. You need it to be C++ (or C) because the form input will be converted into a binary message that is laid out according to the C memory model. It assumes the C++ processes that ultimately consume these message expect them as binary data. The generated CGI uses Enterprise Integration Technologies' libcgi (*http://www.landfield.com/hypermail/source/libcgi/*) to simplify the common CGI tasks such as query-string parsing:

```
<!DOCTYPE xslt [
  <!--Used to control code intenting -->
  <!ENTITY INDENT "    ">
]>
<xsl:stylesheet version="1.1" xmlns:xsl="http://www.w3.org/1999/XSL/Transform">

  <xsl:output method="text"/>
  <xsl:strip-space elements="*"/>

  <!--The message to generate data for. '*' for all -->
  <xsl:param name="message" select=" '*' "/>
  <!--The directory to generate code -->
  <xsl:param name="generationDir" select=" 'src/' "/>
  <!--The C++ header extension to use -->
  <xsl:param name="headerExt" select=" '.h' "/>
  <!--The C++ source extension to use -->
  <xsl:param name="sourceExt" select=" '.C' "/>

  <!--Key to locate data types by name -->
  <xsl:key name="dataTypes" match="Structure" use="Name" />
  <xsl:key name="dataTypes" match="Primitive" use="Name" />
  <xsl:key name="dataTypes" match="Array" use="Name" />
  <xsl:key name="dataTypes" match="Enumeration" use="Name" />


  <!-- Top level template determines which messages to process -->
  <xsl:template match="/">
    <xsl:choose>
        <xsl:when test="$message = '*'">
          <xsl:apply-templates select="*/Messages/*"/>
        </xsl:when>
        <xsl:when test="*/Messages/Message[Name=$message]">
          <xsl:apply-templates select="*/Messages/Message[Name=$message]"/>
        </xsl:when>
        <xsl:otherwise>
          <xsl:message terminate="yes">No such message name
          [<xsl:value-of select="$message"/>]</xsl:message>
        </xsl:otherwise>
    </xsl:choose>
  </xsl:template>
```

```xml
<!-- If the messages data type is contained in the repository then gnerate data
wrapper header and source file for it -->
<xsl:template match="Message">
  <xsl:choose>
    <xsl:when test="key('dataTypes',DataTypeName)">
      <xsl:apply-templates select="key('dataTypes',DataTypeName)" mode="source">
        <xsl:with-param name="msg" select="Name"/>
      </xsl:apply-templates>
    </xsl:when>
    <xsl:otherwise>
          <xsl:message>Message name [<xsl:value-of select="Name"/>] uses data
          [<xsl:value-of select="DataTypeName"/>] that is not defined in the
          repository.</xsl:message>
    </xsl:otherwise>
  </xsl:choose>
</xsl:template>

<!-- We only generate source if a messages data type is a Stucture. -->
<!-- The only other typical message data type is XML. We don't        -->
<!-- generate wrappers for XML payloads.                              -->
<xsl:template match="Structure" mode="source">
  <xsl:param name="msg"/>

  <xsl:document href="{concat($generationDir,Name,'CGI',$sourceExt)}">

<xsl:text>
#include &lt;stdio.h&gt;
#include "cgi.h"
#include "</xsl:text>
<xsl:value-of select="Name"/><xsl:value-of select="$headerExt"/>
<xsl:text>"

void cgi_main(cgi_info *cgi)
{
    </xsl:text>
    <xsl:value-of select="Name"/>
    <xsl:text> data ;
    form_entry* form_data = get_form_entries(cgi) ;
</xsl:text>

  <xsl:for-each select="Members/Member">
    <xsl:apply-templates select="key('dataTypes',DataTypeName)" mode="variables">
      <xsl:with-param name="field" select="concat($msg,'_',Name)"/>
      <xsl:with-param name="var" select="Name"/>
    </xsl:apply-templates>
   </xsl:for-each>

  <xsl:for-each select="Members/Member">
    <xsl:apply-templates select="key('dataTypes',DataTypeName)" mode="load">
      <xsl:with-param name="field" select="concat('data.',Name)"/>
      <xsl:with-param name="var" select="Name"/>
    </xsl:apply-templates>
  </xsl:for-each>
```

```
<xsl:text>
&INDENT;//Enque data to the process being tested
&INDENT;enqueData(data) ;

}</xsl:text>
</xsl:document>
</xsl:template>

<!-- Declare and initialize variables for each field -->
<xsl:template match="Structure" mode="variables">
  <xsl:param name="field"/>
  <xsl:param name="var"/>
      <xsl:for-each select="Members/Member">
            <xsl:apply-templates select="key('dataTypes',DataTypeName)"
                mode="variables">
              <xsl:with-param name="field" select="concat($field,'_',Name)"/>
              <xsl:with-param name="var" select="$var"/>
            </xsl:apply-templates>
      </xsl:for-each>
</xsl:template>

<xsl:template match="*" mode="variables">
  <xsl:param name="field"/>
  <xsl:param name="var"/>

  <xsl:text>&INDENT;const char * </xsl:text>
  <xsl:value-of select="$var"/>
  <xsl:text> = parmval(form_data, "</xsl:text>
  <xsl:value-of select="$field"/>
  <xsl:text>");&#xa;</xsl:text>
</xsl:template>

<!-- Initialize data form the converted value -->
<xsl:template match="Structure" mode="load">
  <xsl:param name="field"/>
  <xsl:param name="var"/>
  <xsl:for-each select="Members/Member">
        <xsl:apply-templates select="key('dataTypes',DataTypeName)" mode="load">
          <xsl:with-param name="field" select="concat($field,'.',Name)"/>
          <xsl:with-param name="var" select="concat($field,'_',Name)"/>
        </xsl:apply-templates>
  </xsl:for-each>
</xsl:template>

<xsl:template match="Primitive" mode="load">
  <xsl:param name="field"/>
  <xsl:param name="var"/>

  <xsl:text>&INDENT;</xsl:text>
  <xsl:value-of select="$field"/>
  <xsl:text> = </xsl:text>
  <xsl:value-of select="Name"/>
  <xsl:text>(</xsl:text>
  <xsl:value-of select="$var"/>
```

```
    <xsl:text>);&#xa;</xsl:text>
</xsl:template>

<xsl:template match="Enumeration" mode="load">
 <xsl:param name="field"/>
  <xsl:param name="var"/>

  <xsl:text>&INDENT;</xsl:text>
  <xsl:value-of select="$field"/>
  <xsl:text> = Enum</xsl:text>
  <xsl:value-of select="Name"/>
  <xsl:text>NameToVal(</xsl:text>
  <xsl:value-of select="$var"/>
  <xsl:text>);&#xa;</xsl:text>
</xsl:template>

</xsl:stylesheet>
```

If run against our repository, this XSLT transformation generates a *cgi* program for each message. For example:

```
#include <stdio.h>
#include "cgi.h"
#include "msg_ids.h"
#include "AddStockOrderData.h"

void cgi_main(cgi_info *cgi)
{
    AddStockOrderData data ;
    form_entry* form_data = get_form_entries(cgi) ;
    const char * symbol = parmval(form_data, "ADD_STOCK_ORDER_symbol");
    const char * quantity = parmval(form_data, "ADD_STOCK_ORDER_quantity");
    const char * side = parmval(form_data, "ADD_STOCK_ORDER_side");
    const char * type = parmval(form_data, "ADD_STOCK_ORDER_type");
    const char * price = parmval(form_data, "ADD_STOCK_ORDER_price");
    data.symbol = StkSymbol(symbol);
    data.quantity = Shares(quantity);
    data.side = EnumBuyOrSellNameToVal(side);
    data.type = EnumOrderTypeNameToVal(type);
    data.price = Real(price);

    //Enque data to the process being tested
    enqueData(ADD_STOCK_ORDER,data) ;

}
```

Discussion

The solution makes several assumptions. First, it assumes that the primitive types (e.g., Shares) are classes with constructors that convert from strings to the type's internal representation (e.g., int). Second, it assumes the existence of conversion functions for converting symbolic names of enumeration constants to their integral values. As you might guess, these functions can be generated easily from information in the repository. We leave that as an exercise. Third, the generated code assumes a function, called enqueData, that knows how to send a message to the correct process under test. The details of how this function interacts with the specific middleware and how it locates the particular queue vary from implementation to implementation.

The bottom line is that you have to tweak this code generator to suit your needs. However, once a sufficiently rich metadata repository is established, a significant amount of automation is possible. The functionality automated in this example and Recipe 10.6 could easily keep a programmer busy full time. This is especially true if the messages the application handles are in constant flux.

10.8   Generating Code from UML Models via XMI

Problem

You want to generate code from Unified Modeling Language (UML) specifications but are unhappy with the results produced by your UML tools' native-code generator.

The State Design Pattern

A *state machine* is a useful design tool that directly models a software system whose behavior changes over time as various events unfold. A state machine is often depicted as a graph where vertices (nodes) designate specific states and where edges (links) specify transitions between states in response to a stimulus or event.

The state design pattern approaches the construction of a state machine by representing the concrete states by distinct classes that derive from an abstract base State class. A separate StateMachine class represents the state machine as a whole and holds a pointer to a concrete State that represents the current state. Methods in the StateMachine defer to the current state to implement state-specific behavior. Invocation of these methods may cause the concrete state class to transition its owning StateMachine to a new state.

Solution

XMI is a standard XML-based representation of UML that many UML modeling tools (such as Rational Rose) support. Although the stated purpose of XMI is to allow interchange of modeling information between different tools, it also can be the basis for code generation.

Most UML tools support code generation but rarely generate more than a skeleton of the object model. For instance, all UML-based generators I am aware of only consider information in class diagrams.

Here you will generate code for the *State Design Pattern*[*] that combines information from both a class diagram (Figure 10-2) and a state chart (Figure 10-3). The code generator assumes that the designer followed these conventions.

1. The state context class has the stereotype StateMachine.

2. The abstract base class of the actual state classes has the stereotype State.

3. All operations in the state context that forward their implementation to the state classes have the stereotype delegate (indicating that they delegate their responsibility to the state).

4. All state context operations used by the states to implement state-machine behavior have the stereotype action.

5. The only exception to (4) is the single operation that should be invoked when the state does not know what to do. This operation has stereotype default and is generally used for error handling.

6. The UML State Chart states use the same names as the concrete classes derived from the State interface (2).

7. The *actions* and *guards* associated with transitions refer to the context and use the exact operation names. An *action* is the code executed upon a transition and a *guard* is a condition that must be true for the transition to be chosen.

The next example shows a state machine that implements the basic functionality of an answering machine when you retrieve your messages.

The XMI generated from this simple design cannot be shown in its entirety because it is huge. XMI uses horrendously long and arduous naming conventions. This chapter shows a fragment containing the AnsweringMachineState class to give the flavor of it. However, even this has been elided:

```
<Foundation.Core.Class xmi.id="S.10011">
  <Foundation.Core.ModelElement.name>AnsweringMachineState
  </Foundation.Core.ModelElement.name>
  <Foundation.Core.ModelElement.stereotype>
    <Foundation.Extension_Mechanisms.Stereotype xmi.idref="G.22"/>
    <!-- state -->
  </Foundation.Core.ModelElement.stereotype>
  <Foundation.Core.GeneralizableElement.specialization>
    <Foundation.Core.Generalization xmi.idref="G.91"/>
    <!-- {Connected-&gt;AnsweringMachineState}{3D6782A402EE} -->
    <Foundation.Core.Generalization xmi.idref="G.92"/>
```

---

[*] *Design Patterns: Elements of Reusable Object-Oriented Software* by Erich Gamma, Richard Helm, Ralph Johnson, and John Vlissides (Addison-Wesley, 1995).

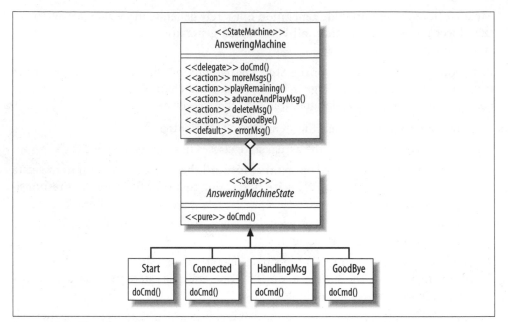

Figure 10-2. Class diagram representing states

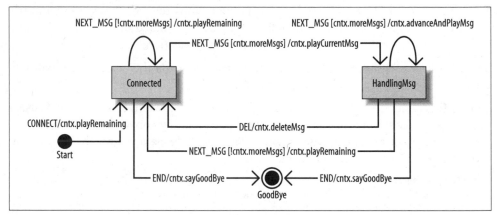

Figure 10-3. State chart for answering machine

```
<!-- {HandlingMsg-&gt;AnsweringMachineState}{3D6782EF0119} -->
<Foundation.Core.Generalization xmi.idref="G.93"/>
<!-- {Start-&gt;AnsweringMachineState}{3D67B2FD004E} -->
<Foundation.Core.Generalization xmi.idref="G.94"/>
<!-- {GoodBye-&gt;AnsweringMachineState}{3D67B31B02AF} -->
</Foundation.Core.GeneralizableElement.specialization>
<Foundation.Core.Classifier.associationEnd>
  <Foundation.Core.AssociationEnd xmi.idref="G.25"/>
</Foundation.Core.Classifier.associationEnd>
<Foundation.Core.Classifier.feature>
  <Foundation.Core.Operation xmi.id="S.10012">
```

```
<Foundation.Core.ModelElement.name>doCmd</Foundation.Core.ModelElement.name>
<Foundation.Core.ModelElement.visibility xmi.value="public"/>
<Foundation.Core.Feature.ownerScope xmi.value="instance"/>
<Foundation.Core.BehavioralFeature.isQuery xmi.value="false"/>
<Foundation.Core.Operation.specification/>
<Foundation.Core.Operation.isPolymorphic xmi.value="false"/>
<Foundation.Core.Operation.concurrency xmi.value="sequential"/>
<Foundation.Core.ModelElement.stereotype>
  <Foundation.Extension_Mechanisms.Stereotype xmi.idref="G.23"/>
  <!-- pure -->
</Foundation.Core.ModelElement.stereotype>
<Foundation.Core.BehavioralFeature.parameter>
  <Foundation.Core.Parameter xmi.id="G.76">
    <Foundation.Core.ModelElement.name>cntx</Foundation.Core.ModelElement.name>
    <Foundation.Core.ModelElement.visibility xmi.value="private"/>
    <Foundation.Core.Parameter.defaultValue>
      <Foundation.Data_Types.Expression>
        <Foundation.Data_Types.Expression.language/>
        <Foundation.Data_Types.Expression.body/>
      </Foundation.Data_Types.Expression>
    </Foundation.Core.Parameter.defaultValue>
    <Foundation.Core.Parameter.kind xmi.value="inout"/>
    <Foundation.Core.Parameter.type>
      <Foundation.Core.Class xmi.idref="S.10001"/>
      <!-- AnsweringMachine -->
    </Foundation.Core.Parameter.type>
  </Foundation.Core.Parameter>
  <Foundation.Core.Parameter xmi.id="G.77">
    <Foundation.Core.ModelElement.name>cmd</Foundation.Core.ModelElement.name>
    <Foundation.Core.ModelElement.visibility xmi.value="private"/>
    <Foundation.Core.Parameter.defaultValue>
      <Foundation.Data_Types.Expression>
        <Foundation.Data_Types.Expression.language/>
        <Foundation.Data_Types.Expression.body/>
      </Foundation.Data_Types.Expression>
    </Foundation.Core.Parameter.defaultValue>
    <Foundation.Core.Parameter.kind xmi.value="inout"/>
    <Foundation.Core.Parameter.type>
      <Foundation.Core.DataType xmi.idref="G.65"/>
      <!-- Command -->
    </Foundation.Core.Parameter.type>
  </Foundation.Core.Parameter>
  <Foundation.Core.Parameter xmi.id="G.78">
    <Foundation.Core.ModelElement.name>doCmd.Return
    </Foundation.Core.ModelElement.name>
    <Foundation.Core.ModelElement.visibility xmi.value="private"/>
    <Foundation.Core.Parameter.defaultValue>
      <Foundation.Data_Types.Expression>
        <Foundation.Data_Types.Expression.language/>
        <Foundation.Data_Types.Expression.body/>
      </Foundation.Data_Types.Expression>
    </Foundation.Core.Parameter.defaultValue>
    <Foundation.Core.Parameter.kind xmi.value="return"/>
    <Foundation.Core.Parameter.type>
```

```
            <Foundation.Core.DataType xmi.idref="G.67"/>
            <!-- void -->
          </Foundation.Core.Parameter.type>
        </Foundation.Core.Parameter>
      </Foundation.Core.BehavioralFeature.parameter>
    </Foundation.Core.Operation>
  </Foundation.Core.Classifier.feature>
</Foundation.Core.Class>
```

The following large XSLT example converts the XMI into a C++ implementation of
this state machine according to the State Design Pattern. Out of sheer desperation, I
use XML entities to abbreviate long XMI names. I don't usually recommend this
practice, but in this case it was the only way to make the XSLT fit reasonably on the
page. It also reduces the inherent noise level of the XMI DTD. You will also notice
that keys are used extensively because XMI makes heavy use of cross references in
the form of xmi.id and xmi.idref attributes:

```
<?xml version="1.0" encoding="UTF-8"?>
<!DOCTYPE xslt [
  <!--=============================================================-->
  <!-- XMI's high level organization constructs            -->
  <!--=============================================================-->
  <!ENTITY BE "Behavioral_Elements">
  <!ENTITY SM "&BE;.State_Machines">
  <!ENTITY SMC "&SM;.StateMachine.context">
  <!ENTITY SMT "&SM;.StateMachine.top">
  <!ENTITY MM "Model_Management.Model">
  <!ENTITY FC "Foundation.Core">
  <!ENTITY FX "Foundation.Extension_Mechanisms">


  <!--=============================================================-->
  <!-- Abbreviations for the basic elements of a XMI       -->
  <!-- file that are of most    interest to this stylesheet.  -->
  <!--=============================================================-->
  <!--The model as a whole -->
  <!ENTITY MODEL "XMI/XMI.content/&MM;">
  <!--Some generic kind of UML element -->
  <!ENTITY ELEM "&FC;.Namespace.ownedElement">
  <!--Elements of state machines -->
  <!ENTITY STATEMACH "&MODEL;/&ELEM;/&SM;.StateMachine">
  <!ENTITY STATE "&SM;.CompositeState">
  <!ENTITY SUBSTATE "&STATE;.substate">
  <!ENTITY PSEUDOSTATE "&SM;.PseudoState">
  <!ENTITY PSEUDOSTATE2 "&SMT;/&STATE;/&SUBSTATE;/&PSEUDOSTATE;">
  <!ENTITY ACTION
"&BE;.Common_Behavior.ActionSequence/&BE;.Common_Behavior.ActionSequence.action">
  <!ENTITY GUARD "&SM;.Transition.guard/&SM;.Guard/&SM;.Guard.expression">
  <!--The association as a whole -->
  <!ENTITY ASSOC "&FC;.Association">
  <!--The connection part of the association-->
  <!ENTITY CONN "&ASSOC;.connection">
  <!--The ends of an association. -->
  <!ENTITY END "&ASSOC;End">
```

```
<!ENTITY CONNEND "&CONN;/&END;">
<!ENTITY ENDType "&END;.type">
<!-- A UML class -->
<!ENTITY CLASS "&FC;.Class">
<!--The name of some UML entity -->
<!ENTITY NAME "&FC;.ModelElement.name">
<!--A operation -->
<!ENTITY OP "&FC;.Operation">
<!-- A parameter -->
<!ENTITY PARAM "&FC;.Parameter">
<!ENTITY PARAM2 "&FC;.BehavioralFeature.parameter/&PARAM;">
<!-- The data type of a parameter -->
<!ENTITY PARAMTYPE "&PARAM;.type/&FC;.DataType">
<!--A UML sterotype -->
<!ENTITY STEREOTYPE "&FC;.ModelElement.stereotype/&FX;.Stereotype">
<!-- A Supertype relation (inheritance) -->
<!ENTITY SUPERTYPE "&FC;.Generalization.supertype">
<!ENTITY GENERALIZATION
"&FC;.GeneralizableElement.generalization/&FC;.Generalization">
<!--=============================================================-->
<!--Formatting                                                  -->
<!--=============================================================-->

<!--Used to control code intenting -->
<!ENTITY INDENT "    ">
<!ENTITY INDENT2 "&INDENT;&INDENT;">
]>
<xsl:stylesheet version="1.0" xmlns:xsl="http://www.w3.org/1999/XSL/Transform">
  <xsl:output method="text"/>

  <!--Index classes by their id -->
  <xsl:key name="classKey" match="&CLASS;" use="@xmi.id"/>
  <xsl:key name="classKey" match="&CLASS;" use="&NAME;"/>

  <!-- Index Stereoptypes by both name and xmi.id -->
  <xsl:key name="stereotypeKey" match="&FX;.Stereotype" use="@xmi.id"/>
  <xsl:key name="stereotypeKey" match="&FX;.Stereotype" use="&NAME;"/>

  <!--Index data types by their id -->
  <xsl:key name="dataTypeKey" match="&FC;.DataType" use="@xmi.id"/>

  <!--Index associations by their end classes -->
  <xsl:key name="associationKey" match="&ASSOC;"
      use="&CONNEND;/&ENDType;/&FC;.Interface/@xmi.idref"/>
  <xsl:key name="associationKey" match="&ASSOC;"
      use="&CONNEND;/&ENDType;/&CLASS;/@xmi.idref"/>

  <!--Index generalizations by their id -->
  <xsl:key name="generalizationKey" match="&FC;.Generalization" use="@xmi.id"/>

  <!--Index states and pseudo states together by their id -->
  <xsl:key name="stateKey" match="&SM;.SimpleState" use="@xmi.id"/>
  <xsl:key name="stateKey" match="&PSEUDOSTATE;" use="@xmi.id"/>
```

```
<!--Index state transitions by their id -->
<xsl:key name="transKey" match="&SM;.Transition" use="@xmi.id"/>

<!--Index transitions events by their id -->
<xsl:key name="eventsKey" match="&SM;.SignalEvent" use="@xmi.id"/>

<!-- The xmi ids of stereoptypes used to encode State Pattern  in UML -->
<xsl:variable name="STATE_MACH"
              select="key('stereotypeKey','StateMachine')/@xmi.id"/>
<xsl:variable name="STATE"
              select="key('stereotypeKey','state')/@xmi.id"/>
<xsl:variable name="DELEGATE"
              select="key('stereotypeKey','delegate')/@xmi.id"/>
<xsl:variable name="ACTION"
              select="key('stereotypeKey','action')/@xmi.id"/>
<xsl:variable name="DEFAULT"
              select="key('stereotypeKey','default')/@xmi.id"/>

<xsl:variable name="PURE"
              select="key('stereotypeKey','pure')/@xmi.id"/>

<!-- We use modes to generate the source in 5 steps -->
<xsl:template match="/">

  <!-- Declare state interface -->
  <xsl:apply-templates mode="stateInterfaceDecl"
      select="&MODEL;/&ELEM;/&CLASS;[&STEREOTYPE;/@xmi.idref =
                                                $STATE_MACH]"/>

  <!-- Declare concrete states -->
  <xsl:apply-templates mode="concreteStatesDecl"
      select="&MODEL;/&ELEM;/&CLASS;[not(&STEREOTYPE;)]"/>

  <!-- Declare state context class -->
  <xsl:apply-templates mode="stateDecl"
      select="&MODEL;/&ELEM;/&CLASS;[&STEREOTYPE;/@xmi.idref =
                                                $STATE_MACH]"/>

  <!--Implement states -->
  <xsl:apply-templates mode="concreteStatesImpl"
      select="&MODEL;/&ELEM;"/>

  <!--Implement context -->
  <xsl:apply-templates mode="stateContextImpl"
      select="&MODEL;/&ELEM;/&CLASS;[&STEREOTYPE;/@xmi.idref =
                                       $STATE_MACH]"/>

</xsl:template>

<!-- STATE CONTEXT DECLARATION -->
<xsl:template match="&CLASS;" mode="stateDecl">

  <!-- Find the class associated with this state context that -->
  <!-- is a state implementation. This is the type of the state -->
```

```
<!-- machines corrent state memeber variable -->
<xsl:variable name="stateImplClass">
  <xsl:variable name="stateClassId" select="@xmi.id"/>
  <xsl:for-each select="key('associationKey',$stateClassId)">
    <xsl:variable name="assocClassId"
                  select="&CONNEND;[&ENDType;/*/@xmi.idref !=
                                     $stateClassId]/&ENDType;/*/@xmi.idref"/>
    <xsl:if test="key('classKey',$assocClassId)/&STEREOTYPE;/@xmi.idref
                                                         = $STATE">
      <xsl:value-of select="key('classKey',$assocClassId)/&NAME;"/>
    </xsl:if>
  </xsl:for-each>
</xsl:variable>

<xsl:variable name="className" select="&NAME;"/>

<xsl:text>&#xa;class </xsl:text>
<xsl:value-of select="$className"/>
<xsl:text>&#xa;{&#xa;public:&#xa;&#xa;</xsl:text>


<!--Ctor decl -->
<xsl:text>&INDENT;</xsl:text>
<xsl:value-of select="$className"/>::<xsl:value-of select="$className"/>
<xsl:text>();&#xa;&#xa;</xsl:text>

<!-- Delegates are operations that defer to the current state -->
<xsl:apply-templates
                  select="*/&OP;[&STEREOTYPE;/@xmi.idref = $DELEGATE]"
                  mode="declare"/>

<!-- void changeState(AbstractState& newState) -->
<xsl:text>&INDENT;void changeState(</xsl:text>
<xsl:value-of select="$stateImplClass"/>
<xsl:text>&amp; newSate) ;&#xa;</xsl:text>

<xsl:text>&#xa;&#xa;</xsl:text>
<!-- Non-Delegates are other operations operations that states -->
<!-- invoke on the context -->
<xsl:apply-templates
          select="*/&OP;[&STEREOTYPE;/@xmi.idref != $DELEGATE]"
          mode="declare"/>
<xsl:text>&#xa;private:&#xa;&#xa;</xsl:text>
<xsl:text>&INDENT;</xsl:text>
<xsl:value-of select="$stateImplClass"/>
<xsl:text>* m_State ;</xsl:text>
<xsl:text>&#xa;&#xa;} ;&#xa;&#xa;</xsl:text>

</xsl:template>

<!-- CONCRETE STATES DECLARATION -->

<xsl:template match="&CLASS;" mode="concreteStatesDecl">
  <xsl:text>class </xsl:text>
```

```
    <xsl:value-of select="&NAME;"/>
      <xsl:call-template name="baseClass"/>
      <xsl:text>&#xa;{&#xa;public:&#xa;&#xa;</xsl:text>
      <!-- Concrete States are Singletons so we generate an -->
      <!-- instance method -->
      <xsl:text>&INDENT;static </xsl:text>
      <xsl:value-of select="&NAME;"/>
      <xsl:text>&amp; instance( ) ;</xsl:text>
      <xsl:text>&#xa;&#xa;private:&#xa;&#xa;</xsl:text>
      <!-- We protect constructors of Singletons-->
      <xsl:text>&INDENT;</xsl:text>
      <xsl:value-of select="&NAME;"/>
      <xsl:text>() {} &#xa;</xsl:text>
      <xsl:text>&INDENT;</xsl:text>
      <xsl:value-of select="&NAME;"/>(const <xsl:value-of select="&NAME;"/>
      <xsl:text>&amp;) {} &#xa;</xsl:text>
      <xsl:text>&INDENT;void operator =(const </xsl:text>
      <xsl:value-of select="&NAME;"/>
      <xsl:text>&amp;) {} &#xa;</xsl:text>
      <xsl:apply-templates select="*/&OP;" mode="declare"/>
      <xsl:text>
} ;

</xsl:text>
  </xsl:template>

  <!-- Templates used to declare classes with all public members -->

  <xsl:template match="&CLASS;" mode="declare">
    <xsl:text>class&#x20;</xsl:text>
    <xsl:value-of select="&NAME;"/>
    <xsl:text>&#xa;{&#xa;public:&#xa;&#xa;</xsl:text>
    <xsl:apply-templates select="*/&OP;" mode="declare"/>
    <xsl:text>&#xa;} ;&#xa;</xsl:text>
  </xsl:template>

  <xsl:template match="&OP;" mode="declare">
    <xsl:variable name="returnTypeId"
                  select="&PARAM2;[&PARAM;.kind/@xmi.value =
                                   'return']/&PARAMTYPE;/@xmi.idref"/>
      <xsl:text>&INDENT;</xsl:text>
    <xsl:if test="&STEREOTYPE;/@xmi.idref = $PURE">
      <xsl:text>virtual </xsl:text>
    </xsl:if>
    <xsl:value-of select="key('dataTypeKey',$returnTypeId)/&NAME;"/>
      <xsl:text>&#x20;</xsl:text>
    <xsl:value-of select="&NAME;"/>
    <xsl:text>(</xsl:text>
    <xsl:call-template name="parameters"/>
    <xsl:text>)</xsl:text>
    <xsl:if test="&STEREOTYPE;/@xmi.idref = $PURE">
      <xsl:text> = 0 </xsl:text>
```

```
    </xsl:if>
    <xsl:text>;&#xa;</xsl:text>
</xsl:template>

<!--Eat extra text nodes -->
<xsl:template match="text()" mode="declare"/>

<!-- STATE INTERFACE DECLARATION -->
<xsl:template match="&CLASS;" mode="stateInterfaceDecl">

    <xsl:text>//Forward declarations&#xa;</xsl:text>
    <xsl:text>class </xsl:text>
    <xsl:value-of select="&NAME;"/>
    <xsl:text>;&#xa;&#xa;</xsl:text>

    <xsl:variable name="stateClassId" select="@xmi.id"/>
    <!-- Find the class associated with the state context that -->
    <!-- is a state. -->
    <xsl:for-each select="key('associationKey',$stateClassId)">
        <xsl:variable name="assocClassId"
                      select="&CONNEND;[&ENDType;/*/@xmi.idref !=
                                        $stateClassId]/&ENDType;/*/@xmi.idref"/>
        <xsl:if test="key('classKey',$assocClassId)/&STEREOTYPE;/@xmi.idref =
                                                                    $STATE">
            <xsl:apply-templates select="key('classKey',$assocClassId)"
                                 mode="declare"/>
        </xsl:if>
    </xsl:for-each>
    <xsl:text>&#xa;&#xa;</xsl:text>
</xsl:template>

<!--Eat extra text nodes -->
<xsl:template match="text()" mode="stateInterfaceDecl"/>

<!-- STATE CONTEXT IMPLEMENTATION -->
<xsl:template match="&CLASS;" mode="stateContextImpl">

    <xsl:variable name="stateImplClass">
        <xsl:variable name="stateClassId" select="@xmi.id"/>
        <xsl:for-each select="key('associationKey',$stateClassId)">
            <xsl:variable name="assocClassId"
                select="&CONNEND;[&ENDType;/*/@xmi.idref !=
                                        $stateClassId]/&ENDType;/*/@xmi.idref"/>
            <xsl:if test="key('classKey',$assocClassId)/&STEREOTYPE;/@xmi.idref
                                                                    = $STATE">
                <xsl:value-of select="key('classKey',$assocClassId)/&NAME;"/>
            </xsl:if>
        </xsl:for-each>
    </xsl:variable>

    <xsl:variable name="className" select="&NAME;"/>
    <xsl:text>//Constructor&#xa;</xsl:text>
    <xsl:value-of select="$className"/>::<xsl:value-of
                                        select="$className"/>
```

```
<xsl:text>()&#xa;</xsl:text>
<xsl:text>{&#xa;</xsl:text>
<xsl:text>&INDENT;//Initialize state machine in start state &#xa;</xsl:text>
<xsl:variable name="startStateName">
  <xsl:call-template name="getStartState">
    <xsl:with-param name="classId" select="@xmi.id"/>
  </xsl:call-template>
</xsl:variable>
<xsl:text>&INDENT;m_State = &amp;</xsl:text>
<xsl:value-of select="$startStateName"/>
<xsl:text>::instance() ;&#xa;</xsl:text>
<xsl:text>}&#xa;&#xa;</xsl:text>

<!-- void changeState(AbstractState& newState) -->
<xsl:text>void </xsl:text>
<xsl:value-of select="$className"/>
<xsl:text>::changeState(</xsl:text>
<xsl:value-of select="$stateImplClass"/>
<xsl:text>&amp; newState)&#xa;</xsl:text>
<xsl:text>{&#xa;</xsl:text>
<xsl:text>&INDENT;m_State = &amp;newState;</xsl:text>
<xsl:text>&#xa;}&#xa;&#xa;</xsl:text>

<xsl:for-each select="*/&OP;[&STEREOTYPE;/@xmi.idref = $DELEGATE]">
  <xsl:variable name="returnTypeId"
                          select="&PARAM2;[&PARAM;.kind/@xmi.value =
                                   'return']/&PARAMTYPE;/@xmi.idref"/>
  <xsl:value-of select="key('dataTypeKey',$returnTypeId)/&NAME;"/>
  <xsl:text>&#x20;</xsl:text>
  <xsl:value-of select="$className"/>::<xsl:value-of select="&NAME;"/>
  <xsl:text>(</xsl:text>
  <xsl:call-template name="parameters"/>
  <xsl:text>)&#xa;</xsl:text>
  <xsl:text>{&#xa;</xsl:text>
  <xsl:text>&INDENT;m_State-></xsl:text>
  <xsl:value-of select="&NAME;"/>
  <xsl:text>(*this, </xsl:text>
  <xsl:for-each select="&PARAM2;[&PARAM;.kind/@xmi.value != 'return']">
    <xsl:value-of select="&NAME;"/>
    <xsl:if test="position() != last()">
      <xsl:text>, </xsl:text>
    </xsl:if>
  </xsl:for-each>
  <xsl:text>);&#xa;</xsl:text>
  <xsl:text>}&#xa;&#xa;</xsl:text>
</xsl:for-each>

<xsl:for-each select="*/&OP;[&STEREOTYPE;/@xmi.idref != $DELEGATE]">
  <xsl:variable name="returnTypeId"
                select="&PARAM2;[&PARAM;.kind/@xmi.value =
                         'return']/&PARAMTYPE;/@xmi.idref"/>
  <xsl:value-of select="key('dataTypeKey',$returnTypeId)/&NAME;"/>
  <xsl:text>&#x20;</xsl:text>
  <xsl:value-of select="$className"/>::<xsl:value-of select="&NAME;"/>
```

```
      <xsl:text>(</xsl:text>
      <xsl:call-template name="parameters"/>
      <xsl:text>)&#xa;</xsl:text>
      <xsl:text>{&#xa;</xsl:text>
      <xsl:text>&INDENT;//!TODO: Implement behavior of this action&#xa;</xsl:text>
      <xsl:text>}&#xa;&#xa;</xsl:text>
    </xsl:for-each>
  </xsl:template>
</xsl:template>
<xsl:template match="text()" mode="stateContextImpl"/>

<!-- CONCRETE STATES IMPLEMENTATION -->
<xsl:template match="&CLASS;" mode="concreteStatesImpl">
  <xsl:variable name="classId" select="@xmi.id"/>
  <xsl:variable name="stateMachine"
                select="/&STATEMACH;[&SMC;/&CLASS;/@xmi.idref =
                                                        $classId]"/>
  <!-- For each state in the machine, generate its implementation -->
  <xsl:for-each select="$stateMachine//&PSEUDOSTATE; |
                                      $stateMachine//&SM;.SimpleState">
    <xsl:call-template name="generateState">
      <xsl:with-param name="stateClass" select="key('classKey',&NAME;)"/>
    </xsl:call-template>
  </xsl:for-each>
</xsl:template>

<!--Eat extra text nodes  -->
<xsl:template match="text()" mode="concreteStatesImpl"/>

<xsl:template name="generateState">
  <!--This is a xmi class corresponding the the state -->
  <xsl:param name="stateClass"/>
  <!-- The current context is some state -->
  <xsl:variable name="state" select="."/>
  <xsl:variable name="className" select="&NAME;"/>
  <xsl:if test="$className != $stateClass/&NAME;">
    <xsl:message terminate="yes">State and class do not match!</xsl:message>
  </xsl:if>
  <xsl:for-each select="$stateClass/*/&OP;">
    <xsl:variable name="returnTypeId"
                  select="&PARAM2;[&PARAM;.kind/@xmi.value =
                                        'return']/&PARAMTYPE;/@xmi.idref"/>
    <xsl:value-of select="key('dataTypeKey',$returnTypeId)/&NAME;"/>
    <xsl:text>&#x20;</xsl:text>
    <xsl:value-of select="$className"/>::<xsl:value-of select="&NAME;"/>
    <xsl:text>(</xsl:text>
    <xsl:call-template name="parameters"/>
    <xsl:text>)&#xa;</xsl:text>
    <xsl:text>{&#xa;</xsl:text>
    <xsl:for-each
        select="$state/&SM;.StateVertex.outgoing/&SM;.Transition">
      <xsl:call-template name="generateStateBody">
        <xsl:with-param name="transition"
          select="key('transKey',@xmi.idref)"/>
      </xsl:call-template>
```

```
      </xsl:for-each>
      <xsl:text>&INDENT2;context.errorMsg() ;&#xa;</xsl:text>
      <xsl:text>}&#xa;&#xa;</xsl:text>
    </xsl:for-each>
  </xsl:template>


  <xsl:template name="generateStateBody">
    <xsl:param name="transition"/>
    <xsl:text>&INDENT;if (cmd == </xsl:text>
    <xsl:variable name="eventId"
        select="$transition/&SM;.Transition.trigger/&SM;.SignalEvent/@xmi.idref"/>
    <xsl:value-of select="key('eventsKey',$eventId)/&NAME;"/>
    <xsl:if test="$transition/&SM;.Transition.guard">
      <xsl:text> &amp;&amp; </xsl:text>
      <xsl:value-of
    select="$transition/&GUARD;/*/Foundation.Data_Types.Expression.body"/>
      <xsl:text>()</xsl:text>
    </xsl:if>
    <xsl:text>)&#xa;</xsl:text>
    <xsl:text>&INDENT;{&#xa;</xsl:text>
    <xsl:text>&INDENT2;</xsl:text>
    <xsl:value-of
        select="$transition/&SM;.Transition.effect/&ACTION;/*/&NAME;"/>
    <xsl:text>() ;&#xa;</xsl:text>
    <xsl:variable name="targetStateId"
                  select="$transition/&SM;.Transition.target/*/@xmi.idref"/>
    <xsl:if test="$targetStateId != $transition/@xmi.id"/>
      <xsl:text>&INDENT2;cntx.changeState(</xsl:text>
      <xsl:value-of select="key('stateKey',$targetStateId)/&NAME;"/>
      <xsl:text>::instance());&#xa;</xsl:text>
    <xsl:text>&INDENT;}&#xa;</xsl:text>
    <xsl:text>&INDENT;else&#xa;</xsl:text>
  </xsl:template>

  <!-- Generate function parameters -->
  <xsl:template name="parameters">
    <xsl:for-each select="&PARAM2;[&PARAM;.kind/@xmi.value != 'return']">
      <xsl:choose>
        <xsl:when test="&PARAMTYPE;">
          <xsl:value-of
                select="key('dataTypeKey',&PARAMTYPE;/@xmi.idref)/&NAME;"/>
        </xsl:when>
        <xsl:when test="&PARAM;.type/&CLASS;">
          <xsl:value-of
                select="key('classKey',
                            &PARAM;.type/&CLASS;/@xmi.idref)/&NAME;"/>
          <xsl:text>&amp;</xsl:text>
        </xsl:when>
      </xsl:choose>
      <xsl:text>&#x20;</xsl:text>
      <xsl:value-of select="&NAME;"/>
      <xsl:if test="position() != last()">
        <xsl:text>, </xsl:text>
```

```
      </xsl:if>
    </xsl:for-each>
  </xsl:template>

  <!-- Generate base classes -->
  <xsl:template name="baseClass">
    <xsl:if test="&GENERALIZATION;">
      <xsl:text> : </xsl:text>
      <xsl:for-each select="&GENERALIZATION;">
        <xsl:variable name="genAssoc"
                      select="key('generalizationKey',@xmi.idref)"/>
        <xsl:text>public </xsl:text>
        <xsl:value-of
      select="key('classKey',
                $genAssoc/&SUPERTYPE;/&CLASS;/@xmi.idref)/&NAME;"/>
        <xsl:if test="position() != last()">
          <xsl:text>, </xsl:text>
        </xsl:if>
      </xsl:for-each>
    </xsl:if>
  </xsl:template>
  <xsl:template name="getStartState">
    <xsl:param name="classId"/>
    <xsl:variable name="stateMachine"
                  select="/&STATEMACH;[&SMC;/&CLASS;/@xmi.idref =
                                                   $classId]"/>
    <xsl:value-of
                  select="$stateMachine/&PSEUDOSTATE2;
                                   [&PSEUDOSTATE;.kind/@xmi.value =
'initial']/&NAME;"/>
  </xsl:template>
</xsl:stylesheet>
```

Here is a portion of the resulting C++ code:

```
//Forward declarations
class AnsweringMachine;

class AnsweringMachineState
{
public:

    virtual void doCmd(AnsweringMachine& cntx, Command cmd) = 0 ;

} ;


class Connected : public AnsweringMachineState
{
public:

    static Connected& instance() ;

private:
```

```cpp
    Connected( ) { }
    Connected(const Connected&) { }
    void operator =(const Connected&) { }
    void doCmd(AnsweringMachine& cntx, Command cmd);

} ;

class HandlingMsg : public AnsweringMachineState
{
public:

    static HandlingMsg& instance( ) ;

private:

    HandlingMsg( ) { }
    HandlingMsg(const HandlingMsg&) { }
    void operator =(const HandlingMsg&) { }
    void doCmd(AnsweringMachine& cntx, Command cmd);

} ;

//!OTHER STATES WERE ELIDED TO SAVE SPACE...

class AnsweringMachine
{
public:

    AnsweringMachine::AnsweringMachine( );

    void doCmd(Command cmd);
    void changeState(AnsweringMachineState& newSate) ;


    bool moreMsgs( );
    void playRemaining( );
    void playCurrentMsg( );
    void advanceAndPlayMsg( );
    void deleteMsg( );
    void sayGoodBye( );
    void errorMsg( );

private:

    AnsweringMachineState* m_State ;

} ;

void Connected::doCmd(AnsweringMachine& cntx, Command cmd)
{
    if (cmd == NEXT_MSG && cntx.moreMsgs( ))
    {
        cntx.playCurrentMsg( ) ;
        cntx.changeState(HandlingMsg::instance( ));
```

```
    }
    else
    if (cmd == NEXT_MSG && !cntx.moreMsgs())
    {
        cntx.playRemaining() ;
        cntx.changeState(Connected::instance());
    }
    else
    if (cmd == END)
    {
        cntx.sayGoodBye() ;
        cntx.changeState(GoodBye::instance());
    }
    else
        context.errorMsg() ;
}

//!OTHER STATES WERE ELIDED TO SAVE SPACE...

//Constructor
AnsweringMachine::AnsweringMachine()
{
    //Initialize state machine in start state
    m_State = &Start::instance() ;
}

void AnsweringMachine::changeState(AnsweringMachineState& newState)
{
    m_State = &newState;
}

void AnsweringMachine::doCmd(Command cmd)
{
    m_State->doCmd(*this, cmd);
}

bool AnsweringMachine::moreMsgs()
{
    //!TODO: Implement behavior of this action
}

void AnsweringMachine::playRemaining()
{
    //!TODO: Implement behavior of this action
}

void AnsweringMachine::playCurrentMsg()
{
    //!TODO: Implement behavior of this action
}

//!OTHER ACTIONS WERE ELIDED TO SAVE SPACE...
```

Discussion

You might want to write your own UML code generation for three reasons. First, you might not like the style or code substance generated by the modeling tool's native code generator. Second, the tool might not generate code in the language you require. For instance, I do not know of a UML tool that generates Python.[*] Third, you want to automate the generation of a higher-level design pattern or software service that you use frequently in development. This last case is the motivation behind the solution section's example.

Building a general-purpose, multilanguage code-generation facility on top of XMI and XSLT is an interesting project, but well beyond the scope of a single example. The example's solution is not intended as a production-ready generator, but it is a start. In particular, four important improvements could be made.

First, the generating XSLT should be broken down into small components that generate portions of the target programming language's various constructs. This is similar to what we did in Chapter 9 with SVG generation.

Second, the generating XSLT should understand more UML information, such as access control, rather than hardcoding these decisions.

Third, the generator should use XSLT 1.0 extensions or XSLT 2.0 to generate code into multiple header and source files, rather than one monolithic source.

Fourth, but least important, several code-layout styles could be supported. For example, the C++ code is in the style of Allman, but many (misguided?) C++ programmers prefer K&R (*http://www.tuxedo.org/~esr/jargon/html/entry/indent-style. html*). Then again, you might just run the output through a separate code beautifier and dispense with all formatting decisions entirely.

10.9   Generating XSLT from XSLT

Problem

You want to generate XSLT from a different XML representation. Alternatively, you want to transform XSLT or pseudo-XSLT into real XSLT.

Solution

Two things about the control structure of XSLT sometimes annoy me. The first is the absence of an if-then-elsif-else construct; the second is the absence of a true looping construct. Of course, I am aware of xsl:choose and xsl:for-each, but each is

---

[*] Not that I am a big fan of this curly-bracket-less language, but it has a large contingent of enthusiastic developers.

lacking to some extent. I find xsl:choose annoying because the choose element serves practically no function, except to force an extra level of nesting. The xsl:for-each is not really a looping construct but an iteration construct. To emulate loops with counters, you have to use recursion or the Piez method (see Recipe 1.5), which is awkward.

This example illustrates an XSLT-to-XSLT generation by pretending that XSLT has the elements xslx:elsif, xslx:else, and xslx:loop. Since it really does not, you will create a stylesheet that generates true XSLT from the following pseudo-XSLT. Having an xsl:if and an xslx:if is awkward, but it would be wrong to use the standard XSLT namespace for your extended elements; these elements might be defined in standard XSLT some day:

```
<xsl:stylesheet version="1.0" xmlns:xsl="http://www.w3.org/1999/XSL/Transform"
 xmlns:xslx="http://www.ora.com/XSLTCookbook/ExtendedXSLT" >

<xsl:output method="text"/>

<xsl:template match="foo">
  <xslx:if test="bar">
    <xsl:text>You often will find a bar in the neighborhood of foo!</xsl:text>
  </xslx:if>
  <xslx:elsif test="baz">
    <xsl:text>A baz is a sure sign of geekdom</xsl:text>
  </xslx:elsif>
  <xslx:else>
    <xslx:loop param="i" init="0" test="$i &lt; 10" incr="1">
      <xsl:text>Hmmm, nothing to say here but I'll say it 10 times.</xsl:text>
    </xslx:loop>
  </xslx:else>
  <xslx:loop param="i" init="10" test="$i >= 0" incr="-1">
    <xslx:loop param="j" init="10" test="$j >= 0" incr="-1">
      <xsl:text>&#xa;</xsl:text>
      <xsl:value-of select="$i * $j"/>
    </xslx:loop>
  </xslx:loop>
  <xslx:if test="foo">
      <xsl:text>foo foo! Nobody says foo foo!</xsl:text>
  </xslx:if>
  <xslx:else>
      <xsl:text>Well, okay then!</xsl:text>
  </xslx:else>
</xsl:template>

</xsl:stylesheet>
```

Here is a transformation that generates true XSLT from pseudo-XSLT. To keep things simple, this example does not include semantic checking such as checks for multiple xsl:else clauses with a single xsl:if or checks for duplication of parameters in nested loops:

```xml
<xsl:stylesheet version="1.0"
 xmlns:xsl="http://www.w3.org/1999/XSL/Transform"
 xmlns:xslx="http://www.ora.com/XSLTCookbook/ExtendedXSLT"
 xmlns:xso="dummy" >

<!-- Reuse the identity transform to copy -->
<!-- regular XSLT form source to destiniation -->
<xsl:import href="../util/copy.xslt"/>


<!-- DO NOT let the processor do the formatting via indent = yes -->
<!-- Because this could screw up xsl:text nodes                -->
<xsl:output method="xml" version="1.0" encoding="UTF-8" />

<!--We use xso as a alias when we need to output literal xslt elements -->
<xsl:namespace-alias stylesheet-prefix="xso" result-prefix="xsl"/>

<xsl:template match="xsl:stylesheet | xsl:transform">
  <xso:stylesheet>
   <!--The first pass handles the if-elsif-else translation -->
   <!--and the conversion of xslx:loop to named template calls -->
   <xsl:apply-templates select="@* | node()"/>

   <!--The second pass handles the conversion of xslx:loop -->
   <!-- to recusive named templates -->
   <xsl:apply-templates mode="loop-body" select="//xslx:loop"/>

  </xso:stylesheet>
</xsl:template>

<!--We look for xslx:if's that have matching xslx:elsif or xslx:else -->
<xsl:template match="xslx:if[following-sibling::xslx:else or
                            following-sibling::xslx:elsif]">
  <xsl:variable name="idIf" select="generate-id()"/>
  <xso:choose>
    <xso:when test="{@test}">
      <xsl:apply-templates select="@* | node()"/>
    </xso:when>
    <!-- We process the xsl:eslif and xslx:else in a special mode -->
    <!-- as part of the xsl:choose. We must make sure to only pick -->
    <!-- up the ones whose preceding xslx:if is this xslx:if -->
    <xsl:apply-templates
     select="following-sibling::xslx:else[
                    generate-id(preceding-sibling::xslx:if[1]) = $idIf] |
             following-sibling::xslx:elsif[
                    generate-id(preceding-sibling::xslx:if[1]) = $idIf]"
     mode="choose"/>
  </xso:choose>
</xsl:template>

<!--Ignore xslx:elsif and xslx:else in normal mode -->
<xsl:template match="xslx:elsif | xslx:else"/>

<!--An xslx:elsif becomes a xsl:when -->
<xsl:template match="xslx:elsif"  mode="choose">
```

```
   <xso:when test="{@test}">
     <xsl:apply-templates select="@* | node( )"/>
   </xso:when>
</xsl:template>

<!--An xslx:else becomes a xsl:otherwise -->
<xsl:template match="xslx:else" mode="choose">
 <xso:otherwise>
   <xsl:apply-templates/>
 </xso:otherwise>
</xsl:template>


<!-- An xslx:loop becomes a call to a named template -->
<xsl:template match="xslx:loop">
   <!-- Each template is given the name loop-N where N is position -->
   <!-- of this loop relative to previous loops at any level -->
   <xsl:variable name="name">
     <xsl:text>loop-</xsl:text>
     <xsl:number count="xslx:loop" level="any"/>
   </xsl:variable>

   <xso:call-template name="{$name}">
     <xsl:for-each select="ancestor::xslx:loop">
       <xso:with-param name="{@param}" select="${@param}"/>
     </xsl:for-each>
     <xso:with-param name="{@param}" select="{@init}"/>
   </xso:call-template>

</xsl:template>

<!-- Mode loop-body is used on the 2nd pass. -->
<!-- Here recursive templates are generated to do the looping.  -->

<xsl:template match="xslx:loop" mode="loop-body">
   <xsl:variable name="name">
     <xsl:text>loop-</xsl:text>
     <xsl:value-of select="position( )"/>
   </xsl:variable>

   <xso:template name="{$name}">
     <!--If this loop is nested in another it must -->
     <!--"see" the outter loop parameters so we generate these here -->
     <xsl:for-each select="ancestor::xslx:loop">
       <xso:param name="{@param}"/>
     </xsl:for-each>
     <!--The local loop parameter -->
     <xso:param name="{@param}"/>
     <!--Generate the recusion control test -->
     <xso:if test="{@test}">
       <!-- Apply template in normal mode to handle -->
       <!-- calls to nested loops while copying everything else. -->
       <xsl:apply-templates/>
       <!--This is the recursive call that applies -->
```

```
        <!--the incr to the loop param -->
        <xso:call-template name="{$name}">
          <xsl:for-each select="ancestor::xslx:loop">
            <xso:with-param name="{@param}" select="${@param}"/>
          </xsl:for-each>
          <xso:with-param name="{@param}" select="${@param} + {@incr}"/>
        </xso:call-template>
      </xso:if>
    </xso:template>
  </xsl:template>

</xsl:stylesheet>
```

Here is the result of the generation:

```
<xso:stylesheet xmlns:xso="http://www.w3.org/1999/XSL/Transform" xmlns:xsl="http://
www.w3.org/1999/XSL/Transform" xmlns:xslx="http://www.ora.com/XSLTCookbook/
ExtendedXSLT" version="1.0">
  <xsl:output method="text"/>
  <xsl:template match="foo">
    <xso:choose>
      <xso:when test="bar">
        <xsl:text>You often will find a bar in the neighborhood of foo!</xsl:text>
      </xso:when>
      <xso:when test="baz">
        <xsl:text>A baz is a sure sign of geekdom</xsl:text>
      </xso:when>
      <xso:otherwise>
        <xso:call-template name="loop-1">
          <xso:with-param name="i" select="0"/>
        </xso:call-template>
      </xso:otherwise>
    </xso:choose>
    <xso:call-template name="loop-2">
      <xso:with-param name="i" select="10"/>
    </xso:call-template>
    <xso:choose>
      <xso:when test="foo">
        <xsl:text>foo foo! Nobody says foo foo!</xsl:text>
      </xso:when>
      <xso:otherwise>
        <xsl:text>Well, okay then!</xsl:text>
      </xso:otherwise>
    </xso:choose>
  </xsl:template>
  <xso:template name="loop-1">
    <xso:param name="i"/>
    <xso:if test="$i &lt; 10">
      <xsl:text>Hmmm, nothing to say here but I'll say it 10 times.</xsl:text>
      <xso:call-template name="loop-1">
        <xso:with-param name="i" select="$i + 1"/>
      </xso:call-template>
    </xso:if>
  </xso:template>
```

```
    <xso:template name="loop-2">
      <xso:param name="i"/>
      <xso:if test="$i &gt;= 0">
        <xso:call-template name="loop-3">
          <xso:with-param name="i" select="$i"/>
          <xso:with-param name="j" select="10"/>
        </xso:call-template>
        <xso:call-template name="loop-2">
          <xso:with-param name="i" select="$i + -1"/>
        </xso:call-template>
      </xso:if>
    </xso:template>
    <xso:template name="loop-3">
      <xso:param name="i"/>
      <xso:param name="j"/>
      <xso:if test="$j &gt;= 0">
        <xsl:text>
</xsl:text>
        <xsl:value-of select="$i * $j"/>
        <xso:call-template name="loop-3">
          <xso:with-param name="1" select="$i"/>
          <xso:with-param name="j" select="$j + -1"/>
        </xso:call-template>
      </xso:if>
    </xso:template>
</xso:stylesheet>
```

Discussion

The xsl:namespace-alias element is the key to generating XSLT with XSLT. Without it, the processor would not be able to distinguish actual XSLT content from content that is meant to be output as literal result elements. Generation of XSLT with XSLT is useful in more contexts then this recipe will cover. Some additional examples include:

Facilitation of literate programming

Literate programming embeds code fragments in human-readable documentation (rather than the usual reverse situation) so that information is presented in the order that best suits people, rather than the order that best suits compilers.

Provision of conditional includes/imports

If this feature were in XSLT, it would probably require awkward extensions to the processing model akin to a C program's preprocessor.

Enabling the dynamic evaluation of XPaths

This category refers to a stylesheet that generates XPaths from an import source and embeds them in another stylesheet that evaluates them statically. The extra level of indirection thus emulates dynamic behavior. Often those XPaths are embedded in a document. For example, you might see a table specification like:

```
<table of="person">
  <column label="Firstname" content="name/firstname" />
  <column label="Surname" content="name/surname" />
  <column label="Age" content="@age" type="number" />
  <sort select="Surname, Firstname, Age" />
</table>
```

It is easier to generate the table described by this XML—by generating XSLT from the table specification and then running that XSLT over the data—than it is to interpret the table specification within the same stylesheet you use to process the data.

See Also

See Oliver Becker's XSLT loop compiler for a similar example that also validates (*http://www.informatik.hu-berlin.de/~obecker/XSLT/#loop-compiler*).

CHAPTER 11

Vertical XSLT Application Recipes

*A newcomer wonders if there's a secret handshake or code required
to delve into its riddles…such as knowing what to bring to a potluck.*
—From a book review of *Potluck: Stories That Taste Like Hawaii*

This chapter differs from the others because the examples represent mini-XSLT applications covering a diverse set of domains (a potluck, if you will). Many examples relate to the use of specific commercial software. As software vendors embrace XML, they provide opportunities for their products to be used in ways they never imagined (or did not get around to implementing).

Microsoft is one vendor that has jumped on the XML bandwagon. The latest versions of Microsoft Visio (Version 10.0) and Excel (Office XP Version 10.0) both support XML output. Visio is a proprietary vector drawing package, and Visio's XML output (called Visio VDX) is also Visio-specific. John Breen has done an admirable job converting this output to Scalable Vector Graphics (SVG). His code is featured in Recipe 11.1.

Microsoft Excel allows spreadsheets to be saved in XML. Unfortunately, the XML directly models the structure of an Excel spreadsheet. Recipe 11.2 shows how to covert them to a more usable form.

Topic Maps are an up-and-coming XML technology for modeling knowledge in a way that makes information published on the Web more useful to both people and machines. XTM is an open standard for representing topic maps in XML. By analogy, software developers model knowledge about systems by using the *Unified Modeling Language* (UML). UML has its own standard XML representation known as *XML Metadata Interchange* (XMI). UML and Topic Maps do not serve the same audience; however, UML is rich enough to capture the concepts addressed by Topic Maps if you follow certain conventions. Since UML has been around longer than Topic Maps, the software tools are more mature. Recipe 11.3 shows how the XMI output of a popular UML authoring tool (Rational Rose) can be converted into XTM Topic Maps.[*]

---

[*] You might call this recipe Acronym Conversion Software (ACS).

One of XTM's most useful features is its ability to generate web sites. Recipe 11.4 addresses this Topic Map application. Nikita Ogievetsky contributed this recipe based on his work on the Cogitative Topic Maps Web Site (CTW) framework

Finally, we clean up the chapter with some SOAP, the W3C's XML format for implementing web services. The Simple Object Access Protocol is a way for software systems to communicate via standardized XML messages. This section addresses a SOAP-related draft specification called *Web Service Definition Language* (WSDL). As its name implies, WSDL is an XML specification for documenting a SOAP service. This discussion shows how to convert WSDL into human-readable documentation.

The examples in this chapter are long, but you can find the full source code at *http:// www.oreilly.com/catalog/xsltckbk/*.

11.1   Converting Visio VDX Documents to SVG

Problem

You want to convert Microsoft Visio XML files (VDX) into more portable SVG files.

Solution

John Breen implemented the following solution. He maps the major Visio elements to SVG as shown in Table 11-1.

Table 11-1. Visio-to-SVG Mappings

Visio element	SVG element
VisioDocument/Colors/ColorEntry	color value
VisioDocument/Stylesheets/StyleSheet	CSS Style
VisioDocument/Pages/Page	Svg
Page/Shapes/Shape	G
Shapes/Shape/@NameU	@id
Shapes/Shape/XForm	transform
XForm/PinX and XForm/PinX	translate()
Shapes/Shape/Fill/FillForegnd	@fill (with lookup)
Shapes/Shape/Geom	Path
Shape/Geom/MoveTo	@d "M"
Shape/Geom/LineTo	@d "L"
Shape/Geom/NoFill(0)	@d "z"

This section goes over only the main stylesheet and select portions of the included ones. The entire source code with examples is available at *http://sourceforge.net/ projects/vdxtosvg/*:

```
<xsl:stylesheet xmlns:xsl="http://www.w3.org/1999/XSL/Transform"
  xmlns:v="urn:schemas-microsoft-com:office:visio"
  xmlns:xlink="http://www.w3.org/1999/xlink"
  xmlns:math="java.lang.Math"
  xmlns:jDouble="java.lang.Double"
  xmlns:saxon="http://icl.com/saxon"
  exclude-result-prefixes="v math saxon jDouble"
  xmlns="http://www.w3.org/2000/svg"
  version="1.0">

<xsl:output method="xml"
  version="1.0"
  omit-xml-declaration="no"
  media-type="image/svg+xml"
  encoding="iso-8859-1"
  indent="yes"
  cdata-section-elements="style"
  doctype-public="-//W3C//DTD SVG 1.0//EN"
  doctype-system="http://www.w3.org/TR/2001/REC-SVG-20010904/DTD/svg10.dtd"
  />
```

The stylesheet uses a parameter pageNumber for specifying what page should be extracted from the VDX, and the parameter userScale specifies by which amount to scale Visio units to user units:

```
<xsl:param name="pageNumber" select="1"/>
<xsl:param name="userScale"  select="100"/>

<!-- ============= Variables (ie, Constants) ===================== -->
<!-- Color map -->
<xsl:variable name="Colors"
              select="//v:Colors[position( )=1]/v:ColorEntry"/>

<!-- Page being processed -->
<xsl:variable name="Page"
        select="/v:VisioDocument/v:Pages/v:Page[number($pageNumber)]"/>

<!-- Template Masters -->
<xsl:variable name="Masters"
              select="//v:Masters[position( )=1]/v:Master"/>

<!-- viewBox Master -->
<xsl:variable name="viewBoxMaster"
              select="$Masters[@NameU='viewBox']"/>

<!-- Ratio of font height to width (fudge factor) -->
<xsl:variable name="fontRatio"
              select="2"/>

<!-- Pi (SVG uses degrees, Visio uses radians) -->
<xsl:variable name="pi" select="3.14159265358979323846264338327"/>
```

The stylesheet is decomposed into several components that are included here. Portions of these modules are discussed later in this section. The stylesheet implements some extensions in JavaScript; however, if your XSLT processor does not support JavaScript, you can still use this code. Some text might not format nicely, however:

```
<!-- Included files -->
<xsl:include href="visio-style.xsl"/>
<xsl:include href="visio-text.xsl"/>
<xsl:include href="visio-masters.xsl"/>
<xsl:include href="visio-nurbs.xsl"/>

 <!-- Scripts -->
<xsl:template name="required-scripts">
  <script xlink:href="wordwrap.js" type="text/ecmascript"/>
</xsl:template>

<xsl:template match="/v:VisioDocument">
  <xsl:apply-templates
    select="$Page"/>
</xsl:template>
```

A Visio page is mapped onto an SVG graphic. Information from the Visio document determines how best to lay out the graphic in a view box:

```
<!-- ============= Page ===================================-->
<xsl:template match="v:Page">
  <xsl:message>
    <xsl:value-of select="@NameU"/>
  </xsl:message>
  <svg id="{@NameU}">
    <xsl:attribute name="xml:space">
      <xsl:value-of select="'preserve'"/>
    </xsl:attribute>
    <xsl:choose>
      <!-- Use viewBox with name 'default' if present -->
      <xsl:when test="//v:Shape[@Master=$viewBoxMaster/@ID
                      and @NameU='default'][1]">
        <xsl:for-each
          select="//v:Shape[@Master=$viewBoxMaster/@ID
                  and @NameU='default']">
          <xsl:attribute name="viewBox">
            <xsl:value-of select="concat(
                            v:XForm/v:PinX*$userScale, ' ',
                            -v:XForm/v:PinY*$userScale, ' ',
                            v:XForm/v:Width*$userScale, ' ',
                            v:XForm/v:Height*$userScale)"/>
          </xsl:attribute>
        </xsl:for-each>
      </xsl:when>
      <!-- Otherwise, center on sheet -->
      <xsl:otherwise>
        <xsl:attribute name="viewBox">
          <xsl:value-of select="concat('0 ',
```

```
                                    -v:PageSheet/v:PageProps/v:PageHeight
                                      *$userScale, ' ',
                                    v:PageSheet/v:PageProps/v:PageWidth
                                      *$userScale, ' ',
                                    v:PageSheet/v:PageProps/v:PageHeight
                                      *$userScale)"/>
          </xsl:attribute>
        </xsl:otherwise>
      </xsl:choose>
      <xsl:call-template name="required-scripts"/>
      <xsl:call-template name="predefined-pattern-fgnds"/>
      <xsl:call-template name="predefined-markers"/>
```

The real meat of the conversion begins here. Start by processing Visio stylesheet elements to convert them into equivalent Cascading Style Sheet directives. Then convert all shapes into their SVG representation:

```
      <xsl:apply-templates select="../../v:StyleSheets"/>
      <xsl:apply-templates select="v:Shapes/v:Shape"/>
    </svg>
  </xsl:template>


  <!-- ============= StyleSheets ================ -->
  <xsl:template match="v:StyleSheets">
    <defs>
      <xsl:for-each select="v:StyleSheet">
        <!-- Line style -->
        <style id="ss-line-{@ID}" type="text/css">
          <xsl:text>*.ss-line-</xsl:text><xsl:value-of select="@ID"/>
          <xsl:text> { </xsl:text>
          <xsl:call-template name="recursive-line-style">
            <xsl:with-param name="ss" select="."/>
          </xsl:call-template>
          <xsl:text> }</xsl:text>
        </style>
        <!-- Fill style -->
        <style id="ss-fill-{@ID}" type="text/css">
          <xsl:text>*.ss-fill-</xsl:text><xsl:value-of select="@ID"/>
          <xsl:text> { </xsl:text>
          <xsl:call-template name="recursive-fill-style">
            <xsl:with-param name="ss" select="."/>
          </xsl:call-template>
          <xsl:text> }</xsl:text>
        </style>
        <!-- Text style -->
        <style id="ss-text-{@ID}" type="text/css">
          <xsl:text>*.ss-text-</xsl:text><xsl:value-of select="@ID"/>
          <xsl:text> { </xsl:text>
          <xsl:call-template name="recursive-text-style">
            <xsl:with-param name="ss" select="."/>
          </xsl:call-template>
          <xsl:text> } </xsl:text>
        </style>
      </xsl:for-each>
```

```
      </defs>
</xsl:template>

<!-- Recurse through StyleSheet inheritance -->
<xsl:template name="recursive-line-style">
  <xsl:param name="ss"/>
  <xsl:if test="$ss/@LineStyle">
    <xsl:call-template name="recursive-line-style">
      <xsl:with-param name="ss"
        select="$ss/../v:StyleSheet[@ID=$ss/@LineStyle]"/>
    </xsl:call-template>
  </xsl:if>
  <xsl:apply-templates select="$ss/v:Line" mode="style"/>
</xsl:template>

<xsl:template name="recursive-fill-style">
  <xsl:param name="ss"/>
  <xsl:if test="$ss/@FillStyle">
    <xsl:call-template name="recursive-fill-style">
      <xsl:with-param name="ss"
        select="$ss/../v:StyleSheet[@ID=$ss/@FillStyle]"/>
    </xsl:call-template>
  </xsl:if>
  <xsl:apply-templates select="$ss/v:Fill" mode="style"/>
</xsl:template>

<xsl:template name="recursive-text-style">
  <xsl:param name="ss"/>
  <xsl:if test="$ss/@TextStyle">
    <xsl:call-template name="recursive-text-style">
      <xsl:with-param name="ss"
        select="$ss/../v:StyleSheet[@ID=$ss/@TextStyle]"/>
    </xsl:call-template>
  </xsl:if>
  <xsl:apply-templates select="$ss/v:Char|$ss/v:Para" mode="style"/>
</xsl:template>

<!-- This template returns a string for the line style -->
<xsl:template match="v:Line" mode="style">
  <xsl:for-each select="v:LineWeight">
    <xsl:text>stroke-width:</xsl:text>
    <xsl:value-of select=". * $userScale"/><xsl:text>;</xsl:text>
  </xsl:for-each>
  <xsl:for-each select="v:LineColor">
    <xsl:choose>
      <xsl:when test="../v:LinePattern > 0">
        <xsl:text>stroke:</xsl:text>
        <xsl:call-template name="lookup-color">
          <xsl:with-param name="c_el" select="."/>
        </xsl:call-template>
      </xsl:when>
      <xsl:when test="../v:LinePattern = 0">
        <xsl:text>stroke:none</xsl:text>
      </xsl:when>
```

```
    </xsl:choose>
    <xsl:text>;</xsl:text>
  </xsl:for-each>
  <xsl:for-each select="v:EndArrow">
    <xsl:choose>
      <xsl:when test=". = 0">
        <xsl:value-of select="string('marker-end:none;')"/>
      </xsl:when>
      <xsl:otherwise>
        <xsl:value-of select="concat('marker-end:url(#EndArrow-', .,
                              '-', ../v:EndArrowSize, ');')"/>
      </xsl:otherwise>
    </xsl:choose>
  </xsl:for-each>
  <xsl:apply-templates select="v:LinePattern[. &gt; 1]" mode="style"/>
</xsl:template>

<!-- This template returns a string for the fill style -->
<xsl:template match="v:Fill" mode="style">
  <xsl:for-each select="v:FillForegnd">
    <xsl:choose>
      <xsl:when test="../v:FillPattern = 1">
        <xsl:text>fill:</xsl:text>
        <xsl:call-template name="lookup-color">
          <xsl:with-param name="c_el" select="."/>
        </xsl:call-template>
      </xsl:when>
      <xsl:when test="../v:FillPattern = 0">
        <xsl:text>fill:none</xsl:text>
      </xsl:when>
      <xsl:otherwise>
        <xsl:text>fill:url(#</xsl:text>
        <xsl:value-of select="generate-id(../..)"/>
        <xsl:text>-pat)</xsl:text>
      </xsl:otherwise>
    </xsl:choose>
    <xsl:text>;</xsl:text>
  </xsl:for-each>
</xsl:template>

<!-- This template returns a string for the text style -->
<xsl:template match="v:Char|v:Para" mode="style">
  <xsl:for-each select="v:Color">
    <!-- I don't think Visio handles filled characters -->
    <xsl:text>stroke:none</xsl:text>
    <xsl:text>;fill:</xsl:text>
    <xsl:call-template name="lookup-color">
      <xsl:with-param name="c_el" select="."/>
    </xsl:call-template>
    <xsl:text>;</xsl:text>
  </xsl:for-each>
  <xsl:for-each select="v:Size">
    <xsl:text>font-size:</xsl:text>
    <xsl:value-of select=". * $userScale"/><xsl:text>;</xsl:text>
```

```
    </xsl:for-each>
    <xsl:for-each select="v:HorzAlign">
      <xsl:text>text-anchor:</xsl:text>
      <xsl:choose>
        <xsl:when test="(. = 0) or (. = 3)">
          <xsl:text>start</xsl:text>
        </xsl:when>
        <xsl:when test=". = 1">
          <xsl:text>middle</xsl:text>
        </xsl:when>
        <xsl:when test=". = 2">
          <xsl:text>end</xsl:text>
        </xsl:when>
      </xsl:choose>
      <xsl:text>;</xsl:text>
    </xsl:for-each>
  </xsl:template>

  <!-- Ignore all other StyleSheet elements -->
  <xsl:template match="*[parent::v:StyleSheet]" priority="-100"/>
```

Here is where shapes are mapped onto an SVG equivalent. Notice how shapes can be associated with masters in a Visio document. Think of a master as a template of a shape from which a shape on a page can inherit attributes and behavior.

Each Visio shape is, by default, translated as a `<g>` element since a Visio shape can contain both graphics and text. Recall that the `<g>` element is SVG's way of specifying a group of graphical elements that can share stylistic traits.

SvgElement is a Visio property that the user can attach to a Visio shape to specify special handling by this translator. For example, svgElement can be set to any other SVG container element, such as `<defs>`. This feature keeps certain shapes from being rendered, such as paths for animateMotion elements. This way, the path can be referenced in the SVG file, but it will not be displayed.

One of the main reasons for using svgElement is to indicate special shapes that are translated to elements that have no correspondence in Visio, such as animate, animateMotion, and viewBox. *visio-master.xsl*, discussed later, handles these elements:

```
  <!-- ============= Shape ==================== -->
  <xsl:template match="v:Shape">

    <xsl:variable name="master"
              select="/v:VisioDocument//v:Masters[1]/
                      v:Master[@ID=current( )/@Master]"/>

    <xsl:variable name="svgElement">
      <xsl:choose>
        <!-- Check for special svgElement property in shape ... -->
        <xsl:when test="./v:Prop/v:Label[.='svgElement']">
          <xsl:value-of
            select="./v:Prop/v:Label[.='svgElement']/../v:Value"/>
        </xsl:when>
```

```
      <!-- ... and in master -->
      <xsl:when test="@Master and
                      $master//v:Prop/v:Label[.='svgElement']">
       <xsl:value-of
         select="$master//v:Prop/v:Label[.='svgElement']/../v:Value"/>
      </xsl:when>

      <!-- The simple case maps a shape onto a svg (g)roup -->
      <xsl:otherwise>
       <xsl:value-of select="'g'"/>
      </xsl:otherwise>
    </xsl:choose>
  </xsl:variable>

  <xsl:choose>

    <xsl:when test="@Master and string($svgElement)
                    and contains($specialMasters, $svgElement)">
      <xsl:call-template name="choose-special-master">
        <xsl:with-param name="master" select="$master"/>
        <xsl:with-param name="masterElement" select="$svgElement"/>
      </xsl:call-template>
    </xsl:when>

    <xsl:when test="($svgElement = 'defs') or ($svgElement = 'g') or
                    ($svgElement = 'symbol')">
      <xsl:choose>
        <xsl:when test="v:Hyperlink">
          <!-- Surround shape with 'a' element -->
          <!-- This is a minimal implementation.  It doesn't support
               multiple links, subaddress, etc. -->
          <a xlink:title="{v:Hyperlink/v:Description}"
             xlink:href="{v:Hyperlink/v:Address}">
            <xsl:if test="v:Hyperlink/v:NewWindow">
              <xsl:attribute name="show">
                <xsl:value-of select="new"/>
              </xsl:attribute>
            </xsl:if>
            <xsl:element name="{$svgElement}">
              <xsl:call-template name="userShape"/>
            </xsl:element>
          </a>
        </xsl:when>
        <xsl:otherwise>
          <xsl:element name="{$svgElement}">
            <xsl:call-template name="userShape"/>
          </xsl:element>
        </xsl:otherwise>
      </xsl:choose>
    </xsl:when>
  </xsl:choose>
</xsl:template>
```

Here the normal shapes created by the user are mapped to SVG, as specified in the Table 11-1:

```
<!-- This does the processing for normal 'user' shapes -->
<xsl:template name="userShape">
  <xsl:variable name="master"
    select="/v:VisioDocument/v:Masters
            /v:Master[(@ID=current( )/@Master)
                      and (current( )/@Type != 'Group')]
            /v:Shapes/v:Shape |
            /v:VisioDocument/v:Masters
            /v:Master[@ID=current( )
            /ancestor::v:Shape[@Master]/@Master]
            //v:Shape[@ID=current( )/@MasterShape] | ."/>

  <xsl:call-template name="setIdAttribute"/>

  <xsl:attribute name="class">
    <xsl:for-each select="($master[@LineStyle])[last( )]">
      <xsl:text> ss-line-</xsl:text>
      <xsl:value-of select="@LineStyle"/>
    </xsl:for-each>
    <xsl:for-each select="($master[@FillStyle])[last( )]">
      <xsl:text> ss-fill-</xsl:text>
      <xsl:value-of select="@FillStyle"/>
    </xsl:for-each>
  </xsl:attribute>
  <xsl:attribute name="style">
    <xsl:for-each select="$master">
      <xsl:apply-templates select="./v:Line" mode="style"/>
      <xsl:apply-templates select="./v:Fill" mode="style"/>
    </xsl:for-each>
  </xsl:attribute>
  <xsl:for-each select="v:XForm">
    <xsl:call-template name="transformAttribute">
    </xsl:call-template>
  </xsl:for-each>
  <!-- This is to create the custom pattern -->
  <xsl:apply-templates select="v:Fill" mode="Shape"/>
  <xsl:for-each select="v:Geom">
    <xsl:apply-templates select="v:Ellipse"/>
    <xsl:if test="v:MoveTo or v:LineTo">
      <xsl:call-template name="pathElement"/>
    </xsl:if>
  </xsl:for-each>
  <xsl:for-each select="($master/v:Text)[last( )]">
    <xsl:apply-templates select="."/>
  </xsl:for-each>

  <xsl:apply-templates select="v:Shapes/v:Shape"/>

  <!-- Add elements from properties -->
  <xsl:for-each select="v:Prop">
    <xsl:choose>
      <xsl:when test="starts-with(v:Label, 'svg-element')">
```

```
            <!-- This is sort of ugly - it may disappear some day -->
            <xsl:value-of disable-output-escaping="yes" select="v:Value"/>
          </xsl:when>
        </xsl:choose>
      </xsl:for-each>
    </xsl:template>

    <xsl:template match="v:Ellipse">
      <!-- This is a somewhat limited translation.  It assumes that the
           axes are parallel to the x & y axes, and the lower-left corner
           of the bounding box is at the origin (which appears to be the
           way Visio draws them by default). -->
      <ellipse id="ellipse-{generate-id(ancestor::v:Shape[1])}"
        cx="{v:X*$userScale}" cy="{-v:Y*$userScale}"
        rx="{v:X*$userScale}" ry="{v:Y*$userScale}"/>
    </xsl:template>

    <!-- ==================  Utility templates ========================= -
  ->

    <!-- Lookup color value in Colors element -->
    <xsl:template name="lookup-color">
      <xsl:param name="c_el"/>
      <xsl:choose>
        <xsl:when test="starts-with($c_el, '#')">
          <xsl:value-of select="$c_el"/>
        </xsl:when>
        <xsl:otherwise>
          <xsl:value-of select="$Colors[@IX=string($c_el)]/@RGB"/>
        </xsl:otherwise>
      </xsl:choose>
    </xsl:template>
```

If a Visio element has a name, use it as the shape ID; otherwise, use generate-id( ):

```
    <xsl:template name="setIdAttribute">
      <xsl:attribute name="id">
        <xsl:choose>
          <xsl:when test="@NameU">
            <xsl:value-of select="@NameU"/>
          </xsl:when>
          <xsl:otherwise>
            <xsl:value-of select="generate-id(.)"/>
          </xsl:otherwise>
        </xsl:choose>
      </xsl:attribute>
    </xsl:template>

    <!-- Translate XForm element into transform attribute -->
    <xsl:template name="transformAttribute">
      <xsl:attribute name="transform">
        <xsl:text>translate(</xsl:text>
        <xsl:value-of select="concat((v:PinX - v:LocPinX)*$userScale,
                              ',', -(v:PinY - v:LocPinY)*$userScale)"/>
        <xsl:if test="v:Angle != 0">
          <xsl:text>) rotate(</xsl:text>
```

```
        <xsl:value-of select="-v:Angle*180 div $pi"/>
        <xsl:value-of select="concat(',', v:LocPinX*$userScale,
                              ',', -v:LocPinY*$userScale)"/>
      </xsl:if>
      <xsl:text>)</xsl:text>
    </xsl:attribute>
  </xsl:template>
```

Visio Geom elements are translated to paths. Most of the mapping is straightforward, except for the handling of Non-Uniform Rational B-Splines (NURBS), which is delegated to a special set of templates in *visio-nurbs.xsl*, which you can peruse in the full distribution:

```
<!-- Translate Geom element into path element -->
<xsl:template name="pathElement">
  <xsl:variable name="pathID">
    <xsl:text>path-</xsl:text>
    <xsl:choose>
      <xsl:when test="ancestor::v:Shape[1]/@NameU">
        <xsl:value-of select="ancestor::v:Shape[1]/@NameU"/>
      </xsl:when>
      <xsl:otherwise>
        <xsl:value-of select="generate-id(ancestor::v:Shape[1])"/>
      </xsl:otherwise>
    </xsl:choose>
  </xsl:variable>
  <path id="{$pathID}">
    <xsl:attribute name="d">
      <xsl:for-each select="v:*">
        <xsl:choose>
          <xsl:when test="name() = 'MoveTo'">
            <xsl:value-of select="concat('M', v:X*$userScale,
                                  ',', -v:Y*$userScale, ' ')"/>
          </xsl:when>
          <xsl:when test="name() = 'LineTo'">
            <xsl:value-of select="concat('L', v:X*$userScale,
                                  ',', -v:Y*$userScale, ' ')"/>
          </xsl:when>
          <xsl:when test="name() = 'EllipticalArcTo'">
            <!-- If we don't have access to trig functions, the
                 arc will just be represented by two line segments-->
            <xsl:choose>
              <xsl:when test="function-available('math:atan2')">
                <xsl:call-template name="ellipticalArcPath"/>
              </xsl:when>
              <xsl:otherwise>
                <xsl:value-of select="concat('L', v:A*$userScale,
                                      ',', -v:B*$userScale,
                                      ' L', v:X*$userScale,
                                      ',', -v:Y*$userScale, ' ')"/>
              </xsl:otherwise>
            </xsl:choose>
          </xsl:when>
          <xsl:when test="(name() = 'NoFill') or (name() = 'NoLine') or
                          (name() = 'NoShow') or (name() = 'NoSnap')">
```

```
              <!-- Ignore these -->
            </xsl:when>
            <xsl:when test="name( ) = 'NURBSTo'">
              <xsl:call-template name="NURBSPath"/>
            </xsl:when>
            <xsl:otherwise>
              <xsl:message>
                <xsl:text>Warning: unsupported path command found:</xsl:text>
                <xsl:value-of select="name( )"/>
                <xsl:text>; replacing with LineTo</xsl:text>
              </xsl:message>
              <xsl:value-of select="concat('L', v:X*$userScale,
                                    ',', -v:Y*$userScale, ' ')"/>
            </xsl:otherwise>
          </xsl:choose>
        </xsl:for-each>
      </xsl:attribute>
      <xsl:if test="v:NoFill = 1">
        <xsl:attribute name="fill"><xsl:text>none</xsl:text></xsl:attribute>
      </xsl:if>
    </path>
</xsl:template>

<!-- This template calculates the path string for an elliptical arc -->

<xsl:template name="ellipticalArcPath">

<!-- Figure sweep based on angle from current point -->
<!-- to (X,Y) and (A,B) -->

<!-- TODO: figure a better way to make sure the preceding
     sibling is a drawing element -->

  <xsl:variable name="lastX"
    select="preceding-sibling::*[1]/v:X"/>
  <xsl:variable name="lastY"
    select="preceding-sibling::*[1]/v:Y"/>
  <xsl:variable name="angle"
    select="math:atan2(v:Y - $lastY, v:X - $lastX)
            - math:atan2(v:B - $lastY, v:A - $lastX)"/>
  <xsl:variable name="sweep">
    <xsl:choose>
      <xsl:when test="$angle &gt; 0
                      and math:abs($angle) &lt; 180">
        <xsl:value-of select='0'/>
      </xsl:when>
      <xsl:when test="$angle &lt; 0
                      and math:abs($angle) &gt; 180">
        <xsl:value-of select='0'/>
      </xsl:when>
      <xsl:otherwise>
        <xsl:value-of select='1'/>
      </xsl:otherwise>
    </xsl:choose>
  </xsl:variable>
```

```
        <xsl:value-of select="concat('A',
                    (preceding-sibling::*[1]/v:X - v:X)*$userScale, ',',
                    (preceding-sibling::*[1]/v:Y - v:Y)*$userScale, ' ',
                    v:C,  ' 0,', $sweep, ' ', v:X*$userScale, ',',
                    -v:Y*$userScale, ' ')"/>
    </xsl:template>

</xsl:stylesheet>
```

Discussion

Visio is a powerful vector graphics editor that, in its current version, does not support SVG. Needless to say, SVG is not powerful enough to represent every Visio construct accurately, but it can come close. Simple Visio diagrams can be translated to SVG almost exactly. More complex SVG may need some touch up in a native SVG editor. The release notes that come with the full distribution identify missing features. Figure 11-1 is a sample of the SVG generated from a Visio file and rendered almost flawlessly.

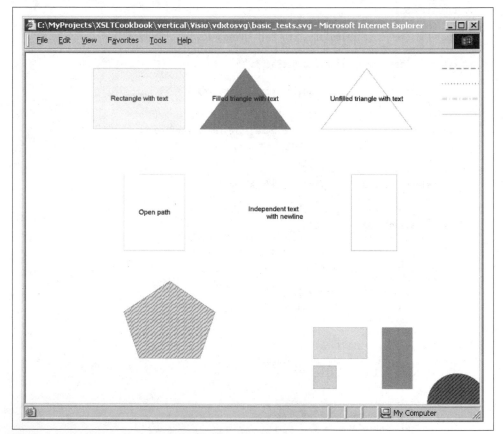

Figure 11-1. Basic SVG shapes and text converted from Visio

The important lesson you should learn from this example goes beyond the details of Visio VDX , SVG, or any special tricks or techniques the author uses. It is simply the fact that this complex transformation was the author's first experience with XSLT. This says something very positive about the power of XSLT's transformational paradigm.

See Also

The source code and some demonstrations are available on Source Forge at *http://sourceforge.net/projects/vdxtosvg/*.

11.2   Working with Excel XML Spreadsheets

Problem

You want to export data from Excel to XML, but not in the native format supported by Microsoft.

Solution

If you have an Excel spreadsheet that looks like this:

Date	Price	Volume
20010817	61.88	260163
20010820	62.7	241859
20010821	60.78	233989
20010822	60.66	387444

Then the Excel XML version looks like this:

```
<?xml version="1.0"?>
<Workbook xmlns="urn:schemas-microsoft-com:office:spreadsheet" xmlns:o="urn:schemas-
microsoft-com:office:office" xmlns:x="urn:schemas-microsoft-com:office:excel" xmlns:
ss="urn:schemas-microsoft-com:office:spreadsheet" xmlns:html="http://www.w3.org/TR/
REC-html40">
  <DocumentProperties xmlns="urn:schemas-microsoft-com:office:office">
    <Author>Salvatore R. Mangano</Author>
    <LastAuthor>Salvatore R. Mangano</LastAuthor>
    <Created>2002-08-18T00:43:49Z</Created>
    <LastSaved>2002-08-18T02:19:21Z</LastSaved>
    <Company>Descriptix</Company>
    <Version>10.3501</Version>
  </DocumentProperties>
```

```
<OfficeDocumentSettings xmlns="urn:schemas-microsoft-com:office:office">
  <DownloadComponents/>
  <LocationOfComponents HRef="/"/>
</OfficeDocumentSettings>
<ExcelWorkbook xmlns="urn:schemas-microsoft-com:office:excel">
  <WindowHeight>9915</WindowHeight>
  <WindowWidth>10140</WindowWidth>
  <WindowTopX>240</WindowTopX>
  <WindowTopY>255</WindowTopY>
  <ProtectStructure>False</ProtectStructure>
  <ProtectWindows>False</ProtectWindows>
</ExcelWorkbook>
<Styles>
  <Style ss:ID="Default" ss:Name="Normal">
    <Alignment ss:Vertical="Bottom"/>
    <Borders/>
    <Font/>
    <Interior/>
    <NumberFormat/>
    <Protection/>
  </Style>
</Styles>
<Worksheet ss:Name="msft">
  <Table ss:ExpandedColumnCount="3" ss:ExpandedRowCount="5" x:FullColumns="1"
  x:FullRows="1">
    <Row>
      <Cell>
        <Data ss:Type="String">Date</Data>
      </Cell>
      <Cell>
        <Data ss:Type="String">Price</Data>
      </Cell>
      <Cell>
        <Data ss:Type="String">Volume</Data>
      </Cell>
    </Row>
    <Row>
      <Cell>
        <Data ss:Type="Number">20010817</Data>
      </Cell>
      <Cell>
        <Data ss:Type="Number">61.88</Data>
      </Cell>
      <Cell>
        <Data ss:Type="Number">260163</Data>
      </Cell>
    </Row>
    <Row>
      <Cell>
        <Data ss:Type="Number">20010820</Data>
      </Cell>
```

```
          <Cell>
            <Data ss:Type="Number">62.7</Data>
          </Cell>
          <Cell>
            <Data ss:Type="Number">241859</Data>
          </Cell>
        </Row>
        <Row>
          <Cell>
            <Data ss:Type="Number">20010821</Data>
          </Cell>
          <Cell>
            <Data ss:Type="Number">60.78</Data>
          </Cell>
          <Cell>
            <Data ss:Type="Number">233989</Data>
          </Cell>
        </Row>
        <Row>
          <Cell>
            <Data ss:Type="Number">20010822</Data>
          </Cell>
          <Cell>
            <Data ss:Type="Number">60.66</Data>
          </Cell>
          <Cell>
            <Data ss:Type="Number">387444</Data>
          </Cell>
        </Row>
      </Table>
      <WorksheetOptions xmlns="urn:schemas-microsoft-com:office:excel">
        <Selected/>
        <Panes>
          <Pane>
            <Number>3</Number>
            <ActiveRow>11</ActiveRow>
            <ActiveCol>5</ActiveCol>
          </Pane>
        </Panes>
        <ProtectObjects>False</ProtectObjects>
        <ProtectScenarios>False</ProtectScenarios>
      </WorksheetOptions>
    </Worksheet>
  </Workbook>
```

which is probably not what you had in mind!

This example conveniently maps an Excel XML file to a simpler XML file. Many spreadsheets created in Excel have a structure in which the first row contains column names and subsequent rows contain data for those columns.

One obvious mapping would convert the column names into element names and the remaining cells into element content. The only missing pieces of information are the names of the top-level element and the element containing each row. This stylesheet takes these names as parameters with some obvious defaults. It converts some of the useful metadata into comments and throws away the Excel-specific stuff. This section provides several other parameters that increase the generality of the conversion, such as which row contains the column names, where the data starts, and what to do about empty cells:

```
<?xml version="1.0" encoding="UTF-8"?>
<xsl:stylesheet version="1.0"
                xmlns:xsl="http://www.w3.org/1999/XSL/Transform"
                xmlns:o="urn:schemas-microsoft-com:office:office"
                xmlns:x="urn:schemas-microsoft-com:office:excel"
                xmlns:ss="urn:schemas-Xmicrosoft-com:office:spreadsheet"
                                  exclude-result-prefixes="o x ss">

<xsl:exclude-result-prefixes >

<xsl:output method="xml" version="1.0" encoding="UTF-8" indent="yes"/>

<!-- The name of the top level element -->
<xsl:param name="topLevelName" select=" 'Table' "/>
<!-- The name of each row -->
<xsl:param name="rowName" select=" 'Row' "/>
<!-- The namespace to use -->
<xsl:param name="namespace"/>
<!-- The namespace prefix to use -->
<xsl:param name="namespacePrefix"/>
<!-- The character to use if column names contain white space -->
<xsl:param name="wsSub" select="'_'"/>
<!--Determines which row contains the col names-->
<xsl:param name="colNamesRow" select="1"/>
<!--Determines which row the data begins -->
<xsl:param name="dataRowStart" select="2"/>
<!-- If false then cells with null or whitespace only content -->
<!-- will be skipped -->
<xsl:param name="includeEmpty" select="true( )"/>
<!-- If false then author and creation meta data will not be put -->
<!-- into a comment-->
<xsl:param name="includeComment" select="true( )"/>

<!--Normalize the namespacePrefix -->
<xsl:variable name="nsp">
  <xsl:if test="$namespace">
    <!-- Only use prefix if namespace is specified -->
    <xsl:choose>
      <xsl:when test="contains($namespacePrefix,':')">
        <xsl:value-of
            select="concat(translate(substring-before(
                                         $namespacePrefix,
                                         ':'),' ',''),':')"/>
      </xsl:when>
      <xsl:when test="translate($namespacePrefix,' ','')">
        <xsl:value-of
            select="concat(translate($namespacePrefix,' ',''),':')"/>
```

```
        </xsl:when>
        <xsl:otherwise/>
      </xsl:choose>
    </xsl:if>
</xsl:variable>

<!--Get the names of all the columns with white space replaced by  -->
<xsl:variable name="COLS" select="/*/*/*/ss:Row[$colNamesRow]/ss:Cell"/>

<xsl:template match="o:DocumentProperties">
  <xsl:if test="$includeComment">
    <xsl:text>&#xa;</xsl:text>
    <xsl:comment>
     <xsl:text>&#xa;</xsl:text>
      <xsl:if test="normalize-space(o:Company)">
        <xsl:text>Company: </xsl:text>
        <xsl:value-of select="o:Company"/>
        <xsl:text>&#xa;</xsl:text>
      </xsl:if>
      <xsl:text>Author: </xsl:text>
      <xsl:value-of select="o:Author"/>
      <xsl:text>&#xa;</xsl:text>
      <xsl:text>Created on: </xsl:text>
      <xsl:value-of select="translate(o:Created,'TZ',' ')"/>
      <xsl:text>&#xa;</xsl:text>
      <xsl:text>Last Author: </xsl:text>
      <xsl:value-of select="o:LastAuthor"/>
      <xsl:text>&#xa;</xsl:text>
      <xsl:text>Saved on:</xsl:text>
      <xsl:value-of select="translate(o:LastSaved,'TZ',' ')"/>
      <xsl:text>&#xa;</xsl:text>
    </xsl:comment>
  </xsl:if>
</xsl:template>

<xsl:template match="ss:Table">
  <xsl:element
      name="{concat($nsp,translate($topLevelName,
                    '&#x20;&#x9;&#xA;',$wsSub))}"
      namespace="{$namespace}">
    <xsl:apply-templates select="ss:Row[position() >= $dataRowStart]"/>
  </xsl:element>
</xsl:template>

<xsl:template match="ss:Row">
  <xsl:element
     name="{concat($nsp,translate($rowName,
                    '&#x20;&#x9;&#xA;',$wsSub))}"
      namespace="{$namespace}">
    <xsl:for-each select="ss:Cell">
      <xsl:variable name="pos" select="position()"/>

      <!-- Get the correct column name even if there were empty -->
      <!-- cols in original spreadsheet -->
```

```
      <xsl:variable name="colName">
        <xsl:choose>
          <xsl:when test="@ss:Index and
                            $COLS[@ss:Index = current( )/@ss:Index]">
            <xsl:value-of
                select="$COLS[@ss:Index = current( )/@ss:Index]/ss:Data"/>
          </xsl:when>
          <xsl:when test="@ss:Index">
            <xsl:value-of
                  select="$COLS[number(current( )/@ss:Index)]/ss:Data"/>
          </xsl:when>
          <xsl:otherwise>
            <xsl:value-of select="$COLS[$pos]/ss:Data"/>
          </xsl:otherwise>
        </xsl:choose>
      </xsl:variable>

      <xsl:if test="$includeEmpty or
                      translate(ss:Data,'&#x20;&#x9;&#xA;','')">
        <xsl:element
            name="{concat($nsp,translate($colName,
                                  '&#20;&#x9;&#xA;',$wsSub))}"
            namespace="{$namespace}">
          <xsl:value-of select="ss:Data"/>
        </xsl:element>
      </xsl:if>

    </xsl:for-each>
  </xsl:element>
</xsl:template>

<xsl:template match="text( )"/>

</xsl:stylesheet>
```

The result of the transformation, with default parameter values, is the much more direct XML representation that follows:

```
<Table>
  <Row>
    <Date>20010817</Date>
    <Price>61.88</Price>
    <Volume>260163</Volume>
  </Row>
  <Row>
    <Date>20010820</Date>
    <Price>62.7</Price>
    <Volume>241859</Volume>
  </Row>
  <Row>
    <Date>20010821</Date>
    <Price>60.78</Price>
    <Volume>233989</Volume>
  </Row>
```

```
      <Row>
        <Date>20010822</Date>
        <Price>60.66</Price>
        <Volume>387444</Volume>
      </Row>
    </Table>
```

Discussion

I almost did not include this recipe in the book because it initially seemed trivial. However, I realized that the book needs to handle many special cases, and many implementations (including my first) would miss them. For example, spreadsheets often contain empty columns used as spacers. You need to know how to handle them by looking for the @ss:Index attribute. This book's initial version also hard-coded many of the choices this version exposes as parameters.

At least one obvious additional extension could be made to this stylesheet: the handling of multiple ss:Worksheet elements. This handling could be done by specifying the worksheet number as a parameter:

```
<xsl:param name="WSNum" select="1"/>

<xsl:variable name="COLS"
        select="/*/ss:Worksheet[$WSNum]/*/ss:Row[$colNamesRow]/ss:Cell"/>

<xsl:template match="ss:Workbook">
  <xsl:element name="{concat($nsp,translate($topLevelName,
                '&#x20;&#x9;&#xA;',$wsSub))}"
              namespace="{$namespace}">
    <xsl:apply-templates select="ss:Worksheet[number($WSNum)]/ss:Table"/>
  </xsl:element>
</xsl:template>
```

A more ambitious solution handles each Worksheet in a multiple Worksheet document as a separate element in the resulting document. This setup means that the column names can no longer be handled as a global variable:

```
<xsl:template match="ss:Workbook">
  <xsl:element name="{concat($nsp,translate($topLevelName,
                '&#x20;&#x9;&#xA;',$wsSub))}"
              namespace="{$namespace}">
    <xsl:choose>
      <xsl:when test="number($WSNum) > 0">
        <xsl:apply-templates
            select="ss:Worksheet[number($WSNum)]/ss:Table">
          <xsl:with-param name="COLS"
            select="ss:Worksheet[number($WSNum)]
                                    /*/ss:Row[$colNamesRow]/ss:Cell"/>
        </xsl:apply-templates>
      </xsl:when>
      <xsl:otherwise>
        <xsl:for-each select="ss:Worksheet">
```

```
        <xsl:element
            name="{concat($nsp,translate(@ss:Name,
                '&#x20;&#x9;&#xA;',$wsSub))}"
            namespace="{$namespace}">
          <xsl:apply-templates select="ss:Table">
            <xsl:with-param name="COLS"
                            select="*/ss:Row[$colNamesRow]/ss:Cell"/>
          </xsl:apply-templates>
        </xsl:element>
      </xsl:for-each>
    </xsl:otherwise>
  </xsl:choose>
 </xsl:element>
</xsl:template>

<xsl:template match="ss:Table">
  <xsl:param name="COLS"/>
    <xsl:apply-templates select="ss:Row[position() >= $dataRowStart]">
      <xsl:with-param name="COLS" select="$COLS"/>
    </xsl:apply-templates>
</xsl:template>

<xsl:template match="ss:Row">
  <xsl:param name="COLS"/>

  <!-- The rest is the same as original ... -->

</xsl:template>
```

The only trouble with this solution is that it assumes that the column names have to be in the same row in each worksheet.

11.3   Generating XTM Topic Maps from UML Models via XMI

Problem

You want to use your favorite XMI-enabled UML modeling tool to author XTM Topic Maps.

Solution

Readers not already familiar with Topic Maps might want to read the "Discussion" section before reviewing this solution.

Since UML was not explicitly designed to represent topic maps, this example works only if certain conventions are adopted. Most conventions revolve around the use of specific UML *stereotypes*. A stereotype is a UML extension mechanism that lets you associate a symbol with any UML classifier that designates that classifier as having user-defined semantics. To implement Topic Maps in UML, refer to the stereotypes listed in Table 11-2.

Table 11-2. Conventions for topic mapping in UML

Stereotype	UML context	Meaning
Topic	Class	Represents a topic. It is the default role of a class in our conventions, so this stereotype is optional.
Subject	Class	Designates that the class models a subject indicator. Designate the class as a subject when it is the target of a `subjectIndentityRef`. Specifically, this stereotype disambiguates the `subjectIndicator` that references a published subject indicator rather than a topic or a resource. See *http://www.topicmaps.org/xtm/index.html#elt-subjectIdentity*.
Resource	Class	Designates that the class represents a resource used as the target of a topic-occurrence association.
Base Name	Class	Designates that the class models an alternate topic base name and therefore implies a scope. The scope elements are associated with the `baseName` class via associations with stereotype *scope*.
Occurrence	Association	Designates that the association points to a resource that is an occurrence of the topic.
Scope	Association	Indicates the association that specifies the scope of the topic map characteristic. The nature of the scope depends on the stereotype of the target class (`topicRef`, `resourceRef`, or `subjectIndicatorRef`).
Variant	Generalization Association and Class	Connects to the topic of which it is a variant via a generalization association with stereotype variant. The parameters controlling the variant's applicability are encoded into the class's attributes. The class itself is also given the stereotype, variant to distinguish it from a topic.

In addition to these stereotypes, the following UML-to–Topic Map mappings are used:

UML class
> Is a Models Topic Map topic, unless a non-topic stereotype is present. The class name is used as the topic base name. If the class has an attribute called ID, its default value is used as the topic ID. If no such ID is present, then the class name is also used as the topic ID.

UML association
> Models a Topic Map association unless a stereotype specifies otherwise. The UML association name is the Topic Map association name. The UML role specifiers are the Topic Map role specifiers.

UML instantiates association
> Models the Topic Map `instanceOf` relationship.

Unadorned UML generalization (inheritance) association
> Used as a shortcut to specify the canonical `superclass-subclass` association where the ends are assigned the roles `superclass` and `subclass` automatically. This same relationship links classes with the `baseName` stereotype to the topic classes for which they represent an alternate scoped name. Generalization with the stereotype variant also specifies topic variants.

If you use Rational Rose and it cannot save models as XMI, you should download the Rose add-in at *http://www.rational.com/support/downloadcenter/addins/rose/index.jsp*. I tested only this example with Rose, but other UML tools such as TogetherSoft's Together Control Center also support XMI, and this example will probably work with these tools as well.

The stylesheet that transforms XMI to XTM is shown here. As was the case when you considered transforming XMI in Recipe 10.8, use several entities to make the long element names of XMI manageable:

```
<?xml version="1.0" encoding="UTF-8"?>
<!DOCTYPE xslt [
  <!--=======================================================-->
  <!-- XMI's high level organization constructs    -->
  <!--=======================================================-->
  <!ENTITY FC "Foundation.Core">
  <!ENTITY FX "Foundation.Extension_Mechanisms">
  <!ENTITY FD "Foundation.Data_Types">
  <!ENTITY MM "Model_Management.Model">
  <!ENTITY ME "&FC;.ModelElement">


  <!--=======================================================-->
  <!-- Abbreviations for the basic elements of a XMI -->
  <!-- file that are of most interest to this        -->
  <!-- stylesheet.                                   -->
  <!--=======================================================-->
  <!--Some generic kind of UML element -->
  <!ENTITY ELEM "&FC;.Namespace.ownedElement">
  <!--The association as a whole -->
  <!ENTITY ASSOC "&FC;.Association">
  <!--The connection part of the association-->
  <!ENTITY CONN "&ASSOC;.connection">
  <!--The ends of an association. -->
  <!ENTITY END "&ASSOC;End">
  <!ENTITY CONNEND "&CONN;/&END;">
  <!ENTITY ENDTYPE "&END;.type">
  <!-- A UML class -->
  <!ENTITY CLASS "&FC;.Class">
  <!--The name of some UML entity -->
  <!ENTITY NAME "&FC;.ModelElement.name">
  <!--A UML sterotype -->
  <!ENTITY STEREOTYPE "&ME;.stereotype/&FX;.Stereotype">
  <!--The place where UML documentation is stored in XMI. -->
  <!-- We use for resource data -->
  <!ENTITY TAGGEDVALUE
      "&ME;.taggedValue/&FX;.TaggedValue/&FX;.TaggedValue.value">
  <!-- A Supertype relation (inheritance) -->
  <!ENTITY SUPERTYPE "&FC;.Generalization.supertype">
  <!ENTITY SUBTYPE "&FC;.Generalization.subtype">
  <!ENTITY SUPPLIER "&FC;.Dependency.supplier">
  <!ENTITY CLIENT "&FC;.Dependency.client">
```

```
<!ENTITY DEPENDENCY
    "/XMI/XMI.content/&MM;/&ELEM;/&FC;.Dependency">
<!ENTITY EXPRBODY
    "&FC;.Attribute.initialValue/&FD;.Expression/&FD;.Expression.body">
<!ENTITY ATTR "&CLASS;ifier.feature/&FC;.Attribute">
<!--Used for pointing at standard XTM PSIs -->
<!ENTITY TM.ORG "http://www.topicmaps.org/xtm/index.html">
]>

<xsl:stylesheet version="1.0"
                xmlns:xsl="http://www.w3.org/1999/XSL/Transform"
                xmlns:xtm="http://www.topicmaps.org/xtm/1.0"
                xmlns:xlink="http://www.w3.org/1999/xlink">

<xsl:param name="termOnErr" select="true()"/>

<xsl:output method="xml" version="1.0" encoding="UTF-8" indent="yes"/>
```

Use keys to simplify the identification of stereotypes and traverse UML associations, which use cross references between xmi.id and xmi.idref attributes:

```
<!--Index classes by their name -->
<xsl:key name="classKey" match="&CLASS;" use="@xmi.id"/>
<!-- Index Stereoptypes by both name and xmi.id -->
<xsl:key name="stereotypeKey"
            match="&FX;.Stereotype" use="@xmi.id"/>
<xsl:key name="stereotypeKey"
            match="&FX;.Stereotype" use="&NAME;"/>

<!-- The xmi ids of stereoptypes used to encode topic maps in UML  -->
<!-- We use these as an efficient means for checking if a sterotype-->
<!--  is attached to an element                                    -->

<xsl:variable name="OCCURANCE_ID"
            select="key('stereotypeKey','occurance')/@xmi.id"/>
<xsl:variable name="RESOURCE_ID"
            select="key('stereotypeKey','resource')/@xmi.id"/>
<xsl:variable name="TOPIC_ID"
            select="key('stereotypeKey','topic')/@xmi.id"/>
<xsl:variable name="SUBJECT_ID"
            select="key('stereotypeKey','subject')/@xmi.id"/>
<xsl:variable name="BASENAME_ID"
            select="key('stereotypeKey','baseName')/@xmi.id"/>
<xsl:variable name="SCOPE_ID"
            select="key('stereotypeKey','scope')/@xmi.id"/>
<xsl:variable name="VARIANT_ID"
            select="key('stereotypeKey','variant')/@xmi.id"/>
```

You can convert a XMI UML model to a topic map in two passes. First, import topics from classes, and then import XTM associations from UML associations:

```
<xsl:template match="/">
  <xtm:topicMap>
    <xsl:apply-templates mode="topics"/>
    <xsl:apply-templates mode="associations"/>
```

```
        </xtm:topicMap>
      </xsl:template>
```

The only classes that should be translated into topic are the ones without a stereo-type or with a topic stereotype. The other classes in the model are representations to which a topic can refer, such as subject indicators and resources:

```
<!--==========================================-->
<!-- UML Classes to TOPICS  Translation  -->
<!--==========================================-->

<xsl:template match="&ELEM;/&CLASS;" mode="topics">
  <!-- Topics are modeled as classes whose      -->
  <!-- stereotype is either empty or 'topic'  -->
  <xsl:if test="not(&STEREOTYPE;/@xmi.idref) or
                    &STEREOTYPE;/@xmi.idref = $TOPIC_ID">
    <xsl:variable name="topicId">
      <xsl:call-template name="getTopicId">
        <xsl:with-param name="class" select="."/>
        <xsl:with-param name="prefix" select="''"/>
      </xsl:call-template>
    </xsl:variable>
    <xtm:topic id="{$topicId}">
      <!--This for-each is solely to change context to the optional -->
      <!-- Core.Attribute attribute named 'subjectIdentityid' -->
      <xsl:for-each select="&ATTR;[&NAME; = 'subjectIdentity']">
        <xtm:subjectIdentity>
          <xtm:subjectIdicatorRef xlink:href="{&EXPRBODY;}"/>
        </xtm:subjectIdentity>
      </xsl:for-each>
      <xtm:baseName>
        <xtm:baseNameString>
          <xsl:value-of select="&NAME;"/>
        </xtm:baseNameString>
      </xtm:baseName>
      <xsl:apply-templates select="." mode="getAlternateBaseNames"/>
      <xsl:apply-templates select="." mode="getVariants"/>
      <xsl:apply-templates select="." mode="getInstanceOf">
        <xsl:with-param name="classId" select="@xmi.id"/>
      </xsl:apply-templates>
      <xsl:apply-templates select="." mode="getOccurances"/>
    </xtm:topic>
  </xsl:if>
</xsl:template>

<!-- Return the topic id of a topic class which is its id -->
<!-- attribute value or its name -->
<xsl:template name="getTopicId">
  <xsl:param name="class"/>
  <xsl:param name="prefix" select="'#'"/>
  <xsl:for-each select="$class">
    <xsl:choose>
      <xsl:when test="&ATTR;/&NAME; = 'id' ">
        <xsl:value-of select="&ATTR;[&NAME; = 'id']/&EXPRBODY;"/>
```

```
      </xsl:when>
      <xsl:otherwise>
        <xsl:value-of select="concat($prefix,&NAME;)"/>
      </xsl:otherwise>
    </xsl:choose>
  </xsl:for-each>
</xsl:template>

<!-- Return the subject identity of a subject class which -->
<!-- is its subjectIdentity attribute value or its name -->
<xsl:template name="getSubjectIdentity">
  <xsl:param name="class"/>
  <xsl:for-each select="$class">
    <xsl:choose>
      <xsl:when test="&ATTR;/&NAME; = 'subjectIdentity' ">
        <xsl:value-of select="&ATTR;[&NAME; =
                              'subjectIdentity']&EXPRBODY;"/>
      </xsl:when>
      <xsl:otherwise>
        <xsl:value-of select="concat('#',&NAME;)"/>
      </xsl:otherwise>
    </xsl:choose>
  </xsl:for-each>
</xsl:template>

<!-- Return the resource identity of a resource class which -->
<!-- is either its resourceName attribute or its name -->
<xsl:template name="getResourceIdentity">
  <xsl:param name="class"/>
  <xsl:for-each select="$class">
    <xsl:choose>
      <xsl:when test="&ATTR;/&NAME; = 'resourceName' ">
        <xsl:value-of select="&ATTR;[&NAME; =
                              'resourceName']/&EXPRBODY;"/>
      </xsl:when>
      <xsl:otherwise>
        <xsl:value-of select="concat('#',&NAME;)"/>
      </xsl:otherwise>
    </xsl:choose>
  </xsl:for-each>
</xsl:template>
```

You can model alternate base names and variants as specializations of the base topic class through the UML generalization association. Depending on your point of view, this may seem natural or an abuse of the concept. Nevertheless, it is effective and allows a visual cue in the UML diagram, rather than relying solely on stereotype tags:

```
<!-- Alternate base names are found by traversing UML -->
<!-- generalization relationships and looking for baseName -->
<!-- sterotypes -->

<xsl:template match="&ELEM;/&CLASS;" mode="getAlternateBaseNames">
  <xsl:variable name="xmiId" select="@xmi.id"/>
  <xsl:for-each select="../&FC;.Generalization
                        [&SUPERTYPE;/&CLASS;/@xmi.idref = $xmiId]">
```

```
        <xsl:variable name="subtypeXmiId"
                    select="&FC;.Generalization.subtype/&CLASS;/@xmi.idref"/>
        <xsl:variable name="class" select="key('classKey',$subtypeXmiId)"/>
        <xsl:if test="$class/&STEREOTYPE;/@xmi.idref = $BASENAME_ID">
          <xsl:variable name="name" select="$class/&NAME;"/>
          <xtm:baseName>
            <xsl:call-template name="getScope">
              <xsl:with-param name="class" select="$class"/>
            </xsl:call-template>
            <xtm:baseNameString>
              <xsl:value-of select="substring-after($name,'::')"/>
            </xtm:baseNameString>
          </xtm:baseName>
        </xsl:if>
    </xsl:for-each>
</xsl:template>

<!-- Variants are found by traversing UML -->
<!-- generalization relationships and looking for baseName -->
<!-- sterotypes -->

<xsl:template match="&ELEM;/&CLASS;" mode="getVariants">
  <xsl:variable name="xmiId" select="@xmi.id"/>
  <xsl:for-each select="../&FC;.Generalization
                          [&SUPERTYPE;/&CLASS;/@xmi.idref = $xmiId]">
    <xsl:variable name="subtypeXmiId"
          select="&FC;.Generalization.subtype/&CLASS;/@xmi.idref"/>
    <xsl:variable name="variantClass"
                  select="key('classKey',$subtypeXmiId)"/>
    <xsl:if test="$variantClass/&STEREOTYPE;/@xmi.idref = $VARIANT_ID">
      <xsl:variable name="name" select="$variantClass/&NAME;"/>
      <xtm:variant>
        <xtm:variantName>
          <xsl:call-template name="resourceRep">
            <xsl:with-param name="class" select="$variantClass"/>
          </xsl:call-template>
        </xtm:variantName>
        <xtm:parameters>
          <xsl:call-template name="getVariantParams">
            <xsl:with-param name="class" select="$variantClass"/>
          </xsl:call-template>
        </xtm:parameters>
        <!-- Change context to this variant to get nested variants, -->
        <!-- if any. -->
        <xsl:apply-templates select="$variantClass" mode="getVariants"/>
      </xtm:variant>
    </xsl:if>
  </xsl:for-each>
</xsl:template>

<!-- Gets a variant's parameters from    -->
<!-- the attibutes of the variant class -->
<xsl:template name="getVariantParams">
  <xsl:param name="class"/>
```

```
    <xsl:if test="not($class/&ATTR;)">
      <xsl:message terminate="{$termOnErr}">
      A variant must have at least one parameter.
      </xsl:message>
    </xsl:if>
    <xsl:for-each select="$class/&ATTR;">
      <!-- A parameter is either modeld as a subject indicator  -->
      <!-- or topic ref                                         -->
      <xsl:choose>
        <xsl:when test="&STEREOTYPE;/@xmi.idref = $SUBJECT_ID">
            <xtm:subjectIdicatorRef xlink:href="{&EXPRBODY;}"/>
        </xsl:when>
        <xsl:otherwise>
            <xtm:topicRef  xlink:href="{&EXPRBODY;}"/>
        </xsl:otherwise>
      </xsl:choose>
    </xsl:for-each>
  </xsl:template>
```

Topic Map occurrences are modeled as associations to classes containing resource references or data. Since inline resource data can be too large to fit nicely as an attribute value, this example allows the attribute description to be used as an alternate container of resource data:

```
<!-- Topic map occurances are modeled as associations to -->
  <!-- classes containing resource references or data -->
  <xsl:template match="&ELEM;/&CLASS;" mode="getOccurances">
    <xsl:variable name="xmiId" select="@xmi.id"/>
    <!--Search over the associations this class participates-->
    <xsl:for-each
          select="../&ASSOC;
                      [&CONN;/*/&ENDTYPE;/&CLASS;/@xmi.idref = $xmiId]">
      <!-- Test for the presence of the occurance stereotype -->
      <xsl:if test="&STEREOTYPE;/@xmi.idref = $OCCURANCE_ID">
        <!--Get the id of the resource by looking at the other end -->
        <!-- of the occurance association -->
        <xsl:variable name="resourceId"
                    select="&CONN;/*/&ENDTYPE;/&CLASS;
                                [@xmi.idref != $xmiId]/@xmi.idref"/>
        <!-- Get the class representing the resource -->
        <xsl:variable name="resourceClass"
                    select="key('classKey',$resourceId)"/>
        <xtm:occurance>
          <xsl:apply-templates select="." mode="getInstanceOf">
            <xsl:with-param name="classId" select="$resourceId"/>
          </xsl:apply-templates>
          <!--TODO: Can't model this yet!
            <xsl:call-template name="getScope">
              <xsl:with-param name="class"/>
            </xsl:call-template>
          -->
          <!-- We either have a resource ref or resource data. -->
          <!-- If the class has a  resourceData attribute it   -->
          <!-- is the later.                                    -->
```

```
            <xsl:call-template name="resourceRep">
              <xsl:with-param name="class" select="$resourceClass"/>
            </xsl:call-template>
          </xtm:occurance>
        </xsl:if>
    </xsl:for-each>
</xsl:template>

<!-- This template determines how the resource is represented -->
<xsl:template name="resourceRep">
    <xsl:param name="class" />
    <xsl:variable name="resourceData">
      <!--for-each to change context -->
      <xsl:for-each select="$class/&ATTR;[&NAME; = 'resourceData']">
        <xsl:choose>
          <!--The resource data was encoded in the UML attr -->
          <!--documentation                              -->
          <xsl:when test="&TAGGEDVALUE;">
            <xsl:value-of select="&TAGGEDVALUE;"/>
          </xsl:when>
          <!--The resource data was encoded in the UML attr value -->
          <xsl:otherwise>
            <xsl:value-of select="&EXPRBODY;"/>
          </xsl:otherwise>
        </xsl:choose>
      </xsl:for-each>
    </xsl:variable>
    <!-- if we found some resource data then use it. -->
    <!-- Otherwise assume the user meant this to be a reference -->
    <xsl:choose>
      <xsl:when test="string($resourceData)">
        <xtm:resourceData>
          <xsl:value-of select="$resourceData"/>
        </xtm:resourceData>
      </xsl:when>
      <xsl:otherwise>
        <xsl:variable name="resource">
          <xsl:call-template name="getResourceIdentity">
            <xsl:with-param name="class" select="$class"/>
          </xsl:call-template>
        </xsl:variable>
        <xtm:resourceRef xlink:href="{$resource}"/>
      </xsl:otherwise>
    </xsl:choose>
</xsl:template>
```

XTM instanceOf relationships are modeled as UML *dependency* associations, also called *instantiates*. This representation of instanceOf is quite natural:

```
<!-- This template finds if a topic class has any instanceOf -->
<!-- associations. -->
<xsl:template match="&ELEM;/&CLASS;" mode="getInstanceOf">
  <xsl:param name="classId"/>
  <!-- We loop of dependency relations and determine  -->
```

```
<!-- how the instance is represented-->
<xsl:for-each
        sclcct="&DEPENDENCY;[&CLIENT;/&CLASS;/@xmi.idref = $classId]">
  <xtm:instanceOf>
    <xsl:variable name="instanceClass"
        select="key('classKey',&SUPPLIER;/&CLASS;/@xmi.idref)"/>
    <!-- Figure out if instance is modeled as a subject or a topic -->
    <xsl:variable name="sterotypeId"
                  select="$instanceClass/&STEREOTYPE;/@xmi.idref"/>
    <xsl:choose>
      <!-- This is the case of a subject indicator -->
      <xsl:when test="$sterotypeId = $SUBJECT_ID">
        <xsl:variable name="subjectIdentity">
          <xsl:call-template name="getSubjectIdentity">
            <xsl:with-param name="class" select="$instanceClass"/>
          </xsl:call-template>
        </xsl:variable>
        <xsl:if test="not(normalize-space($subjectIdentity))">
          <xsl:message terminate="{$termOnErr}">
          Subject with no identity!
          </xsl:message>
        </xsl:if>
        <xtm:subjectIdicatorRef xlink:href="{$subjectIdentity}"/>
      </xsl:when>
      <!-- Otheriwse the instance is represented by a topic -->
      <xsl:when test="not($sterotypeId) or $sterotypeId = $TOPIC_ID">
        <xsl:variable name="topicId">
          <xsl:call-template name="getTopicId">
            <xsl:with-param name="class" select="$instanceClass"/>
          </xsl:call-template>
        </xsl:variable>
        <xsl:if test="not(normalize-space($topicId))">
          <xsl:message terminate="{$termOnErr}">
          Topic with no id!
          </xsl:message>
        </xsl:if>
        <topicRef xlink:href="{$topicId}"/>
      </xsl:when>
      <xsl:otherwise>
        <xsl:message terminate="{$termOnErr}">
          <xsl:text>instanceOf must point to a topic or a subject. </xsl:text>
          <xsl:value-of select="$instanceClass/&NAME;"/>
          <xsl:text> is a </xsl:text>
          <xsl:value-of
              select="key('stereotypeKey',$stereotypeId)/&NAME;"/>
          <xsl:text>.&#xa;</xsl:text>
        </xsl:message>
      </xsl:otherwise>
    </xsl:choose>
  </xtm:instanceOf>
</xsl:for-each>
</xsl:template>
```

```
<xsl:template name="getScope">
  <xsl:param name="class"/>
  <xsl:variable name="classesAssociations"
                select="/*/XMI.content/*/&ELEM;
                        /&ASSOC;
                        [&CONN;/*/
                        &FC;.AssociationEnd.type/
                        &CLASS;/@xmi.idref = $class/@xmi.id]"/>
  <xsl:variable name="scopeAssociations"
                select="$classesAssociations[
                        &FC;.ModelElement.stereotype/
                        &FX;.Stereotype/
                        @xmi.idref = $SCOPE_ID]"/>
  <xsl:if test="$scopeAssociations">
    <xtm:scope>
      <xsl:for-each select="$scopeAssociations">
        <xsl:variable name="targetClassId"
            select="&CONN;/*/&ENDTYPE;/&CLASS;
                        [@xmi.idref != $class/@xmi.id]/@xmi.idref"/>
        <xsl:variable name="targetClass"
                      select="key('classKey',$targetClassId)"/>
        <xsl:call-template name="getScopeRef">
          <xsl:with-param name="class" select="$targetClass"/>
        </xsl:call-template>
      </xsl:for-each>
    </xtm:scope>
  </xsl:if>
</xsl:template>

<xsl:template name="getScopeRef">
  <xsl:param name="class"/>
  <xsl:variable name="stereotypeId"
                select="$class/&FC;.ModelElement.stereotype/
                        &FX;.Stereotype/
                        @xmi.idref"/>
  <xsl:choose>
    <xsl:when test="not($stereotypeId) or $stereotypeId = $TOPIC_ID">
      <xsl:variable name="topidId">
        <xsl:call-template name="getTopicId">
          <xsl:with-param name="class" select="$class"/>
        </xsl:call-template>
      </xsl:variable>
      <xtm:topicRef xlink:href="{$topidId}"/>
    </xsl:when>
    <xsl:when test="$stereotypeId = $SUBJECT_ID">
      <xsl:variable name="subjectId">
        <xsl:call-template name="getSubjectIdentity">
          <xsl:with-param name="class" select="$class"/>
        </xsl:call-template>
      </xsl:variable>
      <xtm:subjectIndicatorRef xlink:href="{$subjectId}"/>
    </xsl:when>
    <xsl:when test="$stereotypeId = $RESOURCE_ID">
      <xsl:variable name="resourceId">
```

```
        <xsl:call-template name="getResourceIdentity">
          <xsl:with-param name="class" select="$class"/>
        </xsl:call-template>
      </xsl:variable>
      <xtm:resourceRef xlink:href="{$resourceId}"/>
    </xsl:when>
    <xsl:otherwise>
      <xsl:message terminate="{$termOnErr}">
      A Scope must be either a topicRef, subjectRef or resourceRef!
      </xsl:message>
    </xsl:otherwise>
  </xsl:choose>
</xsl:template>

<xsl:template match="text()" mode="topics"/>

<!--=========================================-->
<!-- UML ASSOCIATION TO TOPIC ASSOCIATIONS -->
<!--=========================================-->
<xsl:template match="&ASSOC;" mode="associations">
  <!-- Only named UML associations are topic map associations -->
  <xsl:if test="normalize-space(&NAME;)">
    <xtm:asociation id="{&NAME;}">
      <xtm:instanceOf>
        <topicRef
          xlink:href="{key('stereotypeKey',
                          &STEREOTYPE;/@xmi.idref)/&NAME;}"/>
      </xtm:instanceOf>
      <xsl:for-each select="&CONNEND;">
        <xtm:member>
          <xtm:roleSpec>
            <xtm:topicRef xlink:href="{&NAME;}"/>
          </xtm:roleSpec>
          <xsl:variable name="topicId">
            <xsl:call-template name="getTopicId">
              <xsl:with-param name="class"
                      select="key('classKey',
                                  &ENDTYPE;/&CLASS;/@xmi.idref)"/>
            </xsl:call-template>
          </xsl:variable>
          <xtm:topicRef xlink:href="{$topicId}"/>
        </xtm:member>
      </xsl:for-each>
    </xtm:asociation>
  </xsl:if>
</xsl:template>

<xsl:template match="&ELEM;/&FC;.Generalization"
              mode="associations">

  <xsl:variable name="subClassId"
              select="&SUBTYPE;/&CLASS;/@xmi.idref"/>
  <xsl:variable name="subClass"
              select="key('classKey',$subClassId)"/>
```

```
<xsl:variable name="superClassId"
              select="&SUPERTYPE;/&CLASS;/@xmi.idref"/>
<xsl:variable name="superClass"
              select="key('classKey',$superClassId)"/>

<!-- If a generalization relation exists from a topic to a -->
<!-- topic we use this as an indication of a canonical      -->
<!-- superclass-subclass relation, Ideally we would use an -->
<!-- absence of a stereotype on the generalization but the -->
<!-- version of XMI I am using is not storing stereotype    -->
<!-- info for generalizations                               -->
<xsl:if test="(not($subClass/&STEREOTYPE;/@xmi.idref) or
                  $subClass/&STEREOTYPE;/@xmi.idref = $TOPIC_ID) and
                  (not($superClass/&STEREOTYPE;/@xmi.idref) or
                  $superClass/&STEREOTYPE;/@xmi.idref = $TOPIC_ID)">

  <xtm:asociation>
    <xsl:variable name="id">
      <xsl:choose>
        <xsl:when test="normalize-space(&NAME;)">
          <xsl:value-of select="&NAME;"/>
        </xsl:when>
        <xsl:otherwise>
          <xsl:value-of select="@xmi.id"/>
        </xsl:otherwise>
      </xsl:choose>
    </xsl:variable>

    <xsl:attribute name="id">
      <xsl:value-of select="$id"/>
    </xsl:attribute>

    <xtm:instanceOf>
      <subjectIndicatorRef
          xlink:href="&TM.ORG;#psi-superclass-subclass"/>
    </xtm:instanceOf>

    <xtm:member>

      <xtm:roleSpec>
        <xtm:subjectIndicatorRef
                          xlink:href="&TM.ORG;#psi-superclass"/>
      </xtm:roleSpec>

      <xsl:variable name="superClassTopicId">
        <xsl:call-template name="getTopicId">
          <xsl:with-param name="class" select="$superClass"/>
        </xsl:call-template>
      </xsl:variable>
      <xtm:topicRef xlink:href="{$superClassTopicId}"/>

    </xtm:member>
```

```
              <xtm:member>
                <xtm:roleSpec>
                  <xtm:subjectIndicatorRef xlink:href="&TM.ORG;#psi-subclass"/>
                </xtm:roleSpec>

                <xsl:variable name="subClassTopicId">
                  <xsl:call-template name="getTopicId">
                    <xsl:with-param name="class" select="$subClass"/>
                  </xsl:call-template>
                </xsl:variable>

                <xtm:topicRef xlink:href="{$subClassTopicId}"/>
              </xtm:member>

            </xtm:asociation>
          </xsl:if>
        </xsl:template>

        <xsl:template match="text()" mode="associations"/>

      </xsl:stylesheet>
```

These templates are part of the second pass in which UML associations not already
handled due to special stereotypes are converted into topic map associations. Here,
the stereotype of an association is the topicRef that determines what kind of association is modeled. The stereotype entry was abused in this way largely because UML
provided no other natural home for this information. Scoped associations a problem
I chose to ignore (see the "Discussion" section). In all other respects, a UML association matches the topic map concept well:

```
<!--===========================================-->
<!-- UML ASSOCIATION TO TOPIC ASSOCIATIONS -->
<!--===========================================-->
<xsl:template match="&ASSOC;" mode="associations">
  <!-- Only named UML associations are topic map associations -->
  <xsl:if test="normalize-space(&NAME;)">
    <xtm:asociation id="{&NAME;}">
      <xtm:instanceOf>
        <topicRef
          xlink:href="{key('stereotypeKey',
                        &STEREOTYPE;/@xmi.idref)/&NAME;}"/>
      </xtm:instanceOf>
      <xsl:for-each select="&CONNEND;">
        <xtm:member>
          <xtm:roleSpec>
            <xtm:topicRef xlink:href="{&NAME;}"/>
          </xtm:roleSpec>
          <xsl:variable name="topicId">
            <xsl:call-template name="getTopicId">
              <xsl:with-param name="class"
                      select="key('classKey',
                                &ENDTYPE;/&CLASS;/@xmi.idref)"/>
            </xsl:call-template>
```

```
        </xsl:variable>
        <xtm:topicRef xlink:href="{$topicId}"/>
      </xtm:member>
    </xsl:for-each>
  </xtm:asociation>
</xsl:if>
</xsl:template>

<xsl:template match="&ELEM;/&FC;.Generalization"
              mode="associations">

  <xsl:variable name="subClassId"
                select="&SUBTYPE;/&CLASS;/@xmi.idref"/>
  <xsl:variable name="subClass"
                select="key('classKey',$subClassId)"/>
  <xsl:variable name="superClassId"
                select="&SUPERTYPE;/&CLASS;/@xmi.idref"/>
  <xsl:variable name="superClass"
                select="key('classKey',$superClassId)"/>
```

If a generalization relation exists from topic to topic, use it as an indication of a canonical superclass-subclass relation. The XTM specification provides explicit support for this important relationship via published subject indicators (PSI). Ideally, you would use an absence of a stereotype on the generalization, but the version of XMI I use does not store stereotype information for generalizations:

```
  <xsl:if test="(not($subClass/&STEREOTYPE;/@xmi.idref) or
                 $subClass/&STEREOTYPE;/@xmi.idref = $TOPIC_ID) and
                (not($superClass/&STEREOTYPE;/@xmi.idref) or
                 $superClass/&STEREOTYPE;/@xmi.idref = $TOPIC_ID)">

    <xtm:asociation>
      <xsl:variable name="id">
        <xsl:choose>
          <xsl:when test="normalize-space(&NAME;)">
            <xsl:value-of select="&NAME;"/>
          </xsl:when>
          <xsl:otherwise>
            <xsl:value-of select="@xmi.id"/>
          </xsl:otherwise>
        </xsl:choose>
      </xsl:variable>

      <xsl:attribute name="id">
        <xsl:value-of select="$id"/>
      </xsl:attribute>

      <xtm:instanceOf>
        <subjectIndicatorRef
           xlink:href="&TM.ORG;#psi-superclass-subclass"/>
      </xtm:instanceOf>
```

```
    <xtm:member>

      <xtm:roleSpec>
        <xtm:subjectIndicatorRef xlink:href="&TM.ORG;#psi-superclass"/>
      </xtm:roleSpec>

      <xsl:variable name="superClassTopicId">
        <xsl:call-template name="getTopicId">
          <xsl:with-param name="class" select="$superClass"/>
        </xsl:call-template>
      </xsl:variable>
      <xtm:topicRef xlink:href="{$superClassTopicId}"/>

    </xtm:member>

    <xtm:member>
      <xtm:roleSpec>
        <xtm:subjectIndicatorRef xlink:href="&TM.ORG;#psi-subclass"/>
      </xtm:roleSpec>

      <xsl:variable name="subClassTopicId">
        <xsl:call-template name="getTopicId">
          <xsl:with-param name="class" select="$subClass"/>
        </xsl:call-template>
      </xsl:variable>

      <xtm:topicRef xlink:href="{$subClassTopicId}"/>
    </xtm:member>

  </xtm:asociation>
 </xsl:if>
</xsl:template>

<xsl:template match="text()" mode="associations"/>

</xsl:stylesheet>
```

Discussion

Topic Maps represent knowledge about real-world subjects. These techniques enable computers and people to find relevant information faster and with greater precision. Topic Maps were first discussed in 1993, when the ideas were first expressed as a Davenport Group working document.[*] The paradigm was extended in the context of the GCA Research Institute (now called the IDEAlliance) in relation to applications of HyTime (*http://www.hytime.org/papers/htguide.html*). The XTM specification was an offshoot of this work, which was organized under the control of an independent organization called TopicMaps.org.

---

[*] The Davenport Group was founded by a Unix System vendor and others, including O'Reilly & Associates.

A topic is an electronic proxy to a real-world subject. Ozzy Osborne is a real world subject; however, since you can't store the real Ozzy in a computer, you create an Ozzy topic as a surrogate. Topics have names called base names. A topic can have one universal name (properly called *unconstrained*) and several other names that are specific to a scope. A scope is a context in which a topic map characteristic is valid. In the case of a topic name, a scope can indicate that the topic *Ozzy Osborne* is also John Michael Osbourne in the *legal* scope.*

A topic can point to an occurrence, which is a resource that supplies information relevant to a topic. A resource might refer to an addressable content (resourceRef) or the content itself (resourceData).

A topic can participate in a special association called instanceOf that declares this topic to be a specific instance of a more general class of objects. The class can be designated by a reference to another topic or to a subject indicator. *Subject Indicators* are an interesting topic map feature. They facilitate a method that specifies the nature of a subject by associating it with a standard published address, such as one maintained by a government standards body.

Topics can be related by associations. An association is a named relationship between two or more topics in which each topic plays a specified role in the association.

Several other interesting topic map facilities model knowledge about subjects. Readers interested in topic maps are encouraged to read the specification of XTM at *http://www.TopicMaps.org*. Compared to other specifications, this one is especially friendly to the uninitiated. Almost all of XTM's functionality is mapped on to some construct in UML (as explained in the "Solution" section). Dealing with the Topic Map notion of scope is this mapping's main difficulty. In the topic map paradigm, a scope is a method specifying that a topic characteristic is only valid in a particular setting. Scope applies to base names, associations, and occurrences. Although these conventions can deal with scope for base names, they cannot currently handle scopes for associations and occurrences. This is because these conventions are modeled as UML associations, and in UML an association is not normally context sensitive. You can model this feature via UML constraints. Alas, the version of XMI that is available for Rational Rose does not capture information on constraints. In practice, scope is an advanced topic map function that many users will not need, so this problem might not be a major liability, especially for novice topic mappers.

Figure 11-2 is an example of a topic map represented in UML. This topic models information about a tomato in the context of a meal. Although the example is somewhat whimsical, I used it because Sam Hunting used the same example in

---

* Unless John Michael legally changed his name to Ozzy, in which case his mom might be the only one who cares about this scope.

XML Topic Maps: Creating and Using Topic Maps for the Web (Addison Wesley, 2002). In this example, he exercised many of the topic map facilities, which allows you to check the resulting XMI's accuracy.

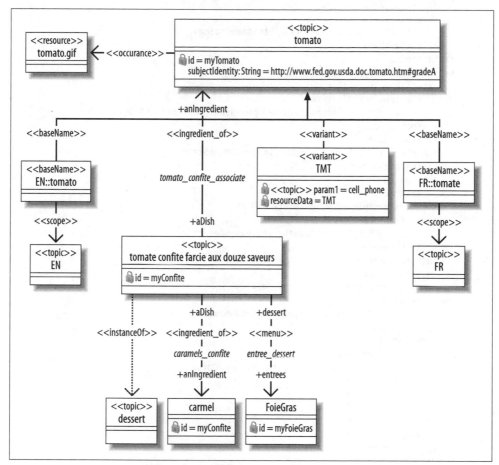

Figure 11-2. UML diagram of a tomato topic map

A portion of the resulting XTM file follows:

```
<xtm:topicMap xmlns:xtm="http://www.topicmaps.org/xtm/1.0" xmlns:xlink="http://www.
w3.org/1999/xlink">
   <xtm:topic id="EN">
      <xtm:subjectIdentity>
         <xtm:subjectIdicatorRef
            xlink:href="http://www.topicmaps.org/xtm/1.0/language.xtm#en"/>
      </xtm:subjectIdentity>
      <xtm:baseName>
         <xtm:baseNameString>EN</xtm:baseNameString>
      </xtm:baseName>
   </xtm:topic>
```

```
<xtm:topic id="FR">
   <xtm:subjectIdentity>
      <xtm:subjectIdicatorRef
          xlink:href="http://www.topicmaps.org/xtm/1.0/language.xtm#fr"/>
   </xtm:subjectIdentity>
   <xtm:baseName>
      <xtm:baseNameString>FR</xtm:baseNameString>
   </xtm:baseName>
</xtm:topic>
<xtm:topic id="myTomato">
   <xtm:subjectIdentity>
      <xtm:subjectIdicatorRef
          xlink:href="http://www.fed.gov/usda/doc/tomato.htm#gradeA"/>
   </xtm:subjectIdentity>
   <xtm:baseName>
      <xtm:baseNameString>tomato</xtm:baseNameString>
   </xtm:baseName>
   <xtm:baseName>
      <xtm:scope>
         <xtm:topicRef xlink:href="#EN"/>
      </xtm:scope>
      <xtm:baseNameString>tomato</xtm:baseNameString>
   </xtm:baseName>
   <xtm:baseName>
      <xtm:scope>
         <xtm:topicRef xlink:href="#FR"/>
      </xtm:scope>
      <xtm:baseNameString>tomate</xtm:baseNameString>
   </xtm:baseName>
   <xtm:variant>
      <xtm:variantName>
         <xtm:resourceData>TMT</xtm:resourceData>
      </xtm:variantName>
      <xtm:parameters>
         <xtm:topicRef xlink:href="cell_phone"/>
         <xtm:topicRef xlink:href="TMT"/>
      </xtm:parameters>
   </xtm:variant>
   <xtm:occurance>
      <xtm:resourceRef xlink:href="#tomato.gif"/>
   </xtm:occurance>
</xtm:topic>
<xtm:topic id="myConfite">
   <xtm:baseName>
      <xtm:baseNameString>tomate confite farcie aux douze saveurs
         </xtm:baseNameString>
   </xtm:baseName>
   <xtm:instanceOf>
      <topicRef xlink:href="#desert"/>
   </xtm:instanceOf>
</xtm:topic>
```

```
<!-- Elided -->

    <xtm:asociation id="tomato_confite_association">
        <xtm:instanceOf>
            <topicRef xlink:href="ingredient_of"/>
        </xtm:instanceOf>
        <xtm:member>
            <xtm:roleSpec>
                <xtm:topicRef xlink:href="anIngredient"/>
            </xtm:roleSpec>
            <xtm:topicRef xlink:href="myTomato"/>
        </xtm:member>
        <xtm:member>
            <xtm:roleSpec>
                <xtm:topicRef xlink:href="aDish"/>
            </xtm:roleSpec>
            <xtm:topicRef xlink:href="myConfite"/>
        </xtm:member>
    </xtm:asociation>
    <xtm:asociation id="caramels_confite">
        <xtm:instanceOf>
            <topicRef xlink:href="ingredient_of"/>
        </xtm:instanceOf>
        <xtm:member>
            <xtm:roleSpec>
                <xtm:topicRef xlink:href="anIngredient"/>
            </xtm:roleSpec>
            <xtm:topicRef xlink:href="myCarmel"/>
        </xtm:member>
        <xtm:member>
            <xtm:roleSpec>
                <xtm:topicRef xlink:href="aDish"/>
            </xtm:roleSpec>
            <xtm:topicRef xlink:href="myConfite"/>
        </xtm:member>
    </xtm:asociation>
    <!-- Elided -->
    </xtm:topicMap>
```

See Also

UML and XMI are standards of the Object Management Group (OMG). More information is available at *http://www.omg.org/uml/* and *http://www.omg.org/technology/xml/index.htm*.

TopicMaps.org (*http://www.topicmaps.org*) is the official site for Topic Map– and XTM-related information.

Recipe 11.4 shows how topic maps generate web sites.

11.4 Generating Web Sites from XTM Topic Maps

Problem

You want to capture knowledge about a subject in a Topic Map. You want to do so in a way that facilitates generation of a web site from the Topic Map using XSLT.

Solution

The solution is based on the Cogitative Topic Maps Web Site (CTW) framework introduced to readers in *XML Topic Maps*, edited by Jack Park (Addison Wesley, 2002). Extreme Markup Languages initially presented this work in 2000.

Readers unfamiliar with Topic Maps may want to read the "Discussion" in Recipe 11.3 first or refer to the "See Also" section of 11.3 and this recipe for more resources.

The CTW uses the following mapping from topic map elements to HTML:

Topic map element	HTML rendering
Topic map	Web site
Topic	Web page
Topic associations	Site map
Topic occurrences	Images, graphics, text, HTML fragments, etc.
Topic names	Page Headers, Titles, Lists, and Hyperlink titles

The Topic Map we create covers the subject of algorithms and, specifically, sorting algorithms. Knowledge represented in this topic map was aggregated from information resources gathered on the Internet and organized as class-subclass associations between algorithms and occurrences of types descriptions, demonstrations, and code examples in several programming languages.

Once the subject and content of the web site were decided, the ontology of the web site subjects and objects followed quite naturally. The CTW ontology layer consists of two main parts: classification of web site's topic subjects and classification of topic characteristics that provide web-page content.

Both classifications play a very important role in controlling a web site's look and feel. Topic types control web-page layouts, and types of topic characteristics control the styling of web-page elements and building blocks. The results are depicted in Figure 11-3.

The following subsections describe the subjects of the Sorting Algorithms web site.

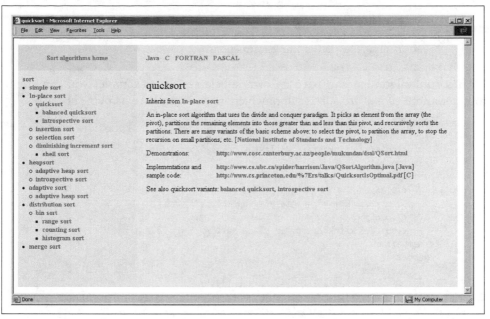

Figure 11-3. The look and feel of a generated site

Sorting algorithms

The main subjects of our web site are the sorting algorithm's various subclasses:

```
<topic id="sort">
    ...
</topic>
<association>
    <instanceOf>
        <topicRef xlink:href="#_class-subclass"/>
    </instanceOf>
    <member>
        <roleSpec>
            <topicRef xlink:href="#_superclass"/>
        </roleSpec>
        <topicRef xlink:href="#sort"/>
    </member>
    <member>
        <roleSpec>
            <topicRef xlink:href="#_subclass"/>
        </roleSpec>
        <topicRef xlink:href="#simplesort"/>
        <topicRef xlink:href="#in-place sort"/>
        <topicRef xlink:href="#heapsort"/>
        <topicRef xlink:href="#adaptivesort"/>
        <topicRef xlink:href="#distributionsort"/>
        <topicRef xlink:href="#mergesort"/>
    </member>
</association>
```

The full version of the topic map and XSLT scripts is available online at *http://www.cogx.com/ctw*. This section provides only some fragments to illustrate example instructions.

Each sorting algorithm can have its own subclasses—for example, you can count four variations of *in-place-sort*, each of which may in turn have its own subclasses:

```
<association>
    <instanceOf>
        <topicRef xlink:href="#_class-subclass"/>
    </instanceOf>
    <member>
        <roleSpec>
            <topicRef xlink:href="#_superclass"/>
        </roleSpec>
        <topicRef xlink:href="#in-place sort"/>
    </member>
    <member>
        <roleSpec>
            <topicRef xlink:href="#_subclass"/>
        </roleSpec>
        <topicRef xlink:href="#quicksort"/>
        <topicRef xlink:href="#insertionsort"/>
        <topicRef xlink:href="#selsort"/>
        <topicRef xlink:href="#dimincrsort"/>
    </member>
</association>
```

The National Institute of Standards and Technology (NIST) maintains an excellent web site on algorithms (*http://www.nist.gov/dads/*) and collects information about various computational algorithms. It maintains a web page devoted to each algorithm. This topic map uses URLs of those pages as algorithm subject identifiers of algorithms:

```
<topic id="insertionsort">
    <subjectIdentity>
        <subjectIndicatorRef
            xlink:href="http://www.nist.gov/dads/HTML/insertsrt.html"/>
    </subjectIdentity>
```

Besides playing roles in class-subclass associations with other algorithms, sorting algorithms have other topic characteristics such as base names and occurrences.

In this topic map, sorting algorithms have names under which they are commonly recognized:

```
<baseName>
    <baseNameString>insertion sort</baseNameString>
</baseName>
```

Sometimes they also have alternative names represented as base names in the also-known-as scope:

```
<baseName>
    <scope>
        <topicRef xlink:href="#also-known-as"/>
    </scope>
    <baseNameString>linear insertion sort</baseNameString>
</baseName>
```

The algorithm's description is represented as a topic occurrence of type description in the scope of the description's source. The following code is a citation from the National Institute of Standards and Technology web site (thus specified in the scope of the nist topic) that can also read, "In the context of NIST, insertion sort is described as..."

```
<occurrence>
    <instanceOf>
        <topicRef xlink:href="#description"/>
    </instanceOf>
    <scope>
        <topicRef xlink:href="#nist"/>
    </scope>
    <resourceData>Sort by repeatedly taking the next item and inserting it into
    the final data structure in its proper order with respect to items already
    inserted. </resourceData>
</occurrence>
```

Links to algorithm demonstrations such as applets and animations are represented as topic occurrences of type demonstration:

```
<occurrence>
    <instanceOf>
        <topicRef xlink:href="#demo"/>
    </instanceOf>
    <resourceRef xlink:href=
    "http://www.cosc.canterbury.ac.nz/people/mukundan/dsal/ISort.html"/>
</occurrence>
```

You can also record links to sorting algorithms implementations and represent them in your topic map as occurrences of type code sample specified in the scope of a programming language in which they are implemented. Programming languages is the other class of topics represented on your web site that constitute an orthogonal navigational dimension:

```
<occurrence>
    <instanceOf>
        <topicRef xlink:href="#code"/>
    </instanceOf>
    <scope>
        <topicRef xlink:href="#fortran"/>
    </scope>
    <resourceRef
    xlink:href="http://gams.nist.gov/serve.cgi/Module/TOMS/505/8547"/>
</occurrence>
```

```
        <occurrence>
            <instanceOf>
                <topicRef xlink:href="#code"/>
            </instanceOf>
            <scope>
                <topicRef xlink:href="#java"/>
            </scope>
            <resourceRef xlink:href=
            "http://www.cs.ubc.ca/spider/harrison/Java/InsertionSortAlgorithm.java"/>
        </occurrence>
    </topic>
```

That is all the information about algorithms that we chose to represent. You will use it to build page headers, links to related algorithms, descriptions, links to pages on the Web defining that algorithm, links to algorithm demonstrations, and code samples with cross links to programming languages in which these examples are implemented.

Programming languages

You only need be interested in the fact that program languages are, in their names and definitions, instances of the programming language class:

```
<topic id="java">
    <subjectIdentity>
        <subjectIndicatorRef
        xlink:href="http://foldoc.doc.ic.ac.uk/foldoc/foldoc.cgi?query=java"/>
    </subjectIdentity>
    <instanceOf>
        <topicRef xlink:href="#plang"/>
    </instanceOf>
    <baseName>
        <baseNameString>Java</baseNameString>
    </baseName>
    <occurrence>
        <instanceOf>
            <topicRef xlink:href="#definition"/>
        </instanceOf>
        <scope>
            <topicRef xlink:href="#cnet"/>
        </scope>
        <resourceData>Sun Microsystems' Java is a programming language for adding
animation and other action to Web sites. The small applications (called applets) that
Java creates can play back on any graphical system that's Web-ready, but your Web
browser has to be Java-capable for you to see it. According to Sun's description,
Java is a "simple, object-oriented, distributed, interpreted, robust, secure,
architecture-neutral, portable, high-performance, multithreaded, dynamic, buzzword-
compliant, general-purpose programming language." </resourceData>
    </occurrence>
</topic>
```

The programming language page shown in Figure 11-4 gathers links to code samples implemented in that language and cross links to the implemented algorithms.

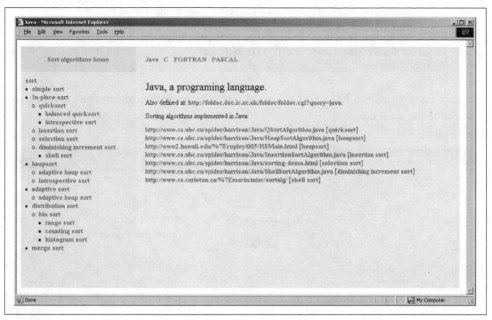

Figure 11-4. Programming languages page

Root topic

In the CTW framework, root is the topic whose subject is indicated by the topic map document itself. In topic map terms, root topic reifies the topic map document to which it belongs:

```
<topic id="default">
    <subjectIdentity>
        <subjectIndicatorRef xlink:href="#map"/>
    </subjectIdentity>
```

When topic maps merge in CTW, this topic is added to the scopes of all topic characteristic assignments. More importantly, this topic corresponds to the home or default page of the CTW web site.

This example displays its hyperlinked name in the upper-left corner of all pages on your web site:

```
<baseName>
    <baseNameString>Sort algorithms home</baseNameString>
</baseName>
```

This is the place to store topic map annotations and assertions about the topic map. This example is limited to the description of project and copyright metadata:

```
<occurrence>
    <instanceOf>
        <topicRef xlink:href="#definition"/>
    </instanceOf>
```

```
        <resourceData><![CDATA[ This web site covers the subject of
        algorithms and specifically sorting algorithms.<br><br>
        It was created for the purposes of a CTW recipe for the
        O'Reilly XSLT Cookbook.]]> </resourceData>
    </occurrence>
</topic>
```

The root page shown in Figure 11-5 shows only the project's description as an introduction to the web site.

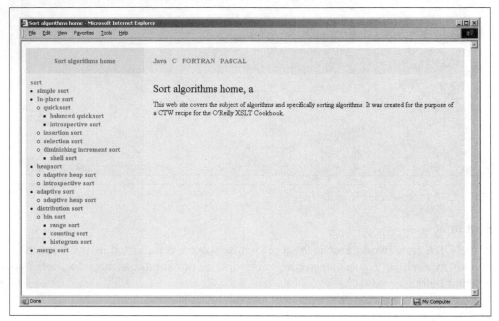

Figure 11-5. Root page of the sort algorithms web site

Page elements and layout

First, define the root variable that represents the root topic: as described earlier, this
topic is indicated by the containing topic map document:

```
<xsl:variable name="root"
    select="//topic[subjectIdentity/subjectIndicatorRef/@xlink:href
                                    = concat('#',/topicMap/@id)]"/>
```

The same node could be matched using the subjectIndicator key that matches topics using addresses of resources that indicate them:

```
<xsl:key
    name = "subjectIndicator"
    match = "topic"
    use = "subjectIdentity/subjectIndicatorRef/@xlink:href" />

<xsl:variable name="root"
            select="key('subjectIndicator',concat('#',/topicMap/@id))"/>
```

First, generate the default page by calling the root-page layout template for the root topic:

```
<xsl:template match="/">
    <xsl:call-template name="root-page">
        <xsl:with-param name="this" select="$root"/>
    </xsl:call-template>
```

Next, the code generates web pages for every subclass of the sorting algorithm. Here you call the algorithm-page layout template with basic sorting algorithm as *this* parameter. The template recursively calls itself to iterate over subclasses of all subclasses:

```
<xsl:call-template name="algorithm-page">
    <xsl:with-param name="this" select="key('topicByID','#sort')"/>
</xsl:call-template>
```

The stylesheet generates pages for every instance of a programming language by calling the lang-page layout template:

```
<xsl:for-each select="key('instanceOf','#plang')">
    <xsl:call-template name="plang-page"/>
</xsl:for-each>
</xsl:template>
```

The instanceOf key returns all topic instances of a class based on the class topic's hashed IDs:

```
<xsl:key
  name = "instanceOf"
  match = "topic"
  use = "instanceOf/topicRef/@xlink:href" />
```

The topicByID key returns all topic elements based on a given topic's hashed IDs:

```
<xsl:key
  name = "instanceOf"
  match = "topic"
  use = "instanceOf/topicRef/@xlink:href" />
```

As you might have noticed in the screenshots, all three layout templates have a common subdivision into four square areas. The common main page-building template controls this. First, instruct the processor to create an output file relative to the output folder specified in the $out-dir parameter, and create the TITLE header with the current topic's base name in the unconstrained scope. The latter is achieved by instantiating template matching <topic> elements in the label mode. Then start the page's subdivision into four parts. In the upper-right corner, create a hyperlink to the home page whose label is the name of root topic in the unconstraint scope. The topic-matching template in the link mode accomplishes this task. In the upper-right part of the page, you'll have a selection of links to programming languages pages. Iterating over all instances of programming-language topic creates this. In the lower-left quarter of the page under the home page link, print the part of the site map corresponding to the sorting algorithms' classification. Finally, in the main part of the page in the lower-right quarter, output the main-page content pertinent to the current topic submitted to the page template as content parameter:

```
<xsl:template name="page">
  <xsl:param name="this"/>
  <xsl:param name="content"/>
  <redirect:write select="concat($out-dir,$this/@id,'.html')">
  <HTML>
    <HEADER>
      <TITLE>
        <xsl:apply-templates select="$this" mode="label"/>
      </TITLE>
    </HEADER>
    <BODY>
    <table width="1000" height="100%" cellspacing="0" cellpadding="10">
    <tr>
      <td width="250" height="20" bgcolor="#ffddbb" align="center">
        <xsl:apply-templates select="$root" mode="link"/>
      </td>
      <td width="750" height="20" valign="top" bgcolor="#eeeeee">
        <table cellspacing="10">
          <tr>
            <xsl:for-each select="key('instanceOf','#plang')">
              <td background="grey">
                <xsl:apply-templates select="." mode="link"/>
              </td>
            </xsl:for-each>
          </tr>
        </table>
      </td>
    </tr>
    <tr>
      <td valign="top" bgcolor="#eeeeee">
        <xsl:call-template name="sitemap">
          <xsl:with-param name="classRef">#sort</xsl:with-param>
          <xsl:with-param name="current" select="$this/@id"/>
        </xsl:call-template>
      </td>
      <td valign="top" bgcolor="#ffeedd" >
       <xsl:copy-of select="$content"/>
      </td>
    </tr></table>
    </BODY>
  </HTML>
  </redirect:write>
</xsl:template>
```

The previous template uses the baseName-matching template in the label mode:

```
<xsl:template match="topic" mode="label">
    <xsl:value-of select="baseName[not(scope)]/baseNameString"/>
</xsl:template>
```

The `baseName` matching template in the `link` mode creates a hyperlink to the topic's web page:

```
<xsl:template match="topic" mode="link">
  <a href="{@id}.html">
    <xsl:value-of select="baseName[not(scope)]/baseNameString"/>
  </a>
</xsl:template>
```

Later in the code, you will use the `baseName`-matching template in the `subject-indicator` mode. This template creates a hyperlink to a resource indicating the matched topic:

```
<xsl:template match="topic" mode="indicator">
  <a href="{subjectIdentity/subjectIndicatorRef/@xlink:href}">
    <xsl:value-of select="baseName[not(scope)]/baseNameString"/>
  </a>
</xsl:template>
```

The `sitemap` template iterates over all subclasses of the sort topic, creates hyperlinks to pages corresponding to derived algorithms, and recursively calls itself to iterate over subclasses of the subclasses:

```
<xsl:template name="sitemap">
  <xsl:param name="classRef"/>
  <xsl:param name="current"/>
  <xsl:variable name="topic" select="key('topicByID',$classRef)"/>
  <xsl:choose>
    <xsl:when test="$topic/@id=$current">
      <span class="A">
       <xsl:apply-templates select="$topic" mode="label"/>
      </span>
    </xsl:when>
    <xsl:otherwise>
      <xsl:apply-templates select="$topic" mode="link"/>
    </xsl:otherwise>
  </xsl:choose>
  <xsl:variable name="aref" select="key('classAssoc',$classRef)"/>
  <xsl:if test="$aref">
    <ul>
      <xsl:for-each
          select="$aref/member
                    [roleSpec/topicRef/@xlink:href=
                     '#_subclass']/topicRef">
        <li>
        <xsl:call-template name="sitemap">
          <xsl:with-param name="classRef" select="@xlink:href"/>
          <xsl:with-param name="current" select="$current"/>
        </xsl:call-template>
        </li>
      </xsl:for-each>
    </ul>
  </xsl:if>
</xsl:template>
```

The classRef key used by the site map template uses the ID of a given topic to match superclass-subclass associations for which the topic plays super-class role:

```
<xsl:key
  name = "classAssoc"
  match = "association[instanceOf/topicRef/@xlink:href=
                        '#_class-subclass']"
  use = "member[roleSpec/topicRef/@xlink:href=
              '#_superclass']/topicRef/@xlink:href" />
```

Later in the code, you will use a subClassRef key that also matches superclass-subclass associations, but this time using member where the topic plays sub-class role:

```
<xsl:key
  name = "subClassAssoc"
  match = "association[instanceOf/topicRef/@xlink:href=
                        '#_class-subclass']"
  use = "member[roleSpec/topicRef/@xlink:href=
              '#_subclass']/topicRef/@xlink:href" />
```

Now you are ready to consider the three layout templates.

The root-page layout template is very simple. Call the page template described earlier and send it the generated HTML code for occurrences of type description in the content parameter:

```
<xsl:template name="root-page">
  <xsl:param name="this"/>
  <xsl:call-template name="page">
    <xsl:with-param name="this" select="$this"/>
    <xsl:with-param name="content">
      <font size="+1">
        <xsl:apply-templates
            select="$this/occurrence
                      [instanceOf/topicRef/@xlink:href='#description']"/>
      </font>
    </xsl:with-param>
  </xsl:call-template>
</xsl:template>
```

The plang-page layout template is a bit more involved. It has a title composed of the name of the current topic followed by the name of topic's type. Then a subject identity line points to a place elsewhere on the Web where the topic's subject is defined. Following it are topic descriptions, if any. Iterate and output a link for each code occurrence implemented in the current language. In square brackets following the resource, place a link to the sorting algorithm implemented in this resource:

```
<xsl:template name="plang-page">
  <xsl:param name="this" select="."/>
  <xsl:call-template name="page">
    <xsl:with-param name="this" select="$this"/>
    <xsl:with-param name="content">
      <font size="+2">
```

```
    <xsl:apply-templates select="$this" mode="label"/>, a
    <xsl:apply-templates mode="label"
  select="key('topicByID',$this/instanceOf/topicRef/@xlink:href)" />.
  </font>
  <br/><br/>
  <xsl:apply-templates select="$this/subjectIdentity"/>
  <xsl:apply-templates
  select="$this/occurrence
                    [instanceOf/topicRef/@xlink:href='#description']"/>
  <xsl:variable name="codes"
    select="key('plang-codes',concat('#',$this/@id))"/>
  <xsl:if test="$codes">
    <span>Sorting algorithms implemented in
      <xsl:apply-templates select="$this" mode="label"/>:</span>
    <ul>
      <xsl:for-each select="$codes">
        <li>
          <a href="{resourceRef/@xlink:href}">
              <xsl:value-of select="resourceRef/@xlink:href"/>
          </a>
          [<xsl:apply-templates select=".." mode="link"/>]<br/>
        </li>
      </xsl:for-each>
    </ul>
    <br/><br/>
  </xsl:if>
  </xsl:with-param>
  </xsl:call-template>
</xsl:template>
```

The plang-codes key used earlier matches all occurrences in the topic map by any of their scope themes:

```
<xsl:key
 name="plang-codes"
 match="occurrence"
 use="scope/topicRef/@xlink:href"/>
```

The algorithm-page layout template comes last. Its title is composed of the current topic's name followed by also-known-as names in square brackets. The subject identity line is followed by the list of superclasses, if any, from which the current sorting algorithm inherits. Then you'll find one or more sorting algorithm descriptions, followed by the list of links to algorithm demonstration occurrences and the list of code samples with cross links to implementing programming languages in square brackets. On the bottom of the page, you'll list subclasses or variations, if any, of the current sorting algorithm. Finally, the algorithm-page layout template calls itself recursively to output pages for subclasses of all its subclasses:

```
<xsl:template name="algorithm-page">
  <xsl:param name="this"/>
  <xsl:call-template name="page">
    <xsl:with-param name="this" select="$this"/>
    <xsl:with-param name="content">
```

```
<font size="+2"><xsl:apply-templates select="$this" mode="label"/>
  <xsl:if test="$this/baseName
                      [scope/topicRef/@xlink:href='#also-known-as']">
    [<xsl:value-of select="$this/baseName
      [scope/topicRef/@xlink:href='#also-known-as']
      /baseNameString"/>]
  </xsl:if>
</font>
<br/><br/>
<xsl:apply-templates select="$this/subjectIdentity"/>
<xsl:variable name="superclasses"
  select="key('subClassAssoc',concat('#',$this/@id))
  member[roleSpec/topicRef/@xlink:href='#_superclass']/topicRef"/>
<xsl:if test="$superclasses">
  Inherits from
  <xsl:for-each select="$superclasses">
    <xsl:apply-templates
      select="key('topicByID',@xlink:href)" mode="link"/>
      <xsl:if test="position() != last()">, </xsl:if>
  </xsl:for-each>
  <br/><br/>
</xsl:if>
<xsl:apply-templates
  select="$this/occurrence
                 [instanceOf/topicRef/@xlink:href='#description']"/>
<xsl:variable name="demos"
   select="$this/occurrence
                 [instanceOf/topicRef/@xlink:href='#demo']"/>
<xsl:if test="$demos">
  <span>Demonstrations: </span>
  <ul>
    <xsl:for-each select="$demos">
      <li>
        <a href="{resourceRef/@xlink:href}"><
         xsl:value-of select="resourceRef/@xlink:href"/>
        </a><br/>
      </li>
    </xsl:for-each>
  </ul>
  <br/>
</xsl:if>
<xsl:variable name="codes"
   select="$this/occurrence[instanceOf/topicRef/@xlink:href='#code']"/>
<xsl:if test="$codes">
  <span>Implementations and sample code: </span>
  <ul>
    <xsl:for-each select="$codes">
      <li>
        <a href="{resourceRef/@xlink:href}">
          <xsl:value-of select="resourceRef/@xlink:href"/>
        </a>
        [<xsl:apply-templates mode="link"
         select="key('topicByID',scope/topicRef/@xlink:href)"/>]
      </li>
```

```
        </xsl:for-each>
      </ul>
      <br/>
    </xsl:if>
    <xsl:variable name="subclasses"
        select="key('classAssoc',
                    concat('#',$this/@id))/member
                                [roleSpec/topicRef/@xlink:href=
                                '#_subclass']/topicRef"/>
      <xsl:if test="$subclasses">
        See also
        <xsl:value-of select="$this/baseName[not(scope)]/baseNameString"/>
        variants:
        <xsl:for-each select="$subclasses">
          <xsl:apply-templates
              select="key('topicByID',@xlink:href)" mode="link"/>
          <xsl:if test="position() != last()">, </xsl:if>
        </xsl:for-each>
      </xsl:if>
    </xsl:with-param>
  </xsl:call-template>
  <xsl:variable name="aref"
              select="key('classAssoc',concat('#',$this/@id))"/>
  <xsl:for-each
    select="$aref/member
            [roleSpec/topicRef/@xlink:href='#_subclass']/topicRef">
    <xsl:call-template name="algorithm-page">
      <xsl:with-param name="this" select="key('topicByID',@xlink:href)"/>
    </xsl:call-template>
  </xsl:for-each>
</xsl:template>
```

Discussion

Topic Maps is a technology that accumulates and manages knowledge about real-world domains. In this case, you represented relationships between algorithms and other objects and resources. If you are careful to follow the conventions of CTW, you'll be able to drive the creation of a web site from the topic map source.

In this solution, you were limited to just a few types of objects and relationships between them. Real-life applications are much more complicated. The main idea was to demonstrate the power and tremendous opportunities provided by the CTW framework.

In the CTW framework, a single topic map document controls both the content and structure of an entire web site. Proper CTW topic map architecture provides robust and intuitive maintenance of links between web pages, web-page content, and meta-data. Web sites built according to CTW are easily merged and immune to dead links. XSLT offers a consistent look and feel, platform independence, and reusability.

You do have to pay to get all these benefits: the CTW framework requires you to think of your content in terms of topics, topic characteristics, and associations. This approach limits you to creating content only in the limits of the chosen ontology, but it helps keep the knowledge represented on the web site well organized and navigable.

XSLT enables the CTW because it provides a modular and maintainable means to transform and stylize the knowledge contained in the topic map. Dynamic CTW solutions created with XSLT scale up to several thousand topics, and static solutions are limited only by the available disk space.

See Also

XML Topic Maps: Creating and Using Topic Maps for the Web, edited by Jack Park, (Addison Wesley, 2002) is an excellent book that covers both the theory and application of topic maps in a very accessible manner.

You can find a good collection of links to resources about topic maps at *http://www. dmoz.org/Computers/Artificial_Intelligence/Knowledge_Representation/Topic_Maps/*.

The author maintains a site at *http://www.cogx.com/ctw* that further discusses topic maps and the cogitative topic maps framework. Slides from the Extreme Markup Languages presentation of CTW are available at *http://www.cogx.com/Extreme2000/*.

11.5   Serving SOAP Documentation from WSDL

Problem

You are using SOAP and WSDL to build a service-based enterprise architecture. You want developers to be able to find complete and pertinent information on available services.

Solution

This solution constructs a WSDL-based service documentation server: a service that provides information about services.* This example will use a Perl-based CGI that invokes XSLT processing on a single WSDL file containing or including information about all services available in an enterprise. Here the CGI invokes the XSLT processor in a `system` call. This clumsy setup is good for prototyping but not production use. A better solution would use the Perl modules `XML::LibXML` and `XML::LibXSLT`. An even better architecture would use a more sophisticated server-side XSLT-enabled

---

* A metaservice, if you will.

solution such as Cocoon. To focus on the XSLT and WSDL aspects of this example, and not the CGI architecture, we took a simplistic approach.

The site's main page is generated by a CGI that shows the user available services and ports. See the discussion for explanations of services and ports. It uses the following Perl CGI frontend to Saxon:

```
#!c:/perl/bin/perl
print "Content-type: text/html\n\n" ;
system "saxon StockServices.wsdl wsdlServiceList.xslt" ;
```

The transformation builds a form containing all available services, ports, bindings, and port types:

```
<?xml version="1.0" encoding="UTF-8"?>
<xsl:stylesheet
    version="1.0"
    xmlns:xsl="http://www.w3.org/1999/XSL/Transform"
    xmlns:wsdl="http://schemas.xmlsoap.org/wsdl/"
    xmlns:soap="http://schemas.xmlsoap.org/wsdl/soap/"
    xmlns:http="http://schemas.xmlsoap.org/wsdl/http/"
    xmlns:mime="http://schemas.xmlsoap.org/wsdl/mime/"
    exclude-result-prefixes="wsdl soap http mime">

  <xsl:output method="html"/>

  <xsl:template match="/">
     <html>
     <head>
       <title>Available Services at ACME Web Services, Inc.</title>
       <xsl:comment>WSDL Documentation: Generated by wsdlServiceList.xslt
       </xsl:comment>
     </head>
     <body>
       <xsl:apply-templates/>
     </body>
     </html>

  </xsl:template>

  <xsl:template match="wsdl:definitions">
    <h1>Available Services at ACME Web Services, Inc.</h1>
    <br/>
    <form name="QueryServiceForm" method="post" action="QueryService.pl">
    <table>
      <tbody>
        <tr>
          <td>Services</td>
          <td>
            <select name="service">
              <option value="ALL">ALL</option>
              <xsl:apply-templates select="wsdl:service"/>
            </select>
          </td>
        </tr>
```

```
        <tr>
         <td>Ports</td>
         <td>
           <select name="port">
             <option value="ALL">ALL</option>
             <xsl:apply-templates select="wsdl:service/wsdl:port"/>
           </select>
         </td>
        </tr>
         <tr>
         <td>Bindings</td>
         <td>
           <select name="binding">
             <option value="ALL">ALL</option>
             <xsl:apply-templates select="wsdl:binding"/>
           </select>
         </td>
        </tr>
         <tr>
         <td>Port Types</td>
         <td>
           <select name="portType">
             <option value="ALL">ALL</option>
             <xsl:apply-templates select="wsdl:portType"/>
           </select>
         </td>
        </tr>
       </tbody>
      </table>
      <br/>
      <button type="submit" name="submit">Query Services</button>
      </form>
    </xsl:template>

  <xsl:template match="wsdl:service | wsdl:port | wsdl:binding | wsdl:portType">
    <option value="{@name}"><xsl:value-of select="@name"/></option>
  </xsl:template>

  </xsl:stylesheet>
```

Users can select a combination of service, port, bind, and port type on which they want more detailed information. When submitted, another small Perl CGI extracts the input and invokes another XSLT transform:

```
#!/perl/bin/perl

use warnings;

use strict;
use CGI qw(:standard);

my $query = new CGI ;
```

```perl
my $service = $query->param('service');
my $port = $query->param('port');
my $binding = $query->param('binding');
my $portType = $query->param('portType');

print $query->header('text/html');

system "saxon StockServices.wsdl QueryService.xslt service=$service port=$port
binding=$binding portType=$portType"
```

This transformation extracts the services that match the user's criteria and displays
detailed information about the service. The first part of the stylesheet normalizes
some parameters. It does so because an attribute reference in a WSDL file could contain a namespace prefix, but the @name attribute of the element it references does not.
The same reasoning applies to key construction:

```xml
<?xml version="1.0" encoding="UTF-8"?>
<!DOCTYPE xslt [
  <!ENTITY TNSPREFIX "'acme:'">
]>
<xsl:stylesheet
     version="1.0"
     xmlns:xsl="http://www.w3.org/1999/XSL/Transform"
     xmlns:xsd="http://www.w3.org/2000/10/XMLSchema"
     xmlns:wsdl="http://schemas.xmlsoap.org/wsdl/"
     xmlns:soap="http://schemas.xmlsoap.org/wsdl/soap/"
     xmlns:http="http://schemas.xmlsoap.org/wsdl/http/"
     xmlns:mime="http://schemas.xmlsoap.org/wsdl/mime/">

<!--Query parameters -->
<xsl:param name="service" select="'ALL'"/>
<xsl:param name="port" select="'ALL'"/>
<xsl:param name="binding" select="'ALL'"/>
<xsl:param name="portType" select="'ALL'"/>

<!-- A technique (or a hack) to make variables empty   -->
<!-- if the corrsponding parameter is ALL or otherwise -->
<!-- the concatenation of &TNSPREFIX and the paramter  -->
<!-- For example, number($service = 'ALL') * 99999 + 1 -->
<!-- will be 1 if $service is not equal to 'ALL' but    -->
<!-- 100000 if it is and hence beyond the lenght of the-->
<!-- string which causes substring to return empty      -->
<!-- This is all to simplify cross-referencing.         -->
<xsl:variable name="serviceRef"
              select="substring(concat(&TNSPREFIX;,$service),
                                number($service = 'ALL') * 99999 + 1)"/>
<xsl:variable name="portRef"
              select="substring(concat(&TNSPREFIX;,$port),
                                number($port = 'ALL') * 99999 + 1)"/>
<xsl:variable name="bindingRef"
              select="substring(concat(&TNSPREFIX;,$binding),
                                number($binding = 'ALL') * 99999 + 1)"/>
```

```
<xsl:variable name="portTypeRef"
              select="substring(concat(&TNSPREFIX;,$portType),
                                number($portType = 'ALL') * 99999 + 1)"/>

<!-- These keys simplify and speed up querying -->
<xsl:key name="bindings_key"
         match="wsdl:binding" use="concat(&TNSPREFIX;,@name)"/>
<xsl:key name="portType_key"
         match="wsdl:portType" use="concat(&TNSPREFIX;,@name)"/>

<xsl:output method="html"/>

  <xsl:template match="/">
      <html>
      <head>
        <title>ACME Web Services, Inc. Query Result</title>
        <xsl:comment>WSDL Documentation: Generated by wsdlServiceList.xslt
        </xsl:comment>
      </head>
      <body>
        <xsl:apply-templates select="wsdl:definitions"/>
      </body>
    </html>
</xsl:template>
```

Here you simplify the problem of determining whether the query found matching
services by capturing the result in a variable and testing its normalized value. If it is
empty, then you know the query failed, and it displays an appropriate message. The
query is a little tricky because the service's portType can be determined only by making two hops from the service to its binding and then to the binding's port type:

```
<xsl:template match="wsdl:definitions">
    <xsl:variable name="result">
        <!-- Query services that match the query parameters        -->
        <!-- The portType match is the only complicated part        -->
        <!-- We need to traverse form the service's port, to the binding-->
        <!-- and then to the binding's type to do the match. Hence   -->
        <!-- the nested key( ) calls                                -->
        <xsl:apply-templates
            select="wsdl:service[
                    (not($serviceRef)  or @name = $service) and
                    (not($portRef)     or wsdl:port/@name = $port) and
                    (not($bindingRef)  or wsdl:port/@binding = $bindingRef)
                    and
                    (not($portTypeRef) or key('portType_key',
                                             key('bindings_key',
                                               wsdl:port/@binding)/@type)
                                                 /@name = $portType)]"/>
    </xsl:variable>
    <xsl:choose>
      <xsl:when test="normalize-space($result)">
        <xsl:copy-of select="$result"/>
      </xsl:when>
```

```
    <xsl:otherwise>
      <p><b>No Matching Services Found</b></p>
    </xsl:otherwise>
  </xsl:choose>
</xsl:template>
```

The rest of the stylesheet is mostly logic that renders the WSDL as HTML table entries. A service may contain more than one port, so be sure to select ports based on the query parameters once more:

```
<xsl:template match="wsdl:service" mode="display">
<h1><xsl:value-of select="@name"/></h1>
<p><xsl:value-of select="wsdl:documentation"/></p>
<table border="1" cellpadding="5" cellspacing="0"  width="600">
  <tbody>
    <xsl:apply-templates
        select="wsdl:port[(not($portRef) or @name = $port) and
                          (not($bindingRef) or @binding = $bindingRef)]"
        mode="display"/>
  </tbody>
</table>
</xsl:template>
```

Use your keys to traverse (do a join) between port and binding, as well as between binding and port type:

```
<xsl:template match="wsdl:port" mode="display">
    <tr>
      <td style="font-weight:bold" colspan="2" align="center">Port</td>
    </tr>
    <tr>
      <td colspan="2"><h3><xsl:value-of select="@name"/></h3></td>
    </tr>
    <tr>
      <td style="font-weight:bold" width="50">Binding</td>
      <td><xsl:value-of select="substring-after(@binding,':')"/></td>
    </tr>
    <tr>
      <td style="font-weight:bold" width="50">Address</td>
      <td><xsl:value-of select="soap:address/@location"/></td>
    </tr>
    <tr>
      <th colspan="2" align="center">Operations</th>
    </tr>
    <xsl:apply-templates select="key('bindings_key',@binding)" mode="display"/>
</xsl:template>

<xsl:template match="wsdl:binding" mode="display">
  <xsl:apply-templates select="key('portType_key',@type)" mode="display">
    <xsl:with-param name="operation" select="wsdl:operation/@name"/>
  </xsl:apply-templates>
</xsl:template>
```

```
<xsl:template match="wsdl:portType" mode="display">
  <xsl:param name="operation"/>
  <xsl:for-each select="wsdl:operation[@name = $operation]">
    <tr>
      <td colspan="2"><h3><xsl:value-of select="@name"/></h3></td>
    </tr>
    <xsl:if test="wsdl:input">
      <tr>
        <td style="font-weight:bold" width="50">Input</td>
        <td><xsl:value-of select="substring-after(wsdl:input/@message,':')"/></td>
      </tr>
      <xsl:variable name="msgName"
          select="substring-after(wsdl:input/@message,':')"/>
      <xsl:apply-templates
          select="/*/wsdl:message[@name = $msgName]" mode="display"/>
    </xsl:if>
    <xsl:if test="wsdl:output">
      <tr>
        <td style="font-weight:bold" width="50">Output</td>
        <td><xsl:value-of select="substring-after(wsdl:output/@message,':')"/></td>
      </tr>
      <xsl:variable name="msgName"
          select="substring-after(wsdl:output/@message,':')"/>
      <xsl:apply-templates
          select="/*/wsdl:message[@name = $msgName]" mode="display"/>
    </xsl:if>
  </xsl:for-each>
</xsl:template>

<xsl:template match="wsdl:message" mode="display">
  <xsl:variable name="dataType"
      select="substring-after(wsdl:part[@name='body']/@element,':')"/>
  <tr>
    <td colspan="2">
      <xsl:apply-templates
          select="/*/wsdl:types/*/*[@name=$dataType]" mode="display">
        <xsl:with-param name="initial-newline" select="false()"/>
      </xsl:apply-templates>
    </td>
  </tr>
</xsl:template>
```

This code renders the messages' XSD schema as XML within HTML. The actual
schema is probably the most informative piece of information you can display in
order to document the data types associated with the service input and output messages:

```
<xsl:template match="*" mode="display">
  <xsl:param name="initial-newline" select="true()"/>

  <xsl:if test="$initial-newline">
    <xsl:call-template name="newline"/>
  </xsl:if>
  <!-- open tag -->
```

```
<a>&lt;</a>
<a><xsl:value-of select="name(.)" /> </a>

<!-- Output attributes -->
<xsl:for-each select="@*">
  <a><xsl:text> </xsl:text><xsl:value-of select="name(.)" />  </a>
  <a>=&quot;</a>
  <xsl:value-of select="." />
  <a>&quot;</a>
</xsl:for-each>

<xsl:choose>
    <xsl:when test="child::node( )">
    <!-- close start tag -->
    <a>&gt;</a>
    <xsl:apply-templates  mode="display"/>
    <xsl:call-template name="newline"/>
    <!-- closing tag -->
    <a>&lt;</a>
    <a>/<xsl:value-of select="name(.)" /></a>
    </xsl:when>
    <xsl:otherwise>
        <a>/</a>
    </xsl:otherwise>
  </xsl:choose>
  <a>&gt;</a>
</xsl:template>

<!-- Add a newline and then indent based on depth within the schema -->
<xsl:template name="newline">
    <br/>
    <xsl:for-each select="ancestor::xsd:*[not(self::xsd:schema)]">
        <xsl:text>    </xsl:text>
    </xsl:for-each>
</xsl:template>

</xsl:stylesheet>
```

Discussion

Chapter 10 spoke of a message repository that can capture metadata about messages exchanged in a client-server architecture. WSDL is an example of a kind of message-repository syntax for a web-service-based architecture. Here you can also use the same WSDL to generate code and documentation. This example focuses on serving up documentation.

WSDL describes web services in terms of associations between services and ports. In WSDL terms, a *port* is a single end point defined as a combination of a binding and a network address. A *binding* is a concrete protocol and data-format specification for a particular port type. A *port type* defines an abstract set of operations supported by one or more end point. An *operation* is an action that a service can perform, and it is defined in terms of a message with a corresponding data payload. The data payload is usually described in terms of an XSD schema. The following code is a partial example of a simple WSDL describing a set of services offered within the Acme Corporation:

```
<definitions name="StockServices" targetNamespace="http://acme.com/services.wsdl"
xmlns:acme="http://acme.com/services.wsdl" xmlns:xsd1="http://acme.com/stockquote.
xsd" xmlns:soap="http://schemas.xmlsoap.org/wsdl/soap/" xmlns="http://schemas.
xmlsoap.org/wsdl/">
```

WSDL uses XSD schema as the default method of specifying the message data types exchanged in a service architecture:

```
<types>
  <schema targetNamespace="http://acme.com/services.xsd"
    xmlns="http://www.w3.org/2000/10/XMLSchema">
    <element name="Ticker">
      <complexType>
        <all>
          <element name="tickerSymbol" type="string"/>
        </all>
      </complexType>
    </element>
    <element name="TradePrice">
      <complexType>
        <all>
          <element name="price" type="float"/>
        </all>
      </complexType>
    </element>
    <element name="CompanyName">
      <complexType>
        <all>
          <element name="company" type="string"/>
        </all>
      </complexType>
    </element>
    <element name="ServicesInfo">
      <complexType>
        <sequence>
          <element name="Services">
            <complexType>
              <sequence>
                <element name="Service" type="string" minOccurs="0"
                         maxOccurs="unbounded"/>
              </sequence>
            </complexType>
          </element>
          <element name="Ports">
            <complexType>
              <sequence>
                <element name="Port" type="string" minOccurs="0"
                         maxOccurs="unbounded"/>
```

```
            </sequence>
          </complexType>
        </element>
        <element name="Bindings">
          <complexType>
            <sequence>
              <element name="Binding" type="string" minOccurs="0"
                       maxOccurs="unbounded"/>
            </sequence>
          </complexType>
        </element>
        <element name="PortTypes">
          <complexType>
            <sequence>
              <element name="Port" type="string" minOccurs="0"
                       maxOccurs="unbounded"/>
            </sequence>
          </complexType>
        </element>
        </sequence>
      </complexType>
    </element>
    <element name="ServicesQuery">
      <complexType>
        <all>
          <element name="Service" type="string"/>
          <element name="Port" type="string"/>
          <element name="Binding" type="string"/>
          <element name="PortType" type="string"/>
        </all>
      </complexType>
    </element>
    <element name="ServicesResponse">
      <complexType>
        <sequence>
          <any/>
        </sequence>
      </complexType>
    </element>
  </schema>
</types>
```

Messages bind names to data types and are used to specify what is communicated within the service architecture:

```
<message name="GetLastTradePriceInput">
  <part name="body" element="xsd1:Ticker"/>
</message>
<message name="GetLastTradePriceOutput">
  <part name="body" element="xsd1:TradePrice"/>
</message>
<message name="GetCompanyInput">
  <part name="body" element="xsd1:Ticker"/>
</message>
```

```
<message name="GetCompanyOutput">
  <part name="body" element="xsd1:CompanyName"/>
</message>
<message name="GetTickerInput">
  <part name="body" element="xsd1:CompanyName"/>
</message>
<message name="GetTickerOutput">
  <part name="body" element="xsd1:Ticker"/>
</message>
<message name="GetServicesInput"/>
<message name="GetServicesOutput">
  <part name="body" element="xsd1:ServicesInfo"/>
</message>
<message name="QueryServicesInput">
  <part name="body" element="xsd1:ServicesQuery"/>
</message>
<message name="QueryServicesOutput">
  <part name="body" element="xsd1:ServicesRespose"/>
</message>
```

The port types specify which operations are available at a particular service end point (port). This section describes two such port types: one that gives stock quote information and another that describes a service discovery service. The service discovery service is the service you implement in this example, except that it would be used by a program other than a browser:

```
<portType name="StockPortType">
  <operation name="GetLastTradePrice">
    <input message="acme:GetLastTradePriceInput"/>
    <output message="acme:GetLastTradePriceOutput"/>
  </operation>
  <operation name="GetTickerFromCompany">
    <input message="acme:GetTickerInput"/>
    <output message="acme:GetCompanyOutput"/>
  </operation>
  <operation name="GetCompanyFromTicker">
    <input message="acme:GetCompanyInput"/>
    <output message="acme:GetTickerOutput"/>
  </operation>
</portType>
<portType name="ServicePortType">
  <operation name="GetServices">
    <input message="acme:GetServicesInput"/>
    <output message="acme:GetServicesOutput"/>
  </operation>
  <operation name="QueryServices">
    <input message="acme:QueryServicesInput"/>
    <output message="acme:QueryServicesOutput"/>
  </operation>
</portType>
```

The bindings tie operations to specific protocols. Here you declare that operations are bound to the SOAP protocol:

```
<binding name="StockQuoteSoapBinding" type="acme:StockPortType">
  <soap:binding style="document" transport="http://schemas.xmlsoap.org/soap/http"/>
  <operation name="GetLastTradePrice">
    <soap:operation soapAction="http://acme.com/GetLastTradePrice"/>
    <input>
      <soap:body use="literal"/>
    </input>
    <output>
      <soap:body use="literal"/>
    </output>
  </operation>
</binding>
<binding name="StockTickerSoapBinding" type="acme:StockPortType">
  <soap:binding style="document" transport="http://schemas.xmlsoap.org/soap/http"/>
  <operation name="GetTickerFromCompany">
    <soap:operation soapAction="http://acme.com/GetTickerSymbol"/>
    <input>
      <soap:body use="literal"/>
    </input>
    <output>
      <soap:body use="literal"/>
    </output>
  </operation>
</binding>
<binding name="StockNameSoapBinding" type="acme:StockPortType">
  <soap:binding style="document" transport="http://schemas.xmlsoap.org/soap/http"/>
  <operation name="GetCompanyFromTicker">
    <soap:operation soapAction="http://acme.com/GetCompanyName"/>
    <input>
      <soap:body use="literal"/>
    </input>
    <output>
      <soap:body use="literal"/>
    </output>
  </operation>
</binding>
<binding name="ServiceListSoapBinding" type="acme:ServicePortType">
  <soap:binding style="document" transport="http://schemas.xmlsoap.org/soap/http"/>
  <operation name="GetServices">
    <soap:operation soapAction="http://acme.com/GetServices"/>
    <input>
      <soap:body use="literal"/>
    </input>
    <output>
      <soap:body use="literal"/>
    </output>
  </operation>
</binding>
```

Two services are advertised here. One is related to stock quotes, and the other to service discovery. Notice how the services organize a set of ports to specify the functionality available though the service:

```
<service name="StockInfoService">
  <documentation>Provides information about stocks.</documentation>
  <port name="StockQuotePort" binding="acme:StockQuoteSoapBinding">
    <soap:address location="http://acme.com/stockquote"/>
  </port>
  <port name="StockTickerToNamePort" binding="acme:StockTickerSoapBinding">
    <soap:address location="http://acme.com/tickertoname"/>
  </port>
  <port name="StockNameToTickerPort" binding="acme:StockNameSoapBinding">
    <soap:address location="http://acme.com/nametoticker"/>
  </port>
</service>
<service name="ServiceInfoService">
  <documentation>Provides information about avaialable services.</documentation>
  <port name="ServiceListPort" binding="acme:ServiceListSoapBinding">
    <soap:address location="http://acme.com/stockquote"/>
  </port>
  <port name="ServiceQueryPort" binding="acme:ServiceQuerySoapBinding">
    <soap:address location="http://acme.com/tickertoname"/>
  </port>
</service>

</definitions>
```

Using your CGI-based server, you get a service-query screen. You can select the parameters of the query as shown in Figure 11-6.

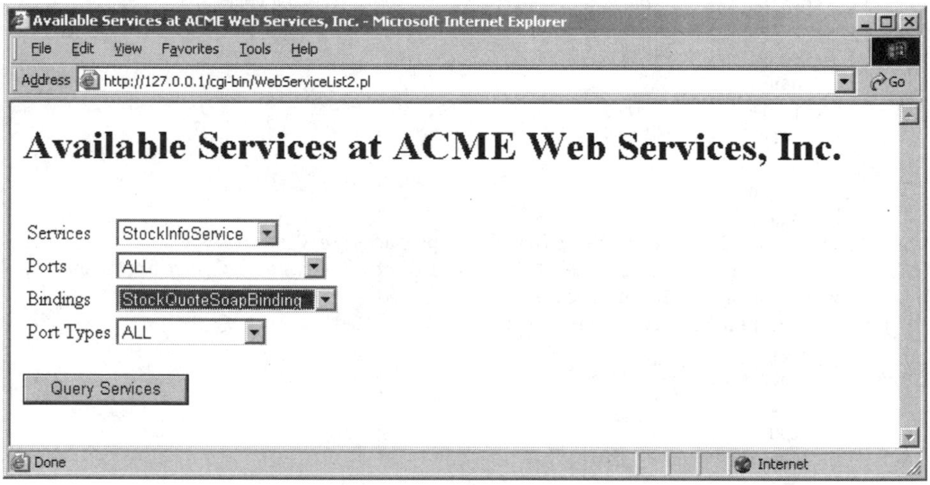

Figure 11-6. WSDL query screen

When you submit the query, you obtain the result shown in Figure 11-7.

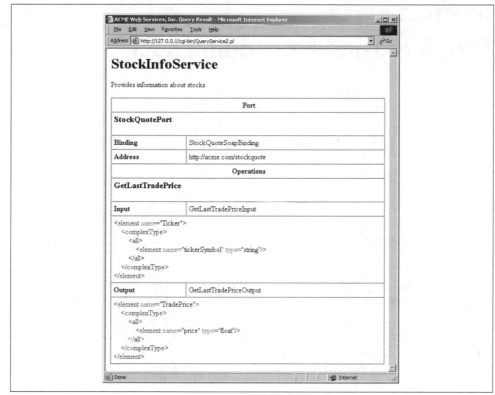

Figure 11-7. WSDL result screen

See Also

The specifications for WSDL are available at *http://www.w3.org/TR/wsdl*. WSDL is not yet an official W3C recommendation; however, it is quickly gaining recognition and support in the industry. An official Web Services Description Working Group (*http://www.w3.org/2002/ws/desc/*) is working on what will eventually be a W3C-sanctioned recommendation.

See Recipe 12.5 for ways of embedding XSLT processing into Perl rather than forking off a separate process.

CHAPTER 12

Extending and Embedding XSLT

I think everybody should have a great Wonderbra.
There's so many ways to enhance them, everybody does it.
—Christina Aguilera

Truly ambitious programmers are never satisfied with what they are given and are obsessively driven to enhance what they have. I say "ambitious" rather than "great" because greatness, in my opinion, comes from knowing when it is wiser to work within the system versus when it is best to extend the system. Nevertheless, this chapter is dedicated to extending the system both from the perspective of XSLT needing functionality best implemented in another language and from the perspective of other languages needing XSLT.

Extending XSLT is, by definition, a facility on the fringes of the specification. Extensions decrease the portability of the XSLT script. This is definitely a hazard when you use extensions provided natively by your XSLT processor or when implementing your own extension. It is true even if you implement your extensions in a highly portable language like Java. The most obvious reason is that some XSLT processors are not written in Java and are thus unlikely ever to support Java-based extensions. However, even if you only want your extensions to work in Java-based XSLT processors, you might still find that the extension mechanism of XSLT was not fully standardized in Version 1.0. This state of affairs improved in Version 1.1, but 1.1 is no longer an official XSLT release and many processors do not support it. Surprisingly, XSLT 2.0 does not promise any standardization with respect to extensions.

EXSLT.org is a portal dedicated to establishing standards XSLT implementers can follow when implementing common extensions. Chapters 2 and 3 mentioned EXSLT with respect to math extensions and date extensions. EXSLT.org also organized other extension categories, some of which this chapter touches upon. It is certainly a site worth visiting before going off and implementing your own extension. There is a good chance that someone either developed such an extension or put some thought into how the extension should work.

In contrast to extending XSLT, *embedding* XSLT involves invoking XSLT transformations from another language without forking your XSLT processor in a separate process. You will see how XSLT can be accessed from within Java- and Perl-based programs.

When writing this chapter, it quickly became apparent that you could easily dedicate a whole book to extension and embedding—especially when you consider the cross between implementations, extension languages, and interesting examples. To keep this chapter manageable, I compromised by alternating between Xalan Java 2 and Saxon and sticking mostly to Java and JavaScript. This chapter also discusses MSXML.

To prevent repetition, this section explains how to use extensions in both Saxon and Xalan Java 2.

Saxon Extension Functions

Saxon lets you access extension junctions written in Java by using the interface defined in the XSLT 1.1 draft standard. Although this feature was dropped from XSLT 2.0, it will probably remain in Saxon since vendors can do what they please on the 2.0 standard's extensibility front. However, the element's namespace could be changed.

Java is the only extension language currently supported by Saxon, so extension function bindings are defined along the lines of the following example:

```
<xsl:stylesheet
  version="1.1"
  xmlns:xsl="http://www.w3.org/1999/XSL/Transform"
  xmlns:Math="java:java.lang.Math"
```

```
                   exclude-result-prefixes="Math">

     <xsl:script implements-prefix="Math"
                      xmlns:Math="java:java.lang.Math"
                      language="java"
                      src="java:java.lang.Math"/>
```

Here the naming convention used for the namespace is not strictly required. However, if followed, it makes the xsl:script element optional. Hence, if you need to access an extension only once, you can write something like:

```
<xsl:stylesheet
  xmlns:xsl="http://www.w3.org/1999/XSL/Transform">

  <xsl:variable name="PI" select="4 * Math:atan(1.0)"
                xmlns:Math="java:java.lang.Math"/>
<!-- ... -->
</xsl:stylesheet>
```

Here the namespace encodes the binding to the Java implementation rather than the xsl:script. Note that these binding techniques are independent; if you use the xsl:script element, then the namespace's content does not matter. On the other hand, if you omit the xsl:script, the namespace has the sole responsibility of binding the Java implementation.

Saxon Extension Elements

Extension elements in Saxon can be implemented only in Java. You must define a namespace that binds the extension to its implementation. However, the rules are more explicit here than with extension functions. The namespace must end in a /, followed by the fully qualified class name of a Java class that implements the interface com.icl.saxon.ExtensionElementFactory:

```
<xsl:stylesheet
xmlns:xsl="http://www.w3.org/1999/XSL/Transform"
xmlns:acmeX="http://www.acmeX.com/com.acemX.SuperExtensionFactory"
extension-element-prefixes="acmeX">

<!-- ... -->
</xsl:stylesheet>
```

The prefix must also be listed in the stylesheet's extension-element-prefixes attribute.

Details of the ExtensionElementFactory are covered in Recipe 12.4.

Xalan Java 2 Extension Functions

Extension functions in Xalan Java 2 are bound using two Xalan extensions, xalan:component and xalan:script, where the relevant Xalan namespace URI is http://xml.apache.org/xslt.

The xalan:component element associates the extension namespace prefix with the names of extension functions or elements that will be defined by the enclosing xalan:script element. The xalan:script element defines the language used to implement the extension and its associated implementation. The choices here vary. Casual users of Java-based extensions should note that Xalan supports an abbreviated syntax that does not require the use of the xalan:component or xalan:script elements. Simply declare the namespace in one of the forms shown here, and invoke the Java function using the appropriate syntax. For scripting languages, this shortcut does not apply.

Java Extension Function Using the Class Format Namespace

```
<xsl:stylesheet
xmlns:xsl="http://www.w3.org/1999/XSL/Transform"
xmlns:xalan="http://xml.apache.org/xslt"
xmlns:Math="xalan://java.lang.Math">

<xalan:component prefix="Math" functions="sin cos tan atan">
 <xalan:script lang="javaclass" src="xalan://java.lang.Math"/>
</xalan:component>

<xsl:variable name="PI" select="4.0 *"/>
```

If you use this form and omit the xalan:component element, then your stylesheet can work with both Saxon and Xalan.

Java Extension Function Using the Package Format Namespace

```
<xsl:stylesheet
xmlns:xsl="http://www.w3.org/1999/XSL/Transform"
xmlns:xalan="http://xml.apache.org/xslt"
xmlns:myJava="xalan://java.lang">

<xalan:component prefix="Math" functions="sin cos tan atan">
 <xalan:script lang="javaclass" src="java.lang"/>
</xalan:component>

<xsl:variable name="PI" select="4.0 * myJava:Math.atan(1.0)"/>

<!-- ... -->

</xsl:stylesheet>
```

This form is useful if you want to reference many classes within the same package.

Java Extension Function Using the Java Format Namespace

```
<xsl:stylesheet
xmlns:xsl="http://www.w3.org/1999/XSL/Transform"
xmlns:xalan="http://xml.apache.org/xslt"
xmlns:java="http://xml.apache.org/xslt/java">

<xalan:component prefix="Math" functions="sin cos tan atan">
 <xalan:script lang="javaclass" src="http://xml.apache.org/xslt/java"/>
</xalan:component>

<xsl:variable name="PI" select="4.0 * java:java.lang.Math:atan(1.0)"/>

<!-- ... -->

</xsl:stylesheet>
```

Use this form if you want to access a wide variety of Java-based extensions with a single namespace declaration. The disadvantage is that each invocation becomes more verbose.

Scripting Extension Function Using Inline Script Code

```
<xsl:stylesheet version="1.0"
xmlns:xsl="http://www.w3.org/1999/XSL/Transform"
xmlns:xalan="http://xml.apache.org/xslt"
xmlns:trig="http://www.acmeX.com/extend/trig">

<xalan:component prefix="trig" functions="sin cons tan atan">
  <xalan:script lang="javascript">
    function sin (arg){ return Math.sin(arg);}
    function cos (arg){ return Math.cos(arg);}
    function tan (arg){ return Math.tan(arg);}
    function atan (arg){ return Math.atan(arg);}
  </xalan:script>
</xalan:component>

<xsl:variable name="PI" select="4.0 * trig:atan(1.0)"/>

<!-- ... -->

</xsl:stylesheet>
```

Saxon currently supports JavaScript, NetRexx, BML, JPython, Jacl, JScript, VBScript, and PerlScript, but appropriate extensions need to be obtained from third parties supporting the respective languages. See *http://xml.apache.org/xalan-j/extensions.html#supported-lang* for details.

Xalan Java 2 Extension Elements

Extension elements in Xalan can be written in Java or in a supported scripting language. Java-based extensions elements also allow the shortcut syntax that dispenses with the xalan:component or xalan:script elements.

Java Extension Element

```
<xsl:stylesheet version="1.0"
xmlns:xsl="http://www.w3.org/1999/XSL/Transform"
xmlns:xalan="http://xml.apache.org/xslt"
xmlns:MyExt="xalan://com.AcmeX.MyExtensionElement">
extension-element-prefixes="MyExt">

<xalan:component prefix="MyExt" elements="superExtension">
  <xalan:script lang="javasclass"
                src=" xalan:// com.AcmeX.MyExtensionElement"/>
</xalan:component>

<xsl:template match="*">
    <myExt:superExtension attr1="val1" attr2="val2">
        <!-- ... -->
    <myExt:superExtension>
</xsl:template>

</xsl:stylesheet>
```

The implementation must be via a Java class and method with the following signature:

```
public class com.AcmeX.MyExtensionElement
{

public SomeType superExtension(
        org.apache.xalan.extensions.XSLProcessorContext ctx,
        org.apache.xalan.templates.ElemExtensionCall extensionElement)
  {
     //...
  }

}
```

where SomeType designates the return type, ctx is a instance of the processing context, and extensionElement is the node corresponding to the stylesheet's extension element. In the method signature, you may also use the indicated types' superclasses. The com.AcmeX.MyExtensionElement base class can be anything you like, including none, as shown here.

Whatever the function returns is put into the result tree, so use void if you do not want this effect. See Recipe 12.4 for further details on the XSLProcessorContext and ElemExtensionCall classes.

Scripting Extension Elements

Scripted extensions are very similar to Java extensions, except the extension is implemented inside of the xalan:script element:

```
<xsl:stylesheet version="1.0"
xmlns:xsl="http://www.w3.org/1999/XSL/Transform"
xmlns:xalan="http://xml.apache.org/xslt"
xmlns:MyExt="xalan://com.AcmeX.MyExtensionElement">
extension-element-prefixes="MyExt">

<xalan:component prefix="rep" elements="repeat">
  <xalan:script lang="javascript">
    function superExtension(ctx, elem)
    {
      /* ... */
      return null ;
    }
  </xalan:script>
</xalan:component>

<xsl:template match="*">
    <myExt:superExtension attr1="val1" attr2="val2">
        <!-- ... -->
    <myExt:superExtension>
</xsl:template>
</xsl:stylesheet>
```

As with Java, the return value is placed into the result tree, but you return null to disable this effect with scripting languages. See Recipe 12.2 for an example.

MSXML Extension Functions

Microsoft's MSXML 3.0, 4.0, and .NET XSLT processor is extensible via Jscript and VBScript. MSXML .NET adds C# extensibility. Extensions in MSXML are specified using the ms:script element:

```
<xsl:stylesheet version="1.0"
  xmlns:xsl="http://www.w3.org/1999/XSL/Transform"
  xmlns:ms="urn:schemas-microsoft-com:xslt"
  xmlns:myExt="urn:AcmeX.com:xslt">

<ms:script language="JScript" implements-prefix="myExt">
  <![CDATA[
  function superExtension(ops) {
      /* ... */
    return result;
  }
  ]]>
</ms:script>

</xsl:stylesheet>
```

See Also

The XSLT C library for Gnome (libxslt) also supports extensibility. See *http://xmlsoft.org/XSLT/extensions.html* for details.

12.1 Using Saxon's and Xalan's Native Extensions

Problem

You want to know how to exploit some of the useful extensions available in these popular XSLT implementations.

Solution

This recipe is broken into a bunch of mini-recipes showcasing the most important Saxon and Xalan extensions. For all examples, the saxon namespace prefix is associated with *http://icl.com/saxon*, and the xalan namespace prefix is associated with *http://xml.apache.org/xslt*.

You want to output to more than one destination

This book has used Saxon's facility several times to output results to more than one file. Saxon uses the saxon:output element. It also provides the xsl:document element, but it will only work if the stylesheet version attribute is 1.1 and is therefore not preferred. The href attribute specifies the output destination. This attribute can be an attribute value template:

```
<saxon:output href="toc.html">
  <html>
    <head><title>Table of Contents</title></head>
    <body>
      <xsl:apply-templates mode="toc" select="*"/>
    </body>
  </html>
</saxon:output>
```

Xalan takes a significantly different approach to multidestination output. Rather than one instruction, Xalan gives you three: redirect:open, redirect:close, and redirect:write. The extension namespace associated with these elements is xmlns: redirect = "org.apache. xalan.xslt.extensions.Redirect". For the most common cases, you can get away with using redirect:write by itself because if used alone, it will open, write, and close the file.

Each element includes a file attribute and/or a select attribute to designate the output file. The file attribute takes a string, so you can use it to specify the output filename directly. The select attribute takes an XPath expression, so you can use it to generate the output file name dynamically. If you include both attributes, the redirect extension first evaluates the select attribute and falls back to the file attribute if the select attribute expression does not return a valid filename:

```
<xalan:write file="toc.html">
  <html>
    <head><title>Table of Contents</title></head>
    <body>
      <xsl:apply-templates mode="toc" select="*"/>
    </body>
  </html>
</saxon:output>
```

By using Xalan's extended capabilities, you can switch from writing a primary output file to other secondary files while the primary remains open. This step undermines the no-side-effects nature of XSLT, but presumably, Xalan will ensure a predictable operation:

```
<xsl:template match="doc">
<xalan:open file="regular.xml"/>
    <xsl:apply-templates select="*"/>
<xalan:close file="regular.xml"/>
<xsl:template/>

<xsl:template match="regular">
  <xsl:write file="regular.xml">
    <xsl:copy-of select="."/>
  </xsl:write>
</xsl:template>

<xsl:template match="*">
  <xsl:variable name="file" select="concat(local-name( ),'.xml')"/>
  <xsl:write select="$file">
    <xsl:copy-of select="."/>
  </xsl:write>
</xsl:template>
```

XSLT 2.0 provides native support for multiple result destinations via a new element called xsl:result-document:

```
<xsl:result-document format="html" href="toc.html">
  <html>
    <head><title>Table of Contents</title></head>
    <body>
      <xsl:apply-templates mode="toc" select="*"/>
    </body>
  </html>
</xsl:result-document>
```

You want to split a complex transformation into a series of transformations in a pipeline

Developers who have worked a lot with Unix are intimately familiar with the notion of a processing pipeline, in which the output of a command is fed into the input of another. This facility is also available in other operating systems, such as Windows. The genius of the pipelining approach to software development is that it enables the assembly of complex tasks from more basic commands.

Since an XSLT transformation is ultimately a tree-to-tree transformation, applying the pipelining approach is natural. Here the result tree of one transform becomes the input tree of the next. You have seen numerous examples in which the node-set extension function can create intermediate results that can be processed by subsequent stages. Alternatively, Saxon provides this functionality via the `saxon:next-in-chain` extension attribute of `xsl:output`. The `saxon:next-in-chain` attribute directs the output to another stylesheet. The value is the URL of a stylesheet that should be used to process the output stream. The output stream must always be pure XML, and attributes that control the output's format (e.g., `method`, `cdata-section-elements`, etc.) have no effect. The second stylesheet's output is directed to the destination that would have been used for the first stylesheet if no `saxon:next-in-chain` attribute were present.

Xalan has a different approach to this functionality; it uses a `pipeDocument` extension element. The nice thing about `pipeDocument` is that you can use it in an otherwise empty stylesheet to create a pipeline between independent stylesheets that do not know they are used in this way. The Xalan implementation is therefore much more like the Unix pipe because the pipeline is not hardcoded into the participating stylesheets. Imagine that a stylesheet called *strip.xslt* stripped out specific elements from an XML document representing a book, and a stylesheet called *contents.xslt* created a table of contents based on the hierarchical structure of the document's markup. You could create a pipeline between the stylesheets as follows:

```
<xsl:stylesheet version="1.0"
      xmlns:xsl="http://www.w3.org/1999/XSL/Transform"
      xmlns:pipe="xalan://PipeDocument"
      extension-element-prefixes="pipe">

<xsl:param name="source"/>
<xsl:param name="target"/>
<!-- A list of elements to preserve. All others are stripped. -->
<xsl:param name="preserve-elems"/>

<pipe:pipeDocument   source="{$source}" target="{$target}">
```

```
  <stylesheet href="strip.xslt">
    <param name="preserve-elems" value="{$preserve-elems}"/>
  </stylesheet>

  <stylesheet href="contents.xslt"/>

 </pipe:pipeDocument>

</xsl:stylesheet>
```

This code would create a table of contents based on the specified elements without disabling the independent use of *strip.xsl* or *contents.xsl*.

You want to work with dates and times

Chapter 3, provided a host of recipes dealing with dates and times but no pure XSLT facility that could determine the current date and time. Both Saxon and Xalan implement core functions from the EXSLT dates and times module. This section includes EXSLT's date-and-time documentation for easy reference. The functions are shown in Table 12-1 with their return type, followed by the function and arguments. A question mark (?) indicates optional arguments.

Table 12-1. EXSLT's date-and-time functions

Function	Behavior
string date: date-time( )	The date:date-time function returns the current date and time as a date/time string. The returned date/time string must be in the format XML schema defines as the lexical representation of xs:dateTime.
string date: date(string?)	The date:date function returns the date specified in the date/time string given as the argument. If no argument is given, the current local date/time, as returned by date:date-time, is used as a default argument.
string date: time(string?)	The date:time function returns the time specified in the date/time string given as the argument. If no argument is given, the current local date/time, as returned by date:date-time, is used as a default argument.
number date: year(string?)	The date:year function returns the date's year as a number. If no argument is given, then the current local date/time, as returned by date:date-time, is used as a default argument.
boolean date: leap-year(string?)	The date:leap-year function returns true if the year given in a date is a leap year. If no argument is given, then the current local date/time, as returned by date:date-time, is used as a default argument.
number date: month-in-year(string?)	The date:month-in-year function returns the month of a date as a number. If no argument is given, then the current local date/time, as returned by date:date-time, is used as the default argument
string date: month-name(string?)	The date:month-name function returns the full name of the month of a date. If no argument is given, then the current local date/time, as returned by date:date-time, is used as the default argument.
string date: month-abbreviation(string?)	The date:month-abbreviation function returns the abbreviation of the month of a date. If no argument is given, then the current local date/time, as returned by date:date-time, is used as the default argument.

Table 12-1. EXSLT's date-and-time functions (continued)

Function	Behavior
number date: week-in-year(string?)	The date:week-in-year function returns the week of the year as a number. If no argument is given, then the current local date/time, as returned by date:date-time, is used as the default argument. Counting follows ISO 8601: Week 1 in a year is the week containing the first Thursday of the year, with new weeks beginning on Mondays.
number date: day-in-year(string?)	The date:day-in-year function returns the day of a date in a year as a number. If no argument is given, then the current local date/time, as returned by date:date-time, is used as the default argument.
number date: day-in-month(string?)	The date:day-in-month function returns the day of a date as a number. If no argument is given, then the current local date/time, as returned by date:date-time, is used as the default argument.
number date: day-of-week-in- month(string?)	The date:day-of-week-in-month function returns the day of the week in a month as a number (e.g., 3 for the third Tuesday in May). If no argument is given, then the current local date/time, as returned by date:date-time, is used as the default argument.
number date: day-in-week(string?)	The date:day-in-week function returns the day of the week given in a date as a number. If no argument is given, then the current local date/time, as returned by date:date-time, is used as the default argument.
string date: day-name(string?)	The date:day-name function returns the full name of the day of the week of a date. If no argument is given, then the current local date/time, as returned by date:date-time, is used as the default argument.
string date: day-abbreviation(string?)	The date:day-abbreviation function returns the abbreviation of the day of the week of a date. If no argument is given, then the current local date/time, as returned by date:date-time, is used as the default argument.
number date: hour-in-day(string?)	The date:hour-in-day function returns the hour of the day as a number. If no argument is given, then the current local date/time, as returned by date:date-time, is used as the default argument.
number date: minute-in-hour(string?)	The date:minute-in-hour function returns the minute of the hour as a number. If no argument is given, then the current local date/time, as returned by date:date-time, is used as the default argument.
number date: second-in-minute(string?)	The date:second-in-minute function returns the second of the minute as a number. If no argument is given, then the current local date/time, as returned by date:date-time, is used as the default argument.

```
<xsl:stylesheet version="1.0"
xmlns:xsl="http://www.w3.org/1999/XSL/Transform"
xmlns:date="http://exslt.org/dates-and-times">

<xsl:output method="html" version="1.0" encoding="UTF-8" indent="yes"/>

<xsl:template match="/">
  <html>
    <head><title>My Dull Home Page</title></head>
    <body>
      <h1>My Dull Homepage</h1>
      <div>It's <xsl:value-of select="date:time( )"/> on <xsl:value-of
      select="date:date( )"/> and this page is as dull as it was yesterday.</div>
```

```
        </body>
      </html>

  </xsl:template>

  </xsl:stylesheet>
```

You need a more efficient implementation of set operations

Chapter 7 investigated various means of implementing set operations other than set union, which XPath supplies natively via the union operator (|). These solutions were not necessarily the most efficient or obvious.

Both Saxon and Xalan remedy this problem by implementing many of the set operations defined by EXSLT's set module (see Table 12-2).

Table 12-2. EXSLT's set module's set operations

Function	Behavior
Node-set set: difference(node-set, node-set)	The set:difference function returns the difference between two node sets— nodes that are in the node set passed as the first argument that are not in the node set passed as the second argument.
Node-set set: intersection(node-set, node-set)	The set:intersection function returns a node set comprising the nodes that are within both the node sets passed to it as arguments.
Node-set set: distinct(node-set)	The set:distinct function returns a subset of the nodes contained in the node set NS passed as the first argument. Specifically, it selects a node N if no node in NS has the same string value as N, and that precedes N in document order.
boolean set: has-same-node(node-set, node-set)	The set:has-same-node function returns true if the node set passed as the first argument shares nodes with the node set passed as the second argument. If no nodes are in both node sets, it returns false.
Node-set set: leading(node-set, node-set)	The set:leading function returns the nodes in the node set passed as the first argument that precede, in document order, the first node in the node set passed as the second argument. If the first node in the second node set is not contained in the first node set, then an empty node set is returned. If the second node set is empty, then the first node set is returned.
Node-set set: trailing(node-set, node-set)	The set:trailing function returns the nodes in the node set passed as the first argument that follow, in document order, to the first node in the node set passed as the second argument. If the first node in the second node set is not contained in the first node set, then an empty node set is returned. If the second node set is empty, then the first node set is returned.

set:distinct is a convenient way to remove duplicates, as long as equality is defined as string-value equality:

```
<xsl:varaible name="firstNames" select="set:destinct(person/firstname)"/>
```

set:leading and set:traling can extract nodes bracketed by other nodes. For example, Recipe 10.9 used a complex expression to locate the xslx:elsif and xslx:else nodes that went with your enhanced xslx:if. Extensions can simplify this process:

```
<xsl:apply-templates
        select="set:leading(following-sibling::xslx:else |
        following-sibling::xslx:elsif, following-sibling::xslx:if)"/>
```

This code specifies that you select all xslx:else and xslx:elseif siblings that come after the current node, but before the next xslx:if.

You want extended information about a node in the source tree

Xalan provides functions that allow you to get information about the location of nodes in the source tree. Saxon 6.5.2 provides only saxon:systemId and saxon:lineNumber. Debugging is one application of these functions. To use the functions, set the TransformerFactory source_location attribute to true with either the command-line utility -L flag or the TransformerFactory.setAttribute( ) method.

systemId( )
systemId(node-set)

> Returns the system ID for the current node and the first node in the node set, respectively.

lineNumber( )
lineNumber(node-set)

> Returns the line number in the source document for the current node and the first node in the node set, respectively. This function returns −1 if the line number is unknown (for example, when the source is a DOM Document).

columnNumber( )
columnNumber(node-set)

> Returns the column number in the source document for the current node and the first node in the node set, respectively. This function returns −1 if the column number is unknown (for example, when the source is a DOM Document):

```
<xsl:stylesheet version="1.0"
 xmlns:xsl="http://www.w3.org/1999/XSL/Transform"
 xmlns:xalan="http://xml.apache.org/xslt"
 xmlns:info="xalan://org.apache.xalan.lib.NodeInfo">

  <xsl:output method="xml" version="1.0" encoding="UTF-8" indent="yes"/>

  <xsl:template match="foo">
    <xsl:comment>Matched a foo on line <xsl:value-of
    select="info:lineNumber()"/> and column <xsl:value-of
    select="info:columnNumber()"/>.</xsl:comment>
    <!-- ... -->
  </xsl:template>

</xsl:stylesheet>
```

You want to interact with a relational database

Interfacing XSLT to a relational database opens up a whole new world of possibilities. Both Saxon and Xalan have extensions to support SQL. If you write stylesheets that modify databases, you violate the XSLT no-side-effects rule.

 Michael Kay has this to say about Saxon's SQL extensions, "These are not intended as being necessarily a production-quality piece of software (there are many limitations in the design), but more as an illustration of how extension elements can be used to enhance the capability of the processor."

Saxon provides database interaction via five extension elements: `sql:connect`, `sql:query`, `sql:insert`, `sql:column`, and `sql:close`. Anyone who ever interacted with a relational database though ODBC or JDBC should feel comfortable using these elements.

```
<sql:connect driver="jdbc-driver" database="db name" user="user name"
password="user password"/>
```
> Creates a database connection. Each attribute can be an attribute value template. The `driver` attribute names the JDBC driver class, and the `database` must be a name that JDBC can associate with an actual database.

```
<sql:query table="the table" column="column names" where="where clause"
row-tag="row element name" column-tag="column element name"
disable-output-escaping="yes or no"/>
```
> Performs a query and writes the results to the output tree using elements to represent the rows and columns. The names of these elements are specified by `row-tag` and `col-tag`, respectively. The `column` attribute can contain a list of columns or use * for all.

```
<sql:insert table="table name">
```
> Performs an SQL INSERT. The child elements (`sql:column`) specify the data to be added to the table.

```
<sql:column name="col name" select="xpath expr"/>
```
> Used as a child of `sql:insert`. The value can be specified by the `select` attribute or by the evaluation of the `sql:column`'s child elements. However, in both cases only the string value can be used. Hence, there is no way to deal with other standard SQL data types.

Xalan's SQL support is richer than Saxon's. This chapter covers only the basics. The "See Also" section provides pointers to more details. Unlike Saxon, Xalan uses extension functions that provide relational database access.

```
sql:new(driver, db, user, password)
```
> Establishes a connection.

```
sql:new(nodelist)
```
Sets up a connection using information embedded as XML in the input document or stylesheet. For example:

```
DBINFO>
    <dbdriver>org.enhydra.instantdb.jdbc.idbDriver</dbdriver>
    <dburl>jdbc:idb:../../instantdb/sample.prp</dburl>
    <user>jbloe</user>
    <password>geron07moe</password>
</DBINFO>

<xsl:param name="cinfo" select="//DBINFO"/>
<xsl:variable name="db" select="sql:new($cinfo)"/>
```

```
query(xconObj, sql-query)
```
Queries the database. The xconObj is returned by new( ). The function returns a *streamable* result set in the form of a row-set node. You can work your way through the row set one row at a time. The same row element is used repeatedly, so you can begin transforming the row set before the entire result set is returned.

```
pquery(xconObj,sql-query-with-params)
addParameter(xconObj, paramValue)
addParameterFromElement(xconObj,element)
addParameterFromElement(xconObj,node-list)
clearParameters(xconObj)
```
Used together to implement parameterized queries. Parameters take the form of ? characters embedded in the query. The various addParameter( ) functions set these parameters with actual values before the query is executed. Use clearParameters( ) to make the connection object forget about prior values.

```
close(xconObj)
```
Closes the connection to the database.

The query( ) and pquery( ) extension functions return a Document node that contains (as needed) an array of column-header elements, a single row element that is used repeatedly, and an array of col elements. Each column-header element (one per column in the row set) contains an attribute (ColumnAttribute) for each column descriptor in the ResultSetMetaData object. Each col element contains a text node with a textual representation of the value for that column in the current row.

You can find more information on using XSLT to access relational data in Doug Tidwell's *XSLT* (O'Reilly, 2001).

You want to dynamically evaluate an XPath expression created at runtime

Saxon and Xalan have a very powerful extension function called evaluate that takes a string and evaluates it as an XPath expression. Such a feature was under consideration for XSLT 2.0, but at this time, the XSLT 2.0 working group decided not to pursue it. Their justification is that dynamic evaluation "...has significant implications on the runtime architecture of the processor, as well as the ability to do static optimization."

Dynamic capabilities can come in handy when creating a table-driven stylesheet. The following stylesheet can format information on people into a table, but you can customize it to handle an almost infinite variety of XML formats simply by altering entries in a table:

```
<xsl:stylesheet version="1.0" xmlns:xsl="http://www.w3.org/1999/XSL/Transform"
 xmlns:saxon="http://icl.com/saxon"
 xmlns:paths="http://www.ora.com/XSLTCookbook/NS/paths"
 exclude-result-prefixes="paths">

<xsl:output method="html"/>

<!-- This parameter is used to specify a document con taining a table that -->
<!-- specifies how to locate info on people -->
<xsl:param name="pathsDoc"/>

<xsl:template match="/">
<html>
  <head>
    <title>People</title>
  </head>
  <body>
  <!-- We load an Xpath expression out of a table [Symbol_Wingdings_224] -->
  <!-- in an external document. -->
  <xsl:variable name="peoplePath"
      select="document($pathsDoc)/*/paths:path[@type='people']/@xpath"/>
    <table>
    <tbody>
      <tr>
        <th>First</th>
        <th>Last</th>
      </tr>
      <!-- Dynamically evaluate the xpath that locates information on -->
      <!-- each person -->
      <xsl:for-each select="saxon:evaluate($peoplePath)">
        <xsl:call-template name="process-person"/>
      </xsl:for-each>
    </tbody>
  </table>
  </body>
</html>
</xsl:template>

<xsl:template name="process-person">
  <xsl:variable name="firstnamePath"
      select="document($pathsDoc)/*/paths:path[@type='first']/@xpath"/>
  <xsl:variable name="lastnamePath"
      select="document($pathsDoc)/*/paths:path[@type='last']/@xpath"/>
  <tr>
    <!-- Dynamically evaluate the xpath that locates the person -->
    <!-- specific info we want to process -->
```

```
      <td><xsl:value-of select="saxon:evaluate($firstnamePath)"/></td>
      <td><xsl:value-of select="saxon:evaluate($lastnamePath)"/></td>
   </tr>
 </xsl:template>

 </xsl:stylesheet>
```

You can use this table to process person data encoded as elements:

```
`<paths:paths
  xmlns:paths="http://www.ora.com/XSLTCookbook/NS/paths">
  <paths:path type="people" xpath="people/person"/>
  <paths:path type="first" xpath="first"/>
  <paths:path type="last" xpath="last"/>
</paths:paths>
```

Add this table to process person data encoded as attributes:

```
<paths:paths xmlns:paths="http://www.ora.com/XSLTCookbook/NS/paths" >
  <paths:path type="people" xpath="people/person"/>
  <paths:path type="first" xpath="@first"/>
  <paths:path type="last" xpath="@last"/>
</paths:paths>
```

You want to change the value of a variable

Almost any book you read on XSLT will describe the inability to change the value of variables and parameters once they are bound as a feature of XSLT rather than a defect. This is true because it prevents a certain class of bugs, makes stylesheets easier to understand, and enables certain performance optimizations. However, sometimes being unable to change the values is simply inconvenient. Saxon provides a way around this obstacle with its saxon:assign extension element. You can use saxon:assign only on variables designated as assignable with the extension attribute saxon:assignable="yes":

```
<xsl:stylesheet version="1.0" xmlns:xsl="http://www.w3.org/1999/XSL/Transform"
xmlns:saxon="http://icl.com/saxon"
extension-element-prefixes="saxon">

<xsl:output method="xml" version="1.0" encoding="UTF-8" indent="yes"/>

<xsl:variable name="countFoo" select="0" saxon:assignable="yes"/>

<xsl:template name="foo">
   <saxon:assign name="countFoo" select="$countFoo + 1"/>
   <xsl:comment>This is invocation number <xsl:value-of select="$countFoo"/> of
template foo.</xsl:comment>
</xsl:template>

<!- ... -->

</xsl:stylesheet>
```

You want to write first-class extension functions in XSLT

Many examples in this book are implemented as named templates accessed via `xsl:call-template`. Often, this implementation is inconvenient and awkward because what you really want is to access this code as first-class functions that can be invoked as easily as native XPath functions. Help is on the way in XSLT 2.0, but in the meantime, you might consider using an EXSLT extension called `func:function` that is implemented by Saxon and the latest version of Xalan (Version 2.3.2). The following code is a template from Chapter 2 reimplemented as a function:

```
<xsl:stylesheet version="1.0"
  xmlns:xsl="http://www.w3.org/1999/XSL/Transform"
  xmlns:func="http://exslt.org/functions"
  xmlns:str="http://www.ora.com/XSLTCookbook/namespaces/strings"
  extension-element-prefixes="func">

  <xsl:template match="/">
    <xsl:value-of
        select="str:substring-before-last('123456789a123456789a123',
                                           'a')"/>
  </xsl:template>

  <func:function name="str:substring-before-last">
  <xsl:param name="input"/>
  <xsl:param name="substr"/>

  <func:result>
    <xsl:if test="$substr and contains($input, $substr)">
      <xsl:variable name="temp"
                    select="substring-after($input, $substr)" />
      <xsl:value-of select="substring-before($input, $substr)" />
      <xsl:if test="contains($temp, $substr)">
        <xsl:value-of
            select="concat($substr,
                           str:substring-before-last($temp, $substr))"/>
      </xsl:if>
    </xsl:if>
  </func:result>
  </func:function>

</xsl:stylesheet>
```

Discussion

Using vendor-specific extensions is a double-edged sword. On the one hand, they can provide you with the ability to deliver an XSLT solution faster or more simply than you could if you constrained yourself to standard XSLT. In a few cases, they allow you to do things that are impossible with standard XSLT. On the other hand, they can lock you into an implementation whose future is uncertain.

EXSLT.org encourages implementers to adopt uniform conventions for the most popular extensions, so you should certainly prefer an EXSLT solution to a vendor-specific one if you have a choice.

Another tactic is to avoid vendor-specific implementations altogether in favor of your own custom implementation. In this way, you control the source and can port the extension to more than one processor, if necessary. Recipes 12.2, 12.3, and 12.4 address custom extensions.

See Also

This book has not covered all of the extensions available in Saxon and Xalan. Additional information and features of Saxon extensions can be found at *http://saxon. sourceforge.net/saxon6.5.2/extensions.html* or *http://saxon. sourceforge.net/saxon7.2/ extensions.html* (the XSLT 2.0 beta version). Additional Xalan extension information can be found at *http://xml. apache.org/xalan-j/extensionslib.html*.

12.2 Extending XSLT with JavaScript

Problem

You want to execute JavaScript to implement functionality missing from XSLT.

Solution

The following examples use Xalan Java 2's ability to invoke scripting languages such as JavaScript. A typical use of a JavaScript-based extension invokes a function that is not native to XSLT or XPath. One common example is trigonometric functions:

```
<xsl:stylesheet version="1.0"
xmlns:xsl="http://www.w3.org/1999/XSL/Transform"
xmlns:xalan="http://xml.apache.org/xslt"
xmlns:trig="http://www.ora.com/XSLTCookbook/extend/trig">

<xsl:output method="text"/>

<xalan:component prefix="trig" functions="sin">
  <xalan:script lang="javascript">
    function sin (arg){ return Math.sin(arg);}
  </xalan:script>
</xalan:component>

<xsl:template match="/">
  The sin of 45 degrees is <xsl:text/>
  <xsl:value-of select="trig:sin(3.14159265 div 4)"/>
</xsl:template>

</xsl:stylesheet>
```

With JavaScript, you can actually implement functions that have side effects and objects that maintain state:[*]

```
<xsl:stylesheet version="1.0"
xmlns:xsl="http://www.w3.org/1999/XSL/Transform"
xmlns:xalan="http://xml.apache.org/xslt"
xmlns:count="http://www.ora.com/XSLTCookbook/extend/counter">

<xsl:output method="text"/>

<xalan:component prefix="count"
                 functions="counter nextCount resetCount makeCounter">
  <xalan:script lang="javascript">


    function counter(initValue)
    {
      this.value = initValue ;
    }

    function nextCount(ctr)
    {
      return ctr.value++ ;
    }

    function resetCount(ctr, value)
    {
      ctr.value = value  ;
      return "" ;
    }

    function makeCounter(initValue)
    {
      return new counter(initValue) ;
    }

  </xalan:script>
</xalan:component>

<xsl:template match="/">
  <xsl:variable name="aCounter" select="count:makeCounter(0)"/>
  Count: <xsl:value-of select="count:nextCount($aCounter)"/>
  Count: <xsl:value-of select="count:nextCount($aCounter)"/>
  Count: <xsl:value-of select="count:nextCount($aCounter)"/>
  Count: <xsl:value-of select="count:nextCount($aCounter)"/>
  <xsl:value-of select="count:resetCount($aCounter,0)"/>
  Count: <xsl:value-of select="count:nextCount($aCounter)"/>
</xsl:template>

</xsl:stylesheet>
```

---

[*] Shame on me for suggesting such a thing! Seriously, though, when you leave the confines of XSLT, you need not play by its rules, but you must accept the consequences.

In most implementations, this code results in:

```
Count: 0
Count: 1
Count: 2
Count: 3
Count: 0
```

A processor that expects no side effects can potentially change the order of evaluation and undermine the expected results. Here you can access JavaScript's regular expression library:

```
<?xml version="1.0" encoding="UTF-8"?>
<xsl:stylesheet version="1.0"
xmlns:xsl="http://www.w3.org/1999/XSL/Transform"
xmlns:xalan="http://xml.apache.org/xslt"
xmlns:regex="http://www.ora.com/XSLTCookbook/extend/regex">

<xsl:output method="text"/>

<xalan:component prefix="regex"
     functions="match leftContext rightContext getParenMatch makeRegExp">
  <xalan:script lang="javascript">

    function Matcher(pattern)
    {
      this.re = new RegExp(pattern) ;
      this.re.compile(pattern) ;
      this.result="" ;
      this.left="" ;
      this.right="" ;
    }

    function match(matcher, input)
    {
      matcher.result = matcher.re.exec(input) ;
      matcher.left = RegExp.leftContext ;
      matcher.right = RegExp.rightContext ;
      return matcher.result[0] ;
    }

    function leftContext(matcher)
    {
      return matcher.left ;
    }

    function rightContext(matcher)
    {
      return matcher.right ;
    }

    function getParenMatch(matcher, which)
    {
      return matcher.result[which] ;
    }
```

```
    function makeRegExp(pattern)
    {
      return new Matcher(pattern) ;
    }


  </xalan:script>
</xalan:component>

<xsl:template match="/">
  <xsl:variable name="dateParser"
      select="regex:makeRegExp('(\d\d?)[/-](\d\d?)[/-](\d{4}|\d{2})')"/>
  Match: <xsl:value-of
            select="regex:match($dateParser,
                      'I was born on 05/03/1964 in New York City.')"/>
  Left: <xsl:value-of select="regex:leftContext($dateParser)"/>
  Right: <xsl:value-of select="regex:rightContext($dateParser)"/>
  Month: <xsl:value-of select="regex:getParenMatch($dateParser, 1)"/>
  Day: <xsl:value-of select="regex:getParenMatch($dateParser,2)"/>
  Year: <xsl:value-of select="regex:getParenMatch($dateParser,3)"/>
</xsl:template>
</xsl:stylesheet>
```

This example results in:

```
Match: 05/03/1964
Left: I was born on
Right:  in New York City.
Month: 05
Day: 03
Year: 1964
```

In addition, Xalan lets you create JavaScript-based extension elements. Here is an extension element that repeats the execution of its content n times. It is useful for duplicating strings, structure, or as a simple looping construct:

```
<?xml version="1.0" encoding="UTF-8"?>
<xsl:stylesheet version="1.0"
xmlns:xsl="http://www.w3.org/1999/XSL/Transform"
xmlns:xalan="http://xml.apache.org/xslt"
xmlns:rep="http://www.ora.com/XSLTCookbook/extend/repeat"
extension-element-prefixes="rep">

<xsl:output method="xml"/>

<xalan:component prefix="rep" elements="repeat">
  <xalan:script lang="javascript">
<![CDATA[
    function repeat(ctx, elem)
    {
      //Get the attribute value n as an integer
      n = parseInt(elem.getAttribute("n")) ;
      //get the transformer which is required to execute nodes
      xformer = ctx.getTransformer() ;
      //Execute content of repeat element n times
      for(var ii=0; ii < n; ++ii)
      {
```

```
          node = elem.getFirstChild() ;
          while(node)
          {
            node.execute(xformer) ;
            node = node.getNextSibling() ;
          }
        }
        //The return value is inserted into the output
        //so return null to prevent this
        return null ;
      }
  ]]>
    </xalan:script>
  </xalan:component>

  <xsl:template match="/">
    <tests>
      <!--Use to duplicate text-->
      <test1><rep:repeat n="10">a</rep:repeat></test1>
      <!--Use to duplicate structure-->
      <test2>
        <rep:repeat n="10">
          <Malady>
            <FirstPart>Shim's</FirstPart>
            <SecondPart>Syndrome</SecondPart>
          </Malady>
        </rep:repeat>
      </test2>
      <!--Use to repeat the execution of xslt code -->
      <!--(which is really what we've been doing in test1 and test2)-->
      <test3>
        <rep:repeat n="10">
          <xsl:for-each select="*">
            <xsl:copy/>
          </xsl:for-each>
        </rep:repeat>
      </test3>
    </tests>
  </xsl:template>

</xsl:stylesheet>
```

Discussion

Creating extensions in JavaScript (or another embedded scripting language) is seductive because although you need to switch languages mentally, there is no need to switch to a different development environment or invoke a separate compiler. However, possibly the greatest benefit is that languages like JavaScript or VBScript are very easy to learn.*

---

* In fact, before writing this book, I could count the number of lines of JavaScript I had written on two hands and a few toes.

The challenge to using scripting-based extensions is that the documentation on how to tie XSLT and the scripts together tends to be thin. A few pointers are in order. Most of this information is available in the Xalan extension documents (*http://xml. apache.org/xalan-j/extensions.html*), but it is easy to miss when you are in a hurry to get something working.

First, script-based extensions are available only in Xalan Java, not Xalan C++.

Second, make sure you add *bsf.jar* and *js.jar* (for JavaScript) to your class path either on the command line when invoking Java from a Unix shell:

```
java -cp /xalan/bin/xalan.jar:/xalan/bin/xercesImpl.jar:/xalan/bin/bsf.jar: /xalan/
bin/js.jar org.apache.xalan.xslt.Process -in input.xml -xsl trans.xslt
```

or in the CLASSPATH environment variable:

```
export CLASSPATH=/xalan/bin/xalan.jar:/xalan/bin/xercesImpl.jar:/xalan/bin/bsf.jar:/
xalan/bin/js.jar
```

For Windows, replace colon path separators with semicolons and use set rather than export.

Third, note that *js.jar* is not part of the Xalan distribution. You must get it separately from Mozilla.org (*http://www.mozilla.org/rhino/*).

Once you configure your environment correctly, you need to specify your stylesheet to conform to Xalan's requirements for script-based extensions. See the introduction of this chapter for the gory details.

Implementing extension functions are much easier than implementing extension elements, and the examples in the "Solution" section (in conjunction with Xalan's documentation) should be sufficient. The rest of this section focuses on extension elements.

When an extension element's associated function is invoked, it is automatically passed two objects. The first is a context of type org.apache.xalan.extensions. XSLProcessorContext. This object is a handle for getting several other useful objects, such as the context node, the Stylesheet object, and the transformer. It also implements a function outputToResultTree(Stylesheet stylesheetTree, java.lang.Object obj) that can output data to the result tree. That fact that all these objects are Java based but accessible from JavaScript is a function of the Bean Scripting Framework (*http://oss.software.ibm.com/developerworks/projects/bsf*), which is contained in *bsf. jar*.

The second object is an instance of org.apache.xalan.templates.ElemExtensionCall. This object represents the extension element itself. From this element, you can extract attributes and child elements that your script needs to interpret to implement the extension's functionality. This is done using standard DOM function calls such as getAttribute( ), getFirstChild( ), getLastChild( ), etc.

There are few limitations on what you can do with a scripting-based extension element. You simply must be capable and willing to dig into the Xalan Java source code and documentation to find out how to make it do what you want. However, you should use scripting-based extensions only for simple tasks because they are significantly slower than native Java extensions.

See Also

The definitive source for information on Xalan extensibility is *http://xml.apache.org/xalan-j/extensions.htm*.

12.3   Adding Extension Functions Using Java

Problem

You want to add your own custom extension functions written in Java.

Solution

This chapter's introduction covered the mechanism for binding the stylesheet to the Java implementations, so this section concentrates on examples.

Chapter 2 showed how to convert numbers from base 10 to other bases (such as base 16 (hex)). You can implement a hex converter in Java easily:

```
package com.ora.xsltckbk.util;

public class HexConverter
{

  public static String toHex(String intString)
  {
    try
    {
       Integer temp = new Integer(intString) ;
       return new String("0x").concat(Integer.toHexString(temp.intValue( ))) ;
     }
     catch (Exception e)
     {
       return new String("0x0") ;
     }
  }
}
```

You can probably tell by the way the return value is formatted with a leading 0x that this particular function will be used in a code-generation application. The following example shows how it might be used:

```
<?xml version="1.0" encoding="UTF-8"?>
<xsl:stylesheet version="1.0" xmlns:xsl="http://www.w3.org/1999/XSL/Transform"
xmlns:xalan="http://xml.apache.org/xslt"
xmlns:hex="xalan://com.ora.xsltckbk.util.HexConverter"
exclude-result-prefixes="hex xalan">

<xsl:template match="group">
enum <xsl:value-of select="@name"/>
{
  <xsl:apply-templates mode="enum"/>
} ;
</xsl:template>

<xsl:template match="constant" mode="enum">
  <xsl:variable name="rep">
    <xsl:call-template name="getRep"/>
  </xsl:variable>
  <xsl:value-of select="@name"/> = <xsl:value-of select="$rep"/>
  <xsl:if test="following-sibling::constant">
    <xsl:text>,</xsl:text>
  </xsl:if>
</xsl:template>

<xsl:template match="constant">
  <xsl:variable name="rep">
    <xsl:call-template name="getRep"/>
  </xsl:variable>
const int <xsl:value-of select="@name"/> = <xsl:value-of select="$rep"/> ;
</xsl:template>

<xsl:template name="getRep">
  <xsl:choose>
    <xsl:when test="@rep = 'hex'">
      <xsl:value-of select="hex:toHex(@value)"/>
    </xsl:when>
    <xsl:otherwise>
      <xsl:value-of select="@value"/>
    </xsl:otherwise>
  </xsl:choose>
</xsl:template>

</xsl:stylesheet>
```

The next example shows how you can construct Java objects and call their methods. Dealing with text layout is difficult when transforming XML to Scalable Vector Graphics. SVG gives you no way to determine how long a string will be when it is rendered. Fortunately, Java provides the functionality you need. The question is whether Java's opinion of how long a string will be when rendered in a particular font matches the SVG engine opinion. Nevertheless, this idea is seductive enough to try:

```
package com.ora.xsltckbk.util ;
import java.awt.* ;
import java.awt.geom.* ;
import java.awt.font.* ;
import java.awt.image.*;

public class SVGFontMetrics
{
  public SVGFontMetrics(String fontName, int size)
  {
    m_font = new Font(fontName, Font.PLAIN, size) ;
    BufferedImage bi
        = new BufferedImage(1, 1, BufferedImage.TYPE_INT_ARGB);
    m_graphics2D = bi.createGraphics() ;
  }

  public SVGFontMetrics(String fontName, int size, boolean bold,
                        boolean italic)
  {
    m_font = new Font(fontName, style(bold,italic) , size) ;
    BufferedImage bi
        = new BufferedImage(1, 1, BufferedImage.TYPE_INT_ARGB);
    m_graphics2D = bi.createGraphics() ;
  }

  public double stringWidth(String str)
  {
    FontRenderContext frc = m_graphics2D.getFontRenderContext();
    TextLayout layout = new TextLayout(str, m_font, frc);
    Rectangle2D rect = layout.getBounds() ;
    return rect.getWidth() ;
  }

  public double stringHeight(String str)
  {
    FontRenderContext frc = m_graphics2D.getFontRenderContext();
    TextLayout layout = new TextLayout(str, m_font, frc);
    Rectangle2D rect = layout.getBounds() ;
    return rect.getHeight() ;
  }

  static private int style(boolean bold, boolean italic)
  {
    int style = Font.PLAIN ;
    if (bold) { style |= Font.BOLD;}
    if (italic) { style |= Font.ITALIC;}
    return style ;
  }

  private Font m_font = null ;
  private Graphics2D m_graphics2D = null;
}
```

Here Java 2's (JDK 1.3.1) Graphics2D and TextLayout classes provide the information you need. You implemented two public constructors to support simple fonts and fonts that are either bold or italic. Two public methods, stringWidth( ) and stringHeight( ), get dimensional information about a how a particular string would be rendered in the font specified by the constructor. This technique is generally accurate on most common fonts, but without precise guarantees, you will have to experiment.

The following stylesheet tests the results:

```
<xsl:stylesheet version="1.0" xmlns:xsl="http://www.w3.org/1999/XSL/Transform"
xmlns:xalan="http://xml.apache.org/xslt"
xmlns:font="xalan://com.ora.xsltckbk.util.SVGFontMetrics"
exclude-result-prefixes="font xalan">

<xsl:output method="xml"/>

<xsl:template match="/">
  <svg width="100%" height="100%">
    <xsl:apply-templates/>
  </svg>
</xsl:template>

<xsl:template match="text">
  <xsl:variable name="fontMetrics"
      select="font:new(@font, @size, boolean(@weight), boolean(@stytle))"/>
  <xsl:variable name="text" select="."/>
  <xsl:variable name="width" select="font:stringWidth($fontMetrics, $text)"/>
  <xsl:variable name="height" select="font:stringHeight($fontMetrics, $text)"/>
  <xsl:variable name="style">
    <xsl:if test="@style">
      <xsl:value-of select="concat('font-style:',@style)"/>
    </xsl:if>
  </xsl:variable>
  <xsl:variable name="weight">
    <xsl:if test="@weight">
      <xsl:value-of select="concat('font-weight:',@weight)"/>
    </xsl:if>
  </xsl:variable>
  <g style="font-family:{@font};font-size:{@size};{$style};{$weight}">
    <!-- Use the SVGFontMetrics info render a rectangle that is -->
    <!-- slightly bigger than the expected size of the text -->
    <!-- Adjust the y position based on the previous text size. -->
    <rect x="10"
          y="{sum(preceding-sibling::text/@size) * 2}pt"
          width="{$width + 2}"
          height="{$height + 2}"
          style="fill:none;stroke: black;stroke-width:0.5;"/>
    <!-- Render the text so it is cenetered in the rectangle -->
    <text x="11"
          y="{sum(preceding-sibling::text/@size) * 2 + @size div 2 + 2}pt">
      <xsl:value-of select="."/>
    </text>
  </g>
```

```
    </xsl:template>

  </xsl:stylesheet>
```

Your test run produced pretty good results on some commonly available fonts, as shown in Figure 12-1:

```
<TextWidthTest>
    <text font="Serif" size="9">M's are BIG; l's are small;</text>
    <text font="Serif" size="10">SVG makes handling text no fun at all</text>
    <text font="Helvetica" size="12">But if I cheat with a little Java</text>
    <text font="Arial" size="14" weight="bold">PROMISE ME YOU WON'T TELL MY MAMMA!
    </text>
    <text font="Century" size="16" style="italic">But if you do, I won't lose cheer.
    </text>
    <text font="Courier New" size="18" weight="bold" style="italic">Its really my tech
editor that I fear!</text>
</TextWidthTest>
```

Figure 12-1. Creating correctly sized text-bounding rectangles with the SVGFontMetrics extension

Discussion

The examples shown in the "Solution" section work unchanged with either Xalan or Saxon (despite the xml.apache.org/xslt namespace). It works because you used the processors' shortcut conventions for encoding the Java class in the namespace.

Notice that constructors are accessed using a function with the name new( ) and that the XSLT processors can figure out which overloaded constructor to call based on the arguments. Member functions of a Java class are called by passing an extra initial argument corresponding to this. The HexConverter example shows that static members are called without the extra this parameter.

The SVGFontMetrics example does not work with older versions of the JDK, but similar results can be obtained if you use the java.awt.FontMetrics class in conjunction with the original java.awt.Graphics class:

```
package com.ora.xsltckbk.util ;
import java.awt.* ;
import java.awt.geom.* ;
import java.lang.System ;

public class FontMetrics
{
  public FontMetrics(String fontName, int size)
  {
    //Any concrete component will do
    Label component = new Label() ;
    m_metrics
      = component.getFontMetrics(
          new Font(fontName, Font.PLAIN, size)) ;
    m_graphics = component.getGraphics() ;
  }

  public FontMetrics(String fontName, int size, boolean bold, boolean italic)
  {
    //Any concrete component will do
    Label component = new Label() ;
    m_metrics
      = component.getFontMetrics(
          new Font(fontName, style(bold,italic) , size)) ;
    m_graphics = component.getGraphics() ;
  }

  //Simple, but less accurate on some fonts
  public int stringWidth(String str)
  {
    return  m_metrics.stringWidth(str) ;
  }

  //Better accuracy on most fonts
  public double stringWidthImproved(String str)
  {
    Rectangle2D rect = m_metrics.getStringBounds(str, m_graphics) ;
    return rect.getWidth() ;
  }

  static private int style(boolean bold, boolean italic)
  {
    int style = Font.PLAIN ;
    if (bold) { style |= Font.BOLD;}
    if (italic) { style |= Font.ITALIC;}
    return style ;
  }
```

```
    private java.awt.FontMetrics m_metrics = null;
    private java.awt.Graphics m_graphics = null ;
}
```

Although these particular examples may not fulfill your immediate needs, they demonstrate the mechanisms by which you can harness your own Java-based extension functions. Other possibilities, in increasing level of difficulty, include:

1. Using Java's Hashtable instead of xsl:key. This allows better control over which elements are indexed and allows the index to be changed during the execution. It overcomes the limitation, whereas xsl:key definitions cannot reference variables. You can also use it to build a master index that spans multiple documents.

2. Implementing a node-sorting function that can compensate for xsl:sort's limitations, for example, constructing a sort based on foreign language rules. Doug Tidwell demonstrates this example with Saxon in *XSLT* (O'Reilly, 2001).

3. Reads and writes multiple file formats in a single stylesheet. For example, it allows the stylesheet to read text files other than XML, such as CSV or proprietary binary files. XSLT 2.0 provides capabilities in this area, but you may not want to wait for it.

4. Processes compressed XML straight from a zip file using java.util.zip.ZipFile. Studying the source code of your XSLT processor's document function would be helpful.

See Also

Chapter 9 punted on the problem of laying out text within your generated SVG tree nodes. You could use SVGFontMetrics as an ingredient in the solution.

Although not specifically related to XSLT extensions, developers interested in Java and SVG should check out Batik (*http://xml.apache.org/batik/index.html*).

12.4   Adding Extension Elements Using Java

Problem

You want to extend the functionality of XSLT by adding elements with custom behavior.

Solution

Prior sections considered how extensions provided by the XSLT implementers could be used to your advantage. This section develops your own extension elements from scratch. Unlike extension functions, creating extension elements requires much more intimacy with a particular processor's implementation details. Because processor designs vary widely, much of the code will not be portable between processors.

This section begins with a simple extension that provides syntactic sugar rather than extended functionality. A common requirement in XSLT coding is to switch context to another node. Using an xsl:for-each is an idiomatic way of accomplishing this. The process is somewhat confusing because the intent is not to loop but to change context to the *single* node defined by the xsl:for-each's select:

```
<xsl:for-each select="document('new.xml')">
    <!-- Process new document -->
</xsl:for-each>
```

You will implement an extension element called xslx:set-context, which acts exactly like xsl:for-each, but only on the first node of the node set defined by the select (normally, you have only one node anyway).

Saxon requires an implementation of the com.icl.saxon.style.ExtensionElement-Factory interface for all extension elements associated with a particular namespace. The factory is responsible for creating the extension elements from the element's local name. The second extension, named templtext, is covered later:

```
package com.ora.xsltckbk;
import com.icl.saxon.style.ExtensionElementFactory;
import org.xml.sax.SAXException;

public class CkBkElementFactory implements ExtensionElementFactory {

    public Class getExtensionClass(String localname)  {
        if (localname.equals("set-context")) return CkBkSetContext.class;
        if (localname.equals("templtext")) return CkBkTemplText.class;
        return null;
    }

}
```

When using a stylesheet extension, you must use a namespace that ends in a /, followed by the factory's fully qualified name. The namespace prefix must also appear in the xsl:stylesheet's extension-element-prefixes attribute:

```
<xsl:stylesheet version="1.0"
 xmlns:xsl="http://www.w3.org/1999/XSL/Transform"
 xmlns:xslx="http://com.ora.xsltckbk.CkBkElementFactory"
 extension-element-prefixes="xslx">

<xsl:template match="/">
  <xslx:set-context select="foo/bar">
    <xsl:value-of select="."/>
  </xslx:set-context>
</xsl:template>

</xsl:stylesheet>
```

The set-context element implementation derives from com.icl.saxon.style. StyleElement and must implement prepareAttributes() and process(), but it will usually implement the others shown in Table 12-3.

Table 12-3. *Important Saxon StyleElement methods*

Method	Effect
isInstruction()	Extensions always return `true`.
mayContainTemplateBody()	Returns `true` if this element can contain child elements. Often returns `true` to allow an `xsl:fallback` child.
prepareAttributes()	Called at compile time to allow the class to parse information contained in the extensions attributes. It is also the time to do local validation.
validate()	Called at compile time after all stylesheet elements have done local validation. It allows cross validation between this element and its parents or children.
process(Context context)	Called at runtime to execute the extension. This method can access or modify information in the context, but must not modify the stylesheet tree.

The `xslx:set-context` element was easy to implement because the code was stolen from Saxon's `XSLForEach` implementation and modified to do what `XSLForEach` does, but only once:

```
public class CkBkSetContext extends com.icl.saxon.style.StyleElement {

    Expression select = null;

    public boolean isInstruction() {
        return true;
    }

    public boolean mayContainTemplateBody() {
        return true;
    }
```

Here you make sure `@select` is present. If it is, call `makeExpression`, which parses it into an XPath expression:

```
public void prepareAttributes()
                throws TransformerConfigurationException {

    StandardNames sn = getStandardNames();
    AttributeCollection atts = getAttributeList();

    String selectAtt = null;

    for (int a=0; a<atts.getLength(); a++) {
        int nc = atts.getNameCode(a);
        int f = nc & 0xfffff;
        if (f==sn.SELECT) {
            selectAtt = atts.getValue(a);
        } else {
            checkUnknownAttribute(nc);
        }
    }

    if (selectAtt==null) {
        reportAbsence("select");
```

```
        } else {
            select = makeExpression(selectAtt);
        }
    }

    public void validate() throws TransformerConfigurationException {
        checkWithinTemplate();
    }
```

This code is identical to Saxon's for-each, except instead of looping selection. hasMoreElements, it simply checks once, extracts the element, sets the context and current node, processes children, and returns the result to the context:

```
public void process(Context context) throws TransformerException
{
    NodeEnumeration selection = select.enumerate(context, false);
    if (!(selection instanceof LastPositionFinder)) {
        selection = new LookaheadEnumerator(selection);
    }

    Context c = context.newContext();
    c.setLastPositionFinder((LastPositionFinder)selection);
    int position = 1;

      if (selection.hasMoreElements()) {
          NodeInfo node = selection.nextElement();
          c.setPosition(position++);
          c.setCurrentNode(node);
          c.setContextNode(node);
          processChildren(c);
          context.setReturnValue(c.getReturnValue());
      }
    }
}
```

The next example extension is not as simple because it extends XSLT's capabilities rather than creating an alternate implementation for existing functionality.

You can see that because a whole chapter of this book is dedicated to code generation, the task interests me. However, although XSLT is near optimal in its XML manipulation capabilities, it lacks output capabilities due to the XML's verbosity. Consider a simple C++ code generation task in native XSLT:

```
<classes>
  <class>
    <name>MyClass1</name>
  </class>

  <class>
    <name>MyClass2</name>
  </class>

  <class>
    <name>MyClass3</name>
```

```
    <bases>
      <base>MyClass1</base>
      <base>MyClass2</base>
    </bases>
  </class>

</classes>
```

A stylesheet that transforms this XML into C++ might look like this:

```
<xsl:stylesheet version="1.0" xmlns:xsl="http://www.w3.org/1999/XSL/Transform">

<xsl:output method="text"/>

<xsl:template match="class">
class <xsl:value-of select="name"/> <xsl:apply-templates select="bases"/>
{
public:

  <xsl:value-of select="name"/>() ;
  ~<xsl:value-of select="name"/>() ;
  <xsl:value-of select="name"/>(const <xsl:value-of select="name"/>&amp; other) ;
  <xsl:value-of select="name"/>&amp; operator =(const <xsl:value-of select="name"/>
&amp; other) ;
} ;
</xsl:template>

<xsl:template match="bases">
<xsl:text>: public </xsl:text>
<xsl:for-each select="base">
  <xsl:value-of select="."/>
  <xsl:if test="position() != last()">
    <xsl:text>, public </xsl:text>
  </xsl:if>
</xsl:for-each>
</xsl:template>

<xsl:template match="text()"/>

</xsl:stylesheet>
```

This code is tedious to write and difficult to read because the C++ is lost in a rat's nest of markup.

The extension xslx:templtext addresses this problem by creating an alternate implementation of xsl:text that can contain special *escapes* and indicate special processing. An escape is indicated by surrounding backslashes (\) and comes in two forms. An obvious alternative would use { and } to mimic attribute value templates and XQuery; however, because you use these common characters in code generators, I opted for the backslashes.

Escape	Equivalent XSLT
\expression\	`<xsl:value-of select="expression"/>`

\expression%delimit\ᵃ	`<xsl:for-each select="expression">`
	`<xsl:value-of select="."/>`
	`<xsl:if test="position( ) !=`
	`    last( )>`
	`    <xsl:value-of select="delimit"/>`
	`</xsl:if>`
	`</xsl:for-each>`

ᵃ XSLT 2.0 will provide this functionality via `<xsl:value-of select="expression" separator="delimit" />`

Given this facility, your code generator would look as follows:

```
<xsl:stylesheet
 version="1.0"
 xmlns:xsl="http://www.w3.org/1999/XSL/Transform"
 xmlns:xslx="http://com.ora.xsltckbk.CkBkElementFactory"
 extension-element-prefixes="xslx">

<xsl:output method="text"/>

<xsl:template match="class">
<xslx:templtext>
class \name\ <xsl:apply-templates select="bases"/>
{
public:

  \name\( ) ;
  ~\name\( ) ;
  \name\(const \name\&amp; other) ;
  \name\&amp; operator =(const \name\&amp; other) ;
} ;
</xslx:templtext>
</xsl:template>

<xsl:template match="bases">
<xslx:templtext>: public \base%', public '\</xslx:templtext>
</xsl:template>

<xsl:template match="text( )"/>

</xsl:stylesheet>
```

This code is substantially easier to read and write. This facility is applicable to any context where a lot of boilerplate text will be generated. An XSLT purist may frown on such an extension because it introduces a foreign syntax into XSLT that is not subject to simple XML manipulation. This argument is valid; however, from a practical standpoint, many developers would reject XSLT (in favor of Perl) for boilerplate generation simply because it lacks a concise and unobtrusive syntax for getting the job done. So enough hemming and hawing; let's just code it:

```
package com.ora.xsltckbk;
import java.util.Vector ;
import java.util.Enumeration ;
import com.icl.saxon.tree.AttributeCollection;
import com.icl.saxon.*;
import com.icl.saxon.expr.*;
import javax.xml.transform.*;
import com.icl.saxon.output.*;
import com.icl.saxon.trace.TraceListener;
import com.icl.saxon.om.NodeInfo;
import com.icl.saxon.om.NodeEnumeration;
import com.icl.saxon.style.StyleElement;
import com.icl.saxon.style.StandardNames;
import com.icl.saxon.tree.AttributeCollection;
import com.icl.saxon.tree.NodeImpl;
```

Your extension class first declares constants that will be used in a simple state machine that parses the escapes:

```
public class CkBkTemplText extends com.icl.saxon.style.StyleElement
{
    private static final int SCANNING_STATE = 0 ;
    private static final int FOUND1_STATE   = 1 ;
    private static final int EXPR_STATE     = 2 ;
    private static final int FOUND2_STATE   = 3 ;
    private static final int DELIMIT_STATE  = 4 ;
```

Then define four private classes that implement the mini-language contained within the xslx:templtext element. The base class, CkBkTemplParam, captures literal text that may come before an escape:

```
private class CkBkTemplParam
{
    public CkBkTemplParam(String prefix)
    {
        m_prefix = prefix ;
    }

    public void process(Context context) throws TransformerException
    {
        if (!m_prefix.equals(""))
        {
            Outputter out = context.getOutputter();
            out.setEscaping(false);
            out.writeContent(m_prefix);
            out.setEscaping(true);
        }
    }

    protected String m_prefix ;
}
```

The CkBkValueTemplParam class derives from CkBkTemplParam and implements the behavior of a simple value-of escape \expr\. To simplify the implementation in this example, the disabled output escaping will be the norm inside a xslx:templtext element:

```
private class CkBkValueTemplParam extends CkBkTemplParam
{
  public CkBkValueTemplParam(String prefix, Expression value)
  {
    super(prefix) ;
    m_value = value ;
  }

  public void process(Context context) throws TransformerException
  {
    super.process(context) ;
    Outputter out = context.getOutputter();
    out.setEscaping(false);
    if (m_value != null)
    {
        m_value.outputStringValue(out, context);
    }
    out.setEscaping(true);
  }

  private Expression m_value ;

}
```

The CkBkTemplParam class implements the of \expr%delimit\ behavior, largely by mimicking the behavior of a Saxon XslForEach class:

```
private class CkBkListTemplParam extends CkBkTemplParam
{
  public CkBkListTemplParam(String prefix, Expression list,
                            Expression delimit)
  {
    super(prefix) ;
    m_list = list ;
    m_delimit = delimit ;
  }

  public void process(Context context) throws TransformerException
  {
    super.process(context) ;
    if (m_list != null)
    {
      NodeEnumeration m_listEnum = m_list.enumerate(context, false);

      Outputter out = context.getOutputter();
      out.setEscaping(false);
      while(m_listEnum.hasMoreElements())
      {
        NodeInfo node = m_listEnum.nextElement();
```

```
      if (node != null)
      {
        node.copyStringValue(out);
      }
      if (m_listEnum.hasMoreElements( ) && m_delimit != null)
      {
        m_delimit.outputStringValue(out, context);
      }
    }
    out.setEscaping(true);
  }
}

private Expression m_list = null;
private Expression m_delimit = null ;
}
```

The last private class is CkBkStyleTemplParam, and it is used as a holder of elements nested within the xslx:templtext, for example, xsl:apply-templates:

```
private class CkBkStyleTemplParam extends CkBkTemplParam
{
  public CkBkStyleTemplParam(StyleElement snode)
  {
    m_snode = snode ;
  }

  public void process(Context context) throws TransformerException
  {
    if (m_snode.validationError != null)
    {
        fallbackProcessing(m_snode, context);
    }
    else
    {
        try
      {
        context.setStaticContext(m_snode.staticContext);
        m_snode.process(context);
      }
      catch (TransformerException err)
      {
        throw snode.styleError(err);
      }
    }
  }
}
```

The next three methods are standard. If you allow the standard disable-output-escaping attribute to control output escaping, you would capture its value in prepareAttributes( ). The Saxon *XslText.java* source provides the necessary code:

```
public boolean isInstruction( )
{
```

```
   return true;
}

public boolean mayContainTemplateBody()
{
  return true;
}

public void prepareAttributes() throws TransformerConfigurationException
{
  StandardNames sn = getStandardNames();
   AttributeCollection atts = getAttributeList();
   for (int a=0; a<atts.getLength(); a++)
  {
     int nc = atts.getNameCode(a);
    checkUnknownAttribute(nc);
  }
 }
```

The validate stage is an opportunity to parse the contents of the xslx:templtext element, looking for escapes. You send every text node to a parser function. Element style content is converted into instances CkBkStyleTemplParam. The member m_TemplParms is a vector where the results of parsing are stored:

```
public void validate() throws TransformerConfigurationException
{
    checkWithinTemplate();
    m_TemplParms = new Vector() ;

    NodeImpl node = (NodeImpl)getFirstChild();
    String value ;
    while (node!=null)
    {
      if (node.getNodeType() == NodeInfo.TEXT)
      {
        parseTemplText(node.getStringValue()) ;
      }
      else
      if (node instanceof StyleElement)
      {
         StyleElement snode = (StyleElement) node;
        m_TemplParms.addElement(new CkBkStyleTemplParam(snode)) ;
      }
      node = (NodeImpl)node.getNextSibling();
    }
}
```

The process method loops over m_TemplParms and calls each implementation's process method:

```
public void process(Context context) throws TransformerException
{
  Enumeration iter = m_TemplParms.elements() ;
  while (iter.hasMoreElements())
```

```
    {
        CkBkTemplParam param = (CkBkTemplParam) iter.nextElement() ;
        param.process(context) ;
    }
}
```

The following private functions implement a simple state-machine-driven parser that would be easier to implement if you had access to a regular-expression engine (which is actually available to Java Version 1.4.1). The parser handles two consecutive backslashes (\\) as a request for a literal backslash. Likewise, %% is translated into a single %:

```java
private void parseTemplText(String value)
{
    //This state machine parses the text looking for parameters
    int ii = 0 ;
    int len = value.length() ;

    int state = SCANNING_STATE ;
    StringBuffer temp = new StringBuffer("") ;
    StringBuffer expr = new StringBuffer("") ;
    while(ii < len)
    {
      char c = value.charAt(ii++) ;
      switch (state)
      {
        case SCANNING_STATE:
        {
          if (c == '\\')
          {
            state = FOUND1_STATE ;
          }
          else
          {
            temp.append(c) ;
          }
        }
        break ;

        case FOUND1_STATE:
        {
          if (c == '\\')
          {
            temp.append(c) ;
            state = SCANNING_STATE ;
          }
          else
          {
            expr.append(c) ;
            state = EXPR_STATE ;
          }
        }
        break ;
```

```
          case EXPR_STATE:
          {
            if (c == '\\')
            {
              state = FOUND2_STATE ;
            }
            else
            {
              expr.append(c) ;
            }
          }
          break ;

          case FOUND2_STATE:
          {
            if (c == '\\')
            {
              state = EXPR_STATE ;
              expr.append(c) ;
            }
            else
            {
              processParam(temp, expr) ;
              state = SCANNING_STATE ;
              temp = new StringBuffer("") ;
                    temp.append(c) ;
              expr = new StringBuffer("") ;
            }
          }
          break ;
        }
      }
    if (state == FOUND1_STATE || state == EXPR_STATE)
    {
        compileError("xslx:templtext dangling \\");
    }
    else
    if (state == FOUND2_STATE)
    {
      processParam(temp, expr) ;
    }
    else
    {
      processParam(temp, new StringBuffer("")) ;
    }
}

private void processParam(StringBuffer prefix, StringBuffer expr)
{
  if (expr.length( ) == 0)
  {
    m_TemplParms.addElement(new CkBkTemplParam(new String(prefix))) ;
  }
  else
```

```
        {
            processParamExpr(prefix, expr) ;
        }
    }

    private void processParamExpr(StringBuffer prefix, StringBuffer expr)
    {
        int ii = 0 ;
        int len = expr.length( ) ;

        int state = SCANNING_STATE ;
        StringBuffer list = new StringBuffer("") ;
        StringBuffer delimit = new StringBuffer("") ;
        while(ii < len)
        {
            char c = expr.charAt(ii++) ;
            switch (state)
            {
            case SCANNING_STATE:
            {
                if (c == '%')
                {
                    state = FOUND1_STATE ;
                }
                else
                {
                    list.append(c) ;
                }
            }
            break ;

            case FOUND1_STATE:
            {
                if (c == '%')
                {
                    list.append(c) ;
                    state = SCANNING_STATE ;
                }
                else
                {
                    delimit.append(c) ;
                    state = DELIMIT_STATE ;
                }
            }
            break ;

            case DELIMIT_STATE:
            {
                if (c == '%')
                {
                    state = FOUND2_STATE ;
                }
                else
                {
```

```
            delimit.append(c) ;
          }
        }
        break ;
      }
    }
    try
    {
      if (state == FOUND1_STATE)
      {
          compileError("xslx:templtext trailing %");
      }
      else
      if (state == FOUND2_STATE)
      {
          compileError("xslx:templtext extra %");
      }
      else
      if (state == SCANNING_STATE)
      {
        String prefixStr = new String(prefix) ;
        Expression value = makeExpression(new String(list)) ;
        m_TemplParms.addElement(
              new CkBkValueTemplParam(prefixStr, value)) ;
      }
      else
      {
        String prefixStr = new String(prefix) ;
        Expression listExpr = makeExpression(new String(list)) ;
        Expression delimitExpr = makeExpression(new String(delimit)) ;
        m_TemplParms.addElement(
           new CkBkListTemplParam(prefixStr, listExpr, delimitExpr)) ;
      }
    }
    catch(Exception e)
    {
    }
  }
  //A vector of CBkTemplParms parse form text
  private Vector m_TemplParms = null;
}
```

You can make some useful enhancements to the functionality of xslx:templtext. For
example, you could expand the functionality of the list escape to multiple lists (e.g.,
/expr1%delim1%expr2%delim2/.). This enhancement would roughly translate into the
following XSLT equivalent:

```
<xsl:for-each select="expr1">
  <xsl:variable name="pos" select="position( )"/>
  <xsl:value-of select="."/>
  <xsl:if test="$pos != last( )">
    <xsl:value-of select="delim1"/>
  </xsl:if>
  <xsl:value-of select="expr2[$pos]"/>
```

```
<xsl:if test="$pos != last( )">
    <xsl:value-of select="delim2"/>
</xsl:if>
</xsl:for-each >
```

This facility would be useful when pairs of lists need to be sequenced into text. For example, consider a C++ function's parameters, which consist of name and type pairs. The XSLT code is only a rough specification of semantics because it assumes that the node sets specified by expr1 and expr2 have the same number of elements. I believe that an actual implementation would continue to expand the lists as long as any set still had nodes, suppressing delimiters for those that did not. Better yet, the behavior could be controlled by attributes of xslx:templtext.

Discussion

Space does not permit full implementations of these extension elements in Xalan. However, based on the information provided in the introduction, the path should be relatively clear.

See Also

Developers interested in extending Saxon should read Michael Kay's article on Saxon design (*http://www-106.ibm.com/developerworks/library/x-xslt2*).

12.5 Using XSLT from Perl

Problem

You have a problem that is more appropriately solved in Perl, but would be easier with a pinch of XSLT.

Solution

There are several choices for embedding XSLT in Perl. XML::LibXSLT and XML::LibXML are Perl frontends to the functionality of GNOME library's SAX and XSLT processors. The following example, borrowed from Erik T. Ray's and Jason McIntosh's *Perl and XML* (O'Reilly, 2002), shows a Perl program that batch-processes several XML files with a single XSLT script, compiled once:

```
use XML::LibXSLT;
use XML::LibXML;

# the arguments for this command are stylesheet and source files
my( $style_file, @source_files ) = @ARGV;
```

```
# initialize the parser and XSLT processor
my $parser = XML::LibXML->new( );
my $xslt = XML::LibXSLT->new( );
my $stylesheet = $xslt->parse_stylesheet_file( $style_file );

# for each source file: parse, transform, print out result
foreach my $file ( @source_files ) {
  my $source_doc = $parser->parse_file( $source_file );
  my $result = $stylesheet->transform( $source_doc );
  print $stylesheet->output_string( $result );
}
```

Parameters to the stylesheet can be passed in as a Perl hash, as shown in the following code:

```
#Similar code from previous example has been elided.

my %params = {
     param1 => 10,
     param2 => 'foo',
} ;

foreach my $file ( @source_files ) {
  my $source_doc = $parser->parse_file( $source_file );
  my $result = $stylesheet->transform($source_doc, %params);
  print $stylesheet->output_string( $result );
}
```

Passing parameters to from Perl to the stylesheet would enable, among other things, a Perl-based CGI program that received input from an HTML form and queried an XML database using XSLT. See Recipe 11.5, where we cheated by forking the XSLT processor rather than embedding.

XML::Xalan is another Perl XSLT module that allows Perl to invoke Xalan's processor. Edwin Pratomo, the author of this module, still considers it alpha-level software.

Using XML::Xalan through external files is your simplest option:

```
use XML::Xalan;

  #Construct the transformer
  my $tr = new XML::Xalan::Transformer;

  #Compile the stylesheet
  my $compiled = $tr->compile_stylesheet_file("my.xsl");

#Parse the input source document
  my $parsed = $tr->parse_file("my.xml");

  my $dest_file = "myresult.xml" ;

  #Execute the transformation saving the result
  $tr->transform_to_file($parsed, $compiled, $dest_file)
    or die $tr->errstr;
```

A more useful mode of usage returns the result into a variable for further processing:

```
my $res = $tr->transform_to_data($parsed, $compiled);
```

You do not need to preparse the input or precompile the stylesheet, since either can be passed as files or literal strings:

```
my $res = $tr->transform_to_data($src_file, $xsl_file);
```

This returns the literal result as a string, so this usage probably makes most sense when the output format is text that you want to post-process in Perl.

Alternatively, you can receive the results in an event-driven manner:

```
#Create a handler sub
$out_handler = sub {
    my ($ctx, $mesg) = @_;
    print $ctx $mesg;
};
#Invoke the transformation using the handler
$tr->transform_to_handler(
    $xmlfile, $xslfile,
    *STDERR, $out_handler);
```

Discussion

Many Perl developers have not fully embraced XSLT because once you master Perl, it is difficult to do something in anything but the Perl way. To be fair, most Perl developers realize that other languages have their place, and XSLT certainly can simplify a complex XML transformation even if most of the overall program remains purely Perl.

See Also

Other Perl XSLT solutions include T. J. Mather's XML::GNOME::XSLT, which is a Perl frontend to libXSLT, a C-based XSLT processor from GNOME. You can also use the native Perl XSLT implementation XML::XSLT by Jonathan Stowe. Currently, it does not implement many of XSLT 1.0's most advanced features, including xsl:sort, xsl:key, and xsl:import, and it has only partial support in several other areas. A third option is Pavel Hlavnicka's XML::Saboltron, which is a Perl frontend to the Ginger Alliance's C++-based XSLT offering. Information on these modules can be found at *http://www. cpan.org.*

Another solution that mixes Perl with XSLT is AxKit, an XML Application server for Apache. AxKit uses a pipelining processing model that allows processing of content in stages. It uses the Sablotron processor for XSLT functionality.

12.6   Using XSLT from Java

Problem

You want to invoke XSLT processing from within a Java application.

Solution

You can invoke XSLT functionality from Java in three basic ways.

- Using the native interface of your favorite Java-based XSLT implementation
- Using the more portable TrAX API
- Using JAXP 1.1 (a superset of TrAX)

If you are familiar with the internals of a specific Java-based XSLT implementation, you might be tempted to use its API directly. However, this solution is not desirable, since your code will not be portable.

An alternative is Transformation API for XML (TrAX), an initiative initially sponsored by Apache.org (*http://xml.apache.org/xalan-j/trax.html*). The philosophy behind TrAX is best explained by quoting the TrAX site:

> The Java community will greatly benefit from a common API that will allow them to understand and apply a single model, write to consistent interfaces, and apply the transformations polymorphically. TrAX attempts to define a model that is clean and generic, yet fills general application requirements across a wide variety of uses.

TrAX was subsumed into Java's JAXP 1.1 (and more recently 1.2) specification, so there are now only two ways to interface Java to XSLT: portably and nonportably. However, the choice is not simply a question of right and wrong. Each processor implementation has special features that are sometimes needed, and if portability is not a concern, you can take advantage of a particular facility that you require. Nevertheless, this section covers only the portable JAXP 1.1 API.

You can implement a simple XSLT command-line processor in terms of JAXP 1.1, as shown in an example borrowed from Eric M. Burke's *Java and XSLT* (O'Reilly, 2001):

```
public class Transform
{

  public static void main(String[ ] args) throws Exception
  {
    if (args.length != 2)
    {
      System.err.println(
        "Usage: java Transform [xmlfile] [xsltfile]");
      System.exit(1);
    }
```

```
        //Open the source and style sheet files
        File xmlFile = new File(args[0]);
        File xsltFile = new File(args[1]);

        //JAXP uses a Source interface to read data
        Source xmlSource = new StreamSource(xmlFile);
        Source xsltSource = new StreamSource(xsltFile);

        //Factory classes allow the specific XSLT processor
        //to be hidden from the application by returning a
        //standard Transformer interface
        TransformerFactory transFact =
          TransformerFactory.newInstance();
        Transformer trans = transFact.newTransformer(xsltSource);

        //Applies the stylesheet to the source document
        trans.transform(xmlSource, new StreamResult(System.out));
    }
}
```

In addition to a StreamResult, a DOMResult can capture the result as a DOM tree for further processing, or a SAXResult can be specified to receive the results in an event-driven manner.

In the case of DOM, the user can obtain the result as a DOM Document, DocumentFragment or Element, depending on the type of node passed in the DOMResult constructor.

In the case of SAXResult, a user-specified ContentHandler is passed to the SaxResult constructor and is the object that actually receives the SAX events. Recall that a SAX content handler receives callbacks for events such as startDocument( ), startElement( ), characters( ), endElement( ), and endDocument( ). See *http://www.megginson.com/SAX* for more information on SAX.

Discussion

The beauty of accessing XSLT transformation capabilities from Java is not that you can write your own XSLT processor frontend, as you did in the solution section, but that you can extend the already formidable capabilities of Java to include XSLT's transformational abilities.

Consider a server process written in Java that must deal with constantly changing XML files stored in an XML database or XML arriving in the form of SOAP messages. Perhaps this server needs to support multiple versions of document schema or multiple SOAP clients for backward compatibility. Thus the server must handle several schemas transparently. If data in an older schema can be transformed to newer ones, then the server code will be that much simpler.

The nice thing about using XSLT via the JAXP interface is that instances of transformers can be reused so you need to parse the stylesheet only once, when the server loads. However, if your server is multithreaded and each thread must handle transformations, different instances will be required per thread to ensure thread safety.

See Also

Eric M. Burke's *Java and XSLT* (O'Reilly, 2001) contains extensive coverage of Java and XSLT integration, especially via JAXP 1.1. It includes several complete application examples, such as Discussion Forum and Wireless Markup Language (WML) applications.

CHAPTER 13

Testing and Debugging

*Frequently, crashes are followed with a message like
"ID 02." "ID" is an abbreviation for idiosyncrasy and
the number that follows indicates how many more
months of testing the product should have had.*
—Guy Kawasaki

Many XSLT scripts you write will be so-called one-offs that transform well-defined input. Here testing does little more than execute the transformation against the input and inspect the output. However, even in this simple case, how do you best deal with a stylesheet that does not do what you expect? Usually, simple inspection of the code reveals the offending lines. However, debugging by code inspection is often not effective for developers new to XSLT—including those who are seasoned in manipulating XML in more procedural languages. This chapter demonstrates basic debugging techniques that offer quicker solutions to common coding mistakes and enhance your understanding of XSLT.

Many examples in this book emphasize the creation of reusable XSLT. Authors of reusable code must subject that code to more rigorous testing. By definition, reusable code is often deployed in contexts of which the author cannot have full knowledge. You should ensure that the code performs as advertised for typical inputs and boundary conditions. Reusable code should also behave predictably in the face of illegal inputs.

Developers are more likely to test when it is easy. Interpreted languages such as XSLT are typically easier to test because there is no compile and link cycle. XSLT has a further advantage in that it is *homoiconic*—the syntax of the language and its data are identical. This feature allows easy embedding of test data into the stylesheet, thus creating completely self-contained tests.

All recipes in this chapter are based purely on facilities in XSLT. However, nothing beats a native debugger. The following is a list of commercial products in this space. I have not tried all the products, so do not interpret the list as an endorsement. Many products do much more than debug XSLT.

- Active State's Visual XSLT (*http://www.activestate.com/Products/Visual_XSLT/*)
- Altova's XML Spy Version 5.0 (*http://www.xmlspy.com/products_ide.html*)
- MarrowSoft's Xselerator 2.5 (*http://www.topxml.com/xselerator/*)

Treebeard (*http://treebeard.sourceforge.net/*) is an open source project that is written in Java and works with Xalan, Saxon, jd, and Oracle XSLT processors. It is more of a visual XSLT development environment than a full-fledged debugger, but it can help debug XPath expressions.

13.1 Using xsl:message Effectively

Problem

You want to inspect your stylesheet to determine why it does not do what you expect.

Solution

The simplest tool in your debugging arsenal is `xsl:message`, which is often used to figure out if you are executing a particular template:

```
<xsl:stylesheet version="1.0" xmlns:xsl="http://www.w3.org/1999/XSL/Transform">

<!-- ... -->

<xsl:template match="someElement[someChild = 'someValue']">
  <xsl:message>Matched someElement[someChild = 'someValue']</xsl:message>

  <!-- ... -->

</xsl:template>

</xsl:stylesheet>
```

The technique is even more useful when you display relevant data. Be sure to surround the output with known, descriptive text so you can disambiguate the output from other occurrences of `xsl:message` and detect when a message was executed (but the results were empty):

```
<xsl:stylesheet version="1.0" xmlns:xsl="http://www.w3.org/1999/XSL/Transform">

<xsl:template match="someElement[someChild = 'someValue']">
  <xsl:param name="myParam"/>
  <!-- This is not an effective debugging technique. If you run a test and see
       nothing it might be because the template was never matched or it might be
       because it was matched with $myParam empty -->
  <xsl:message><xsl:value-of select="$myParam"/></xsl:message>
</xsl:template>
```

```
<xsl:template match="someElement[someChild = 'someOtherValue']">
  <xsl:param name="myParam"/>
  <!-- This is better -->
  <xsl:message>Matched someElement[someChild = 'someOtherValue']</xsl:message>
  <xsl:message>$myParam=[<xsl:value-of select="$myParam"/>]</xsl:message>
</xsl:template>

</xsl:stylesheet>
```

Use a debugging parameter to preserve xsl:message-based instrumentation in your stylesheet. Place the parameter in your own namespace if you want to distribute the code to others without interfering with their own debug instrumentation:

```
<xsl:stylesheet version="1.0" xmlns:xsl="http://www.w3.org/1999/XSL/Transform"
                xmlns:dbg="http:www.ora.com/XSLTCookbook/ns/debug">

<xsl:param name="dbg:debugOn" select="false()"/>

<xsl:template match="someElement[someChild = 'someValue']">
  <xsl:param name="myParam"/>
  <xsl:if test="$dbg:debugOn">
    <xsl:message>Matched someElement[someChild = 'someValue']</xsl:message>
    <xsl:message>$myParam=[<xsl:value-of select="$myParam"/>]</xsl:message>
  </xsl:if>
</xsl:template>

</xsl:stylesheet>
```

Discussion

Before debuggers, there were print statements. Although some interactive XSLT debuggers are now available, none that I know of are free.

In addition to the previous usage of xsl:message, you might consider using assertions to test preconditions, postconditions, or invariants that must be true at some point in the stylesheet:

```
<xsl:if test="debugOn>
  <xsl:if test="insert some invariant test">
    <xsl:message terminate="yes">
      Message describing the violation or failure.
    </xsl:message>
  </xsl:if>
</xsl:if>
```

Assertion style tests typically use terminate="yes" because they are fatal errors by definition.

An important consideration when debugging with xsl:message is that the output's destination varies, depending on the environment in which the XSLT script is executed. For example, you may not be able to see the output at all if the transformation runs in a browser client. It is usually advisable to test stylesheets using a command-line processor before moving to the target environment.

When the output is XML or HTML, an alternative to xsl:message is to emit debugging comments into the result document using xsl:comment. In particular, you can begin each template in your stylesheet with an xsl:comment to trace back from the output to the templates that generated it:

```
<xsl:template match="*">
    <xsl:comment>Generated by the wild card match</xsl:comment>
 ...
</xsl:template>


 ...


<xsl:template match="*" mode="foo">
    <xsl:comment>Generated by the mode=foo wild card match</xsl:comment>
 ...
</xsl:template>
```

13.2   Tracing the Flow of Your Stylesheet Through Its Input Document

Problem

You want to trace your stylesheet's navigation through the XML document.

Solution

You should first consider the trace options available in your XSLT processor. Saxon has a -t option that displays timing information about various processing stages and a -T option that causes the output of trace information. Xalan has -TT, which traces the templates as they are called; -TG, which traces each generation event; -TS, which traces each selection event; and -TTC, which traces template children as they are called.

If your processor does not support trace output or you need higher degrees of control over the output, you can consider a solution based on xsl:message. With xsl:message, it is easy to generate debug output that lets you trace the flow of control through the stylesheet. It is also useful to trace the flow of the stylesheet through the document. Here is a utility you can import into any stylesheet for this purpose:

```
<!-- xtrace.xslt -->

<xsl:stylesheet version="1.0" xmlns:xsl="http://www.w3.org/1999/XSL/Transform"
                              xmlns:dbg="http://www.ora.com/XSLTCookbook/ns/debug">

<xsl:param name="debugOn" select="false()"/>

<xsl:template match="node()" mode="dbg:trace" name="dbg:xtrace">
<xsl:param name="tag" select=" 'xtrace' "/>
<xsl:if test="$debugOn">
  <xsl:message>
      <xsl:value-of select="$tag"/>: <xsl:call-template name="dbg:expand-path"/>
```

```
    </xsl:message>
  </xsl:if>
</xsl:template>

<!--Expand the xpath to the current node -->
<xsl:template name="dbg:expand-path">
  <xsl:apply-templates select="." mode="dbg:expand-path"/>
</xsl:template>

<!-- Root -->
<xsl:template match="/" mode="dbg:expand-path">
  <xsl:text>/</xsl:text>
</xsl:template>

<!--Top level node -->
<xsl:template match="/*" mode="dbg:expand-path">
  <xsl:text>/</xsl:text><xsl:value-of select="name()"/>
</xsl:template>

<!--Nodes with node parents -->
<xsl:template match="*/*" mode="dbg:expand-path">
  <xsl:apply-templates select=".." mode="dbg:expand-path"/>/<xsl:value-of
select="name()"/>[<xsl:number/>]<xsl:text/>
</xsl:template>

<!--Attribute nodes -->
<xsl:template match="@*" mode="dbg:expand-path">
  <xsl:apply-templates select=".." mode="dbg:expand-path"/>/@<xsl:value-of
select="name()"/>
</xsl:template>

<!-- Text nodes (normalized for clarity) -->
<xsl:template match="text()" mode="dbg:expand-path">normalized-text(<xsl:value-of
select="normalize-space(.)"/>)</xsl:template>

</xsl:stylesheet>
```

When you place calls to dbg:xtrace in your stylesheet, you will generate a message
containing the path to the current node. For example, this code instruments an identity stylesheet with xtrace:

```
<xsl:stylesheet version="1.0" xmlns:xsl="http://www.w3.org/1999/XSL/Transform"
                                         xmlns:dbg="http://www.ora.com/
XSLTCookbook/ns/debug">

<xsl:include href="xtrace.xslt"/>

<xsl:template match="/ | node() | @* | comment() | processing-instruction()">
  <xsl:call-template name="dbg:trace"/>
  <xsl:copy>
    <xsl:apply-templates select="@* | node()"/>
  </xsl:copy>
</xsl:template>

</xsl:stylesheet>
```

Using this test input:

```
<test foo="1">
  <someElement n="1"/>
  <someElement n="2">
    <someChild>someValue</someChild>
  </someElement>
  <someElement n="3">
    <someChild>someOtherValue</someChild>
  </someElement>
  <someElement n="4">
    <someChild>someValue</someChild>
  </someElement>
</test>
```

you produce the following debug output:

```
xtrace: /
xtrace: /test
xtrace: /test/@foo
xtrace: normalized-text( )
xtrace: /test/someElement[1]
xtrace: /test/someElement[1]/@n
xtrace: normalized-text( )
xtrace: /test/someElement[2]
xtrace: /test/someElement[2]/@n
xtrace: normalized-text( )
xtrace: /test/someElement[2]/someChild[1]
xtrace: normalized-text(someValue)
xtrace: normalized-text( )
xtrace: normalized-text( )
xtrace: /test/someElement[3]
xtrace: /test/someElement[3]/@n
xtrace: normalized-text( )
xtrace: /test/someElement[3]/someChild[1]
xtrace: normalized-text(someOtherValue)
xtrace: normalized-text( )
xtrace: normalized-text( )
xtrace: /test/someElement[4]
xtrace: /test/someElement[4]/@n
xtrace: normalized-text( )
xtrace: /test/someElement[4]/someChild[1]
xtrace: normalized-text(someValue)
xtrace: normalized-text( )
xtrace: normalized-text( )
```

Discussion

To get the biggest bang for your buck, combine this tracing technique with debugging output that indicates where you are in the stylesheet. You can do that with a separate message, but xtrace has a parameter named tag, which, if set, will be output instead of the default tag.

This example outputs text nodes as normalized so the trace output does not span multiple lines. You can easily remove this filtering if you prefer to see the actual text.

When you use document tracing, think carefully about where to place the calls to trace. The most useful place is at the point or points where the processing of the current node effectively takes place. Consider the following post-order traversal stylesheet borrowed from Recipe 4.6 and instrumented with trace:

```
<xsl:stylesheet version="1.0" xmlns:xsl="http://www.w3.org/1999/XSL/Transform"
    xmlns:dbg="http://www.ora.com/XSLTCookbook/ns/debug">

  <xsl:include href="xtrace.xslt"/>

  <xsl:output method="text"/>

  <xsl:strip-space elements="*"/>

  <xsl:template match="/employee" priority="10">
    <xsl:apply-templates/>
    <xsl:call-template name="dbg:trace"/>
    <xsl:value-of select="@name"/>
    <xsl:text> is the head of the company. </xsl:text>
    <xsl:call-template name="reportsTo"/>
    <xsl:call-template name="HimHer"/>
    <xsl:text>. </xsl:text>
    <xsl:text>&#xa;&#xa;</xsl:text>
  </xsl:template>

  <xsl:template match="employee[employee]">
    <xsl:apply-templates/>
    <xsl:call-template name="dbg:trace"/>
    <xsl:value-of select="@name"/>
    <xsl:text> is a manager. </xsl:text>
    <xsl:call-template name="reportsTo"/>
    <xsl:call-template name="HimHer"/>
    <xsl:text>. </xsl:text>
    <xsl:text>&#xa;&#xa;</xsl:text>
  </xsl:template>

  <xsl:template match="employee">
    <xsl:call-template name="dbg:trace"/>
    <xsl:text>Nobody reports to </xsl:text>
    <xsl:value-of select="@name"/>
    <xsl:text>. &#xa;</xsl:text>
  </xsl:template>

<!-- Remainder elided ... -->

</xsl:stylesheet>
```

Notice how you call trace when you act on the current node, not as the first statement of each template. This placement results in the following trace, which accurately reflects the post-order traversal:

```
xtrace: /employee/employee[1]/employee[1]
xtrace: /employee/employee[1]/employee[2]/employee[1]
xtrace: /employee/employee[1]/employee[2]
xtrace: /employee/employee[1]
xtrace: /employee/employee[2]/employee[1]
xtrace: /employee/employee[2]/employee[2]/employee[1]
xtrace: /employee/employee[2]/employee[2]/employee[2]
xtrace: /employee/employee[2]/employee[2]/employee[3]
xtrace: /employee/employee[2]/employee[2]
xtrace: /employee/employee[2]
xtrace: /employee/employee[3]/employee[1]/employee[1]
xtrace: /employee/employee[3]/employee[1]/employee[2]
xtrace: /employee/employee[3]/employee[1]/employee[3]
xtrace: /employee/employee[3]/employee[1]
xtrace: /employee/employee[3]/employee[2]/employee[1]/employee[1]
xtrace: /employee/employee[3]/employee[2]/employee[1]
xtrace: /employee/employee[3]/employee[2]/employee[2]/employee[1]
xtrace: /employee/employee[3]/employee[2]/employee[2]/employee[2]
xtrace: /employee/employee[3]/employee[2]/employee[2]
xtrace: /employee/employee[3]/employee[2]/employee[3]/employee[1]
xtrace: /employee/employee[3]/employee[2]/employee[3]
xtrace: /employee/employee[3]/employee[2]
xtrace: /employee/employee[3]
xtrace: /employee
```

Had you simply placed the trace at the first line, you would have output the following misleading trace that reflects a preorder traversal:

```
xtrace: /employee
xtrace: /employee/employee[1]
xtrace: /employee/employee[1]/employee[1]
xtrace: /employee/employee[1]/employee[2]
xtrace: /employee/employee[1]/employee[2]/employee[1]
xtrace: /employee/employee[1]/employee[2]
xtrace: /employee/employee[1]
xtrace: /employee/employee[2]
xtrace: /employee/employee[2]/employee[1]
xtrace: /employee/employee[2]/employee[2]
xtrace: /employee/employee[2]/employee[2]/employee[1]
xtrace: /employee/employee[2]/employee[2]/employee[2]
xtrace: /employee/employee[2]/employee[2]/employee[3]
xtrace: /employee/employee[2]/employee[2]
xtrace: /employee/employee[2]
xtrace: /cmployee/employee[3]
xtrace: /employee/employee[3]/employee[1]
xtrace: /employee/employee[3]/employee[1]/employee[1]
xtrace: /employee/employee[3]/employee[1]/employee[2]
xtrace: /employee/employee[3]/employee[1]/employee[3]
xtrace: /employee/employee[3]/employee[1]
xtrace: /employee/employee[3]/employee[2]
xtrace: /employee/employee[3]/employee[2]/employee[1]
xtrace: /employee/employee[3]/employee[2]/employee[1]/employee[1]
xtrace: /employee/employee[3]/employee[2]/employee[1]
xtrace: /employee/employee[3]/employee[2]/employee[2]
```

```
xtrace: /employee/employee[3]/employee[2]/employee[2]/employee[1]
xtrace: /employee/employee[3]/employee[2]/employee[2]/employee[2]
xtrace: /employee/employee[3]/employee[2]/employee[2]
xtrace: /employee/employee[3]/cmployee[2]/employee[3]
xtrace: /employee/employee[3]/employee[2]/employee[3]/employee[1]
xtrace: /employee/employee[3]/employee[2]/employee[3]
xtrace: /employee/employee[3]/employee[2]
xtrace: /employee/employee[3]
```

See Also

catchXSL! (*http://www.xslprofiler.org/overview.html*) is a freely downloadable tool that profiles XSL transformations in a processor-dependent manner. In the course of the transformation, every XSLT instruction is recorded and logged as a *style event* provided with a timestamp. The resulting statistics give information about the transformation proceedings and deliver useful hints for stylesheet improvements. A detailed listing of the style events gives information about each step and its duration. A template-oriented listing shows the time spent in each template and may thus indicate time-consuming "hot spots" in the stylesheet.

13.3   Automating the Insertion of Debug Output

Problem

You want to transform your stylesheet into another stylesheet that is instrumented with debug traces.

Solution

Oliver Becker developed a handy stylesheet transformation that takes any input stylesheet and produces an output stylesheet with trace instrumentation:

```
<!--
    Trace utility, modifies a stylesheet to produce trace messages
    Version 0.2
    GPL (c) Oliver Becker, 2002-02-13
    obecker@informatik.hu-berlin.de
-->

<xsl:transform version="1.0"
  xmlns:xsl="http://www.w3.org/1999/XSL/Transform"
  xmlns:trace="http://www.obqo.de/XSL/Trace"
  xmlns:alias="http://www.w3.org/TransformAlias"
  exclude-result-prefixes="alias">

  <xsl:namespace-alias stylesheet-prefix="alias" result-prefix="xsl" />

  <!-- <xsl:output indent="yes" /> -->
```

```
<!-- XSLT root element -->
<xsl:template match="xsl:stylesheet | xsl:transform">
  <xsl:copy>
    <!-- We need the trace namespace for names and modes -->
    <xsl:copy-of select="document('')/*/namespace::trace" />
    <!-- dito: perhaps a namespace was used only as attribute value -->
    <xsl:copy-of select="namespace::*|@*" />
    <xsl:apply-templates />
    <!-- append utility templates -->
    <xsl:copy-of
        select="document('')/*/xsl:template
                            [@mode='trace:getCurrent' or
                             @name='trace:getPath']" />
    <!-- compute the lowest priority and add a default template with
         a lower priority for element nodes -->
    <xsl:variable name="priority"
                  select="xsl:template/@priority
                          [not(. &gt; current()/xsl:template/@priority)]" />
    <xsl:variable name="newpri">
      <xsl:choose>
        <xsl:when test="$priority &lt; -1">
          <xsl:value-of select="$priority - 1" />
        </xsl:when>
        <!-- in case there's only a greater or no priority at all -->
        <xsl:otherwise>-2</xsl:otherwise>
      </xsl:choose>
    </xsl:variable>
    <!-- copy the contents only -->
    <alias:template match="*" priority="{$newpri}">
      <xsl:copy-of select="document('')/*/xsl:template
                            [@name='trace:defaultRule']/node()" />
    </alias:template>
  </xsl:copy>
</xsl:template>

<!-- XSLT templates -->
<xsl:template match="xsl:template">
  <xsl:copy>
    <xsl:copy-of select="@*" />
    <!-- first: copy parameters -->
    <xsl:apply-templates select="xsl:param" />
    <alias:param name="trace:callstack" />
    <xsl:choose>
      <xsl:when test="@name">
        <alias:variable name="trace:current"
                        select="concat($trace:callstack,'/{@name}')" />
      </xsl:when>
      <xsl:otherwise>
        <alias:variable name="trace:current"
              select="concat($trace:callstack,
                      '/{count(preceding-sibling::xsl:template)+1}')" />
      </xsl:otherwise>
    </xsl:choose>
```

```
        <!-- emit a message -->
        <alias:message>
          <alias:call-template name="trace:getPath" />
          <alias:text>&#xA;    stack: </alias:text>
          <alias:value-of select="$trace:current" />
          <xsl:if test="@match or @mode">
            <alias:text> (</alias:text>
            <xsl:if test="@match">
              <alias:text>match="<xsl:value-of select="@match" />"</alias:text>
              <xsl:if test="@mode">
                <alias:text><xsl:text> </xsl:text></alias:text>
              </xsl:if>
            </xsl:if>
            <xsl:if test="@mode">
              <alias:text>mode="<xsl:value-of select="@mode" />"</alias:text>
            </xsl:if>
            <alias:text>)</alias:text>
          </xsl:if>
          <xsl:apply-templates select="xsl:param" mode="traceParams" />
        </alias:message>

        <!-- process children except parameters -->
        <xsl:apply-templates select="node( )[not(self::xsl:param)]" />
      </xsl:copy>
    </xsl:template>

<!-- add the callstack parameter for apply-templates and call-template -->
<xsl:template match="xsl:apply-templates | xsl:call-template">
  <xsl:copy>
    <xsl:copy-of select="@*" />
    <alias:with-param name="trace:callstack" select="$trace:current" />
    <xsl:apply-templates />
  </xsl:copy>
</xsl:template>

<!-- output parameter values -->
<xsl:template match="xsl:param" mode="traceParams">
  <alias:text>&#xA;    param: name="<xsl:value-of select="@name" />"
                   value="</alias:text>
  <alias:value-of select="${@name}" />" <alias:text />
  <!--
  <alias:copy-of select="${@name}" />" <alias:text />
  -->
</xsl:template>

<!-- output variable values -->
<xsl:template match="xsl:variable">
  <xsl:copy>
    <xsl:copy-of select="@*" />
    <xsl:apply-templates />
  </xsl:copy>
  <xsl:if test="ancestor::xsl:template">
    <alias:message>    variable: name="<xsl:value-of select="@name" />"
                   value="<alias:text />
```

```
      <alias:value-of select="${@name}" />" </alias:message>
  </xsl:if>
</xsl:template>

<!-- copy every unprocessed node -->
<xsl:template match="*|@*">
  <xsl:copy>
    <xsl:apply-templates select="@*" />
    <xsl:apply-templates />
  </xsl:copy>
</xsl:template>

<!-- ************************************************************ -->
<!-- The following templates will be copied into the modified    -->
<!-- stylesheet                                                   -->
<!-- ************************************************************ -->

<!--
 | trace:getPath
 | compute the absolute path of the context node
 +-->
<xsl:template name="trace:getPath">
  <xsl:text>node: </xsl:text>
  <xsl:for-each select="ancestor::*">
    <xsl:value-of
        select="concat('/', name(), '[',
        count(preceding-sibling::*[name()=name(current())])+1, ']')" />
  </xsl:for-each>
  <xsl:apply-templates select="." mode="trace:getCurrent" />
</xsl:template>

<!--
 | trace:getCurrent
 | compute the last step of the location path, depending on the
 | node type
 +-->
<xsl:template match="*" mode="trace:getCurrent">
  <xsl:value-of
      select="concat('/', name(), '[',
      count(preceding-sibling::*[name()=name(current())])+1, ']')" />
</xsl:template>

<xsl:template match="@*" mode="trace:getCurrent">
  <xsl:value-of select="concat('/@', name())" />
</xsl:template>

<xsl:template match="text()" mode="trace:getCurrent">
  <xsl:value-of
      select="concat('/text()[', count(preceding-sibling::text())+1,
                                                      ']')" />
</xsl:template>

<xsl:template match="comment()" mode="trace:getCurrent">
  <xsl:value-of
```

```
        select="concat('/comment( )[',
                    count(preceding-sibling::comment( ))+1, ']')" />
  </xsl:template>

  <xsl:template match="processing-instruction( )" mode="trace:getCurrent">
    <xsl:value-of
        select="concat('/processing-instruction( )[',
        count(preceding-sibling::processing-instruction( ))+1, ']')" />
  </xsl:template>

  <!--
   | trace:defaultRule
   | default rule with parameter passing
   +-->
  <xsl:template name="trace:defaultRule">
    <xsl:param name="trace:callstack" />
    <xsl:message>
      <xsl:call-template name="trace:getPath" />
      <xsl:text>&#xA;    default rule applied</xsl:text>
    </xsl:message>
    <xsl:apply-templates>
      <xsl:with-param name="trace:callstack" select="$trace:callstack" />
    </xsl:apply-templates>
  </xsl:template>

</xsl:transform>
```

Discussion

Here is a sample of the debug output produced when this transformation was applicd to *postorder.orgchart.xslt* from Recipe 4.6:

```
node: /employee[1]
   stack: /1 (match="/employee")
node: /employee[1]/employee[1]
   stack: /1/2 (match="employee[employee]")
node: /employee[1]/employee[1]/employee[1]
   stack: /1/2/3 (match="employee")
node: /employee[1]/employee[1]/employee[2]
   stack: /1/2/2 (match="employee[employee]")
node: /employee[1]/employee[1]/employee[2]/employee[1]
   stack: /1/2/2/3 (match="employee")
node: /employee[1]/employee[1]/employee[2]
   stack: /1/2/2/reportsTo
node: /employee[1]/employee[1]/employee[2]
   stack: /1/2/2/HimHer
node: /employee[1]/employee[1]
   stack: /1/2/reportsTo
node: /employee[1]/employee[1]
   stack: /1/2/HimHer
node: /employee[1]/employee[2]
   stack: /1/2 (match="employee[employee]")
node: /employee[1]/employee[2]/employee[1]
   stack: /1/2/3 (match="employee")
```

```
node: /employee[1]/employee[2]/employee[2]
   stack: /1/2/2 (match="employee[employee]")
node: /employee[1]/employee[2]/employee[2]/employee[1]
   stack: /1/2/2/3 (match="employee")
node: /employee[1]/employee[2]/employee[2]/employee[2]
   stack: /1/2/2/3 (match="employee")
node: /employee[1]/employee[2]/employee[2]/employee[3]
   stack: /1/2/2/3 (match="employee")
node: /employee[1]/employee[2]/employee[2]
   stack: /1/2/2/reportsTo
node: /employee[1]/employee[2]/employee[2]
   stack: /1/2/2/HimHer
node: /employee[1]/employee[2]
   stack: /1/2/reportsTo
node: /employee[1]/employee[2]
   stack: /1/2/HimHer
node: /employee[1]/employee[3]
   stack: /1/2 (match="employee[employee]")
node: /employee[1]/employee[3]/employee[1]
   stack: /1/2/2 (match="employee[employee]")
node: /employee[1]/employee[3]/employee[1]/employee[1]
   stack: /1/2/2/3 (match="employee")
node: /employee[1]/employee[3]/employee[1]/employee[2]
   stack: /1/2/2/3 (match="employee")
node: /employee[1]/employee[3]/employee[1]/employee[3]
   stack: /1/2/2/3 (match="employee")
node: /employee[1]/employee[3]/employee[1]
   stack: /1/2/2/reportsTo
node: /employee[1]/employee[3]/employee[1]
   stack: /1/2/2/HimHer
node: /employee[1]/employee[3]/employee[2]
   stack: /1/2/2 (match="employee[employee]")
node: /employee[1]/employee[3]/employee[2]/employee[1]
   stack: /1/2/2/2 (match="employee[employee]")
node: /employee[1]/employee[3]/employee[2]/employee[1]/employee[1]
   stack: /1/2/2/2/3 (match="employee")
node: /employee[1]/employee[3]/employee[2]/employee[1]
   stack: /1/2/2/2/reportsTo
node: /employee[1]/employee[3]/employee[2]/employee[1]
   stack: /1/2/2/2/HimHer
node: /employee[1]/employee[3]/employee[2]/employee[2]
   stack: /1/2/2/2 (match="employee[employee]")
node: /employee[1]/employee[3]/employee[2]/employee[2]/employee[1]
   stack: /1/2/2/2/3 (match="employee")
node: /employee[1]/employee[3]/employee[2]/employee[2]/employee[2]
   stack: /1/2/2/2/3 (match="employee")
node: /employee[1]/employee[3]/employee[2]/employee[2]
   stack: /1/2/2/2/reportsTo
node: /employee[1]/employee[3]/employee[2]/employee[2]
   stack: /1/2/2/2/HimHer
```

```
node: /employee[1]/employee[3]/employee[2]/employee[3]
    stack: /1/2/2/2 (match="employee[employee]")
node: /employee[1]/employee[3]/employee[2]/employee[3]/employee[1]
    stack: /1/2/2/2/3 (match="employee")
node: /employee[1]/employee[3]/employee[2]/employee[3]
    stack: /1/2/2/2/reportsTo
node: /employee[1]/employee[3]/employee[2]/employee[3]
    stack: /1/2/2/2/HimHer
node: /employee[1]/employee[3]/employee[2]
    stack: /1/2/2/reportsTo
node: /employee[1]/employee[3]/employee[2]
    stack: /1/2/2/HimHer
node: /employee[1]/employee[3]
    stack: /1/2/reportsTo
node: /employee[1]/employee[3]
    stack: /1/2/HimHer
node: /employee[1]
    stack: /1/reportsTo
node: /employee[1]
    stack: /1/HimHer
```

The modified stylesheet outputs trace messages via the xsl:message mechanism. The format for every processed node is as follows:

```
node: [XPath to this node]
    stack: [call stack of the templates invoked]
    param: name="[parameter name]" value="[parameter value]"
    more parameters ...
    variable: name="[variable name]" value="[variable value]"
    more variables ...
```

The call stack takes the form of a path (with / as separator) and includes all passed templates. If a template has a name attribute, then this name is used. Otherwise, the number (position) of the template appears within the stack. If the current template does not have a name, the match attribute is displayed. If a mode attribute is specified, its value is displayed.

One known problem is that the output for parameters or variables is their *string value* (produced with xsl:value-of). That's not reasonable for node sets and result-tree fragments. However, using xsl:copy-of results in an error if the variable contains attribute or namespace nodes without parents.

See Also

The *trace.xslt* source and further examples can be found at *http://www.informatik.hu-berlin.de/~obecker/XSLT/#trace*.

13.4 Including Embedded Unit Test Data in Utility Stylesheets

Problem

You want to package tests with your utility stylesheets so they can verified at any time.

Solution

The following stylesheet is meant to be included as a utility. However, this example provides the capability of testing the stylesheet by executing it as its own input document:

```
<!-- math.max.xslt -->

<xsl:stylesheet version="1.0" xmlns:xsl="http://www.w3.org/1999/XSL/Transform"
 xmlns:math="http://www.exslt.org/math" exclude-result-prefixes="math"
xmlns:test="http://www.ora.com/XSLTCookbook/test" id="math:math.max">

<xsl:template name="math:max">
    <xsl:param name="nodes" select="/.."/>
    <xsl:param name="max"/>
  <xsl:variable name="count" select="count($nodes)"/>
  <xsl:variable name="aNode" select="$nodes[ceiling($count div 2)]"/>
  <xsl:choose>
    <xsl:when test="not($count)">
      <xsl:value-of select="number($max)"/>
    </xsl:when>
    <xsl:when test="number($aNode) != number($aNode)">
      <xsl:value-of select="number($aNode)"/>
    </xsl:when>
    <xsl:otherwise>
      <xsl:call-template name="math:max">
        <xsl:with-param name="nodes" select="$nodes[not(. &lt;= number($aNode))]"/>
        <xsl:with-param name="max">
          <xsl:choose>
            <xsl:when test="not($max) or $aNode > $max">
              <xsl:value-of select="$aNode"/>
            </xsl:when>
            <xsl:otherwise>
              <xsl:value-of select="$max"/>
            </xsl:otherwise>
          </xsl:choose>
        </xsl:with-param>
      </xsl:call-template>
    </xsl:otherwise>
  </xsl:choose>
</xsl:template>
```

```
<!-- TEST CODE: DO NOT REMOVE! -->
<xsl:template match="/xsl:stylesheet[@id='math:math.max'] | xsl:include[@href='math.
max.xslt'] " priority="-1000">
<xsl:message>
TESTING math.max
</xsl:message>

<xsl:for-each select="document('')/*/test:test">
    <xsl:variable name="ans">
        <xsl:call-template name="math:max">
            <xsl:with-param name="nodes" select="test:data"/>
        </xsl:call-template>
    </xsl:variable>
    <xsl:if test="$ans != @ans">
        <xsl:message>
            math:max TEST <xsl:value-of select="@num"/> FAILED [<xsl:value-of
select="$ans"/>]
        </xsl:message>
    </xsl:if>
</xsl:for-each>

<!-- Test with Infinity -->
<xsl:variable name="ans1">
    <xsl:call-template name="math:max">
        <xsl:with-param name="nodes" select="document('')/*/test:test[@num=1]/test:
data"/>
        <xsl:with-param name="max" select="1 div 0"/>
    </xsl:call-template>
</xsl:variable>
<xsl:if test="$ans1 != Infinity">
    <xsl:message>
        math:max Infinity Test FAILED [<xsl:value-of select="$ans1"/>]
    </xsl:message>
</xsl:if>

<!-- Test with -Infinity -->
<xsl:variable name="ans2">
    <xsl:call-template name="math:max">
        <xsl:with-param name="nodes" select="document('')/*/test:test[@num=1]/test:
data"/>
        <xsl:with-param name="max" select="-1 div 0"/>
    </xsl:call-template>
</xsl:variable>
<xsl:if test="$ans2 != document('')/*/test:test[@num=1]/@ans">
    <xsl:message>
        math:max -Infinity Test FAILED [<xsl:value-of select="$ans2"/>]
    </xsl:message>
</xsl:if>

</xsl:template>
```

```
<test:test num="1" ans="9" xmlns="http://www.ora.com/XSLTCookbook/test">
    <data>9</data>
    <data>8</data>
    <data>7</data>
    <data>6</data>
    <data>5</data>
    <data>4</data>
    <data>3</data>
    <data>2</data>
    <data>1</data>
</test:test>

<test:test num="2" ans="1" xmlns="http://www.ora.com/XSLTCookbook/test">
    <data>1</data>
</test:test>

<test:test num="3" ans="1" xmlns="http://www.ora.com/XSLTCookbook/test">
    <data>-1</data>
    <data>1</data>
</test:test>

<test:test num="4" ans="0" xmlns="http://www.ora.com/XSLTCookbook/test">
    <data>0</data>
    <data>0</data>
</test:test>

<test:test num="5" ans="NaN" xmlns="http://www.ora.com/XSLTCookbook/test">
    <data>foo</data>
    <data>1</data>
</test:test>

<test:test num="6" ans="NaN" xmlns="http://www.ora.com/XSLTCookbook/test">
    <data>1</data>
    <data>foo</data>
</test:test>

<test:test num="7" ans="NaN" xmlns="http://www.ora.com/XSLTCookbook/test">
</test:test>

</xsl:stylesheet>
```

Discussion

The xsl:stylesheet element has an optional attribute called id. This attribute iden-
fities stylesheets that are embedded in larger documents. However, here the ID is
used for testing purposes. You want to package test code with the stylesheet but
make reasonably certain that this test code does not interfere with the normal usage
of the stylesheet. Do this by creating a template that will match only when the
stylesheet processes itself:

```
<xsl:template match="/xsl:stylesheet[@id='math:math.max'] |
    xsl:include[@href='math.max.xslt']">
```

This explains the /xsl:stylesheet[@id='math:math.max'], but what about the xsl:include[@href='math.max.xslt'] part? To see the value of this, here is a stylesheet that packages all your math utilities into a single file for easy inclusion. You would like an easy way to test the entire package too:

```
<!-- math.xslt -->

<xsl:stylesheet version="1.0" xmlns:xsl="http://www.w3.org/1999/XSL/Transform"
    xmlns:math="http://exslt.org/math"
    extension-element-prefixes="math" id="math:math">

<xsl:include href="math.abs.xslt"/>
<xsl:include href="math.constant.xslt"/>
<xsl:include href="math.exp.xslt"/>
<xsl:include href="math.highest.xslt"/>
<xsl:include href="math.log.xslt"/>
<xsl:include href="math.lowest.xslt"/>
<xsl:include href="math.max.xslt"/>
<xsl:include href="math.min.xslt"/>
<xsl:include href="math.power.xslt"/>
<xsl:include href="math.sqrt.xslt"/>

<!--TEST CODE -->
<xsl:template match="xsl:stylesheet[@id='math:math'] | xsl:include[@href='math.
xslt']">

<xsl:message>
TESTING math
</xsl:message>

    <xsl:for-each select="document('')/*/xsl:include">
        <xsl:apply-templates select="."/>
    </xsl:for-each>
</xsl:template>

<xsl:template match="xsl:include" priority="-10">
    <xsl:message>
    WARNING: <xsl:value-of select="@href"/> has no test code.
    </xsl:message>
</xsl:template>

</xsl:stylesheet>
```

Here you see that the test code for a package simply loops over all its xsl:include elements and applies templates to them. This step causes each included stylesheet tests to be exercised due to the aforementioned xsl:include[@href='*filename*'] part of the match.

Notice the template <xsl:template match="xsl:include" priority="-10">. This template causes emission of a warning if an included file does not contain test code. This concept is important for quality control, since forgetting to create tests is easy.

If you object to packaging the tests with the actual code, you can achieve the same effect by creating separate test files for each utility. In this case, there is no need to use the id attribute of the stylesheet; simply match against the root:

```
<!-- math.max.test.xslt-->

<xsl:stylesheet version="1.0" xmlns:xsl="http://www.w3.org/1999/XSL/Transform"
  xmlns:math="http://www.exslt.org/math" exclude-result-prefixes="math"
xmlns:test="http://www.ora.com/XSLTCookbook/test">

<xsl:include href="../math/math.max.xslt"/>

<!-- TEST CODE: DO NOT REMOVE! -->
<xsl:template match="/ | xsl:include[@href='math.max.test.xslt']">
<xsl:message>
TESTING math.max
</xsl:message>

<xsl:for-each select="document('')/*/test:test">
    <xsl:variable name="ans">
        <xsl:call-template name="math:max">
            <xsl:with-param name="nodes" select="test:data"/>
        </xsl:call-template>
    </xsl:variable>
    <xsl:if test="$ans != @ans">
        <xsl:message>
            math:max TEST <xsl:value-of select="@num"/> FAILED [<xsl:value-of
select="$ans"/>]
        </xsl:message>
    </xsl:if>
</xsl:for-each>

<!-- ... Same as math.max.xslt above ... -->

</xsl:stylesheet>
```

You would then create separate test packages:

```
<!-- math.test.xslt -->

<xsl:stylesheet version="1.0" xmlns:xsl="http://www.w3.org/1999/XSL/Transform"
    xmlns:math="http://exslt.org/math"
    extension-element-prefixes="math">

<xsl:include href="math.max.test.xslt"/>
<xsl:include href="math.min.test.xslt"/>

<!-- ... Same as math.xslt, above ... -->

</xsl:stylesheet>
```

If you separate your tests in this way, be sure to ship the test code with the actual implementations. Doing so allows your clients to verify tests for themselves. The test code also doubles as an example of how to use the templates.

13.5 Structuring Unit Tests

Problem

You want to structure tests to simplify testing.

Solution

Notice how Recipe 13.4 embedded test data in the test stylesheets. Each test element contains a test num attribute and the correct result in the form of an ans attribute. The test driver then extracts these test elements from the stylesheet, executes the test, and compares the expected answer against the actual answer. The most important aspect of the test driver is that it produces no output when the test succeeds.

Discussion

Some of the best advice on automating testing is in Brian W. Kernighan's and Rob Pike's *The Practice of Programming* (Addison Wesley, 1999). The authors state that test programs should produce output only when tests *fail*. Why? Who wants to wade through pages of test output to look for cases where the test fail? If you expect test code to produce no output, you will quickly notice failures when there *is* output. Of course, you should test your test code to make sure it actually executes before relying on this testing technique.

The method that stores the answer as an attribute in the test element works for simple tests that produce a primitive result. However, some templates produce node sets. In this case, you might need to store the correct answer as child elements in the tests. You can then use the value set operations of Recipe 7.2 to compare results. However, sometimes you can test node-set producing templates more simply. Consider the test driver for the math:lowest template. Recall that math:lowest returns a node set consisting of all instances of the lowest number in an input node set:

```
<xsl:stylesheet version="1.1" xmlns:xsl="http://www.w3.org/1999/XSL/Transform" xmlns:
math="http://www.exslt.org/math" exclude-result-prefixes="math test" xmlns:
test="http://www.ora.com/XSLTCookbook/test" id="math:math.lowest">

<xsl:import href="math.min.xslt"/>

<xsl:template name="math:lowest">
    <xsl:param name="nodes" select="/.."/>

    <xsl:variable name="min">
        <xsl:call-template name="math:min">
            <xsl:with-param name="nodes" select="$nodes"/>
        </xsl:call-template>
    </xsl:variable>
    <xsl:choose>
        <xsl:when test="number($min) = $min">
            <xsl:copy-of select="$nodes[. = $min]"/>
```

```
          </xsl:when>
          <xsl:otherwise/>
      </xsl:choose>
</xsl:template>

   <!-- TEST CODE: DO NOT REMOVE! -->
   <xsl:template match="xsl:stylesheet[@id='math:math.lowest'] |
       xsl:include[@href='math.lowest.xslt'] " xmlns:exsl="http://exslt.org/common">
      <xsl:message>
TESTING math.lowest
</xsl:message>
      <xsl:choose>
         <xsl:when test="function-available('exsl:node-set')">
           <xsl:for-each select="document('')/*/test:test">
              <xsl:variable name="ans">
                <xsl:call-template name="math:lowest">
                   <xsl:with-param name="nodes" select="test:data"/>
                </xsl:call-template>
              </xsl:variable>
               <xsl:variable name="$ans-ns" select=" exsl:node-set($ans)"/>
               <xsl:if test="not($ans-ns/* != test:data[. = current()/@ans]) and
                   count($ans-ns/*) != count(test:data[. = current()/@ans])">
                 <xsl:message>
                     math:lowest TEST <xsl:value-of select="@num"/> FAILED
                     [<xsl:copy-of select="$ans-ns"/>]
                     [<xsl:copy-of select="test:data[. = current()/@ans]"/>]
                 </xsl:message>
                 </xsl:if>
             </xsl:for-each>
          </xsl:when>
          <xsl:otherwise>
            <xsl:message>
               WARNING math.lowest test code requires exsl:node-set
               THIS VERSION=[<xsl:value-of select="system-property('xsl:version')"/>]
               VENDOR=[<xsl:value-of select="system-property('xsl:vendor')"/>]
               </xsl:message>
           </xsl:otherwise>
        </xsl:choose>
    </xsl:template>

   <test:test num="1" ans="1" xmlns="http://www.ora.com/XSLTCookbook/test">
     <data>9</data>
     <data>8</data>
     <data>7</data>
     <data>6</data>
     <data>5</data>
     <data>4</data>
     <data>3</data>
     <data>2</data>
     <data>1</data>
   </test:test>

  <!-- more tests here ... >

</xsl:stylesheet>
```

The comparison relies on the behavior of != when both sides are node sets: the result is true if a pair of nodes, one from each node set, have different string values. You can make sure that the nodes returned by selecting the answer nodes from the test set are the same as the nodes returned by math:lowest. You can also make sure that the counts are the same.

Some forms of computation (especially mathematical approximations) produce results that are correct even when the value produced is not exactly equal to the theoretically correct answer. In this case, you can include an error tolerance in the test data and make sure the computed answer is identical to the correct answer within the stated tolerance.

See Also

Brian W. Kernighan's and Rob Pike's *The Practice of Programming* (Addison Wesley, 1999), although not specifically written for XSLT, contains relevant advice for testing and debugging all kinds of programs.

13.6   Testing Boundary and Error Conditions

Problem

You are writing utility templates to be used by others, and you want them to be robust.

Solution

Boundary-condition testing

In all programming languages, bugs most often appear at boundary conditions. Thus, you should choose test data in which values lie along data extremes. Boundary values include maximum, minimum, and just inside/outside boundaries. If your templates work correctly for these special values, then they will probably work correctly for all other values. It is impossible to provide an exhaustive list of boundary conditions because they vary from problem to problem. Below is a list of typical cases you should consider.

If a template acts on node sets, then be sure to test the following cases:

- An empty node set
- A node set with one element
- A node set with two elements
- A node set with an odd number of elements other than 1
- A node set with an even number of elements other than 2

If a template acts on a string, be sure to test the following cases:

- The empty string
- A string of length 1
- Other strings of varying sizes

If your template uses `substring-before` or `substring-after` for searches, be sure to test the following cases:

- Strings that do not contain the test string
- Strings that start with the search string
- Strings that end with the search string
- Strings that contain only the search string

If a template acts on numbers, be sure to test:

- The number 0
- The number 1
- Negative numbers
- Fractional numbers ($0 < x < 1$)
- Numbers with whole and fractional parts
- Prime numbers
- Other special boundary numbers that are unique to your problem

If a template compares two numbers X and Y, be sure to test cases in which:

- $X < Y$, especially $X = Y - 1$ and $X = Y - d$, where d is a small fraction
- $X = Y$
- $X > Y$, especially $X = Y + 1$ and $X = Y + d$, where d is a small fraction

When you know or have access to the schema of a document that a stylesheet will process, be sure to test inputs where:

- Optional elements are absent
- Optional elements are present
- Unbounded elements have only one instance
- Unbounded elements have several instances

Error-condition testing

A robust reusable template or stylesheet should fail gracefully in the face of erroneous input. Here you often use `xsl:message` with `terminate=yes` to report illegal parameter values.

If a template acts on numbers, be sure to test error handling for:

- NaN (0 div 0)
- Infinity (1 div 0)
- –Infinity (–1 div 0)
- Zero when undefined (e.g., logarithms)
- Negative numbers when undefined (e.g., for factorial)
- Non-numeric input (e.g., "foo")

When templates or stylesheets use parameters, be sure to test what happens when:

- Parameters without default values are not set
- Parameters receive out-of-bound values
- Parameters receive values of the wrong type

You can check for parameters that aren't set by using the following trick:

```
<xsl:param name="param1">
   <xsl:message terminate="yes">
      $param1 has not been set.
   </xsl:message>
</xsl:param>
```

However, this trick is not guaranteed to work because nothing in the standard setup states the value of a parameter not evaluated if a value is passed for that parameter. However, most XSLT processors are friendly to this technique. If you wanted to be absolutely safe, you could set the value to an illegal value (such as 1 div 0) and test for it in the body of the template:

```
<xsl:param name="param1" select="1 div 0" />

<xsl:if test="$param1 = 1 div 0">
  <xsl:message terminate="yes">
    $param1 has not been set, or has been set to Infinity, which is
    invalid.
  </xsl:message>
</xsl:if>
```

When you know or have access to the document's schema a stylesheet is expected to process to see how the stylesheet responds to that input:[*]

- Completely violates the schema (e.g., an unrelated XML document as input)
- Contains some elements that violate the schema
- Violates minOccurs and maxOccurs constraints
- Violates data type constraints

---

[*] This test assumes that the XSLT processor uses a nonvalidating parser or that you remove the schema reference from the input document.

Discussion

When developing XSLT for your own consumption, you are free to choose just how robust you want the code to be. However, when others use your code, it is a good practice to include reasonable error handling. Your clients will also thank you for delivering code that works for legal but unusual input.

When you create templates that use recursion, dividing the implementation into two templates is a good idea. The main template does the error checking and, if no errors are detected, calls an implementation template that computes the result recursively. Recipe 2.5 used this tactic for logarithms.

CHAPTER 14

Generic and Functional Programming

*The brilliant moves we occasionally make would not
have been possible without the prior dumb ones.*
—Stanley Goldstein

This chapter renders all previous chapters moot. Okay, maybe this is a slight exaggeration. The fact is that the examples in previous chapters solve the particular problems they address. They are also useful for didactic purposes. If an example does not solve a problem you face, it might point the way to a solution. The desired solution could be a small modification of the code or a reapplication of the same techniques.

This chapter sets its goals a little higher. It presents examples that solve a very broad range of problems without requiring customization of the example's core code. Those of you who are familiar with C++, and specifically the *Standard Template Library* (STL), already know the power you can obtain by creating generic code (generic algorithms) and reusing them in various contexts. Others who use functional programming languages (e.g., Lisp, ML, or Haskell) also know of the great power obtained through the creation of higher-order functions: general-purpose functions that are specialized by accepting special purpose functions as arguments. This chapter shows that XSLT, although not specifically designed as a generic or functional language, has inherent capabilities to enable similar usage.

The techniques used in this chapter stretch the abilities of XSLT quite a bit. Not everyone will want to use the examples, some of which are complex and slow. Nevertheless, I am reminded of the days before C++ had native support for templates. You could fake generic programming by using macros, but the results were awkward. However, enough people saw the potential, and templates soon became a first-class feature in C++, and possibly one of C++'s most important characteristics, despite the proliferation of other OO languages. Pushing the language envelope in this way puts pressure on the language and possibly makes it evolve faster. This faster development is good because languages that cease to evolve often die out.

Before diving into the examples, let's first discuss some of the general techniques used in this chapter. This will allow the examples to concentrate on the application of the techniques rather than their mechanics.

Extending the Content of Global Variables

This chapter extensively uses XSLT's ability to import (xsl:import) and override templates, variables, and other top-level elements in the importing spreadsheet.

 I like to use the object-oriented term *override* when discussing xsl:import; however, a more technically correct explanation notes that some top-level elements in the importing stylesheet have higher import precedence than matching elements in the imported stylesheet. You can find a complete explanation of how each XSLT top-level element works with respect to xsl:import in Michael Kay's *XSLT Programmer's Reference* (Wrox, 2001).

This chapter takes advantage of the ability to combine a global variable's contents defined in an imported stylesheet with one defined in an importing stylesheet.

The following stylesheet defines two variables. The first, $data1-public-data, is unique to this stylesheet. The second, $data, is defined in terms of the first, but can be overridden:

```
<!-- data1.xslt -->

<xsl:stylesheet version="1.0"
  xmlns:xsl="http://www.w3.org/1999/XSL/Transform"
  xmlns:d="http://www.ora.com/XSLTCookbook/NS/data">

<xsl:output method="xml" indent="yes"/>

<d:data value="1"/>
<d:data value="2"/>
<d:data value="3"/>

<xsl:variable name="data1-public-data" select="document('')/*/d:*"/>
<xsl:variable name="data" select="$data1-public-data"/>

<xsl:template match="/">
  <demo>
    <xsl:copy-of select="$data"/>
  </demo>
</xsl:template>

</xsl:stylesheet>
```

Now define another stylesheet that extends the value of $data. It too defines a unique variable that is the union of the first stylesheet's public data and locally defined data. It then redefines $data in terms of this union:

```
<!-- data2.xslt -->

<xsl:stylesheet version="1.0"
 xmlns:xsl="http://www.w3.org/1999/XSL/Transform"
 xmlns:d="http://www.ora.com/XSLTCookbook/NS/data">

<xsl:import href="data1.xslt"/>

<xsl:output method="xml" indent="yes"/>

<d:data value="5"/>
<d:data value="7"/>
<d:data value="11"/>

<xsl:variable name="data2-public-data"
     select="document('')/*/d:* | $data1-public-data"/>

<xsl:variable name="data" select="$data2-public-data"/>

</xsl:stylesheet>
```

The output of data1.xslt is:

```
<demo xmlns:d="data">
    <d:data value="1"/>
    <d:data value="2"/>
    <d:data value="3"/>
</demo>
```

The output of data2.xslt is:

```
<demo xmlns:d="data">
    <d:data value="1"/>
    <d:data value="2"/>
    <d:data value="3"/>
    <d:data value="5"/>
    <d:data value="7"/>
    <d:data value="11"/>
</demo>
```

Defining the second stylesheet's $data in terms of the first's, without the need for the extra variables, would be convenient; however, XSLT treats this definition circularly. The technique defines a named set that is operated on by templates in a core stylesheet but allows importing stylesheets to expand the set. The motivation for this will become clearer as you proceed.

Using Template Tags

XSLT provides no direct way to pass the name of a template to another template so that the second template can invoke the first indirectly. In other words, the following code is illegal in XSLT 1.0 and 2.0:

```
<xsl:stylesheet version="1.0" xmlns:xsl="http://www.w3.org/1999/XSL/Transform">

<!-- THIS IS NOT LEGAL XSLT -->

<xsl:template match="/">
  <!-- We can call templates by name ...-->
  <xsl:call-template name="sayIt">
    <xsl:with-param name="aTempl" select=" 'sayHello' "/>
  </xsl:call-template>

  <xsl:call-template name="sayIt">
    <xsl:with-param name="aTempl" select=" 'sayGoodby' "/>
  </xsl:call-template>
</xsl:template>

<xsl:template name="sayIt">
  <xsl:param name="aTempl"/>
  <!--But not when the name is indirectly specified with a variable -->
  <xsl:call-template name="{$aTemple}"/>
</xsl:template>

<xsl:template name="sayHello">
  <xsl:value-of select=" 'Hello!' "/>
</xsl:template>

<xsl:template name="sayGoodby">
  <xsl:value-of select=" 'Goodby!' "/>
</xsl:template>

</xsl:stylesheet>
```

As it turns out, you can create some powerful and reusable code if you can figure out how to achieve this level of indirection within the confines of XSLT. Fortunately, you can achieve this goal by using matching instead of naming. The trick is to define a template that can match only one particular piece of data. That piece of data is called a template tag, and by convention, you define the tag directly above the template it matches:

```
<xsl:stylesheet version="1.0" xmlns:xsl="http://www.w3.org/1999/XSL/Transform"
 xmlns:f="http://www.ora.com/XSLTCookbook/namespaces/func">

<xsl:output method="text"/>

<xsl:template match="/">
  <xsl:call-template name="sayIt">
    <xsl:with-param name="aTempl" select=" 'sayHello' "/>
  </xsl:call-template>
  <xsl:call-template name="sayIt">
    <xsl:with-param name="aTempl" select=" 'sayGoodbye' "/>
  </xsl:call-template>
</xsl:template>
```

```
<xsl:template name="sayIt">
  <xsl:param name="aTempl"/>
  <!--Applay templates selecting a tag element that is unique to the template we want
  to invoke -->
  <xsl:apply-templates select="document('')/*/f:func[@name=$aTempl]"/>
</xsl:template>


<!-- A tagged template consists of a tag element and a template that matches that
tagged element -->
<f:func name="sayHello"/>
<xsl:template match="f:func[@name='sayHello']">
  <xsl:text>Hello!&#xa;</xsl:text>
</xsl:template>


<!-- Another tagged template -->
<f:func name="sayGoodby"/>
<xsl:template match="f:func[@name='sayGoodby']">
  <xsl:text>Goodby!&#xa;</xsl:text>
</xsl:template>

</xsl:stylesheet>
```

In this particular case, these contortions are pure overkill because you could simply create a template that takes the output string as data. The true power of this technique is only realized when the tagged functions compute something the caller can use.

When using this technique, use a sanity-checking template that will match when no tagged template matches:

```
<xsl:template match="f:func">
    <xsl:message terminate="yes">
  BAD FUNC! Template may not match generic:func declaration.
    </xsl:message>
</xsl:template>
```

Mike Kay points out that another generic programming technique has the templates match themselves, as in:

```
<xsl:template name="f:sayHello"
              match="xsl:template[@name='f:sayHello']">
  <xsl:text>Hello!&#xa;</xsl:text>
</xsl:template>

<xsl:template name="f:sayGoodbye"
              match="xsl:template[@name='f:sayGoodbye']">
  <xsl:text>Goodbye!&#xa;</xsl:text>
</xsl:template>
```

By using this technique, you can still call the template by name without any problems, and it still looks like a normal template. This chapter does not use this technique because we sometimes like to associate other data with the template tags and thus prefer them to be separate elements.

Generic Programming Versus Functional Programming

Generic programming is a method of organizing highly reusable components that can be customized with little or no loss of runtime performance. You can reuse generic components (classes and functions) by instantiating them with particular types and/or objects.

Functional programming programs with higher-order functions: functions that can take other functions as parameters and return functions as values.

You can interpret the template tagging technique in two ways. If you put on your Generic programming hat, you can claim that the sayIt template is a generic template that is parameterized with another template. However, if you put on your functional programming hat, you can claim that the sayIt template is a higher-order function that takes another function as an argument. Those familiar with C++'s style of generic programming will probably argue that the second interpretation is more accurate because the parameterization occurs at a runtime rather than at compile time. However, I do not believe that generic programming language must be a compile-time construct. Later you will see that the element tags can actually do more than serve as a proxy for the name of a function; these tags can also carry data reminiscent of the traits technique used in C++-style generic programming.

See Also

Dimitre Novatchev was the first person, to my knowledge, to discover techniques for generic and functional programming in XSLT. He wrote several articles on the topic. See *http://topxml.com/members/profile.asp?id=i1005*. The generic programming recipes in this chapter were developed before I discovered Dimitre's work and vary in some ways from Dimitre's approach. I would recommend viewing Dimitre's work only after you are comfortable with these examples. Dimitre pushes the edge of what can be done further than I do, and his techniques are thus somewhat more challenging. Dimitre has an XSLT library called *FXSL - an XSLT functional programming library* that can be downloaded from *http://topxml.com/xsl/articles/dice*.

14.1   Creating Polymorphic XSLT

Problem

You want to create XSLT that performs the same function on disparate data.

Solution

There are two kinds of polymorphic behavior in XSLT. The first form is reminiscent of *overloading*, and the second is similar to *overriding*.

Some modern languages, notably C++, let you create overloaded functions: functions that have the same name but take different types as arguments. The compiler figures out which version of the function to call based on the type of data passed to it at the point of call. XSLT does not have this exact capability; however, consider the following stylesheet:

```
<xsl:stylesheet version="1.0" xmlns:xsl="http://www.w3.org/1999/XSL/Transform">

<xsl:output method="html" />

<xsl:template match="/">
  <html>
    <head>
      <title>Area of Shapes</title>
    </head>
    <body>
      <h1>Area of Shapes</h1>
      <table cellpadding="2" border="1">
        <tbody>
          <tr>
            <th>Shape</th>
            <th>Shape Id</th>
            <th>Area</th>
          </tr>
          <xsl:apply-templates/>
        </tbody>
      </table>
    </body>
  </html>
</xsl:template>

<xsl:template match="shape">
  <tr>
    <td><xsl:value-of select="@kind"/></td>
    <td><xsl:value-of select="@id"/></td>
    <xsl:variable name="area">
      <xsl:apply-templates select="." mode="area"/>
    </xsl:variable>
    <td align="right"><xsl:value-of select="format-number($area,'#.000')"/></td>
  </tr>
</xsl:template>

<xsl:template match="shape[@kind='triangle']" mode="area">
  <xsl:value-of select="@base * @height"/>
</xsl:template>

<xsl:template match="shape[@kind='square']" mode="area">
  <xsl:value-of select="@side * @side"/>
</xsl:template>

<xsl:template match="shape[@kind='rectangle']" mode="area">
  <xsl:value-of select="@width * @height"/>
</xsl:template>
```

```
<xsl:template match="shape[@kind='circle']" mode="area">
  <xsl:value-of select="3.1415 * @radius * @radius"/>
</xsl:template>

</xsl:stylesheet>
```

Notice that several templates have an area mode. These templates differ in what types of shapes they except and compute a different function based on the particular shape. If you equate mode to function name and the match pattern to the data type, you will immediately see this technique as an instance of polymorphic overloading.

Overriding is the second form of polymorphism. You can see numerous examples of overriding in this book's examples. In XSLT, you use xsl:import to achieve this form of polymorphic behavior. The following example is a rewrite of the DocBook stylesheet from Recipe 8.1. It was engineered for extensibility in the following ways:

- It uses variables to define primitive components of otherwise monolithic attribute content. The variables can be redefined when importing stylesheets.

- It uses attribute sets, which can be augmented with additional attributes or have existing attributes overridden in importing stylesheets.

- It uses simple templates for each section of the document that can be overridden in importing stylesheets.

- It provides a *hook* via a call to the named template extra-head-meta-data whose default implementation does nothing.

```
<xsl:stylesheet version="1.0" xmlns:xsl="http://www.w3.org/1999/XSL/Transform">
<xsl:output method="html"/>

<!-- Variables defining various style components -->
<xsl:variable name="standard-font-family" select=" 'font-family:
Times serif; font-weight' "/>

<xsl:variable name="chapter-label-font-size" select=" 'font-size : 48pt' "/>
<xsl:variable name="chapter-title-font-size" select=" 'font-size : 24pt' "/>
<xsl:variable name="epigraph-font-size" select=" 'font-size : 10pt' "/>
<xsl:variable name="sect1-font-size" select=" 'font-size : 18pt' "/>
<xsl:variable name="sect2-font-size" select=" 'font-size : 14pt' "/>
<xsl:variable name="normal-font-size" select=" 'font-size : 12pt' "/>

<xsl:variable name="normal-text-color" select=" 'color: black' "/>
<xsl:variable name="chapter-title-color" select=" 'color: red' "/>

<xsl:variable name="epigraph-padding" select=" 'padding-top:4;
padding-bottom:4' "/>

<xsl:variable name="epigraph-common-style" select="concat($standard-font-
family,'; ', $epigraph-font-size, '; ', $epigraph-padding, '; ',$normal-text-
color)"/>
<xsl:variable name="sect-common-style" select="concat($standard-font-family,';
font-weight: bold', '; ',$normal-text-color)"/>
```

```
<!-- Attribute sets -->
<xsl:attribute-set name="chapter-align">
  <xsl:attribute name="align">right</xsl:attribute>
</xsl:attribute-set>

<xsl:attribute-set name="normal-align">
</xsl:attribute-set>

<xsl:attribute-set name="chapter-label" use-attribute-sets="chapter-align">
  <xsl:attribute name="style">
    <xsl:value-of select="$standard-font-family"/>;
    <xsl:value-of select="$chapter-label-font-size"/>;
    <xsl:value-of select="$chapter-title-color"/>
    <xsl:text>; padding-bottom:10; font-weight: bold</xsl:text>
  </xsl:attribute>
</xsl:attribute-set>

<xsl:attribute-set name="chapter-title" use-attribute-sets="chapter-align">
  <xsl:attribute name="style">
    <xsl:value-of select="$standard-font-family"/>;
    <xsl:value-of select="$chapter-title-font-size"/>;
    <xsl:value-of select="$chapter-title-color"/>
    <xsl:text>; padding-bottom:150; font-weight: bold</xsl:text>
  </xsl:attribute>
</xsl:attribute-set>

<xsl:attribute-set name="epigraph-para" use-attribute-sets="chapter-align">
  <xsl:attribute name="style">
    <xsl:value-of select="$epigraph-common-style"/><xsl:text>;
    font-style: italic</xsl:text>
  </xsl:attribute>
</xsl:attribute-set>

<xsl:attribute-set name="epigraph-attribution"
use-attribute-sets="chapter-align">
  <xsl:attribute name="style">
    <xsl:value-of select="$epigraph-common-style"/>
  </xsl:attribute>
</xsl:attribute-set>

<xsl:attribute-set name="sect1">
  <xsl:attribute name="align">left</xsl:attribute>
  <xsl:attribute name="style">
    <xsl:value-of select="$sect-common-style"/>;
    <xsl:value-of select="$sect1-font-size"/>
  </xsl:attribute>
</xsl:attribute-set>

<xsl:attribute-set name="sect2">
  <xsl:attribute name="align">left</xsl:attribute>
  <xsl:attribute name="style">
    <xsl:value-of select="$sect-common-style"/>;
    <xsl:value-of select="$sect2-font-size"/>
  </xsl:attribute>
</xsl:attribute-set>
```

```xsl
<xsl:attribute-set name="normal">
  <xsl:attribute name="align">left</xsl:attribute>
  <xsl:attribute name="style">
    <xsl:value-of select="$standard-font-family"/>;
    <xsl:value-of select="$normal-font-size"/>;
    <xsl:value-of select="$normal-text-color"/>
  </xsl:attribute>
</xsl:attribute-set>

<!-- Templates -->
<xsl:template match="/">
  <html>
    <head>
      <xsl:apply-templates mode="head"/>
      <xsl:call-template name="extra-head-meta-data"/>
    </head>
    <body style=
    "margin-left:100;margin-right:100;margin-top:50;margin-bottom:50">
      <xsl:apply-templates/>
      <xsl:apply-templates select="chapter/chapterinfo/*" mode="copyright"/>
    </body>
  </html>

</xsl:template>

<!-- Head -->

<xsl:template match="chapter/title" mode="head">
    <title><xsl:value-of select="."/></title>
</xsl:template>

<xsl:template match="author" mode="head">
    <meta name="author" content="{concat(firstname,' ', surname)}"/>
</xsl:template>

<xsl:template match="copyright" mode="head">
    <meta name="copyright" content="{concat(holder,' ',year)}"/>
</xsl:template>

<xsl:template match="text()" mode="head"/>

<!--Override in importing styleshhet if necessary -->
<xsl:template name="extra-head-meta-data"/>

<!-- Body -->

<xsl:template match="chapter">
  <div xsl:use-attribute-sets="chapter-label">
    <xsl:value-of select="@label"/>
  </div>
  <xsl:apply-templates/>
</xsl:template>
```

```xsl
<xsl:template match="chapter/title">
  <div xsl:use-attribute-sets="chapter-title">
    <xsl:value-of select="."/>
  </div>
</xsl:template>

<xsl:template match="epigraph/para">
  <div xsl:use-attribute-sets="epigraph-para">
    <xsl:value-of select="."/>
  </div>
</xsl:template>

<xsl:template match="epigraph/attribution">
  <div xsl:use-attribute-sets="epigraph-attribution">
    <xsl:value-of select="."/>
  </div>
</xsl:template>


<xsl:template match="sect1">
  <h1 xsl:use-attribute-sets="sect1">
    <xsl:value-of select="title"/>
  </h1>
  <xsl:apply-templates/>
</xsl:template>

<xsl:template match="sect2">
  <h2 xsl:use-attribute-sets="sect2">
  <xsl:value-of select="title"/>
  </h2>
    <xsl:apply-templates/>
</xsl:template>

<xsl:template match="para">
  <p xsl:use-attribute-sets="normal">
    <xsl:value-of select="."/>
  </p>
</xsl:template>

<xsl:template match="text( )"/>

<xsl:template match="copyright" mode="copyright">
  <div style="font-size : 10pt; font-family: Times serif; padding-top : 100">
    <xsl:text>Copyright </xsl:text>
    <xsl:value-of select="holder"/>
    <xsl:text> </xsl:text>
    <xsl:value-of select="year"/>
    <xsl:text>. All rights reserved.</xsl:text>
  </div>
</xsl:template>

<xsl:template match="*" mode="copyright"/>

</xsl:stylesheet>
```

Discussion

Calling XSLT an object-oriented language would stretch the truth. The behavior of xsl:import is only loosely similar to inheritance, and it operates at the level of the entire stylesheet. Furthermore, it has no notion of encapsulation or data abstraction. However, XSLT developers who already have an object-oriented mindset can often leverage that experience to the creation of more modular and reusable stylesheets.

Consider the example of overloading in the "Solution" section. Whenever you need to perform similar operations on disparate data, you will often want to structure your stylesheet in this manner. Of course, you could achieve the same result using conditional logic:

```
<xsl:template match="shape">
  <tr>
    <td><xsl:value-of select="@kind"/></td>
    <td><xsl:value-of select="@id"/></td>
    <xsl:variable name="area">
      <xsl:call-template name="area"/>
    </xsl:variable>
    <td align="right"><xsl:value-of select="format-number($area,'#.000')"/></td>
  </tr>
</xsl:template>

<xsl:template name="area">
  <xsl:choose>

    <xsl:when test="@kind='triangle' ">
      <xsl:value-of select="@base * @height"/>
    </xsl:when>

    <xsl:when test="@kind='square' " >
      <xsl:value-of select="@side * @side"/>
    </xsl:when>

    <xsl:when test="@kind='rectangle' ">
      <xsl:value-of select="@width * @height"/>
    </xsl:when>

    <xsl:when test="@kind='circle' ">
      <xsl:value-of select="3.1415 * @radius * @radius"/>
    </xsl:when>

  </xsl:choose>

</xsl:template>
```

In a simple case such as this, it is difficult to argue that the overloading method is superior to the conditional one. However, consider cases when someone needs to reuse the stylesheet, except that he must deal with triangles encoded in terms of sides and angles. If the stylesheet is written using separate templates for each shape, then importing the stylesheet and extending its behavior is simple. However, if the logic for each shape is written in a monolithic conditional manner, then the user must either copy the entire stylesheet and edit the parts that must change or extend the original and risk breaking it unintentionally.

Overriding is the key to creating modular and reusable XSLT. Nevertheless, reuse does not come for free; it requires planning. Specifically, you must think about three things:

1. What clients of your stylesheet might want to alter
2. What you may *not* want them to alter
3. What they are unlikely to alter

Failing to think about Item 1 results in an inflexible stylesheet that can be reused only by the cut, paste, and edit mechanism. Failing to think about Item 2 could create pitfalls for the client of your stylesheet. Failing to think about Item 3 results in overly complicated stylesheets with potentially poor performance and low maintainability.

In the DocBook stylesheet, we made it convenient to override font and other text attributes individually. We made it less convenient to override alignment attributes in a way that would create inconsistent or poor alignment choices between text elements where you desire consistency or a particular alignment. For example, it is more difficult to change the alignment of section and normal text elements by specifying their alignment separately. Finally, we did not try to make it easy for particular HTML element names to be overridden because doing so would have complicated the stylesheet in a way that adds little value.

See Also

Chris Rathman has a more extensive example of polymorphic XSLT at *http://www. angelfire.com/tx4/cus/shapes/xsl.html*.

14.2 Creating Generic Element Aggregation Functions

Problem

You want to create reusable templates that perform a wide variety of node-set aggregation operations.

Solution

A fully generic extensible solution exploits the template-tagging method discussed in this chapter's introduction:

```
<xsl:stylesheet version="1.0"
  xmlns:xsl="http://www.w3.org/1999/XSL/Transform"
  xmlns:generic="http://www.ora.com/XSLTCookbook/namespaces/generic"
  xmlns:aggr="http://www.ora.com/XSLTCookbook/namespaces/aggregate"
  extension-element-prefixes="generic">

  <xsl:variable name="generic:public-generics"
                select="document('')/*/generic:*"/>

  <xsl:variable name="generic:generics" select="$generic:public-generics"/>


  <!-- Primitive generic functions on x -->

<generic:func name="identity"/>
  <xsl:template match="generic:func[@name='identity']">
      <xsl:param name="x"/>
      <xsl:value-of select="$x"/>
  </xsl:template>

  <generic:func name="square"/>
  <xsl:template match="generic:func[@name='square']">
      <xsl:param name="x"/>
      <xsl:value-of select="$x * $x"/>
  </xsl:template>

  <generic:func name="cube"/>
  <xsl:template match="generic:func[@name='cube']">
      <xsl:param name="x"/>
      <xsl:value-of select="$x * $x * $x"/>
  </xsl:template>

  <generic:func name="incr" param1="1"/>
  <xsl:template match="generic:func[@name='incr']">
      <xsl:param name="x"/>
      <xsl:param name="param1" select="@param1"/>
      <xsl:value-of select="$x + $param1"/>
  </xsl:template>

<!-- Primitive generic aggregators -->

  <generic:aggr-func name="sum" identity="0"/>
  <xsl:template match="generic:aggr-func[@name='sum']">
      <xsl:param name="x"/>
      <xsl:param name="accum"/>
      <xsl:value-of select="$x + $accum"/>
  </xsl:template>

  <generic:aggr-func name="product" identity="1"/>
  <xsl:template match="generic:aggr-func[@name='product']">
      <xsl:param name="x"/>
      <xsl:param name="accum"/>
      <xsl:value-of select="$x * $accum"/>
  </xsl:template>
```

```
<!-- Generic aggregation template -->
<xsl:template name="generic:aggregation">
  <xsl:param name="nodes"/>
  <xsl:param name="aggr-func" select=" 'sum' "/>
  <xsl:param name="func" select=" 'identity' "/>
  <xsl:param name="func-param1"
             select="$generic:generics[self::generic:func and
                                       @name = $func]/@param1"/>
  <xsl:param name="i" select="1"/>
  <xsl:param name="accum"
             select="$generic:generics[self::generic:aggr-func and
                                       @name = $aggr-func]/@identity"/>

  <xsl:choose>
    <xsl:when test="$nodes">

      <!--Compute func($x) -->
      <xsl:variable name="f-of-x">
        <xsl:apply-templates
             select="$generic:generics[self::generic:func and
                                       @name = $func]">
          <xsl:with-param name="x" select="$nodes[1]"/>
          <xsl:with-param name="i" select="$i"/>
          <xsl:with-param name="param1" select="$func-param1"/>
        </xsl:apply-templates>
      </xsl:variable>

      <!-- Aggregate current $f-of-x with $accum -->
      <xsl:variable name="temp">
        <xsl:apply-templates
            select="$generic:generics[self::generic:aggr-func and
                                      @name = $aggr-func]">
          <xsl:with-param name="x" select="$f-of-x"/>
          <xsl:with-param name="accum" select="$accum"/>
          <xsl:with-param name="i" select="$i"/>
        </xsl:apply-templates>
      </xsl:variable>

      <!--We tail recursivly process the remaining nodes using position( )
      -->
      <xsl:call-template name="generic:aggregation">
        <xsl:with-param name="nodes" select="$nodes[position( )!=1]"/>
        <xsl:with-param name="aggr-func" select="$aggr-func"/>
        <xsl:with-param name="func" select="$func"/>
        <xsl:with-param name="func-param1" select="$func-param1"/>
        <xsl:with-param name="i" select="$i + 1"/>
        <xsl:with-param name="accum" select="$temp"/>
      </xsl:call-template>
    </xsl:when>
    <xsl:otherwise>
      <xsl:value-of select="$accum"/>
    </xsl:otherwise>
  </xsl:choose>
</xsl:template>

</xsl:stylesheet>
```

The generic code has three basic parts.

The first part consists of tagged generic functions on a single variable x. These functions allow performance of aggregation operations on functions of an input set. The simplest such function is identity, which is used when you want to aggregate the input set itself. Square, cube, and incr functions are also predefined. Users of the stylesheet can define other functions.

The second part consists of tagged generic aggregator functions. You will see two common implemented aggregators: sum and product. Again, importing stylesheets can add other forms of aggregation.

The third part consists of the generic aggregation algorithm. It accepts as parameters a set of nodes to aggregate, the name of an aggregator function (default is sum), and the name of a single element function (the default is identity). The $i parameter keeps track of the position of the currently processed node and is made available to both the element and aggregation functions, should they desire it. The $accum keeps a working value of the aggregation. Notice how the default value is initialized from the @identity attribute kept with the aggregate function's tag. This initialization demonstrates a powerful feature of the generic approach with which metadata can be associated with the function tags. This feature is reminiscent of the way C++-based generic programming uses traits classes.

The first step to understanding this code is to show a simple application that both uses and extends the aggregation facilities, as shown in Example 14-1.

Example 14-1. Using and extending generic aggregation

```
<xsl:stylesheet version="1.0"
  xmlns:xsl="http://www.w3.org/1999/XSL/Transform"
  xmlns:generic="http://www.ora.com/XSLTCookbook/namespaces/generic"
  xmlns:aggr="http://www.ora.com/XSLTCookbook/namespaces/aggregate"
  extension-element-prefixes="generic aggr">

<xsl:import href="aggregation.xslt"/>

<xsl:output method="xml" indent="yes"/>

<!-- Extend the available generic functions -->
<xsl:variable name="generic:generics" select="$generic:public-generics | document('')/*/
generic:*"/>

<!--Add a generic element function for computing reciprocal -->
<generic:func name="reciprocal"/>
<xsl:template match="generic:func[@name='reciprocal']">
    <xsl:param name="x"/>
    <xsl:value-of select="1 div $x"/>
</xsl:template>

<!--Add generic agregators for computing the min and the max values in a node set-->
<generic:aggr-func name="min" identity=""/>
```

Example 14-1. Using and extending generic aggregation (continued)

```
<xsl:template match="generic:aggr-func[@name='min']">
    <xsl:param name="x"/>
    <xsl:param name="accum"/>
  <xsl:choose>
    <xsl:when test="$accum = @identity or $accum >= $x">
      <xsl:value-of select="$x"/>
    </xsl:when>
    <xsl:otherwise>
      <xsl:value-of select="$accum"/>
    </xsl:otherwise>
  </xsl:choose>
</xsl:template>

<generic:aggr-func name="max" identity=""/>
<xsl:template match="generic:aggr-func[@name='max']">
    <xsl:param name="x"/>
    <xsl:param name="accum"/>
  <xsl:choose>
    <xsl:when test="$accum = @identity or $accum &lt; $x">
      <xsl:value-of select="$x"/>
    </xsl:when>
    <xsl:otherwise>
      <xsl:value-of select="$accum"/>
    </xsl:otherwise>
  </xsl:choose>
</xsl:template>

<!--Test aggregation functionality -->
<xsl:template match="numbers">

<results>

  <!-- Sum the numbers -->
  <sum>
    <xsl:call-template name="generic:aggregation">
      <xsl:with-param name="nodes" select="number"/>
    </xsl:call-template>
 </sum>

  <!-- Sum the squares -->
  <sumSq>
    <xsl:call-template name="generic:aggregation">
      <xsl:with-param name="nodes" select="number"/>
      <xsl:with-param name="func" select=" 'square' "/>
    </xsl:call-template>
  </sumSq>

  <!-- Product of the reciprocals -->
  <prodRecip>
    <xsl:call-template name="generic:aggregation">
      <xsl:with-param name="nodes" select="number"/>
      <xsl:with-param name="aggr-func" select=" 'product' "/>
```

Example 14-1. Using and extending generic aggregation (continued)

```
      <xsl:with-param name="func" select=" 'reciprocal' "/>
   </xsl:call-template>
</prodRecip>

<!-- Maximum -->
<max>
   <xsl:call-template name="generic:aggregation">
   <xsl:with-param name="nodes" select="number"/>
   <xsl:with-param name="aggr-func" select=" 'max' "/>
   </xsl:call-template>
</max>

<!-- Minimum -->
<min>
   <xsl:call-template name="generic:aggregation">
   <xsl:with-param name="nodes" select="number"/>
   <xsl:with-param name="aggr-func" select=" 'min' "/>
   </xsl:call-template>
</min>

</results>

</xsl:template>

</xsl:stylesheet>
```

Example 14-1 shows how new element and aggregation functions can be added to those prepackaged with *aggregation.xslt*. You might not initially expect that computing minimums and maximums can be accomplished with this generic code, but it is quite easy to do.

You can test this code against the following input:

```
<numbers>
   <number>1</number>
   <number>2</number>
   <number>3</number>
</numbers>
```

The result is:

```
<?xml version="1.0" encoding="utf-8"?>
<results>
   <sum>6</sum>
   <sumSq>14</sumSq>
   <prodRecip>0.16666666666666666</prodRecip>
   <max>3</max>
   <min>1</min>
</results>
```

Discussion

The "Solution" section shows only the tip of the iceberg in relation to what can be done with this generic aggregation framework. For example, nothing says you must aggregate numbers. The following code shows how this generic code can be applied to strings as well:

```
<strings>
  <string>camel</string>
  <string>through</string>
  <string>the</string>
  <string>eye</string>
  <string>of</string>
  <string>needle</string>
</strings>

<!DOCTYPE stylesheet [
    <!ENTITY % standard SYSTEM "../strings/standard.ent">
    %standard;
]>
<xsl:stylesheet version="1.0"
  xmlns:xsl="http://www.w3.org/1999/XSL/Transform"
  xmlns:generic="http://www.ora.com/XSLTCookbook/namespaces/generic"
  extension-element-prefixes="generic">

<xsl:import href="aggregation.xslt"/>

<xsl:output method="xml" indent="yes"/>

<!-- Extend the available generic functions -->
<xsl:variable name="generic:generics" select="$generic:public-generics |
document('')/*/generic:*"/>

<!--Add a generic element function for converting first character of $x to uppercase
-->
<generic:func name="upperFirst"/>
<xsl:template match="generic:func[@name='upperFirst']">
    <xsl:param name="x"/>
  <!-- See Recipe 1.8 for an explantion of LOWER_TO_UPPER -->
    <xsl:variable name="upper"
        select="translate(substring($x,1,1),&LOWER_TO_UPPER;)"/>
    <xsl:value-of select="concat($upper, substring($x,2))"/>
</xsl:template>

<!--Add generic agregator that concatenates -->
<generic:aggr-func name="concat" identity=""/>
<xsl:template match="generic:aggr-func[@name='concat']">
    <xsl:param name="x"/>
    <xsl:param name="accum"/>
    <xsl:value-of select="concat($accum,$x)"/>
</xsl:template>
```

```
<!--Test aggregation functionality -->
<xsl:template match="strings">

<results>

  <camelCase>
    <xsl:call-template name="generic:aggregation">
      <xsl:with-param name="nodes" select="string"/>
      <xsl:with-param name="aggr-func" select=" 'concat' "/>
      <xsl:with-param name="func" select=" 'upperFirst' "/>
    </xsl:call-template>
  </camelCase>

</results>

</xsl:template>

</xsl:stylesheet>

<results>
    <camelCase>CamelThroughTheEyeOfNeedle</camelCase>
</results>
```

Aggregation can also compute the statistical functions' average and variance. Here you exploit the $i index parameter. You need to be a little crafty to compute variance; you need to maintain three values in the $accum parameter—the sum, the sum of the squares, and the running variance. You can do this by using an element with attributes. The only downside is that you are forced to use a node-set function in XSLT 1.0:

```
<?xml version="1.0" encoding="UTF-8"?>
<xsl:stylesheet version="1.0"
  xmlns:xsl="http://www.w3.org/1999/XSL/Transform"
  xmlns:generic="http://www.ora.com/XSLTCookbook/namespaces/generic"
  xmlns:exslt="http://exslt.org/common"
  extension-element-prefixes="generic exslt">

<xsl:import href="aggregation.xslt"/>

<xsl:output method="xml" indent="yes"/>

<!-- Extend the available generic functions -->
<xsl:variable name="generic:generics" select="$generic:public-generics |
document('')/*/generic:*"/>

<!--Add generic agregators for computing the min and the max values in a node set-->
<generic:aggr-func name="avg" identity="0"/>
<xsl:template match="generic:aggr-func[@name='avg']">
    <xsl:param name="x"/>
    <xsl:param name="accum"/>
    <xsl:param name="i"/>
    <xsl:value-of select="(($i - 1) * $accum + $x) div $i"/>
</xsl:template>
```

```
<generic:aggr-func name="variance" identity=""/>
<xsl:template match="generic:aggr-func[@name='variance']">
  <xsl:param name="x"/>
  <xsl:param name="accum"/>
  <xsl:param name="i"/>

  <xsl:choose>
    <xsl:when test="$accum = @identity">
      <!-- Initialize the sum, sum of squares and variance.
           The variance of a single number is zero -->
      <variance sum="{$x}" sumSq="{$x * $x}">0</variance>
    </xsl:when>
    <xsl:otherwise>
      <!-- Use node-set to convert $accum to a nodes set containing
           the variance element -->
      <xsl:variable name="accumElem" select="exslt:node-set($accum)/*"/>
      <!-- Aggregate the sum of $x component -->
      <xsl:variable name="sum" select="$accumElem/@sum + $x"/>
      <!-- Aggregate the sum of $x squared component -->
      <xsl:variable name="sumSq" select="$accumElem/@sumSq + $x * $x"/>
      <!-- Return the element with attributes and the current variance
           as its value -->
      <variance sum="{$sum}" sumSq="{$sumSq}">
        <xsl:value-of
              select="($sumSq - ($sum * $sum) div $i) div ($i - 1)"/>
      </variance>
    </xsl:otherwise>
  </xsl:choose>

</xsl:template>

<xsl:template match="numbers">

<results>

  <!-- Average -->
  <avg>
    <xsl:call-template name="generic:aggregation">
      <xsl:with-param name="nodes" select="number"/>
      <xsl:with-param name="aggr-func" select=" 'avg' "/>
    </xsl:call-template>
  </avg>

  <!-- Average of the squares -->
  <avgSq>
    <xsl:call-template name="generic:aggregation">
      <xsl:with-param name="nodes" select="number"/>
      <xsl:with-param name="func" select=" 'square' "/>
      <xsl:with-param name="aggr-func" select=" 'avg' "/>
    </xsl:call-template>
  </avgSq>

  <!-- Variance -->
  <variance>
```

```
          <xsl:call-template name="generic:aggregation">
            <xsl:with-param name="nodes" select="number"/>
            <xsl:with-param name="aggr-func" select=" 'variance' "/>
          </xsl:call-template>
        </variance>

      </results>

    </xsl:template>

  </xsl:stylesheet>
```

This example shows how you can use your aggregation facilities to compute sums of polymorphic functions:

```
<?xml version="1.0" encoding="UTF-8"?>
<xsl:stylesheet version="1.0" xmlns:xsl="http://www.w3.org/1999/XSL/Transform" xmlns:
generic="http://www.ora.com/XSLTCookbook/namespaces/generic" xmlns:aggr="http://www.
ora.com/XSLTCookbook/namespaces/aggregate" xmlns:exslt="http://exslt.org/common"
extension-element-prefixes="generic aggr">

  <xsl:import href="aggregation.xslt"/>

  <xsl:output method="xml" indent="yes"/>

  <!-- Extend the available generic functions -->
  <xsl:variable name="generic:generics"
      select="$generic:public-generics | document('')/*/generic:*"/>

  <!-- Extend the primitives to compute commision-->
  <generic:func name="commision"/>
  <xsl:template match="generic:func[@name='commision']">
    <xsl:param name="x"/>
    <!-- defer actual computation to a polymorphic template using mode commision -->
    <xsl:apply-templates select="$x" mode="commision"/>
  </xsl:template>

  <!-- By default salespeople get 2% commsison and no base salary -->
  <xsl:template match="salesperson" mode="commision">
    <xsl:value-of select="0.02 * sum(product/@totalSales)"/>
  </xsl:template>

  <!-- salespeople with seniority > 4 get $10000.00 base + 0.5% commsison -->
  <xsl:template match="salesperson[@seniority > 4]" mode="commision" priority="1">
    <xsl:value-of select="10000.00 + 0.05 * sum(product/@totalSales)"/>
  </xsl:template>

  <!-- salespeople with seniority > 8 get (seniority * $2000.00) base + 0.8%
commsison -->
  <xsl:template match="salesperson[@seniority > 8]" mode="commision" priority="2">
    <xsl:value-of select="@seniority * 2000.00 + 0.08 *
          sum(product/@totalSales)"/>
  </xsl:template>
```

```
<xsl:template match="salesBySalesperson">
  <results>
    <result>
      <xsl:text>Total commision = </xsl:text>
      <xsl:call-template name="generic:aggregation">
        <xsl:with-param name="nodes" select="*"/>
        <xsl:with-param name="aggr-func" select=" 'sum' "/>
        <xsl:with-param name="func" select=" 'commision' "/>
      </xsl:call-template>
    </result>
    <result>
      <xsl:text>Min commision = </xsl:text>
      <xsl:call-template name="generic:aggregation">
        <xsl:with-param name="nodes" select="*"/>
        <xsl:with-param name="aggr-func" select=" 'min' "/>
        <xsl:with-param name="func" select=" 'commision' "/>
      </xsl:call-template>
    </result>
    <result>
      <xsl:text>Max commision = </xsl:text>
      <xsl:call-template name="generic:aggregation">
        <xsl:with-param name="nodes" select="*"/>
        <xsl:with-param name="aggr-func" select=" 'max' "/>
        <xsl:with-param name="func" select=" 'commision' "/>
      </xsl:call-template>
    </result>
    <result>
      <xsl:text>Avg commision = </xsl:text>
      <xsl:call-template name="generic:aggregation">
        <xsl:with-param name="nodes" select="*"/>
        <xsl:with-param name="aggr-func" select=" 'avg' "/>
        <xsl:with-param name="func" select=" 'commision' "/>
      </xsl:call-template>
    </result>
    <result>
      <xsl:text>Avg sales = </xsl:text>
      <xsl:call-template name="generic:aggregation">
        <xsl:with-param name="nodes" select="*/product/@totalSales"/>
        <xsl:with-param name="aggr-func" select=" 'avg' "/>
      </xsl:call-template>
    </result>
    <result>
      <xsl:text>Min sales = </xsl:text>
      <xsl:call-template name="generic:aggregation">
        <xsl:with-param name="nodes" select="*/product/@totalSales"/>
        <xsl:with-param name="aggr-func" select=" 'min' "/>
      </xsl:call-template>
    </result>
    <result>
      <xsl:text>Max sales = </xsl:text>
      <xsl:call-template name="generic:aggregation">
        <xsl:with-param name="nodes" select="*/product/@totalSales"/>
        <xsl:with-param name="aggr-func" select=" 'max' "/>
      </xsl:call-template>
```

```
    </result>
   </results>
  </xsl:template>

 </xsl:stylesheet>
```

The result when run against *salesBySalesperson.xml* (see Chapter 4) is:

```
<results xmlns:exslt="http://exslt.org/common">
    <result>Total commision = 471315</result>
    <result>Min commision = 19600</result>
    <result>Max commision = 364440</result>
    <result>Avg commision = 117828.75</result>
    <result>Avg sales = 584636.3636363636</result>
    <result>Min sales = 5500.00</result>
    <result>Max sales = 2920000.00</result>
</results>
```

This section has demonstrated that many of the recipes implemented separately in Chapter 2 can be implemented easily in terms of this single generic example. In fact, this generic example can compute an infinite range of aggregation-like functions over a set of nodes. Unfortunately, this flexibility and generality is not free. A generic implementation will typically be 40% slower than a custom hand-coded solution. If speed is the most important consideration, then you may want to consider an optimized hand-coded solution. However, if you need to implement a complex piece of XSLT rapidly that performs a wider variety of aggregation operations, a generic solution will speed up development substantially.* One of the tricks of getting the most mileage out of this approach is to have many common generic element and aggregation functions that are ready to be used. In the actual implementation of *aggregation. xslt*, I have all the functions from this example (and several others). You can access the complete code at the book's web site (*http://www.oreilly.com/catalog/xsltckbk*).

In cases when the aggregate function is not symmetric, you might need to aggregate over a node list in reverse order. This aggregation requires only a minor change to the generic aggregation function:

```
<xsl:template name="generic:reverse-aggregation">
  <xsl:param name="nodes"/>
  <xsl:param name="aggr-func" select=" 'sum' "/>
  <xsl:param name="func" select=" 'identity' "/>
  <xsl:param name="func-param1" select="$generic:generics[self::generic:func and
                                        @name = $func]/@param1"/>
```

---

* Not everyone would agree with this assessment. In fact, some would argue that using this approach slows down development because of the complexity caused by extra levels of indirection. However, repeated usage often makes the complex appear idiomatic. For example, recall how you felt when you first struggled with vanilla XSLT.

```
    <xsl:param name="i" select="1"/>
    <xsl:param name="accum" select="$generic:generics[self::generic:aggr-func and
                                @name = $aggr-func]/@identity"/>

  <xsl:choose>
    <xsl:when test="$nodes">

      <!--Compute func($x) -->
      <xsl:variable name="f-of-x">
        <xsl:apply-templates select=
        "$generic:generics[self::generic:func and @name = $func]">
          <xsl:with-param name="x" select="$nodes[last()]"/>
          <xsl:with-param name="i" select="$i"/>
        </xsl:apply-templates>
      </xsl:variable>

      <!-- Aggregate current $f-of-x with $accum -->
      <xsl:variable name="temp">
        <xsl:apply-templates
            select="$generic:generics[self::generic:aggr-func and
                                @name = $aggr-func]">
          <xsl:with-param name="x" select="$f-of-x"/>
          <xsl:with-param name="accum" select="$accum"/>
          <xsl:with-param name="i" select="$i"/>
        </xsl:apply-templates>
      </xsl:variable>

      <xsl:call-template name="generic:aggregation">
        <xsl:with-param name="nodes"
                        select="$nodes[position()!=last()]"/>
        <xsl:with-param name="aggr-func" select="$aggr-func"/>
        <xsl:with-param name="func" select="$func"/>
        <xsl:with-param name="func-param1" select="$func-param1"/>
        <xsl:with-param name="i" select="$i + 1"/>
        <xsl:with-param name="accum" select="$temp"/>
      </xsl:call-template>
    </xsl:when>
    <xsl:otherwise>
      <xsl:value-of select="$accum"/>
    </xsl:otherwise>
  </xsl:choose>
</xsl:template>
```

See Also

FXSL (see the "See Also" section of this chapter's introduction) has fold and foldr
functions that are similar to generic:aggregation and generic:reverse-aggregation,
respectively.

14.3 Creating Generic Bounded Aggregation Functions

Problem

You want to create reusable templates for performing a wide variety of bounded aggregation operations.

Solution

```
<xsl:template name="generic:bounded-aggregation">
  <xsl:param name="x" select="0"/>
  <xsl:param name="func" select=" 'identity' "/>
  <xsl:param name="func-param1"/>
  <xsl:param name="test-func" select=" 'less-than' "/>
  <xsl:param name="test-param1" select="$x + 1"/>
  <xsl:param name="incr-func" select=" 'incr' "/>
  <xsl:param name="incr-param1" select="1"/>
  <xsl:param name="i" select="1"/>
  <xsl:param name="aggr-func" select=" 'sum' "/>
  <xsl:param name="aggr-param1"/>
  <xsl:param name="accum"
             select="$generic:generics[self::generic:aggr-func and
                                       @name = $aggr-func]/@identity"/>


  <!-- Check if aggregation should continue -->
  <xsl:variable name="continue">
    <xsl:apply-templates
        select="$generic:generics[self::generic:func and
                                  @name = $test-func]">
      <xsl:with-param name="x" select="$x"/>
      <xsl:with-param name="param1" select="$test-param1"/>
    </xsl:apply-templates>
  </xsl:variable>

  <xsl:choose>
    <xsl:when test="string($continue)">
     <!--Compute func($x) -->
      <xsl:variable name="f-of-x">
        <xsl:apply-templates select="$generic:generics[self::generic:func
                                                       and
                                                       @name = $func]">
          <xsl:with-param name="x" select="$x"/>
          <xsl:with-param name="i" select="$i"/>
          <xsl:with-param name="param1" select="$func-param1"/>
        </xsl:apply-templates>
      </xsl:variable>
```

```
<!-- Aggregate current $f-of-x with $accum -->
<xsl:variable name="temp">
  <xsl:apply-templates
      select="$generic:generics[self::generic:aggr-func and
                                @name = $aggr-func]">
    <xsl:with-param name="x" select="$f-of-x"/>
    <xsl:with-param name="i" select="$i"/>
    <xsl:with-param name="param1" select="$aggr-param1"/>
    <xsl:with-param name="accum" select="$accum"/>
  </xsl:apply-templates>
</xsl:variable>

<!-- Compute the next value of $x-->
<xsl:variable name="next-x">
  <xsl:apply-templates
      select="$generic:generics[self::generic:func and
                                @name = $incr-func]">
    <xsl:with-param name="x" select="$x"/>
    <xsl:with-param name="param1" select="$incr-param1"/>
  </xsl:apply-templates>
</xsl:variable>

  <!--We tail recursivly process the remaining nodes using
      position( ) -->
  <xsl:call-template name="generic:bounded-aggregation">
    <xsl:with-param name="x" select="$next-x"/>
    <xsl:with-param name="func" select="$func"/>
    <xsl:with-param name="func-param1" select="$func-param1"/>
    <xsl:with-param name="test-func" select="$test-func"/>
    <xsl:with-param name="test-param1" select="$test-param1"/>
    <xsl:with-param name="incr-func" select="$incr-func"/>
    <xsl:with-param name="incr-param1" select="$incr-param1"/>
    <xsl:with-param name="i" select="$i + 1"/>
    <xsl:with-param name="aggr-func" select="$aggr-func"/>
    <xsl:with-param name="aggr-param1" select="$aggr-param1"/>
    <xsl:with-param name="accum" select="$temp"/>
  </xsl:call-template>
</xsl:when>
<xsl:otherwise>
  <xsl:value-of select="$accum"/>
</xsl:otherwise>
</xsl:choose>
</xsl:template>
```

This template does not aggregate a node set, but rather aggregates over a set of values defined by an initial value, an increment function, and a predicate that determines when the aggregation should terminate. The incrementing function and test function each can take their own parameters. The other generic:bounded-aggregation parameters are the same as generic:aggregation in Recipe 14.2.

Discussion

Recipe 14.2 addresses the problem of aggregating XML content generically. However, sometimes you need to perform aggregation-like operations on mathematically synthesized data.

The simplest thing to do with this generic bounded aggregation function is to implement the factorial and prod-range templates from Recipe 2.5:

```
<xsl:stylesheet version="1.0"
  xmlns:xsl="http://www.w3.org/1999/XSL/Transform"
  xmlns:generic="http://www.ora.com/XSLTCookbook/namespaces/generic"
  xmlns:aggr="http://www.ora.com/XSLTCookbook/namespaces/aggregate"
  xmlns:exslt="http://exslt.org/common"
  extension-element-prefixes="generic aggr exslt">

<xsl:import href="aggregation.xslt"/>

<xsl:output method="xml" indent="yes"/>

<xsl:template name="factorial">
  <xsl:param name="n" select="0"/>

  <xsl:call-template name="generic:bounded-aggregation">
    <xsl:with-param name="x" select="$n"/>
    <xsl:with-param name="test-func" select=" 'greater-than' "/>
    <xsl:with-param name="test-param1" select="0"/>
    <xsl:with-param name="incr-func" select=" 'decr' "/>
    <xsl:with-param name="aggr-func" select=" 'product' "/>
  </xsl:call-template>

</xsl:template>

<xsl:template name="prod-range">
  <xsl:param name="start" select="1"/>
  <xsl:param name="end" select="1"/>

  <xsl:call-template name="generic:bounded-aggregation">
    <xsl:with-param name="x" select="$start"/>
    <xsl:with-param name="test-func" select=" 'less-than-eq' "/>
    <xsl:with-param name="test-param1" select="$end"/>
    <xsl:with-param name="incr-func" select=" 'incr' "/>
    <xsl:with-param name="aggr-func" select=" 'product' "/>
  </xsl:call-template>

</xsl:template>

<xsl:template match="/">

  <results>
```

```
    <factorial n="0">
      <xsl:call-template name="factorial"/>
    </factorial>

    <factorial n="1">
      <xsl:call-template name="factorial">
        <xsl:with-param name="n" select="1"/>
      </xsl:call-template>
    </factorial>

    <factorial n="5">
      <xsl:call-template name="factorial">
        <xsl:with-param name="n" select="5"/>
      </xsl:call-template>
    </factorial>

    <factorial n="20">
      <xsl:call-template name="factorial">
        <xsl:with-param name="n" select="20"/>
      </xsl:call-template>
    </factorial>

    <product start="1" end="20">
      <xsl:call-template name="prod-range">
        <xsl:with-param name="start" select="1"/>
        <xsl:with-param name="end" select="20"/>
      </xsl:call-template>
    </product>

    <product start="10" end="20">
      <xsl:call-template name="prod-range">
        <xsl:with-param name="start" select="10"/>
        <xsl:with-param name="end" select="20"/>
      </xsl:call-template>
    </product>

  </results>

  </xsl:template>

  </xsl:stylesheet>
```

The resulting output is:

```
<results>
    <factorial n="0">1</factorial>
    <factorial n="1">1</factorial>
    <factorial n="5">120</factorial>
    <factorial n="20">2432902008176640000</factorial>
    <product start="1" end="20">2432902008176640000</product>
    <product start="10" end="20">6704425728000</product>
</results>
```

However, this is only the tip of the iceberg! You can also use generic:bounded-aggregation for numeric integration:

```
<xsl:stylesheet version="1.0"
  xmlns:xsl="http://www.w3.org/1999/XSL/Transform"
  xmlns:generic="http://www.ora.com/XSLTCookbook/namespaces/generic"
  xmlns:aggr="http://www.ora.com/XSLTCookbook/namespaces/aggregate"
  xmlns:exslt="http://exslt.org/common"
  extension-element-prefixes="generic aggr exslt">

  <xsl:import href="aggregation.xslt"/>

  <xsl:output method="xml" indent="yes"/>

<!-- Extend the available generic functions -->
<xsl:variable name="generic:generics" select="$generic:public-generics |
document('')/*/generic:*"/>

  <xsl:template name="integrate">
    <xsl:param name="from" select="0"/>
    <xsl:param name="to" select="1"/>
    <xsl:param name="func" select=" 'identity' "/>
    <xsl:param name="delta" select="($to - $from) div 100"/>

    <xsl:call-template name="generic:bounded-aggregation">
      <xsl:with-param name="x" select="$from"/>
      <xsl:with-param name="func" select=" 'f-of-x-dx' "/>
      <xsl:with-param name="func-param1">
        <params f-of-x="{$func}" dx="{$delta}"/>
      </xsl:with-param>
      <xsl:with-param name="test-func" select=" 'less-than' "/>
      <xsl:with-param name="test-param1" select="$to"/>
      <xsl:with-param name="incr-func" select=" 'incr' "/>
      <xsl:with-param name="incr-param1" select="$delta"/>
      <xsl:with-param name="aggr-func" select=" 'sum' "/>
    </xsl:call-template>

  </xsl:template>

  <xsl:template name="integrate2">
    <xsl:param name="from" select="0"/>
    <xsl:param name="to" select="1"/>
    <xsl:param name="func" select=" 'identity' "/>
    <xsl:param name="delta" select="($to - $from) div 100"/>

    <xsl:call-template name="generic:bounded-aggregation">
      <xsl:with-param name="x" select="$from"/>
      <xsl:with-param name="func" select=" 'f-of-x-dx-2' "/>
      <xsl:with-param name="func-param1">
        <params f-of-x="{$func}" dx="{$delta}"/>
      </xsl:with-param>
      <xsl:with-param name="test-func" select=" 'less-than' "/>
      <xsl:with-param name="test-param1" select="$to"/>
      <xsl:with-param name="incr-func" select=" 'incr' "/>
```

```
      <xsl:with-param name="incr-param1" select="$delta"/>
      <xsl:with-param name="aggr-func" select=" 'sum' "/>
   </xsl:call-template>

</xsl:template>

<generic:func name="f-of-x-dx"/>
<xsl:template match="generic:func[@name='f-of-x-dx']">
    <xsl:param name="x"/>
    <xsl:param name="param1"/>

    <xsl:variable name="f-of-x">
     <xsl:apply-templates select="$generic:generics[self::generic:func
     and @name = exslt:node-set($param1)/*/@f-of-x]">
       <xsl:with-param name="x" select="$x"/>
     </xsl:apply-templates>
     </xsl:variable>

    <xsl:value-of select="$f-of-x * exslt:node-set($param1)/*/@dx"/>
</xsl:template>

<generic:func name="f-of-x-dx-2"/>
<xsl:template match="generic:func[@name='f-of-x-dx-2']">
    <xsl:param name="x"/>
    <xsl:param name="param1"/>

    <xsl:variable name="func" select="exslt:node-set($param1)/*/@f-of-x"/>
    <xsl:variable name="dx" select="exslt:node-set($param1)/*/@dx"/>

    <xsl:variable name="f-of-x">
     <xsl:apply-templates
         select="$generic:generics[self::generic:func and
                                   @name = $func]">
       <xsl:with-param name="x" select="$x"/>
     </xsl:apply-templates>
     </xsl:variable>

    <xsl:variable name="f-of-x-plus-dx">
     <xsl:apply-templates select="$generic:generics[self::generic:func
                                            and @name = $func]">
       <xsl:with-param name="x" select="$x + $dx"/>
     </xsl:apply-templates>
     </xsl:variable>

    <!-- This is just the absolute value of $f-of-x-plus-dx - $f-of-x -->
    <xsl:variable name="abs-diff"
              select="(1 - 2 *(($f-of-x-plus-dx - $f-of-x) &lt; 0)) *
                      ($f-of-x-plus-dx - $f-of-x)"/>

    <xsl:value-of select="$f-of-x * $dx + ($abs-diff * $dx) div 2"/>

</xsl:template>
```

```
<xsl:template match="/">

<results>

  <integrate desc="intgr x from 0 to 1">
    <xsl:call-template name="integrate"/>
  </integrate>

  <integrate desc="intgr x from 0 to 1 with more precision">
    <xsl:call-template name="integrate">
      <xsl:with-param name="delta" select="0.001"/>
    </xsl:call-template>
  </integrate>

  <integrate desc="intgr x from 0 to 1 with better algorithm">
    <xsl:call-template name="integrate2"/>
  </integrate>

  <integrate desc="intgr x**2 from 0 to 1">
    <xsl:call-template name="integrate">
      <xsl:with-param name="func" select=" 'square' "/>
    </xsl:call-template>
  </integrate>

  <integrate desc="intgr x**2 from 0 to 1 with better algorithm">
    <xsl:call-template name="integrate2">
      <xsl:with-param name="func" select=" 'square' "/>
    </xsl:call-template>
  </integrate>

</results>

</xsl:template>

</xsl:stylesheet>
```

The challenge here is that you want the user of the integrate templates to pass in any old function of x. However, you need to compute a sum that is a function of that function. Hence, you need a way to define a higher-order function. In addition, you must pass the higher-order function an additional parameter—in this case, the delta used to approximate the integration. You can do this by passing an element that you synthesize on the fly, `<params f-of-x="{$func}" dx="{$delta}"/>`. This compound parameter is used in the higher-order functions `f-of-x-dx` and `f-of-x-dx-2`. Unfortunately, XSLT 1.0 forces you to use `exsl:node-set` to extract information from the compound parameter.

Here is the output of the stylesheet shown earlier:

```
<results>
  <integrate desc="intgr x from 0 to 1">
    0.4950000000000004
  </integrate>
```

```
   <integrate desc="intgr x from 0 to 1 with more precision">
     0.4995000000000005
   </integrate>
    <integrate desc="intgr x from 0 to 1 with better algorithm">
      0.5000000000000001
      </integrate>
    <integrate desc="intgr x**2 from 0 to 1">
      0.32835000000000036
    </integrate>
    <integrate desc="intgr x**2 from 0 to 1 with better algorithm">
      0.33335000000000037
    </integrate>
  </results>
```

You are unlikely to need numerical integration in XSLT. Numerical integration is not the point of this example. Instead, it demonstrates the power of the generic programming style to accomplish much by using generic reusable code.

14.4 Creating Generic Mapping Functions

Problem

You want to create reusable templates for performing operations on items in a node set.

Solution

The solution involves recursively processing the elements in $nodes and invoking the generic function, $func, on each element. You allow the possibility that the function specified by $func is parameterized. This parameter can be specified by $func-param. You further state that the default value of the $func-param is obtained from an attribute, @param1, in the generic functions tag. This stipulation allows the default to be a function of the specified generic:

```
<xsl:template name="generic:map">
  <xsl:param name="nodes" select="/.."/>
  <xsl:param name="func" select=" 'identity' "/>
  <xsl:param name="func-param1"
      select="$generic:generics[self::generic:func and @name = $func]/@param1"/>
  <xsl:param name="i" select="1"/>
  <xsl:param name="result" select="/.."/>

  <xsl:choose>
    <xsl:when test="$nodes">
      <xsl:variable name="temp">
        <xsl:apply-templates
            select="$generic:generics[self::generic:func and
                                   @name = $func]">
          <xsl:with-param name="x" select="$nodes[1]"/>
          <xsl:with-param name="i" select="$i"/>
```

```
                    <xsl:with-param name="param1" select="$func-param1"/>
                </xsl:apply-templates>
            </xsl:variable>

            <xsl:call-template name="generic:map">
                <xsl:with-param name="nodes" select="$nodes[position( ) > 1]"/>
                <xsl:with-param name="func" select="$func"/>
                <xsl:with-param name="func-param1" select="$func-param1"/>
                <xsl:with-param name="i" select="$i +1"/>
                <xsl:with-param name="result"
                                select="$result | exslt:node-set($temp)"/>
            </xsl:call-template>
        </xsl:when>
        <xsl:otherwise>
            <xsl:apply-templates select="$result" mode="generic:map"/>
        </xsl:otherwise>
    </xsl:choose>
</xsl:template>

<xsl:template match="/ | node( ) | @*" mode="generic:map">
    <node>
        <xsl:copy-of select="."/>
    </node>
</xsl:template>
```

You can see the effect of this process by considering the incr generic function:

```
<generic:func name="incr" param1="1"/>
<xsl:template match="generic:func[@name='incr']">
    <xsl:param name="x"/>
    <xsl:param name="param1" select="@param1"/>
    <xsl:value-of select="$x + $param1"/>
</xsl:template>
```

The incr generic function's parameter specifies the amount by which to increment and is defaulted to one. Here you create a stylesheet that maps incr across a node set of numbers, first using the default parameter and then by setting it to 10. For good measure, you also extend the set of generics to include a reciprocal function and map the numbers using that function:

```
<xsl:stylesheet version="1.0"
  xmlns:xsl="http://www.w3.org/1999/XSL/Transform"
  xmlns:generic="http://www.ora.com/XSLTCookbook/namespaces/generic"
  xmlns:exslt="http://exslt.org/common"
  extension-element-prefixes="exslt" exclude-result-prefixes="generic">

<xsl:import href="aggregation.xslt"/>

<xsl:output method="xml" indent="yes"/>

<!-- Extend the available generic functions -->
<xsl:variable name="generic:generics" select="$generic:public-generics |
document('')/*/generic:*"/>
```

```
<!--Add a generic element function for computing reciprocal -->
<generic:func name="reciprocal"/>
<xsl:template match="generic:func[@name='reciprocal']">
    <xsl:param name="x"/>
    <xsl:value-of select="1 div $x"/>
</xsl:template>

<!--Test map functionality -->
<xsl:template match="numbers">

<results>

<incr>
  <xsl:call-template name="generic:map">
    <xsl:with-param name="nodes" select="number"/>
    <xsl:with-param name="func" select=" 'incr' "/>
  </xsl:call-template>
</incr>
<incr10>
    <xsl:call-template name="generic:map">
      <xsl:with-param name="nodes" select="number"/>
      <xsl:with-param name="func" select=" 'incr' "/>
      <xsl:with-param name="func-param1" select="10"/>
    </xsl:call-template>
</incr10>
<recip>
    <xsl:call-template name="generic:map">
      <xsl:with-param name="nodes" select="number"/>
      <xsl:with-param name="func" select=" 'reciprocal' "/>
    </xsl:call-template>
</recip>
</results>

</xsl:template>

</xsl:stylesheet>
```

This results in the following output:

```
<incr>
    <node>11</node>
    <node>4.5</node>
    <node>5.44</node>
    <node>78.7777</node>
    <node>-7</node>
    <node>2</node>
    <node>445</node>
    <node>2.1234</node>
    <node>8.77</node>
    <node>4.1415927</node>
  </incr>
  <incr10>
      <node>20</node>
      <node>13.5</node>
      <node>14.440000000000001</node>
```

```
        <node>87.7777</node>
        <node>2</node>
        <node>11</node>
        <node>454</node>
        <node>11.1234</node>
        <node>17.77</node>
        <node>13.1415927</node>
    </incr10>
    <recip>
        <node>0.1</node>
        <node>0.2857142857142857</node>
        <node>0.2252252252252252</node>
        <node>0.012857155714298572</node>
        <node>-0.125</node>
        <node>1</node>
        <node>0.0022522522522522522</node>
        <node>0.8901548869503294</node>
        <node>0.1287001287001287</node>
        <node>0.31830988148145367</node>
    </recip>
</results>
```

Discussion

Map can extract a subset of a node set that meets specified criteria. Here you use a generic function that is a predicate. You achieve the desired effect by structuring your predicates so that they return their input when the predicate is true and nothing when the predicate is false. For example:

```
<generic:func name="less-than"/>
<xsl:template match="generic:func[@name='less-than']">
    <xsl:param name="x"/>
    <!-- limit -->
    <xsl:param name="param1"/>
    <xsl:if test="$x &lt; $param1"><xsl:value-of select="$x"/></xsl:if>
</xsl:template>
```

You then capture the nodes of the result with a simple filtering template:

```
xsl:template match="/ | node() | @*" mode="generic:map">
  <xsl:if test="string(.)">
    <node>
      <xsl:copy-of select="."/>
    </node>
  </xsl:if>
</xsl:template>
```

Here is a sample of the technique in action:

```
<xsl:stylesheet version="1.0"
  xmlns:xsl="http://www.w3.org/1999/XSL/Transform"
  xmlns:generic="http://www.ora.com/XSLTCookbook/namespaces/generic"
  xmlns:exslt="http://exslt.org/common"
  extension-element-prefixes="exslt" exclude-result-prefixes="generic">

<xsl:import href="aggregation.xslt"/>
```

```
<xsl:output method="xml" indent="yes"/>

<!--Test map functionality -->
<xsl:template match="numbers">

<results>

<less-than-5>
  <xsl:call-template name="generic:map">
    <xsl:with-param name="nodes" select="number"/>
    <xsl:with-param name="func" select=" 'less-than' "/>
    <xsl:with-param name="func-param1" select="5"/>
  </xsl:call-template>
</less-than-5>

<greater-than-5>
  <xsl:call-template name="generic:map">
    <xsl:with-param name="nodes" select="number"/>
    <xsl:with-param name="func" select=" 'greater-than' "/>
    <xsl:with-param name="func-param1" select="5"/>
  </xsl:call-template>
</greater-than-5>

</results>


</xsl:template>

<xsl:template match="/ | node() | @*" mode="generic:map">
  <xsl:if test="string(.)">
    <node>
      <xsl:copy-of select="."/>
    </node>
  </xsl:if>
</xsl:template>
```

A test of this stylesheet produces the following output:

```
<results>
    <less-than-5>
        <node>3.5</node>
        <node>4.44</node>
        <node>-8</node>
        <node>1</node>
        <node>1.1234</node>
        <node>3.1415927</node>
    </less-than-5>
    <greater-than-5>
        <node>10</node>
        <node>77.7777</node>
        <node>444</node>
        <node>7.77</node>
    </greater-than-5>
</results>
```

Mapping is not limited to numerical processing. Consider the following stylesheet that finds the length of all <para> elements in a DocBook document:

```
<xsl:stylesheet version="1.0"
  xmlns:xsl="http://www.w3.org/1999/XSL/Transform"
  xmlns:generic="http://www.ora.com/XSLTCookbook/namespaces/generic"
  xmlns:exslt="http://exslt.org/common"
  extension-element-prefixes="exslt" exclude-result-prefixes="generic">

<xsl:import href="aggregation.xslt"/>

<xsl:output method="xml" indent="yes"/>

<!-- Extend the available generic functions -->
<xsl:variable name="generic:generics" select="$generic:public-generics |
document('')/*/generic:*"/>

<!--Add a generic element function for computing reciprocal -->
<generic:func name="length"/>
<xsl:template match="generic:func[@name='length']">
  <xsl:param name="x"/>
  <xsl:value-of select="string-length($x)"/>
</xsl:template>

<!--Test map functionality -->
<xsl:template match="/">

<para-lengths>
    <xsl:call-template name="generic:map">
      <xsl:with-param name="nodes" select="//para"/>
      <xsl:with-param name="func" select=" 'length' "/>
    </xsl:call-template>
</para-lengths>

</xsl:template>

<xsl:template match="/ | node() | @*" mode="generic:map">
  <length>
    <xsl:copy-of select="."/>
  </length>
</xsl:template>

</xsl:stylesheet>
```

Or this example, which creates a document summary by extracting the first three sentences of each paragraph:

```
<xsl:stylesheet version="1.0"
  xmlns:xsl="http://www.w3.org/1999/XSL/Transform"
  xmlns:generic="http://www.ora.com/XSLTCookbook/namespaces/generic"
  xmlns:exslt="http://exslt.org/common"
  extension-element-prefixes="exslt" exclude-result-prefixes="generic">
```

```
<xsl:import href="aggregation.xslt"/>

<xsl:output method="xml" indent="yes"/>

<!-- Extend the available generic functions -->
<xsl:variable name="generic:generics" select="$generic:public-generics |
document('')/*/generic:*"/>

<!--A generic function for extracting sentences -->
<generic:func name="extract-sentences" param1="1"/>
<xsl:template match="generic:func[@name='extract-sentences']" name="generic:extract-
sentences">
  <xsl:param name="x"/>
  <xsl:param name="param1" select="@param1"/>
   <xsl:choose>
    <xsl:when test="$param1 >= 1 and contains($x,'.')">
      <xsl:value-of select="substring-before($x,'.')"/>
      <xsl:text>.</xsl:text>
      <xsl:call-template name="generic:extract-sentences">
        <xsl:with-param name="x" select="substring-after($x,'.')"/>
        <xsl:with-param name="param1" select="$param1 - 1"/>
      </xsl:call-template>
    </xsl:when>
    <xsl:otherwise/>
   </xsl:choose>
</xsl:template>

<xsl:template match="/">

<summary>
    <xsl:call-template name="generic:map">
      <xsl:with-param name="nodes" select="//para"/>
      <xsl:with-param name="func" select=" 'extract-sentences' "/>
      <xsl:with-param name="func-param1" select="3"/>
    </xsl:call-template>
</summary>

</xsl:template>

<xsl:template match="/ | node() | @*" mode="generic:map">
  <para>
    <xsl:copy-of select="."/>
  </para>
</xsl:template>

</xsl:stylesheet>
```

These examples are convoluted ways of creating results that can easily be obtained
with more straightforward stylesheets. Creating stylesheets that perform transformations a node at a time is easy. For example, the summary stylesheet is more clearly
implemented as follows:

```
<xsl:stylesheet version="1.0" xmlns:xsl="http://www.w3.org/1999/XSL/Transform">
    <xsl:output method="xml" version="1.0" encoding="UTF-8" indent="yes"/>
```

```
<xsl:template name="extract-sentences">
  <xsl:param name="text"/>
  <xsl:param name="num-sentences" select="1"/>
   <xsl:choose>
     <xsl:when test="$num-sentences >= 1 and contains($text,'.')">
       <xsl:value-of select="substring-before($text,'.')"/>
       <xsl:text>.</xsl:text>
       <xsl:call-template name="extract-sentences">
         <xsl:with-param name="text" select="substring-after($text,'.')"/>
         <xsl:with-param name="num-sentences" select="$num-sentences - 1"/>
       </xsl:call-template>
     </xsl:when>
     <xsl:otherwise/>
   </xsl:choose>
</xsl:template>

<xsl:template match="/">
  <summary>
    <xsl:apply-templates select=".//para"/>
  </summary>
</xsl:template>

<xsl:template match="para">
  <para>
      <xsl:call-template name="extract-sentences">
        <xsl:with-param name="text" select="."/>
        <xsl:with-param name="num-sentences" select="3"/>
      </xsl:call-template>
    </para>
</xsl:template>

</xsl:stylesheet>
```

However, if in a single stylesheet you need to perform several map-like operations, then the generic implementation could result in less custom-written code.

An alternate mapping generic function is generic:map2. Rather than applying a unary function to a single node set, generic:map2 applies a binary function to the elements of two node sets and returns the resulting node set:

```
<xsl:template name="generic:map2">
  <xsl:param name="nodes1" select="/.."/>
  <xsl:param name="nodes2" select="/.."/>
  <xsl:param name="func" select=" 'identity' "/>
  <xsl:param name="func-param1" select="$generic:generics[self::generic:func and
@name = $func]/@param1"/>
  <xsl:param name="i" select="1"/>
  <xsl:param name="result" select="/.."/>

  <xsl:choose>
    <xsl:when test="$nodes1 and $nodes2">
      <xsl:variable name="temp">
        <xsl:apply-templates
            select="$generic:generics[self::generic:aggr-func and
                                      @name = $func]">
```

```
          <xsl:with-param name="x" select="$nodes1[1]"/>
          <xsl:with-param name="accum" select="$nodes2[1]"/>
          <xsl:with-param name="i" select="$i"/>
          <xsl:with-param name="param1" select="$func-param1"/>
      </xsl:apply-templates>
    </xsl:variable>

    <xsl:call-template name="generic:map2">
      <xsl:with-param name="nodes1" select="$nodes1[position( ) > 1]"/>
      <xsl:with-param name="nodes2" select="$nodes2[position( ) > 1]"/>
      <xsl:with-param name="func" select="$func"/>
      <xsl:with-param name="func-param1" select="$func-param1"/>
      <xsl:with-param name="i" select="$i +1"/>
      <xsl:with-param name="result" select="$result | exslt:node-set($temp)"/>
    </xsl:call-template>
  </xsl:when>
  <xsl:otherwise>
    <xsl:apply-templates select="$result" mode="generic:map"/>
  </xsl:otherwise>
  </xsl:choose>
</xsl:template>
```

generic:map2 operates on two independent node sets in parallel and thus can apply
any binary generic operation to the successive nodes. As with generic:map, the utility
is a function of the frequency of usage.

14.5   Creating Generic Node-Set Generators

Problem

You want to create reusable templates for generating a node set computationally.

Solution

The first generic function in this category generates a node set by executing a function over successive values, as defined by an incrementing function, until an upper
bound is reached:

```
<xsl:template name="generic:gen-set">
  <xsl:param name="x" select="1"/>
  <xsl:param name="func" select=" 'identity' "/>
  <xsl:param name="func-param1"
      select="$generic:generics[self::generic:func and @name = $func]/@param1"/>
  <xsl:param name="test-func" select=" 'less-than' "/>
  <xsl:param name="test-param1" select="$x + 1"/>
  <xsl:param name="incr-func" select=" 'incr' "/>
  <xsl:param name="incr-param1" select="1"/>
  <xsl:param name="i" select="1"/>
  <xsl:param name="result" select="/.."/>

  <!-- Check if aggregation should continue -->
  <xsl:variable name="continue">
```

```
    <xsl:apply-templates
        select="$generic:generics[self::generic:func and
                 @name = $test-func]">
      <xsl:with-param name="x" select="$x"/>
      <xsl:with-param name="param1" select="$test-param1"/>
    </xsl:apply-templates>
  </xsl:variable>

  <xsl:choose>
    <xsl:when test="string($continue)">
      <!--Compute func($x) -->
      <xsl:variable name="f-of-x">
        <xsl:apply-templates
            select="$generic:generics[self::generic:func and
                                      @name = $func]">
          <xsl:with-param name="x" select="$x"/>
          <xsl:with-param name="i" select="$i"/>
          <xsl:with-param name="param1" select="$func-param1"/>
        </xsl:apply-templates>
      </xsl:variable>

      <!-- Compute the next value of $x-->
      <xsl:variable name="next-x">
        <xsl:apply-templates
            select="$generic:generics[self::generic:func and
                                      @name = $incr-func]">
          <xsl:with-param name="x" select="$x"/>
          <xsl:with-param name="param1" select="$incr-param1"/>
        </xsl:apply-templates>
      </xsl:variable>

        <xsl:call-template name="generic:gen-set">
          <xsl:with-param name="x" select="$next-x"/>
          <xsl:with-param name="func" select="$func"/>
          <xsl:with-param name="func-param1" select="$func-param1"/>
          <xsl:with-param name="test-func" select="$test-func"/>
          <xsl:with-param name="test-param1" select="$test-param1"/>
          <xsl:with-param name="incr-func" select="$incr-func"/>
          <xsl:with-param name="incr-param1" select="$incr-param1"/>
          <xsl:with-param name="i" select="$i + 1"/>
          <xsl:with-param name="result"
                          select="$result | exslt:node-set($f-of-x)"/>
        </xsl:call-template>
      </xsl:when>
      <xsl:otherwise>
        <xsl:apply-templates select="$result" mode="generic:gen-set"/>
      </xsl:otherwise>
    </xsl:choose>
</xsl:template>

<xsl:template match="node()" mode="generic:gen-set">
  <gen-set>
    <xsl:copy-of select="."/>
  </gen-set>
</xsl:template>
```

Here you use this template to generate a list of squares of the first ten integers:

```
<xsl:stylesheet version="1.0" xmlns:xsl="http://www.w3.org/1999/XSL/Transform"
   xmlns:generic="http://www.ora.com/XSLTCookbook/namespaces/generic">

<xsl:import href="aggregation.xslt"/>

<xsl:output method="text" />

<xsl:template match="/">
  <xsl:call-template name="generic:gen-set">
    <xsl:with-param name="x" select="1"/>
    <xsl:with-param name="func" select=" 'square' "/>
    <xsl:with-param name="incr-param1" select="1"/>
    <xsl:with-param name="test-func" select=" 'less-than-eq' " />
    <xsl:with-param name="test-param1" select="10"/>
  </xsl:call-template>
</xsl:template>

<xsl:template match="node()" mode="generic:gen-set">
<xsl:value-of select="."/>
<xsl:text> </xsl:text>
</xsl:template>
```

```
1 4 9 16 25 36 49 64 81 100
```

The second generic function in this category generates a node set by n successive applications of a function starting with an initial seed value:

```
<xsl:template name="generic:gen-nested">
  <xsl:param name="x" select="1"/>
  <xsl:param name="func" select=" 'identity' "/>
  <xsl:param name="func-param1"
             select="$generic:generics[self::generic:func and
                        @name = $func]/@param1"/>
  <xsl:param name="i" select="1"/>
  <xsl:param name="n" select="2"/>
  <xsl:param name="result">
    <xsl:value-of select="$x"/>
  </xsl:param>

  <xsl:choose>
    <xsl:when test="$i &lt;= $n">
    <!--Compute func($x) -->
      <xsl:variable name="f-of-x">
        <xsl:apply-templates
            select="$generic:generics[self::generic:func and
                                 @name = $func]">
          <xsl:with-param name="x" select="$x"/>
          <xsl:with-param name="i" select="$i"/>
          <xsl:with-param name="param1" select="$func-param1"/>
        </xsl:apply-templates>
      </xsl:variable>

      <xsl:call-template name="generic:gen-nested">
        <xsl:with-param name="x" select="$f-of-x"/>
```

```
            <xsl:with-param name="func" select="$func"/>
            <xsl:with-param name="func-param1" select="$func-param1"/>
            <xsl:with-param name="i" select="$i + 1"/>
            <xsl:with-param name="n" select="$n"/>
            <xsl:with-param name="result"
                            select="exslt:node-set($result) |
                                    exslt:node-set($f-of-x)"/>
          </xsl:call-template>
        </xsl:when>
        <xsl:otherwise>
          <xsl:apply-templates select="$result" mode="generic:gen-nested"/>
        </xsl:otherwise>
      </xsl:choose>
    </xsl:template>

    <xsl:template match="node( )" mode="generic:gen-nested">
      <gen-nested>
        <xsl:copy-of select="."/>
      </gen-nested>
    </xsl:template>
```

Here you use this template to build the series 2, 2 ** 2, (2 ** 2) ** 2, ((2 ** 2) ** 2) ** 2, (((2 ** 2) ** 2) ** 2) ** 2, where ** means to the power of:

```
<xsl:stylesheet version="1.0" xmlns:xsl="http://www.w3.org/1999/XSL/Transform"
  xmlns:generic="http://www.ora.com/XSLTCookbook/namespaces/generic">

  <xsl:import href="aggregation.xslt"/>

  <xsl:output method="text" />

  <xsl:template match="/">
    <xsl:call-template name="generic:gen-nested">
      <xsl:with-param name="x" select="2"/>
      <xsl:with-param name="func" select=" 'square' "/>
      <xsl:with-param name="n" select="4"/>
    </xsl:call-template>
  </xsl:template>

<xsl:template match="node( )" mode="generic:gen-nested">
  <xsl:value-of select="."/>
  <xsl:text> </xsl:text>
</xsl:template>

</xsl:stylesheet>

2 4 16 256 65536
```

Discussion

Recipes 14.2 and 14.3 were many-to-one generic transformations, and Recipe 14.4 explained many-to-many transformations. Naturally, this chapter would not be complete without a one-to-many generic transform.

With a generator, you can create random numbers that can select random nodes from an XML document. This chapter uses a simple *linear congruential* generator (see, for example, *http://www.taygeta.com/rwalks/ node1.html*). Here is a stylesheet that displays a random selection of names from an input document:

```
<xsl:stylesheet version="1.0" xmlns:xsl="http://www.w3.org/1999/XSL/Transform"
  xmlns:generic="http://www.ora.com/XSLTCookbook/namespaces/generic">

<xsl:import href="aggregation.xslt"/>

<xsl:output method="xml" indent="yes"/>

<!-- Extend the available generic functions -->
<xsl:variable name="generic:generics" select="$generic:public-generics
| document('')/*/generic:*"/>

<!-- These values give good random results but you can tweak -->
<xsl:variable name="a" select="16807"/>
<xsl:variable name="c" select="0"/>
<xsl:variable name="m"  select="2147483647"/>

<!-- Store the root for later use -->
<xsl:variable name="doc" select="/"/>

<!-- The random generator -->
<generic:func name="linear-congruential"/>
<xsl:template match="generic:func[@name='linear-congruential']">
    <xsl:param name="x"/>
    <xsl:value-of select="($a * $x + $c) mod $m"/>
</xsl:template>

<xsl:template match="/">
<names>
    <xsl:call-template name="generic:gen-nested">
      <xsl:with-param name="x" select="1"/>
      <xsl:with-param name="func" select=" 'linear-congruential' "/>
      <xsl:with-param name="n" select="100"/>
      <!-- Don't include initial seed -->
      <xsl:with-param name="result" select="/.."/>
    </xsl:call-template>
  </names>
</xsl:template>

<xsl:template match="node( )" mode="generic:gen-nested">

  <!-- Restrict the range to 1 through 100 -->
  <xsl:variable name="random" select=". mod 99 + 1"/>

   <name>
    <xsl:value-of select="$doc/names/name[$random]"/>
   </name>

</xsl:template>

</xsl:stylesheet>
```

Index

We'd like to hear your suggestions for improving our indexes. Send email to *index@oreilly.com*.

B

bar charts, creating, 342–347
barStyle template, 344
base classes, CkBkTemplParam, 555
base conversions, 39–43
base name models, 475
baseName stereotype, 471
batching, 55
Bézier curves, 348
binary messages, rendering, 412–419
binary trees, 134
bindings, 511
    encoding, 520
    names, 513
    ports, 509
bit masks, 69–74
bits, testing, 69–74
boilerplate, SVG, 325–332
boundary conditions, testing, 591–594
building service-based enterprise
    architecture, 504–517

C

calendars
    Hebrew, 92–100
    Islamic, 90–92
    ISO, 87–90
    Julian, 86
    last day of the month, calculating, 78, 90,
        95
capturing nodes, 630
case (of characters), changing, 17–19
catchXSL!, 577
CGI (common gateway interface)
    building architecture, 504–517
    test data entry, 421–426
characters
    Arabic number formatting, 34
    case, changing, 17–19
    counting number of occurrences in a
        string, 23
    removing from strings, 3
charts
    bar, 342–347
    pie, 353–360
    reusable SVG generation
        utilities, 332–368
CkBkTemplParam base class, 555

classes
    AnsweringMachineState, 427
    CkBkTemlParam, 555
    data wrappers, 408–412
    Graphics2D, 546
    java.awt.FontMetrics, 548
    programming language, 494
    TextLayout, 546
    topics, 474
    UML, 471
    XslForEach, 556
clients, test data entry tools, 420
client-side XSLT processing with
    frames, 305–308
Cocoon, 505
code
    embedding, 447
    generating, 388–396
    generic, 595
    inline script, 522
    packaging tests, 588
    stub, 405–408
    switching, 400–405
    Xsltext.java, 557
Cogitative Topic Maps Web Site
    (CTW), 490
colors, customizing, 342
columnar reports, creating, 170–179
    column major mappings, 173
    row major mappings, 173
columns, 469
    major mappings, 173
    (see also Excel)
combinatorial functions, 68
Comma Separated Values (see CSV)
comments, debugging, 572
common gateway interface (see CGI)
compressing files, 549
computing sums of polymorphic
    functions, 616
concat( ) function, 7
conditional imports, 447
conditional includes, 447
conditions, testing, 591–594
constants, generating, 396–400
contains( ) function, 15
context-sensitive variables, 119
conventions
    naming, 520
    topic mapping in UML, 471

E

elements
    converting to attributes, 204–206
    encoding, 535
    Geom, 460
    Java extensions, 523–525
    joins, 255–260
    merging, 221–222
    renaming, 207–212
    Saxon extensions, 520
    Saxon StyleElement method, 551
    ss:Worksheet, 469
    svgElement, 456
    web sites, 496–503
    Xalan Java 2, 520–537
    xsl:include, 587
    xslx:templtext, 556
embedding, 519
    code, 447
    unit test data, 584–588
emulating loops, 442–448
enabling XPaths, 447
encoding
    bindings, 520
    elements, 535
endpoints, services, 514
entities, 18
equi-joins, 258
error conditions, testing, 591–594
escapes, 553
    disable-output-escaping attribute, 557
    state machines, 555
European money format, 31
evaluating XPath expressions, 533–535
events, style, 577
Excel
    exporting data to XML, 463–470
    importing, 596
execution
    JavaScript, 537–543
    templates, 570–572
exporting
    as delimited data, 155–170
    Excel data to XML, 463–470
expr%delimit behavior, 556
expressions, XPath, 533–535, 551
EXSLT, 2
    set operations on nodes, 239
    string functions, 23
extensibility, 519
extension-element-prefixes attribute, 550

extensions, 519
    functions, 23–25
    Java, 522
        customizing, 543–563
        elements, 523–525
    Saxon, 519, 525–537
    scripting, 522
    Xalan Java 2, 520–537

F

factorial, calculating, 52
fields, test data entry web client, 420
files
    constants, 396–400
    cpp, 411
    zip, 549
flattening XML hierarchies, 224–228
floor( ) function, 77
fonts, testing, 547
format-number( ) function, 27
    rounding with, 36
formatting, 607–639
    data wrappers, 408–412
    dates and times, 101–105
    four-quadrant plots, 340
    generic code, 595
    grids, 339
    namespaces, 522
    numbers (see formatting numbers)
    shapes, 458
    stylesheets, 443
    SVG
        bar charts, 342–347
        libraries, 332–368
        Open-Hi-Lo-Close plots, 360–363
        pie charts, 353–360
        tree diagrams, 368–378
        web pages, 378–387
        XY plots, 348–353
    text
        into columns, 170–179
        hierarchical displays, 180–188
        indentation, 180
        managing whitespace, 150–155
        sequential numbering, 188–197
        wrapped text, 197, 200
    Topic Maps, 490
    web sites, 496–503
    X and Y axes, 336
    (see also templates)

HTML (*continued*)
    XML-to-HTML
        transformations, 288–323
        self-contained, 314–318
    (see also web pages, interactive)
hyperlinks, 293–296

I

IDEAlliance, 485
identification of stereotypes, 473
identity transforms, 201
implementing
    Java extensions, 523–525
    Saxon extensions, 520
    set operations, 530
    summary stylesheets, 633
    Topic Maps, 470–489
importing
    spreadsheets, 596
    stylesheet template tags, 597–600
incr generic function, 628
indentation in text output, 180
indexes, 117, 293, 549
inline script code, 522
in-order traversals, 134–138
instanceOf relationships, 478
instantiation, 478
    UML association, 471
integer arithmetic, emulating, 77
integration, numeric, 624
interaction with relational databases, 532
interactive SVG-enabled web pages,
        creating, 378–387
interfaces
    API, 566
    data wrappers, 408–412
    get, 411
    State, 427
    test data entry web CGI, 421–426
interprocess message repository, 390
intersections of nodes, finding, 237–249
invariants, testing, 571
invoking
    Java, 566–568
    scripting languages, 537–543
Islamic calendar, 90–92
    converting to Absolute day numbers, 91
    last day of the month, calculating, 90
ISO calendar, 87–90

J

Java
    extensions, 522
        customizing, 543–563
        elements, 523–525
    invoking, 566–568
    Saxon extensions, 519, 525–537
    Xalan Java 2 extensions, 520–537
java.awt.FontMetrics class, 548
JavaScript, executing, 537–543
joins, 255–260
    equi-joins, 258
    with large number of members, 257
    ports and bindings, 509
    with relations other than equality, 258
Julian calendar, 86
Julian day numbers
    Absolute day numbers, versus, 82
    Absolute days, converting to, 84
    calculating, 82–85
    Gregorian date, converting to, 83

K

key( ) function, 117
keys, 430
    identification of stereotypes, 473

L

labels, aligning, 341
last( ) function, 143
last day of the month, calculating, 78, 95
    Hebrew calendar, 95
    Islamic calendar, 90
layouts
    TextLayout class, 546
    web sites, 496–503
level-order traversals, 138–143
libraries
    bar charts, 342–347
    SVG (see SVG)
line styles, customizing, 351
links (see hyperlinks)
literate programming, 447
local-name( ) function, 127
logarithms, calculating, 45
loops, emulating, 442–448

M

maps
    Excel XML files, 465
    Topic Maps, 470–489
    Visio-to-SVG, 451
masters, Visio documents, 456
matching
    operations, 22
    templates, 598
math functions, 43–74
    absolute value, 43
    addition, 54–57
    averages, 65
    combinatorial functions, 68
    factorial, 52
    integer arithmetic, emulating, 77
    logarithms, 45
    minimums and maximums, 58–65
    multiplication, 54–57
    permutations, 68
    powers, 48
    square root, 44
    standard deviation, 67
    statistical functions, 65–67
    variance, calculating, 67
    (see also numbers)
math:highest function, 58
math:log( ) function, 45
math:log10( ) function, 45
math:log10-util template, 47
math:lowest function, 58, 61
math:max function, 58
math:min function, 58
math:power( ) function, 48
math:power-f( ) function, 49
math:power-frac template, 51
maximums, finding, 58–65
merging documents
    into container documents, 218
    with identical schema, 212–217
    merging elements, 221–222
    more than two documents, 216
    removing duplicate entries, 213–216
    with unlike schema, 217–222
    weaving documents, 219–221
messages
    binary, 412–419
    converting, 421–426
    data wrappers, 408–412
    detecting, 570
    handlers, 405–408

routing, 400–405
    test data entry web clients, 420
methods
    Saxon StyleElement, 551
    stringHeight( ), 546
    stringWidth( ), 546
    xslx:et-context, 550
Metonic cycles, 93
minimums, finding, 58–65
models, 475
    base names, 475
    instanceOf relationships, 478
modes, 295
modifying
    databases, 532
    grids, 340
    values, 535
Muenchian Method for reorganizing
        hierarchies, 234
multiple destinations, outputting Saxon
        to, 525
multiple plots, generating, 353
multiplication, 54–57

N

name( ) function, 127
namespaces
    Java, 522
    re-namespacing, 207
    stripping namespaces from
        documents, 212
naming
    base name models, 475
    bindings, 513
    conventions, 520
    data wrappers, 408–412
    shapes, 459
    templates, 597–600
National Institute of Standards and
        Technology (NIST), 492
navigating stylesheets, 572–577
newline characters, adding, 152
NIST (National Institute of Standards and
        Technology), 492
nodes, 24
    capturing, 630
    comparing using union (|) operator, 120
    determining if two nodes are the
        same, 120–123
    extended information about, 531
    filtering, 114

About the Author

Sal Mangano has been developing software for over 12 years and has worked on many mission-critical applications, especially in the area of financial-trading applications. He currently is working at Morgan Stanley after leaving a long-term consulting assignment at the NYSE. For much of this time, Sal has been passionately interested in data and object-oriented modeling, as well as data transformation and code generation from data models. Unlike many XML/XSLT developers, he did not approach the technology solely from the standpoint of the Internet and web development alone but rather from the broader need for a general-purpose data-transformation framework. This experience has given him a unique perspective that has influenced many of the recipes in this book. Sal has a master's degree in computer science from Polytechnic University.

When not mushing bits around, Sal spends his time with the other two loves of his life: his wife, Wanda, and two-and-a-half-year-old son, Leonardo.

Colophon

Our look is the result of reader comments, our own experimentation, and feedback from distribution channels. Distinctive covers complement our distinctive approach to technical topics, breathing personality and life into potentially dry subjects.

The animals on the cover of *XSLT Cookbook* are red mullet fish. These colorful striped fish are native to warm European seas. They are bottom dwellers who feed on small invertebrates such as crustaceans, worms, and mollusks, along with the occasional small fish. Red mullet are also called goatfish, as they have two flexible whisker-like appendages that hang from their chin. These organs, called barbels, are covered with taste buds to help red mullet locate their food and dig into ocean sand. The fish usually weigh one-half to two pounds and can grow as long as two feet, but most are much smaller. They have a deeply forked tail fin, two dorsal fins, and corresponding pectoral and anal fins. Red mullet are indeed pink to bright red in color, with three or four yellow stripes running lengthwise along their side. Considerable changes in color occur depending on the time of day, stress factors, and age.

Seafood chefs have always prized the red mullet for its firm, lean flesh, subtle flavor, and intense color. The fish is found on menus throughout Europe, but is rarely available in the United States. Red mullet is sometimes called the woodcock of the sea because, like the woodcock, it can be eaten with its innards intact. There are around forty known subspecies, but two types are most popular for food: *Mullus surmuletus* is commonly found in the Atlantic, around the south coast of Britain, and *Mullus barbatus* is a more delicate Mediterranean variety. The latter fish was a favorite of ancient Romans, who proudly displayed live red mullet on the dinner table immediately before handing them over to the cook. Stock was kept in large lagoons, and zealous gourmands paid fabulous prices for any specimen above average size.

Jeffrey Holcomb was the production editor and proofreader for *XSLT Cookbook*. Ann Schirmer was the copyeditor. Matt Hutchinson and Claire Cloutier provided quality control. Indexing services were provided by Octal Publishing.

Ellie Volckhausen designed the cover of this book, based on a series design by Edie Freedman. The cover image is a 19th-century engraving from the Dover Pictorial Archive. Emma Colby produced the cover layout with QuarkXPress 4.1 using Adobe's ITC Garamond font.

David Futato designed the interior layout. This book was converted to FrameMaker 5.5.6 with a format conversion tool created by Erik Ray, Jason McIntosh, Neil Walls, and Mike Sierra that uses Perl and XML technologies. The text font is Linotype Birka; the heading font is Adobe Myriad Condensed; and the code font is Lucas-Font's TheSans Mono Condensed. The illustrations that appear in the book were produced by Robert Romano and Jessamyn Read using Macromedia FreeHand 9 and Adobe Photoshop 6. The tip and warning icons were drawn by Christopher Bing. This colophon was written by Philip Dangler.

Other Titles Available from O'Reilly

XML

XML in a Nutshell, 2nd Edition

*By Elliotte Rusty Harold &
W. Scott Means
1st Edition December 2000
400 pages, ISBN 0-596-00058-8*

This powerful new edition provides
developers with a comprehensive
guide to the rapidly evolving XML
space. Serious users of XML will find
topics on just about everything they need, from fundamental syntax rules, to details of DTD and XML Schema
creation, to XSLT transformations, to APIs used for processing XML documents. Simply put, this is the only reference of its kind among XML books.

Learning XML

*By Erik T. Ray with
Christopher R. Maden
1st Edition January 2001
368 pages, ISBN 0-596-00046-4*

XML (Extensible Markup Language) is
a flexible way to create "self-describing
data"—and to share both the format
and the data on the World Wide Web, intranets, and elsewhere. In *Learning XML*, the authors explain XML and
its capabilities succinctly and professionally, with references to real-life projects and other cogent examples.
Learning XML shows the purpose of XML markup itself,
the CSS and XSL styling languages, and the XLink and
XPointer specifications for creating rich link structures.

Java & XML, 2nd Edition

*By Brett McLaughlin
2nd Edition September 2001
528 pages, ISBN 0-596-00197-5*

New chapters on Advanced SAX,
Advanced DOM, SOAP, and data binding, as well as new examples throughout, bring the second edition of *Java
& XML* thoroughly up to date. Except for a concise introduction to XML basics, the book focuses entirely on using
XML from Java applications. It's a worthy companion for
Java developers working with XML or involved in messaging, web services, or the new peer-to-peer movement.

XML Schema

*By Eric van der Vlist
1st Edition June 2002
400 pages, 0-596-00252-1*

The W3C's XML Schema offers a powerful set of tools for defining acceptable XML document structures and
content. While schemas are powerful,
that power comes with substantial complexity. This book
explains XML Schema foundations, a variety of different
styles for writing schemas, simple and complex types,
datatypes and facets, keys, extensibility, documentation,
design choices, best practices, and limitations. Complete
with references, a glossary, and examples throughout.

XSLT

*By Doug Tidwell
1st Edition August 2001
473 pages, ISBN 0-596-00053-7*

XSLT (Extensible Stylesheet Language
Transformations) is a critical bridge
between XML processing and more
familiar HTML, and dominates the
market for conversions between XML vocabularies. Useful as XSLT is, its complexities can be daunting. Doug
Tidwell, a developer with years of XSLT experience, eases
the pain by building from the basics to the more complex and powerful possibilities of XSLT, so you can jump
in at your own level of expertise.

O'REILLY®

To order: *800-998-9938* • *order@oreilly.com* • *www.oreilly.com*
Online editions of most O'Reilly titles are available by subscription at *safari.oreilly.com*
Also available at most retail and online bookstores.

How to stay in touch with O'Reilly

1. Visit our award-winning web site

http://www.oreilly.com/

★ "Top 100 Sites on the Web"—PC Magazine
★ CIO Magazine's Web Business 50 Awards

Our web site contains a library of comprehensive product information (including book excerpts and tables of contents), downloadable software, background articles, interviews with technology leaders, links to relevant sites, book cover art, and more. File us in your bookmarks or favorites!

2. Join our email mailing lists

Sign up to get email announcements of new books and conferences, special offers, and O'Reilly Network technology newsletters at:

http://elists.oreilly.com

It's easy to customize your free elists subscription so you'll get exactly the O'Reilly news you want.

3. Get examples from our books

To find example files for a book, go to:

http://www.oreilly.com/catalog

select the book, and follow the "Examples" link.

4. Work with us

Check out our web site for current employment opportunities:

http://jobs.oreilly.com/

5. Register your book

Register your book at:

http://register.oreilly.com

6. Contact us

O'Reilly & Associates, Inc.
1005 Gravenstein Hwy North
Sebastopol, CA 95472 USA
TEL: 707-827-7000 or 800-998-9938
          (6am to 5pm PST)
FAX: 707-829-0104

order@oreilly.com
For answers to problems regarding your order or our products. To place a book order online visit:

http://www.oreilly.com/order_new/

catalog@oreilly.com
To request a copy of our latest catalog.

booktech@oreilly.com
For book content technical questions or corrections.

corporate@oreilly.com
For educational, library, government, and corporate sales.

proposals@oreilly.com
To submit new book proposals to our editors and product managers.

international@oreilly.com
For information about our international distributors or translation queries. For a list of our distributors outside of North America check out:

http://international.oreilly.com/distributors.html

adoption@oreilly.com
For information about academic use of O'Reilly books, visit:

http://academic.oreilly.com

O'REILLY®

To order: *800-998-9938* • *order@oreilly.com* • *www.oreilly.com*
Online editions of most O'Reilly titles are available by subscription at *safari.oreilly.com*
Also available at most retail and online bookstores.